Bible Answers for 1000 Difficult Questions

Bible Answers for 1000 Difficult Questions

by George Sandison and Staff

WORLD
Bible Publishers, Inc.
Iowa Falls, Iowa

ISBN: 0-529-06934-2

Printed in the United States of America

Contents

FOREWORD

THIS volume is the outcome of Biblical research covering a period of almost a quarter of a century, and represents the combined labors of careful and painstaking scholars, pastors, professors and theologians of all denominations. Their investigations have been conducted along the lines followed by the ablest orthodox expositors of the present day. To the average student and Bible reader, it will be found a valuable means of reference, and a source of constant edification, enlightenment and education.

The contributors to the book have not merely traveled along the ordinary highways of Biblical literature; they have found in rarely trodden footpaths and byways much that is valuable and known only to the few. They have carefully weighed and tested their authorities and, with infinite labor, have here set down only that which has appealed to them as worthy of preservation and likely to be of service to earnest Bible students everywhere. It is humbly hoped that the book will be found worthy of a place on the student's table as a companion to the Bible, since it serves to shed the light of the best modern interpretation upon a very large number of obscure passages, many of which are liable to be misunderstood by the ordinary reader. It is supplementary to the Sacred Book in the sense that it presents, from trustworthy sources, more or less difficult of access, much that is in the nature of corroborative evidence. It also gives, in many instances, renderings of difficult passages with a closer and truer relation to the original test.

In the domain of practical everyday Christian living, and particularly in dealing with problems that are constantly arising for consideration, it will be found especially helpful. Many of the questions with which it deals are such as are familiar to the average man or woman, and they will find in it material aid toward their solution.

In view of the steadily growing interest in all forms of Bible study, and with a sincere desire to be of service to the multitudes who yearn to know more of God's Word, and to place at their disposal a means of real help which we are led to hope will be welcomed and appreciated, the present volume is respectfully submitted by the compiler.

FACTS ABOUT THE BIBLE

1 Who wrote the various books in the Bible?

Genesis, Exodus, Leviticus, Numbers, Deuteronomy—Moses (scholarly opinions differ here, but so far no thoroughly convincing arguments have been advanced to disprove the Mosaic authorship of large portions of these books); Joshua—Joshua (also ascribed in Phineas, Eleazar, Samuel and Jeremiah); Judges—ascribed by Jewish tradition to Samuel; Ruth—unknown; I and II Samuel unknown (probably the work of Samuel, Nathan and others); I and II Kings—unknown; I and II Chronicles—probably Ezra; Ezra—probably Ezra; Nehemiah—Nehemiah; Esther—probably Mordecai, or Ezra; Job—uncertain (has been attributed to Moses, or Job); the Psalms—David, Moses, and others; Proverbs—Solomon and others; Ecclesiastes formerly ascribed to Solomon, now thought by many to belong to a later period; Song of Solomon—Solomon; Isaiah—Isaiah; Jeremiah—Jeremiah; Lamentations—Jeremiah; the remaining books of the Old Testament were written by the prophets whose names they bear, with the probable exception of Jonah; Matthew—Matthew; Mark—Mark; Luke—Luke; John—John; Acts—Luke; Romans to Philemon—Paul; Hebrews—unknown (has been ascribed to Paul, Luke, Apollos, Barnabas); James—James; I and II Peter—Peter; I, II and III John—John; Revelation—John.

2 What is meant by the inspiration of the Bible?

The question is asked, "How can I know that the Bible is inspired?" Even in this late day, when the number of Christians has multiplied from a mere handful to four hundred and seventy millions, or fully one-fourth of the entire population of the globe, there are people who doubt the inspiration of the Bible. At different times during the last twenty centuries assaults have been made against the Sacred Book, which Gladstone termed the "'Impregnable Rock of Holy Scripture," but without avail. It has a firmer hold on the hearts of men than in any previous age. Mr. Moody, the greatest of American evangelists, was once asked whether he regarded the Bible as inspired, and his answer was brief and to the point: "I know the Bible is inspired," he said, "because it inspires me!" There are countless thousands who will echo this answer and whose lives have been transformed by the same inspiration. Not only the great religious scholars, but the masters of secular literature regard the Bible as unapproachable in its high standard of expression, its magnificent imagery, the transcendent nobility of its rhetoric, the authority with which it appeals to the hearts of men, the universality of its application and the power it exercises over the souls of men. It bears within itself the evidence of inspiration, and wherever it is known and read and its precepts followed, its influence is uplifting and inspiring. The theory of inspiration does not exclude, but rather implies, human agency, however. "Holy men of God spake as they were moved by the Holy Spirit." (II Peter I:21).

3 What is higher criticism?

The ordinary study or criticism is directed to finding out the meaning of the passages, their correct translation and their significance and bearing on doctrines. The higher critics go above and back of all that, applying to the books of the Bible the same tests and methods of examination as are applied to other ancient books. They try to find out who were really the authors of the books and when they were written and whether any changes have been made in them since they were written. This latter question they try to solve by a close examination of the text. When they find, for example, such an expression as "There was no king in Israel in those days" (Judges 17:6), they conclude that that sentence was inserted as explanatory, by some one who edited the book after the contemporaneous historian had finished it. Or to take an example of a different kind: There is a statement in Psalm 51:16 that God desires not sacrifice, while in the nineteenth verse it is said that he will be pleased with sacrifice. The explanation the higher critics give is that probably the latter verse was added later, by some priest who did not wish the people to cease bringing sacrifices. The best scholars of the present day believe that many of the conclusions reached by the higher critics are erroneous, and that others are mere guesses for which there is not sufficient evidence.

4 What are the proofs of Bible authenticity?

"Can we prove the authenticity of the Bible by outside evidence ?" is a frequent question. The authenticity of the Bible is being proved by the old records on monuments, by tablets recently deciphered, and by discoveries in Bible lands. That is if by authenticity you mean its historical truth. As to inspiration, the best evidence is its effects. The man who loves the Bible and tries to conduct his life according to its precepts is a better man for the effort. The Bible-reading nation advances in the best line of civilization, caring for its poor and afflicted, and becoming in all ways better. Another evidence of its being inspired is the revelation it gives a man of himself, holding a mirror to his gaze by which he recognizes himself. Another evidence is its survival. No book was ever more violently attacked, no book was ever more misused, yet it has outlived the attacks of foes and the faults of friends and is read today more widely than ever. These are a few of the reasons for believing it came from God.

5 Can we find any reference to Christ in contemporaneous secular writers?

Yes. There are references to Christ in connection with Christians, by several historians. Tacitus, who was praetor under Domitian in A.D. 88, only fifty-eight years after the Crucifixion, refers to Christ (Annal XV:44). Pliny the younger, who was tribune in Syria about the same time, also refers to him (Epistle X:97). There are also references in Lucian, who lived about the middle of the second century. He states explicitly the fact of Christ having been crucified. Suetonius and Eusebius also refer to Christ. Besides these evidences, there was the persecution of the Christians under Nero, which is recorded by all historians. Nero died A. D. 68, only thirty-eight years after the Crucifixion. It is therefore clear that there were many Christians before that time. How could the sect have come into existence without a founder? If you saw an oak growing in a place where there was no tree fifty years before, you would suspect that some one had planted an acorn there, and if four men told you how, when and by whom it was planted, you would be prepared to believe them. So there is good reason for believing the Gospel narratives, when you read in secular history of the existence of the Christian Church fifty years after the Crucifixion. Their stories are a credible explanation of a well-established fact.

6 Does the Bible teach science?

It is not a scientific textbook, nor was it written to teach science, but religion. The discrepancies between the story of creation as given in the Bible and that given by the scientists are very much such as we should find in two descriptions of a great battle, if one of them was written by a clergyman who knew nothing of military tactics, and the other by a military expert who knew nothing of religion. The important fact for us—the fact that is of more momentous interest than all the discoveries of science—is that God made the universe. For this knowledge we are not indebted to science, which has not yet attained it, but we do get it from the Bible. A person who wants to know the latest discoveries of science as to geology and astronomy, should study the recent books of science; but if he wants to know the way to God and eternal happiness, he should go to the Bible. Each has its own sphere.

7 Why should we believe the Scriptures?

Some people answer this query by saying that the reason is found in the fact that the Bible is the only book handed down to us through the ages. That is not the best answer. Some ancient writings, like the Vedas, for instance, are almost as ancient as the Bible. And many tablets and monuments are in existence containing words written as long ago as the writings of the Scriptures. There are many powerful arguments for the Bible, but the greatest is that every person who will really study it finds that it does tell the truth about the human soul. When a man reads in an arithmetic that two and two make four, he does not stop to ask himself why he should believe the arithmetic. He knows instinctively and intuitively that the arithmetic is telling him the truth. So when an honest man studies the Bible he finds it full of truths about himself. The Bible tells him he is a sinner, and he knows that is true. The Bible tells him about God, and he finds in his heart a deep conviction that just such a God exists. The Bible offers forgiveness, and the man knows he needs it. Step by step, and point by point, the Bible shows the man what he is and what he needs and points the way to finding the fulfillment of his needs and desires. People find in the Bible help for bearing their trials, power to resist temptation, assurance of immortality and friendship with God. A man who never saw the Bible before, when he reads of God in it, realizes that he always needed and longed for God, but did not know how to find him till the Bible showed him the way. Particularly does it show him how to find God in Christ. That, after all, is the supreme mission of the Bible—to lead men to Christ. But, again, taking the Bible as literature, we find that it hangs together, that it bears within itself the evidence that it is true. Start with the writings of Paul. Here is a levelheaded, highly educated, practical man who has left to the world's literature certain letters to groups of friends. These letters tell about Paul's personal knowledge of Christ, his personal friendship for him, his personal endeavors to forward the work of Christ which he had formerly antagonized until Christ himself appeared to him and set him right. Paul tells of becoming acquainted later with men who had known Christ in the flesh—Peter, James, John and others. We find that these men also wrote about Jesus, John writing three letters and a narrative of his life; Peter writing two letters, and apparently giving much of the information to his nephew Mark, who wrote another version of the life of Jesus. Luke, another friend of Paul, and probably also a personal friend of Jesus, wrote another version of his life and wrote the history of what his apostles did through his power after he had risen from the dead and gone back to the heavenly world. These were all good, honest, intelligent men. We may believe what they wrote about Christ and his salvation, just as we believe what Caesar wrote about the Gallic Wars. Further, we find that Christ came from a people whose history is recorded in the books of the Bible and whose prophets uttered messages from God. Peter connects the messages of the prophets with those of himself and the other apostles in II Peter 3:2: "That ye may be mindful of the words which were spoken before by the holy prophets, and of the commandment of us the apostles of our Lord and Saviour." The Bible holds together about the person of Christ as the great divine-human document which reveals him to the world.

8 Has Bible history been substantiated?

Yes, to a very notable extent by investigations in Bible lands. Excavations of ancient Babylonian tablets have corroborated the Biblical story of the Flood. The discovery of Assyrian inscriptions has proved the identity of Sargon, one of the greatest of the kings of that nation (see Isa. 20:1-4); identification of the site of Nineveh and of the Tower of Babel or "Birs Nimrud." Many facts concerning kings, nations, cities and events have been brought to light in these ancient records of brick, stone or papyrus, confirming Scripture history.

9 Were the Gospels written by the men whose names they bear?

Presumption based on internal evidence is in favor of that theory. There has been no serious question as to the authorship of Matthew. Mark is supposed to have derived his knowledge of the events he recorded from Peter. Our knowledge of Peter's character leads us to believe that if he undertook to write a Gospel it would be such an one as the Gospel according to Mark. Such an expression as that in Mark 14:72, "When he thought thereon he wept," implies an intimate knowledge of him such as would be written by Peter himself, or by a close associate. The introduction to Luke's Gospel shows that many Gospels were in existence when Luke wrote, and as he knew of them, he may have availed himself of the material they contained. His remark about writing "in order" suggests compilation. The authorship of the fourth Gospel has been hotly disputed, chiefly because some critics held that the writer of Revelation could not have written the elegant and cultured Greek of the Gospel. The majority of the commentators now, however, are in favor of the belief that John wrote it.

10 When were the Gospels written?

The genuineness of the four Gospels rests upon better authority than that of any other ancient writings. It is the general conclusion of the most eminent scholars that all four were written during the latter half of the first century. Before the end of the second century they were in general use and acceptance as one collection. They are mentioned by Tertullian, in a book written about A. D. 208, as being the work of two apostles and two disciples of apostles. Marcion also mentions their apostolic origin. Origen (who lived A. D. 185-253) refers to them as "the four elements of the church's faith." Theophilus, Bishop of Antioch (A. D. 168), also mentions the Gospels in his writings, and Jerome tells us that Theophilus arranged the four into one work. Tatian (who died about A.D. 170) compiled a Harmony of the Gospels. Justin Martyr (A.D. 99-165) gives many quotations from the Gospels. Many other witnesses might be cited to the same purpose. None of the original manuscripts are now in existence.

11 What are the curiosities of the Scriptures?

In the Bible the word "Lord" is found 1,853 times. The word "Jehovah" 6,855 times.

The word "Reverend" but once, and that in the 9th verse of Psalm III.

The 8th verse of the 97th Psalm is the middle verse of the Bible.

The 9th verse of the 8th chapter of Esther is the longest.

The 35th verse of the 11th chapter of St. John is the shortest.

In the 107th Psalm four verses are alike: The 8th, 15th, 21st and 31st.

Ezra 7:21 contains all the letters of the alphabet except J.

Each verse of the 136th Psalm ends alike.

No names or words of more than six syllables are found in the Bible.

The 37th chapter of Isaiah and 19th chapter of II Kings are alike.

The word "girl" occurs but twice in the Bible, and that in the 3rd verse of the 3rd chapter of Joel and Zechariah 8:5.

There are found in both books of the Bible 3,538, 483 letters, 773,693 words, 31,373 verses, 1,189 chapters and 66 books.

The 26th chapter of the Acts of the Apostles is the finest chapter to read.

The most beautiful chapter is the 23rd Psalm.

The four most inspiring promises are John 14:2-6, 37; Matthew 11:28; Psalm 37:4.

The 1st verse of the 51st chapter of Isaiah is the one for the new convert.

All who flatter themselves with vain boasting should read the 6th chapter of Matthew.

All humanity should learn the 6th chapter of St. Luke from the 20th verse to its ending.

12 What are the symbols for Christ?

"What symbols are used for both Christ and his people?" is a frequent question. There are six symbols used for both Christ and his people.

1. A BRANCH. *For Christ*, in Is. 11:1-4, "A branch out of his roots shall bear fruit," and "with the breath of his lips shall he slay the wicked;" in Zech. 6:12, 13, Heb. 3:1-4, Is. 4:2, Zech. 3:8, Jer. 23:5, 33:15, 16. *For his People.* John 15:5, "Ye are the branches;" Is. 60:21, "The people also shall be all righteous, the branch of my planting;" also, Rom. 11:16, Ps. 80:11, 15.

2. LIGHT. *For Christ.* In John 8:12, Jesus spake, "I am the light of the world;" also, in John 9:5. Luke 2:32, and I John 1:5, "God is light." *For his People.* Phil. 2:15, "Among whom ye are seen as lights in the world," Matt. 5:14, Eph. 5:8, Acts 13:47, Is. 42:6, Prov. 4:18.

3. A STONE. *For Christ* in I Pet. 2:4, 6, 7, 8, "A living stone," "A chief corner-stone," "the stone which the builders rejected," "a stone of stumbling;" also, Ps. 118:22, Eph. 2:20, Matt. 21:42. *For his People.* I Pet. 2:5, "Ye also as living stones are built up a spiritual house;" also, Eph. 2:21, 22.

4. A TEMPLE. Used *for Christ* in Rev. 21:22, "And I saw no temple therein for the Lord God the Almighty and the Lamb are the temple thereof;" also, John 2:19, 21. *For his People.* I Cor. 3:16, 17, "For the temple of God is holy which temple ye are," and I Cor. 6:19, II Cor. 6:16.

5. A SUN. *For Christ.* Ps. 84:11, "For the Lord God is a sun and shield;" also, Mal. 4:2, Rev. 21:23, 22:5. *For his People.* Judges 5:31, "Let them that love thee be as the sun;" also, Matt. 13:43.

6. A STAR. *For Christ.* Rev. 22:16, "I am the bright and morning star," II Pet. 1:19, "Until the day dawn and the day-star arise in your hearts;" also, Num. 24:17. *For his People.* Dan. 12:1-3, "And they that be wise shall shine," "and they that turn many to righteousness as the stars for ever and ever."

13 What are the sacred or symbolical numbers in Scripture?

There are certain numbers employed in Scripture that are known as sacred or symbolical numbers. Among these are *seven* (perfection), as the triune symbol of deity and the four quarters of the earth; *forty,* a "round number," signifying duration, distance, quantity; *ten* (completeness); *five,* as used in offerings etc.; *four,* related to the quarters of the globe, the shape of the holy of holies in the temple, etc.; *three,* symbol of supreme divinity; *twelve,* which derives its significance from the twelve tribes and which has been called the "square number," the "zodiacal number," the "apostolic number." 12X12 means, symbolically, fixity and completeness, and taken a thousand-fold, it gives the grand multiple of 144,000 (otherwise a countless multitude), one thousand symbolizing the world wholly pervaded by the divine—a world redeemed!

14 Why in Scripture is seven used more than any other number?

The symbolism of "seven" should be traced back to the symbolism of its component elements, "three" and "four," which represent divinity and humanity. Hence, "seven" represents the union between God and man. Among the Persians, the Greeks, the ancient Indians, the Romans, and all nations where seven days in the week were recognized, the influence of the number seven prevailed. It was called by Cicero "the knot and cement of all things," because in "seven" the spiritual and natural world were comprehended in one idea. Some writers claim that the Hebrews borrowed it from their heathen neighbors. The Sabbath, being the seventh day, suggested seven as the appointment for all sacred periods. The seventh month was ushered in by the Feast of Trumpets; seven weeks was the interval between the Passover and the Pentecost, and so on, recognizing seven as the symbol of all connected with the Divinity.

15 What is the significance of the number forty in Scripture?

It is not merely an arbitrary period or a "round number," but is chosen to convey the sense of fullness. Some of its prominent Scriptural uses are: Moses was forty days on the mount (Ex. 24:18, etc.); Elijah, strengthened by angel food, fasted for forty days (I Kings 19:8); the rain of the flood fell for forty days (Gen. 7:12); Noah opened the window of the ark after forty days (Gen. 8:6); the spies spent forty days in searching Canaan (Num. 13:25); Moses twice fasted and prayed for forty days (Deu. 9:18-25); Ezekiel bore the iniquities of Judah forty days (Eze. 4:6); Nineveh was allowed forty days to repent (Jonah 3:4); the Israelites wandered forty years in the wilderness (Num. 34:33); Goliath defied Saul's army for forty days (I Sam. 17:16); forty days was the period of embalming (Gen. 50:3); the Lord fasted for forty days (Matt. 4:2, etc.); the arisen Lord was seen for forty days (Acts 1:3); the Jews were forbidden to inflict more than forty stripes (Deu 25:3). It is noteworthy that Jerusalem was destroyed forty years after Christ's ascension, and tradition says Jesus was forty hours in the tomb. Lent lasts for forty days, as does also quarantine. St. Swithin betokens forty days' rain, while many ancient laws concerning physicians, knights, husbands, wives, widows, sanctuary privileges, fines, etc., all cluster about this number.

16 Who compiled the Old Testament?

It is claimed that the books of the Old Testament were collected and arranged under the supervision of Ezra, though modern scholarship disputes the claim. The epistles of Paul to the various churches were collected and incorporated with the other epistles and the Gospels and Revelation into one book during the first half of the second century, and as we learn from Eusebius, were in general use soon after the year 300 A.D.

17 Have some books of the Bible been excluded?

The excluded books are known as "Apocrypha," and are as follows: I Esdras, II Esdras, Tobit, Judith, several chapters of Esther which are found neither in the Hebrew nor the Chaldee, The Wisdom of Solomon, The Wisdom of Jesus, son of Sirach, or Ecclesiasticus, Baruch, The Song of the Three Holy Children, The History of Susanna, The History of the Destruction of Bel and the Dragon, The Prayer of Manasseh, I Maccabees, II Maccabees. They were excluded by the early Christian Church on the ground that they were of doubtful authority and not tending to spiritual edification. This decision has never been reversed, although in some periods of the Church's history a number of the apocryphal writings were published in smaller type after the regular books in the Bible. At one time the volume of apocryphal writings was even larger than the genuine, but very many of them, being rejected, quickly perished.

18 What are the famous songs of the Bible?

The great songs of the Old Testament, besides the Psalms and certain metrical passages in Job, are: Lamech's Sword Song, Gen. 4:23, 24; Noah's Song, Gen. 9:25-27; Moses' and Miriam's Song, Ex. 15:1-19, 21; War Songs, etc., Num. 21:14, 15, 17, 18, 27-30; Moses' Prophetic Song, Deut. 32:1-43; Song of Deborah and Barak, Judg. 5:2-21; Samson's Riddle Song, Judg. 15:16; Hannah's Magnificat, I Sam. 2:1-10; David's Song of the Bow, II Sam. 1:19-27; David's Song over Abner, II Sam. 3:33, 34; David's Thanksgiving, I Chron. 16:8-36; Hezekiah's Song, Isa. 38:10-20; Jonah's Prayer Song, Jonah 2:2-9; Habakkuk's Prayer Song, Hab. 3:2-19; and the four original songs in the New Testament: Luke 1:46-55; Luke 1:68-80; Luke 2:14; Luke 2:20-33.

19 Who was the author of Revelation?

"Was the Book of Revelation written by the same John who wrote the Gospel and the Epistle?" This question has been long disputed by scholars. Dionysius, in A.D. 240, was one of the earliest to express a doubt. It was attributed to John Mark, the companion of Paul and Barnabas and the author of the Gospel of Mark; to John the Presbyter, to Cerinthus, and others. The majority of German scholars agree with Luther in denying that Revelation was written by the apostle. On the other hand, there is internal evidence of John's authorship. His description of himself is in the manner of John. The apostle was the only man of prominence of that name who was banished to Patmos. The addresses to the seven churches of Asia show a knowledge of them consistent with the fact that the apostle was their overseer. On the whole, therefore, there seems good reason to believe that it was written by the Apostle John. The differences in the style of the Gospel and the Revelation, which are very marked, doubtless first gave rise to the doubt of the apostolic authorship. These are accounted for by the age of the author and by his perturbation of mind under the excitement of the visions.

OLD TESTAMENT PERSONS
AND THINGS

20 What were the meaning and result of Abraham's sacrifice?

The story of Abraham will ever be an important one, and particularly that part of it dealing with the memorable doings at the place he named "Jehovahjireh," where, as related in Genesis 22, he showed his wonderful obedience to God. Whatever may be conjectured to the contrary, the record in Genesis is clear and unmistakable. It was a test of Abraham's faith in God. Some critics want to know why, if God is all knowing, he should have said to Abraham: "For now I know that thou fearest God" (Gen. 22:12). The problem of foreknowledge is an extremely difficult one, and discussion about it is usually fruitless. (God in this case speaks of the test of Abraham as though it had been an experiment. He proved him and found him firm in faith and perfect in obedience. It was in obedience to the Lord's command that he stood ready to offer up his son Isaac, and not because he himself had chosen such a sacrifice, in order to be like his idolatrous neighbors, who offered up their children to Moloch. Genesis 22:2 dismisses this latter suggestion altogether.

The immediate effect of Abraham's successful test was the great blessing which God bestowed on him (verse 16), which, together with God's covenant, made Abraham the most important Biblical character and his name better known than that of any other human being on earth. All the promises to Abraham have been fulfilled, except the return of his descendants to the promised land. His seed is past all reckoning. Not only have all the Jews been his offspring, but Christians as well are in a sense his spiritual children. Their faith in Christ brings them into his family and makes them heirs of the promises made to him. The land of Canaan was promised to his seed forever. Since they are not in possession of it now we must believe they will return, as many other prophecies also declare. The promise was, however, not made to Abraham alone, but to him and his seed, which includes Christ—to the literal Israel and also to the spiritual Israel. The complete fulfillment of the covenant awaited the coming of Christ, "the seed," concerning whom it was made. See Galatians 3:16.

**21 Did Abraham see God in one of the three
men who visited him?**

There is doubtless difficulty in reconciling the passage in Genesis 18
with the statement in John 1:18, that "No man hath seen God at any
time." Authorities regarded the Genesis passage as relating to one of the
"theophanies" of the Old Testament; that is, a real appearance of God
to man. It is believed, however, that these appearances were of Christ
the Son, rather than God the Father. The New Testament teaches that
Christ existed co-eternally with the Father, and it is not inconceivable
that he would at times take the appearance of humanity when he wished
especially to make himself known to men. This explanation reconciles
all these occurrences with the statement of John that no one has seen
God; that is, God the Father. Christ is the personal manifestation of
God to man.

22 How should we interpret the miracle at Ajalon

The passage in Joshua, 10th chapter, describing the miracle of the
sun and moon at the time of the battle in the vale of Ajalon, has been
much discussed. Some commentators hold that it is a passage in which
the inspired historian departs from his narrative to introduce a highly
poetic quotation, in other words, a poetical figure of speech, not to be
interpreted literally—as though one might say that "God and all nature
fought on the side of Joshua." Again, the reference to the poetical book
of Jasher as the source of this passage lends color to this explanation
(see verse 13). Others prefer the literal view, regarding it as a miracle in
which the hours when sun and moon were both visible (the sun on the
heights of Gibeon at noon and the moon in the valley) were extended
into a whole day, or twelve hours of light (see Macdonald's *Principia
and the Bible*), the continued radiance of both orbs lighting the battle-
ground. Still another interpretation is that the sun and moon were heavily obscured by storm clouds (see verse 11), and that Joshua's prayer
was that they should withhold their light and that the gloom or semi-
darkness of the storm might last until the battle was fought, giving the
Israelites the advantage of a surprise with smaller numbers, the strength
of which the enemy could not properly estimate.

**23 Did Adam and Eve actually eat fruit,
or is the story a parable?**

The only source of information is the Bible narrative and it contains
no intimation that it is to be understood otherwise than literally. Theologians who have preferred to regard the narrative as a parable or allegory have usually been led to do so by the suggestion that the eating of
fruit which was "good for food," and "pleasant to the eyes," and was
moreover within reach, was an offense too venial to have been justly vi-

sited with a punishment so severe and far-reaching. The objection, however, is not well founded, because it ignores the main point involved. The gravity of the offense consisted, not in the act itself, but in the fact that Adam and Eve in committing it were consciously and wilfully violating God's explicit and emphatic command. They were punished for disobedience. Even if we should hold that it took some other form than the actual and literal eating of fruit, the principle is the same. There is no valid reason for rejecting the Bible narrative or putting any other construction on the words than is there implied.

24 Was Adam a red man?

Adam means "red" and so also does the word Edom, both having relation to the ruddiness of flesh and the color of the clayey soil. (See Gen. 2:7.) Some commentators hold that Adam, the first man, was probably of the complexion of the Arabs, or Edomites, ruddy though dark, while others take a different view. No definite theory can be formed on this subject.

25 What language did Adam and Eve speak?

There are many mundane things beyond the reach of present human knowledge and the site of Eden and the language of our first parents are among the number. Some philologists have ventured the conjecture that the primeval language must have been a simple vocabulary whose formation is indicated in Gen. 2:19, and which was strictly limited to the natural requirements of our first progenitors; in other words, signs and sounds apprehensible by the senses. All agree that speech, or the power of expressing emotions, or desires, was coeval with the creation of man. The earliest monuments and inscriptions yet discovered do not reach as far back into antiquity as the confusion of tongues at Babel (about B.C. 2200), previous to which (Gen. 2:1), the Biblical record states that "the whole earth was of one language and one speech," although probably there were many variations and dialects, each containing some element of the original tongue. Man's first utterances were probably what philologists term a "physical language," limited to the expression of simple needs and afterwards expanded to meet man's growing experience with his own nature and the world around him.

26 What became of Aaron's rod?

It was preserved in the tabernacle and, according to Paul (see Heb. 9:4), it was kept in the Ark, beside the two tablets of stone and the pot of manna. There is no mention of any other receptacle. The statement in I Kings 8:9 implies that by Solomon's time these relics had disappeared. It is possible, however, for a different interpretation to be placed on Deut. 31:26, which may mean that the rod was kept beside the Ark, and not within it.

27 What was the name of Cain's wife?

The name of Cain's wife is nowhere mentioned in the Bible. Arab traditions are preserved in one of which she is called *Azura*, in another *Save*, but these are not seriously regarded by scholars.

28 Who was David's mother?

Her name is not given in Scripture. The reference to Abigail, one of the members of Jesse's family, in II Sam. 17:25, is frequently misunderstood. The Nahash there mentioned is either another name for Jesse or it refers to Nahash, king of Ammon, one of whose wives afterward became the wife of Jesse, as stated in the chronicles of the Jewish church.

29 Who named Eve?

Adam bestowed upon his companion the name of "Eve" (Gen. 3:20).

30 What is the date of the great famine in Egypt?

Began approximately 1875 B.C.

31 When did Joseph come to Egypt?

Believed to be about 1895 B.C.

32 Was Ham the first black person?

Ham, one of the sons of Noah, was the progenitor of the black race (see Gen. 9:18-27).

33 What is the date of Jacob's journey to Egypt?

About 1874 B.C. Date of his death, 1857 B.C.

34 How many walls did Jerusalem have?

There were three walls about Jerusalem. The first was built by David and Solomon; the second, enclosing one of the northern sections of the city, was built by Uzziah, Jotham and Manasseh, and restored by Nehemiah; the third was built by Herod Agrippa, and was intended to enclose the hitherto unprotected suburbs which had grown out from the northern part of the city. According to Josephus, who is not always thoroughly reliable, the circumference of the city, evidently including all the sections enclosed by the three walls he describes, was thirty-three stadia, a little less than four English miles.

35 What is the origin of the name "Jew"?

The appellation "Jew" is derived from the patriarch Judah, and was originally applied to all members of that tribe and also to subjects of the separate kingdom of Judah, in contradistinction to the seceding ten tribes, who retained the name of Israelites. During the captivity and ever since, the term "Jew" seems to have been applied indiscriminately to the whole race.

36 Who were the kings of Judah in succession?

The names of the kings of Judah in their canonical order are: Rehoboam, Abijah, Asa, Jehoshaphat, Jehoram, Ahaziah, Athaliah (queen), Joash, Amaziah, Uzziah, Jotham, Ahaz, Hezekiah, Manasseh, Amon, Josiah, Jehoahaz, Jehoiakim, Jehoiachin, Zedekiah.

37 What was manna?

It is supposed that the manna of the Israelites was a saccharine exudation of a species of tamarisk, the sap of which was set flowing by an insect. Several trees yield manna, as the flowering ash of Sicily and the eucalyptus of Australia. In India a sweet exudation comes from the bamboo, and a similar substance is obtained from the sugar-pine and common reed of our own country.

38 What is the meaning of "Mizpah"?

Mizpah, or Mizpeh, was the name of several localities in Old Testament history. The word means "a watch-tower," and in literature the whole of the beautiful remark made by Laban to Jacob (Gen. 31:49) has been included in its meaning: "The Lord watch between me and thee when we are absent one from the other."

39 Who was Moses' Ethiopian wife?

Commentators hold that the Ethiopian (or Cushite) woman mentioned in Num. 12 as the wife of Moses, against whom Aaron and Miriam complained, was Zipporah. Their opposition is believed to have been caused by jealousy of her relatives and their influence.

40 What became of Moses' rod?

There is nothing to show what became of Moses' rod. Aaron's rod, however, is said (in Heb. 9:4) to have been preserved in the sacred Ark of the Jews along with the tables of the law and the pot of manna.

41 What was the name of Potiphar's wife?

Her name is not given in the Bible, although it has been preserved in tradition. The Koran gives her name as Zuleika, and certain Arab writers call her Raïl.

42 What two Bible chapters are alike?

The two chapters in the Bible that are alike are II Kings 19 and Isa. 37. Both are regarded as the work of Isaiah, relating a series of events which in one book are placed in their proper historical setting and in the other find their true place among the prophecies.

43 Was Sarai a relative of Abram?

In Gen. 20:12 Abram speaks of Sarai as his halfsister, the daughter of the same father, but not the same mother. The common Jewish tradition referred to by Josephus (*Antiquities* 1, 6, 6) and also by Jerome, is that Sarai was identical with Iscah (see Gen. 11:29), daughter of Haran and sister of Lot, who is called Abraham's "brother."

44 What is the meaning of *selah*?

The word "Selah," which occurs a number of times in the Psalms, was a musical or liturgical sign, whose meaning is unknown. Some regard it as a pause in the music, to mark a transition in the theme or composition. It seems to have no grammatical connection with the sentence after which it appears, and has therefore nothing to do with the meaning of the passage. It was a note to the singers of the psalm, or to those who were accompanying the singing with instruments.

45 What was the fate of Amalek?

The Amalekites were a wicked, oppressive war-like and cruel people. They were powerful and influential and possessed cities in the south of Canaan. (See I Sam. 15:18; Judg. 10:12; Num. 24:7.) They were the first to oppose Israel (Exo. 17:8); Saul overcame them (I Sam. 14:48); David invaded their land (I Sam. 30:1-2), and what was left of them was completely destroyed during the reign of Hezekiah (I Chron. 4:41-43)

46 Who were called "the children of Lot"?

The Ammonites were so called (Deu. 2:19). They were a cruel, covetous, proud, reproachful, vindictive, superstitious and idolatrous nation (see Amos 1:13; Zep. 2:10; Eze. 25:3, 6; Judg. 10:6; Jer. 27:3). Their chief city was Rabbah (II Sam. 12:26-27), where they were governed by hereditary kings (II Sam. 2:20-21). They had various encounters with Israel. With the Philistines they oppressed Israel for eighteen years (Judg. 10:6-9). Saul suceeded against them as did David, and Joab overcame them (I Sam. 11:11; II Sam. 10:7-14) . Solomon intermarried with them and introduced their idols into Israel (I Kin. 11:1-5).

47 Who were the Amorites?

They were one of the seven nations of Canaan and were governed by many independent kings (Josh. 5:1; Josh. 9:10). They originally inhabited a mountain district in the south (Num. 13:29), but later acquired an extensive tract from Moab, east of Jordan (Num. 21:26, 30). They had many strong cities (Num. 32:17, 33). They were profane, wicked and idolatrous (Gen. 15:16; Josh. 24:15). They interfered with Israel (Num. 21:21) at times, again were peaceful, but were finally brought into bondage by Solomon (I Kin. 9:20-21).

48 Where was the first altar built?

In Genesis 8:20 we find the first reference to an altar, namely that one on which Noah offered his sacrifice to God for deliverance from the danger of the Flood. Armenian tradition says it was built on Mount Ararat.

49 What language was spoken at Babel?

The tower of Babel is always an interesting subject for discussion. Philologists are divided concerning the language spoken before the "Confusion of Tongues" at Babel. What little we know of it is learned at second-hand from the testimonies of classical authorities. The Babylonians called the locality of Babel "Barsip" (the Tower of Tongues). A French expedition to Mesopotamia found a clay cake or tablet, which showed that the language at some indefinitely remote period was written in the form of signs and hieroglyphics; but even this was probably long after the dispersion at Babel. What universal language was spoken by prehistoric man thousands of years ago will probably never be definitely known. It may have been Babylonian or Arabic in character, but this is mere conjecture. Supplementary to the Bible record, there are many traditions preserved concerning the Tower and its fate, and these mostly claim for it a Babylonian origin, holding that Babylonia was the cradle of the human race. The site of the tower, according to modern opinion, is identified as *Birs Nimrud*, a huge mound covering gigantic ruins and situated at Felujiah in Mesopotamia; but this identification is by no means certain.

50 What was the cause of the Babylonian captivity of Judah?

The political cause of the captivity was the repeated revolt of Judah against the power of Babylon. Relying on the help of Egypt, the king broke his promise of fidelity and refused to pay the tribute he had promised to pay. The prophets uttered many warnings against this suicidal course, and still more against the idolatry and accompanying immorality which prevailed. They assured the nation that, beset as Judah was by dangers from her powerful neighbors, she would be safe, if only she would be faithful to God. But the king and people were continually forsaking him and turning to evil courses, until at last God gave them up to their enemies. This was the spiritual cause of the captivity. The neglect of the Sabbatic years, mentioned II Chronicles 36:21, was only one of many provocations. The writer mentions it incidentally, to show that what the people would not do voluntarily, was done when they were carried away and the land rested seventy years.

51 Why was God angry with Balaam?

You need to read the entire story in Numbers 22 to get a complete idea of the situation. Balaam was in the first instance forbidden to go. That answer should have been sufficient for Balaam, but when the princes came with alluring offers of gifts and office and honors, he bade them remain to see whether there might be any fresh instructions. He obviously hoped that permission would be given. He showed his ignorance of God's ways in supposing that Barak's gifts and promises could make any difference to God's decision. His answers to the men also showed that he would like to comply if God would let him. Probably, too, God read in his mind an intention to pronounce the curse for which Barak was willing to pay. Hence the warning by the way, which would brace up his wavering resolution to utter the word of the Lord even if it was disagreeable to Barak.

**52 In what language was the message
      on the wall of Belshazzar written?**

The words, as they are found in Daniel, are pure Chaldee, and if they appeared in the Chaldean characters on the wall, might have been read by any person present who understood the alphabet of the Babylonian language. Authorities differ as to the language in which the famous *Mene, Mene, Tekel, Upharsin* appeared. Dr. Hales suggests that it may have been in primitive Hebrew; Josephus implies that it was in Greek. Another explanation is that while the observers may have been familiar with the language, its meaning or signification may have been hidden from them, until explained by the prophet.

53 What are the essential facts about Cain?

The Genesis narrative tells us that the Lord had no respect for Cain's offering, as he had that of Abel, his brother's. The reason for this must have been a wrong spirit in Cain (Gen. 4:3-7). Verse 7 states: "If thou doest well, shalt thou not be accepted? And if thou doest not well sin lieth at the door." There have been many interpretations suggested for the last part of this verse; but whatever translation may be given the specific words, the whole narrative implies that the trouble with Cain was with his motive. He did not come humbly, worshipfully, as Abel did, and probably his offering was less costly, less of a real sacrifice. Again, it has been thought that in the acceptance of the animal sacrifice and the rejection of the fruit sacrifice there was a suggestion of the fact that sin requires death for an atonement. Abel's was the first of the long line of offerings for sin in which blood was shed, culminating in the sacrifice of Christ's body on the cross.

The mark upon Cain has been a fertile subject of conjecture among Biblical scholars. Some hold that it was probably a sign given to Cain as assurance that no man should kill him, but the nature of the sign, and whether it was something perceptible to others, are left in uncertainty. One commentator suggests that it may have been an aspect of such ferocity that he became an object of horror and avoidance.

Lastly, the question is asked about the land of Nod, to which Cain was banished after the murder of Abel and where he found his wife. The land of Nod means simply "land of exile." We may gather from Gen. 4:14-15 that at the time referred to, the human family had multiplied considerably. Cain's wife was doubtless some blood relative, probably a sister. An ancient Arab tradition states that her name was Azura. From the account in Genesis, we may conjecture that although only four persons are mentioned in the sacred narrative up to this point, the human race had increased rapidly (Josephus says that the Jews held a tradition that Adam had thirty-three sons and twenty-three daughters). Cain's fear of punishment may therefore have been directed toward his own relatives.

54 How many of the children of Israel entered Canaan?

The number of adults over twenty years of age who left Egypt is stated in Exodus 12:37, at about six hundred thousand. Allowing the normal proportion of children to such a host we may infer that the total number was probably between one and two millions. Three or four months later, when they were at Sinai, a more careful count was made and the number of adults is then given (Ex. 38:26) at 603,550. Two years later another census was taken and the number is stated (Num. 2:32) at exactly the same figure, but as the Levites were not included and there were 22,000 of them, we may assume that by that time the adults numbered about 625,000. Thirty-eight years later, immediately after a pestilence had swept away 'arge numbers and just before entering Canaan, another census was taken. The figures are given (Numbers 26:21) at 601,730, which shows a slight decrease. Of these only two— Joshua and Caleb—were left of the adults who crossed the Red Sea. With these exceptions, the entire adult generation died in the wilderness.

55 What was the sin of the Canaanites?

The Canaanites were descendants of Ham (Gen. 10:6) and comprised seven distinct nations (Deu. 7:1). Though great and mighty (Num. 73:28) they were idolatrous, superstitious, profane and wicked (Deu. 29:17, Deu. 18:9-11, Lev. 18:21). They had many strong cities (Num. 13:28). Israel was warned against making league or intermarrying with them or following their idols or customs (Deu. 7:2; Jos. 23:12, Ex. 23:24; Lev. 18:26, 27). They were partially subdued by Israel (Josh. 10, Josh. 11, Judg. 1). Some of their descendants were still found in the time of Jesus (Matt. 15:22; Mark 7:26).

56 Can the approximate date of creation be established?

An ever fruitful topic is the date of Creation. The chronology which one finds in the marginal columns of many of the older Bibles, notably in the Authorized Version of King James, is not a part of the Bible itself by any means. It is the work of Archbishop Ussher, an illustrious prelate of the Irish Church, who lived 1580-1656. His chronological labors were directed towards affording an idea of the time that elasped between certain events in recorded history. For this purpose he took the year 1 A.D. the beginning of the Christian era as his starting point, and reckoned backwards as far as reliable recorded history afforded good working ground. He reckoned as far back as 4,000 years before Christ, and then finding no more available material in the form of history, either written or inscribed, he had necessarily to stop. He did not by any means imply, however, nor are his figures interpreted by Biblical scholars to mean, that he had reached the point of Creation. On the contrary, he had simply gone as far as recorded history enabled him to go. The Mosaic books in the Old Testament did not claim, in any sense, that the world was created in 4,000 B.C. The first line, first verse, and first chapter of Genesis distinctly tells us that "in the beginning" God created the heaven and the earth. Moses was educated at the court Egypt and imbibed all that was worth learning of the Egyptian civilization, which was old even at that date. But before Egypt there had been still older kingdoms and civilizations. Any one looking up the history in any good encyclopedia of Babylonia, Phoenicia, Chaldea and other ancient nations will form some idea of the great antiquity of that portion of the world's history which has not yet been definitely written. In the last century, the world has yielded up many of its secrets to excavators, and consecrated scholarship has made unquestioned discoveries, which are accepted by all the churches, showing that recorded time must now be pushed back to a period at least 2,000 years earlier than Ussher's computation. How far beyond this we have to travel to get at the date of Creation is as much a conjecture as ever. Science tells us that countless ages may have passed in the early stages of the world's geological development; and even before man appeared on the scene. It is true that scientists differ in this as they do in many other things, but the essential fact remains that the world is far older by many thousands of years than our forefathers supposed. We have better light on the subject than they had, and yet in no vital sense does that light conflict with the words of Scripture "in the beginning." In the New Testament also the same identical language is used at the opening of John's Gospel, chapter 1, verse 1, "In the beginning was the Word." Thus we see in both dispensations, the old and the new, a recognition of the fact that the date of the world's creation is far beyond man's computation.

57 How much time was consumed in the work of creation?

Many have asked: "How long did it take God to create the world and what was the order in which the various beings and things were brought forth?" There are many theories propounded concerning Creation. Some interpreters contend that the Bible account should be taken as meaning literal days, while others, remembering that a day is as a thousand years in God's sight, interpret them as meaning periods of indefinite duration. This problem has been a theme of endless discussion and science is powerless to decide it. The first three days of Creation comprise the inorganic era and the last three days the organic era. The first two chapters of Genesis are repetitive of the story of Creation, the first seven verses of chapter 2 reciting more briefly what was already stated in the first chapter in a somewhat different literary form. As to the order in which Creation proceeded, we have nothing else to guide us than Genesis and the order there given is: first day, light (general); second day, earth and water divided; third day, land and water outlined and vegetation created; fourth day, light (direct); fifth day, lower animals created; sixth day, mammals and man created; seventh day, rest.

As to the length of time between the Creation of Adam and of Eve, that is one of the disputed points on which no one can speak conclusively. Theorizing is futile and traditions (such as some found in Jewish literature) do not avail.

58 Was David justified in ordering Solomon to have Joab and Shimei executed?

Dean Stanley, strange to say, avers that in the order given to Solomon (I Kings 2:5-9) King David "bequeathed a dark legacy of long cherished vengeance." Dr. Terry's view seems more probable, that "this dying charge was not the offspring of personal revenge, but a measure of administrative wisdom." "David," says Wordsworth, "does not mention among Joab's sins that which caused him personally the most poignant grief, the murder of Absalom." He dwells on the fact that Joab had treacherously slain Abner and had also assassinated Amasa, shedding the blood of war in peace. Shimei had blasphemously insulted the royal majesty of Israel. David, it is true, had sworn to spare Shimei, but this oath was not binding on Solomon. David seems to feel that he had been too lax in punishing crime. His own guilt, though repented of, may have made him feel that the son of Zeruiah, in particular, was too strong for him. Hence this charge to Solomon as keeper of God's law and guardian of the kingdom's safety. In one sense, the execution of these men may be looked upon as an act of retributive justice (they being the enemies of the king), yet in the view of some commentators, the personal vindictiveness that David cherished in the matter, and the absence of a disinterested purpose to secure justice and the welfare and security of Israel, his kingdom, call for condemnation of David in his instructions to his son.

59 Were Daniel's companions in the lions' den his brothers?

In Dan. 1:6 the companions and Daniel are spoken of as the children of Judah. This means of the tribe of Judah. There is no evidence that they were brothers in the sense of blood relationship. Shadrach was the Chaldee name of Hananiah, the chief of the "three children," or young men of the tribe of Judah, who were Daniel's companions. He was taken captive with Daniel and a number of others at the first invasion of Judah by Nebuchadnezzar about B.C. 606. All four were young men of kingly bearing of the royal tribe of Judah and of superior understanding or education. Meshach was the Chaldee name given by the Babylonian court to Mishael, and Abednego was the name similarly bestowed on Azariah.

60 Who were King David's wives?

He had a number of wives, but those that are known chiefly to history are Abigail of Carmel (I Chron. 3:1); Michal, the daughter of Saul (II Sam. 3:13); and Bathsheba (I Chron. 3:5).

61 Why was King David "a man after God's own heart"?

This question has often been asked, both by scoffers and the serious. David, it is true, had fallen into deep sin many times; but his struggles, his remorse, his repentance, his efforts at reparation—these also must be considered. He lived in a rude and warlike age. His whole life, as one biographer says, was "the faithful struggle of an earnest human soul toward what was good and best—a struggle often baffled, yet never ended." This was the character of the man who was illustrious as soldier, shepherd, poet, king, prophet; who kindled patriotism, united Israel, and made it a great nation, and who drove out the worship of strange gods in the land. In view of all the blessings that came to the Hebrew race through David's reign; in view also of "the oath sworn unto David," and of the many evidences of his repentance and his trust in God, as expressed in the Psalms, his career must be regarded as a whole rather than judged of by specific acts, if we would try to find out how David in any degree merited the commendation which the sacred historians accord him.

62 From whom were the Edomites descended?

They were descendants of Esau. They inhabited a fertile and rich country specially given to them (Deu. 2:5; Gen. 27:39). Their country was traversed by roads though it was mountainous and rocky (Num. 20:17; Jer. 49:16). They were governed by dukes and later by kings (Gen. 36:15-30; Num. 20:14). In character they are said to have been wise, proud and self-confident, strong and cruel, vindictive, idolatrous and superstitious (Jer. 49:7, 16, 19; Eze. 25:12; II Chron. 25:14, 20; Jer. 27:3). They inhabited the cities of Avith, Pau, Bozrah, Teman and others. Though they were implacable enemies of Israel, it was forbidden to hate them (Deu. 23:7) or to spoil, and they might be received into the congregation in the third generation (Deu. 23:8). Saul made war against them and David conquered them (I Sam. 14:47; II Sam. 8:14). They took refuge in Egypt and returned after David's death (I King 11:17-22) when they confederated with Israel's enemies only to again be overthrown (2 Chron. 20:10) but finally aided Babylon against Judah (Psa. 137:7, Oba. 11).

63 What became of Elijah's body?

The bodies of Elijah and Enoch were doubtless changed or transformed as Paul describes in I Cor. 15:51, 52—the verses immediately following the well-known passage, that flesh cannot inherit the kingdom. They were changed into spiritualized bodies like in some degree that with which Christ rose from the dead. His resurrection body seemed to be made of flesh, but it was clearly different from that which he possessed before his death. All the redeemed, the saints who have died before Christ's coming and those who are alive when he comes, are promised these new "celestial" bodies for the heavenly life. These are the views of commentators who have discussed the subject.

64 Was there rain before the flood?

Read Genesis 2:4-6. This, according to some geologists, indicates that the earth, being then in a cooling condition, had no rain; and they also affirm that there may have been none until the great precipitation at the Flood cleared the atmosphere, and established new conditions. (See chapters 8 and 9.) Of course, these are merely scientific speculations or conjectures, but they are not opposed to Scripture.

65 What was the population of earth before
and after the flood?

All the information we have in Scripture concerning the population of the earth before the Flood is contained in Genesis chapters 4, 5 and 6. It is made clear in Gen. 5:4 that Adam had a numerous progeny. Jewish tradition says he had thirty-three sons and twenty-three daughters. Chapter 5:1 tells of the increased population. There must have been intermarriages. This is the view generally accepted by commentators, as the only reasonable explanation, where no other light can be had on the subject. The only record we have of the repopulation of the world after the Flood is that found in Genesis, ninth, tenth and eleventh chapters.

66 Was the rainbow visible before the flood?

There is no recorded evidence that a rainbow was visible from the earth before the Flood. Some commentators hold that the conditions described in Genesis 2:6, "But there went up a mist from the earth," etc., lasted until the atmospheric change wrought by the Flood and that the rainbow was a natural consequence of such change. This, however, despite the fact that scientific support is claimed for such view, is merely conjecture. The Bible (Gen. 9:13-17) is very clear to the effect that God established the rainbow at that time as "the token of the covenant" between Him and mankind and hence we need no conjecture.

67 How soon after Adam's fall did idolatry begin?

Adam and some of his descendants as late as the time of the Flood, are believed to have lived under a revealed system, in which, through their patriarchs and otherwise, they had a knowledge of God sufficient for their condition. Afterwards there arose the nature-worship, called *Fetishism*, consisting of the setting up and worshipping of animals, trees and stones, etc.—an idolatry invented by those who for their sins had been forsaken of God (Romans 1:28). There is no distinct mention in the Bible of any idols prior to the time of the Flood, but it is reasonable to suppose that idolatry was one of the abominations for which that terrible punishment was visited on the earth. The first positive indications of idolatry which appear in history are found in the worship of *Set* or *Sitekh* (equivalent to the Hebrew Patriarch, *Seth*), to whom divine honors were paid by the Egyptians. Some Jewish writers interpret Genesis 4:26 to mean that *Enos*, the son of *Seth*, was the originator of idolatry in that he paid divine honors to the host of heaven instead of to God alone.

68 What is known of the Hittites?

They were descendants of Canaan's son Heth. One of the seven Canaanitish nations, they dwelt in Hebron and were governed by kings (Deu. 7:1; Gen. 23:2, 3, 19; I Kin. 10:29). Their land was promised to Israel and it was commanded to destroy them; but Israel did not destroy them entirely (Deu. 7:1, 2, 24; Josh. 14:13; Judg. 3:5) . Among their prominent personages were Ephron, Ahimelech and Uriah (Gen. 49:30; I Sam. 26:6; II Sam. 11:6, 21). Esau, Solomon and many other Israelites intermarried with the Hittites. They were a warlike people and made many conquests.

69 What is known of the Hivites?

They formed one of the seven nations of Canaan, descended from Canaan (Gen. 10:15, 17). They dwelt near Lebanon. The Shechemites and Gibeonites were affiliated with them (Judg. 3:3; Gen. 34:2; Josh. 9:3-7). Esau intermarried with them. Their land was promised to Israel and it was commanded to destroy them (Deu. 7:1, 2, 24). In the reign of Solomon, a remnant of the Hivites was made tributary to Israel (I Kin. 9:20, 21).

70 Who were the Ishmaelites?

They were descendants of Ishmael, Abraham's son, and were divided into twelve tribes (Gen. 25:16; Gen. 16:15, 16). They were also called Hagarites, Hagarenes and Arabians (I Chron. 5:10; Psa. 83:6; Isa. 13:20). They were governed by kings, were rich in cattle and dwelt in tents (Jer. 25:24; Isa. 13:20; I Chron. 5:21). Though they were the merchants of the East and traveled around in large caravans (Gen. 37:25; Job 6:19), they were frequently lawless and would waylay and plunder travelers (Jer. 3:2). After harassing Israel, they were overcome by Gideon (Judg. 8:10-24; II Chron. 5:10; II Chron. 26:7). It would seem that later they became more peacefully inclined, as they sent presents to Kings Solomon and Jehoshaphat (I Kin. 10:15; II Chron. 17:11).

**71 When did the change in Jacob's
      spiritual nature occur?**

It began at Bethel but the change there was extremely slight. Jacob regarded his vision there very much as a business arrangement. If God would help him and give him bread to eat and bring him back safe, then God should be his God and he would give him a tenth of all. At Jabbok the crisis was much more far-reaching. He realized there his danger and his need of a blessing. He no longer bargained with God, he saw that his own strength was futile, he was a humble suppliant for God's favor. From that night on he was a different man, by no means perfect, but far better than before.

**72 Did Jephthah really offer up
      his daughter as a sacrifice?**

Both the Authorized and Revised Versions leave the question in doubt, and commentators have been divided in opinion as to whether she was sacrified or doomed to live the life of a recluse. Human sacrifices are an abomination unto the Lord. A new reading or translation which several notable scholars have urged as the correct one is: "It shall surely be the Lord's *or* I will offer up to him a burnt offering." Hebrew scholars declare this to be the more accurate rendering. (See Judges 11:30, 31, 39.) It changes the aspect of the case and makes Jephthah to say practically that if the first living thing that came forth from his house to meet him was one that would be unacceptable, then a burnt offering of an acceptable character would be substituted. This would lead to the conclusion that the daughter was not sacrificed, but condemned to a life of perpetual virginity and a burnt offering offered up in her stead. Several eminent writers, including Joseph Kinchi, Ben Gerson and Bechai (Jewish authorities) and a number of Christian authors, held that instead of being sacrificed she was shut up in a house specially prepared by her father and visited there by the daughters of Israel four days in a year as long as she lived. In support of this theory it is pointed out that the Hebrew term employed to express Jephthah's vow is the word *neder*, which means a "consecration" and not *che-rem*, which means "destruction."

73 Why do the Jews always face the east when praying?

In Jerusalem, the Jews always turned their faces toward the "holy hill" of the temple while praying (see Dan. 6:10; II Chron. 6:34). The Samaritans, on the contrary, faced Mt. Gerizim. In the court of the temple, the Jews in prayer faced the temple itself (see I Kings 8:38) to the Holy of Holies (see Ps. 5:8). Daniel, while praying in exile, opened his window toward Jerusalem (see Dan. 6:10). Modern Jews in Europe and America customarily face the East in prayer. It was a custom among the early Christians to face the East but that has long been discontinued. Mohammedans face in the direction of Mecca.

74 Will the Jews be restored to Palestine at Christ's second coming?

Students of prophecy are not agreed on the subject. The majority infer, from various passages, that they will be restored before the coming of Christ in the second stage of that coming. The first stage is thought to be in the air to summon those Christians who are looking for him, to meet him (see I Thess. 4:16, 17). The second stage is after the great tribulation when he comes to reign.

75 How often was Jerusalem destroyed?

The Holy City has been captured and recaptured many times by contending forces. In several of the sieges it has been partially ruined, but in at least four it has been practically destroyed, the first about 1400 B.C., when captured by the tribes of Judah and Simeon; the second in 586 by Nebuchadnezzar; the third in 170 B.C. by Antiochus Epiphanes; the fourth, and doubtless most terrible, in 70 A.D., by Titus. The city was restored by Hadrian in 135 A.D., and since then has changed hands many times. It now belongs to Turkey, and has about 60,000 inhabitants.

76 Why was the temple built in Jerusalem?

In II Sam. 24:16-25 we learn how the threshing floor of Araunah came to be chosen for the site of an altar of commemoration and sacrifice. Moreover, Scripture and Jewish tradition unite in pointing to that threshing floor as the spot upon which Abraham prepared to offer Isaac (although some eminent authorities have disputed this). Read also the account of the purchase of the site from Ornan (Araunah) in I Chron. 21:26-28; and in the next chapter (I Chron. 22:1, 9, 10) which shows how David had a divine revelation that his son should build the temple there.

77 Who was Job?

According to leading commentators, Job was a personage of distinction, wealth and influence who lived in the north of Arabia Deserta, near the Euphrates, some 1800 B.C. His life was patriarchal, his language the Hebrew of that early day, when it was interspersed with Syriac and Arabic. He lived before Moses. His book is probably the oldest book in the world. It is now interpreted as a public debate in poetic form, dealing with the Divine government. It abounds in figurative language. The "day" mentioned in Job 2:1 was one appointed for the angels to give an account of their ministry to God. Evil is personified in Satan, who also comes to make report. The question to Satan and his response are simply a dramatic or poetic form of opening the great controversy which follows.

78 Did God give Job into the hands
    of Satan to be tempted?

"Tempted" is scarcely the word to use in that case. Job was tried or tested. The question was what his motive was in serving God. Satan with his natural doubt about any one having pure motives, asserted that Job served God only for what he gained by it, and that if his property was taken away from him, he would curse God. So Job was put to the proof, to see what he would do under trial, and whether he was really as disinterested as God believed him to be. The object of the author appears to have been to correct a false view of adversity, which view was prevalent in his time. People had the idea that severe calamities were punishments dealt out by God because of sin. When a man of good moral character, therefore, was in trouble, people suspected that he had sinned secretly, and that God was punishing him for it. It was often a cruel and unjust suspicion. In writing this description, the author evidently was trying to eradicate it. After reading such a book, a man who saw another in trouble, instead of despising him as a sinner, might say, "Perhaps he is being tried as Job was," and so might sympathize instead of blaming him. Our concern should be to learn the lesson the book was designed to teach, rather than to discuss the question whether it is history or parable, for that question cannot now be authoritatively answered.

79 Did God "blot out" the day on which Job was born?

This question is doubtless prompted by the ancient tradition or superstition that we have less days in February than any other month, as Job was born in February. This of course is a fallacy. There was no February in the time of Job, 1520 B.C. The months, or divisions of time, were not as we have them now. The year of the Jews consisted of twelve lunar months of twenty-nine and thirty days alternately, a thirteenth being from time to time introduced to accommodate it to the sun and seasons. Let it be noted that while Job cursed his birthday, he did not curse his Maker, so why should the Lord drop a day on account of a little weakness in his servant, who, despite his great sufferings, never uttered any reproach against the Author of his being? Our months as at present, we have from the Romans. With those people February had originally twenty-nine days in an ordinary year, but when the Roman Senate decreed that the eighth month should bear the name of Augustus, a day was taken from February and given to August, which had then only thirty, that it might not be inferior to July, named in honor of Julius Caesar.

80 Are the speeches of Job's friends to be regarded as inspired?

This question is answered authoritatively in the book itself (see Job 42:7), where God is represented as saying, "My wrath is kindled against thee and thy two friends; for ye have not spoken of me the thing that is right." One gets a clearer idea of the book by regarding it as a symposium on the problem of suffering, each speaker being a representative of a school of thought. Each speaker keeps to the same aspect of the subject but all agree in regarding unusual suffering as an evidence of unusual sin. They imply that in Job's case, he being outwardly so good a man, his sin was aggravated by hypocrisy. This was unjust, because, as we learn by the first chapter, it was precisely because he was so good a man that his affliction came upon him. The author of the book evidently wished to administer a warning to the people of his time against being uncharitable in their inferences.

81 Is the Book of Job real history or a dramatic allegory?

Job is believed to have been a real personage—a type of the earliest patriarchs, a man of high intelligence and great faith. The story is cast in dramatic form. Professor S. S. Curry, of Yale and Harvard Divinity

Schools, thus outlines it: the place, a hill outside the city; a rising storm, flashing lightning, rolling thunder and a rainbow; the speakers, God, the patriarch Job, his friends, and Satan; the theme, the mystery of human suffering, and human existence." To which may be added, a sublime faith in the divine wisdom, righteousness and justice. The book of Job is regarded by the highest Bible scholarship as a spiritual allegory. The name Job is derived from an Arabic word signifying "repentance," although Job himself is held to be a real personage. (See Ezek. 14:14 and James 5:11.)

82 Why did the wicked kings of Judah let their sons pass through fire?

It was a heathen form of worship to Molech, Milcom or Chemosh, which the Israelites had borrowed or adapted from the Moabites and Amnonites. Human sacrifices were made in high places to Molech. The chief interpreters Jarchi, Kimchi and Maimonides wrote that in the worship of Molech, the children were not burned, but were made to pass before two burning pyres as a purificatory rite. It is quite clear, however, that in many cases lives were actually sacrificed (see Psalm 106:37, 38; Jer. 7:31). It was assumed that by this rite the victims were purged from dross of the body and attained union with the deity.

83 Who were the "lost tribes"?

The "lost tribes," so-called, were the Jews carried into captivity by Shalmaneser (II Kings 17:6), and chiefly belonging to Israel or the ten tribes. Many theories as to their location and their descendants have been ventilated, and they have been successively located (by ingenious investigators) in Hindustan, Tartary, China, Africa, Great Britain and among the aborigines of North America. More reasonable conjectures hold that while some returned after the exile, and others were left in Samaria, many remained in Assyria and afterward joined with the Jews in forming colonies throughout the East, so that, in a certain sense, they shared the ultimate history of their brethren of Judah.

84 What secular evidence have we of the fate of Lot's wife?

The pillar which is mentioned in the story concerning the fate of Lot's wife, in Genesis 19, is referred to by a number of writers. Josephus (in *Antiquities* I, 11, 4) wrote that it still remained in his day, and he had seen it—*i.e.*, the peculiar formation of crumbling, crystalline rock associated by tradition with the event. Clemens Romanus, Irenaeus and Benjamin of Tudela also wrote of the strange formation as visible in their day, but later writers stated that it had ceased to exist. It is related that, by a singular coincidence, Lieutenant Lynch, who led an

American exploring party around the Dead Sea, found on the southwestern shore, at a place called by the Arabs Usdum, a pillar some forty feet high, composed of salt crystals, capped with carbonate of lime, which he assumed to have been detached by the action of the winter rains upon the rock-salt hills. Professor Palmer claims in one of his books to have seen this same formation, which the Arabs, in their usual manner, had connected with the Bible story, although it is not at all certain that the locality is identical with that indicated in Genesis. Several commentators hold that the geological character of the rocks and the prevalence of salt crystals justify the conclusion that the Bible passage might be interpreted to mean "*like* a pillar of salt," and that the body of Lot's wife "had become fixed for a time to the soil by saline or bituminous incrustations."

85 Who and what was Melchisedek?

It is in the fourteenth chapter of Genesis that Melchisedec is historically presented to us. The incident and its record, although so brief, and standing in such singular isolation from the thread of the history which it interrupts, is not only in itself most striking and interesting, but also in its typical teaching profoundly instructive. How suddenly and altogether unexpectedly does Melchisedec here appear before us—a most kingly and majestic form, yet clad in priestly robes, and with the mystic emblems of eucharistic offering—bread and wine—in his hands. We see those priestly hands raised in blessing; we observe the great patriarch, Abraham—the father of the faithful and the Friend of God—bowing before the mysterious priest-king, and presenting to him the tithes of all his spoil; and then, as abruptly as it appeared, the vision passes away, and for nearly a thousand years the voice of inspiration utters not again the name of Melchisedec. Then, however, in an ecstatic Psalm of a most distinctly Messianic character, and descriptive of our Lord's exaltation in the day of his power, we meet with it once more in the solemn declaration: "The Lord hath sworn and will not repent, thou art a priest forever, after the order of Melchisedec (Ps. 110:4). Again, something like a thousand years pass away, and then, once more, the writer of the Epistle to the Hebrews take up the subject of this mysterious personage, who, "Without father, without mother, without genealogy, having neither beginning of days, or end of life; but made like unto the Son of God; abideth a priest continually" (Heb. 7:3); and on the two brief references to him, above given, which are all that the Scriptures contain, founds an argument to show the superiority of Christ's priesthood, as being "after the order of Melchisedec," to that of Aaron, or Levi, which it had superseded.

Who was Melchisedec? Much labor has been wasted in attempts to answer the question. Later Jewish tradition identified him with Shem;

and it is certain that that patriarch was not only alive in the days of Abraham, but even continued to live till Jacob was fifty years old. (Compare Gen. 11:11 with verses 12:26, 21:5, 25:7-26.) According to others he belonged to the family of Ham, or of Japheth; and it has been said that this is necessarily implied by the language of the Apostle when drawing a parallel between Melchisedec and Christ, he says that our Lord belonged to "a tribe of which no man gave attendance at the altar." Some, again, have suggested that he was an incarnate angel, or other superhuman creature, who lived for a time among men. Others have held that he was an early manifestation of the Son of God; and a sect, called the Melchisedecians, asserted that he was "an incarnation of the Holy Ghost." But, in all these conjectures, the fact has been strangely overlooked that the reticence of Scripture on the point is typical and significant, for, could it be determined who Melchisedec really was, it could no longer be said that he was "Without father, without mother, without genealogy"; which statement is to be understood, not as implying that he was not a natural descendant of Adam, but that he designedly appears and disappears in the sacred narrative without mention either of his parentage or death.

There can, however, be no question that, whoever Melchisedec may have been, he was an eminent type of Christ. This is placed beyond doubt, not only by the language of the 110th Psalm—the Messianic character of which has ever been recognized by Jews and Christians alike—but especially by the argument of the Apostle, in the seventh chapter of the Epistle to the Hebrews, in the course of which there occurs the explicit declaration that he was—in the various respects mentioned—"made like unto the Son of God."

86 Who were the Moabites?

They were the descendants of Lot and were neighbors of the Amorites on the opposite side of the River Arnon (Num. 21:13). They were governed by kings and possessed many great cities (Num. 21:28-30; Is. 15-1; Num. 23:7). They were proud, arrogant, idolatrous, superstitious, rich, confident and prosperous. They were mighty men of war (Is. 16:6; I Kin. 11:7; Jer. 27:3; Jer. 48:7, 11, 14). The Amorites deprived them of a large part of their territory (Num. 21:26). The Moabites refused to let Israel pass through their country and were so greatly impressed and alarmed by the multitude of the Israelitish host that, with Midian, they sent Balaam to curse it (Num. 22 to 24). Subsequently, Israel was enticed into their idolatry and even intermarried with them. They were always hostile to Israel until Saul subdued them (I Sam. 14:47) and were later made tributary to David and the Jewish kings (II Sam. 8:2-12; II Kin. 3:4), but finally joined Babylon against Judah (II Kin. 24:2).

87 Why did Moses strike the rock?

The account in Num. 20 very clearly shows that Moses disobeyed the divine command in striking the rock as he did. For the moment he apparently lost his faith, and his temper as well. He had been explicitly instructed to "speak unto the rock" (verse 8) instead of which he addressed the people in hasty and passionate words and smote the rock twice. (See Ps. 106:32, 33.) His whole attitude betrayed his doubt not of God's power, but of his will to help a people who had been rebellious. Further, Moses was irreverent (see verse 12) in that his language and bearing detracted from the sanctity of the occasion and was therefore displeasing to God. He had been entrusted with a great enterprise and his perfect obedience to and implicit faith in God were indispensable. As the result showed, his failure involved serious consequences for the whole nation.

88 What was the dispute over Moses' body
between Michael and Satan?

The passage in Jude 1:9 referring to the dispute between Michael and Satan over the body of Moses, is regarded by Vitringa, Lardner, McKnight and other distinguished commentators as symbolical, "the body of Moses" being intended to represent the Mosaic law and institutions (see Zech. 3:1), in the same manner in which modern Christians call the Church "the body of Christ." According to others, it has reference to a Jewish legend connected with the secret burial of the great lawgiver (Deu. 34:6). The *Targum* of Jonathan attributes the burial of Moses to the hands of angels, led by Michael as the guardian of Israel. Other views set forth in the Hebrew books are that Satan disputed the burial, claiming the body because of the blood of the Egyptian whom Moses slew, and because of the leader's sin at Meribah. Having "the power of death," he opposes the raising of Moses' body again for these reasons, but the latter's visible presence with Enoch and Elijah at the Transfiguration gave evidence of Michael's triumph, and was also a pledge of the coming resurrection. Josephus, the Jewish historian (in *Antiquities* 4:8), states that God hid the body of Moses, lest it should be worshiped by the people.

89 Did Nebuchadnezzar literally eat grass?

We do not know any more on the subject than is related in the Bible. The natural inference from the narrative is that the king was temporarily deprived of his reason, and insane people often do things as unnatural as eating grass. There is nothing improbable in the Biblical statement. On the other hand, some authorities suggest that the narrative means nothing more than that the king left his palace and the cares of state

and lived the life of a peasant for seven years; or, as we might say, vege-
tated in rural seclusion; but the plain statement of the text is that generally accepted. Daniel 4:35-37 indicates that he became, at least
outwardly, a believer in the true God.

90 What were the dimensions
and material of Noah's ark?

According to the directions in Genesis 6:15, the Ark was 300 cubits
long, 50 cubits broad and 30 cubits high. Bible students have been
greatly puzzled over the length of the cubit, which seems to have varied
greatly in ancient times. It is evident, however (from Deu. 3:11), that it
was taken as a measure from the human body, and may have been
either from the wrist to the end of the third figure, or the entire length
of the lower or forearm, from the elbow to the wrist, or even from the
elbow to the finger-point. One authority, Celsus, says the cubit was
identified with the *ulna*, or under and larger of the two bones of the
arm. The Egyptian cubit, which the Hebrews may have taken, measured six hand-breadths and the Jewish rabbins (as the *Mishna* states)
assigned six hand-breadths to the Mosaic cubit, while Josephus says a
cubit was equal to two spans, the span being equal to three hand-
breadths. Ezek. 40:5, 43:13 speaks of the cubit "which was a cubit and a
hand-breadth" which was the Babylonian cubit. It would thus seem
that the Ark, though its size cannot be confidently stated, was a very
spacious vessel, probably exceeding 500 feet in length, fully 85 feet
broad and over 52 feet high. In 1609 Peter Jansen of Horn, in Holland,
built a vessel of these proportions and found that it would stow fully a
third more cargo than ships of its size built in the ordinary manner. It
had 3,600,000 cubic feet of space, and after nine-tenths had been assigned for food storage there was still room for 7,000 pairs of animals,
each with 50 cubic feet of space. It was, in fact, a huge floating storehouse, rather than a shlp.

As to the materials of which the Ark was built, we find in Genesis
6:14 that Noah is told to make an ark of "gopher" wood. There are various conjectures as to what kind of wood this was. Bunsen holds that it
was a wood found only in Egypt; Dietrich believes it was a heavy reed-
like growth; Gesenius affirms that it was pine, fir or cedar, and Bochart
says cypress. Chaldee translators declare it to have been the *sissu*, a
dark-colored wood of Arabian growth and highly valued. A majority
hold to the opinion that cypress was meant, on account of its enduring
qualities.

As to the time occupied in building it, much has been said but little
of real worth. The only Bible passage supposably referable to this question is Genesis 6:3. This passage is variously interpreted. By some it is
held to refer to a shortening of human life; by others it is interpreted as

meaning that the period stated would be further granted as a respite—an opportunity for repentance—failing which the divine presence (the Shecinah, which had hitherto continued at the gate of Eden) would be withdrawn from the world on account of its wickedness. The best answer is that nowhere is it stated in the Bible how long Noah was engaged in building the Ark. The Lord had offered a respite of 120 years, after the warning to the human race (see I Peter 3:20; II Peter 2:5), and it was during this period that Noah, who was a "preacher of righteousness," not only labored in the work of awakening the people to the enormity of their sin and of urging them to repentance, but also used a portion of that period in preparing the Ark for the emergency that would arise, if the people did not listen to his cry for repentance.

91 What were the "bitter herbs" used at the Passover?

Since endive, chicory, wild lettuce, or nettles, were important articles of food to the ancient Egyptians, it is likely that these were the bitter herbs of the Passover feast, more especially so, as they are at the present time eaten by the Jews in the East.

92 Were the patriarchs really as old as the Bible record states?

Some of the "higher critics" claim that the ancient calendar of the antediluvians made the year really a month, or lunar period. Others, with somewhat more reason, assert that a year was a season of growth equal to three of our months. Hensler and Hufeland, two German authorities, claim that the patriarchal year was three months till Abraham's time, eight months till Joseph's time, and thereafter twelve months. One eminent Bible scholar has pointed out that if we accept the monthly year theory, Mahalaleel's sixty-five years before the birth of his son Jared would make him a parent at five years and three months of our reckoning; Enoch would be the same age when his son Methuselah was born, and the ages of the other patriarchs at the birth of their children would be equally preposterous. Of course, such conclusions absolutely condemn the monthly year theory. Conditions among the antediluvians were totally different from those after the Flood. There had been no rain, and the sun and planets were not visible; in the moist atmosphere, growth was greatly stimulated and all natural conditions tended to animal and vegetable longevity, precisely as the Bible indicates. Besides, as that period produced animal types of giant proportions, created for strength and endurance, the analogy of nature would seem to demand that man should bear some harmonious proportion to his surroundings. Genesis 6:4 (first clause) clearly implies this. Age and stature, not only human but otherwise, became greatly diminished after the Flood.

93 Was Pharaoh drowned in the Red Sea?

All the evidence is against the theory that he was drowned in the Red Sea. Some very interesting information, furnishing striking confirmation of the Bible narrative, has recently been obtained, by deciphering the inscriptions on ancient Egyptian monuments. From these it appears that the Pharaoh who "refused to let the people go" was named Menephthah. He was the youngest son of the great Pharaoh, Rameses II, the Pharaoh who oppressed the Hebrews and ordered the killing of the male infants, and whose death is mentioned in Exodus 2:23. Menephthah was an old man, at least sixty, when he came to the throne, and was constitutionally timid and feeble. He joined with him in the government his brilliant son Seti, a young man resembling in person and character his grandfather, the great Rameses. Seti was virtually king though his father, Menephthah, was king in name. The Bible alludes to Seti as "the firstborn of Pharaoh who *sat on the throne*" (Ex. 12:29). This young man's tomb has been found, and a record of his achievements, showing him to have been a great general and administrator. But his name does not appear in the list of the Pharaohs and the inscription on his tomb shows that he never became king, but died suddenly, while still only a prince. The Bible tells us how he died. It was on the night when the angel slew the firstborn. Menephthah, as we know by the Bible narrative, pursued the Hebrews. He had no son now to take command as on former occasions. He was then an old man eighty-two years of age. What more likely than that, when he saw the Israelites descend into the Red Sea, he should send on his army and stay behind himself, not caring at his age, and at night, to undertake so perilous a journey. The Egyptian records state that once before, on the eve of battle, when he should have led his army, the old man had a convenient vision, ordering him not to enter the battle but to give the command to his son. He doubtless excused himself on this occasion and so saved his life. A parallel case of a father and son reigning simultaneously is found in Belshazzar, who, though exercising kingly functions, does not appear on the list of kings. He was associated in government with his father, Nabonnidus, and, like Seti in Egypt, died before his father.

94 What is meant by, "I will harden Pharaoh's heart"?

This expression in Exodus 7:3 has been a stumbling block to many. There is a point reached by those who have long persisted in wicked courses which is known as judicial blindness, a point at which—God's restraining spirit being withdrawn—they became unable to distinguish right from wrong or good from evil. They grow hardened and morally incorrigible. (See Mark 3:5; Rom. 11:25; II Cor. 3:14; Eph. 4:18.) Under such circumstances, the offender turns even blessings into sin by abusing them, and unless overtaken by some great adversity, continues in his course, blind to consequences. This was doubtless the case with Pharaoh. Egypt had sinned deeply, and so long as its rulers were unchecked by some stronger power, they would continue to sin. Pharaoh, long accustomed to the abuse of power, steeled himself against all sense of justice and mercy, and this the "permissive act of providence" allowed, in order that the culminating punishment should be the more severe. In other words, Pharaoh was permitted to go on in his sin, in order that his fate might be made an awful example to the whole world.

95 If God "hardened" Pharaoh's heart, was it possible for him to do otherwise than he did?

The true interpretation is that the divine message of warning and the plagues which followed were the occasion of Pharaoh's heart being hardened. Thus the expression which has been translated as "hardened," is, in Hebrew, "strong," implying that the influence of the events had been to make the king's heart stubborn or rebellious. (See Ex. 7:13, 14, 8:19, and 9:35.) Elsewhere in the same narrative the Hebrew expression is capable of being translated "made heavy" (as in Ex. 7:14 and 8:15 and 32, also Ex. 9:34). The passage in Exodus 7:23, which may be rendered as in the Authorized Version, and also as "he (Pharaoh) set his heart even to this," expresses the condition of Egypt's ruler, who had set his face like a flint against Jehovah, and was alternately depressed and defiant, but not repentant.

96 Who were the Philistines?

Their origin is nowhere expressly stated in the Bible; but since the prophets describe them as "the Philistines from Caphtor" (Amos 9:7), and "the remnant of the maritime district of Caphtor" (Jer. 47:4), it is probable that they were the "Caphtorim which came out of Caphtor," and who expelled the Avim from their lands and occupied them (Deu. 2:23), and that they were the Caphtorim mentioned in the Mosaic genealogical table among the descendants of Mizraim. There is equal authority for believing Caphtor to have been the island of Cyprus, or a land somewhere between Egypt and Ethiopia, or a part of Northern Egypt. Some have claimed that Caphtor and the modern island of Crete are identical; but the best authorities do not agree with this conclusion.

97 Who wrote the poetical books of Proverbs and Psalms?

Some ancient authorities, rabbins and others attribute Proverbs to Solomon; others hold that it has a composite origin and is the work of a number of writers. The ablest modern critics hold the latter opinion. It is probable that Solomon was the author of the portion beginning with the first verse of the tenth chapter and ending with the sixteenth verse of the twenty-second chapter. As we learn from the first verse of the twenty-fifth chapter, the collection of proverbs extending to the end of the twenty-ninth chapter was also attributed to him, but was not compiled until 250 years after his death. The remainder of the book appears to be composed of six portions by different hands at different periods. One of these is the introduction, which occupies the first nine chapters. This was probably written by the man who compiled the whole book, but whose name is unknown.

The Book of Psalms (which is the Psalter of the Hebrews) has many authors, the principal one being David. Some are attributed to Hezekiah, Josiah, and Zerubbabel, two (the 72nd and 127th) to Solomon, several to the Levites and the Asaphites, one, at least, to Jeduthun, eleven to the sons of Korah, one to Ethan (Psalm 89), while many are of uncertain authorship. Moses is given by tradition as the author of Psalm 90, being the only contribution of which his authorship is reasonably certain. The Psalms cover a period of a thousand years. They were composed at different remote periods, by various poets; David, the most prolific contributor, being indicated as the author of seventy-three Psalms in the Hebrew text and eleven in the Septuagint.

98 What figure is conveyed by the words "Rachel weeping for her children"?

The passage in Matthew 2:18 relates to the Babylonian captivity. Rachel, the wife of Jacob, and mother of Joseph and Benjamin, is figuratively represented as rising from the tomb and lamenting over the loss of her children. Ramah in Benjamin was a scene of pillage and massacre in Jeremiah's time (see Jer. 31:15), and hence is chosen by the prophet in his figurative scene of lamentation.

99 What was the width of the Red Sea at the point where Israel crossed?

It is generally held by a majority of writers and travelers that the passage was made at Ras Atakah Point, about six miles south of Suez, and opposite the southern end of Jebel Atakah. At Ras Atakah, the land runs out in the form of a promontory for fully a mile into the sea beyond the regular shore line. Beyond this, there is a shoal for nearly a mile more, over which the water at low tide is usually about fourteen feet deep. Beyond this, and before the true channel or center is reached, there are two other comparative shoals; the channel itself is somewhere about fifty feet deep and three-quarters of a mile wide. There is another succession of shoals on the eastern shore. The distance from shore to shore is about five and a half miles.

100 From where did the Queen of Sheba come?

It is supposed by well-informed authorities that she came from Yemen, in Arabia Felix. In Matthew 12:42 she is referred to as the "Queen of the South," who came from "the uttermost parts of the earth," a term applied by the ancients to southern Arabia. Not improbably she was a lineal descendant of Abraham by Keturah, whose grandson, Sheba, peopled that part of the then known world. The Arabic account of this queen gives her the name of Bilkis or Yelkamah, a monarch of the Himyerites; but their account is probably more legendary than accurate as to detail.

101 What problems did the Queen of Sheba
pose to prove the wisdom of Solomon?

The Bible here gives us no clue but tradition has preserved some of the questions which she is said to have put to Solomon to test his wisdom. These, we believe, are principally found in the Talmudical writings. It is said she introduced a party of children all dressed alike, and asked the king to tell which were boys and which girls. King Solomon ordered vessels to be brought that the children might wash their hands. The girls rolled up their sleeves, but the boys plunged their hands into the water at once, and were easily detected by the king. The queen next ordered her attendants to set before Solomon a number of beautiful bouquets and asked him to indicate which were the real flowers and which the false. Solomon ordered the keeper of his gardens to bring in a hive of bees, and they almost instantly settled upon the natural flowers and began to extract the sweets from them, leaving the artificial flowers untouched. Other traditions illustrative of Solomon's wisdom are told by the ancient writers.

102 What was the chief sin of King Saul
(I Samuel 13:13, 14)?

His chief sin was disobedience. Samuel, the recognized representative of God in the nation, had commanded him to wait till he arrived in Gilgal, saying he would come in seven days. Saul did not wait till the end of the seventh day, thereby showing an impatient and disobedient spirit. God demands that men obey Him implicitly. "To obey is better than sacrifice," Samuel said to Saul on another occasion of his disobedience. Probably, also, Saul had no right to conduct the ritual of sacrifice. As to Samuel's doing so, he may simply have ordered it done, directing Eleazar the priest to conduct the ceremony; or his office of prophet may have given him the authority to act also as priest. Furthermore, though not a descendant of Aaron, he belonged to the priestly tribe of Levi.

103 Why were "shepherds" an abomination to the Egyptians?

The reason of the Egyptian hatred of the shepherds is a historic one. The Hyksos or Shepherd Kings, hundreds of years before Joseph's time, had invaded and conquered Lower Egypt and ruled the Delta, although they never occupied the whole country. They came from the East and were probably Arabians, and are represented as having been a cruel and arrogant race, who subjected the Egyptians to great hardships. (See Gen 46:34.) They were finally driven out of the country by a coalition of forces under several kings. They were probably called Shepherds because of the simplicity of their life, which was largely pastoral and semi-barbaric. Manetho, the Egyptian historian, says that they were the builders of Jerusalem, but his reference is probably to the Canaanites rather than the Jews. Some writers suggest that they were the progenitors of the Bedouins, and that the Amalekites, Midianites, and other hostile nations who opposed the Israelites after the Exodus were also descended from the stock of the expelled Shepherds. It is not improbable that the Philistines may also have been a branch of the same Shepherd family.

104 Who were the Sidonians?

These people were descendants of Sidoa, a son of Canaan, and were formerly a part of the Phoenician nation (Matt. 15:21, 22; Mark 7:24, 26). They dwelt on the sea-coast in the cities of Zidon and Zarephath (Josh. 11:8; I Kin. 17:9; Luke 4:26), and were governed by kings. In character they were careless, idolatrous, superstitious, wicked and unpenitent (Judg. 18:7; I Kin. 11:5; Jer. 27:3-9; Matt. 11:21, 22). Their business was commerce and of course they were skillful sailors (Is. 23:2; Eze. 27:8). They supplied the Jews with timber, who in turn supplied them with provisions (I Chron. 22:4; Acts 12:20; Eze. 27:17). Although they were hostile and oppressive to God's people, Solomon and Abijah intermarried with them, and Israel followed the Sidonian idolatry (Judg. 10:12; Eze. 28:22-24; I Kin. 11:1, 16:31).

105 What is known of the city of Sodom outside the Bible?

Comparatively little. Sodom was a small but populous country, and according to Josephus (*Antiquities*, chapter 9, book 1) was rich and flourishing, with five kings controlling its affairs and with a certain degree of ancient civilization. Doubtless they were idolaters, but they had an opportunity, through the presence of Lot and his household, of knowing the true God. In chapter 11, book 1 of the *Antiquities* the historian tells of their great wealth and pride, their injustice toward men, their impiety and peculiar vices. So persistent were they in wickedness that the overthrow of their chief city and the destruction of the people came upon them as a punishment.

**106 Can any spiritual lesson be drawn
from Solomon's song?**

Undoubtedly, as from every other part of the Bible. The difficulties in regard to it arise from the various views as to its plan and purpose. No less than sixteen of these have been advanced by expositors. Three only, however, have commended themselves to any large number of Bible students. One of them regards it as the yearning of God's people, when separated from the Temple and the ordinances of the Jewish service. A second view is that it represents, under the image of an intense love, the relation of Christ and his people. Paul uses the same symbol in Eph. 5:22-23. This was evidently the view taken by the men who put the headings to the chapters in the King James Version of the Bible, which headings have been discarded in the Revised Version. The third view is the literal, which is taken by modern scholars and is growing in favor. It is that the poem celebrates the trials and triumph of a country maiden, who when carried away from her humble home and her rustic lover to become an inmate of the king's harem, rejects with scorn the magnificence and luxury offered her and remains faithful to her lover, with whom she returns. The lesson is obvious. It is the lesson of a fidelity to truth and righteousness which no offer of wealth and luxury can disturb.

**107 Where was the twelfth tribe at the time
of the Jewish kings?**

Rehoboam reigned over one and Jeroboam over ten. (I Kings 11:31-35, 12:21.) The tribe of Levi was not counted because it had no land possessions (Num. 18:20-24), except cities for dwellings, with their outlying fields for pasturage (Num. 35:1-8). The tribe of Joseph was divided into two parts, Ephraim and Manasseh, which are usually spoken of as two distinct tribes. But in this division Joseph seems to have been counted as but one tribe, making Jeroboam's ten. Although Rehoboam at first retained only Judah, most of the tribe of Benjamin soon joined his kingdom. Simeon and Dan also became part of the kingdom of Judah.

108 What was the real sin of Uzzah?

The sin of Uzzah (I Chron. 13:9, 10) and its sudden punishment have been a subject of much discussion. None but priests of Aaron's family (that is, of the priest's household) were permitted to touch the Ark. Uzzah was of a Levitical family. In the house of his father, Abinadab, the Ark had rested for twenty years. When Uzzah put forth his hand to prevent the Ark from falling he was smitten, Josephus explains, because he touched it, "not being a priest." Others, however, have taken the view that Uzzah's sin was not that of laying unordained and unconsecrated hands upon the Ark in a moment of excitement, but rather—if the real reason lay in this direction at all—because he recklessly and sacrilegiously appropriated to himself powers and privileges which he well knew belonged to higher persons. One commentator writes: "The whole proceeding was disorderly and contrary to the distinct and significant regulations of the law which prescribed that the Ark should be carried on the shoulders of the Levites (Ex. 25:14), whereas it was here conveyed in a cart drawn by oxen. Besides, it should have been covered. There seems to have been no priest in charge, and it would appear that the sacred vessel was brought forth naked to the common gaze." Uzzah as a Levite should have observed and remedied these things, but his growing familiarity with the mysteries of the Jewish religion had made him careless, and the punishment came upon him at a time when it would most effectually check the evils among the people. That it had this effect is evident from I Chron. 15:2-13

109 Did the Witch at Endor really raise the spirit of Samuel?

Much has been written on the question whether, in the scene at Endor, an imposture or a real apparition appeared. Eustathius and a majority of the early Christian fathers held the former opinion, and represent it as a deception of the evil one; Origen held the latter view. It should be remembered that Saul, at the time was forsaken of God and that, rendered desperate by his sins, he had recourse to this woman, who in the Hebrew writings is described as "a mistress of Ob" or a necromancist (not a "witch") who obtained a living by pretending to have intercourse with spirits, while the Greek writers describe her as a ventriloquist. Josephus, the Jewish historian, describes her as one of a class of fortune-tellers who had been banished by the king. Saul's highly wrought nervous condition at the time, combined with the fact that he himself saw no vision or spirit, but simply listened to and accepted the necromancer's description of an aged man of godlike appearance, should be taken into consideration, and these facts doubtless influenced the early fathers in reaching the conclusion that the wretched king had been the victim of an imposition.

110 What is the real meaning of the visions described by Zechariah?

The chapters containing the visions are chiefly concerned with the hope founded on the approaching end of the seventy years, which, as Jeremiah predicted, would be the period of the captivity in Babylon. These are the meaning of the visions, according to some interpreters: The flying roll, a huge book with wings, contained the record of sin and curse. The prophet sees it flying from the Holy Land, destroying on its way the houses of the thieves and perjurers. The woman in the ephah (5:5-11) represents the principle of evil and of temptation. She, too, like sin and the curse, must be removed from the land, and she is carried away to the land of Shinar, which the Jews regarded as the fit abode of wicked things. The chariots of the winds (6:1-8) are God's messengers commissioned to avenge Israel. The black horses go north, that is to punish Persia; the dappled, south, that is against Egypt; and the white, west, that is against Greece, then becoming formidable. The horses of the fourth chariot have a general commission for any part of the world in which enmity to Israel might develop.

NEW TESTAMENT PERSONS
AND THINGS

111 How was the Apostles' Creed formulated?

According to one ancient writer who quotes from tradition, it was Peter who contributed the first sentence—"I believe in God the Father Almighty"; John added—"Maker of heaven and earth"; James—"And in Jesus Christ, his only Son our Lord"; Andrew—"Who was conceived by the Holy Ghost, born of the Virgin Mary"; Philip—"Suffered under Pontius Pilate; was crucified dead and buried"; Thomas—"He descended into hell; the third day he rose again from the dead"; Bartholomew—"He ascended into heaven and sitteth at the right hand of God the Father Almighty"; Matthew—"From whence he shall come to judge the quick and the dead." The other clauses were contributed by James (son of Alpheus), Simon Zelotes, Jude and Matthias. It should be remembered, however, that neither Luke nor any ecclesiastical writer before the fifth century makes mention of an assembly of the apostles to formulate a creed, and the early fathers never claimed that the apostles framed it. Its date and the circumstances of its origin are uncertain.

112 Did the Apostle John write the last
chapter of his Gospel?

We know that it has been asserted by some critics that this chapter must have been added by another hand, because the evangelist concluded his work in the previous chapter. This, however, is not accepted by sound scholarship, for the reason that it is not unusual in the New Testament writings and in other good books, for authors to insert supplementary matter, to which class the chapter in question clearly belongs. There is no evidence that John's Gospel was ever known in the early Church without this chapter. John, it is true, refers to himself in the third person; but he did so also in chapter 19:35 in practically the same terms as in 21:24. The best commentators agree as to the genuineness on *prima facie* evidence.

113 What were the locusts that became
the food of John the Baptist?

Some writers think it may have been the common locust or green grasshopper, which, when prepared and dried, tastes somewhat like a shrimp. Many ancient authors mention them as food. Diodorus Siculus refers to a people of Ethiopia, who were called *acridophaghi*, or locust eaters. Porphryius says that whole armies have been saved from starvation by eating locusts. Aristotle and Aristophanes assert that they were relished by the Greeks, and Layard, the discoverer, found evidence that they were eaten in a preserved state by the Assyrians. Later commentators, however have conjectured that the "locust" mentioned in Mark's Gospel as being the food of John the Baptist, was the carob, the fruit of a tree of the locust family, which is a sort of sweetish bean, in pods, much used by the poorer classes.

114 What is known of John's birth and early training?

He was of the priestly race by both parents, his father, Zacharias, being a priest of the course of Abijah, and Elisabeth a descendant of Aaron. Of the first thirty years of his life, the only history we have is contained in a single verse, Luke 1:80. But it is a reasonable presumption that he received the Jewish ecclesiastical training of that period. He was the chosen forerunner of the Messiah (Luke 1:76). Dwelling alone in the desert region westward of the Dead Sea, he prepared himself for his work by discipline and constant prayer. One of his instructors, Banus (mentioned by Josephus, the Jewish historian), tells how he lived with John in the desert, eating the sparse food and bathing frequently by day and night. At last (about A.D. 25) John came forth from his hermit-like seclusion in the wild mountainous tract in Judea lying beyond the desert and the Dead Sea, and took up the work of his real office, preaching repentance and baptism, and attracting great multitudes.

115 Was John the Baptist sentenced to death before the dance of Salome?

While there is no record to prove it, the presumption is that Herod, in his mind, had already condemned John on political grounds as one whose existence endangered his position and authority, but his awakened conscience and the fear inspired by John's teachings restrained him. He had kept John in the prison of Machaerus nearly a year when the Salome incident occurred, which gave Herodias her opportunity to be revenged upon the Baptist, who had rebuked both her and Herod for their sinful relations. It cannot be asserted that Herod would have executed John had not the king been caught by his pledge to Salome. On the contrary Mark 6:26 tells us that he "was exceeding sorrowful."

116 When did John the Baptist die?

The date is somewhat difficult to determine with any degree of reliability. The first Passover of Jesus' ministry is believed to have occurred in A.D. 27. His baptism at John's hands took place immediately before that time. John's imprisonment in the tower of Machaerus in all probability began in A.D. 27 and in the first half of that year, but Herod's unwillingness to put him to death may have delayed the climax until the beginning of A.D. 28. Tradition says he was buried in Samaria.

117 Was John the Baptist Elijah?

The statement in the affirmative is made a number of times in the New Testament. (See Matt. 11:14, 17:10-12; Mark 9:12, 13. See also Mal. 4:5.) But some of the ablest commentators hold that we must interpret the connection figuratively, and that there is no reason for believing that this means any more than that he was the new Elijah of his time, a rugged prophet, like Elijah in temperament, habits and speech, unafraid even of kings. He himself said distinctly that he was not Elijah (John 1:21). The sense in which the expression was used is made clear in Luke 1:17: "He shall go before him in *the spirit and power* of Elijah." In the narrative of Elijah's appearance at the transfiguration there is no suggestion that he was John the Baptist, whom all the men present had known and seen, and who had only recently died. One of the things that distinguishes the philosophy of the Bible from that of uninspired teachings is that it never confuses or obscures personal identity. Each soul has a distinct personality, which can never be merged or changed into another.

118 What was John the Baptist's place in prophecy?

"Who was the last prophet of the old dispensation?" John the Baptist came as the forerunner of Christ, and so may be considered the last prophet of the old dispensation. Christ said: "All the prophets and the law prophesied until John" (Matt. 11:13). Otherwise, if you regard him as belonging to an intermediate dispensation, the last would be the prophet called Malachi, the writer of the last book in the Old Testament. It is not certain that Malachi was his name, as the word may be translated, "My messenger."

119 Why was twelve the full number of the apostles?

All of the twelve disciples were Jews. Their number was doubtless fixed upon after the analogy of the twelve tribes. They were mostly Galileans, taken from the common people, and some at least had been disciples of John the Baptist. (See Matt. 12:25; John 1:35; Matt. 19:28.)

120 Have we historical records of the deaths of the apostles?

The records of their end are found in traditions preserved by the early Church. Matthew was martyred in Ethiopia; Mark in Alexandria, Egypt; Luke was hanged on an olive tree in Greece; John, after many perils, died a natural death in Ephesus; Peter was crucified in Rome, head downwards; James the Great beheaded at Jerusalem; James the Less beaten to death with a fuller's club in the temple grounds; Philip hanged at Hieropolis; Bartholomew flayed alive; Thomas slain with a lance at Coromandel; Jude killed with arrows; Simeon crucified in Persia; Andrew crucified; Matthias stoned and beheaded; Barnabas stoned to death by Jews at Salamis; Paul beheaded at Rome under Nero.

121 If Paul had not expected a resurection would he have lived a self-indulgent life?

No, he was not that kind of man. In the passage in I Cor. 15:32 he is considering the attitude of an opponent, and is stating such an argument as might be made by one who believed there was no life beyond the grave. In effect he says: "A man who does not believe in immortality might naturally say, in considering such a life as mine, that it is folly. Instead of fighting with beasts as I did at Ephesus, and enduring all kinds of hardship and persecution, it would be better for me if I simply enjoyed the good things of life. Such a man could never be persuaded to become a Christian, if there was no prospect of a future life.

122 Is it known who were Paul's parents?

The name of Paul's parents are not given in the Scriptures. The only mention of his blood relations is in Acts 23:16 and Rom. 16:7, 11, but whether Andronicus, Junia and Herodion were really relatives or simply friends is an open question.

123 What are the dates of the thirteen Pauline epistles?

According to the best authorities the epistles of Paul were written at about the following times:

Romans	58 A.D. at Corinth.
I Corinthians	57 A.D. at Ephesus.
II Corinthians	58 A.D. at Philippi.
I Thessalonians	52 A.D. at Corinth.
II Thessalonians	52 or 53 A.D. at. Corinth.
Philippians	61 A.D. at Rome.
Colossians	63 A.D. at Rome.
Ephesians	63 A.D. at Rome.
Galatians	58 A.D. at Corinth.
Philemon	63 A.D. at Rome.
I Timothy	65 A.D. in Macedonia.
II Timothy	67 A.D. in Rome.
Titus	66 A.D. in Macedonia.

124 What do we know of Paul's personal appearance?

All we know of it, from his own writings, is found in II Cor. 10:10, which indicates that he did not possess the advantage of a distinguished or imposing presence. His stature was somewhat diminutive, his eyesight weak (see Acts 23:5 and Gal. 4:15) nor did he regard his address as impressive. Much of this personal criticism, however, may have been the outcome of the apostle's desire to avoid magnifying himself or his own talents. A fourth century tablet represents him as venerable-looking and dignified, with a high, bald forehead, full-bearded, and with features indicating force of character. One ancient writer says Paul's nose was strongly aquiline. All the early pictures and mosaics, as well as some of the early writers (among them Malalus and Nicephorus) agree in describing the apostle as of short stature, with long face, prominent eyebrows, clear complexion and a winning expression, the whole aspect being that of power and dignity. The oldest known portrait is the Roman panel of the fourth century, already referred to above.

125 What was the cause of the dispute between Peter and Paul at Antioch?

"When Peter was come to Antioch, I withstood him to the face, because he was to be blamed," wrote Paul in Gal. 2:11. In view of this statement of Paul, some have questioned whether we may regard both Paul and Peter as having been acting under inspiration. The question of inspiration is not involved in the incident that took place at Antioch, when Paul rebuked Peter for his inconsistency. It is simply a question of human weakness. While under the influence of certain High Church Jewish-Christians, who came from James, Peter withdrew and separated himself from the Antioch Christians, "fearing them of the circumcision." The result was that Barnabas, and doubtless many others, were affected by his example, which became a scandal in the community. To save the Church from an apostasy, Paul took Peter to task for his conduct and rebuked him openly, as his conduct was an attack on Gospel liberty. The writings of Paul and Peter that have found their way into the New Testament Canon are, beyond doubt, inspired, but to say that every word they uttered during their Christian lives was inspired is what we do not believe. Paul and Peter had human weaknesses and limitations, like other men. But when they wrote authoritatively under the guidance of the Holy Ghost, they were kept free from errors and mistakes, and in this way were inspired.

126 Was Paul familiar with the Scriptures?

It is made clear in Acts 27 that Paul was familiar with "all the learning of the Greeks." Tarsus, his native city, was a famous seat of learning and philosophical research, and he probably had the advantage of training in its schools. The son of a Pharisee and trained from boyhood to the pursuits of a doctor of Jewish law, he presumably was instructed in the elements of Rabbinical lore, including of course the Jewish Scriptures. These are the inferences of those writers who have studied his life career. This could not apply to the New Testament writings as we now know them, for they were only in the making, and must have been very incomplete; but it is a fair presumption that in his later career, as an apostle, he was not ignorant of such writings as may then have been in existence, dealing with the events of Jesus' life and ministry. There was no New Testament, in the modern meaning of the term, in Paul's day, and could not have been, for obvious reasons.

127 What part did Paul have in the stoning of Stephen?

Paul, at the time of Stephen's martyrdom, was more than a mere spectator; he was an active assistant. There is nothing in the Scripture to show that before his miraculous conversion, he had shown or expressed regret at his participation in Stephen's death. On the contrary, he had become, and was, up to the moment when he was stricken down, one of the bitterest and most relentless persecutors of the Christians. (See Acts 26:10, 12.) What he may have thought, in his own heart at times, of his share in the tragedy, or what influence it may have had upon him, can only be a matter of surmise. There was nothing to outwardly reveal that he brooded over it or that he repented at all, before his own transformation.

128 Was Paul ever married?

There is no evidence in the New Testament to show that he was ever married, and commentators have held that various passages in which he urges celibacy, show him to have remained single by choice. But this is only an inference. Others take the opposite view, pointing out that at the age of thirty, he was a member of the Sanhedrin (Acts 26:10); as such he "gave his vote" against the followers of Jesus. Being the youngest of the judges, he was appointed "judicial witness" of the execution of Stephen. According to Maimonides, and the Jerusalem *Gemara*, it was required of all who were to be made members of that Council that they should be married, and fathers of families, because such were supposed to be more inclined to merciful judgment. (See *Life of St. Paul*, by Conybeare and Howson, volume 1, chapter 2.)

129 What were the dates of Paul's missionary journeys?

Paul's introduction by the sacred historian (when he was a witness of Stephen's martyrdom), is supposed to have been about A.D. 36. At that time he was probably between thirty and forty years of age. His conversion took place A.D. 37. He left Damascus A.D. 37. First missionary journey undertaken A.D. 44; his second, three years later, and his third, four years after the second.

130 When did Paul go to Rome and how long did he stay?

According to the best available information, the shipwreck occurred in the year 56 A.D., and late in the autumn of that year Paul reached Rome as a prisoner. The length of his stay is uncertain. Acts 28:30 says two years, and the author probably knew. It is probable that Paul was then set at liberty and made another preaching tour, going farther west than before. He was afterwards again seized and taken back to Rome. How long a time elapsed between his second arrival and his execution there no one knows.

131 Did Paul baptize?

He answers this question himself (I Cor. 1:17). He implies that he had something better to do. Christ sent him not to baptize but to preach the Gospel. The value of baptism in the case of the Corinthian converts was that it was a public profession of their faith—it placed them on record. This result would be attained whoever administered the rite, and, therefore, Paul relegated the duty to some other Christian. After he left, the Corinthians began to think there was some special significance about it, and for this Paul reproves them.

132 Did Peter go to Rome?

There is nothing in the book of Romans to indicate Peter's presence in Rome at any time, but that is merely negative evidence. If he ever visited Rome, it was probably during the last year of his life, although Eusebius in the *Chronicon* says he visited it in A.D. 42. Jerome also mentions Peter's visit to Rome. Catholic writers assert that he was there for a number of years. There is no evidence of the fact in the New Testament books. It is generally accepted, however, that he was in Rome in his last year when he became a martyr as our Lord predicted (John 21:18, 19). Dionysus of Corinth writes that Peter and Paul suffered martyrdom in Italy together. Irenaeus confirms his presence in Rome. Caius, Origen, Tertullian and others bear similar testimony.

133 Was Peter converted before his denial of Christ?

Peter was a man of resolute character, bold and decisive. He was easily the leader of the twelve. Honest-hearted and warmly attached to Christ, he believed himself immovably loyal; yet in the hour of temptation he proved unstable and weak. Jesus knew his heart and warned him against over-confidence in his own loyalty. "I have been praying for thee," he said, "that thy faith fail not." He needed this divine strengthening. His faith had failed once before in a crisis (see Matt. 14:29), and what he needed to confirm him now was the "power from on high" which would come later. The tempter was to sift all the disciples, and Jesus foresaw Peter's weakness, but he was preserved from falling by this special intercession. His case shows, perhaps more completely than any other in the New Testament, the weakness of the natural and the strength of the spiritual man. Even at the moment of his denial of Christ, it needed but a glance from the eye of his Lord to make him instantly repentant. After the enduement with the Holy Ghost, he stood forth as the leader of the apostles, faithful unto death.

134 What was Paul's "thorn in the flesh"?

It referred to some bodily affliction affecting him individually and physically, but not his work as an apostle. In Gal. 4:13, 14 he refers to it as an "infirmity of my flesh"—some form of bodily sickness which had detained him among the Galatians. It was probably something that caused him acute pain, and also some degree of shame, since it "buffeted" him (I Pet. 2:20). There have been many conjectures as to its real character. Some have imagined it to be blasphemous thoughts, and others, remorse for his former life; but the most probable view is that it was an affliction which caused him physical annoyance, possibly a disorder of the eyes, or some nervous ailment. At all events, we are assured that it was so persistent and recurrent that he speaks of it in terms of apology and mortification.

135 For what purpose was Judas chosen as a disciple?

He was attracted, as the others were, by the preaching of the Baptist or by his own Messianic hopes. It can be imagined, however, that baser motives may have mingled with his faith and zeal. He must have possessed some qualifications, probably plausibility being one, and he may even have excelled the rest of the twelve in business ability. Again, he may have joined the twelve in all sincerity, and yielded to temptation only when he found the handling of the money made him covetous. It was evident that Jesus knew from the beginning what Judas would do (John 6:64). Volumes have been written in the futile effort to explain why Judas was chosen.

136 In what sense was Judas a devil?

Little is known of the life of Judas before his appearance among the apostles. He was probably drawn by the Baptist's preaching, or by his own ambitious hopes of the coming of a Messianic kingdom, in which he might play an important and lucrative part. He seems to have declared himself a disciple of Jesus, as the others did, and as he was intrusted with the finances of the little company, we may judge that he enjoyed a measure of confidence, although this seems to have been undeserved. (See John 12:6.) That Jesus himself knew the heart of Judas from the beginning is made clear from the text. (See also John 6:64-71.) Our Lord knew his inmost thoughts. He knew Judas to be deceitful and treacherous. He knew of his criminal confidences with the priests, which culminated in the betrayal. (See John 18:3-5.) The act of betrayal was not the outcome of a sudden impulse at the Last Supper, but was the closing scene in a long career of deceit and treachery. Judas was probably ambitious, and like several other apostles believed that Jesus would set up an earthly kingdom in which he himself might have an influential part. Of his early history before his name appeared in the list of the apostles, nothing is known. The name "Iscariot" is variously explained, some writers holding that he was so called because he belonged to Kerioth in the tribe of Judah.

137 How did Judas die?

Several explanations of the apparent discrepancy between Matt. 27:3-10 and Acts 1:18, 19 have been offered. The first, with relation to the death of Judas, is that the word translated as "hanged" in Matt. 27:5 is capable of a different interpretation, *i.e.*, death by a sudden spasm of suffocation, which might have been accompanied by a fall before the spasm spent itself. Another suggestion, which has been made by some eminent scholars, is that the work of suicide was but half accomplished when, the halter parting, Judas fell with the result stated in Acts 1:18.

138 Was it repentance or remorse that drove Judas to suicide?

All we know is what the Scripture tells us. It may have been remorse, or chagrin over the failure of his plans, but it could hardly have been repentance. It was suggested by DeQuincey, with some plausibility, that in betraying Christ, he was seeking to precipitate a crisis, out of which he expected to see Christ emerge triumphant. He thought Christ would use his miraculous power to save himself, and when in danger of death, would declare himself King, and would set up his kingdom, in which the disciples would hold high office. When he found that Christ intended to submit, he perceived that his scheme to force his hand had failed, and he was overwhelmed by the catastrophe he had precipitated. The suggestion is not sustained by the conception we gain of him in the Gospels, but it is possible to imagine an ambitious and avaricious man acting in that way; if, as is possible, he was impatient with Christ, who had powers so great and yet was so slow to use them to advance his own interests and those of the men who had left all to follow him, he may have tried this scheme. The suggestion, however, is pure conjecture. No one has been able to analyze satisfactorily the character of Judas.

139 Were the apostles converted
before the day of Pentecost?

Jesus had said many things to and about His disciples before his death, which indicated that they were converted men: "Rejoice, because your names are written in heaven," Luke 10:20; "Now ye are clean through the word that I have spoken unto you," John 15:3; "Ye know him" (the Spirit of truth), "for he dwelleth with you, and shall be in you." In the last verse he distinguishes them from "the world." The world, he said, cannot receive the Spirit; but the Spirit was already with the disciples, and was to come into their hearts in greater fullness, as he did on the day of Pentecost. In the high-priestly prayer Jesus said: "I pray not for the world, but for them which thou hast given me; for they are thine;" "They are not of the world, even as I am not of the world;" "Thine they were, and thou gavest them me; and they have kept thy word," John 17:9, 14, 16, 6. Although Peter was a converted man, he fell into sin and denied his Master. It is the common experience of justified Christians that, while they do not habitually sin, they slip occasionally into transgression. But after the fullness of the Spirit had been received on the day of Pentecost, Peter and the other apostles stood firm. This also has been the experience of many Christians since the apostles' time, who have found, in a larger blessing, sanctifying and keeping grace. Jacob's experience was the same. Before his blessing at Jabbok, he had met God at Bethel and received the promise: "I will not leave thee" (Gen. 28:15); God had spoken to him again, while he dwelt with Laban (Gen. 31:3-11); the angels of God met him at Mahanaim (Gen. 32:2). But after the experience at Jabbok, or Peniel, he lived to the end of his days a purer, higher spiritual life.

140 Was the gift of tongues retained by the apostles
until their death?

The endowment of the "gift of tongues" was apparently continued to the Christians during the apostolic age. Jesus before his ascension breathed upon his disciiples and said "Receive ye the Holy Ghost." Fifty days after the crucifixion, the disciples received special power, when the Holy Ghost came upon them. It was to be a sign—to belong to only a few—the apostles and evangelists and with this gift they went forth to preach to the nations. Later, Paul wrote that he "spake with tongues more than all." In I Cor. 13:8, however, we see that "tongues" were already ceasing, as belonging to the past. Many times since then the question has arisen whether the gift of tongues was continued to succeeding generations. The attitude of the early Church, neither to quench nor forbid them (see I Thess. 5:19), yet not to invite or excite them, was a safe one. If they were of God, the fact would make itself apparent; if they were simply hysterical jargon, they would quickly subside. Throughout Church history, there were many spurious instances. Irenaeus wrote of some in his time who spoke with tongues, but Eusebius hardly referred to the subject, and Chrysostom mentions it only to discourage what he considered as an ecstatic indulgence of doubtful spiritual profit.

141 Were any of the disciples married?

Very little is known regarding the domestic relations of the apostles beyond what is disclosed in the Gospels. Matt. 8:15 clearly implies that Peter was married. Bartholomew is said by tradition to have been the bridegroom at the wedding at Cana, and Philip is mentioned by Clement of Alexandria as having had a wife and children. Nothing definite can be asserted concerning the others, although they are generally assumed to have been unmarried.

142 Who were the Essenes?

A small community of Jews in the time of Christ, who led a pastoral life and did not marry. They held their goods and took their meals in common, strictly observed the Sabbath, prayed before sunrise with their faces to the East, bathed daily in cold water, never swore, sacrificed no animals, and believed in immortality without a resurrection of the body.

143 Who were the Gentiles?

Gentiles, which means simply "peoples," was a term applied indiscriminately by the Jews to all other nations than themselves. After a time it acquired a hostile meaning, as the Jews gradually drew themselves apart as a "holy nation." The term is used of "Galilee of the Gentiles," where some five nations other than the Jews were represented; the "Court of the Gentiles" outside the Temple area; the "isles of the Gentiles," etc.

144 Who were the Pharisees?

The Pharisees were a Jewish sect deriving their name from a word which means "separate" or "distinct." They were disciples of the Jewish sages, who held themselves aloof and claimed to keep rigidly the Mosaic laws of purity. They had many religious observances and believed in a future life of rewards and punishments.

145 Who were the Sadducees?

The Sadducees were a sect of free-thinkers, differing greatly from the Pharisees on many points. They rejected the oral law and the prophets and only accepted the Pentateuch, and Josephus says they denied the resurrection from the dead.

146 Who were the Herodians?

The Herodians were a class of Jews in the time of Christ, who were partisans of Herod, either of a political or religious sort, or both. It appears that when the ecclesiastical authorities of Judea held a council against the Saviour, they associated with themselves the Herodians, and sent an embassy to Jesus designing to trap him in his speech. As tetrarch of Galilee, Herod Antipas was the ruler of the province which was Jesus' home, and the Jews doubtless argued that Herod would be pleased if they could convict Jesus of being a rival claimant to the crown. The Pharisees were a Jewish sect who held rigidly aloof from other sects, claimed to be free from every kind of impurity and united to keep the Mosaic laws, to which they gave the closest study. They were frequently denounced by our Saviour for their self-righteousness and their assumption of superior piety. The Sadducees were another sect, originally a religious body, but which had developed into a body of free-thinkers. They rejected the oral law and the prophets, but believed in the Pentateuch; they denied the resurrection and they held different views from other Jews on various other important points while claiming to be the most aristocratic and conservative of all the bodies.

**147 What is known of the early life
of the author of the Epistle of James?**

Nothing authoritative. He was probably brought up with Jesus and the other children in the Nazareth home. It is believed that he did not become a follower of Christ until after the resurrection. Christ seems to have appeared specially to him, and as Paul mentions the fact (I Cor. 15:7) we may presume it was generally known, though it is not related in any of the Gospels. James was a strict Jew before becoming a Christian, and was highly esteemed among the Jews for his piety. It looks as though he never quite shook off his Jewish ideas (Gal. 2:12), and his epistle shows that he could not cordially endorse Paul's way of stating the Gospel.

148 Was it a whale that swallowed Jonah?

Nowhere in the book of Jonah are we told that the fish that swallowed Jonah was a whale. In Matt. 12:40 the word "whale" is used, but the revised version gives "sea monster" in the margin. There is absolute proof that sea monsters large enough to swallow a man have been found in the Mediterranean and other seas.

149 Who were the Karaites, or Readers?

They were a small remnant of the Sadducees, "the Protestants of Judaism," formed into a sect by Ananben-Daniel in the eighth century. They rejected the rabbinical traditions and the Talmud, and accepted the Scriptures alone. The origin of their name is uncertain. Some of the sect exist in the Crimea, Poland and Turkey.

150 How long did Lazarus live after being raised from the dead?

There are no authoritative data on the subject. An old tradition, mentioned by Epiphanius, says that Lazarus was thirty years old when restored from death and that he lived thirty years thereafter. Still another tradition declares that he traveled to Southern Europe, accompanied by Mary and Martha, and preached the Gospel in Marseilles.

151 Who was Lydia?

She is mentioned in Acts 16:15 and was a resident of Thyatira, a city celebrated for its purple dyes. She seems to have been a business woman, engaged in the sale of dyed goods, and she evidently had an extensive establishment, as she was able to accommodate the missionary party. She was a proselyte to the Jewish faith, but became a believer under Paul's ministry.

152 Was Mary, the mother of Jesus, of the tribe of Judah?

It is not proved, except inferentially. The Jews, in constructing their genealogical tables, reckoned wholly by males. Some of the best modern authorities, however, observing all the rules followed by the Hebrews in genealogies, have reached the conclusion that in Zorobabel the lines of Solomon and Nathan unite, and that Joseph and Mary are therefore of the same tribe and family, being both descendants of David in the line of Solomon and that both have in them the blood of Nathan. David's son, Joseph, has descent from Abiud (Matt. 1:13) and Mary from Rhesa (Luke 3:27), sons of Zorobabel. The genealogies of Matthew and Luke are parts of one perfect whole; the former bearing the descent of Mary and Joseph from Solomon—the latter the descent of both from Nathan.

153 Who were the parents of Mary?

Many scholars are of opinion that she was the daughter of the Heli mentioned in Luke 3:23. As the Jews reckoned their genealogy by the male side only, it was customary to set a man's son-in-law down as his son. This would account for Joseph being described by one evangelist as the son of Jacob and by the other as the son of Heli. Apart from that theory there are no data for ascertaining the parentage of Mary.

154 How many Marys are there in the Bible?

The Marys spoken of in the New Testament are: Mary the mother of Christ, Mary Magdalene, Mary the sister of Lazarus, Mary the wife of Cleophas (John 19:25) and Mary the mother of John (Acts 12:12).

155 Who are the Nestorians?

They are the descendants of a sect of early Christians, named after Nestorius, a theologian of the fifth century A.D. They claim also to be descended from Abraham, and sometimes call themselves Chaldeans. They are probably the oldest of the Oriental churches. They are found in Persia, in India, East Indies, Syria, Arabia, Asia Minor, and even in Cochin China, the principal settlements, however, being in and near Persia. They believe Christ to be both divine and human—two persons, with only a moral and sympathetic union. They do not believe in any divine humiliation nor any exaltation of humanity in Christ. They acknowledge the supreme authority of the Scriptures and believe they contain all that is essential to salvation. The main body of Nestorians is nominally Christian, but it is a lifeless Christianity. They have no images, but they invoke the Virgin and the saints and are ignorant and superstitious.

156 Who were the Nicolaitans?

Though they are mentioned in Rev. 2:15 it is not positively known, but from the context it would appear that they were people who abused Paul's doctrine of Christian liberty, which they turned into license. It is supposed that Jude 4 refers to them. They appear to have attended the heathen rites and shared in the abominations there practised. Some suppose them to have been followers of Nicolas of Antioch, but if so, they falsely claimed that he taught such things. It is more probable that the name, if relating to a person at all, has been confused with some other Nicolas.

WORDS AND TERMS

**157 What significance has the word *Abba*
when it precedes the word *Father*?**

"Abba" is the Hebrew word for "father," in the emphatic or definite state, as "thy father." Its use in referring to God was common among the Jews; but in order that it might not seem too familiar or irreverent, the New Testament writers gave it the two-fold form, which has become a recognized phrase in Christian worship. It is as though they said: "Father, our Father."

**158 What are we to understand by the
Battle of Armageddon, referred to
in the Book of Revelation?**

Armageddon is the name given to the last great battle to be fought in the world's history, in which the whole human race is arrayed on one side or the other. It is to be the final struggle of Antichrist. When it will be fought no one can tell; but that there will be a great struggle we are assured. Before that day comes "many false prophets shall arise and lead many astray . . . iniquity shall be multiplied and the love of many shall wax cold." There are to be false Christs, false teachers doing signs and wonders, and leading astray "even the elect if such were possible." It is to be preceded by a period of apostasy, in which the authority of the wicked one will be fully demonstrated, with the assumption of divinity and the demand for universal worship as God. In the present stage of the conflict between good and evil, when mighty forces are arrayed on both sides, we can see the foreshadowing of the fierce struggle that is to come; but we may rest assured that righteousness will triumph in the end. (See the parallel passage in Joel 3:2-12.) Armageddon is "the mountain of Megiddo," west of the Jordan, a scene of early historic battles and the place that would naturally suggest itself to the mind of a Galilean writer to whom the place and its associations were familiar.

**159 What is meant by the terms "prince of the power
of the air" and "baptized for the dead"?**

It refers to Satan (Eph. 2:2), the "prince of evil," who assails men on earth with trials and temptations. The word "power" is used here for the embodiment of that evil spirit which is the ruling principle of all unbelief, especially among the heathen. (See I Tim. 4:1; II Cor. 4:4; John 12:31.)

Beuzel translated the familiar passage in I Cor. 15:29 thus: "Over the dead," or "immediately upon the dead," meaning those who will be gathered to the dead immediately after baptism. Many in the ancient church put off baptism till near death. The passage probably referred to some symbolical rite of baptism or dedication of themselves to follow the dead even to death. Another view held by some expositors is that it was a custom to baptize certain persons with the names of the dead, in the hope that they might inherit their spirit and carry on their work.

160 What is the baptism of fire?

It has been variously interpreted to mean: (1) the baptism of the Holy Spirit, (2) the fires of purgatory, and (3) the everlasting fires of hell. Modern theologians take the view that the baptism of fire and that of the Holy Ghost are the same, and that it may be rendered "baptized with the Holy Ghost through the outward symbol of fire," or "as with the cloven tongues of fire," referring to the Pentecostal baptism.

161 Have automobiles and airplanes been the subject of biblical prophecy?

Nahum 2:4 has been quoted as referring to automobiles, but this appears to strain the meaning of the passage, which was written as a direct prophecy of the destruction of Nineveh. The verse describes the mad rush of those in chariots to escape the enemy. Isa. 60:8 has been thought by some to be a reference to the coming use of airships, but here again the direct meaning is obvious, that in the time of Judea's prosperity ships shall flock to her shores as doves to the windows of their dovecotes. Hab. 1:8 might be thought to presage manflight, but the figure is used to express the terrific haste with which the Chaldeans shall come against Judea.

162 What is meant by the "beast and his mark" in the Book of Revelation?

The Seer of Revelation appears to have had his visions in the form of a series of scenes, as in a panorama. Almost at the close (Rev. 14:9) he saw the beast you refer to. It is evidently identical with the beast described by Daniel (7:7). It is representative of the power which is said to have throughout the world's history opposed God. It appears in John's narrative in a series of forms, and is sometimes identified with a persecuting church, and sometimes is the civil power. At the culmination of its career, John saw it as the great Antichrist, who is yet to arise, who would attain to such power in the world that he would exclude any many from office and from even engaging in trade, who did not acknowledge him. Only those who bear the mark of the beast can buy or sell in that time. This mark may be a badge to be worn on forehead or hand, or as some scholars think, merely the coins to be used in business, which will bear Antichrist's title symbolized by the number 666.

163 How was the brazen serpent a type?

"As the serpent was lifted up in the wilderness, so must the son of man be lifted up." These were the Saviour's words. Jesus' death on the cross was an uplifting, and in this sense it is compared to the uplifting of the brazen serpent. In both cases the remedy is divinely provided and there is another striking similarity: As death came to the Israelites in the wilderness by the serpent's sting and life came by the uplifting of a serpent, so, in redemption, by man came death, and by the death of the God-man in the likeness of sinful flesh comes life eternal. In the first instance the cure was effected by directing the eye to the uplifted serpent; in the other, it takes place when the eye of faith is fixed upon the uplifted Christ.

164 Were the giants mentioned in Genesis 6:4 the descendants of angels, as some fanciful interpreters claim?

This has been answered by a notable authority as follows: "Gen. 6:1-4 forms the introduction to the story of the Flood. All races have preserved the tradition of a flood; whether it was universal or local is a moot point. The Jewish Scriptures leave the investigation of natural phenomena to human research. The Bible is not a scientific treatise. Its sole concern is religious and moral. Its aim is to justify the ways of God to man, and to show that natural phenomena, being controlled by God, are in harmony with divine justice. Hence, before relating the story of the Flood, Holy Writ sets forth the universal corruption which justified the destruction of the human race, with the exception of one family. Chapter 6:1-4 describes the violence and immorality prevalent in the antediluvian period. Mankind had, in course of time, fallen into two divisions—the classes and the masses. The masses were the common multitude of toilers, the ordinary 'sons of men.' The classes were the 'supermen,' 'the sons of God,' 'the mighty heroes.' The latter formed the aristocracy; they were the ruling class, the children of judges and princes. Small in number, they were physically strong and mentally vigorous, and had, moreover, appropriated a large portion of the wealth of the then known world. They should have used their power and position for the benefit of their kind, and set an example in chastity, temperance, selfrestraint, justice and kindliness. Instead, they gave way to unbridled lust, to indulge which they resorted to violence. 'They saw that the daughters of men (*i.e.*, the common folk) were fair, and they took (*i.e.*, by force) whomsoever they chose.' This abuse of power was punished by the destruction of the race. 'The Eternal said: My spirit shall not abide in man forever.' The Hebrew word may mean 'abide as a sword in a sheath'; or it may mean 'contend with man'—the higher with the lower nature—the spirit of heaven with the body formed of dust and its instincts, of the earth, earthy; or it may mean 'My spirit shall not rule in man.' The struggle is too severe. 'Since he is but flesh, his days shall be one hundred and twenty years.' On account of the moral infirmity incident to human nature, time will be given for repentance. If the opportunity is not taken, destruction will follow the respite. *Nephilim* literally means 'the fallen.' On the principle of *lucus a non lucendo*, the term refers to the men of gigantic stature who existed in ancient times. They were the mighty men who yielded to licentious passions. The children of these illegitimate unions were also, for some generations, Nephilim of gigantic stature, famed for their physical and mental development, but morally degenerate. They were the renowned heros of old—the mighty warriors, like the berserkers of the northern sagas."

Another view is that "the sons of God" were the Sethites, who had mantained in some measure the filial relationship to God, and who now intermarried with the Cainites, who had been spiritually disowned on account of their godlessness and unbelief. All the evidence leads to the conclusion that the whole arraignment of wickedness upon the earth related to beings of flesh and blood (see Gen. 6:3) and not to supernatural beings, who, we are elsewhere told distinctly, have no distinction of sex and never marry (see Luke 20:35, 36). In this view, which seems to be the correct one, the appellation "sons of God" refers to men's moral and in no sense to their physical state. There are many passages elsewhere that bear out this belief. (See Acts 17:28; Ex. 4:22, 23; Deut. 14:1; Hosea 11:1, etc.)

165 What is meant by "casting out devils"?

The question has been the subject of dispute for many generations. The plain meaning of the narrative, however, seems to us to be that Satan had gained absolute possession and control of the afflicted persons and that Christ evicted him by his superior power. It seems to us impossible on any other assumption to satisfactorily explain the words of exorcism Christ used, the words uttered by the afflicted persons and the effects which followed. The symptoms described very closely resemble those of some forms of epilepsy and insanity of our time. Science, however, does not now ascribe the affliction to demoniacal possession. Nevertheless some of the patients do occasionally display a degree of malignity and cunning which could scarcely be exceeded if they were really possessed by the devil.

166 What and where is the "kingdom of God"?

There are several senses in which the word "kingdom" is used. It may be taken in general terms as the kingdom which is set up in the heart (as Christ told the Pharisees, Luke 17:21, "The kingdom of God is within you") and the kingdom which is set up in the world (see Daniel 2:44) and the kingdom Christ will establish at his second coming (II Timothy 4:1), and there is the kingdom in heaven where God reigns. In the first of these senses we enter the kingdom at conversion when we give our allegiance to Christ.

167 What is being "baptized unto death"?

The passage in Rom. 6:3, 4, 5 implies that those who have gone through this experience have formally surrendered the whole state and life of sin, as being dead in Christ. Verse 4 is more accurately interpreted "by the same baptism which makes us sharers in his death we are made partakers of his burial also," thus severing our last link of connection with the sinful condition and life which Christ brought to an end in his death. Possibly immersion was alluded to in this verse as symbolical of burial and resurrection. Verse 5 is self-explanatory.

168 In what sense is the believer "in Christ"?

The reference is exclusively to the relation of the believer to the risen Lord, and expresses a peculiar spiritual connection. Rev. David Smith, the distinguished theologian, defines it as a spiritual way of four connecting links, viz.: (1) Christ for us (see II Cor. 5:21), which is substitution; (2) We in Christ (II Cor. 5:7; Rom. 6:11), which is justification; (3) Christ in us (Rom. 8:11; II Cor. 13:5; Gal. 2:20), which is sanctification, and (4) We for Christ (II Cor. 5:10), which is consecration. This is the condition of Christ's true disciple. He stands in the world as representative and witness-bearer for Christ. It is not merely a question of his own salvation; he must be a shining light to guide others, and must live the Christ-life, under whatever circumstances he may be placed. One who lives the Christ-life and all of whose thoughts, acts, influences and hopes are centered on carrying on the work of Christ, and who is guided by his will, can be said to be truly "in Christ."

169 What is it to be "risen with Christ"?

Paul had described himself as having been crucified with Christ (Gal. 2:20). He was dead to the world through the death of Christ, dead to sin, to worldly ambition, and to all the worldly principles and motives. But he might have been asked, "Was he really dead?" and, in Col. 3:1, he answers that, like Christ, he had received a new life, having been raised with him, as he had been crucified with him. This was the resurrection life by which he had become transformed, and was a new creature in Christ Jesus. It was this that Augustine meant when he was greeted by a dissolute companion of his youth, whom he had passed on the street without recognition. "August, it is I, do you not know me?" He replied: "I am August no longer." Having become a Christian (risen with Christ) he had abandoned all his old life with its companions and associations.

170 What is the Biblical definition of a Christian?

A Christian is (1) one who believes in Jesus Christ the divine Son of God, and that through his life and atonement we have everlasting life; (2) the Christian through his fellowship with Christ receives the adoption of a child of God (see I John 3:2 and 5:1); (3) he enters into fellowship and communion with God. See Heb. 2:11, 16; I John 1:3; Prov. 18:24. (4) He is sanctified and separated. See Rom. 1:7; I Pet. 1:14, 15; I Thess. 5:23. (5) He is a soldier. I Tim. 6:12; II Tim. 2:3, 4. (6) He is an heir of glory. Rom. 8:17; Gal. 3:29; Gal. 4:7; Titus 3:7; I Pet. 1:3, 4.

171 Who were the first Christians?

See Acts 11:26; 26:28 and I Peter 4:16 which make the earliest mention of the term "Christian" being used to distinguish this from other religious sects. Thus, though the three Magi or Eastern princes, who came, led by the star, to worship the infant Christ (see Matt. 2:1-5), and the shepherds who also worshiped (see Luke 2:15, 16, 17) and the aged Simeon and Anna (same chapter) doubtless believed, they were not Christians in name; nor does it appear that either the divine nature of the Master or his mission were clearly comprehended until John the Baptist proclaimed him as Messiah. His disciples were *literally* the first Christians, being both believers and followers. The first Christians known as such by name, were those of the church founded by Paul and Barnabas at Antioch about A.D. 34. The term "Christian" is said to have been first used in the Episcopate of Evodius at Antioch, who was appointed by the Apostle Peter as his own successor.

172 When was the first "church" so called?

The word "church" is first applied by Luke the evangelist to the company of original disciples at Jerusalem at Pentecost (Acts 2:47), and is afterwards applied in Acts, Epistles and Revelation to the whole Christian body or society, as well as the sanctified of God (Eph. 5:27), and to those who profess Christian faith under pastors (I Cor. 12:28). It was also applied to early societies of Christians in cities and provinces (Acts 8:1), to Christian assemblies (Rom. 16:5), and to small gatherings of friends and neighbors in private houses (I Cor. 11:18 and 14:19, 28). In those early days and for a long time afterward, there was no distinctive body and certainly no denomination; the church was simply an appellation describing groups of believers anywhere. Later, these groups were organized into congregations and districts and parishes were defined. Then they were called "Christians," the first use of this appellation being at Antioch. The Romanist claim to priority is an old one, but it does not stand the test of history. The title "Catholic Church" (meaning the "church universal") was originally given to the Christian Church on account of its not being confined to Jews but embracing other nationalities. The earliest use of this title was about 166 A.D., whereas the Roman Catholic Church as such did not come into existence until several centuries afterward, when the original church divided in consequence of the rivalry between the bishops of Rome and Constantinople.

173 Who first fixed the date of Christmas day on December 25th?

There does not seem to have been any special observance of the nativity until the celebration in the Eastern Church (or Greek Christian Church) in A.D. 220. The Western (or Latin) Church began to celebrate it about a century later. Both adopted the uniform date about A.D. 380. There are some writers, however, who affirm that it was solemnly celebrated among the early Christians in the second century. Chronologists disagree as to the exact year of the nativity, but the majority believe it was B.C. 5. The celebration was at first held on January 6, but toward the end of the fourth century it was changed to December 25. The Christmas tree, it is said, was first used in Europe in the eighth or ninth century, and was introduced by a German or Hungarian princess.

174 How are we to understand and interpret the act of creation?

"Creation" means, in the orthodox sense, that God of his own free will and by his absolute power, called the whole universe into being, evoking into existence that which before was nonexistent. See Rom. 4:17; Ps. 33:6, 9; Heb. 3:4; Acts 17:24; Acts 14:15; Ps. 102:5; Jer. 10:12; John 1:3; Rev. 4:11. It is needless to speculate on these matters. If we concede the absolute power of God, we must accept his power both to create and annihilate, as stated in the Scriptures. There are many problems which the finite mind cannot wholly grasp and which must be accepted by faith or left alone.

175 What is demoniac possession?

Whether or not there are evil spirits and the fact of demon possession has often proved baffling to believers. Ephesians 6:12, for instance, is a recognition of the existence and power of evil spirits. It is intimated that there are kingdoms of evil, ruled by wicked beings, which are fighting the powers of good. Against these forces the Christian, protected by the armor of God, is called to fight. The expression "in high places," or as translated in the margin, "heavenly places," may mean in the "upper air," as some interpret it, or as others hold, that even in the highest Christian experiences we are subject to temptation (which is, of course, the case), and that we must contend with the evil spirits for the possession of these high places in the spiritual world.

Although many rationalistic teachers have held that the Biblical cases of demon possession were nothing more than forms of epilepsy, violent hysteria, lunacy and other kinds of permanent or temporary mental derangement known at the present day, nothing has been actually proven which discredits the Scripture accounts and statements. Specialists today recognize the existence of recurrent mania, which sometimes assumes a destructive character. The Bible recognizes a form of lunacy different from demon possession. See Matt. 4:24. We know there are evil persons who, while alive in the flesh, do harm to others. Some have the definite experience of feeling themselves impelled to do wrong by an influence outside their own minds or bodies. Some present-day cases of insanity are really cases in which there are features that furnish a close parallel to demon possession. It is only fair to state, however, that present-day theological opinion is divided on the subject. It is certain that the belief in demon possession was held in early Christian times, and for long ages thereafter, and included at one time almost every form of mental disorder. On the other hand, it is urged that it is just as rational to believe in devils as to believe in angels. Angels are a race of personal holy beings; demons a race of personal vicious beings, both existing in a form other than human and corporeal.

176 In what sense was man created in the divine likeness?

Man's likeness to God, referred to in Gen. 1:26, is the great fact which distinguishes him from the rest of creation. He is a "person" with power to think, feel and will, and with the capacity for moral life and growth. Still further, at the beginning, man had not only the capacity for moral life, but his moral disposition was such that he loved God, loved the right, and hated the wrong. The tragedy of the fall reversed this. Man was still a person and still had the capacity for righteousness, but his spirit was so changed that he feared and distrusted God, and, to a greater or less extent, loved the evil and disliked the good. Jesus came to undo this calamity and to restore us to a moral likeness to God.

177 What is meant by the "elect"?

"Elect" is a term variously applied. It sometimes meant the ancient church, and the whole body of baptized Christians; again, it was those elected to baptism; and still again, it was the newly baptized who had just been admitted to full Christian privileges. Further it is applied to those especially chosen for the Lord's work, like his prophets and evangelists, and to those who had undergone tribulation and even martyrdom. It has been applied to the whole Jewish people as chosen of God. Finally, it is applied to individuals who, not of their own merit, but through God's grace, through Jesus Christ, are chosen not only to salvation, but to sanctification of the spirit and who are holy and blameless before the Lord. They are individuals specially chosen out of the world to be heirs of salvation and witnesses for God before men. This is not of works, but of free grace. In a general way, the "elect" are the sanctified—those chosen to salvation through sanctification of the spirit, as explained in Peter 1:2 and similar passages. They are the special vessels of the Spirit chosen in God's good pleasure to carry out his purposes. This election is of grace and not of works (see Rom. 9:18, 22, 23). In all ages such men have been evidently chosen by the Lord as his witnesses. This choice is at once an expression of his sovereignty and his grace. Paul himself was so chosen. On the other hand it should not be forgotten that salvation is by grace. The whole subject of election has been one of acute controversy for ages and has given rise to many differences of opinion. The attitude of Christians with regard to the Second Coming should be one of prayer, expectancy and constant preparation.

178 What is meant by the phrase, "saved, yet as by fire"?

The apostle in I Cor. 3:15 speaks of mistaken teachings and concludes that the man whose work was not of genuine character, who had been seeking worldly gain and popularity and not trying to win and build up souls, would lose the reward which would be given to the preacher who built on the foundation of Christ, "gold, silver, and precious stones." The unprofitable worker's work he likens to wood and stubble which would not stand the day of judgment. Even though his soul should be saved, he would miss the reward promised to the faithful worker, while his own work, being false, will not escape the destruction.

179 What is meant by "strange fire"?

The "strange fire" mentioned in Lev. 10:1, 2 is understood to mean that Nadab and Abihu, instead of taking fire into their censers from the brazen altar, took common fire which had not been consecrated, and thus were guilty of sacrilege. They had witnessed the descent of the miraculous fire from the cloud (see chapter 9:24), and they were under solemn obligation to use that fire which was specially appropriated to the altar service. But instead of doing so, they became careless, showing want of faith and lamentable irreverence, and their example, had it been permitted to pass unpunished, would have established an evil precedent. The fire that slew them issued from the most holy place, which is the accepted interpretation of the words, "from the Lord." Besides, the two young priests had already been commanded (or warned) not to do the thing they did (verse 2). They had undertaken to perform acts which belonged to the high priest alone, and even to intrude into the innermost sanctuary. See the warnings in Ex. 19:22 and Lev. 8:35.

180 What was the forbidden fruit?

There have been many interpretations of the Fall, and the books on the subject would fill a small library. The majority of the early Christian fathers held the Mosaic account to be historical, and interpreted it literally, believing that an actual fruit of some kind, not definitely known, was eaten by our first parents. A few early writers, Philo among them, regarded the story of the Fall as symbolical and mystical, shadowing forth allegorical truths, and that the serpent was the symbol of pleasure, and the offense was forbidden sensuous indulgence. Whatever the "fruit" may have been, its use was plainly the violation of a divine prohibition, the indulgence of an unlawful appetite, the sinful aspiration after forbidden knowledge. Professor Banks, several years ago, while traveling in the region of the Tigris and Euphrates, found in a little known district a place which the natives declared to be the traditional site of Eden and a tree (name and species unknown) which they believed to be the successor of the original tree of knowledge, and it was venerated greatly. It bore no fruit.

181 What are spiritual gifts?

For an enumeration of the spiritual gifts see Acts 11:17; I Cor. 12 and 13; I Peter 4:10. The gift of healing is held by some denominations as having belonged exclusively to apostolic times, while others claim that it is granted even now to those who have sufficient faith.

182 What is a "generation"?

"Generation" is used in a variety of senses in the Scriptures. In some cases, it means a period of limitless duration; in others it means the past (Isa. 51:8), and still others the future (Ps. 100:5); again, it means both the past and future (Ps. 102:24). In Gen. 6:9 it means all men living at any given time. In Prov. 30:11, 14 it refers to a class of men with some special characteristics, and in Ps. 49:19 it may be interpreted to mean the "dwelling-place." A generation, in modern phraseology, means thirty to thirty-five years, but there is no instance of the word being used in this particular sense in the Bible. Thus, "the book of the generation of Jesus Christ" is a genealogical record extending back to Abraham. In I Peter 2:9 it means an elect race.

183 What was the "gift of tongues"?

It is understood to have been not only the power of speaking various languages which the speaker had not previously studied or acquired, but also the power to speak a spiritual language unknown to man, uttered in ecstasy and understood only by those enlightened by the Holy Spirit. Paul, in I Cor. 12:10, is writing not to depreciate this gift, but to warn the Corinthians not to be led away by unprofitable or doubtful manifestations of it. Even in those early days of the Church, the leaders had difficulty in controlling the tendency to fanaticism among its adherents. The gift of tongues at Pentecost was given because of a great and urgent need. It is supposed by some authorities to have been speaking so that under the direction of the Holy Spirit it sounded to the ear of every auditor as though it were his own mother-tongue. There were many nationalities represented in the throng, but no confusion or misunderstandings. The gift of tongues on this particular occasion was the miraculous method employed to bring into the Gospel fold the strangers from other lands. The lesson is that God is not the author of confusion, and he never gives a message to his children that is unintelligible. Any "gift" or message that is incapable of being understood is *not of God*. We should try the spirits by this simple but decisive test.

184 What does the term "God's image" mean?

In discussing spiritual things, to be right, no one can go beyond the word of Scripture. The Bible tells us that God gave to man a living soul. In this sense he was in the image of his Maker in his dispositions, temperament and desires, and in his obedience to the divine will; but this condition was forfeited through sin. It could only be said thereafter of those who walked uprightly before God and were inspired of him, that they were "his offspring." (Matt. 13:38; Mark 7:10. See John 12:36; Acts 13:10; Col. 3:6.) Jesus himself drew the distinction when he told the wicked scribes and Pharisees that they were the children of the evil one, and this is the actual condition of every one living in sin, unrepentant and unforgiven. Thus while in his perfect condition man was like his Maker, in a condition of sin he is no longer so, nor has he any of the spiritual attributes and qualities that belong to the perfect condition, or even of the pardoned sinner, who has the hope through Christ of reconciliation and restoration. The Bible nowhere declares that man is of himself and inherently immortal. "The soul that sinneth, it shall die." When sin entered, then came physical decay and death; man's first condition was lost and with the continuance of sin, and unrepentant and unforgiven, he also forfeited spiritual immortality. Eternal life is the gift of God. Paul declares that Jesus, through his Gospel, brought life and immortality to light for fallen man and showed the path to restoration through repentance, forgiveness and acceptance.

**185 Where and when did the Jews
   get the name "Hebrews"?**

It is held by the best authorities and by the Jews themselves that the name is derived from Heber, or Eber (which means "from the other side," or a sojourner, or immigrant). Heber was the son of Salah and the father of Peleg (see Gen. 10-24, 11:14, and I Chron. 1:25). Abram was the first to be called a Hebrew (Gen. 14:13), presumably in the immigrant sense. The name is seldom used of the Israelites in the Old Testament, except when the speaker is a foreigner, or when the Israelites speak of themselves to one of another nation. Some writers have held that Hebrew is derived from Abraham (Abrai), but this explanation is not generally adopted.

**186 What were the "heresies" of apostolic times
   (Galatians 5:20)?**

The Greek word translated "heresies" in Gal. 5:20 means either an opinion or a party. As used in the New Testament it stands for an opinion "varying from the true exposition of the Christian faith" (as in II Peter 2:11), or a body of men following mistaken or blameworthy ideas, or, as a combination of these two meanings, "dissensions." This latter definition "dissensions" is the rendering given by Thayer in this passage. The American revision translates the word "parties," leaving, however, the expression "heresies" as the marginal reading. The three last words of the verse, "strife," "seditions," "heresies," are, in the American revision, "factions, divisions, parties."

187 What is an indulgence?

An "indulgence" is a spiritual bill of health or official act of pardon granted by the Church of Rome. It has no warrant in Scripture. There are indulgences to ease the way of souls out of purgatory, indulgences for the living, permitting them to eat meat on holy days; indulgences for the forgiveness of past sins, and, in Spain at least, and probably in other countries, indulgences for those who have committed crimes, by which they are relieved of the responsibility of their acts. Indulgences are usually purchased with a fee, although in some cases they are granted in consideration of undergoing some form of penance. A recent illustration is the distribution of indulgences during the Eucharistic Congress in Vienna, where they seem to have been granted free to many people as a reward for their loyalty and devotion to the Catholic Church on that occasion.

**188 What is meant by "because thou hast
   left thy first love"?**

These words (in Rev. 2:4) were addressed to the Christian believers at Ephesus. The "first love" does not refer to any person or influence other than Christ, but simply means that the Ephesians had lost the intensity of their affection and zeal for Christ. The Ephesian Church had had special opportunities and blessing. Under Paul's ministrations its members had received the gift of the Holy Spirit (Acts 19:1-6); the apostle had resided with them for three years (Acts 20:31); he had later written to them what is perhaps his most spiritually exalted epistle. Their experience of love ior Christ had been warm and keen. In his message sent them through John the Master is reproving them for having allowed their love for him to grow weak and cold.

189 How did Satan, the evil one, receive the name "Lucifer"?

There have been at different times various interpretations of the famous passage in Isa. 14:12: "How art thou fallen from heaven, O Lucifer, son of the morning! how art thou cut down to the ground, which didst weaken the nations!" "Lucifer" means "lightbringer," and has also been translated "son of the morning," "morning star," "brilliant," "splendid," "illustrious." Tertullian and Gregory the Great interpreted the passage in Isaiah as referring to the fall of Satan, and, since their time, the name "Lucifer" has been almost universally held by the Christian Church to be an appellation of Satan before the fall. Dr. Henderson, a famous commentator, simply interprets it "illustrious son of the morning," and holds that it has no reference to the fall of the apostate angels. Some later authorities claim that the passage has a prophetic reference to the fall from power of the great and illustrious King of Babylon, who surpassed all other monarchs of his time in splendor.

190 What were the "marks of the Lord Jesus"?

It was a practice to brand slaves with their owners' initials. A slave by showing the brand proved to whom his service was due and that no one else had a claim upon him. The marks of the Lord Jesus which Paul bore (Gal. 6:17) were the scars received in his service—the marks of the rods with which he was beaten and the wounds he received in fighting with wild beasts. He showed them as evidence that he belonged to the Lord Jesus.

191 Who were the Magi?

These wise men were from either Arabia, Mesopotamia, Egypt, or somewhere else in the East. "East" is not to be understood in our wide, modern sense, but referred to those countries that lie to the east as well as north of Palestine. Thus, Persia is referred to as the "East" (Isa. 46:11). While it is true that the Gospel account does not state the number of wise men, but simply says they were from the East, many ancient traditions have been preserved from the early days of the Christian Church, among them one which states that there were three Magian princes, and gives their names as Caspar, Melchior and Balthasar, who came with a large retinue of servants and camels. Magism is supposed to have originated in Chaldea and thence spread to the adjacent countries. The Magians are believed to have been originally Semitic. Among the Greeks and Romans they were known as Chaldeans. Daniel sympathized with the order during his exile, and probably became one of their number. They believed in God, hated idolatry and looked for a Messiah. The latter fact alone would almost be regarded as conclusive evidence of their Semitic descent. There are no absolute data, however, for asserting it positively. For many generations the Magi has looked for the fulfillment of the prophecy contained in Numbers 24:17 ". . . there shall come a star out of Jacob . . ." and when the light as guiding star indicated the direction of Judea they knew the prophecy had been fulfilled. "His star" can be interpreted as "his sign." Whatever form it assumed, it was sufficiently marked as an astronomical phenomenon to claim attention. Some writers have contended that it was visible to the Magi alone; others hold that it was a heavenly light, standing as a beacon of glory over the manger; still others, that it was the luminous figure of an angel. Tradition asserts that "the star" guided the Magi both by day and by night. The infant Saviour was probably over two months old when the visit of the Magi took place. They had seen the phenomenon of the star long before their arrival in Jerusalem, two months after Jesus had been presented in the temple, and it was some time after this that the Magi arrived in Jerusalem and went thence to Bethlehem to worship him and offer gifts. It must have taken them many months to accomplish the journey from their own country to Palestine. The Magi brought the first material Christmas gifts when they presented their love offerings.

192 What did Paul mean by "the revelation of the man of sin"?

Paul evidently believed that immediately before the second coming of Christ there would be fierce temptation and persecution (II Thess. 2:3). Christ referred to the same event (see Matt. 24:20-25). The man of sin is the Antichrist or Pseudo-Christ, who is to deceive many. He is described in Rev. 13:11-18.

193 When was the Sabbath changed from the seventh to the first day of the week?

The New Testament indicates that the Jewish Christians held both days holy. Paul evidently preached in the synagogues on the Sabbath, but it was on the first day of the week that the Gentile Christians met to break bread (Acts 20:7). This second sacred day was called the Lord's Day to distinguish it from the Sabbath, and was probably the only one observed by the Gentile converts. There is a hint of their being called to account for observing that day only, in Col. 2:16, where Paul bids them pay no heed to their critics. *The Teaching of the Twelve Apostles*, written certainly before the year 100 A.D., speaks of the Lord's Day and refers to it as a day of holy meeting and the breaking of bread (chapter 14). The primitive Christians everywhere kept it so solemnly. Pliny, the historian, refers to this fact in his letter to Trajan about A.D. 100. Justin Martyr (A.D. 140) describes the religious worship of the early Christians, their sacramental observances, etc., on the "First Day." Other early writers who make clear and unmistakable reference to the Lord's Day are Dionysius of Corinth, Irenaeus of Lyons (who asserted that the Sabbath was abolished), Clement of Alexandria, Tertullian, Origen, Cyprian, Commodian, Victorinus, and lastly Peter of Alexandria (A.D. 300), who says: "We keep the Lord's Day as a day of joy because of him who rose thereon." These evidences cover the first two centuries after our Lord's death and indicate that the Lord's Day is an institution of apostolic sanction and custom. All grounds of doubt are swept away by the fact that Constantine in an edict issued in A.D. 321 honored that day by recognizing it as one sacred to the Christians, and ordered that business should be intermitted thereon. Finally, the Council of Nicaea (A.D. 325) in its official proceedings gave directions concerning the forms of Christian worship on that day, and the Council of Laodicea (A.D. 364) enjoined rest on the Lord's Day. Thus by apostolic usage, by law and custom, by imperial edict and by the highest councils of the early Christian Church the change has been accepted and approved.

194 What is the distinction between the Sabbath, Sunday, and the Lord's Day?

The word "Sabbath" is derived from the Hebrew "Shabua," meaning "seven," or a heptad of seven days. It was employed to designate the seventh day of the Jewish week (from sunset on Friday to sunset on Saturday). Under the Christian dispensation the day of rest is changed from the seventh to the first day of the week, in memory of Christ's resurrection, and its true designation therefore is neither Sabbath (which is the ancient Jewish term) nor Sunday (which is the heathen appellation, *i. e.*, "the day of the sun"), but "the Lord's day." It is not with us, as with the Jews, a day of rest and absolute abstention from all employment, but a day of spiritual recuperation and religious activities in a thousand different directions, and a period of withdrawal from secular pursuits. Under the Mosaic law, one might not walk beyond a certain distance, nor light a fire, nor even carry a handkerchief. With us it is rather a day of celebration and glad Christian work, wholly unhampered by the ancient restrictions and obligations which were designed to apply to a dif-

ferent age and dispensation. The use of any one of the three terms—
Sunday, Sabbath or Lord's Day—is, however, with most people, rather
a matter of habit than of principle, as the historical facts are thoroughly
well established.

195 What are we to understand
by the "secret place"?

The "secret place" (see Ps. 91:1) is interpreted as meaning "the co-
vert" of his tabernacle—"the beatitude of the inner circle, or secret
shrine, to which that select company of the faithfull have access, and
where they may taste the hidden wisdom." One commentator writes
that this passage applies "to those who are more at home with God than
other Christians, and who are also more alone with God. In this inner
circle the childlike spirit is made one with the will and the love of the
almighty Father. It is a security and a refuge against whatsoever may
await us in this world or elsewhere, and those who belong to it bear on
their countenances the seal that they are free from fear of evil and that
they have gained the victory over terror and dismay." In brief, it is only
those who live closely to God who find those divine attributes which to
others are majestic and overpowering, transformed into a sure shelter
and a joy that lifts all care forever from the soul.

196 Who were the "sleeping saints"?

The "sleeping saints" (see Thes. 4:14 and Matt. 27:52, 53) are held to
be Old Testament believers who, having served the Lord faithfully according to their lights, and who looked forward to the promise of the
Messiah's coming, were quickened at the moment of Jesus' death, although they did not come out of their graves until his resurrection. The
opening of the graves was symbolic proclamation that death was "swallowed up in victory"; and the rising of the saints after Jesus' resurrection fittingly showed that the Saviour of the world was to be the "first"
that should rise from the dead. (See Acts 26:23; Col. 1:18; Rev. 1:5.)

197 How are we to understand
the "spirits in prison"?

The passage in I Peter 3:19, 20 is one which has been much discussed.
It is generally interpreted as meaning that the preaching to the spirits
"in prison" implies not the preaching of the Gospel, but the announcement of Christ's finished work. Nor does it imply a second day of grace.
The spirits were clearly those of the Antediluvians. The passage, however, is mysterious and has puzzled Bible students in all times. Peter is
the only Bible writer who mentions the occurrence, whatever it may
have been, so that there are no other passages to shed light upon it. The
apostle was speaking in the context of the operation of the Holy Spirit
and it has been generally thought by Augustine among the Fathers and

by Dr. Adam Clarke and other modern commentators that he referred to the Antediluvians as having, like others who lived before Christ, been under the Spirit's influence, though they repelled it. In that case his meaning would be that Christ had from the beginning been preaching through, or by, the Spirit, to men in all ages, as he preaches to men now by his Spirit through his ministers. Other theologians, Dean Alford among them, contend that somewhere in the universe these Spirits were imprisoned and that Christ preached to them in the interval between his death and resurrection, though that view is surrounded by other difficulties which are obvious. The reference is incidental and does not practically concern us so much as does the lesson Peter is enforcing, that through the Holy Spirit we are enabled to live to the spirit and not to the flesh.

198 What is the Biblical and theological meaning of the word *spiritual*?

The word is one which Christians ought to guard zealously in religious phraseology. There is a recent tendency to use the word in a loose sense, giving it merely its philosophical or scientific meaning rather than its real Bible and theological significance. In secular phraseology the word means: relating to spirit, rather than to matter. Many varying shades of meaning grow out of this basic idea: one poet may be more spiritual than another; one artist than another; one musician than another. In this sense the word implies a relation to thoughts, emotions, impulses, connected with the soul of a man rather than his body. But the Christian use of the word is distinctive. It is given as the third definition of the word in the Standard Dictionary: "Of or relating to the soul as acted on by the Holy Spirit." An apt quotation from Henry Drummond is given: "The *spiritual* life is the gift of the living Spirit. The *spiritual* man is no mere development of the natural man. He is a new creation, born from above." In Christian phraseology, then, a man is spiritual as he is possessed, filled and dominated by the Holy Spirit.

199 What was the purpose of the "tree of knowledge"?

The tree of knowledge of good and evil (Gen. 2:8) was designed as a test of obedience by which our first parents were to be tried, whether they would be good or evil; whether they would chose to obey God or break his commandments, and the eating of the fruit of the tree revealed to them their new condition as sinners under divine displeasure.

200 What is known concerning the "tree of life"?

Gen. 2:9 and 3:22, 24 tells practically all that we know of the "tree of life," although a vast amount of speculative literature has appeared on the subject. Various references to the "tree of life" elsewhere in Scripture show that it was regarded as the means provided by divine wisdom as an antidote against disease and bodily decay. Access to it was conditioned upon our first parents obeying the injunction against eating the forbidden fruit of the "tree of knowledge," which was the test of obedience. Certain Hebrew writers have called the two trees "the trees of the lives," holding that the wondrous property of one in perpetuating physical life and conferring perennial health was in direct contrast with the other, the "tree of knowledge," which was sure to occasion bodily suffering and death. "The tree of life was, in short, a sacramental tree," writes one commentator, "by the eating of which man, in his state of innocence, kept himself in covenant with God."

201 What is it to be "unequally yoked"?

The passage in II Cor. 6:14 may have a wide interpretation. "Unequally yoked" may mean bound together with one who is alien in spirit, although it might also mean that the disparity in culture or possessions, the difference in race, or in religious belief, are to be regarded as insurmountable barriers. In early Israelitish times, marriages with heathen were forbidden; so in Christian times, unions of believers and infidels, or unbelievers in any form, were to be avoided. Righteousness and wickedness cannot pull in the same harness, and as our first duty is to God, we should put away from us all avoidable contact that would hinder its performance. Paul in the passage in question clearly had in mind the union of believers with unbelievers.

202 Who are the "witnesses" who surround the believers?

They are probably the worthies referred to in Heb. 11 chapter, whose triumph through faith are recalled. The word "witnesses" (Heb. 12:1) has two meanings and it is not certain which of the two the writer of the epistle had in his mind. A witness may be a spectator, or he may be one who testifies as in a court of justice. If the word in this passage is used in the former sense, it implies that departed and glorified saints are observing the trials and victories of the Christian on earth. If the word refers to a testifier, it means that the Christian has good reason for making the effort mentioned in the passage, because of the testimony of the Old Testament saints cited in the previous chapter.

JESUS' LIFE AND DEATH

203 Does the doctrine of Jesus' divinity depend
on the miraculous conception?

Even if the doctrine of the miraculous conception were abandoned, it would be difficult, if not impossible, to account for the facts of Christ's life, by any other theory than that of his being the incarnation of God. If you regard him as man, you must explain how he, a plain peasant, trained as a carpenter, brought up in an obscure Oriental town, could live such a life as he undoubtedly lived, and give utterance to truths which have thrilled the world for nineteen hundred years. Besides this he spoke with authority, making claims to a higher nature, which if he did not consciously possess that higher nature, would be false claims. His whole life was consistent with his divinity, and, therefore, even persons who reject his miraculous conception, have good ground for believing him to be divine. It is the only theory that explains such a life. There is no need, however, to reject the doctrine of the miraculous conception. The more you study the life of Jesus, the less you will be surprised to learn that the promise of God through the prophets, of the union of divinity and humanity, was literally fulfilled in him.

204 Was Christ, the Saviour, born in the year 1
or in 5 B.C.?

As we are told in the Gospels that Herod was living and slaughtered the children after Jesus was born (see Matt. 2:16), and as it is claimed by chronologists to be a matter of record that he died in 750 U.C., which corresponds to B.C. 4, it is obvious that Jesus was born before that date. Then, on the other hand, he was born after the decree for the census (Luke 2:1) was issued. From Tertullian we learn that the decree was issued in 748 and the enrollment began in 749 U.C., which corresponds to B.C. 5. Thus the birth is fixed by those two occurrences.

205 Is there a real conflict in the evangelists'
genealogies of Christ?

The purpose of publishing the Saviour's genealogy was to show that he had descended from David. If the genealogy of Mary had been given, it would have carried no weight with the Jews, as they would not admit the divine conception, and regarded Joseph as the head of the family. It was necessary, on their account, to show that Joseph had descended from David. It really, however, includes the others, as the descendants of David were so proud of their distinction, and of the Messianic promise involved, that no man of that family would take a wife of any other family. Mary, undoubtedly, therefore, was descended from David. The theory has been propounded and supported by Weiss and other scholars that the genealogy of Luke is that of Mary. Luke says (3:23) that Joseph was the son of Heli, whereas Matthew says (1:16) that he was the son of Jacob. It is suggested that Luke's statement should read, "who was the son-in-law of Heli," that is, married the daughter of Heli. Luke traces the descent through David's son Nathan, while Matthew traces it through Solomon. Even that explanation, however, has its incongruities, of which there is no clear explanation. The fact that Mary before her marriage went to Bethlehem to be taxed or registered (Luke 2:5), would indicate that she was of David's house. It is noteworthy, too, that Christ's claims to Messiahship were never challenged on that ground. If there had been any flaw in his pedigree, the Jews would have seized upon it without a doubt, because the prophecies clearly stated that Messiah would be descended from David.

206 Who were the brothers of Jesus?

The brethren of Jesus are named in the New Testament as James, Joses, Simon and Judas. In Matt. 12:46; Matt. 13:55; John 2:12, and Acts 1:14 they are generally understood to be proper brothers, all being named together conjointly with the mother of Jesus, and the same is inferred from John 7:5. Some of the early church writers, however, held that they were merely relatives or cousins (sons of Mary the sister of Jesus' mother), it being a common custom to call all immediate relatives, nephews, cousins and half-brothers, by the general designation of "brothers" or "brethren." Further, the early fathers of the church held that Mary, the mother of Jesus, had no other children. The question still remains open whether they were not the sons of Joseph by a former marriage, and therefore half-brothers to Jesus. On the other hand Matt. 1:25 and Luke 2:7 favor the view that they were brothers and that Jesus was the "first-born." Sisters of Jesus are also mentioned in Matt. 13:56 and Mark 6:3, but their names are not given. Much has been written on the subject without positive determination, although most modern commentators hold to the opinion that the "brethren" in question were the sons of Joseph and Mary, and that Mary's mother's sister had two sons, named James and Joses.

207 Is there a rational explanation
of the Star of Bethlehem?

There was a remarkable conjunction of Jupiter and Saturn about that time, which must have been a very brilliant spectacle, and which would be very impressive to astrologers. It might lead them to the belief that some mighty potentate was born, and probably to make inquiry as to such birth. The fact, that would doubtless be known to all Orientals, that the Jews expected a Messiah, may have led the Magi to Palestine. Their inquiry for "the King of the Jews" seems to imply that it was there they expected to find such a being as the conjunction portended. The difficulty, however, is to explain the star going before them (Matt. 2:9). As they traveled westward, it might have had that appearance, but not so definitely as the account implies. Another explanation is that it was possibly a meteor divinely directed.

208 Did the parents of our Lord take him after his birth to Jerusalem or to Egypt?

According to some, the accounts in Matthew and in Luke do not agree. But there is really no discrepancy. After the birth of Jesus, the parents remained at Bethlehem until the time arrived for presenting the Babe in the Temple, being the end of the days of purification. After the presentation, Joseph and Mary with the child went to Nazareth, adjusted their affairs and returned to Bethlehem, where they were dwelling—no longer in a stable but in "a house"—when the incident of the Magis' visit occurred. These wise men had first gone to Jerusalem, whence they were directed to Bethlehem. After their visit Joseph was warned by an angelic messenger and the flight into Egypt followed. To get a clear idea of the order of events, the records of the four evangelists must be taken as a whole, as one records incidents which another omits. Thus Mark and John contain nothing relative to the childhood of Jesus, while Matthew and Luke taken together, give a clear outline of these events, though Luke omits all reference to the return to Bethlehem and the journey into Egypt, the latter of which Matthew relates with considerable detail. In no sense did any one of the four evangelists intend to present a complete chronological record of the Saviour's earthly life, but each designed rather to supplement what the others had written.

209 How could Jesus, being already perfect, increase in wisdom?

The statement in Luke 2:52 is explicit and there is no reason for doubting it. Jesus was subject to human conditions and limitations so far as the divine nature could be subjected. We read of His being weary, of his being hungry and thirsty, and we are assured that He was tempted in all points like as we are, which all show that in His physical nature He was human. Doubtless He would be educated like other boys, and probably His consciousness of divinity would be gradual, and possibly not complete until the forty days in the desert. His questioning the doctors in the Temple (Luke 2:46) is supposed by some authorities to have been not catechizing them but to obtain information.

210 How old was Jesus when he began to understand the nature of his mission?

Although one cannot trace with any degree of precision the various stages of development of the consciousness of his mission, it is evident from the Gospel record that it must have begun early and gradually increased to complete appreciation as manhood approached. We are told that even in childhood he "grew and waxed strong in spirit, filled with wisdom," and the "grace of God was upon him." (Luke 2:40.) In youth we find him questioning and expounding to the rabbis in the temple and "increasing in stature and in wisdom and in favor with God and man." His wonderful knowledge, his amazing questions and his discerning answers to the elders must have become more and more accentuated during the passage of these early years, and we may gather that Mary had already premonitions of the future career of her Divine Son, since she pondered over and "hid all these things in her heart." There are indications that seem to warrant the conclusion that long before the opening of his public ministry, Jesus was absorbed by the thought of the mission to which he was destined. He knew his Father's business and did it, and he frequented his Father's house. His life and surroundings in Nazareth brought him in contact with a simple, earnest people and with sorrow and suffering. These were years of character-building and development. They bore fruit when the time was ripe for his public ministry and prepared him for the baptism at John's hands. This was the last act of his private life and the first that marked the beginning of his public mission, when the heavenly voice proclaimed him as the "Beloved Son" and the Baptist bare record that he was the Son of God.

211 Why is Christ described as a high priest after the order of Melchizedek?

The writer of the Epistle to the Hebrews, whether Paul or some other person, was showing the superiority of Christianity to Judaism. It too had its priest and sacrifice. The Jew might answer that Christ could not be a high priest as he did not come of the tribe of Levi, to which the priesthood was confined. The answer is that there was another order of priesthood—that of Melchizedek, which Abraham recognized (Gen. 14:20) by paying him tithes. Christ belonged to that order as the Psalmist had predicted (Ps. 110:4), and Levi, through his ancestor, had thus indicated his superiority. It is an argument that would have weight with a Jew. It is a curious fact, that among the recently discovered Tel el-Amarna tablets, are letters from one Ebed-tob, King of Uru Salim (Jerusalem), who describes himself as not having received the crown by inheritance from father or mother, but from the mighty God. We know nothing of Melchizedek beyond the scanty references in Genesis, but this tablet appears to intimate that the ancient Kings of Jerusalem claimed this divine right.

212 As God, how could Jesus be weary, hungry and thirsty?

In his divinity, no; but in his humanity he could be all of these. Scripture tells us that in his human aspect he was "in all things as we are." What we have in the Gospels is the report by his hearers of what he said. As John tells us (21:25), it is a very imperfect and meagre report, but sufficient for the purpose the writers had in view. At the same time, it is doubtful how much of the Godhead Jesus may voluntarily have laid aside when he became man. Paul says (Phil. 2:7, R.V.) that "he emptied himself," from which we infer that in order fully to enter into human feeling he divested himself of such qualities as would have kept him from feeling hunger, etc. It behooved him to be made in all things like unto his brethren, and he could not be that unless he temporarily relinquished some portion of his divinity.

213 Why was Jesus baptized?

The Saviour evidently ranked baptism as one of the acts inseparable from his Messianic calling (see John 1:31). By being publicly baptized he entered into John's community, which was introductory to his greater Messianic work. Further, it was the means of revealing himself to the Baptist and through him to the people. John was the forerunner of the Messiah, and it was especially fitting that he should personally serve at Jesus' consecration to his Messianic work, and assist at the beginning of his public career.

214 Did Christ make wine at the Cana feast or was it grape juice?

The fact that the ruler of the feast pronounced the miraculous wine "the best," showed that it was really wine, but we are not justified in concluding that it was alcoholic or intoxicating. There has been endless discussion on this point, but we are satisfied that divine power never gave any gift to man that would degrade or hurt him.

215 What was Jesus' first sermon?

Luke tells us (Luke 3:23) that Jesus was about thirty years of age when he began his ministry. During his sojourn in Galilee (chap. 4, v. 14) he had already spoken in the synagogues. Mark 1:14, 15 mentions these instances, though very briefly, and so also does John 2:11. His first recorded sermon is mentioned in Luke 4:16-28. It was on the Sabbath day, and he took his text from the prophet Esais. He had passed through his forty days' preparatory vigil in the wilderness and was filled with the Spirit, and ready for his work.

216 Did Christ sing any hymns?

While there is no record of such a thing, in Scripture, or anywhere else, it does not seem improbable. See the passage in Matt. 26:30 and Mark 14:26. The closing hymn here referred to was probably the chant called by the Jews "the great Hallel," and which consists of parts of Psalms 115, 116, 117 and 118, these parts being sung at the close of the Passover. "It is hardly conceivable," writes one commentator, "that the eleven disciples should have been singing to cheer their sorrowing hearts and that their Lord should have stood silent beside them."

217 Was Jesus really tempted as we are?

Unquestionably he submitted to all the liabilities of the human condition; we are told expressly that he "was in all things as we are." The appeal of the tempter was to his ambition, and the purpose, as some commentators conclude, was to excite in his mind the desire for worldly power and dominion. Even his own followers had cherished visions of an earthly kingdom. The question whether he could by any possibility have yielded has often been asked, but it is one that must remain unanswered. To say that it was impossible would imply that he was not wholly subject to human conditions and temptations; while to admit its possibility would make him less than divine. The incident shows to us that while the vision of sudden power may have been alluring, it could not move him from the fixed and beneficent purpose of his great mission, which was to establish his kingdom in the hearts of men by love and sacrifice, and by the example of his perfect humanity. Contrasted with such a kingdom, all the glory of worldly pomp and power are trivial, transient and unsatisfying.

218 Could Jesus sin?

The Christian Church has always held that Christ was absolutely free from sin. This is in accordance with the explicit teachings of Scripture, which states that he was in all things "as we are, yet without sin." (Heb. 4:15.) He is also described as the Holy One, the Just and Righteous (Acts 3:14, 22:14; I Peter 3:18; I John 2:29, 3:7). See also I Peter 11:21, 22; I Peter 1:19; II Cor. 5:21 and other passages. One of the earliest of Church councils (A.D. 451) formulated the doctrine of his sinlessness thus: "Truly man, with a rational soul and body, with like essence with us as to his manhood, and in all things like us, with sin excepted," and this has remained unchanged as the accepted Christological doctrine of the Christian Church. Whether he *could not* sin has been much discussed. Doubtless he *could* have yielded; but the fact remains that he *did not* yield to temptation and continued to the end an example of perfect purity and sinlessness—the condition of man before his fall.

219 Did Satan own the kingdoms which he offered in the temptation?

No; Satan did not own them. But it is still true that they were in his hands to offer to Christ; he had usurped them. At Creation, Man was placed in the Garden of Eden as lord over all. "Thou hast put all things under his feet," was true of the first Adam (see Ps. 8:4-9), while it will only be carried out permanently under the second Adam. (See I Cor. 15:25; Eph. 1:22; Heb. 2:6-9.) But when Adam listened to Satan and fell, he transferred his allegiance, and through that Satan became the "prince of this world." (See John 14:30; 16:11; 18:36; Luke 22:53; II Cor. 4:4). The consequence of this has been that the empires of the world have been truly delineated as wild beasts. (Dan. 7:3.) It was universal empire Satan offered to Jesus, but which he refused to take from his hand. When Satan said, "to whomsoever I will I give it" (Luke 4:6), the Lord did not deny it, but was content to go on in the path of obedience until the time should come for the Father to give it to him. (Matt. 11:27.) Then "the kingdoms of this world shall become the kingdoms of our Lord and of his Christ, and he shall reign for ever and ever" (Rev. 11:15). The fact that "the powers that be are ordained of God" (Rom. 13:1), does not conflict with this. God did put authority in the hands of Noah, Gen. 9:6, but this has been usurped by Satan, through the willingness of man to be led by him. The fact that the devil has so much to do with the affairs of men in the world is a proof of this. On the other hand, the kingdoms and glory of the world were not his to give. He has no valid claim or right to anything in God's material universe. "The earth is the Lord's and the fulness thereof." The temptation of Christ in the wilderness, according to the best critical authorities was of a subjective character. That is to say, it was a mental appeal to do wrong. It was a phantasy, a deception, a sham. This is the way Satan tempts us, and Christ was in all points tempted as we are. Satan does not need to take us up on a high mountain to show us the kingdoms of the world. He can put a mental picture before us. When we are tempted to do as he bids us and think that certain things will come to pass, we soon discover that the devil has deceived us. When he speaketh a lie he speaketh of his own, for he is a liar, and the father of lies. His tempting promises of glory, greatness and prosperity are all false. Obedience to him, in the end only pierces the soul with many sorrows. He makes the thief believe that his acts will never be known. But God says, "Be sure your sin will find you out." The sensualist, who gratifies his lust, in the end becomes a moral leper. Lastly, he makes the sinner believe a lie that he may be eternally ruined.

220 What became of the nine lepers who did not return after being cleansed?

The inference to be drawn from the Gospel narrative (Luke 17:11-19) is that the nine, being healed merely in body, were so elated and over-joyed with their newfound health that they ungratefully forgot the source of their restoration, whereas the one leper who returned, had learned the deeper lesson of Christ's divinity, and had experienced that inner cleansing and clearness of spiritual vision which, after the first ex-uberant outburst was over, brought him back grateful and loving to the Saviour's feet to pour out his thanks. The nine are not again mentioned.

221 In what kind of a body did Moses appear at the transfiguration?

Probably the spiritual body, to which Paul refers (I Cor. 15:44). It is difficult for us to conceive of such a body because we are so accus-tomed to recognize the soul only as it manifests itself through the senses. But it would be rash to conclude that the soul is dependent on the physical senses for its powers. It may have, or may acquire after the death of the body, new and perhaps superior means of communicating thought and feeling.

222 Were there two different anointments by two different Marys, Mary of Bethany and Mary Magdalene?

There have been many conflicting interpretations of the Scripture narrative concerning Mary of Bethany and the woman spoken of in Luke 7:37. The majority agree that there were two anointings, one dur-ing Jesus' Galilean ministry (Luke 7), the other at Bethany before the last entry into Jerusalem (Matt. 26, Mark 14, John 12). There is not the slightest trace in the Scripture story of any blot on the life of Mary of Bethany. The epithet, Magdalene, seems to have been chosen for the especial purpose of distinguishing the one to whom it was applied from other Marys. Mary or Maryam was a common name, which seems to have led to misunderstanding. Some of the earliest Church writers en-tirely reject the identification of the two Marys, although it is an error into which not a few have fallen. It is to be noted that Luke 7:37 speaks of a woman "which was a sinner," but gives no name, while Luke 10:38, 39 speaks of Mary and Martha as though neither had been named be-fore and without any evidence of previous reference. The whole ques-tion is one concerning which no one can speak with final authority although the reasonable inference is, as we have said, that they were dif-ferent individuals.

223 What prayer did our Saviour offer at the last supper?

The words Jesus employed are not recorded, but the blessing pronounced may have been that which was customarily asked by the head of the household at all Hebrew paschal feasts. It is in these words: "Blessed art thou, O Lord our God, King of the universe, who hast created the fruit of the vine! Blessed art thou, O Lord our God, King of the universe, who hast chosen us above all nations, and exalted us above all peoples, and hast sanctified us with thy commandments. Thou hast given us, O Lord our God, appointed seasons for joy, festivals and holy days for rejoicing, such as the feast of unleavened bread, the time of our liberation, for holy convocation, to commemorate our exodus from Egypt." As Jesus gave to the Last Supper a broader spiritual significance than the Passover possessed, it is probable that he gave to the opening words of blessing a character in keeping with his high purpose. The new Passover was not to be for the Jewish nation alone, but for the whole world.

224 Was Judas at the institution of the Lord's Supper?

It is doubtful whether Judas was present at the institution of the Lord's Supper. He was present at the foot-washing and at the early part of the feast, but he could not remain after Christ spoke of his imminent betrayal and showed his knowledge of the identity of the guilty man. Then Judas went out, but we do not know whether the breaking of the bread and the blessing of the cup had already taken place: from Luke's narrative it would appear that they had; Matthew and Mark, however, mention the ceremony after the conversation about the betrayal, which would imply that Judas was not present at the ceremony. The Evangelists were concerned more about the spiritual significance of the events of that agitating night than about presenting those events in consecutive order.

225 What was the value of the thirty pieces of silver that Judas received?

The pieces of silver were probably shekels. The value of the whole sum in our modern reckoning was about eighteen dollars. Zechariah had predicted the whole transaction (see Zech. 11:12, 13): "They weighed for my price thirty pieces of silver and the Lord said cast it unto the potter," etc. It is not likely that Judas acted from avarice only, though he was fond of money. He probably meant to force Christ's hand. He may have thought him backward in claiming the kingdom, and supposed that if he was driven to bay, he would deliver himself by a miracle and declare himself king. That theory is confirmed by his committing suicide when he discovered the consequences of his act.

226 How did the sleeping disciples know what words Jesus uttered in the garden?

One of the functions of the Holy Spirit was to bring all things to the remembrance or knowledge of the Apostles. Though the Evangelists record most fully the events they witnessed, they record other matters of which they could have had no knowledge except by revelation. This may have been one of them. But it is not stated that they slept all the time they were with Christ in the Garden. The account rather implies men struggling to keep awake. Christ said of them that their spirit was willing. They may have heard the few words they record, though missing the remainder of what may have been, and probably was, a long prayer.

227 Who was the "certain young man" of Mark 14:51?

There has been much speculation as to who this young man was. It has been suggested by some commentators, perhaps rightly, that inasmuch as he is mentioned only by Mark, he was Mark, the evangelist; himself. Mark's family was prominently connected with incidents of the Lord's last days and following the resurrection. Thus the "upper room" where the Last Supper was eaten and which later witnessed the descent of the Holy Spirit was in the ownership of that family and Mark's mother was the sister of Barnabas, a wealthy Levite of Cypress.

228 Was the pain the Saviour suffered on Calvary physical or mental?

Pain is a difficult thing to measure. The sorrow of Jesus will always be one of the awe-inspiring, baffling events of the world story. It is impossible to read the Bible deeply, particularly after one has become personally acquainted with Jesus and observed the amazing power that the facts of his suffering and death possess over human souls, without realizing that there must have been far deeper anguish than can be accounted for by the mere facts of his humiliation, rejection, torture and death. If we consider the merely physical pain we must acknowledge that others have apparently borne as much, though we must also acknowledge that there are almost infinite degrees of susceptibility to pain. A wound which will cause little pain to a man of a certain temperament and organization may be excruciating to one of finer and more acute sensitiveness. But the real agony of Jesus must have been different from either physical or mental. There is a sane note, a moral note in his suffering that puts it altogether beyond our comprehension. Matthew, Mark and Luke all record the fact that as he died he cried out with a loud voice. That seems strange from what we know of the dauntless courage of Jesus. Some immeasurable, inconceivable suffering must lie back of that cry. So also his appeal in the garden for deliverance at the last hour. There must have been an infinite anguish ahead to compel him to ask for another way. We get the clearest hint in the grievous prayer from the cross: "My God, my God, why hast thou forsaken me?" There must have been some definite, conscious, agonizing break in the eternal love which had bound the Father and the Son together. Perhaps there was deeper truth than the ancient formulators of the creed knew in those strange words: "He descended into hell." No—of all the griefs in the world that of Jesus while he was on the cross and while his body lay in the grave, is unique. Its depth, its duration, none can know. They counted the hours he spent on the cross and the hours in the grave. But what eternities of spirit anguish he underwent we may never know. But, praise God! they were enough to shock every penitent soul that hears of it into a new life, a life in which sin is hated and righteousness loved, a life of which the crucified and risen Saviour is the eternal Light and the never-failing hope and joy.

229 Why was the inscription "The King of the Jews" used on the cross?

From the fact that the evangelists give us three different forms for the inscription over the cross it has been argued that they were not accurate in their portrayal of things and events. There is, however, nothing here to disturb anyone. Matthew 27:37 has it, "This is Jesus the King of the Jews," using probably the Greek form; St. Mark 15:26, "The King of the Jews," and Luke 23:38, "This is the King of the Jews," availed themselves of the Roman form, and John 19:19, "Jesus the Nazarene, the King of the Jews," probably employed the Hebrew form. Since the four accounts of the inscription do not differ in import the exact language of the insulting designation is of little or no consequence.

230 How many hours was Jesus on the cross?

It is uncertain how long Jesus lived after he was nailed to the cross. At the longest it could not have been more than six hours. Mark says (15:25), "It was the third hour (or nine o'clock), and they crucified him"; and again (15:34), "And at the ninth hour (3 p. m.), Jesus cried," etc. John, on the other hand, describing the proceedings before Pilate (19:14), says: "It was about the sixth hour." But John was probably reckoning the hours by the Roman method from midnight, which, allowing for the subsequent judicial farce and the journey to Golgotha, would bring him into accord with Mark. Matthew also (27:46), represents Jesus as being alive at the ninth hour (three o'clock). Matthew, Mark and Luke, referring to the darkness, say that it lasted from the sixth hour (noon), till the ninth hour (3 p.m.), but it does not appear to have begun until Jesus had been some time on the cross. The ancients had not the means that we have of accurately reckoning time; so that we cannot be certain of the hour, and it may have been later than nine when Jesus was nailed to the cross. He evidently did not live long after three, probably not many minutes.

231 At what hour did the crucifixion of Jesus take place?

Mark says (15:25) it was about the third hour, or, as we should say, nine o'clock. Again, the sixth hour is referred to by three of the evangelists (Matt. 27:45; Mark 15:33; Luke 23:44), when Jesus had apparently been three hours on the cross. In the next verses, in all three cases, the ninth hour is mentioned as the time of death, which would be three o'clock. The statement of John (19:14) is believed to be due to a copyist's error, or to his using the Roman method of reckoning.

232 Was Jesus happy or sorrowful on his way to the cross?

We cannot suppose so, although some have held that, because he was doing the Father's will, therefore he must have been happy even in the midst of suffering. But in the narratives of the evangelists we find only the impression that he was filled with sorrow. From the time of the agony in the garden (see Matt. 26:37) till the last cry on the cross, this cloud was not lifted. On the way to Calvary, together with his sorrow for the people who "knew not what they did"—who were now as ready to mock and revile him as they were only a short time before to joyfully acclaim him—there must have been a deeper burden of sadness for his base betrayal and for his utter desertion by all of his panic-stricken disciples, even by Peter, that weighed down at every step. Yet, wounded, bleeding, and subjected to the worst indignities, he bore it all without a murmur even while his heart was breaking. He was sustained by the sense of his high mission and bore his suffering with such fortitude that even his enemies remarked it (Luke 23:47). Thus, to the last moments of his earthly life, he was "a man of sorrows and acquainted with grief."

233 Who were the more guilty of Christ's death, the Jews or the Romans?

Both were guilty, although the onus of the malevolent persecution of Christ rests with the Jews. When they brought him before Pilate and that official, although representing the power of Rome, and even admitting that he could "find no fault" in Jesus weakly yielded to the fanatical clamor for the sacrifice, he became a principal with a full share of responsibility for the tragedy that followed. A stronger man, backed by the Roman authority and convinced of the injustice of the mob's demand, would have resolutely refused to permit the innocent to suffer. History is full of passages recording the nobility and justice of men whose firmness checked the commission of crimes in the name of law.

Roman justice, even in that day, was proverbial. It was therefore the duty of Pilate to have executed justice as Governor of Judea. When he had examined Christ and declared that he "found no fault in him" (John 19:6), and again when he declined to acknowledge responsibility for the "blood of this just person," he was pledged by his judicial oaths to execute not injustice in obedience to clamor, but justice, even in the face of the whole Jewish nation. Roman laws governed Judea; the native laws, secular and ecclesiastical, could only be recognized and enforced where they did not conflict with those of Rome. Pilate stifled the voice of conscience, set aside the result of his judicial inquiry, disregarded the warning of his wife, and basely consented to a murder in obedience to Jewish clamor. The priests, it is true never wavered in their demand for the Saviour's death, and even warned Pilate that if he refused to order the execution he would not be Caesar's friend. This touched the Governor's weak point: his ambition. To stand well with Caesar he gratified the populace and ordered his troops to carry out their wishes.

234 What became of Pontius Pilate
after he judged Jesus?

There are various legends and traditions concerning Pilate's further history. The *Acta Pilati*, an apocryphal work still extant, contains some of these. One tradition is to the effect that the Emperor Tiberius, alarmed at the universal darkness which had suddenly fallen on his empire upon the day of the crucifixion, summoned Pilate to Rome to answer for having caused it. Pilate was condemned to death, but pleaded ignorance as his excuse. His wife died at the moment of his execution. Another tradition is that Tiberius, having heard of Christ's miracles, wrote to Pilate bidding him send Jesus to Rome. Pilate was compelled to confess that he had crucified him, and was thrown into prison and committed suicide. Earth and sea refused to receive his body, and it was repeatedly cast up, finally being sunk in a pool at Lucerne, under the shadow of Mount Pilatus. Josephus, the Jewish historian (in *Antiquities*, 18 chap. 4:1), states authoritatively that Pilate met with political disaster. The Samaritans complained against him to Vitellius, president of Syria, who sent Pilate to Rome to answer to Caligula, the successor of Tiberius, and he soon afterward killed himself. The scene of this act is uncertain.

235 Could Pilate have done other than
condemn Jesus to death?

Yes, as Pilate told Jesus (John 19:10), he had power to release him. His difficulty lay in his own bad record. If he refused to oblige the Jews in this matter, they might go to Rome and accuse him before the Emperor of many acts of misgovernment. It would have done him no harm for them to complain of his letting Jesus go. In that matter, his defense that the prisoner was innocent, would have been sufficient. But they would probably say nothing about Jesus; they would bring charges against him for which he had no defense and he would lose his office. He concluded that he could not afford to set them at defiance, although he ought to have done so.

236 Could Christ actually have come down from the cross?

Christ had done many miracles, as when he healed the blind, stilled the storm and raised the dead. His remark to Peter (Matt. 26:53) that his Father would give him twelve legions of angels if he asked for deliverance, showed that he believed he could be delivered if he wished. The only reason why he had no desire to come down from the cross was that love of the human race held him there. He knew that his voluntary sacrifice was essential to the great atonement for the sins of the world. He had foreseen his own death on the cross and on several occasions had spoken of it.

237 How many appearances are recorded of Christ after his resurrection?

Eleven. I Mark 16:9-11; John 20:11-18; 2 Matt. 28:8-10; Mark 16:8; Luke 24:9-11; 3 Luke 24:34; 4 Mark 16:12, 13; Luke 24:13-35; 5 Mark 16:14; Luke 24:36-49; John 20:19-23; 6 John 20:24-29; 7 Matt. 28:16-20; Mark 16:15-18; 8 John 21:1-24; 9 Matt. 28:16; 10 Acts 1:3-8; 11 Acts 9:4; I Cor. 15:8.

238 Where did Christ get the garments which he wore when he appeared to Mary on resurrection morn?

The question has often been asked, but never satisfactorily answered. We must conclude, in the absence of any Scriptural statement about the garments, that they belonged to that strange mysterious life on which Christ entered when he rose from the dead. That they were not of the ordinary materials seems clear from the Gospel narratives, which represent Christ as "vanishing out of their sight" (Luke 24:31), appearing among his disciples in a room the doors of which were shut (John 20:19), and being seen now at Jerusalem, now at Emmaus, and in Galilee, at least forty miles distant. Whatever the garments were, and wheresoever they came from, they were clearly not of the substantial kind, which would have prevented these disappearances.

239 In what body did Jesus appear after the resurrection?

The language of Luke 24:39 is clear and explicit. The resurrection body proved that Jesus was "the Son of God with power" in taking to himself the same identical body which had been crucified and laid in the grave, and yet which had been glorified "by some such inscrutable change as took place at the transfiguration." The very fact attests him as the Master of life and death and as divine. He continued forty days on earth after the resurrection, taking again to himself that life which he had laid down, in order that his followers and the whole world might be convinced of the completeness of his triumph over the grave and that he had not "seen corruption." He ascended to heaven a spiritual body. (Phil. 3:21, Col. 3:4.)

240 How long was Jesus in the grave?

In Matthew 12:40 he said that he would be three days and three nights in the heart of the earth. The passage has long perplexed Biblical students. The most probable explanation is that Christ adopted a mode of expression common among the Jews, and said that he should be in the grave three "evening-mornings," which the translators rendered three days and nights. The Jews also had a rule, of which there are several examples in other parts of the Bible, that any part of the *onah*, or period, counted as the whole. Thus the interval between the crucifixion and the burial on the Friday would be part of Friday, and would count as one "evening-morning"; from sunset on Friday to sunset on Saturday would count as the second; and from Saturday sunset to the resurrection on Sunday morning as the third. The disciples evidently regarded the Sunday as the third day, as is seen by the conversation on the way to Emmaus, when Cleopas said: "This is the third day since these things were done." (Luke 24:21.)

Professor Wescott, a great New Testament scholar and one of the editors of the most widely used text of the Greek New Testament, held the view that crucifixion and burial occurred on Thursday; but practically every other authority disagrees with him. The celebration of Friday as the day of our Lord's death and burial dates back to extremely early times in Church history. It is true that the expression "three days and three nights" in the passage you mention sounds very emphatic to our Western ears, accustomed to the sharp distinction conveyed by the words in our time and speech. But, as Dr. Whedon comments here, "the Jews reckoned the entire twenty-four hours in an unbroken piece as a *night-and-day*. They counted the odd fragment of a day, in computation, as an entire night-and-day. Our Lord, therefore, was dead during three night-and-days."

241 Did Jesus die of a broken heart?

That is the opinion of many who have written on the subject, physicians included. It is certain that the crucifixion did not kill him, as that was a death by exhaustion. Jesus was not exhausted, for we are told (Matt. 27:50) that he "cried with a loud voice" when he yielded up the ghost. The fact that when the soldier pierced his side there came thereout blood and water (John 19:34) indicates, according to eminent surgeons, that the heart was ruptured. The most probable way of accounting for the blood and water flowing from a wound in the side of a dead body is that the spear pierced the pericardium—or sac which contains the heart—which would contain blood and water if the heart were ruptured. The severe strain in the Garden the night before, the intensity of which was indicated by a sweat of blood, probably prepared the physical nature of Jesus for the sudden collapse, which caused Pilate to "marvel that he was dead already." (Mark 15:44.)

242 Why did the soldiers cast lots for Christ's garment?

When the soldiers cast lot for the Saviour's garment (John 19:24) they had no design to fulfill a prediction of the Old Testament. They had probably never heard of the prophecy. They simply perceived that if they tore the garment into four pieces they would spoil it, and it would be of no value. It was the most natural course for such men to cast lots for it. The evangelist, in writing that it was done "that the Scripture might be fulfilled" meant that in God's providence the fulfilment took place. The soldiers were unconsciously doing the thing that it was predicted they would do. John was anxious to show that Christ was the predicted Messiah, and he mentions this incident to show that the details of the prophetic writings were fulfilled in him.

243 Why did Jesus after his resurrection say, "Touch me not"?

It was not a time for the old familiar greeting or handclaspings. He had not come to renew the former human associations with his followers. A great change had taken place. The crown of his life-work was not yet complete. He must show himself in his resurrected body to his disciples before he ascends to the Father. Mary evidently comprehended the significance of the change and went and told the disciples.

244 Was the ascension in human form?

The visible resurrection was essential as a demonstration of his victory over death. The facts of the ascension are so well authenticated in numerous passages, that they are accepted by all denominations of the Christian Church. It was a bodily ascension, visible to the multitudes, as far as human eye could penetrate. What change may have occurred in the spiritualizing of his body, in its preparation for his place on God's right hand, we may only conjecture. The best commentators hold that "though Christ rose with the same body in which he died, it acquired, either at his resurrection or at his ascension, and without the loss of identity, the attributes of a spiritual body, as distinguished from a natu-

ral body; of an incorruptible, as distinguished from a corruptible, body."
See Phil. 3:21; Col. 3:4

245 What were some of the particular characteristics of Jesus that made him so worthy of following?

He was altogether lovely, Song of Solomon 5:16; holy, righteous, good, faithful, true, just, guileless and sinless, spotless, innocent, harmless (Luke 1:35; Acts 4:27; Is. 53:11; Matt. 19:16; Is. 11:5; John 1:14; John 7:18; Zec. 9:9; John 5:30; Is. 53:9; I Pet. 2:22; John 8:46; I Pet. 1:19; Matt. 27:4). He was forgiving, Luke 23:34; merciful, Heb. 2:17, and loving, John 13:1, 15:13; compassionate and benevolent, Is. 40:11; Luke 19:41; Matt. 4:23, 24; Acts 10:38. He was meek, lowly in heart; patient, humble and long suffering, Matt. 11:29, 27:14; I Tim. 1:16; Luke 22:27. Though zealous, he was resigned, resisted temptation and was obedient to God the Father, even as he had been subject to his parents in his youth (Luke 2:49, 22:42; John 4:34, 15:10; Luke 2:57).

246 Why is Jesus sometimes called the Son of Man and sometimes the Son of God?

It is held that Jesus, in applying to himself the title Son of Man, intended to emphasize his humanity and his representative character. The Jews were looking for a Messiah who would raise Israel to the head of the nations; Jesus wished to impress the disciples with the fact that he was representative of the whole human race and not of the Jews only. Then, too, to have spoken openly of himself as the Son of God would have been at once to exasperate the Jews and bring upon himself a charge of blasphemy, as in the end it did (see John 10:36). The title, Son of Man, was not open to that danger, as it was expressive of lowliness, humility and identification with humanity. In using it, however, Jesus did not withdraw his claim to be the Son of God. When the High Priest put him on his oath (see Matt. 26:63-65) he acknowledged that he was the Son of God.

JESUS—SAYINGS OF JESUS

247 What is the meaning of the name "Jesus"?

The name "Jesus" is the name by which the Saviour is preferably known in the Gospels. "Christ" is used as a proper name in the Epistles, but in the Gospels, except in rare instances, such as Matt. 1:1; Mark 1:1; Luke 11:11; John 1:17, there is found not the familiar "Christ" but "The Christ." The later combination of the two names, "Jesus Christ," is found only in John (John 17:3) and after the resurrection (Acts 2:38, 3:6). "Jesus" is the Greek form of the Hebrew name "Jehoshua," or in its abbreviated form "Joshua." Its variants are found in "Jeshua" and "Hoshea." "Jesus" means Deliverer and the divine selection of the name is indicated in Matt. 1:21—"He shall save his people from their sins."

248 In what language did Christ speak?

The common language of Palestine at that time was Aramaic, a Syro-Chaldaic dialect. After the Babylonian captivity it supplanted the original Hebrew, although the latter continued in use for ecclesiastical documents. It is reasonable to believe that Christ used the Aramaic, as the people would not have understood him had he spoken any other language. Matthew is commonly believed to have been written in Aramaic and the other three in Greek. The commercial and literary language of the day was Greek. Neither Luke nor John was an uneducated man. Both would be likely to know Greek. Mark, too, as a young Jew of some standing, would probably know the language.

249 Why have we differing versions
of the Lord's Prayer?

There is no absolute evidence that the prayer was taught on one occasion only. Matthew reports it as given during the Sermon on the Mount, and Luke (who was not one of the twelve) places its delivery after the close of the Galilean ministry, but mentioning no time or place. Many of the best scholars regard the position of the prayer in Matthew as unhistorical and give the preference to Luke, although it by no means follows that even he gives the original form. If delivered on more than one occasion, the prayer may have had one form for a small group of disciples, and another form for the whole body of Jesus' followers. And this might account for the presence of a clause in one version which was absent in the other. The word "trespasses" may be regarded simply as a variant. Furthermore, it is conjectured that Luke made certain changes in the expressions of the prayer, to make its meaning clearer to Gentile hearers. Cyril, Bishop of Jerusalem, is the first writer who expressly mentions the use of the Lord's Prayer in religious worship, but it was not generally used in Christian churches during the early days. There is no evidence that it was employed by the apostles. Luke omits the closing doxology, and although it appears in Matthew's Gospel as we now have it, it is not to be found in any of the early manuscripts, and is probably an interpolation due to liturgical use.

250 Have there been any parallels to the Lord's Prayer?

Some commentators have claimed that the Prayer is based upon expressions and sentiments already familiar to the Jews, and that parallel phrases may be found in the Talmud, but this does not detract from its beauty and originality as a whole.

251 What is implied in Jesus' words, "See the Son of Man coming in his kingdom"?

This passage is frequently misunderstood. Mark has the better version: "Till they see the Kingdom of God come with power" (which is the more explicit), and Luke: "Till they see the Kingdom." Jesus is believed to have had reference to the realization of the firm establishment and victorious progress of the new Kingdom of Christ during the lifetime of some then present. He did not refer here to his second coming, but to the founding and triumphant extension of that work, the acceptance of which by the world was to be the grand pledge of his return.

252 What is meant by "poor in spirit"?

The simple meaning of this passage (Matt. 5:3) is that it is the humble soul that gets blessed. And the higher a saint gets in the divine life the more humble he will be. Spiritual progress which is not accompanied by humility is progress in the wrong direction. This is one of the distinctive points of Christ's doctrine; at the very threshold of the Christian life the Christian gives up his self-confidence; he surrenders all hope of making himself righteous, and gives himself to Christ to be made righteous. And his highest attainment can be expressed in the words of Paul: "I am crucified with Christ; nevertheless I live, yet not I, but Christ liveth in me."

253 Did Jesus abrogate the law?

In Matt. 5:17-20 Jesus was exlaining that he did not come to abrogate but to fulfil the law—to unfold its true spiritual meaning. In verse 19, the thing spoken of, as commentators explain, is not "the practical

breaking or disobeying of the law, but annulling or enervating its obligation by a vicious system of interpretation and teaching others to do the
same; so the thing threatened is not exclusion from heaven and still less
the lowest place in it, but a degraded and contemptuous position in the
present stage of the kingdom of God—in other words, they shall be reduced, by the retributive providence that overtakes them, to the same
condition of dishonor to which their false system of teaching has brought
down the eternal principles of God's law." On the other hand, those
who so teach that they exalt and honor God's authority, shall be honored in the kingdom in due proportion. It is therefore a rebuke to the
outward and formal righteousness of the Scribes and Pharisees, who
neglect the inward, vital and spiritual.

254 What is meant by "whosoever therefore shall break one of these least commandments"?

The meaning of the passage in Matt. 5:19 is: Whosoever shall break,
or make invalid through deliberate misinterpretation, one of the least of
these commandments and shall teach men so (as the Pharisees were doing), shall be called the least in the kingdom of heaven. The penalty was
not exclusion from heaven, but the loss of the position of honor in
God's kingdom, which they might have enjoyed. On the other hand,
whosoever shall teach men to obey the law in its right interpretation,
looking to the glory and honor of God, should be honored in heaven. It
was a warning to the Scribes and Pharisees that righteousness must be
inward, vital and spiritual, instead of *outward* and formal.

255 What are we to understand by, "Lead us not into temptation"?

God does not tempt any one. He may permit us to be placed in positions where, if left to our own resources, we would fall; but he does not
tempt us to evil. Eve said, "The serpent beguiled me." (See Gen. 3:1, 4,
5, 13.) She yielded in her weakness and suffered accordingly (vs. 14, 15,
16). In Matt. 4:1, and parallel passages, it is distinctly stated that the
devil was the tempter of Jesus. In I Cor. 10:13, also, it is made clear that
though God may permit us to be tempted, he is not the tempter. See
James 1:13, where it is emphatically asserted that God tempts no man.
The withdrawal of the Holy Spirit exposes us to temptation, by leaving
the heart open to the attack of the tempter; but nothing is more erroneous than to assume that temptation, or the placing of any agent in
man's spiritual path which may cause him to fall, comes from God. If
this were true, he would be the author of eternal ruin to multitudes who
rush into sin by yielding to temptation. See also Job, 1st and 2nd chapters, where Satan is shown as the tempter who pleads to be allowed to
test the spiritual stability of the patriarch. The only sources of tempta-

tion in any case are the evil spirit, the world and the flesh. Unless we are fortified by the presence of the Divine Spirit, when these assail, we are especially exposed and liable to fall. See further on the subject Rev. 12:9; John 8:44; II Cor. 11:3; I John 3:8; Mark 1:13; Luke 4:2; Acts 5:3; Matt. 26:41. Even when God has made a trial of man's faith, he has done so in every instance by the removal of spiritual safeguards and leaving man to his own resources, when the tempter availed himself of the opportunity. In this sense, it is evident that a test is not a temptation.

Some cannot reconcile the statement that God did tempt Abraham, Gen. 22:1, with the assertion of James 1:13 that God tempts no man. James refers to allurements to sin. Abraham was not tempted in that sense. He was tried and tested. Temptation is a trial and a test because when a man is tempted he learns his strength and weakness, hence the confusion in the meanings of the word. It is obvious, however, that the trial may come in different ways. In Abraham's case he was ordered to do something that was against his nature, and the question was whether he would do what he did not wish to do at the command of God. James, on the other hand, is speaking of a case in which a man is prompted to follow his own inclinations and to commit sin. God tempts no man to commit sin, but he does test our faith in him and love for him by trials. Job must have been tempted to take his wife's advice and curse God; but his trials, as we know, were tests of his disinterested allegiance, not such temptations as James refers to.

256　Who are the "angels of the little ones"?

The reference in Matt. 8:10 has caused discussion among divines in all periods of the Christian Church, and is by no means satisfactorily explained. Jesus seems to have lifted for a moment the veil over the unseen state, and to have spoken of a matter familiar to him, but incomprehensible to us. The apparent meaning is that even the humblest followers of Christ are ministered to by angels, who have access to the presence of God himself.

257　What is meant by, "The children of the kingdom shall be cast out into outer darkness"?

In this passage (Matt. 8:11-12) Christ was evidently referring to the Jews. His remark was called forth by a Roman officer exhibiting more faith in him than had ever been done by a Jew. He therefore warned his Jewish hearers that, although they prided themselves on being children of the kingdom of God, through their descent from Abraham, they might be excluded from the kingdom because of personal unfitness; while others, who could not claim that illustrious pedigree, would be admitted because of their personal fitness. The present application of his words appears to us to be not to converted persons, but to nominal

Christians, who have never been converted, but expect to enter heaven because they belong to Christian families, have been baptized and admitted to membership in a Christian church, but have not the spirit of Christ and Christ's words here also apply to people in Christian countries who having a knowledge of the things of God, do not live according to their knowledge. They, too, will see people who had not their advantages admitted, while they themselves are excluded.

258 What is meant by, "Let the dead bury their dead"?

The language employed by Christ (Matt. 8:22) on the occasion in question is to be accepted figuratively as in many other instances of his teachings. He was speaking of the characteristics of true discipleship, and particularly referred to those who permitted themselves to become so entangled in worldly affairs, that they persistently procrastinated in spiritual things. To these, Jesus showed that all other claims were inferior to the divine claim upon their energies and the paramount command to "preach the kingdom of God." These should take precedence even of the highest claims of nature. While immortal souls are in peril, the true disciple must not hesitate, but must go even at the sacrifice of all he holds dear. Those who remain, being dead to the spiritual call, may well be relied upon to fulfill all needful natural duties to the dead or the dying among themselves. The disciple's duty is to obey the call, leaving the consequences with God.

259 Why did Jesus want the news of his miracles kept quiet?

It was probably out of consideration for his followers, as there might be a popular rising which might lead to slaughter. The people were expecting the Messiah to be a king, and, if they had recognized Christ, and still held that notion they would probably have risen in rebellion against Rome. On one occasion (John 6:15), he hid himself to prevent such a rising. It was safe after his death to preach him as the Christ, because then the spiritual nature of his kingdom would be understood; but while he lived, it was necessary to avoid publicity. Even the disciples expected that he would make himself king and did not understand his real purpose until after the resurrection.

260 What is meant by, "Who is able to destroy both soul and body in hell"?

Stier and some other writers contend that it is Satan to whom Christ refers in Matt. 10:28, but the context disproves this theory. The whole tenor of the chapter is directed to encouraging men to trust in God and to fear offending him. Christ shows in the following verse how God's control covers all life, and that without his permission no life is lost.

Christ does not teach us anywhere to fear Satan, but to rejoice that, through himself, Satan has been overcome. In this passage the contrast is between the fear of man on the one hand, which might lead us to keep away from Christ or desert him lest we should be persecuted; and the fear, on the other hand, of God whose power is infinite in extent, and whom we should dread to displease.

261 What is meant by, "I came not to send peace, but a sword"?

Christ's work on the individual soul may help you to understand his meaning (Matt. 10:34). The converted soul enjoys a peace passing all understanding; but how is it attained? The first stages of the process are those of fierce conflict. See the agony, the distress, that the majority of men pass through when they are under conviction. It is through conflict that peace is attained. It is so with the evil in the world. Christ's kingdom is one of peace; but not the despicable peace with wickedness and oppression. With those evils there must be war. If a father wisely loves his son, he does not ignore that son's bad ways; he punishes him in order to save him. You may say how do we reconcile the rod in the father's hand with his love for his child. There is no need to reconcile. The rod is a sign and proof of the father's love. So Christ's coming brought a sword to smite the evil that is cursing the world.

262 What is meant by, "For I am come to set a man at variance with his father"?

This statement (Matt. 10:35) showed the result of his coming, not the purpose of it. Christ was warning the people who came to him of the sufferings they would have to endure, among which was this of the hostility of their near relatives. Many were offering themselves as his disciples who expected that he would become the King of Israel, and that they would share his glory, and he wished none to come with any such idea. He wanted them to count the cost, and he told them of the trials awaiting them if they followed him. They must be quite sure that they loved him so well that if their fathers or their brothers cast them off for being Christians they would be faithful to Christ, even at the cost of losing the love of their relatives.

263 What is meant by, "This is Elias which was to come"?

There was a prophecy that God would send Elijah or Elias to turn the hearts of the people (Malachi 4:5). When John appeared the Jews asked him if he was Elias, and he answered that he was not (John 1:21). They evidently expected that the literal Elijah, who is represented as ascending to heaven without dying (II Kings 2:11), would be sent to earth. John knew he was not that. He regarded himself as a humble messenger, a mere voice, with no distinction but that of preparing the way. The character of his preaching, however, shows that, like other messengers from God, he underestimated his dignity. When Christ spoke of him he settled the question definitely in the passage you refer to. John, he said, was the Elias to whom the prophecy referred.

264 What are the "idle words" that men shall give account of?

The passage in Matt. 12:36 means unseemly or improper conversation, levity, slander, scoffing, boasting, swearing, mocking at sacred things. The Saviour had been speaking of blasphemy and of the scoffing attitude of the Pharisees, who imputed his miracles to Beelzebub. The "idle words" presumably referred more particularly to their sceptical way of accounting for the miracles, of which they had spoken slightingly.

265 What are we to understand by Christ's parable of the return of the unclean spirit?

Its first application, as the closing words show, is to the Jews of that time. (See Matt. 12:43, 45.) They were rid of the evil of idolatry, but were worse than their fathers, who worshiped idols, in that they rejected Jesus and finally crucified him. In modern times, the same evil is seen when a nation abandons its superstitions, but instead of turning to Christ, and becoming Christian, becomes atheistic. Its application to individuals is of the same character. Christianity is positive as well as negative in its effects. It forbids and condemns sin (that is negative); it also enjoins love, kindness, service (that is positive). If, for example, a man who has been a drunkard overcomes his propensity, that is, gets rid of his unclean spirit, but does not go forward to faith in Christ, he is liable to become Pharisaic and intolerant, and perhaps sceptical. In that condition he is liable to fall into worse sin. The throne of the soul is never empty. If Christ does not rule, some evil spirit takes possession.

266 What are the tares mentioned in Matthew 13:25?

The tares in the parable refer to the seed called "darnel," a rank and widely distributed grass, and the only species that has deleterious properties. It is poisonous and its grains, if eaten, produce vomiting, purging, convulsions and sometimes even death. Before it comes into the ear it resembles the wheat so closely that it can hardly be distinguished from the latter, hence the command to leave it to the harvest. Grain-growers in Palestine believe the tares, or *zuwan*, to be a diseased or degenerate wheat. The seed resembles wheat in form, but is smaller and nearly black.

267 What was the power conferred on Peter by Christ's commission of the keys?

The keys and the power of binding and loosing referred to a common Jewish custom. When a man had passed his examinations for the high position of a doctor of the law, he received as his diploma, a key which was handed to him with the words, "Receive authority to bind and to loose," that is to permit or forbid. Having mastered the law, he could say whether some act was lawful or unlawful. Peter's declaration that Jesus was the Son of God was the evidence of his having reached a state of spiritual faith and percept on which Christ recognized (Matt. 16:18, 19). The keys may also have had reference to Peter's opening the doors of Christ's kingdom to the multitude on the day of Pentecost and to the Gentiles by preaching to Cornelius. It is clear that the Apostles did not recognize Peter as superior to themselves. It was James who passed sentence in the council (Acts 15:13, 19) although Peter was present; and Paul "withstood Peter to the face." (Gal. 2:11.)

268 What is meant by Jesus' advice, "Turn to him the other cheek also"?

Christ's teaching in this and other passages was intended to inculcate principles, rather than blind, literal, servile obedience. He would have his followers patient, gentle, non-resistant, forbearing, submitting to be wronged rather than resisting. His own example in yielding himself to death, when by the exercise of his miraculous powers he could have delivered himself, is an illustration of his meaning. Yet he scourged the traders in the Temple, and in denouncing the Scribes and Pharisees he showed that he was not deficient in vigor. There have, however, been many instances of men literally obeying the command to turn the other cheek, and in some, the effect on the striker was to produce shame and humiliation greater than could have resulted from a fight. There have been many, too, who after painful experience have wished they had submitted to a wrong instead of going to the courts. (See Matt. 18:15, 16, 17.)

269 Who are the people to whom Christ referred as being "joined together of God"?

We may understand the remark better by reading the whole passage (Matt. 19:1-12). The Pharisees were trying to draw Christ into a controversy which, at the time, was raging between the schools of different Jewish teachers. One school contended that a man was justified in divorcing his wife for any cause as, for instance, if she burnt the food she was cooking for his dinner. Another school held that physical defects alone justified divorce. There were other schools holding other opinions. Christ refused to identify himself with any and lifted the question into the higher plane by showing the origin of marriage in divine institution.

270 What was the "needle's eye"?

The "'needle's eye" (Matt. 19:24) was the small gate or wicket at the side of the big gate at the entrance to the city wall. When the big gate closed for the day, all entrance had to be gained through the small gate, and to a loaded camel, or indeed to any body of considerable size, passage was impossible.

271 What is meant by, "A rich man shall hardly enter the kingdom of God"?

To rightly understand the full significance of the passage in Matt. 19:23 read Luke 18:24-27. It may be liberally interpreted: "How hard it is for those who trust in riches to enter! Unless this idolatrous trust and confidence in mere wealth is overcome, they cannot enter" except by a miracle of divine grace, which changes the heart. Jesus found no fault with the young man because of his riches, since wealth, and the power and influence it brings, may be made a means of great blessing if used in the right spirit as a trust committed to our stewardship. He found, however, that the young man's wealth was to him of greater moment than his eternal welfare, since he could not grasp the great opportunity offered him by the Master. Paul in I Cor. 6:10 also has a bearing upon the love of wealth and the hard and merciless means that are sometimes adopted to acquire it. Where extortion begins may be defined by statute, but, it must really be determined by the conscience, since what is a fair return in one case may be a cruel extortion in another. We must carry the Christ idea into our business relations, and deal not only justly but generously and humanely, never making gain of another's necessity, and if with all we pile up riches, we are apt to rely on them to put us into heaven. This was the case of the young man who came to Christ. The sincerity of the young man was obvious; yet he himself felt that although he had lived a clean, moral life, keeping the letter of the law in absolute strictness, there was yet something wanting. He was not satisfied with his own blameless life. It was to find out what this hidden need was that he came to the Master, and asked, "What lack I yet?" Jesus, reading his heart, knew that his wealth stood as a barrier between him and the spiritual life he craved; that the influence and social position it gave were so dear to him that he could not bear to part with them, even to attain his ideal of a perfect life. His riches were his idol, and this the Master knew. So when Jesus in his wisdom put the test, forcing the young man to choose between riches and heaven—that he must himself cast aside the stumbling-block in his spiritual path—he failed at the crisis, turned his back upon the Master, and went away sorrowful. Jesus demanded an absolute surrender of the heart and the whole life, the placing of all in the scale as a heart offering. Good works could not save, but sacrifice of our works and our wealth brings us into a new and divine relationship as true heirs to the kingdom. See Matt. 19:29, in which the spiritual compensation for such sacrifice is promised. The rich young ruler came very near to the kingdom, but without entering in. His own estimate of his obedience was not justified, for if he had indeed kept the first commandment he would have placed God first, above even his much-prized earthly treasures, and he would never have gone away from Christ.

272 What is the parable of the laborers in Matthew 20:1-6 intended to teach?

There has, probably, been more difference in explaining this parable than any other. To us it appears that the incidents of it are not intended as laying down a business principle, but as a commentary on the events in the preceding chapter. Peter had asked, "What shall we have, therefore?" showing a bargaining spirit. Christ shows him by this parable that, not they who stipulate for reward, but they who trust in God, leaving their reward for him to fix are treated best. That was a prominent characteristic of Christ. He craved personal trust and personal faith in himself. Where does the injustice of the householder come in? He kept his agreement with the early laborers, who had stipulated for a penny a day. They had the amount they had demanded and had no grievance. The householder chose to deal more liberally with the others, who had left their remuneration to him, but that was in no sense a wrong to the early laborers. If an employer knows something about one of his employees—perhaps that he has been sick, or that he has a large family— and chooses to give him a double wage, is he bound to go all round his factory and double the wages of every man in his employ? It is the hireling spirit, the spirit of the man who bargains, who resents the kindness done to another as a wrong to himself, that Christ reproves here. He condemns it, as he condemned the elder brother in the parable of the Prodigal Son, who resented the feast to the prodigal and reminded the father of his own claims. Many of the first (not all) shall be last because of the spirit in which they have performed their work.

273 In the parable of the laborers what is the principle taught?

This parable in Matt. 20:1-16 stands in close connection with the preceding chapter, and its evident purpose was to illustrate the sentiment of the closing verse: "Many that are first shall be last, and the last shall be first." The parable has reference to rewards, and illustrates the method of their bestowment upon the followers of Christ, namely, in such a way that the last shall be equal to the first, and the first last—a way that rewards faithfulness of service, rather than length of service or the amount accomplished in the service. The purpose of the parable, being understood, it cannot properly awaken any question as to discrimination in the matter of the pay of the laborers. As to the transaction of the householder, as represented in the parable, there was no injustice in it. He agreed with the first laborers for "a penny a day," while with the others no specified amount was agreed upon, and he could pay them what he pleased. Further, the Saviour does not necessarily approve the course of the householder, and we are not required to show that it was either right or wise, as an act of man toward men, but only that rewards in the kingdom of God are thus bestowed without reference to the time of service, another and very different consideration actuating our Heavenly Father in this matter—namely, faithfulness.

The parable was an answer to Peter's question (Matt. 19:27), "Behold, we have forsaken all and followed thee: what shall we have therefore?" In a word, it was a rebuke of the bargaining spirit. Those who follow Christ for the sake of the reward, and not from love of him, will not be defrauded. They will have all that God has promised them, but they are not those whom he most loves. A parent who promises a child a reward for a certain service, or for good behavior, and notices that the child performs the task or behaves himself better than at other times, when no reward is promised, does not approve of the child's spirit. He does not like to see the child doing for money the thing that he does not do for love, as he ought to do. Still, he keeps his promise and pays, as he agreed. But the child who does cheerfully and readily, as the parent requests, without any promise of reward, is the one whom the parent approves. That child would surely be rewarded, though no reward had been promised.

The householder in the parable makes his bargain with the first party of laborers. The phrase, "when he had agreed with them," clearly implies negotiation. With the others he made no bargain, merely giving his promise to pay whatsoever was right. They trusted him, and went to work. He liked the confidence they showed, and he gave them more than they expected. The early morning laborers had no just ground of complaint. They received all they had stipulated for. All through Christ's ministry he showed the same spirit. He craved personal love and confidence. He wanted people, above all things, to trust in him. Peter's question must have chilled Christ's spirit. It might have been interpreted as showing that this man who Christ supposed was following him for love, was there for what he could make out of it. Hence, the rebuke of the parable.

**274 How are we to interpret Jesus' words,
"The Son of Man came not to be
ministered unto, but to minister"?**

This passage in Matt. 20:28, is the elevation of the duty of Christian service. Of course Christ did come to earth to win all men to his service, but it was for their sakes rather than his own. To serve him meant salvation; it was sin that kept them from their allegiance to him. And he came to save them from their sins. All the time he was in the flesh he gave rather than accepted service. He was moved by love. Even when the people would have taken him by force to make him king he would not accept it. That was not the kind of service he wanted. He wanted men to serve him, in holiness and spiritual power. He gave his body in humiliation and sacrifice in order that they might be lifted up to this higher plane of service. The whole message of the New Testament is that Christ came to earth for the sake of mankind, not for his own sake. And he taught by example the life of humility, self-sacrifice and service which he wishes all men to lead.

**275 What did Jesus mean by "faith
that could remove mountains"?**

This is the language of similitude and figure which Jesus frequently employed to illustrate and emphasize his teaching. A leading commentator writes of this passage (Matt. 21:21): "From the nature of the case supposed—that they might wish a mountain removed and cast into the sea (a thing very far from anything which they could be thought to actually desire)—it is plain that not physical but moral obstacles to the progress of his kingdom were in the Saviour's mind." What he designed to teach was the great lesson that no obstacle should be able to stand before a firm faith in God—that it would enable us to overcome all difficulties, if we absolutely trusted in him.

**276 Was the man without the wedding
garment harshly dealt with?**

No; he was treated as he deserved. At a wedding feast in an Oriental land such as Christ was describing, the king would provide garments for his guests, suitable to the occasion. A guest who declined to wear the wedding garment and went in wearing his ordinary attire, would be conspicuous and his conduct would be an affront to the king. He would naturally be considered as despising the dress which the king had provided and preferring his own. Christ, in the passage in Matt. 22:11-13, was warning his hearers against trusting in their own righteousness and rejecting God's way of salvation.

277 Why should we call Jesus "Master"?

Because he himself has told us to do so. It is a very beautiful and inspiring title which Christians everywhere may apply to their beloved Lord. (See Matt. 23:10.) This passage is a part of Jesus' denunciation of the Scribes and Pharisees, who were given over to formalism and regarded the *letter* rather than the *spirit* of Scripture. They sought personal honors and the applause of the multitudes. They carried strips of parchment of Scripture texts, bound to arm, forehead and side, in time of prayer, and they loved to be addressed by ecclesiastical titles. *Rabbi* (Master) was a title which they particularly affected and which their whole spiritual conduct discredited. Had they been true teachers and guides, instead of false, he would not have reprobated them, nor would they have belied the title they bore. Titles in the modern Christian Church are vain distinctions, except where they are worthily worn. All should be brethren in Christ, the highest dignitary of the church and the humblest follower. Unfortunately, in every age there has been a desire for ecclesiastical distinctions and, while in many cases these have been merited and gladly accorded, in others the honors were not deserved. The ecclesiastical system of the Jews lent itself to this vanity to such an extent as to arouse the divine indignation. The title "Rab" was originally Babylonian and that of "Rabbi," Palestinian. It was given to learned men, authorized teachers of the law and spiritual heads of the community.

**278 What is meant by, "Heaven and earth
    shall pass away"?**

The expressions "heaven" and "the heavens" mean not only the spiritual, eternal world, but also the stars and the spaces of ether surrounding the earth. Jesus used the word frequently in both these senses. He spoke of "the kingdom of heaven," signifying the eternal kingdom, and then spoke of the stars as "heaven" or "the heavens" in passages like the one you mention. Paul speaks of "the house not made with hands eternal in the heavens." (II Cor. 5:1.) The teaching of the Bible is that the material universe, including the earth itself, will be transformed, but that the spiritual universe will endure forever.

279 What is the lesson of the parable of the talents?

The parable in Matt. 25 was given to explain the principle of the judgment. From one who had been well endowed much would be expected, and a smaller result would be looked for from one who had received less. Only he would be punished who had made no effort to turn his talents to account. Christ probably intended it to apply to every kind of gift. Men of wealth, of education, of spiritual privilege, with any kind of opportunity for doing good, were affected by it. A man must do the best he could in his circumstances, and if he could not do as well, or as much as, another who was better equipped, he would not be blamed. The distinction between worldly and spiritual is somewhat vague in this instance. The man who gives to a starving family is not exactly doing spiritual work, but it is the kind of work that this parable would apply to.

280 Was the story of the rich man and Lazarus a parable or an actual fact?

It was a parable—an illustration of the kind made familiar in the teachings of Christ. It is the only parable in which a proper name is employed, and Lazarus was probably chosen because it was a common name. By some both men in the parable have been considered as real personages, and one tradition even gives the name of the rich man as Dobruk, while another gives it as Nimeusis. Neither tradition is deserving of credit, and the best commentators agree that the two characters were described by the Saviour simply to illustrate two type of men.

281 Did Jesus in any of his parables make allusion to historical characters?

He is thought by some to have done so in the parable of the talents (Matt. 25). Dean Farrar points this out as follows: "It is the only instance in which we can connect a parable of the Gospel with historical events. The man who goes into another country to seek a kingdom is Archelaus, son of Herod the Great. Left heir of the chief part of Herod's kingdom by the last will of his father, altered within five days of his death, Archelaus had to travel to Rome to obtain from the Emperor Augustus the confirmation of his heritage. During his absence he had to leave the kingdom under commission to his kinsmen and servants, some of whom were wise and faithful, and others much the reverse. The circumstances of the succession of Archelaus would be recalled to Christ's memory as he passed the magnificent palace which the tyrant had built at Jericho. Archelaus was absent at Rome for some months. Jesus calls him a 'hard man.' The grasping character of Archelaus made him unpopular from the first, and the hatred felt for him was increased by his deadly cruelties. The event to which our Lord here distinctly refers had occurred in his own infancy."

282 What is meant by "new wine in old bottles"?

Mark 2:21, 22, is designed to illustrate the difference between the old and new economies, and the result of mixing up one with the other. The "new wine" was the evangelical freedom which Christ was introducing into the old spirit of Judaism. It was as though he had said, "These inquiries about the difficulty between my disciples and the Pharisees, and even John's disciples, serve to point out the effect of a natural revulsion against sudden change, which time will cure and which will be seen to be to the better advantage."

283 What is meant by Jesus' words, "Unto them that are without, all these things are done in parables"?

In the passage in Mark 4:11, 12 Jesus meant apparently that he made the difference between his teaching of disciples and of the ordinary people because of the spiritual insight of the former. It was of no use to give the latter the direct teaching that he gave the disciples. But he taught them by illustrations to which they would listen and which would remain in their minds. They would thus learn more than they knew at the time. The meaning of the stories was not clear to them then, and they probably thought there was no particular moral to them, but the influence of the teaching would be felt afterwards. Sometimes a child may play at a game that may teach him geography or history and his teacher is aware that the child has learned more than he has any idea of. The child may be interested in a fable and see nothing in it applicable to himself, but in future years the moral meaning of the fable may be perceptible to him.

284 What did our Lord mean when he spoke of "the mystery of the kingdom"?

The word "mystery," found in Mark 4:11, 12 as in certain other places in Scripture, is not used in the classical sense of religious secrets or things incomprehensible, but of things of purely divine revelation—matters foreshadowed in the ancient economy and then only partially understood, but now fully published under the Gospel (see 1 Cor. 2:6, 10; Eph. 3:3, 6, 8, 9). The mysteries of the kingdom meant those great Gospel truths which at that time none but the disciples could appreciate, and even they only in part, while to those without (whose hearts had not yet been opened to the Gospel) they were like tales and fables, subjects of entertainment rather than divine truths. Such persons saw but recognized not, and heard but understood not, for their spiritual sight and understanding were judicially sealed by sin. From obdurate rejection of the Gospel, and their obstinacy in preferring darkness to light, they had become morally incapable of acceptance and totally indifferent. (See prophecy of Is. 6:9, 10, then read contrasting passage in Matt. 13:16.)

285 How should we interpret Jesus' words, "The damsel is not dead, but sleepeth"?

The Saviour's language in Mark 5:39 was as though he had used the familiar figure "she hath fallen asleep"—the same figure that is frequently employed in the Scriptures in describing death as sleep. (See

Acts 7:60; I Cor. 15:6, 18; II Peter 3:4.) Some have interpreted the language of Mark 5 to mean that the maid was in a trance or swoon; but most commentators agree that Mark 5:35 is a clear affirmation that all the signs of death were evident, that the life had already fled and that the reassuring words of the Master (in verse 36) before he had even seen the maid, were intended to strengthen the ruler's faith and prepare him for the manifestation of divine power that followed. The last nine verses, read as a whole, bear out this conclusion.

286 What kind of baskets were used in the miracle of the loaves and fishes?

The Gospel accounts say: "They took up what remained over of the broken pieces twelve baskets full" (Matt. 14:20). "They took up of the broken meat that was left seven baskets" (Mark 8:8). There have been some differences among scholars as to the translation of the word (in the original) denoting "baskets." In describing the earlier miracle, that of the feeding of five thousand, a word is used which indicates large fishing baskets made of rope, while in the narrative of the later miracle, there is used a term which translated means smaller hand-baskets. It might well be asked how could the apostles have carried around with them seven large fishing baskets? A comparison between the two accounts will clear up a seeming difficulty. Many Jews carried small hand-baskets in which they kept their food supplies free from pollution. Each apostle may have carried such a small hand-basket and in the party of apostles there may have been one who carried a large fishing basket. This large fishing basket was filled seven times and again twelve times, for the phraseology used seems to indicate that, whereas in the one instance each apostle filled his small hand-basket with broken pieces, in the other the one large fishing basket was filled seven times.

287 Who was the little child that Jesus took up and blessed?

The details of these incidents in the life of Jesus have been preserved to us only by tradition. It is said that the little child of whom the Saviour remarked, "of such is the kingdom of heaven" (Mark 9:36), afterwards became known to the Christian Church as Ignatius, Bishop of Antioch. He was one of the great company of martyrs who gave their lives for the faith in the time of Trajan, being torn to pieces by lions in the amphitheatre at Rome.

288 What did Jesus mean by saying, "Why callest thou me good"?

The true meaning of the much discussed passage (Mark 10:17) quoted is thus explained by very good authority. Professor David Smith, who writes: " 'Master' or 'Teacher' was the regular appellation of a Jewish

Rabbi, and it was accounted so honorable that it always stood alone without qualification. It was a deliberate departure from the established usage, an intentional improvement on the common style, when the young ruler addressed our Lord as 'Good Master.' It showed that he had recognized him as more than a teacher; and when our Lord fastened upon the epithet, his purpose was to elicit what his questioner really meant. He said in effect: 'You have gone a long way in calling me "good." That epithet belongs only to God. You have recognized me as more than a teacher: are you prepared to go farther, and recognize me as divine?' Hence it appears that our Lord's question is not a repudiation of the attribute of deity. On the contrary, it is an assertion of his title to it. It is a gracious attempt to bring home to that anxious inquirer, in conscious realization, the truth which he had dimly perceived and was groping for."

289 Why was the fig tree blighted?

The fig tree incident related in Mark 11:13 has been a subject of much controversy, and the passage in Mark 11:13 has been claimed by some to be a mistake in the transcription of the record as to the words, "He found nothing but leaves, for the time of figs was not yet." It is explained by some writers (including Pliny and Macrobius) that the fig tree in Palestine produces fruit at two or even three seasons of the year, and Hackett (in his *Scripture Illustrations*) tells us that the fruit precedes the leaves. One might infer from this that if a tree had leaves it might be expected to give evidence at least of having had fruit. In the case of this particular tree, having leaves in advance of the regular time (which "was not yet come") yet with no sign of having borne fruit, it was condemned, as some commentators interpret the case, because of its uselessness. Trench and several others hold that the blighting of the precocious and fruitless tree was designed to convey a rebuke to "the barren traditions of the Pharisees, their ostentatious display of the law, and their vain exuberance of words without the good fruit of works." Still others believe that our Lord, seeing the early leaves, had a right to expect that they would be accompanied by fruit.

290 Was Christ omniscient in the flesh?

It is reasonable to suppose that in the days of his flesh Christ experienced some curtailment of divine attributes. We read of his being weary, of his weeping, of his praying, being hungry and thirsty, and being tempted. We read also of his increasing in wisdom (Luke 2:52). We infer from all these that the divine nature did not have full scope for its powers in the human form or could only express them partially owing to the obvious limitations. Christ seems to have been aware of this while on the earth, for he said, "My Father is greater than I." (John

14:28.) We conclude, therefore, that a part of his humiliation was his voluntarily divesting himself of some part of his divine nature and this may account for such a passage as Mark 13:32. It is impossible for the human mind to fully comprehend the mystery of the Trinity, but we can imagine that Christ in his loving compassion, voluntarily put from him certain attributes of the Godhead while on earth in order that in all things he might be made like unto his brethren. In what way or to what extent, if at all, the incarnation limited the divine attributes cannot be defined, and the fact of his praying to his Father indicated that in the days of his flesh there was a distinction between them that is incomprehensible to us.

291 Does Christ's admission that he did not know the time of the end imply that he was not divine?

No, the inference (to be drawn from Mark 13:32) does not appear logical. We do not understand the union of the two natures in our Lord's person, and therefore cannot explain many of the difficulties which are presented. If, however, we take the conception that is given in the first chapter of John's Gospel, of an incarnation, we can perceive how there may have been restriction in the exercise of divine power operating by a human brain. The instrument would be necessarily inadequate. The assumption of an unrestricted divine nature would imply perfect knowledge in boyhood, yet we know that as a boy Christ did not know all things; for Luke says explicitly (2:52) that he increased in wisdom, which he could not have done had he been omniscient from birth. In taking our nature he voluntarily submitted to the imperfections of our condition, otherwise he would not have been made "like unto his brethren."

292 If Jesus Christ knew all things, did he not know and realize that Judas Iscariot was not a true believer?

Christ did not claim to know all things. He mentioned one thing that he did not know (Mark 13:32). At the same time he is said to have known what was in man (John 2:25), so he may have been aware of the possibilities of evil in Judas, which were probably not developed when he was chosen as an apostle. Christ knew of his intended treachery before it was committed. Doubtless Judas himself, at the time of his call, had no idea that he would commit such a crime. Even at the last, he may have expected that Christ would deliver himself by his miraculous power. He was evidently horror-stricken when he learned the result of what he had done, as is proved by his committing suicide.

**293 What are the signs which Jesus said
"shall follow them that believe"?**

Jesus did not promise that the signs referred to in Mark 16:17 should always follow. The speaking with tongues, casting out devils, taking up serpents, etc., were signs suitable for that age when the people, being densely ignorant, expected miracles and signs. Christ reproved the tendency, and on more than one occasion refused to gratify them. He wanted them to learn from the sign to seek spiritual blessings at his hands, which were of much greater value to them. We have entered into that higher and better understanding of him. It is much more wonderful to see a drunkard reclaimed, a vicious man reformed, than it was to see a lame man healed. The power to cast out devils and to speak with tongues and take up serpents would not be nearly so valuable to us as is the power he gives to transform evil lives.

**294 Why did Jesus say to his disciple John,
"He that is least in the kingdom
of God is greater than he"?**

The passage in Luke 7:28 is frequently misunderstood, as being spoken in derogation of John, because of the doubt his messengers had implied in their question (verse 20). The true meaning, as Weiss and other commentators believe, is that Jesus was speaking of the differences in the success of the Baptist with certain classes. The common people and the publicans, who had repented under John's ministry, and had been baptized by him, understood the meaning of Jesus and were glad (verse 29), but the Pharisees and Scribes—the very class who should have been models of righteousness, had rejected and despised John. That Jesus spoke with this contrast in view is made clear in verses 30 to 35 inclusive. He was speaking of the advancement of the kingdom in the hearts of men.

**295 What was the special value and object
of Jesus' parables?**

"But unto others in parables that seeing they might not see and hearing they might not understand" Luke 8:10. Dean Farrar says on this passage: "Lord Bacon says, 'A parable has a double use; it tends to veil and it tends to illustrate a truth; in the latter case it seems designed to teach, in the former to conceal.' Our Lord wished the multitude to understand, but the result and profit depended solely on the degree of their faithfulness. The parables resembled the Pillar of Fire, which was to the Egyptians a Pillar of Cloud."

The truth veiled in the form of parable was withheld from the people because their minds had grown too gross to receive it. "Had the parable of the mustard seed, for instance," says Dr. Whedon, "been explained to the Pharisees as indicating that the Gospel would yet fill the earth, it would only have excited their additional hostility and hastened their purpose of accusing him as intending to subvert the existing government." They themselves, as we learn from Matt. 13:15, had wilfully closed their eyes to the Gospel, and so its real principles must be withheld from them. To some this may have been a mercy, preventing them from using the truth to evil purposes. To others it may have been simply the penalty due them for having insulted the truth and become unworthy of it. While, however, the parable veiled the truth from cavillers, it unveiled it to the disciples (Matt. 13:11). The unreceptive people, "seeing" the narrative, saw "not" the doctrine embodied; "hearing" the literal parable, they understood "not" the secret meaning. "The whole Gospel is a parable to him whose heart has not the key." This solemn teaching is found also in the law and the prophets. Deu. 29:3, 4; Is. 6:9; Jer. 5:21; Ezek. 12:2.

296 How are we to understand, "Whosoever hath, to him shall be given"?

This expression (Luke 8:18) occurs in a number of New Testament passages, Matt. 13:12, Mark 4:25, etc. Its meaning is most evident in Matt. 25:29, and Luke 19:26, in connection with the parable of the talents, or pounds. Christ is stating in these words two laws which are universal. First, a man must have something to start with before he can do any work. Second, if he does not make good use of what is given he loses it. In other words: something never comes from nothing; neglect means loss. Every man is given something to start with for working out his life plan. If he neglects to use what he has he loses it. It cannot be said that God takes it away from him; the man simply lets it slip through his fingers. Helen Keller had very little to begin with, but she made such amazingly faithful use of that, that she gained much more. She used and developed the sense of touch till it has become almost equal to sight and hearing. But a sense or a muscle unused becomes useless. A man has only to stop walking and he will soon lose the power to walk. It is ridiculous to say that there is anything cruel about this. It is simply the law of life. And the law works no hardship to any one who has a desire to make good use of life. In the passage (Luke 8:18) the law is applied to hearing. When a man hears a truth he must follow it and apply it quickly. If he does not he will forget it, or cease to believe it, or lose it in some other way.

297 Why did Jesus allow evil spirits to enter the herd of swine?

According to the law of Moses, swine were unclean, and any Jew owning them or using them as food violated this law. The destruction of the herd (Luke 8:26, 36) and the question of the destination of the evil spirits has been well explained by Trench in his famous book on *Miracles*. He wrote: "A man is of more value than many swine," and added that it is not necessary to suppose that our Lord *sent* the devils into the swine, but merely *permitted* them to go, adding further that if those Gadarene villagers who owned the swine were Jews, as may be supposed, they were properly punished by the loss of that which they ought not to have had at all. As for the evil spirits, it is reasonable to conclude that they found a congenial refuge somewhere else. With regard to their recognition of Jesus as divine, we have Scripture assurance that "the devils believe and tremble."

298 What did Jesus mean by, "Take no thought for your life, what ye shall eat, neither for your body what ye shall put on"?

This was a part of the "Sermon on the Mount," and Luke 12:19-34 is intended to illustrate heavenly-mindedness and confidence in God's providence. The particular passage quoted admonishes the believer not to be too anxiously concerned or worried about things that are purely temporal. It is right to make due provision for our own needs and the needs of those dependent upon us; but when we have done so, we should not fret and doubt and make ourselves and others miserable because of our fears of coming trouble. This applies to our food, our clothing and our worldly affairs generally. All such doubts and worries spring from unbelief, and are after the manner of the world. If we really believe and trust our heavenly Father, he will provide all we need. This promise, however, does not relieve us from the natural duty of making reasonable provision, though there are some people who mistakenly think so. The whole passage, broadly interpreted, means that we are to do our work here properly and cheerfully and to trust the Father for the rest and never worry, always keeping in view the greater duty of "seeking first the kingdom," beside which all other things are insignificant. Worry in the sense involved in the passage is a sin against God since it shows absolute lack of faith in his promised providential care.

299 What is meant by hating father and mother and wife for Jesus' sake?

In Luke 14:26 our Lord asserts his claim to our most loyal service and our supreme affection. In taking up one's cross to follow him, we must be prepared for trials for his sake, and to break even the nearest and dearest ties, if need be. He must have the first place in our hearts. It may come to choosing between Christ and our nearest relations. Compare Matt. 10:37 with the passage in Luke 14. "Hate" is not the preferable word, as the passage in Matthew shows. The passage in Luke obscures the true form of the expression and invests it with harshness while Matthew makes the true meaning clear, that we are to love him better than all else, even those who are nearest and dearest to us, and that this love must assert itself loyally at the crisis, no matter what it may cost us. A loyal soldier will give up all to serve his country; so we too must be prepared to give up all, if need be, to serve Christ.

300 What was meant by the "ninety and nine just persons which need no repentance"?

There was a tendency among the Pharisees (see Luke 15:2) to despise the sinner and make no effort for his reclamation. They prided themselves on their scrupulous observance of the law and on their lives being free from open sin. Christ met them on their own ground, and showed them that the recovery and reformation of the sinner was pleasing to God. He desires that none should perish, but that all should forsake sin and return. They thought that as there were no flagrant sins in their lives to be repented of, that they were God's favorite children. Christ showed them that if, as they contended, they were free from such sins, their self-righteous attitude was not so pleasing to God as was the attitude of the man who knew he had done wrong, and abjured it and asked pardon. There was need for repentance on the part of those who claimed to be just persons, as Christ showed them over and over again; but he was teaching another lesson at that time, and was proving to them, that, even assuming that they were sinless, as they claimed, they were wrong in the position they took toward the sinner.

301 What actually were the "husks that the swine did eat"?

The husks (see Luke 15:16), were the fruit of the carob tree, which is common in Palestine and is used by the poor as food and for the fattening of swine or cattle. When ripe, it is like a cooked beanpod, brown, glossy, and filled with seeds. Children eat it readily and seem to thrive on it. The carob is of the same family as the American locust tree. Its fruit is sometimes called "St. John's bread," as John the Baptist is thought to have lived upon it in the wilderness.

302 Who is represented by the "elder brother" in the prodigal parable?

Primarily, the Pharisees and chief priests, who were scandalized by seeing Christ associate with the lower classes and notorious sinners. It was a rebuke to selfishness and formalism—to those who believe they have the spiritual right of way and that less worthy persons, who had been basking in the divine goodness should be envious or critical of the cordial welcome that is extended to a redeemed sinner. The lesson applies to people in our own day who have no sympathy with the work going on at rescue missions, and are sceptical about the conversion of evildoers. The parable was a reproof to such persons, but it also conveyed a weighty lesson as to the evil of sin. Although the father forgave his younger son and gave him joyful welcome, he said to the elder, "All that I have is thine," thereby intimating that the younger son's lost patrimony could not be restored. The sinner is urged to repent, and is promised pardon, but the time he has wasted, and the health he has injured, and the mischief his example has done, are irreparable evils.

303 What did our Lord mean by saying to Peter, "When thou art converted, strengthen thy brethren"?

The revised version renders the passage (Luke 22:32): "When thou hast turned again, stablish thy brethren." We cannot suppose that after Peter's fall, he needed conversion in the sense in which we use the word. He needed repentance and restoration. His words, his actions, and the intense devotion he had previously shown to Christ, all indicated a man already converted. He fell under temptation as Christ had foreseen, but it was a backsliding which Christ forgave. At Pentecost their experience was not conversion, but an enducment of power for service, notably the power of speaking foreign tongues.

304 What is meant by the "impassable gulf"?

The "impassable gulf," in Luke 16:26, is a figure employed by the Saviour in describing the eternal separation of the good and the evil in the future life. In his parables and discourses, in order to impress upon the minds of his hearers the central objects of the lessons, he invested them with such natural and harmonious surroundings as the subject and the occasion demanded; and to interpret such surroundings literally would be as futile as to translate literally any of the multitudinous passages, full of similar imagery, that abound in Oriental oratory.

305 What classes of mankind did Dives and Lazarus represent?

In the parable of the rich man and Lazarus (Luke 16:19), the object was to illustrate the result of neglect of duty in commiserating and relieving the sufferings of others; to show how wealth hardens the heart, shuts up the springs of human sympathy and makes the possessor selfish and indifferent to the wants of his fellowmen. The rich man was a type of those who, while possibly generous at times, were yet so centered upon worldly pleasures and self-indulgence that all else was a mere incident. Riches that are used only for our own aggrandizement and gratification become a curse, while the man who employs his wealth in dispensing aid and comfort to those around him and relieving the distressed is a blessing to the land in which he lives. This was the distinction which the Saviour drew in his parable of the division of the sheep and the goats, when the King repudiated those that stood on his left hand with the words: "Inasmuch as ye did it not to one of the least of these ye did it not to me" (Matt. 25:45). Lazarus was a type of the hopeless, helpless, friendless poor who are to be found all over the world, and whose lot could be greatly benefited if people of means held their wealth as a beneficent stewardship. Nothing can be clearer than that it was the Saviour's intention to emphasize by these parables the divine law of love and sympathy which he came to teach the children of men by his own example.

**306 What is meant by the statement that it is
      "easier for heaven and earth to pass,
      than one tittle of the law to fail"?**

The law, in its literalness, endured until the time of John the Baptist. After him the kingdom of heaven was preached, the new kingdom whose law is love, whose king is Christ, and whose members are empowered by the Spirit of Christ to keep the greater and more comprehensive law of love, the law which includes and intensifies all the details of the ancient moral law. The law, while in Jesus it loses some of its ceremonial details, loses nothing of its real power; it is no less powerful, even by the tiniest measurement, than it was before, Luke 16:17. Matt. 5:17-19: Christ fulfilled the ceremonial law; he kept its authenticated details, and in his death all the requirements for sacrifice were satisfied and ended. While he kept the law and was to fulfill it, the Scribes and Pharisees were evading the law. By their interpretations and additions they really deprived it of authority. Jesus told them they must not dodge the law but keep it. He even indicated that those who kept the old law most carefully, as Paul did, would be given high places in the work of his new kingdom. Matt. 19:17: This again was counsel given *before* the Atonement. The way of life then was to seek to keep the law. Rom. 3:31: Here the declaration is made that the Gospel establishes the law. Men without the Gospel had little power to keep the law; the Gospel gives them power to keep it, and thus gives the law its rights, establishes it, makes it possible for its authority to assert itself. Rom. 8:7: The carnal mind is Paul's expression for the natural, evil, willful state of humanity. In that sinful, natural state a man cannot keep God's spiritual law. Paul uses also the term "old man" in the same sense. His teaching is that this "old man" is to be "destroyed" (Rom. 6:6), "put off" (Col. 3:8, 9; Eph. 4:22). James 2:10: This verse is undoubtedly true whether it is applied to law either before or after the Gospel. The judgment of the whole law as an institution came upon the man who violated any part of it; and under the Gospel a man is under the same obligation to keep the whole spirit of the moral law and to obey the words of Christ. We dare not disobey or displease Christ. I John 2:3, 4: These verses make a good climax.

John tells about the "perfect love," which enables humble Christians really to keep Christ's law of kindness. That is the great secret. Paul declares: "Love is the fulfilling of the law." If we love Jesus perfectly we shall not displease him by disobedience; if we really love our neighbor we will do him no harm but all the good we can.

307 What is meant by "making friends of mammon of unrighteousness"?

Probably no passage has been so often the subject of dispute as this in Luke 16:8, 9. The Revised Version renders it, "Make to yourselves friends by means of the mammon of unrighteousness." Luther thought it was a caution against avarice. Farrar regarded it as an injunction to care and faithfulness. Taking account of the parable that precedes the passage, it would appear that Christ was showing how a wicked man succeeded in getting friends at his employer's expense. Good men were not nearly so much in earnest in their godly affairs as the worldly men in their business affairs. If they used their money in relieving the needs of the poor they would make friends in heaven. It would not open the door of heaven, but it would cause those who had been benefited to give a warm welcome, thus enhancing the joy of that state. Dr. William Taylor used to illustrate it thus: A man whose house has been broken into naturally condemns the burglar; but he would be justified in pointing out to a lazy or incompetent workman, that if he had half the ingenuity the burglar had displayed he would soon make a fortune. We cannot imagine sorrow in heaven, but if there is any man who feels regret, it is he who on earth saw his poor brother suffer for the lack of money that he might have given out of his abundance. In heaven he cannot ease the burden of earth, but he must regret that when it was in his power he did not do it.

In the passage in Luke our Lord was showing how worldly people, "in their generation" and for their own selfish purposes, were prudent and sagacious in the worldly sense, and showed energy and determination in carrying out their mercenary plans, none of which, however, were for God and eternity. They were types of the money-makers of that day. Even from them, selfish and worldly though they were, the children of light might learn the lesson of concentration—not in relation to worldly, but to spiritual, things. It should be noted also that (verse 8) it was not Jesus, but the "lord" of the steward who commended the latter. The Revised Version corrects verse 9, which, accurately translated, reads: "Make to yourself friends by means of the mammon of unrighteousness," etc., implying that they, "the children of light," should use money not as the steward did, for selfish purposes, but in doing good to others. (See Luke 6:38 and Matt. 25:34-40.)

**308 When Jesus asked, "Woman, what have I
to do with thee?" was he being
ungracious to his mother?**

These seemingly harsh words (in John 2:4) addressed by the Saviour
to his mother at the feast of Cana, have been a subject of much speculation. In English they have a harsher sound than they have in the original. Thus "woman" is in Greek a mode of address used with respect and
used even to those high in authority, such as queens. What the Saviour
intended by this address was to call his mother's attention to the fact
that it was his work he was doing and not one in which she had any
concern. He no doubt used a gentle inflection of the voice, and her remark to the servants showed that not only was she not hurt or offended, but that she fully understood.

**309 How are we to understand Jesus' proclamation,
"The zeal of thine house hath eaten me up"?**

The passage in John 2:17 is an expression which graphically describes
the tremendous and inspiring enthusiasm of one who is aflame with a
righteous purpose. The disciples were doubtless surprised at the courage of One whom they had regarded as so meek and gentle, setting
himself to a task from which the bravest might have shrunk. It was a
new side to their Master's character, but thinking it over, they realized
that it was one that the prophets had predicted of him. His indignation
at seeing the house that had been dedicated to God so prostituted made
him regardless of his own safety. It absorbed him, or as John says, "ate
him up"—made him forget everything else.

**310 What is meant by, "Except a man be
born of water and of the spirit"?**

This passage in John 3:5 has given rise to much controversy and
theologians are by no means agreed as to its meaning. Our opinion is
that Christ had reference to the topic then agitating such men as the
one he was speaking to. They had a ceremony by which the Gentile was
admitted to the privileges of Judaism, part of which was baptism,
which signified purification from the sins of his old life. To the aston-
ishment of the Pharisees, John the Baptist had insisted that even they
were in need of baptism, just as the proselyte was. But as John intimated that was not enough. There was One coming who would baptize
with the Holy Spirit. Therefore Nicodemus would understand Christ's
meaning, when he spoke of being born of water and of the spirit. To the
new birth it was necessary that a man be purified in heart, his past sins
blotted out, which was symbolized by the water, and he must be quickened to a new life, which was done by the Spirit. Both are still necessary
to conversion. They are called in theological parlance, justification and

sanctification. This element of water and the operation of the spirit are the subject of prediction in Ezekiel 36:25-27.

311 What is the "new birth"?

It is an expression frequently used instead of "regeneration," to express the change from the natural state of sin to the new spiritualized life of the Christian. It is dying unto sin and being born again unto righteousness, a complete transformation of our moral nature, a new heart. Following after conversion and justification, the new birth or regeneration brings about a complete change of heart (see Heb. 10:22; Gal. 6:15; II Cor. 5:17; Col. 3:9; Eph. 4:22-24 and other passages).

312 What is the "witness of the spirit"?

The "witness of the Spirit" is the inward assurance which the believer enjoys of his filial relation to God, namely, that the Holy Spirit witnesses to and with his spirit that he is a child of God, and that his sins are forgiven. The immediate results of this witness of the Spirit are set forth in Gal. 5:22, 23.

313 In what sense is meekness a virtue?

It is a comprehensive virtue. It includes gentleness, readiness to do good to all men, to walk humbly before God and man, and not to overrate ourselves; to be loving as well as lowly-minded, not given to worldly ambition, but zealous to yield willing obedience to God's will; quiet, self-possessed, never quarrelsome nor disputatious. See Matt. 5:5; Matt. 11:29; II Cor. 10:1; I Peter 3:4; I Cor. 6:7; Rom. 12:19; I Peter 2:19-22; Rev. 21:7. Thus the meek, though the "only rightful occupants of a foot of ground or a crust of bread here," are the heirs of all things hereafter.

314 Why did Jesus give an evasive answer to the question, "Who art thou"?

When the question was prompted by mere curiosity, or when it was asked with the object of getting evidence from his own lips for the purpose of prosecuting him, it would have been unwise to satisfy the questioner. When, however, he was speaking to the woman of Samaria (John 4:26), there was no ambiguity: "I that speak unto thee am he." Under the adjuration of the High Priest, too, he answered plainly (Mark 14:62).: "Art thou the Christ the Son of the Blessed? And Jesus said, I am."

315 What were the "greater works" which the disciples of Jesus would do after He had left them?

Christ always objected to being regarded as a mere wonder-worker. He wanted the people to look upon his miracles merely as his credentials, and to argue from them that he who could do such things was sent from God. The miracles were intended to lead them to trust in him for eternal life. Consequently when, as he said, he went to the Father and the Holy Spirit was given to his disciples, they were enabled to do those greater works such as the conversions at Pentecost, which Christ held to be of a far higher order than miracles (John 14:12).

316 Do our public prayers violate Christ's specific injunction to enter into the closet when we pray?

No. Christ referred to the ostentatious devotion of the Pharisees who chose a public place for their devotions, with the motive that men might see them and honor them as pious people (John 16:23). There are many intimations in the New Testament that God approves of his people meeting together for prayer.

317 To what did Christ refer when he asked his disciple Peter whether he loved him "more than these"?

Peter had made himself conspicuous by his protestations of affection, as when he had said (Mark 14:29), "Although all should be offended, yet will not I." The form in which Christ put the question would appear to imply a delicate reminder of Peter's boast. Did he indeed love Christ more than did the other disciples? When Peter again avowed his love, Christ gave him a new commission to feed or shepherd the sheep and lambs (John 21:15). A commission not of authority, but of service.

318 What did Jesus mean by "if I will that he tarry till I come"?

This passage in John 21:20, 22 is frequently misunderstood. John alone of all the disciples survived the destruction of Jerusalem and so witnessed the beginning of that series of events which belong to what are known as the "last days" of that particular age. He may thus be said to have witnessed the foundation of the kingdom in men's hearts, in a greater measure than any of his associates. The language of Jesus (in verse 22) was not a prediction, but a question in which there was, however, an assertion of his divine power to dispose of human life as he willed. It has been made the basis of a tradition which treats it mistakenly as a prophecy.

319 What is the lesson conveyed in the passage on foot washing in John 13:10?

The saying like the act was symbolical. A different word is used in the original to express the washing, in the phrase "he that is washed," from that in the other phrase about the washing of the feet. The former refers to the bath, or the washing of the entire body, while the latter refers to the rinsing of the feet, as of one who had soiled them in walking from the bath. The body having been washed, he was clean every whit, when the dirt subsequently collected on the feet was removed. The teaching is obvious. The Christian who falls into sin does not need another regeneration, but the cleansing of these later sins.

320 Are the verses, "For God so loved the world," etc, the words of Christ or John?

Some scholars have thought that John wrote those verses as a commentary and that they were not spoken by Christ; but the number of such scholars was small and has become smaller as the discussion proceeded. Their theory was based on the fact that there is a change of tense in the verses in question; that the phrase "onlybegotten" was a favorite one with John; and that no further interruption from Nicodemus is reported. These reasons do not appear to us of serious weight. The change of tense occurs only when the topic requires it, and if the words are Christ's the change would occur as certainly as if they were John's. The phrase, "onlybegotten" was, it is true, a favorite one with John, but probably because he had heard it so frequently from his Master. And as to the third reason, it is not likely that Nicodemus broke in on that wonderful revelation, or that if he did, John would interrupt it to report his questions. We cannot believe that Christ ended his talk with the fifteenth verse, because if he had done so, Nicodemus would not have heard the essential facts. Neither would statements so authoritative have been made by John, unless he had distinctly indicated that it was he and not Christ who was speaking. The subject was fully discussed some years ago and scholars so eminent as Alford, Lange and Stier then expressed their conviction that the whole passage, from the beginning of the tenth to the end of the twenty-first verse, was spoken by Christ.

321 How should we interpret, "Take no thought for the morrow"?

Jesus did not have a word to say against industry or prudence. His words in this instance were directed against the anxiety, worry, and foreboding which afflict so many people. Trust in God, he said in effect, do not spoil your lives by this distressing fear. At the worst, you will have clothing and food. Do not be grasping or selfish, but give to those in need. Solomon said a similar thing (Prov. 11:24). The one man whom Christ advised to sell all he had and give to the poor, was a boastful man who wanted to be perfect. Jesus saw the fault in his character and told him that his way to perfection was to eliminate that fault. To other men he probably gave no such advice. He laid his finger on the weak place. The apostles, it is true, were bidden leave all and follow him; but that was necessary to the work to which they were called; yet even with them Peter seems to have kept his house as did John.

322 Who are the "false prophets in sheep's clothing"?

The warning is against teachers who come, claiming to be authorized interpreters of the mind of God and expounders of his Word, yet who are false leaders, having no spiritual light in themselves and being unfitted to guide others into the light of truth. Coming in sheep's clothing implies that they present a plausible exterior, their lips filled with smooth, persuasive words; but they do not teach nor do they themselves know the Gospel of Jesus. They teach instead a manmade Gospel, and make a great show of liberal ideas. The "old paths" they discard for new ways of reaching heaven. They cast doubt upon the essentials of the faith and teach the doctrines of error. Any teacher who does not hold fast to the cardinal points of the Gospel, or who does not emphasize the divine nature and the mediatorial office of Christ and his sacrifice and atonement; who would exalt works above faith; who belittles the importance of the revealed Word, and casts doubt upon its genuineness and authority; who compromises with sin and the weakness of our nature; who leads his flock to regard with doubt all that pertains to the invisible realm of faith and the supernatural; who attaches more importance to the operations of the human mind than to all else such a person is not calculated to lead others in the way of life everlasting. It is therefore of the very first importance that the pastor who is chosen for a church should himself be a Christian, living the Christian life, else, however sincere he may be in his efforts, he will not be able to lead others aright.

323 What does the parable of the ten virgins intend to teach?

The duty of watchfulness and unworldliness. In the East, to this day, at a wedding ceremony, the approach of the bridegroom's procession is heralded by the cry, "The bridegroom cometh," and those who have been invited come out of their houses to join it, and go with him to attend the ceremony. In Christ's time, apparently, they were expected to carry lamps. All the virgins in the parable slept while the bridegroom tarried; but five of them were prepared with oil to trim their lamps, and the others were not. Thus, when the bridegroom came they were ready to meet him, while the others were not. Professing Christians would be similarly divided if Christ were to come to the world now. Some would rejoice and be ready to welcome him, while others, who are leading worldly lives and are not cultivating Christian character, would be unprepared and would be stricken with consternation.

324 What is meant to be taught by the case of the evil spirit which brought into the unguarded heart "seven other spirits more wicked than himself"?

The corresponding passage, Matt. 12:43-45, appears to indicate that primarily the meaning applied to the Jewish nation. It had repented or reformed under the preaching of the Baptist, "cleaned up," as the modern phrase has it, but had not gone on as it should, to acceptance of Christ and righteousness toward God. The negative goodness was to be followed by a worse national condition, in which the Lord would be crucified. It is as if a nation was led to forsake idols, but instead of becoming Christian became atheistic. In the individual the reference is to a man weaned from some besetting sin, but not taking the grace of God into his heart, and replacing the love of sin with love of God and holiness, leaves the heart unoccupied ready for a return of the sin he had quitted, or the fall into something still worse.

325 What are we to understand by, "Many are called, but few are chosen"?

This is one of Christ's terse and memorable sayings, several times uttered. It is interpreted to mean that many receive the invitation of the Gospel who never reach the stage of spiritual progress where they can be said to be "chosen" to salvation through sanctification of the Spirit and belief on the truth." (See II Thes. 2:13.) The "chosen" were those who were set apart for special duty to become living examples of devoted service. Paul was such an illustration of God's sovereignty in choosing his instrument. It should not be held to imply, however, that salvation is forfeited, except through the fault and wickedness of those who are rejected. Christ's death was all-sufficient, and it is not the divine will that any should perish. Many controversies have arisen over this passage, but we can safely rest upon the language of the Saviour himself, who said: "Whosoever will may come" . . . . and "Him that cometh I will in no wise cast out." This promise is absolute and assures us that saving grace is within the reach of all who will forsake sin and accept salvation through Christ. The broad interpretation of the passage would seem to be that while many are called, or set in the way of salvation, the invitation alone does not save them; they must themselves comply with all the conditions. Thus a means is provided for the salvation of all, except those who willfully reject it. This is the true grace of the Gospel and it is so clear and unmistakable that no human doctrine or interpretation can change it.

326 Why did Jesus instruct his disciples to buy swords?

He wished them to be forewarned of the world's hostility to the Gospel. He spoke in figurative language, as he frequently did, and they, misunderstanding him, interpreted his words literally, supposing he alluded to present defense. Seeing that they misinterpreted his language about the swords, he closed the conversation with the words: "It is enough." His healing of the high priest's servant's ear simply emphasized the fact that he had not intended to counsel physical violence.

327 Was there heartlessness in Jesus' words, "Let the dead bury their dead"?

No. He meant to convey that the proclaiming of the Kingdom of God was more important even than to bury the dead—an office which could be performed by those spiritually dead as well as by one who had been called to the Master's service. He did not belittle the office of burial, but simply put it in contrast with the more imperative duty of preaching the Gospel.

328 In what sense is "the kingdom of God within you"?

The words "the kingdom of God is within you" are to be interpreted in the sense that those who follow Christ and believe in him as Saviour, and whose lives are guided by his example, have already in this life a part and share in his kingdom, which is eternal.

329 What is the "sin unto death"?

It is believed to be the sin against the Holy Spirit which tends toward or is destined to result in spiritual death. Several commentators make it quite distinct from what is known as the "unpardonable sin"—which is believed to have been attributing the Spirit's marvelous work to Satanic agencies. Alford makes it the act of "openly denying Jesus to be the Christ, the Son of God." Such willful deniers are not to be received into one's house (see II John verses 10 and 11). The apostle's meaning is evidently that this chief sin is one by which faith and love are destroyed and the new life killed by a palpable rejection of grace. When such a person knowingly thrusts spiritual life from him, no human intercession can avail. See James 5:14, 18; Matt. 12:31, 32, as to the obstinate rejection of the Holy Ghost's plain testimony to the Divine Messiah. Jesus on the cross pleaded for those who knew not what they did in crucifying him, not for those willfully resisting grace.

330 What is to be understood by putting "new cloth on an old garment"?

The new is really the unshrunken cloth which, when it became wet and dried, would draw and strain the old garment, making a greater rent. The meaning was that at that time the most intelligent Jews, such as Nicodemus, were hailing Christ as a reformer. They were mistaken. His religion was not a new patch on the old. The old could not be mended, but must give place to his new religion. A specimen of this futile attempt was seen in the struggle to force the old Jewish laws on the Gentiles, which was repudiated (see Acts 15:1-21).

331 Did an angel actually come down and disturb the pool at Bethesda?

It should be noted that the evangelist, in giving an account of the pool, does nothing more than to state the popular belief (probably a legend) as he found it, without vouching for it except so far as it explained the invalid's presence there. Jesus simply put aside as of no moment the alleged healing virtues of the pool, and aroused the man's faith in that power which alone could minister to his need.

A CHRISTIAN'S PROBLEMS

332 Is being killed in an accident a punishment for wrongdoing?

No, it is not right even to think such a thing, and it is a gross slander on God to say it. Jesus was very explicit on that subject. (See Luke 13:1-5.) The tower of Siloam had fallen and had killed eighteen persons and Jesus was told of it. He took occasion to disabuse his hearers' minds of the idea that accidents were to be regarded as punishments. There was another case in which the question was put to him directly. He was asked who had sinned, a blind man or his parents, that he was born blind, and he answered, neither (John 9:2, 3). The whole book of Job is devoted to the subject. Job's friends thought that his affliction was punishment for hidden sin. God himself interferes to reprove them. It is a wicked and a cruel thing to add to the affliction of a bereaved family by suggesting that their loss is a punishment of the dead or the living.

333 Does Paul imply we should endure uncongenial associations?

In I Cor. 7:15 the bondage of uncongenial association is meant. In Corinth, unbelievers were of a particularly vicious type. The newly converted Christian would be pained day by day by the conduct of an unbelieving husband or wife. The members of the church inquired of Paul whether it was their duty to separate in such cases. He advised their remaining together, and for the believer to try to lead the unbeliever to Christ. But if the unbeliever went away, the believer was not bound to seek a renewal of relations. Let the unbeliever go. There was no compulsion in cases requiring the believer and the unbeliever to live together.

334 How can one have absolute assurance of forgiveness of sin?

The absolute inward assurance of forgiveness is to be obtained by a perfect surrender of our lives to God. If this is done in prayer, and without one reservation, the Holy Ghost performs its part as surely as God's promises stand. There is an expansion, an uplifting, an inward illumination that ever after establishes an assurance of forgiveness of sin to the individual soul. It is "the Spirit witnessing with our spirit that we are the sons of God." This is the new birth. This assurance of God's for-giveness of sins is given in answer to prayer through Jesus, and is com-municated to our souls by the Holy Spirit. The degree or clearness of this assurance is according to our faith. Doubts cloud this conscious-ness of God's favor. The Holy Spirit imparts to the believer an assu-rance of pardon and adoption into God's family. "Ye have received the Spirit of adoption, whereby we cry, Abba, Father. The Spirit itself beareth witness with our spirit, that we are the children of God." "He that believeth on the Son of God hath the witness in himself." God "that cannot lie" says through the inspired apostle, "If we confess our sins, he is faithful and just to forgive us our sins and to cleanse us from all unrighteousness." When the conditions are fully met, faith springs up in the human heart, and to believe "that my sins are forgiven" is without effort, the same as to breathe. Some obtain "absolute inward assurance" of sins forgiven more readily than others. Some souls are most trustful. The doubting and despondent may never in this life have assurance "absolute," yet even these may possess "assurance." The first step to "absolute assurance" is to believe that it is not assurance that saves, but faith. We may not see the bridge over which the train is safely carrying us. So faith saves, though we may not feel safe. The second step is to trust oneself to Christ, as a child lets his father take him in his arms. The third step is to willingly do and bear whatever Christ im-poses. Absolute conviction will be found in your own heart after you have questioned it and can truthfully say these words: "I believe in and love the Lord Jesus Christ, enough to lay down my life, if need be, for his sake. I love him well enough, to live as long as he wants me to, a life of idleness or of labor, a life in prison or a life of freedom, a life of suf-fering or a life free from all care, a life wholly devoid of companionship, wealth, worldly pleasures and friends. I love him well enough to go down to my grave, if need be, branded by the world." When you can freely give such a pledge, then you will feel the blessed peace enter your heart, and God will come and talk with you.

335 Was the atonement an
Old Testament belief?

The expectation of the coming Messiah, who should redeem his peo-ple and should suffer for their sakes, is as old as the beginnings of He-brew nationality. See Isa. 53; Zech. 11:13. The idea of propitiation, reconciliation and expiation was associated with his coming, and al-though substitution is not mentioned it is implied. In connection with the sacrificial offerings similar terms are sometimes used, but the broader view of vicarious sacrifice, with special reference to the Messianic atonement, is most fully set forth in Isa. 53. The Messianic mission was the salvation of the race (Isa. 11). This expectation was not wholly confined to the Jewish people. The Samaritans held it; the Magi knew of it; even in the days of Melchizedek and Job it was understood by inquiring souls (Job 19:25) . The very first recorded Scriptural allusion to it is in Gen. 49:10. See also Isa. 9:1-7; Isa. 40; Micah 5:2. There were periods in Jewish history during which the Messianic predictions and expectations temporarily ceased, but they were never wholly extinguished. It should be admitted, however, that while some of the Jewish Targumistic writings refer to a suffering Messiah, the greater number deal with a powerful and conquering Messiah. Faith in God, belief in his word and a willing obedience were accounted for righteousness in the old dispensation. See Gen. 15:8 and Rom. 4:3-6, 20, 25 and other passages. Incidentally it may be mentioned that Job is supposed to have lived about the time of Isaac, some 1800 B.C., Daniel 600 B.C., Micah 950 B.C., Isaiah 750 B.C., Zechariah, 520 B.C.

336 Is the efficacy of the atonement of Christ limited to those who accept it?

The subject has been discussed for generations, and with no practical benefit. It brings up the old and profitless question of foreordination, which is better left alone. It is sufficient for us to know that whosoever avails himself of the offer of salvation through Christ will be saved. If the ruler of a rebellious people proclaimed amnesty to all who laid down their arms, it would apply to all who complied with the conditions, but those who did not comply would have no part in the amnesty. The limit would not be in the offer but in the disposition of the people.

337 Is celibacy commanded in the Bible?

Certainly not, and no enforced celibacy was known in the Church until long after the apostolic age. Chrysostom opposed it, Polycarp, Eusebius, Cyprian, and other early writers mention priestly marriage as a common thing, and in fact, during the first three centuries there is no evidence of celibacy as a rule of clerical life. The Council of Trent (1545-1563) established the rule of celibacy. It originated officially with the edict of Siricius, bishop of Rome (A.D. 385), who argued that the reason why priests in Old Testament times were allowed to marry was that they might be taken exclusively from the tribe of Levi; but as no such exclusive limitation prevailed in the Roman Catholic priesthood, marriage was unnecessary and inconsistent with the priestly office. The Roman bishops who succeeded Siricius sustained this contention and a long line of Popes confirmed it in their decretals. For centuries, however, there was a continuous struggle over it among the Romanist clergy and many lived openly in wedlock in spite of the decrees. Finally, about the sixteenth century it became a fixed rule of the Roman Church. It is a system which ever since its introduction has given rise to many abuses.

**338 How far may people be compelled
    to accept Christianity?**

It is the mission of Christianity to preach the Gospel to all nations, but this does not imply the employment of force to compel a people to adopt the Christian religion against their will. In our own land, freedom of worship is guaranteed under the constitution. Any attempt to force the adoption of a religion would be a violation of the constitution. Lawful persuasion may be used, and there is, of course, no bar to discussion, but the individual and the community must be left wholly free. The attempt to force religion upon any people, and especially to force it upon any nation as such with the ultimate end in view of establishing a religious power in the State or nation, is in conflict with Christ's own declaration that his kingdom is "not of this world."

339 What is a spiritual church?

In order to have a spiritual church, it is essential that there should be spiritually-minded leaders, men of ripe Christian experience and earnest faith, who can communicate their own enthusiasm for service and soul-winning to their fellow members. The true spiritual church is an active, working church, where the congregation vie with each other not merely in living up to their privileges in the matter of church attendance, but in active personal effort in their neighborhood, drawing others under the influence of the Gospel and organizing themselves for works of charity and kindness. An inactive church cannot have spiritual growth. The church should be directly connected with the work of home and foreign missions, hospital and sick visitation, shepherding of the children, keeping up the Sunday School, and doing good at every opportunity. Neglect of prayer meetings marks a decline of spirituality in a church which no amount of social attractions will repair. The ideal church is one in which every member has a share in the general activities of the organization. This means all, large and small, young and old, learned and ignorant for too often the educated try to obtain an ascendency. Intellectuality is not always an aid to spiritual life; on the contrary, there are very many cases in which it has proved a barrier. One does not perceive God through the intellect alone, and this is shown in the fact that many of the most spiritual natures have been found among the simple and unlearned. Intellectual vanity and self-sufficiency—an overweening confidence in the powers of the finite mind—are among the strongest impediments to faith. "Ye must become as a little child."

**340 Will the whole world be converted
    before the second coming?**

There is nothing in Scripture to make one believe that the whole world will be converted before the Second Coming. On the contrary, we are told that up to and immediately preceding that event, there will be widespread apostasy and spiritual decline, with false Christs and misleaders of men. We should not overlook the fact, however, that the duty is imposed on all Christians to spread the Gospel throughout the world, and to do everything that lies in our power for the conversion of the nations, but the complete harvest can come only in God's own time.

341 Does the rule laid down by Apostle James (2:10) imply that all crimes are equal in guilt?

No; it means that the violation of any of God's laws places the offender in the category of sinners. The writer is arguing with proud, self-righteous people who take credit to themselves for not committing certain sins. He shows them that in committing other sins that are not accounted by men so disgraceful, they are nevertheless sinners against God as surely as if they had committed the sins they condemn. A man who tells a lie has broken God's law and in that respect is under condemnation as the man is who commits a murder. Not that both are equally heinous, but that both stand on an equality in not being able to plead inncence before God. Both are sinners in need of mercy.

342 Why did the Apostle Paul advise Timothy to drink wine?

We suppose he thought it would do him good. He evidently believed that Timothy's ailment, whatever it was, would be relieved by a stimulant. Perhaps if Paul had known as much as modern physicians do of the human constitution, he would not have given the advice. Drinking habits, in our day, do so much harm, that if he were alive now, we do not think he would counsel a young minister to drink wine. He was too much concerned about the general good to suggest an example which would be mischievous.

343 Can evil emanate from God?

This is a topic that has caused much controversy. Evil is the negation of good. God is the source of all goodness, and no evil dwells in him; but with the withdrawal of his guiding and protecting spirit from man, evil comes. In I Sam. 16:14, we are distinctly told that this was the case with Saul. The Spirit of God had forsaken him, and then his soul was an easy prey to the Spirit of Evil. He was hypochondriac and his distemper was aggravated by his wicked temper and his consciousness that as the result of his own sin and folly he was in danger of losing his throne. The passage in Is. 45:7 "I form the light and create darkness; I make peace and create evil" does not refer to moral evil, but to discord or disturbance in the order of the universe as a whole. Thus, as light and darkness are opposites, so in the next clause of the verse, peace and disorder are opposites. Evil is the negation of good and distinction must be made between natural and moral evil. Among natural evils are wars, earthquakes, storms, plagues or whatever disturbs or disarranges the perfection of natural things; whereas moral evil is thought, word or act that is contrary to the revealed law of God and is therefore sin. It is the peculiarity of Hebrew writing to delight in contrasts. You find a long series of them in Proverbs. They are always of the same nature of parallelisms. Thus, in the passage in Isaiah 45, the prophet used the converse of the peace he has been talking of. We should say war or physical disturbance. He uses the word evil in the sense of punishment or misery. It is the state of the nation that he is considering. It serves God and is faithful to him and is prosperous. The prosperity comes from God. It deserts him and disobeys him and is punished by captivity and oppression. They also come from God. In that sense he creates the condition which they regard as an evil. There is a similar argument in Romans 11:22. Moral evil he never creates.

344 Does God choose people for destruction?

Peter was right in saying (II Peter 3:16) that in Paul's epistles there were some things hard to be understood. The verses in Rom. 9:15-20 are confessedly difficult. They appear to be contradictory to the conclusion which Paul reaches at the close of his argument (Romans 11:32) "God hath concluded them all in unbelief, that he might have mercy upon all." Perhaps we would understand his argument better if we knew more of the people to whom he was writing. It may have been, that among them were some who had the audacity to criticize God's method of government, and Paul wanted them to realize that God was not under obligation to save any who rebelled against him. That fact we must admit. No man can claim as a right that God shall forgive him. We know, from Christ's own words and from Paul's own letters, that God does forgive all who come to him in penitence. But when a man defies him, as Pharaoh did, Paul contends that God makes an example of him, that men of all times may see what is the end of defiance of his rule. We do not imagine that Paul meant that God directly hardened Pharaoh, but that the hardening was the effect of the removal of the plagues and was "permitted." The very mercy had the opposite effect on the man that it should have had. Pharaoh misunderstood it, as men now misunderstand God's longsuffering, and think they will escape altogether. Our side of the question is not God's sovereignty, which we can never understand, but the sublime fact that "whosoever will" may come to Christ and be saved.

345 Does Satan interfere with God's children?

Paul, in common with the people of his time, had a firm belief in the interference of Satanic influence in human life. Not only in I Thess.

2:18, but in II Cor. 12:7, he refers to it. The "thorn in the flesh," whatever that affliction was, he regarded as a messenger from Satan. The writer of Samuel took another view. He said the evil spirit that troubled Saul was from the Lord. (See I Sam. 16:14, 18:10 and other passages.) The writer of the book of Job thought that the evil fortune might be the work of Satan under express permission of God. The origin of evil has always been a mystery and it is not solved yet. Though we cannot understand it, we may be sure that vexations and hindrances and temptations do not come to us without the divine permission, and they are intended to strengthen the character. Paul himself said that all things work together for good to them that love God. (Rom. 8:28.)

346 What was the "sentence of the serpent"?

The "sentence of the serpent" as the passage in Gen. 3:15 is called, was a far-reaching one. The prophecy concerning the posterity of the woman, who were to be at enmity with the seed of the serpent, "points to the continual struggle between the woman's offspring and the grand enemy of God and man—the mighty conflict, of which this world has ever since been the theater," between sin and righteousness. In the clause in question perhaps the more accurate reading would be: "I will *permit* enmity between thee and the woman," etc. God is not the author of evil; but when his holy Spirit is withdrawn from a man or a community or a nation, evil comes and takes the place of good.

347 Who created the devil?

This question has puzzled theologians for ages, and has occasioned discussions which have had no profitable issue. There is no source of reliable information but that contained in Scripture and that is of a very meagre character. See Rev. 12:7, 9, and II Peter 2:4. The inference from those and other passages is that Satan was created by God as man was, that he was pure and innocent, but, like man, liable to fall. That he did fall and was cast out of heaven. It cannot be conceived that God created an evil being, though, as we know to our sorrow, he did create a being who became evil. The whole subject is wrapped in mystery and the Bible writers are more intent on the practical question of teaching us how to be delivered from the power of Satan than in giving us his biography. The less we know of him and have to do with him the better for us. That Satan was an angel of high estate, who fell through ambition, leading to rebellion, is the concrete form of a history which is a combination of Scripture and tradition. See John 8:44; Matt. 4:1-11; Matt. 25:41; Luke 8:12; Luke 10:18; Acts 13:10; Eph. 6:11; I Pet. 5:8; I John 3:8 and other passages. In Job he is the adversary and the tempter. See also I Chron. 21:1. Milton the poet described him as "the prince or ruler of the demons." See Dan. 7:10 and Jude 6. These passages leave much unexplained and conjecture here is useless. His final overthrow and punishment are predicted in Rev. 20.

348 Are we as Christians bound to keep the Ten Commandments?

The Christian is not under the law but under grace. That however does not free him from obligation. More is expected of him in the way of righteousness than if he were under the law. You lay down rules for your child and make him obey, but when he grows to manhood he is free from your rules. Do you not expect that he will behave without rules? That was your object in training him, to produce in him a disposition which would keep him right when he became his own master. Now, which of the Commandments do you as a Christian, free from law, feel that you are at liberty to break? You would keep them out of love for God, whether you were bound or not. As to commands and injunctions of the Old Testament, when the question was considered in the first apostolic council (Acts 15:5-29) it was decided that Gentile converts were not to be bound by the Levitical law. Christ, also, in his sermon on the mount, said: "It hath been said by them of old time," and went on to say, "but I say unto you," etc., clearly regarding the law as it stood to be subject to his abrogation. It must not, however, be supposed that the Christian dispensation is less stringent. The man who obeys Christ is under obligations higher than those of the law. As an example, the law forbade murder and Christ forbade the anger that leads to murder. As love is higher than law, so Christ, by setting his people free of law and placing them under the obligation of love, inculcated a higher morality.

349 Who are those who "fall away"?

The passage in Heb. 6:6, like that about the unpardonable sin, has caused much discussion and apprehension. The description in the previous verses of the persons to whom it refers, appears to indicate a condition of enlightenment and of personal experience such as some attain who do not become true Christians, but return to the world. The writer appears to be speaking of a fact rather than enunciating a doctrine. Every Christian minister and worker knows how difficult it is to win a backslider, especially one who has become a scoffer. The truth seems to have no effect upon them. Any person who fears having fallen into that condition can disprove the theory by going to Christ and asking forgiveness. Christ will receive him. The very fact of his being distressed about it indicates that he has not fallen beyond hope. The man who has need to fear, is he who does not trouble about his state.

350 Is there any hope for the backslider?

See Heb. 10:26-29; John 6:37; Heb. 6:4-6, and I John 1:9. The passage in Heb. 10 refers to those who sin after receiving "full knowledge" of the truth (see I Tim. 2:4), and who after having been "enlightened" and tasting a certain measure of grace and the spirit of truth (see John 14:17-29), apostatize to Judaism, or infidelity. Such is not a sin of ignorance or error, but the result of moral wickedness or a deliberate sin against the Spirit—a presumptuous sin against Christ's redemption for us and the spirit of grace in us. Having fully known the one sacrifice for sin, and having a certain experience of the efficacy of that sacrifice, they have now rejected it. In Heb. 6:4, 6, the same idea is emphasized. Such sinners crucify Christ anew, instead of crucifying the world (see Gal. 6:14). The passage in John 6:37 expresses the glorious certainty of eternal life to those who believe and stand firm—those who are given him of the Father and come to him with full surrender. Not the simply willing, but the actually faithful; not the waverers, but the true and abiding, are to realize the promise. In the backslider there has been no complete dedication, otherwise there would be no apostasy. I John 1:9 emphasizes the assurance of forgiveness and acceptance of the faithful ones. Concerning the possibilities of a return to Christ on the part of a backslider, we can only assert that what to man may and often does seem impossible, is possible with God, and that his grace is boundless. Peter backslid in a most grievous way, and yet was forgiven. By a miracle of divine grace, the backslider, although beyond human hope of recall, may in God's abundant mercy find refuge and forgiveness.

351 Does every good thing come from God?

It is impossible to say just what impulses proceed from self and what are the direct influence of God in the unconverted soul. Some impulses to kindness seem purely natural, such as the instinctive care of a mother for her child, which is found in beasts as well as in human kind. The affection of animals for people, like the affection of a dog for his master, is sometimes tremendously strong. While all these noble and beautiful things come from God, they do not necessarily indicate the presence of God in the soul. He has planted certain admirable traits both in the instincts of animals and the minds of men; he also has, of course, the power of communicating with men, speaking to their minds and consciences by his Spirit and by his Word. Reason is higher than instinct and conscience is higher than both, but even conscience may not mean that God is dwelling in the soul. Only when it is enlightened or quickened by the divine power does it become a safe guide. Conscience, therefore, is not so much the voice of God as the human faculty of hearing that voice. But at conversion God's Spirit comes into a man's soul. He is no longer outside, but within; mystically though actually linked to the man himself. The great change then is that a man finds himself loving God, eager to get his messages, anxious to please him. The impulses to do good, instead of being vague and weak, become definite and intense. The converted man feels that God is within him, making suggestions, awakening holy, unselfish, beautiful desires, and giving him power to carry out these good desires in vigorous and successful action.

352 Why do some passages of the New Testament use the neuter pronoun in referring to the Holy Spirit?

In the New Testament references to the Holy Spirit the masculine form is used almost without exception. In John 14:26 and 15:26 the relative pronoun "which" is employed, a word that in present-day English is always neuter. At the time the Bible was translated, however, the form "which" was used of persons as well as things, for example: "Our Father which art in heaven" (Matt. 6:9) and "these . . . which have received the Holy Ghost." (Acts 10:47.) As a matter of fact it would not have been surprising if the neuter form had crept into the translation of some other passages, as the Greek word for spirit (pneuma) is neuter. This makes it all the more remarkable that throughout the Greek New Testament the pronouns referring to this neuter word are masculine. The fact of the Greek noun itself being neuter has no bearing whatever on the question of personality or sex, as is well understood by any one familiar, for instance, with German, in which the same thing is often true.

353 Will the Jews ever return to Palestine?

Will the Jews return to the Holy Land, and will they ever, as a nation, acknowledge Christ as the Messiah? is often asked, and again it is sought to be known how they can be God's chosen people when they reject Christ. There is no doubt that the Jews were God's chosen people and Paul says (Romans 11:1) that He has not cast them off. In that and the two preceding chapters the apostle fully discusses the question. The prophets assure us that they will return to the Holy Land. There are predictions, dating before and during the captivity in Babylon, which were fulfilled when they returned under the edict of Cyrus, but there are others indicating a later and permanent restoration. The passages in Isaiah 2:2-4, Jeremiah 3:18, 16:14, 15; Ezekiel 36:24, 37:21, 25, 39:28, and many others have not yet been fulfilled. They will probably return in unbelief but will be, converted later (see Rom. 11:26).

354 Is justification the same under the old and new dispensations?

Justification is the act of God and has ever been so, under both the Old and New Dispensations. Under the Old, those were accepted who rendered a faithful and willing obedience; thus we read, in Gal. 3:6, that Abraham believed God, and this belief (*i.e.*, faith) was accounted to him for righteousness. Under the New Dispensation, Jesus "came to bring life and immortality to light," that is, to give us a spiritual illumination which would disclose to man the great scheme of redemption ordained from the beginning. The contention, therefore, that none save those who are in the New Dispensation can attain immortality is untenable. Besides, the evidence of Scripture itself is against such a conclusion. Moses and Elijah were seen at the transfiguration. Paul held that while the race, as a whole, died in Adam's sin, as a whole it received life through Christ's redemptive work.

355 How can the kingdom of God be established before the judgment day?

The Kingdom of the Messiah, which was foretold by many of the prophets and is further explained in the New Testament, is a divine, spiritual kingdom, to be built up in the hearts of men and ultimately to become universal. It is described in the early prophecies as a coming golden age, when the true religion should be re-established and universal peace and happiness should prevail. Unquestionably, it was regarded by the Jews in a temporal sense only, but the Saviour himself declared it to be a spiritual kingdom, and his followers look forward to its highest realization only after his return. Meanwhile, it is being established now; from the beginning of the Christian dispensation, it has progressed in the hearts of men. That Jesus himself intended to convey this is made clear in Matt. 8:12, 11:12, 11:28; Mark 12:34; Luke 11:9, 11, and many other passages which deal with the various phases of the same subject. Matt. 24 describes the condition of the believers at the judgment and their welcome to the *fulness* of the completely established kingdom, with all its blessings and rewards.

356 Can a Christian keep the moral law?

To unfallen man, obedience to the moral law would undoubtedly have been within human reach, but to fallen man it stands as an unattainable ideal, to which he may strive, but in vain. There is none without sin (I John 1:8), and as a perfect obedience to God's law implies entire sinlessness, it is obviously impossible that such obedience can be rendered by mortal man. But to those who are in Christ this difficulty is overcome. (Rom. 4:7.) They are not under the law and consequently are not to be judged by the law. (Rom. 6:15; I John 3:9.) Christ, by his perfect obedience, and his sufferings for their sins, has satisfied the law in their behalf. (II Cor. 5:21.) Thus, when grace enters the heart, its sinfulness is removed. The righteousness and perfect obedience of Christ being imputed to his people, they are accepted of God. (Rom. 3:24; II

Cor. 12:9.) Christians, therefore, should not serve in the bondage of fear, as under the law (I Tim. 1:9), but in love, as under grace in Christ Jesus. (Rom. 8:1-15.)

357 Does the Bible say anything about life insurance?

There is nothing in Scripture bearing on the subject of life insurance, but there are various passages on thrift and on making provision for old age. If you turn to I Tim. 5:8 you will find a very definite statement on the subject. Evidently Paul did not believe that any man claiming to be a Christian was justified in leaving his dependent ones to be a burden on the community, either during his life or afterward. There are birds and other animals that give improvident man a lesson by the way they lay up a store of food against the winter season. Jesus in Matt. 6:31-34 was not rebuking thrift, but worldly-mindedness and vanity. He was referring to those who pursued the things of this life as the supreme object. He wanted his followers to "take no thought (anxious care or worry) for the morrow." He had no word of condemnation for attention to business, but business gains, wealth, possessions, etc., are all of secondary importance, and worry about them springs from the heart's distrust of God, and does no good, but rather evil.

358 Is the love of God toward man to be interpreted individually?

This question has often disquieted Christians under affliction. It has often appeared to the godly man, as it did to Job, that the children of God fare no better in the world than the wicked. But we are taught in a multitude of passages in the Bible, that God does know and care for the individual. Christ was very explicit on the subject. (See Matt. 10:29-31.) The promise in the New Testament to Christ's followers is not of prosperity, but that they shall receive strength to bear their afflictions and that those afflictions shall work for good to them. Our prayers would be simple mockeries if we did not believe in God's care for the individual. The Christian, like the worldling, is subject to natural law and other things being equal, a blow that would kill a worldling would kill him. It is often difficult to understand why so many afflictions fall to the righteous which the wicked escape, but God does not explain these particular trials. He expects us to trust him and to be assured that "he does not willingly afflict nor grieve" us, and to patiently wait the revelation which will make all things clear.

359 Does God work miracles at the present time as he did in Biblical times?

This is a question often asked. The arm of Omnipotence is not shortened that it cannot save. Thousands have been restored in mind and body in answer to the prayer of faith. Yet he never works *unnecessary* miracles. God has given us means and endowed us with intelligence to use these means, and he will not withhold his blessing upon their use when we ask it in faith. We ask him to feed us, but we must labor with our hands and not expect him to bless our idleness nor our lack of effort. So, if we ask him to heal us, we must use in faith the means he has supplied, with all the intelligence he has given us. It is simply "tempting God" to neglect his means. Jesus himself applied the clay and the spittle to the eyes of the blind. Naaman had to bathe in the Jordan. Even in the healing of the soul, which is an operation of the Holy Spirit, we must co-operate, and while he works in us, we ourselves must work with "fear and trembling." And if Divine wisdom should see fit to withhold the boon we crave in the form we ask, we must submit in faith to his will, as he knows what is best for us. Strength is often made perfect in weakness and many things we mistakenly call evils are blessings in disguise.

360 Did Paul discourage marriage?

In the 7th chapter of I Cor., Paul had apparently been asked questions by the Church in Corinth which tended to disparage marriage and to regard it as an undesirable state when one of the parties is an unbeliever. His long reply may be summed up in a few words: "Abide in your present station, for the time is short." He believed that, by remaining single, he could devote himself more acceptably to his Gospel work. The passage in I Tim. 5:14 is not inconsistent with the other, for the circumstances of the two cases were different, and in the latter he commends marriage under certain conditions, as an antidote to certain temptations.

361 What has the Bible to say about
marriage and divorce?

The Bible law on marriage and divorce may be learned from the following passages: Gen. 3:24; Matt. 19:5; by Peter in Mark 10:7, 8; Eph. 5:31; Matt. 19:6; Mark 10:8; Mark 10:9; Mal. 2:16; Matt. 5:32, 19:9; I Cor. 7:11; Matt. 19:9; Luke 16:18; Mark 10:11; Luke 16:18; Matt. 5:32; I Cor. 7:11; Rom. 7:2; I Cor. 7:39; Rom. 7:3; I Cor. 7:39.

362 Does God approve of the marriage
of an unbeliever to a believer?

The whole question at issue is fully and fearlessly discussed in II Cor. 6:14-18. This is Paul's interpretation and it stands good today as a general rule of Christian conduct. Nevertheless, we are not to judge those who may ignore the injunction, for in I Cor. 7:14, the apostle shows how such a union may after all accomplish beneficent results. From this verse to chapter 7:1, inclusive, the apostle seems to forbid too much social intercourse generally with idolatrous and heathenish people, rather than to have in view the marriage relation especially. In I Cor. 7:12-16, separation from the unbelieving husband or wife is discountenanced, because the believing spouse may be able to sanctify—that is, make holy—the unregenerate mate, and may effect conversion to salvation. In the same chapter and other passages of the apostolic writings marriage is encouraged without any restrictions. In Gal. 5:1, and Acts 15:10, the word "yoke" is used in a somewhat similar connection to that supposed to contain the implied prohibition. In Phil. 4:3, Paul addresses some unknown individual as "yoke-fellow," and it is quite certain he does not mean his wife. But if it is admitted that the text cited prohibits intermarriage between Christians and unbelievers, it must be construed with reference to the conditions of sensual idolatry universally prevailing at that period in the city of Corinth. Paul was addressing a small community of Christians in a very large heathen city, and it is as if we should advise Christians in China and India not to intermarry with Buddhists and Mohammedans, only more aggravated.

363 Is it possible that the miracle of the incarnation may be repeated?

The word "possible" is inappropriate in such connection, because nothing is impossible with God; but when we hear of his doing something utterly inconsistent with his ways, we know that it cannot be true, because he would never contradict himself. All the teaching of the Bible, the Epistle to the Hebrews especially, leads to the conclusion that Christ is the one and final incarnation of God. There is no need of another, because he fully satisfied the Divine purpose and has been found to fully satisfy the need of man. Many have arisen since his time, as he warned us there would, who have claimed to be God in human form, like some who even in recent years have made such a claim; but they were and are impostors. They are deceiving many, as Christ said impostors would (see Matt. 24:24), but not those who look to Christ for light and guidance.

364 What is the "call" to the ministry?

One of the best evidences of a genuine call is the possession of those special qualifications which add in marked degree to the usefulness of the Christian. If, under his addresses in Sunday School, or at prayer-meetings, or at mission churches God has acknowledged his work and souls are led to Christ, there is strong reason to believe that it may be his duty to devote all his time to preaching and pastoral work. A man's own intense desire to preach and the concurrent opinion of experienced Christians that his work would be useful in the pulpit, are also indications. The basis of all qualifications for the ministry, however, is that there must be in the heart an intense love of souls, consecration to Gospel service, and a sense of personal acceptance, pardon and regeneration through Christ. None but one who has himself traveled the road that leads to the Cross can guide others along the same path. See Col. 1:28; Matt. 15:14; Luke 6:39.

365 What are the qualifications of a minister?

A true minister of the Gospel must possess, above everything else, an intense love for Christ and a great love for his fellowmen. These two qualifications will necessarily give him an intense passion to save souls, and this is the true secret of success. He must love Christ so much and love people so much that he will long to proclaim Christ's message to men and win them to him. He must understand the Gospel—must feel its operation in his own heart and must know that "it is the power of God unto salvation, to every one that believeth." He must understand that the Gospel is the message of God's free grace to men by which he forgives and sanctifies them, and he must know how to lead men, not to try to save themselves by efforts and vows, but to accept humbly God's infinite gift of a present salvation. A minister should have common sense and a well-balanced mind. He should have a clear voice and the ability to express himself clearly and forcibly in speech; if eloquently, so much the better. He should have modesty and tact, and these even without much social experience, will lead him to conduct himself correctly and winsomely. His studies should lead him to know more of Christ, to know more of the Gospel, to know more of men, and to acquire more skill in delivering the message. He must study voice culture, rhetoric and some elocution—though this last is dangerous, as it is apt to make a speaker affected, which is fatal to real success. He must study the Bible and should study theology, and psychology. Special emphasis must be laid upon understanding people. A technical theological education sometimes lifts a man away from the people he must help instead of putting him into closer touch with them. He must understand how people live and work and suffer and think and must be sympathetic with and well informed about the movements they are making toward greater liberties and better social conditions. This understanding of people, individually and in groups, will help him to convince them of their need of Christ for their souls and for society. He should, if possible, also have some knowledge of business affairs so that in the conduct of his church he will not fall into financial and legal snares.

366 How long have we had a trained and educated ministry?

The Bible informs us that even in the days of Samuel there were "schools of the prophets," in which men were trained for the high function of moral and spiritual teaching. The priests and Levites were trained in the knowledge of the ecclesiastical law and the ceremonies. In later Jewish history, twelve great institutions for educating priests, teachers and elders existed. Jesus himself passed a considerable portion of his ministry in instructing and training his disciples. We read in Acts that the apostles imitated his example in personally instructing the younger disciples. John spent his later years teaching at Ephesus, qualifying youths for the ministry, and Mark did likewise at Alexandria. Early Christian training schools were established in Cesarea, Antioch, Laodicea, Nicomedia, Athens, Edessa, Seleucia, Carthage and in Mesopotamia and there were many minor institutions of the same class. Thus all the evidence goes to show that even from the earliest days, those who were designed to convey God's message to the hearts of men were set apart, consecrated, and fitly prepared. It is so today. A trained and educated ministry is essential to the advancement of religion just as training and preparation are needed in other vocations. The apostles, even if they had nothing more, had a course of several years' personal training with the great Master as their teacher before they were sent out on their full mission. It is true that many converted laymen, and women, too, have done and are doing noble work in soul saving, but they are exceptional and the fact that their labors are owned and blessed of God is not a valid argument against a trained ministry, but rather the reverse. With due training they might have accomplished even more.

367 Is misfortune a "judgment of God"?

We have no right to sit in judgment on others, and when some people censoriously announce that a misfortune which befalls a person or a community is "a judgment" of God, they assume undue authority. We are distinctly warned against judging others. See Christ's teaching on this subject. Luke 13:4.

368 Does a Christian have two natures?

In Rom. 7:25 Paul says: "So then with the mind I myself serve the law of God, but with the flesh the law of sin." The argument of the preceding verses has been the hopelessness of the struggle which that man must fight who strives to obtain salvation through the law. He is defeated by his own body, or the flesh, as Paul calls it. It drags him down and forces him to obey and to yield to its cravings; so that in his despair he cries, "What I would I do not; but what I hate that do I." The picture is one that appeals to every unconverted man's experience. His reason, his pride, his manliness direct him to renounce some sin, such as drunkenness or lust. He resolves, but suddenly the craving arises, and in spite of the resolves of his mind—his real ego—he is swept off his feet, and yields to his passion. The revelation of Christ as a helper crosses Paul's mind, and he thanks God. In the eighth chapter he is going to explain this at length, but he halts here at verse 25, to mark the stage reached by the man he is describing. "With the mind, I myself," the real ego am serving God; while with the flesh, the animal nature, I am serving sin. In Romans 8:10 this problem is solved. Through Christ the spirit is strengthened, and the flesh is controlled and sudued. He is freed by the spirit of life (Romans 8:3).

369 Does the Bible speak of the black race?

The ablest scientists hold to the unity of the race, and in this they are in accord with Scripture, which declares that the Creator "hath made of one blood all nations of men, for to dwell on all the face of the earth" (Acts 17:26), and that the "free gift comes upon all men to justification to life." Climatic variations extending over long periods account for physical differences. Blacks are the descendant of Ham, the head of one of the three great divisions of the human race. He was the progenitor of the Egyptians, the Cushites and the African nations, and his descendants were the founders of great empires in Ethiopia, Babylonia, Arabia, Abyssinia and, according to some authorities, in a considerable part of Asia, as far as the Euphrates and the Persian Gulf. No one has the slightest warrant for asserting that the black has not a soul. Christian converts from Cyrene in Upper Libya were among those who were identified with the formation of the first Gentile church in Antioch. Mark the evangelist labored during a large part of his missionary career in Africa. Simon, who bore our Saviour's cross (Matt. 27:32), was a Cyrenian and a native of Libya. The Copts, who were active in the early days of Christianity, were a mixed race, chiefly black. The Coptic Christian Church is one of the oldest in existence and possesses some of the most valuable early Christian manuscripts.

370 Do the Pauline epistles contain all that is essential to salvation?

It is quite proper to lay special emphasis upon the writings of Paul, because he was especially chosen of God to interpret the life and death of the Saviour to the hearts and minds of men, particularly of those who were not Jews. Furthermore, Paul was authorized to show that the requirements of the ceremonial law, as recorded by Moses, were done away with by the sacrifice of Christ. In this way it is easy to see that the explanation of the salvation wrought by the atonement is of more spiritual value than the precepts of the old law of sacrifices and ceremonies, which are no longer in force. The tremendous value of Paul's writings lies in the fact that he shows men the practical, immediate way of receiving salvation, not by the keeping of commandments, but by faith in the crucified Saviour. Granting all this, however, it is great folly to say that the other parts of the Bible are unimportant. The Pentateuch is full of flashes of God's presence and God's will, containing holy principles which are eternal, and recording the experiences of men who knew God; the historical books show God working in the life of a nation; the poetical and wisdom books give us inspiration and instruction for daily living; the prophetic books give us glimpses of the coming Saviour and are pulsating with direct, personal messages from God to the human soul; the Gospels help us to get acquainted with the Redeemer and to understand the kind of life he wants us to live and his hope for the world; the Acts give us clear pictures of men who were impelled by the power of the Holy Ghost and challenge us to let the risen Christ work through us as he worked through them; the other epistles are full of spiritual help, and the book of Revelation gives us visions of the life to come. All are important; all help us to know Christ better; all lead us to God. We must not slight these other books, even while agreeing that Paul is the direct messenger to us Gentiles to show us the way of salvation by faith.

371 Why was polygamy allowed among the patriarchs and why is it wrong now?

Jesus, in speaking of certain provisions of the Mosaic law on the marriage question, said: "From the beginning it was not so." Matt. 19:8. He referred to the original creation of one man and one woman as fixing the moral law that a man should have but one wife. The fact that Abraham and the other patriarchs had more than one wife does not make polygamy right any more than the fact that they owned slaves makes slavery right. The Bible is a truthful record of the lives of the people of whom it tells. They did many things that were wrong; God dealt gently and patiently with his people, leading them by a long process of teaching and development toward the full understanding of his perfect will. There was no particular time at which polygamy became wrong, but it was the teaching of Jesus, more than any other influence, that showed mankind that it is wrong. In the New Testament the love of husband and wife is presented as the highest form of love; it is inconceivable that any outsider, or third person, can enter into this sacred fellowship. Polygamy means injustice to women; the plural wives are outsiders, deprived from the Christian point of view, of real wifehood.

372 Does God answer prayers?

Most assuredly he does, but his ways are not as our ways. We are at best but children in spiritual things. Yet there is nothing in this world so clear and so well attested by Christian evidence, as that if we pray with believing hearts and in the right spirit, he will hear us and do what is best for us. No such prayer goes unanswered. The answer may not be as we expected, nevertheless it will be for the best and to the purpose. Says Professor Denney: "When we pray in Jesus' name there is nothing which we may not ask. Whatever limitations there may be, they are covered by the name of Jesus itself. We must not ask what is outside of that name, not included in its promise. We must not ask a life exempt from labor, from self-denial, from misunderstanding, from the Cross; how could we ask such things in His Name? But ignoring this self-evident restriction, Jesus expressly, emphatically and repeatedly removes every other limit. There is nothing which the name of Jesus puts into our hearts which we may not, with all assurance, put into our prayers." In his name, we can ask with assurance for pardon from God; we can ask to be strengthened in temptation and to be kept from falling, and restored when through human weakness we do fall, for we have the assurance that he will not let us be utterly cast down; we can ask for the sanctifying work of the Holy Spirit in our lives. We can ask that our material wants as well as our spiritual needs may be fully supplied. But, in asking, we must have the faith to lay hold, and when we pray with this faith, we shall never pray amiss.

373 Do prayers for the unconverted help?

The most definite Bible passage on this subject is I John 5:16: "If any man see his brother sin a sin which is not unto death, he shall ask, and he shall give him life." The words of Paul in Acts 16:31, "Thou shalt be saved, and thy house," probably mean simply that if all the members of the household believed they would be saved. But we have positive Scripture warrant for praying for our unconverted friends, and countless incidents from present day life and earlier times prove that many hearts have been won to Christ through prayer. The assurance may not always come that those for whom we pray will yield to God, but sometimes the assurance does come very definitely. Prayer for others should be personal, definite, earnest. S. D. Gordon in his *Quiet Talks on Prayer* takes the position that prayer for others, offered in the name of Jesus, has the effect of driving off evil influences from the persons for whom the prayer is being made. It projects the personal influence of the one who is praying to the one prayed for, and clears the spiritual atmosphere so that the voice of God can be heard and the power of God felt. Just as by talking to a person one may be able to persuade him to listen and yield to God, so by prayer one may influence another to submit himself to God. Most important of all is love. We must love ardently, steadily, those for whom we pray. Love will prevent us from doing things that would mar our influence over them or spoil their conception of the religious life. If our friends know that we love them deeply and constantly our words and prayers will have an almost irresistible power.

374 Should we pray for one from whom the Holy Ghost has departed?

Who are you, to assume to judge that such a one has been forsaken by the Holy Spirit? It would be a fearful responsibility to act on such a conclusion. Of one thing you may rest assured: if the person is at all concerned about his spiritual condition, no matter how deeply he has offended, that very fact is conclusive evidence that the Holy Spirit has not abandoned him, but is still striving with him. When the Holy Spirit leaves a man, that man becomes careless and indifferent and has no desire to pray. It is difficult—almost impossible—for us to understand the operations of the Spirit, but you may be assured that the love and compassion and long-suffering of God are infinite. Christ said that he would cast out none who came to him. With such an assurance, no man need wait to try to solve the mysteries of the Holy Spirit's work. The practical duty of closing with Christ's offer of salvation is the first thing for him to do.

375 Should we persistently ask for blessings?

By all means. The three passages, Matt. 11:12; Luke 11:5-10 (the parable of the friend at night seeking loaves from his neighbor), and Luke 18:1-8 (the parable of the unjust judge), all relate to the subject of earnestness and perseverance in prayer. The argument is that if the unfriendly neighbor and the unjust judge will grant the requests made to them because of the petitioner's insistance, God will surely grant our requests when he sees that we are in desperate earnestness. Matt. 11:12, "the kingdom of heaven suffereth violence, and the violent take it by force," agrees with these two parables in teaching that intensity, of desire and faith and effort, is required for spiritual victory. Faith seems to have two phases: the quiet, restful trust in God; and the aggressive, enthusiastic, energetic, insistent belief that pushes forward through all sorts of obstacles and delays to the victory desired. It is not because God is unjust or unfriendly that he does not answer at once. But our souls are strengthened by the test of waiting, and often human relationships and circumstances are changed as time passes so that the answer is better for the delay than if granted at the first request. God wants to train giants to help him in his work, giants who will believe in him and fight for the right, no matter what obstacles are in the way. And the saints who are strong and rich in faith accomplish most for his kingdom.

376 Is it right to ask for definite blessings?

There are many passages, such as John 16:23, which warrant definiteness in prayer. Indeed, if a man needs something very badly, and is sure that it would be a blessing to him, he would show a lack of faith if he did not pray for it. There are many, however, who shrink from praying for definite blessings, after a painful experience. They have prayed for some blessing, and God has heard them, and granted their request, and it has proved to be a curse. Emerson said, in a passage which we cannot find, but the gist of which we quote from memory, that all prayers are answered, therefore we ought to be very careful for what we pray. A celebrated divine wrote: "There are millions of Christians day by day imploring God for the salvation of the whole world, and the supplication has never been answered. Does God, then, keep his promise? Is prayer a dead failure? Does God mock the Christian Church? Are we told to bring all our gifts into the storehouse and prove him, only to find out that he breaks his promise? The answer to prayer is only a question of time. So far from there ever having been a million prayers lost, *there has never been one prayer lost.* God not only keeps one promise, but he keeps all the promises, and never since the moment we first breathed the Christian life, have we ever offered an unavailing prayer."

377 Why should we agree with our adversary quickly?

The passage is a part of the Sermon on the Mount in Matt., 5th chapter. Jesus had been speaking about quarrels between brothers, and urging reconciliation of such differences in the spirit of love, before coming to the throne of grace. Then (verse 25) he diverges to the question of lawsuits, which were common then as now, and advises his hearers to keep out of the hands of the law and to escape its penalties by settling their disputes between themselves. But he went further than this, for his language pointed to a higher tribunal, to which all must come for judgment and where condemnation awaits them which can only be escaped by their repentance and acceptance of divine mercy.

378 Will God give us anything we ask?

In John 14:14 (which should be read in connection with its surroundings), Jesus was speaking (in the discourse at table after the Supper) of the way, the truth, and the life, and of how his disciples might render acceptable service for the advancement of God's kingdom on earth. He was about to leave them and he gave them the assurance that they would be endowed with power, after his departure, to do the works that he had done. Verse 14 gave them the assurance of his continuous intercession and that their prayers would be heard and answered. He had already told them that they should seek first the kingdom and all things would be added unto them. This verse also shows his divine equality, in the words "I will do it." Our own prayers should be, as far as we are able to make them so, in line with God's will. There are many of us who may ask for things that would be for our own harm; but if we "seek first the kingdom," we have then the assurance that he will care for all our other needs, supply our wants, comfort our sorrows, relieve our hardships and take us safely through the difficult places of life. We have a right to ask for these, if we have acquired this right by belief on the Son of God and by acting in accordance with the divine will. See John 14:12.

379 Does God regard our "little things" in prayer?

Christ assumes toward all his followers the attitude of a friend. He said to his disciples: "Henceforth I call you not servants, but I have called you friends." We "work together" with him as friend with friend; our interests are identical with his and his with ours. On this basis it is perfectly rational to believe that he will give us all the help we need in the work we are trying to do for him; Christ certainly knows all about all the "little things" that come into our lives; also he will allow nothing to happen which will spoil or seriously hinder our work. Paul believed that Satan was trying to hamper him; in one place he says definitely that Satan hindered him, really prevented him from getting where he wanted to go (I Thess. 2:18). The right attitude is to ask God to further our tasks and then heroically and patiently keep at them. We must remember, too, that a certain amount of hardship and suffering is really necessary to develop the most stalwart Christian character. (See Heb. 12:1-11; II Tim. 2:3; Heb. 11, etc.) The Christian must beware of praying selfishly. A brave soldier would hardly pray for fair weather, except as it would aid the battle. We may certainly pray for strength; and the joy will come as we forget self in loving and serving the Master. But we should not forget that when God in his wisdom gave us eyes to see, a tongue to speak, a brain to think and reason to discriminate and guide us in our judgment, he meant these faculties to be of service. He gives us the fertile soil, but we must do the plowing and the planting. Faith in God does not imply that we should look to him to do for us what he has made us capable of doing for ourselves. When we do our part, then we can reach out the hand of faith and grasp his leading hand, which will carry us through in all we cannot do for ourselves.

380 Does God hear the prayer of the wicked?

We have precedent for such a belief. A striking example is that of Manasseh (II Chron. 33:18). A greater sinner than he it would be difficult to imagine. We can understand prayers of sinners for temporal blessings being unheard; "their sacrifice" and perhaps their prayers, too, "are an abomination" (Prov. 15:8); but when the sinner cries to God for pardon and for help to quit his sins, he is surely heard. God does not mock the wicked man when he bids him "seek the Lord." Let the wicked forsake his way and return, for he will abundantly pardon

(Isa. 55:6, 7). God heard the prayers of the people of Nineveh (Jonah 3:7-10). The way of approach to God is by repentance and that God gives (Acts 5:31). When the wicked man prays for that, he gets it; then God forgives him and he is in a position to ask for and receive all other blessings.

381 Was the prohibition against eating pork ever revoked?

At what is known as the first church council, described in Acts 15, the decision was definitely made that Gentile Christians were not to be compelled to keep the Jewish ceremonial law. The council sent a letter to the new converts setting them free from all these ceremonial requirements. This was the great burden of Paul's preaching, namely, that we are saved not by keeping the law of Moses but by faith in Christ. Circumcision was the sign of submission to the Mosaic law, and Paul, greatly to the displeasure of the Jews, taught that this was not necessary. The vision of Peter (Acts 10:9-16) while given for the purpose of making him willing to associate intimately with Gentiles, seems also to teach definitely that the Old Testament distinction between clean and unclean meats is no longer in force.

382 When and why was the Sabbath changed to the first day of the week?

There is no command recorded, and probably none was given to change, but the change was made in celebration of Christ's rising from the dead. At the first great council of the Church, when the question was discussed whether the Gentile converts should be required to obey the Jewish law, it was decided that only four observances should be required of them. (See Acts 15.) The observance of the Jewish Sabbath was not one of the four, and the Gentile Christians do not appear to have ever kept it. The Rabbis had made it ridiculous by a host of absurd regulations about what a man might, or might not, do on that day. Christ was frequently accused of breaking the Sabbath. The Jewish observance was most vexatious and onerous, and the Apostles very wisely did not attempt to bring the Gentiles under the bondage. The writings of the early Fathers show that very early in the Christian era, if not in Apostolic times, the first day of the week was uniformly the day of religious meeting and abstinence from secular labor, thus celebrating the new Creation as the Jewish Sabbath celebrated the old. Several incidental allusions in the Acts show that even in Apostolic times, the custom was prevalent. But we do not observe Sunday as the Sabbath. It is seldom a day of rest to the earnest Christian, but of holy activity in his Master's service.

383 Is suicide wrong?

Life is a precious gift from God and should be so valued. Pain and suffering are to be regarded as discipline. There is no Scriptural authority to justify the view that we have a right to shorten or terminate our existence. Suicide is a crime under human law, and in the early Church it was condemned by repudiation and the denial of Christian burial. See Paul's advice to the Philippian jailer. (Acts 16:28; also Job 14:14.)

384 Is being tempted a sin?

The sin does not consist in the temptation itself, but in inviting it, or yielding to it. Jesus himself was tempted "in all things as we are; yet without sin." Doubtless Satan, in the passage to which you refer, knew that Jesus had been fasting and so tried to tempt him to turn stones into bread. Again, believing that the desire for worldly power might influence him, he tried to tempt him by offering him the dominion of the whole earth, but again failed. It is not strictly correct to say that one cannot be tempted unless he has wrong desires. The tempter is always ready with his lures; but, if we rebuke our own desires and repel the temptation, asking divine strength to do this, the danger will pass. After conversion comes regeneration, and we are enabled to overcome sin. We may still be conscious of a struggle within, but we get strength to stand firm against it. The truly converted man is no longer the slave or bondman of sin, but is kept day by day from its power ever again having dominion over him.

385 What is the Trinity, how is it possible,
and what proof is there of it?

Are questions that have bothered thousands of earnest believers. No one should feel discouraged if the doctrine of the Trinity seems difficult, because as must be remembered, the facts about God are so much bigger than the brain of man that we cannot be expected in our present human state to comprehend them. The orthodox faith is that God is Triune in person. Christians feel by experience that God is their Father, that Christ is their divine Saviour, that the Holy Spirit is their Comforter, Sanctifier and Strengthener. The Father is a person; the Son is a person; the Holy Spirit is a person; three distinct persons in one eternal undivided and indivisible essence. How this is possible is not beyond comprehension to him that has learned to believe and know that to God all is possible and all doubts may be banished by the beautiful thought that to all others there is here one more glorious mystery into the depths and wherefores of which we are to be introduced in the happy beyond. And the proof! What more convincing proof can be asked than the words of him whom no one doubts, the Son of God and of Man. He tells us "I and my Father are one," "He that seeth me seeth him that sent me." In his farewell address to his disciples he speaks of the Comforter which is the Holy Ghost whom the Father will send in my name. At his baptism, the Father's voice is heard from heaven and the Holy Spirit descends in the form of a dove and lights upon him. Yes, at the very beginning of things God speaks of himself in the plural, "Let us make man after our image," while all the while "the Spirit of God moved upon the face of the waters." Truly proof sufficient for all who would believe.

386 Is trouble sent as punishment?

The Bible does not teach that all trouble comes from God as a punishment. It recognizes the fact that trouble is in the world, and, while it has some very definite things to say about it, it does not attempt to give a complete solution of the whole problem. Hebrews 12:5-11 declares that God does in some instances, discipline or "chasten," those whom he loves, but this could hardly be called punishment. (See also Deu. 8:5; Ps. 94:12; John 15:2.) Sometimes, however, calamity is a definite punishment, as in many cases during the history of Israel, and particularly in their exile. The book of Job is a beautiful explanation of a form of suffering which has the double purpose of disciplining the soul and glorifying God. Nothing can bring such credit to God as the demonstration made by a soul that trusts and praises him in the midst of misfortune. Paul and the other apostles glorified in their opportunities to suffer for Jesus' sake. They rejoiced "that they were counted worthy to suffer shame in his name" (Acts 5:41). They felt that he had borne so much for them that they wanted to bear something for him. The Bible nowhere encourages people to dodge suffering; it exhorts them to bear it, while at the same time it exhorts them to lessen the sufferings of others, and help them bear their woes. See James 1:2-5; I Pet. 4:12-19; Gal. 6:2.

387 Why does not God save the
entire human race?

It is contrary to the Divine method of dealing with the human race, as we understand it, for him to use compulsion with men. Apparently, his desire is to have a people who, being left free to choose, voluntarily choose righteousness. He draws them, he yearns over them, applies discipline, offers them his help, but beyond this he will not go in this life. A man who is good only because he is compelled to be good, is of a much lower type than he who, being free to become evil, seeks of his own accord to become good. It is this higher type that, as we believe, God is trying to produce.

**388 Can a good, honest, moral,
       upright life save any one?**

People are constantly being misled in this matter because they fail to understand what salvation really is. Salvation is personal friendship and companionship with God. It is hard to see how a man who is not a friend of God at death will become one immediately after death. Being honest and upright does not really get us acquainted with God. Paul was intensely moral before his conversion, but he found out later that he had been an enemy of God all the time. Then, too, salvation means humility and meekness. The man who believes he can save himself puts himself out of the kingdom of heaven by that very attitude of mind. For the kingdom of heaven is made up of people with childlike hearts, who have given up their pride and self-will. Nor will the mere naming of the name of Christ and making a public confession make the necessary change. Jesus said very distinctly: "Ye must be born again." It is extremely unwise and unsafe to quarrel or argue with Jesus. He knows all about the human heart and all about the kingdom of heaven. The only thing to do is to accept his plan of salvation and let him give us the new heart, the heart that is humble and obedient, that is not self-confident but trustful, the heart that loves God and so will feel at home in God's heaven.

Scripture and experience alike teach that it is possible for one to have all the outward marks of religion, yet fail of possessing the real and vital thing. Saul of Tarsus was a most zealous man, trying to do the will of God, but after his conversion he felt that his former life had been very sinful, because he had not submitted himself to the will of God and accepted Christ's righteousness as his own. John Wesley's experience was similar, and countless others of this and earlier days. It must be remembered that it is not outward conduct that makes the real Christian; it is the inner life, the humility, the glad surrender to God's will, the warm love felt for God and for the souls for whom Christ died. It is not our good works that save us, but a simple, self-forgetful trust in Jesus. This faith brings the life and love which constitute religion.

A simple trust in the death of Jesus as the remedy for our sin. A simple acceptance of Christ to be our righteousness and our salvation will bring the joy and power of a new life of real sonship of God and fellowship with Christ. See Rom. 10:1-4; Phil. 3:3-9.

**389 Is it possible for one to be saved
       without knowing it?**

Among the children of Christian homes or among conscientious heathen (see Rom. 2:14, 15; Acts 10:34, 35), there may be cases in which a soul has salvation and is not definitely conscious of it. In the vast majority of cases, however, since the turning toward sin has been definite and voluntary, so the turning from sin and the receiving of forgiveness and a new nature are so definite as to be matters of plain knowledge. The New Testament clearly teaches that those who become converted may receive the witness of the Spirit, assuring them that they have been born again (see Rom. 8:16; I John 5:10). Any one who wants to be a Christian or hopes he is a Christian may receive this assurance if he persists in trusting Christ. Our salvation depends, not upon our feeling, but upon the unchangeable fact of the atonement and upon the plain promises of God's Word. When we definitely trust we become conscious of certain definite changes in our experience. Fear of God changes to love of God; we love God's people and his work. If we continue faithful the witness of the Spirit will be added to these signs and we shall know that we are children of God.

390 What is meant by transfiguration?

"Transfiguration" signifies a change of form or appearance. The forms of Moses and Elijah, when they appeared on the Mount, were spiritualized. Luke 9:31 speaks of the subject of their converse. Some commentators hold that both Moses and Elijah were honored with an anticipatory resurrection, which would seem to be borne out by the fact of their presence at the transfiguration.

391 What is transubstantiation?

Transubstantiation (the term applied to the change of the substance of the bread and wine into the body and blood of Jesus Christ at the Sacrament) is a doctrine held by some, but not all, of the Christian churches. The Church of England and a large number of Protestant bodies hold that the bread and wine are sanctified symbols. Chrysostom wrote that after divine grace had sanctified the bread, "it is no longer called bread, but dignified with the name of the body of the Lord, although the nature of bread remains in it." Theodoret declared that the bread and wine remain still in their own nature, after consecration. Augustine taught that what they saw upon the altar was bread and the cup, as their own eyes could testify; but that their faith required to be instructed that the bread is the body of Christ; and he added, "These things are therefore called sacraments, because in them one thing is seen and another is understood. That which is seen has a bodily appearance; that which is understood has a spiritual fruit." Isidore of Seville said: "These two things are visible, but being sanctified by the Holy Ghost, they become the sacrament of the Lord's body." Luther held the doctrine of the true presence of the body and blood of Christ, saying, "The bread is the body, the wine is the blood of the Lord," according to a sacramental union, but not in the manner of transubstantiation, adhering literally to the language of the Scriptures. The Catholic

Church has always held the doctrine of the real, corporeal presence. With a few exceptions, the Protestants interpret the Saviour's language figuratively, and hold that Jesus intended to convey to men the lesson that unless they voluntarily appropriated to themselves his death and sacrifice, so that they become their very life and nourishment, they can have no spiritual and eternal life at all.

392 Can a wealthy business man be a practical Christian?

Jesus said it was a hard thing for a rich man to enter into the kingdom; but he also showed, in the parable of the talents and other parables, that riches, properly regarded, and not held as a personal possession to be used for selfish and worldly purposes, but as a trust to be applied conscientiously, may be made a source of blessing. There are many men of large wealth who are useful members of society and who administer their means wisely and conscientiously. Besides, we are not to be the judges of the hearts of men. It has become a habit with many to condemn wealth and its possessors indiscriminately; and it is true that there is much in the present conditions of society that is open to legitimate criticism, but honest men of strict integrity can be found in every honorable line of business, and an active life is as much respected today as when Prov. 22:29 was written. A man who directs his efforts mainly to the acquisition of wealth, without regard to its responsibilities, incurs great spiritual danger. For the use we make of our talents and opportunities we shall be held strictly accountable.

393 Is wealth an evil or a blessing?

There are many passages in the Bible relative to riches and its opposite, poverty. Nowhere is poverty spoken of as a blessing, but rather as a trial and discipline; yet wealth is to be regarded either as a blessing or the reverse, according to circumstances. Riches that are gotten and not by right can never bring happiness or satisfaction, and therefore result in sorrow or disappointment (Jer. 17:11). Christ taught his followers not to lay up for themselves "treasures on earth." He repeatedly warned them against the allurements of wealth. He declared wealth to be a great barrier to many—a hindrance to their eternal welfare. He taught his followers to set their minds on things above, and to take no thought of amassing riches or goods. Usurers, brokers, exchangers, and mere money-getters—those who set their hearts on wealth and made gold their god—he specially denounced. Yet he never spoke, even by implication, a word against the reward of honest industry, but on the contrary commended it. Voluntary poverty was assumed by the earliest disciples and fathers in the Christian Church. There is no duty of this character specifically enjoined, and we are told to "seek first the kingdom" and all needful things will be added. "Neither riches nor poverty" is the ideal meant for a contented Christian life. This is finely set forth in the beautiful prayer in Proverbs 30:8, Agur, the supplicant, being, as is supposed, a symbolical name for Solomon.

394 How do I know that I am saved?

There are two kinds of "assurance," as taught by the creeds, and both of them are matters of ordinary, everyday experience by many Christians. There are certain clear statements in the Bible as to the kind of person a Christian is. He must bear certain signs and marks and do certain things. He must love God and his neighbor; he must love the Church; he must be earnest and patient and bear the various "fruits of the Spirit." Now, a person can tell whether he is doing those things, whether his soul has these marks or not. Added to this test, however, is the direct "witness of the Spirit," the Spirit himself "bearing witness with our spirit that we are the children of God" (Rom. 8:16; II Cor. 1:22; Eph. 1:13). This is the voice of God, assuring us that we are his. It is important to remember that we should not wait for assurance, but must persistently and with determination believe God's word. Any one who is in doubt whether he is a child of God or not should insist immediately upon beginning to trust him. We become Christians by believing that Christ really does forgive our sins and receive us, remembering that he said: "Him that cometh unto me I will in no wise cast out" (John 6:37). As we continue to trust him we shall find ourselves manifesting the fruits of the Spirit, and God will whisper to us that we are his.

395 Why is it wrong to harbor feelings of anger and resentment?

God forbids it (Ecc. 7:9; Matt. 5:22; Rom. 12:19); it is a characteristic of fools and a work of the flesh (Gal. 5:20; Prov. 12:16; Prov. 14:29; Prov. 27:3; Ecc. 7:9). Anger is connected with pride, cruelty, clamorous and evil speaking, malice and blasphemy, strife and contention (Prov. 21:24; Gen. 49:7; Eph. 4:31; Col. 3:8; Prov. 21:19; Prov. 29:22), and brings its own punishment (Job 5:2; Prov. 19:19). Scripture teaches us that grievous words stir up anger, that it may be averted by wisdom and that meakness pacifies (Judg. 12:4; Prov. 29:8, 15:1). We are enjoined to be slow to anger, to avoid those given to it, to be free from it in prayer and not to provoke children to it (Prov. 15:18, 16:32; Tit. 1:7; Jas. 1:19, I Tim. 2:8; Eph. 6:4).

CHRISTIAN LIVING

396 Can one be converted and saved without baptism?

Christ commanded baptism, and we cannot understand any person who really desires to serve him neglecting to obey him in so simple a matter. Still, it lowers the reverence we have for God to believe that he would exclude any really repentant, believing person from heaven simply because he had not been baptized. The person might have been converted on his death-bed, or if he was among Baptists he might die between the time of his conversion and the time set for administering the rite. God is not unjust, and would not hold a man responsible in such circumstances. Do you suppose the thief who repented on the Cross was baptized? Yet Jesus promised him an entrance into Paradise. Baptism generally followed conversion in the time of the Apostles, as it does now generally in heathen lands.

397 Can a person become a Christian without the baptism of the Holy Spirit?

As the word is usually understood, the baptism of the Holy Spirit was to confer special gifts for Christ's service. We have no reason to suppose that any man becomes a Christian without the influence of the Holy Spirit. The question is profitless, inasmuch as God gives the Holy Spirit freely. It would be impossible to state positively in what way the first impression comes in any individual case, but we may be sure that in some way the Holy Spirit's power has operated. This does not relieve any one from responsibility, because God is more willing to impart than men are to receive; but he does not force his gifts upon men.

398 What is the personal examination necessary prior to eating and drinking worthily at communion?

A personal self-examination of the heart. If a man is conscious of hatred toward any one, of malice, of sinful purposes, of sinful connections which he ought to sever, but has not severed, or of cherishing any feeling inconsistent with his relation to Christ, he should not partake of the communion. This does not imply that only perfect persons should do so. If a man is honestly and earnestly striving after holiness and doing all that lies in him to live consistently; and sincerely deplores every failure and means to strive to avoid them in the future; if he loves Christ and is trusting in him for salvation, he is right in partaking of the communion although he may be conscious of having fallen into sin. (I Cor. 11:26, 28.)

399 Should all believers confess Christ?

Yes. There are very many good Christian people who never realize the true joy that belongs to the followers of Jesus, because they do not live in the sunlight. Some are so exceedingly sensitive about personal religion that they shrink to talk of it, even to their intimate friends. Even though they believe, they yet stand "afar off"; they have not been sufficiently drawn by love for the Master, or by zeal for his service, to come near enough to the Cross to feel the glow that stimulates the ardent believer. When once these timid souls can shake off their reticence and come boldly forward and confess Christ before the world, a transformation takes place. There is a very real blessing which follows the confession of our faith before men. Jesus himself said "Every one who shall confess me before men, him will I also confess before my Father, which is in heaven." (Matt. 10:32.) The knowledge of such recognition, following our open acknowledgment of Jesus as a Saviour, gives courage to the Christian and, like a loyal soldier who sees the flag of his country waving above him and who salutes it, his whole being thrills with zeal for service for the Great Captain of Salvation Thus, at every fitting opportunity the believer should run up the flag, and let the world see whom he is serving.

400 What does believing in Christ imply?

Believing in Christ does not mean merely believing that he is the Son of God. "The devils believe and tremble" (James 2:19). It means true repentance, contrition and an earnest desire for forgiveness, which leads us to look to Christ as the only way by which such forgiveness may be attained. To believe in him means that we are not only to believe in his divine mission and in the efficacy of his atonement for our sins, but to follow in his footsteps and emulate his example in all things wherever possible and to pray for the guidance of the Holy Spirit in our daily lives. Forgiveness is granted to all those who repent and believe and ask in faith. True repentance leads not merely to conviction of sin and to sorrow for our past offenses, but to a complete change in our life, *i. e.*, a turning away from sin to holiness and gradual growth in grace through living near to Christ.

401 Should believers in Christ associate with unbelievers?

See II Cor. 6:14; Heb. 3:12; Acts 14:2; II Peter 2:1, 2; also Ch. 3:3, 17. It is not intended, however, that the believer should hold no communication with those who are still in the darkness of unbelief, otherwise he would not be fulfilling the divine command to spread the Gospel, and, "show forth Christ," at all seasons. He should, however, avoid all such associations and relationships—business, social and otherwise—as would bring a discordant element into his own home or business life, and thus antagonize spiritual growth. To put such people on the level of home acquaintances and intimate friends, would be very likely to prove spiritually disastrous to some member of your household.

402 Who are the "blessed" we so often read about in the Bible?

They are whom God chooses and calls (Ps. 65:4; Is. 51:2; Rev. 19:9); they know Christ and his Gospel, believe and are not offended at Christ (Matt. 16:16, 17; Ps. 89:15; Matt. 11:6; Luke 1:45). Their sins are forgiven and God imputes to them righteousness without works (Ps. 32:1, 2; Rom. 4:6-9). But at times they are chastened, and suffer for Christ, but they are not hurt thereby as they trust in God, fear him, yes have their strength in him (Job 5:17; Luke 6:22; Ps. 2:12; Jer. 17:7; Ps. 112:1; Ps. 84:5). Therefore they delight in his commandments and keep them, they hunger and thirst after righteousness, frequent the house of the Lord waiting for him (Ps. 112:1; Rev. 22:14; Matt. 5:6; Ps. 65:4; Is. 30:18). When in contact with the world they avoid the wicked, endure temptation, watch against sin: are undefiled, pure in heart, just, righteous, faithful, poor in spirit, meek, merciful, bountiful and are peacemakers (Ps. 1:1; Jas. 1:12; Rev. 16:15; Ps. 119:1; Matt. 5:8, Ps. 106:3; PS. 5:12; Prov. 28:20; Matt. 5:3; Matt. 5:31; Matt. 5:5; Matt. 5:7; Luke 14:13, 14; Matt. 5:9). Watching for the Lord, they die in him, have part in the first resurrection and shall eat bread in the kingdom of God (Luke 12:37; Rev. 14:13; Rev. 20:6; Luke 14:15; Rev. 19:9).

403 What is Christian conduct?

Believing, fearing, loving, following, obeying and rejoicing in God (Mar. 11:22; Ecc. 12:13; I Pet. 2:17; Deu. 6:5; Eph. 5:1; Luke 1:6; Ps. 33:1). Believing in, loving, obeying, rejoicing in, and following the example of Christ (John 6:29; John 21:15; John 14:21; Phil. 3:1; Phil. 4:4). Walking and living soberly, righteously and godly, honestly, worthy of the Lord God, in the Spirit, in newness of life, worthy of our vocation as children of light (Tit. 2:12; I Thess. 4:12; I Thess. 2:12; Col. 1:10; Gal. 5:25; Rom. 6:4; Eph. 4:1; Eph. 5:8). Then, when we are striving for the faith, putting away all sin, abstaining from all appearance of evil, perfecting holiness, hating defilement, following after that which is good, overcoming the world, adorning the Gospel (Phil. 1:27; I Cor. 5:7; I Thess. 5:22; Matt. 5:48; Jude 23; Phil. 4:8; I John 5:4, 5; Matt. 5:16; Tit. 2:10), we will show a good example, by abounding in the work of the Lord, shunning the wicked, controlling the body, subduing the temper and living peaceably with all men (I Cor. 15:58; Ps. 1:1; Cor. 9:27; Eph. 4:26; Rom. 12:18; Heb. 12:14). Then, too, we will attain the Christ-like ability to submit to injuries and forgive them (Matt. 5:39-41; I Cor. 6:7; Matt. 6:14; Rom. 12:20) and by visiting the afflicted, sympathizing with others, submitting to authorities, being liberal to and honoring others, being contented and by doing as we would be done by (Matt. 25:36; Gal. 6:2; Rom. 12:10; Acts 20:35; Rom. 13:17; Phil. 4:11; Heb. 13:5); attain blessedness (Ps. 1:1-3; Matt. 5:3-12; John 15:10).

404 Is joining the Christian church a means of salvation?

Christ demands that his followers confess him before men (see Luke 12:8, 9), and joining the church is the recognized method of doing so. We are ordered not to forsake "the assembling" of ourselves together in the Lord's House. It places us on record. Beside this, it is a means of grace. One who turns his back on God's Church and his people would be a very singular Christian, indeed. In associating with God's people there is mutual help and reinforced service. Then, too, the Christian would naturally wish to obey Christ's request, that his friends would remember him by partaking together of the bread and wine. There may be obstacles in the way of a Christian joining a church, and we would not judge any man for holding aloof, but he should have very weighty reasons to justify him in doing so. Leading a good moral life and believing in God are not, however, sufficient of themselves for salvation. God is not pleased when men ignore the way of salvation he has provided. Jesus saith, "No man cometh unto the Father but by me" (John 14:6).

405 Does the Bible urge church attendance?

Yes. In both the Old and New Testaments there are numerous passages enjoining attendance in God's house as a duty, a delightful pleasure and a great spiritual privilege. See Lev. 8:3; Deu. 4:10; Psalms 23:6; 26:8; 27:4; 84:1, 4, 10; 122:1; Neh. 13:11; Micah 4:2; Matt. 18:19, 20; Acts 4:31; 15:25; Heb. 10:25. Take your reference Bible and look up, through the marginal notes, still other references. Churchgoing is both a duty and a privilege, and he who neglects it misses a great blessing and much of the enjoyment of spiritual life and growth. The Psalmist tells us that a day in God's courts is "better than a thousand." We are frequently reminded in the Scriptures that it is a duty. See Heb. 10:25; Psalms 111:1; Matt. 18:20, and other passages. True, there are other forms of public confession besides that of joining a church, but that is the ordinary and recognized mode. It is the duty of every Christian to identify himself with a Christian church, that he may make it known where he stands, that he may help in advancing Christ's kingdom and that his own soul may be nourished by the association with other Christians.

406 Is the increase of church wealth and worldly resources to be regarded as a healthy spiritual sign?

History indicates that it is not a healthy sign. The periods of the church's worldly prosperity have usually been periods of moral decadence. There has been a tendency in such times to say, as did the church of Laodicea (Rev. 3:17), "I am rich and increased with goods, and have need of nothing." At the same time, the possession of riches is not incompatible with spirituality. There are, as we in this country have good reason to acknowledge, wealthy men who consecrate their wealth to God. A sincere Christian in business may prosper through the principles of Christianity, which conduce to industry, integrity and clean living. We can imagine a church composed of wealthy men being a church of great power, contributing liberally to the advance of Christ's Kingdom, and doing an immense amount of good in alleviating the burdens of the poor. There is nothing in wealth itself to render a man unfit for the Kingdom of God. It is hard for him to enter, as Christ said, because human nature is apt to love its wealth and to trust in it; but when a wealthy man really gives himself to the Lord, he has opportunities for service which do not lie within reach of the poor man; and if he uses them faithfully, he is more useful, and accomplishes more good. There have been such men, and there still are such men. The church, like the individual, may trust in its riches; and if it does, it is in an unhealthy condition; but it may consecrate its riches, and then it is capable of better service. We must look to other signs to learn if the possession of wealth has eaten into its soul, making it proud, arrogant and sordid, or helpful, beneficent and compassionate, before we can say whether it is the better or the worse for its wealth.

407 Is confession a Christian duty?

"Confess your faults one to another" James 5:16. It makes the whole problem of confession simple to remember that the duty is to confess to those whom we have wronged. If we have done any wrong to any person, we must confess it to him, and ask him to forgive us. A wrong that affects no one but God and ourselves needs to be confessed only to God. Often, however, a public confession is helpful. Under the awakening of conscience a Christian may be led to feel that he has been living under false pretenses, and will find a relief in saying so, and in making a new start. After all, we ought not to dread confession so much as we do. The Christian has no righteousness of his own to uphold; his righteousness consists in, trusting Christ. Paul liked to declare that he was, to all intents and purposes, so far as the law was concerned, a dead man; he had been crucified with Christ, and Christ lived in him. He had no reputation to sustain. He liked to speak of himself as having been the chief of sinners. Then, too, people are apt to be kinder than we think; our friends will not want to condemn us, but help us. But, on the other hand, this is often a fruitful source of cruel temptation to sensitive souls. They imagine they ought to speak of things which no one but God needs to know about. Remember that God is never unreasonable, nor harsh. Tell him all about it, and then he will tell you plainly and kindly whether any other confessions are necessary.

408 Is there any Scriptural authority for the rite of confirmation?

The Apostle Paul is represented as confirming the souls of the disciples (Acts 14:22), and again as confirming the churches (Acts 15:41); Judas and Silas did the same thing (Acts 15:32). It does not in these cases appear to have been a rite or ceremony. But there appears to have been some rite of the kind in the early church. The writer of Hebrews speaks (6:2) of "the doctrine of baptisms and of laying on of hands." He may have had reference to the laying on of hands, implying the gift of the Holy Spirit, as in Acts 8:17, and as Paul did (Acts 19:6). It seems to have been a Jewish idea of ancient date, as Jacob thus blessed Joseph's children (Gen. 48:14). The custom continued in Christ's time (see Matt. 19:13), when "there were brought unto him little children that he should put his hands on them, and pray."

409 Is it not obligatory to use unleavened bread at communion?

Nothing could be more foreign to Christ's spirit and teaching than the character which certain churches give to this simple meal. There is nothing occult or mysterious about it. Christ was founding a kingdom or society, and wished his followers to have some way of showing their membership in it. He would not have them forget that they were Christians. He bade them join together in a simple meal, which was a common way of acknowledging equality and brotherhood. They were to come as Christians and eat and drink together in token of their being united in a common bond of love for him. It was not to be an elaborate feast, but to consist of the common constituents of the ordinary meal of that time. As they ate the broken bread they were to think of his body which was broken for them, and as they drank the wine they were to remember how his blood was shed for them. To make a mass of it and invest the details with a significance never intended is to miss the majestic simplicity of Christ's conception and his purpose in instituting the ordinance.

410 What is conscience?

It is the moral sense in man, by which he judges between right and wrong, and which approves or condemns his conduct. A man is bound to obey it in all his actions. He must, therefore, be careful to see that it is guided by right principles, that it is educated, and is not biased or warped by sophistry, or prejudice, or by impure motives. It has a standard in the Bible which should keep it true and firm. It is, however, quite possible for a man to do wrong conscientiously; in other words, his unenlightened conscience may mislead him. Paul gives an illustration (Acts 26:9) "I thought with myself that I ought to do many things contrary to the name of Jesus." The revelation on the way to Damascus changed that judgment of conscience and gave him a new principle on which he acted. Peter was conscientious in his idea of food and of associating with Gentiles. It took a miracle to open his eyes (Acts 10:28). The inquisitors were probably conscientious in persecuting protestants; Calvin was conscientious in burning Servetus, and the Puritans were conscientious in executing witches. But we see now, in our more enlightened age, that they erred. When a man is uncertain as to the right course to take, he should pray for guidance and direction, should see what principles the Bible lays down in similar matters, and then let his conscience decide. He will be held responsible for obeying his conscience.

411 Does conscience ever approve anything that is wrong? If so, how can it be the voice of God in the soul?

Certainly, conscience may, and often does, approve things that are wrong. A conspicuous instance (as already noted), is that of the Apostle Paul, who verily thought that in persecuting the Christians he was doing God service. Many since his time have erred in the same way, while sincerely believing at the time that they were doing right. Conscience is the faculty of the mind which discerns the moral quality of a course of conduct, and passes judgment upon it, according to the standard of right and wrong which it has. If the standard be wrong, the decisions of conscience will be wrong. "There is a way," says Solomon, "that seemeth right unto a man; but the end thereof are the ways of death." Conscience needs to be educated; it must rely on knowledge and reason for its data; it has to avoid being warped by self-interest and being blunted by its environment. Paul speaks (I Cor. 8:7) of a weak conscience, that is one that sees wrong where there is no wrong. As a judge, it represents

God in the soul, but it never exercises infallible judgment. It needs divine enlightenment and the development which comes from Bible-reading and prayer. It is, however, the "voice of God" within us in this respect, that it bids us do the right, so far as we can discern it, at any cost; and as we obey or disobey, it rewards or punishes with sweet approval or stern condemnation.

412 Is the voice of conscience that of the Holy Spirit?

The facts of experience do not bear out the conclusion that conscience and the Holy Spirit are the same. Conscience is a faculty of the soul which approves or condemns according as one has or has not done what he believes to be right. By study of the Bible, prayer and the counsel of Christian friends one often finds that what seemed formerly to be right was in reality wrong. Paul believed he was doing right while persecuting the Christians. The Hindu mother throwing her babe in the Ganges believes she is doing right, and her conscience approves; but when she becomes a Christian she knows that such a sacrifice is wicked. In all nations and times certain souls have been alert and humble enough to hear the direct messages of the Holy Spirit, but it is through the written Word, the message of the Gospel and the knowledge of Jesus that the Holy Spirit comes to be a positive and constant fact of experience. The Christian tests the messages that seem to come from him by the Bible, by the personality of Christ, by the advice of Christian friends (see I John 4). The messages of the Holy Spirit are clear and positive, not hesitating and confusing. In the enlightened Christian, the voice of conscience and the voice of the Spirit will always agree.

413 How can consecration be accomplished?

This question of consecration is one that frequently arises, yet when we stop to analyze it, it seems strange that there should be any difficulty about it. If you possess anything which you wish to give to another, you simply give it to him; it is just as simple as that to give your whole heart and life to God. We already belong to him absolutely; in consecration we are only returning what is his. This is the "one thing" lacking in countless lives to give them full spiritual meaning and direction. (See Rom. 12:1). The question how we can take ourselves out of God's hands should really be more difficult than the question how we may submit ourselves to him. Remember that God is always reasonable, always kind. Many of the things sometimes suggested to our minds when the subject of consecration is brought up are not the suggestion of the Holy Spirit, but of our own minds, or of disturbing spirits. There is no uncertainty about the voice of God. He only asks us to obey him when he makes duty clear, and has promised to give us grace and power always for the duties he lays upon us. There surely should be no unwillingness to submit our lives to him; he can care for them and direct them much better than we. Consecration becomes simple when we approach the cross of Christ. We realize there that he gave himself for us because we were sinners because of this very unwillingness in our hearts to surrender ourselves to him. Knowing this it is not hard to commit ourselves absolutely to his love, trusting him to forgive our sins, to cleanse our hearts, to guide and to keep us.

414 Is conversion the same as regeneration?

Conversion, when the term is used theologically, is the turning away from sin to God. It is the reversal of a man's course of life. After his conversion his desires and aims and principles of life cease to be toward enjoyment or self-gratification or worldly ambition and tend toward God and holiness. Regeneration is the new birth wrought by the Spirit of God upon the man. Thus conversion supposes some activity on the man's part, while in regeneration he is passive. As the Spirit operates on the spirit of man "making it willing in the day of his power," the difference between the two terms is not of moment.

415 How is conversion accomplished?

By prayer, by repentance of our sins, by sincerely accepting Christ as Saviour, by surrendering ourselves to him in all things as our guide, and by proclaiming our new allegiance and striving, with his help and in his strength, to regulate our lives according to his teachings. Conversion is a turning from sin to righteousness, producing thus a change in our thoughts, desires, dispositions and daily lives, which is the work of the Holy Spirit upon the heart as the result of saving faith. Conversion, however, in the sense of turning from sin and accepting Christ as Saviour, is distinct from regeneration, which is the work of the Spirit only.

416 Are impure thoughts a sign of an unconverted person?

Every man has some avenue by which temptation most easily besets him. His duty is to exercise special vigilance at that avenue. He should study himself and find out how best to deal with the temptation. It is well to ascertain by recalling our periods of trial, what were the exciting causes, and avoid them in future. Plenty of hard work, physical and mental, the pursuit of some absorbing subject of study, constant occupation, the avoidance of reverie, and of suggestive books, a careful attention to diet, and, above all, earnest prayer, especially whenever the evil thoughts arise, are the means we should use. But we must be continually on our guard against sudden temptation. We have to fight our battle, and it will be a hard one, but we may count on divine help, and if we are really in earnest, we will win the victory. We must act intelligently, as we would if we were afflicted with some physical disease and were seeking a cure. Thousands have fought the same battle and have won it. We should not doubt the reality of our conversion. That would undermine our strength.

417 Does the Bible anywhere prohibit all kinds of dancing?

Not specifically, but it condemns frivolity, folly and wickedness in every form. There are various points of Christian behavior applicable to modern life for which no specific rule or authority can be found in the Bible, as social conditions have greatly changed. Modern vices and indulgences have sprung up and these must be dealt with by the Christian as his conscience and judgment dictate. Dancing, though not in itself necessarily sinful, is exceedingly apt to degenerate into sin. Had promiscuous dancing, as it exists in society today, been prevalent in Bible times (instead of the comparatively innocent amusement then known, and the ceremonial or religious dances), it would unquestionably have been a subject of denunciation as sweeping as that applied to any of the vices of the time. The purpose of the Scriptures is to give general principles for the new life and so leave us the great benefit of deciding for ourselves how to apply them. In modern dancing, the evil so far overbalances the good that it is indefensible and should not be sustained by Christians.

418 Does God send disease?

God governs the world by the natural laws which he has established, and it would be impossible to define the extent to which he uses those laws to work out his providential purposes. It is probable that, in some cases, where he sees that a child of his needs discipline, or to be laid aside from worldly work and association so as to be drawn nearer to him, he may permit sickness to come upon him. In some passages sickness is threatened as a punishment. (See Deu. 28:27, 59, 60 and 61.) An instance is mentioned in Acts 12:23. On the other hand, it is certain that many diseases which afflict humanity are the result of disregard of sanitary laws, and although they may be used for the spiritual benefit of the sufferer, should not be attributed to God.

419 How can I get rid of doubt?

The only way out of any form of spiritual darkness is a firm faith in Christ. Spiritual darkness always means that in some way or other we are doubting him. We are often tempted to think that something else is necessary to be done before we begin to trust him, some sacrifice to make, some duty to perform, some problem to be solved. But these things come after faith, not before it. Of course, if some positive wrong has been committed this wrong must be righted before we can believe that Christ fully saves us. But where no such positive wrong has been done and no clear duty neglected, the first, and indeed the only requirement is to trust in Christ. Any other advice would be false. "Christ died for the ungodly." There is our only place of peace and light. When you believe that he died for you, that he died to make possible the forgiveness of your sins and the cleansing of your heart; when you believe that because he died your sins are forgiven and your heart is cleansed, you will have peace, and you will find the Saviour near you, with his light and comfort and power. After all, it is no wonder that we feel sad while we are doubting him. You would feel sad if you were doubting your friend, your brother, your parent. And remember that he, too, is saddened by our doubt. Read some of the rich promises of God's Word, and refuse any longer to doubt that they were written to you as well as to any other of his children: Isa. 55; Ezek. 36:25-27; Matt. 5:8, 10; Matt. 7:7-11; John 7:38, 39; John 8:36; Acts 2:14, 16-21, 39; Rom. 6; Rom. 8:11; II Cor. 7:1; Gal. 3; Eph. 3:14-21; Col. 3; I Thess. 5:23; Heb. 4:9-11, 7:25, 99:11-14; Heb. 10:1-22, 35; Heb. 11; I John 3:1-9, 22; I John 5:4; Jude 24, 25.

420 Does a truly converted person have evil thoughts?

Thoughts of evil may enter the minds of even the most saintly. So long as we are in the body we are subject to temptation, and there can be no temptation without a thought of the evil that is suggested. Every time we hear or see or read of an evil word or act we have the thought of evil. These thoughts are stored in the brain, become items in the great storehouse of memory, and are apt to recur to us at any time. There can be no sin in a thought itself; it is only our feeling about the thought and our decision what to do with it that has any moral quality. When our hearts have been filled with love for God and love for people we find this love making us repel the evil thought and turn toward the good. It is helpful to remember that what makes a thing evil is that it will harm somebody. When we love people, we shall not want to harm them in body, mind or soul, and the thought of love will conquer and expel the thought of evil. It is in this sense that "love is the fulfilling of the law," and that "perfect love casteth out fear," as well as other sinful emotions. We may thus *bring into captivity* every thought to the obedience of Christ.

421 Is it possible to rid oneself of inherited evil tendencies?

We are not quite sure that we are justified in holding our ancestors altogether responsible for our evil tendencies. Some people like to hold

Satan responsible for a share. It is, however, always advisable to inquire how far a man himself is deserving of blame. Probably, if it can be proved that he had nothing to do with the origin of them, still he may have assisted in their development. There is no doubt that he can, at least, be delivered from indulging his evil tendencies, even if they are not entirely extirpated. That is what Christ came to do. He offers us the power we need to bring our natures under subjection. The Holy Spirit in the heart so reinforces the better part of our nature that it gains power enough to hold the evil tendencies in subjection. They then so lose their power that they cease to be a danger, and, like any other part of our being that is not used, become weak. We must help in working out our own salvation. We must avoid temptation, and must be vigilant in preventing outbreaks. God will help us if we are sincere, and with Almighty help, what is there that is not possible?

422 What does faith do for us?

"Faith is the substance of things hoped for, the evidence of things not seen" (Heb. 11:1). We are commanded to have faith in God and in Christ (John 14:1; John 6:29) and yet it, of itself, is the gift and work of God in us, through the Holy Ghost by the Scriptures and preaching and other means (Rom. 12:3; Eph. 2:8; Acts 11:21; I Cor. 2:5; Heb. 12:2; I Cor. 12:9; John 20:31; John 17:20), causing by these means of grace, repentance and thereafter conversion (Mark 1:15; Acts 11:21). Through faith we obtain remission of sins, justification, salvation, sanctification, adoption of and access to God, the gift of the Holy Ghost, spiritual light and life, edification, preservation, eternal life and rest in heaven (Acts 10-43; Rom. 3:25; Acts 13:39; Mark 16:16; Acts 15:9; John 1:12; Gal. 3:26; Rom. 5:2; Eph. 3:12; Acts 11:15-17; John 12:36, 46; John 20:31; Gal. 2:20; John 3:15-16; Heb. 4:3). Faith is essential to the profitable reception of the Gospel; it makes the Gospel effectual in those who have faith; it is necessary in the Christian warfare, and without it it is impossible to please God (Heb. 4:2; I Thess. 2:13; I Tim. 1:18, 19; Heb. 11:6). The effect of faith in us is to produce hope, peace, confidence, boldness in preaching and testifying and, as Christ is precious to those having faith and dwells in their heart, they live, stand, walk, obtain a "good report," work in love, overcome the world, resist the devil (Rom. 5:2; Acts 16:34; Rom. 15:13; Is. 28:16; I Pet. 2:6; I Pet. 2:7; Eph. 3:17; Gal. 2:20; Rom. 4:12; Heb. 11:2, I John 5:4, 5; I Pet. 5:9; Ps. 27:13; I Tim. 4:10). Therefore we should be sincere, strong and steadfast; holding our faith with a good conscience and not only praying for the increase, but having full assurance of it (I Tim. 1:5; II Cor. 8:7; Acts 14:22; Rom. 4:20-24; I Cor. 16:13; Col. 1:23; I Tim. 1:19; Luke 17:5; II Tim. 1:12). Then will we be known by our fruits, as without fruits our faith is dead (Jas. 2:21-25; Jas. 2:17, 20, 26), and as all difficulties are overcome by faith, so all things should be done by it, never fearing as we are fully protected by our shield and breastplate (Matt. 17:20, 21:21; Rom. 14:22; Eph. 6:16; 1 Thess 5:8).

423 What is faith?

Faith is trust. It is the gift of God, wrought in the heart by the Holy Spirit, which quickens and directs all our faculties toward the one object. We must pray to have faith, and to have our faith increased. It will be strengthened, too, by the frequent remembrance of Christ's repeated promises that our prayers to the Father, in his name, would assuredly be heard and answered, if we asked in faith, and believed while we asked. See Matt. 7:7; Luke 11:9; John 14:13, 15, 16; James 4:2; I John 3:22, 5:14; Luke 11:10. Faith has been defined as "the substance of things hoped for, the evidence of things not seen" (Heb. 11:1); it is that operation of the soul in which we are convinced of the existence and truth of something that is not before us, or perceptible to the human senses. Every one entertains faith of some kind, which he would find it difficult if not impossible to demonstrate by visible means. It is the practice of faith the voluntary exercise of it—which enables us to rise to the belief in those great truths which God has been pleased to reveal. Paul says that "we walk by faith, not by sight" (II Cor. 5:7). Jesus himself said (John 20:29), "Blessed are they that have not seen and yet have believed." Thus, while believing what we see and comprehend may have its merits, believing what is *not* seen and but dimly comprehended is a greater merit. There are many things in nature which we believe, yet without being able to fully grasp them with our minds; we believe because we have the evidence of others, though not of our own senses. The faith which simply believes what it can see, understand, define and demonstrate is not real faith at all. "No man hath seen God at any time," yet all men believe in a God. The things of the spiritual world cannot be demonstrated by mere material agencies, but only through spiritual agencies. The exercise of faith increases our spirituality, enables us to comprehend things which without such exercise would be incomprehensible. Paul said that to the learned Greek skeptics the Gospel was "foolishness." Pride of intellect is one of the greatest barriers to spiritual growth.

424 Is a falsehood ever justifiable?

One who makes faith in God and obedience to his will the supreme rule of his life, will never find excuse or justification for a lie. Man's extremity is God's opportunity and it is in such crises, when our faith is put to the ultimate test, that the Almighty reaches out and succors our weak nature with his Divine strength and help. We are distinctly told not to do evil that good may come and that all liars "shall have their place in hell fire, which is the second death." God can deliver those who trust in him in every conflict and those who are so situated are safe according to the measure of their faith. See Is. 26:4; Psalm 3:5 and 118:8; also Psalm 15. Lying in all its forms is expressly forbidden by the Lord. (Lev. 19:11; Col. 3:9.) It is hateful to him. (Prov. 6:16-19.) It shuts out the liar from heaven (Rev. 21:27), and those who are guilty of it find their ultimate abode in hell. (Rev. 21:8.) A full faith, such as that of the glorious men and women who have illumined the world with their lives, will not hesitate to tell the truth and leave the result in God's hands, trusting to the Omnipotent arm for safety.

425 What is the effect of forgiveness?

Some may ask: "Has God forgotten all about my sins now that they are forgiven, and if so why do we not forget?" God says in Is. 43:25 and Jer. 31:34 that he will not remember our transgressions. The sense of "remember" in these passages is clearly that God does not remember the sin *against* the sinner. The account is canceled; the sins are no longer imputed to him. Since the revelation of God's plan of the atonement, we see that the debt is paid. When a debt is paid it is forgotten, though the record of the transaction may remain in the memory of the people concerned. In this sense God forgets our sins, but there is no reason for supposing that he undoes or limits his omniscience by literally not knowing that certain past events have occurred. We know of them, and God cannot observe our own minds without seeing there the record of our sin. There are various passages in Scripture in which God recalls his forgiveness of the iniquities of his people, but the remembrance is not an accusation but rather a testimony of forgiveness. We cannot, by the exercise of the will, make ourselves forget anything. It would be a subtle and almost inconceivable miracle for God to disentangle from our brains the memory of our sins and yet leave there the memory of other acts and events of the same days and hours. While we know that, in every sense of debt or blame, God forgets our sins when he forgives us, it should help to restrain people from sin to recognize the fact that a sin once committed will probably never be erased from our memory, at least in this life, and that it can never be lost from the simple, truthful record of the world's events. This is good for us as a reminder and as a stimulant. Seeing the dangers we have escaped helps us against having serious lapses. Not that we are become sinless, but, thanks to the promises in I John 3:9, we are rid of the dominion of sin, and the lapses we do have are not inputed. Therefore, let none despair in the thought that anything in the past, great or small, can prevent them from having God's peace in their souls just now. Salvation is a present matter. So far as our present standing in Christ is concerned it does not make any difference whether we were converted at the time we were baptized or not. The only question is: "Will we trust Christ just now to forgive all the sins of the past and to make us truly his?" There are promises in the Bible, by the score, of forgiveness for any sinner who will ask for it. Murderers, thieves, drunkards, all sorts of sinners, have found these promises true and received God's peace in their souls. God will forgive and forget, and let you start all over again now? Cease doubting him. Begin to trust him and your trouble will disappear. Read Gal. 5:6; II Cor. 7:2; Is. 55:7; Is. 1:18; Is. 43:25.

426 Is it right to "fear" God?

The word "fear," as used in the Bible, has two distinct meanings—fear in the sense of dread or fright, and fear in the sense of reverence and sincere obedience. It is not easy to determine which meaning is intended for the two Hebrew words most used have both meanings. In the New Testament the Greek word used has more generally the sense of fright or dread. The whole message of the Bible is that what God most earnestly desires from mankind is their love. But sin keeps them from loving him, so he reveals to them, through conscience, and through the law, the fearful results of sin. This awakens a fear which drives them to him for pardon and safety. A man who is living in sin, when his conscience is aroused, is afraid of the power and the justice of God. After he is pardoned he feels a reverence for God and the beginnings of love for him. As he progresses in the Christian life all fear of God, in the sense of terror, is removed. John speaks of the "perfect love which casteth out fear." (I John 4:18.) Throughout the Christian life reverence abides, but love grows more and more dominant. The wonderful word is "friendship." God wants us to be friends of his, as Abraham and Moses were, to serve him because we love him, to be glad in the gifts his love bestows. Christ would like to lead us all to the place where he can say to us as he said to his disciples: "Henceforth, I call you not servants, but I have called you friend." (John 15:15.)

427 Why was not foot-washing kept up as well as the Lord's supper?

Foot-washing in the early centuries and in Oriental lands stood for kindly service and for comfort and hospitality. A guest would wash the dust from his visitor's feet, after removing his sandals, just as we take a friend's coat and hat and hang them up for him. Of course, the specific acts change with changing customs and even with climatic conditions, but the spirit is the same. We want to show our friends that we are willing to serve them. Christ emphasized this by his performing this service (a universal one in the East) for the disciples, though he was recognized as their Teacher, Master and Leader. It was a concrete sign of his whole message that his followers must be humble, and quick to serve others.

He did not limit this spirit and motive to one act of life, but insisted that it become the principle of action for our whole lives. The courtesies and kindnesses that hosts show to guests Christians must show to one another at all times and in all ways, and to all whom they meet.

428 Are we to forgive the wrongdoer if he does not ask it?

Christ inculcates the forgiving spirit, the spirit which loves even an enemy. It is the spirit he displayed on the cross when he prayed to his Father for the soldiers who nailed him to the cross, though they did not pray for themselves nor express contrition. Resentment is forbidden, but on the other hand, we have a right to expect regret on the part of the wrongdoer. He has no right to assume that we shall pass over his wrong as if he had never done it. If he wants our forgiveness he should ask for it; but even before he asks we must be ready to grant it. In our hearts we may already have forgiven him, but the outward and formal reconciliation waits his contrition. In Matt. 18:15 there is an intimation that the one who has suffered the wrong should seek to bring about the contrition of the wrongdoer by going to him and telling him his fault. If after all he withholds it, we are not required to treat him as a brother, but even then we are not to cherish resentment and especially not retaliation, but rather to return good for evil. In Matt. 5:23, 24 it would seem to have been quarrels that our Lord had in mind, rather than injuries. The brother who has aught against you appears to indicate a grudge, or a debt, as the following verses suggest. In any case, there is to be no quarrel. There must be reconciliation first.

429 In what sense is godliness profitable in this present life?

Since God's Word declares that godliness is profitable for the life that now is, it must affect favorably a man's temporal affairs. The necessities of life are promised to those who seek first the kingdom of God. He who contemplates being godly for the sake of gain does not know what true godliness is (see I Tim. 6:5; also Acts 8:19). Under the old covenant, godliness in the nation assured national prosperity. Better blessings are promised under the New Testament dispensation. Temporal prosperity is, however, still a rational sequence of godliness. The higher the tone of the mental and moral qualities the better the business qualifications. Godliness demands industry, economy, honesty, courtesy, patience, hope—all most useful in temporal affairs. "The supplication of a righteous man availeth much in its working" (James 5:16), and he is permitted to pray for prosperity in temporal affairs. We are encouraged to bring everything, by prayer, unto God (Phil. 4:6).

430 How can we grow in grace?

A fair equivalent of the word "grace" is "blessing." Grace means, in the first place, the disposition which God has toward us; that is, his willingness to bless us; his love and favor. It means, also, the blessing received, the state or experience into which we are brought by God's blessing. There is always in the word "grace" the idea of something bestowed entirely without merit or payment on the part of the one who receives it. God's blessings are bestowed freely; we do not earn them; he blesses us because he loves us, because he is gracious. All he asks is that we shall be willing to receive his grace. This promise to Paul means that God will give him the necessary strength to bear the affliction, and also, as Paul implies in the remainder of the verse, that the happiness of the blessing will balance the distress of the thorn.

To grow in grace means to advance and develop in spiritual experience and power. The Christian grows in grace in the first place by growing in faith. The more we believe, the more complete we entrust our souls and all the details of our lives to God, the more we are blessed. We grow in grace by our work for God. Religious work develops spiritual muscle just as physical work develops physical muscle. The more we do the more we can do. Prayer, study of the Bible, fellowship with spiritually-minded people, attendance at divine worship and prayer services, taking part in these services, will help us to grow in grace. We should remember, however, that all grace is bestowed by God himself; as we meet the conditions and enlarge our capacity he gives us more grace, just as he gives us more physical and mental strength when we meet the conditions for physical and mental growth.

431 What is the "blessing of giving"?

The generous heart is commended in many passages in the Scripture, and especially where that generosity has the poor for its object. We are told to remember the poor (see Lev. 25:35; Deu. 15:7), to be a helper to the fatherless (see Ps. 68:5; Ps. 10:14), and the widow (Is. 1:17), to visit those in affliction (James 1:27), and let them share our abundance (Deu. 14:29); and many blessings are promised to those who do these things. The bountiful are especially blessed wherever they give to any worthy cause or person (Deu. 15:10). Remember also that remarkable promise, "He that hath pity on the poor lendeth to the Lord" (see Prov. 19:17). It is a fine thing to lay up treasure in heaven, and we can do this only by doing God's work with the means at our disposal here. If we use his gifts for our own indulgence and pleasure, it will profit us nothing in the end; but if we apply them to his glory and the benefit of our fellow beings who need help more than we do, we shall then be doing his work, and shall receive his approval. In II Cor. 8:12 the apostle speaks of the cheerfulness and willingness with which believers should give to the Lord's work. He does not limit the giving to a tenth, but urges them to give freely and to spare not, that their abundance may make up for the lack in others. The widow's mite (Luke 21:3, 4) was the largest offering in a sense, for she gave all she had, and her faith and generosity were commended above those that gave far richer gifts. There are many worthy people who practice tithing and we would not dissuade them, and there are others who do not limit their gifts to a tenth, but exceed it, and they, too, are worthy of commendation. God looks at the spirit of the gift more than at the gift itself. There are cases in which a tenth might work hardship and, on the other hand there are many where a tenth would be a small offering.

432 What does "loving God" mean?

The duty and privilege of loving God become clear and simple when we think of Christ. Aside from him, the human conceptions of God are such that it is difficult to realize just what it would mean to love him. But friendship for Christ can be very real and precious. This is a definite part of God's whole wonderful plan. He came to earth in the person of Jesus and won just a few friends. These men and women loved him ardently. They loved him as a companion and friend. When he had gone away they loved him with the same definiteness and intensity and felt that he was still with them. Paul, who had never seen him in the flesh, loved him with just the same passion and fervor as did Peter and John, who had seen him. And all these early Christians knew that in loving Jesus they were loving God. As Professor Herrmann of Marburg says: "In their minds all difference between Christ and God himself vanished." He was God; they knew it. And as they loved him and labored for him and went toward death for him, they knew that they were fulfilling the old command, that had been so strange and difficult before, to love the Lord their God with all their heart and with all their soul and with all their mind and with all their strength. This same experience is possible today for every believer. Christ can be to every one of us that ever present Friend in whose companionship we delight and for whom we live and should be willing to die.

433 How may we "reflect" God?

The marginal reading in the Revised Version (II Cor. 3:18) gives "reflecting" instead of beholding. This makes the meaning much clearer. Christians should be mirrors, reflecting the glory of God. Visitors to the Sistine Chapel in the Vatican procure small mirrors which enable them to enjoy the great paintings of Michelangelo on the ceiling without discomfort. Worldly people will not look at God, but they do look at us, and they should see God reflected in us, as the great master's paintings are reflected in the mirror. As we thus behold and reflect God we become constantly more like him ("are transformed into the same image") going from one glorious stage of experience to another ("from glory to glory"). "Even as from the Lord the Spirit" (R.V.) means in a manner that befits the character and manner of the Holy Spirit. He works this transformation in us in the same perfect, adequate, godlike manner in which he always works. Compare Ex. 34:29-35; Ps. 34:5; Acts 4:13. Read the whole of this chapter and the next, II Cor. 3 and 4.

434 How is one to know that he is living close to God?

If we ask, in the name of his dear Son, for a daily infusion of strength and grace sufficient for our needs, he will grant our petition. Perhaps nowhere is the Christian life better expressed than in these lines from Professor David Smith. He is speaking of Christian duty: "The man who bravely goes his hard way by and by discovers God by his side. But there is a richer discovery—the love of God in Christ Jesus our Lord; and it is revealed through love of one's fellow creatures. Keep your heart sweet and gentle; refrain from contention; look with kindly and sympathetic eyes on your fellow creatures, men and beasts and birds; consider their griefs and sufferings, and lend them your best comfort and succor. It is only as we love like him that we know the wonder and glory of his love. There lies the twofold secret of reconciliation, of the linking of our little lives with the eternal order. Obey, and you will know; love, and the love of Christ will be shed abroad in your heart. And once the love of Christ takes possession of you, life will be more precious and wonderful in your eyes, and you will understand what St. Peter means by 'joy unspeakable and full of glory'—that deep, strong gladness which comes of the persuasion that the ultimate fact in the universe is the Love of God in Christ Jesus our Lord, the love which died on the cross for pity of the world's woe."

435 What does adoption by God involve?

"And I will be a Father unto you and ye shall be my sons and daughters, saith the Lord Almighty" (II Cor. 6:18). Such adoption is according to promise, by God's grace, through Christ, and we take it by faith (Gal. 3:7, 26; Rom. 9:8; Eze. 16:3-6; Rom. 4:16, 17; John 1:12). Saints are predestinated unto adoption and are gathered together in one by Christ (Rom. 8:29, John 11:52), whereupon they become his brethren (John 20:17). Our new birth is connected with our adoption, the Holy Spirit is a witness of it, and by leading us gives us evidence of it (John 1:12, 13; Rom. 8:15, 16; Rom. 8:14). This adoption should lead to holiness and should work in us likeness to God and childlike confidence in God (Matt. 5:44, 45, 48; Matt. 6:25-34); a desire for God's glory, love of peace, spirit of prayer, forgiveness and mercy (Matt. 5:16, 7:7-11, 5:9, 6:14; Luke 6:35, 36).

436 How and where does the Bible describe "loving God"?

Love to God is commanded (Deu. 11:1) and is, indeed, the one great commandment (Matt. 22:38). It should be with all the heart, and is better than sacrifice (Deu. 6:5; Mark 12:33). It is produced by the Holy Ghost and engendered by God's love to us and by answers to prayer (Gal. 5:22; I John 4:19; Ps. 116:1). Christ gave us an example of it, and it is a characteristic of saints (John 14:31; Ps. 5:11). Those who have this love are known to God, and are preserved and delivered by him; they partake of his mercy and all things work together for their good (I Cor. 8:3; Ps. 145:20; Ps. 91:14; Ex. 20:6; Rom. 8:28). When persevering (Jude 21), and exhorting one another (Ps. 31:23), saints will have joy, they will have a hatred of sin. In their hearts will be obedience to God, and he, besides being faithful to those who love him, will fulfill in them his promises (Ps. 5:11; I John 5:1; Ps. 97:10; Deu. 30:20; Deu. 7:9; Deu. 13:3; Deu. 11:13; Ps. 69:36; Jas. 1:12). This love to God naturally leads to love to Christ. Here again we have a good example set by God himself and by the saints (Matt. 17:5; John 5:20; I Pet. 1:8). Such love to him should be manifested in seeking, obeying, ministering, preferring him to all others, and in taking up his cross (John 14:15; Matt. 27:55; Matt. 10:37; Matt. 10:38). It is characteristic of saints and an evidence of adoption. Those who have it are loved by both God and Christ, and enjoy communion with them (Song of Sol. 1:4; John 8:42; John 14:21, 23; John 16:27; John 14:23). Such love should be sincere, ardent, supreme, unquenchable and "unto death" (Eph. 6:24; Song of Sol. 1:7; Matt. 10:37; Song of Sol. 2:5, 8:7; Acts 21:13; Rev. 12:11).

437 Why should we praise God, and how should we do so?

We should praise God because he is worthy of and glorified by our praise (II Sam. 22:4; Ps. 22:23). We should praise him because it is due to his majesty, glory, excellency, greatness, holiness, wisdom, power, goodness, mercy, loving-kindness, truth and his wonderful works (Ps. 96:1, 6; Ps. 138:5; Ex. 15:7; I Chron. 16:25; Ex. 15:11; Dan. 2:20; Ps. 21:18; Ps. 107:8; II Chron. 20:21; Ps. 138:2; Is. 25:1; Ps. 89:5). Also on account of his gifts to us, as are, consolations, judgment, counsel, fulfilling of his promises, pardon of sin, spiritual health, constant preservation, deliverance, protection, answering prayer, the hope of glory, and all temporal and spiritual blessings (Ps. 42:5; Ps. 101:1; Ps. 16:7; I Kin. 8:56; Ps. 103:1-3; Ps. 103:3; Ps. 71:6-8; Ps. 40:1-3; Ps. 28:7; Ps. 28:6; Ps. 118:21; I Pet. 1:3, 4; Ps. 103:2; Eph. 1:3; Ps. 104:1, 14; Ps. 136:25). Such praise of God is obligatory on angels, saints, gentiles, children, high and low, young and old, small and great, all men and all creation (Ps. 103:20; Ps. 30:4, 117:1, 8:2, 148:1, 12; Rev. 19:5; Ps. 107:8, 148:1-10).

This praise is good and comely (Ps. 33:1; Ps. 147:1) and should be offered with the understanding, soul, heart, with uprightness, joy, gladness, thankfulness (Ps. 47:7, 103:1, 9:1, 119:7, 63:5; II Chron. 29:30; I Chron. 16:4). It should be offered continually, more and more, day and night, forever and forever (Ps. 35:28, 104:33, 71:14; Rev. 4:8; II Chron. 30:26; Ps. 145:1, 2). And may be expressed in psalms and hymns, accompanied with musical instruments (Ps. 105:2; I Chron. 16:41, 42) and as a part of public worship (Ps. 9:14, 100:4, 118:19, 20). In this worship we should glory, triumph, express our joy by it, declare, invite others to it, pray for ability to offer it, be embued with the spirit of praise under all circumstances, even under afflictions (I Chron. 16:35; Ps. 106:47; Jas. 5:13; Is. 42:12; PS. 34:3, 51:15; Is. 61:3). This praise has ever been highly thought of triumph, voice of melody, voice of psalm, sacrifice of praise and of joy (Heb. 13:15; Ps. 66:8, 47:1; Is. 51:3; Ps. 98:5; Heb. 13:15; Ps. 27:6).

438 What is God's pardon and to what should it lead?

Pardon for our sins was promised to us (Is. 1:18; Jer. 31:34; Heb. 8:12). There can be none without the shedding of blood and legal sacrifices and outward purifications are ineffectual as only through the blood of Christ is it efficacious (Lev. 17:11; Heb. 9:22; Heb. 10:4; Jer. 2:22; Zec. 13:1; I John 1:7). God alone can grant this pardon and does so by and through Christ and his blood (Dan. 9:9; Mark 2:7; Luke 7:48; Luke 1:69, 77; Matt. 26:28). He grants it for Christ's sake, freely, abundantly, readily to those who confess their sins, repent and believe (I John 2:12; Is. 43:25; Neh. 9:17; Is. 55:7; I John 1:9; Acts 2:38; Acts 10:43). By so doing God shows his compassion, grace, mercy, forbearance, loving kindness, justice and faithfulness (Mic. 7:18, 19; Rom. 5:15; Ex. 34:7; II Chron. 30:18; Rom. 3:25; Ps. 51:1; I John 1:9). The result of such pardon is the forgiving, removing and blotting out of transgression, the covering of, and blotting out of sin and not mentioning or remembering transgressions any more (Ps. 32:1, 103:12; Is. 44:22; Ps. 32:1; Acts 3:19; Eze. 18:22; Heb. 10:17). This great and free gift should lead us to return to God, love him, fear and praise him (Is. 44:22; Luke 7:47; Ps. 130:4; Ps. 103:2, 3). It should also induce us to pray for it for ourselves and for others and to strive to become worthy of it as the unforgiving, unbelieving and impenitent cannot share in it (Ps. 25:11; Jas. 5:15; Mark 11:26; John 8:21, 24; Luke 13:25).

439 What is meant by "devotedness to God"?

We should be devoted to God because of his mercies (Rom. 12:1), of his goodness (I Sam. 12:24) and because of the call with which he invites us to him. The death of Christ and our redemption should be compelling forces. Our devotedness should be unreserved (Matt. 6:24), abounding (I Thess. 4:1), persevering (Luke 1:74, 75; Luke 9:62), and in life and death (Rom. 14:8). It should be with our whole being, thus, with our spirit (I Cor. 6:20), with our bodies (Rom. 12:1; I Cor. 6:20), with our members (Rom. 6:12, 13), and with our substance (Ex. 22:29; Prov. 3:9). This devotedness we should show by loving God (Deu. 6:5), serving him (I Sam. 12:24; Rom. 12:11), walking worthy of him (I Thess. 2:12), doing all to his glory (I Cor. 10:31); bearing the cross (Mark 8:34), by self-denial (Mark 8:34), and by giving up all for Christ (Matt. 19:21, 28, 29).

440 Does God communicate his will in any other way than by his Word?

We believe that there are special cases of extreme difficulty in which, when guidance is sought, God does reveal to his children the way in which he wishes them to walk. This he does by interpositions of his providence. If we ask him for guidance in our troubles, in the name of his dear Son, he will not deny it. There are some who think they receive direction in dreams, or by casting lots, or by opening a Bible at random and noticing the first passage that catches the eye. It is unwise to give heed to intimations supposed to reach us in such ways. They are utterly untrustworthy and should be disregarded.

441 What is grace?

In theology, the word "grace" has been the hinge of three great historical controversies, and it is still a subject of varied interpretation. In the spiritual sense, it is divine favor or condescension to mankind individually or collectively. In the concrete Gospel sense, it is the unmerited love and favor of God in Christ, as shown in the salvation freely provided for mankind (see Eph. 2:9). It may also be described as the divine influence acting within the heart, regenerating, sanctifying and keeping it. Grace brings the peace and joy of assurance. It is "the life of the soul, as the soul is the life of the body."

442 Can the church heal by faith today?

There are several religious bodies which teach faith-healing by prayer and the laying on of hands. It is not general, however, among the denominations. But while the divine power is as great today as in the time of the early Church, and while many remarkable instances of healing through faith and prayer are adduced, the usual teaching in the regular denominations is that, in cases of sickness, we should employ the remedies at hand through medical skill or otherwise, and ask God's blessing on these means to effect a cure. There is no passage in the Scriptures, however, which indicates that Christ intended the gift of faith-healing to cease with the apostles. On the contrary, the inference is quite clear, throughout the whole New Testament, that this gift was to remain in the Church. We have so largely lost the gift because of our lack of faith, but there are numerous incidents being reported every day of miraculous healing in answer to prayer in the name of Christ. That there are not more cases is not proof that God's power is shortened, but results are proportioned to our faith. There are many instances in the Church today of wonderful answers to the prayer of faith. It is well to remember, however, that God has placed certain means within our reach and we should employ these means and ask his blessing upon them. Jesus himself never said anything in disparagement of the profession of Luke the "beloved physician." In James 5:15 it should be noted that the writer does not say that the *oil* will save; it is merely a symbol. The healing here mentioned in the first clause of the verse is of the *body*; the second clause implies that the prayer of faith for one who has sinned will bring forgiveness. The same connection of sin and sickness is employed in Is. 33:24; Matt. 9:2-5, and John 5:14. See also Ps. 103:3. The application is found in the next verse, which speaks of repentant confession. The oldest versions of this passage read, "*Therefore*, confess your faults one to another," showing that it must be a precedent condition. This does not justify what is known as the confessional, however, in the sense in which it is employed in the Church of Rome. There, all confessions must be made to the priests. Confession, in the apostolic sense, may be made to any one who is godly and who can pray. It is to be an open confession and not one whispered into the ear of a priest.

443 How can one obtain a "new heart"?

The sole resource is prayer and a constant striving against indulgence in sin. God is able to give a new heart, and when a man is sincerely desirous of obtaining that blessing there is no doubt of its being granted to him. God is more ready to bless us than we are to seek his blessing. But he does not confer his gifts unless they are sincerely sought. And there must be proof of sincerity by co-operation. If a man prayed that he might reach the top of a mountain, God would not take him bodily there, but he would give him the strength to climb. If you read the description of the condition of a man struggling against sin in Romans 7, you will see that victory is obtained through the power that Christ gives. This power is freely granted to all who seek it, and through it any one may overcome evil.

444 What are the consequences of resisting the Holy Spirit?

We are warned against the danger of resisting the Holy Spirit, and Paul (Eph. 4:30) admonishes the believer not to grieve the Holy Spirit. It is possible for one to refuse to obey the call of the Spirit, yet without placing himself outside of the pale of redemption. The Bible itself furnishes several instances of this character. We should advise any one who feels that he may have refused the call at one time to take a hopeful attitude, and to seek God's mercy and forgiveness with a contrite heart, remembering that the promise of forgiveness extends to "whosoever" may come. Jesus saves to the uttermost, and has assured us that he will not reject any one who comes to him in this spirit. We can not set limits to God's mercy, and he is at all times more ready to forgive than we are to seek his forgiveness.

445 In what sense is the Holy Spirit a guide?

The Holy Spirit is certainly promised in answer to believing prayer. (See Luke 11:13.) See an account of his work in John 16:7-15. But the fact should not lead any one to be intolerant, or unreasonable. It is conceivable that a man might be so convinced that he is led of the Spirit to believe or do certain things, as to make grievous errors. He might believe himself infallible. The best and wisest men have in the past made that mistake. The humble, childlike believer seeks enlightenment and it may come to him through a preacher, or through private study, but he should keep his mind open to new light and should never assume, because he has reached a certain conclusion after prayer, that he is necessarily right. He may have been misled by ignorance or prejudice. In his talk with Nicodemus (John 3:8), Christ compared the operations of the Spirit to the movement of the wind, which could not be controlled or directed. We see this sometimes in revivals where we cannot account for one person being converted while another remains unmoved. But we may be quite sure that whenever any one sincerely desires the Holy Spirit's influence, God is more ready to bestow it than we can be to receive it.

446 Should a Christian be joyful?

God gives joy and Christ was appointed to give it, since the Gospels, which treat of him, are the "good tidings" (Ecc. 2:26; Is. 61:3; Luke 2:10, 11) and God's Word affords joy (Neh. 8:12; Jer. 15:16). Joy is promised to saints, prepared for them and enjoined on them (Ps. 132:16; Is. 35:10; Ps. 97:11; Ps. 32:11; Phil. 3:1). It is experienced by believers, peacemakers, the just, the wise, and discreet (Luke 24:52; Prov. 12:20; Prov. 21:15; Prov. 15:23). The joy of the saints is in God. Christ and the Holy Ghost; for their election, salvation, deliverance from bondage, manifestations of goodness, temporal blessings, supplies of grace, divine protection and support and the hope of glory (Ps. 89:16; Rom. 5:11; Luke 1:47; Rom. 14:17; Luke 10:20; Ps. 21:1; Ps. 105:43; II Chron. 7:10; Joel 2:23; Is. 12:13; Ps. 5:11; Ps. 28:7; Rom. 5:2). These being grand blessings and advantages, their joy should be great, abundant, exceeding, animated, unspeakable, full, constant (Zec. 9:9; II Cor. 8:2; Ps. 21:6; Ps. 32:11; I Pet. 1:8; II Cor. 6:10: I Thess. 5:16) and it should be manifest in every condition of life, such as in hope, sorrow, under trials and persecutions, in calamities and afflictions (Rom. 12:12; II Cor. 6:10; Jas. 1:2; I Pet. 1:6; Matt. 5:11, 12; Hab. 3:17, 18). Such joy is made complete by the favor of God, by faith in Christ, the abiding in him and his Word, and by answer to prayer (Acts 2:28; Rom. 15:13; John 15:10, 11; John 17:13; John 16:24). When so conceived and practiced, the saints will serve God with gladness (Ps. 100:2). It will strengthen them (Neh. 8:10); they will use it in all their religious services, have it in all their undertakings, and it shall finally be their reward at the judgment day (Eze. 6:22; Deu. 12:18; Matt. 25:21).

447 Is it wrong to judge others?

It is a common failing in humanity to pass judgment upon others and it is frequently attended by unfortunate results. We are expressly told in Scripture that judgment belongs to God. (See Matt. 7:1-5.) No matter what the occasion, it becomes the Christian to withhold his judgment, and particularly the open expression of it, lest he should be doing an injustice. There are cases, of course, where an act is so palpably wrong and so obviously done with wicked purpose, that we feel naturally disposed to condemn; but even here we may make a mistake, unless we are thoroughly familiar with all the antecedent circumstances. This reservation of judgment does not relate to the operation of the statute law, but to the individual. Paul tells us, in Romans 14:4, that we ought not to assume the right to condemn. Therefore, to tell a person that he is not a Christian, if he has a ring on his finger, is to assume a position to which we have no right. There may be a reason for his wearing it that we do not know; it may be the gift of some relative or friend, or a memorial. To men impressed with the urgent need there is in the world for money to use for charity and religion, it would appear a duty to give all the money available to these causes and not to spend any of it on personal adornment. Arriving at such a conclusion, let him act upon it himself, and not hastily denounce others who may have different ideas of their duty. Above all, we should refrain from censorious gossip, which is a fruitful cause of ill-founded and wicked judgment of others.

448 Why is liberality to be commended?

It is pleasing to God. He never forgets it. Christ set an example of it and it is characteristic of Saints (II Cor. 9:7; Heb. 6:10; II Cor. 8:9; Ps. 112:9). This good quality should be exercised in the service of God towards all men, such as saints, servants, the poor, strangers, and towards enemies (Ex. 35:21-29; Gal. 6:10; Rom. 12:13; Deu. 15:12-14; Lev. 25:35; Prov. 25:21). It should be demonstrated by lending to those in want, in giving alms, relieving the destitute, and in rendering personal services (Matt. 5:42; Luke 12:33; Is. 58:7; Phil. 2:30). In practice, however, we should be guided by these restrictions. We should be liberal without ostentation, with simplicity, should be willing and give abundantly (Matt. 6:1-3; Rom. 82:8; Deu. 16:10; Mat. 6:1-8; II Cor. 8:12; II Cor. 8:7). Its exercise provokes others to like goodness whereas the want of, while bringing to many a curse, is proof of not loving God, and of not having faith (II Cor. 9:2; Prov. 28:27; I John 3:17; Jas. 2:14-16). Liberality is highly commended, blessings are connected with it and promises are given to those who practice it (Luke 3:11, 11:41; I Cor. 16:1; Ps. 41:1; Ps. 112:9; Prov. 11:25). God's people were always noted for having this virtue, as see Prince of Israel, Num. 7:2; Boaz, Ruth 2:16; David, II Sam. 9:7-10; Zacchaus, Luke 19:8; First Christians, Acts 2:45; Barnabas, Acts 4:35, 37; Cornelius, Acts 16:2; Lydia, Acts 16:15; Paul, Acts 20:34.

449 How does Christ influence and change the lives of men?

It is one of the most definitely and positively attested facts of history and of present-day life that multitudes of people have an experience of peace, power, purity and joy which grows out of their belief that God as manifested in the flesh of Jesus of Nazareth died for their sins. This experience is real, is tangible, is witnessed to; it makes the lives of those who possess it altogether different from what they were before. When we ask if such an experience was possible before Christ died, the answer is very clear—No. Many Old Testament saints had a very beautiful and exalted spiritual experience, but they could not have the experience of knowing that God in the flesh had died for their sins. The question of the relation of these facts to sin and the deliverance from it presents some philosophical difficulties, but no really practical difficulties. We can be sure that if any persons found deliverance from sin before Christ came they were comparatively few; but now the deliverance is offered to all. A few saints may have looked forward and grasped the glories of the atonement by faith; we look back upon it as a historic fact and so appropriate its benefits. Again, it is undeniably true that since the incarnation men have been able to get a totally new and infinitely clearer idea of God than if he had not manifested himself in the flesh. He has been interpreted to them in terms of human life, so it is now easy for them to comprehend how God thinks and acts and speaks. It is a higher revelation than that which came through the prophets: "God, who at sundry times and in divers manners spake in time past unto the fathers by the prophets, hath in these last days spoken to us by his Son" (Heb. 1:1, 2). It must certainly be true that the experience of loving Christ as a divine-human friend is different from the experience of loving God as he was revealed in Old Testament times. And when, as has already been suggested, there is added the knowledge that he died to save us, there is a power and depth to the love that would otherwise have been impossible. The one which fully believes in Christ receives fully the benefits of his life, death and resurrection. The one who doubts must continue to miss them.

450 Is fasting necessary to Christian living?

Fasting was voluntary in the early Christian Church. It was charged by his enemies that Christ's disciples "fasted not," while those of John did fast (Matt. 11:18, 19). Our Lord did not positively enjoin religious fasting, and indeed he alluded in terms of censure to the frequent fasts of the Pharisees. His reference to the time which would come when, being deprived of the personal presence of the bridegroom, his disciples would fast, implied rather a season of general mourning than of self-denial. In the Sermon on the Mount (Matt. 6:17) he recognizes the practice, but leaves the frequency and extent to the individual judgment. Fasts were undoubtedly observed by the early Christians (see Acts 13:2, 14:23,; II Cor. 6:5), but these were probably a recognition of old established usage, handed down through generations. When it is remembered that a very large portion of the Christian Church was originally Jewish, it is not surprising that fasting, which was so marked a feature under the old dispensation, should have been handed down from age to age and that it should be occasionally found to some extent in the church even at the present day. That it has merits, both spiritual and physical, may not be gain-said. A sincere fast, which while mortifying the flesh, aided in concentrating the mind upon the things of the Spirit, is especially adapted to certain great emergencies. Our Saviour himself set us the example.

451 May a Christian marry a non-Christian?

Paul gives direct teaching on the subject. He says (II Cor. 6:14), "Be ye not unequally yoked together with unbelievers," etc. In the case of the Corinthians, such a union must have been exceedingly uncongenial, as the unbeliever was usually an idolater. The disparity is not so marked in our day, but it is sufficient still to produce a lack of real harmony. Religion should be to the Christian the first and fundamental element of life. To have a partner who has no sympathy with it is to raise a barrier between the two which keeps them separate in the highest and holiest spheres of life. Generally it leads to the Christian forsaking his faith.

452 How can the unbelieving husband be sanctified by the believing wife?

This probably was never designed for general application. It was meant to meet very special conditions. Paul, in I Cor. 7:14, was writing to Christians newly won from a corrupt and debasing form of heathenism. The converts were disposed to separate from their pagan partners and they wrote for Paul's approval. He told them not to do so. If the pagan husband or wife chose to leave, there was to be no restraint. The Christian must not be the one to seek separation. Rather he should remain in conjugal relations in the hope of saving his pagan wife (see verse 16). His example and tender affection and Christian kindness might win her to Christianity—might be the means of sanctifying her. So the believing wife might influence the pagan husband. Besides, there was the consideration of the children, who, if the believer remained, would be brought up under holy influences.

453 Is it possible to be so trained and nutured from childhood up that a "new birth" is unnecessary?

We believe that Christ's statement, "Ye must be born again," applies to every human being. The most carefully trained child needs it. It is true that there are many so good by nature and training, that they pass through the process almost unconsciously. They do not go through the sorrow and anxiety and distress that precede conversion in the case of people who have led openly wicked lives. They come to God as to a Father, and having learned to love him from their earliest years, they are changed imperceptibly into his image. But, none the less, the change takes place, and the child yields itself by a definite act to Christ as a Saviour. These are beautiful characters, and they have reason to thank God for giving them parents so good and wise. They are, however, very rare. The best trained child is often conscious of having lied, or committed other sins which need to be forgiven, and of having a nature that is prone to sin, which needs to be changed by the Holy Spirit.

454 Who is my neighbor?

The practical question, "How shall I carry out the commandment to love one's neighbor as one's self" is constantly facing the Christian. In the parable of the Good Samaritan, Jesus taught that our neighbor is any one to whom we can be of service. There are no limits as to social standing, or creed, or race, or habitation. Any one whom we can reach has a claim upon our help, which is sanctioned by God himself. The teachings of both Jesus and Paul are plain that a man should care, with special earnestness and affection, for the members of his own household. To be sweet and kind, patient and helpful at home is the first neighborly duty of the Christian. Then the people to whom one is nearest in his daily life have the next claim upon his service. He should be on the lookout for persons and families who are in need and whom he can help. The Christian should make his influence felt for the benefit of his neighborhood, his town, and his state. Mails and express routes have knit the whole world into so compact a neighborhood that every one must feel that the needy in any corner of the world have a claim upon his charitable consideration. Needless to say the joy of such service always far outweighs whatever sacrifice may be involved. Matt. 19:19, 22:39; Luke 10:36, 37; Rom. 13:10.

455 Why and in what ways should we love our fellow man?

God and Christ commanded us to love man. The Saviour gave us an example in doing it (I John 4:7, 21; John 13:34; John 15:12, I John 3:23). It is taught by God and is a fruit of the Spirit (I Thes. 4:9; Gal. 5:22; Col. 1:8). Without it, gifts and sacrifices are as nothing. Love is the great commandment (I Cor. 13-1, 2, 3; Matt. 22:37-39; I Tim. 1:5). This love we should put on, follow after, abound and continue in, and, while provoking each other to it, we should be sincere, disinterested and fervent in it (Col. 3:14; I Cor. 14:1; Phil. 1:9; I Thes. 3:12; II Tim. 2:15; II Cor. 8:7; Rom. 12:9; I Cor. 10:24; I Pet. 1:22). This virtue should be connected with brotherly kindness and should be practiced with a pure heart. We should show it toward saints, ministers, our families, our fellow countrymen, strangers, enemies; yes, to all men! (I Pet. 2:17; I Thess. 5:13; Eph. 5:25; Ex. 32:32; Lev. 19:34; Ex. 23:4-5; Matt. 5:44; Rom. 12:14, 20; Gal. 6:10), and demonstrate it by ministering to the wants of others, relieving strangers, visiting the sick, clothing the needy, sympathizing with and supporting the weak, covering the faults of others, forgiving, forbearing (Matt. 25:35; Gal. 5:13; Lev. 25:35; Is. 58:7; Job 31:16; Jas. 1:27; Rom. 12:15; Gal. 6:2; Prov. 10:12; Eph. 4:32, 4:2). This love to man is evidence of our being in the light of our discipleship with Christ and of spiritual life (I John 2:10; John 13:35; I John 3:14). It is the fulfillment of the Law, is good and pleasant, is a bond of union and perfectness and necessary to true happiness (Rom. 13:8-10; Ps. 133:1-2; Col. 2:2; Col. 3:14; Prov. 15:17).

456 In what sense is our "overcoming" like that of Jesus?

There is more in the statement in Rev. 3:21 than a comparison of our victories with those of Christ. It is rather a statement of similarity in the whole sequence of struggle, victory, and reward in the case of the Christian and of Christ. He struggled, triumphed, and was enthroned; we, too, shall struggle, triumph, and be enthroned. This does not mean that at every step, or necessarily at any step, our experiences shall be identical with his or equal to his. His struggles, his victories, and his rewards are greater than ours can be. Nevertheless we find it to be true, comparing this passage with others, that, whatever struggles we may meet, our victories may be as complete as his. (See I John 2:6, 4:17; II Cor. 2:14, etc.) And this is true because it is his very strength that is available for us in our times of need.

457 What should be the Christian's attitude toward pleasures?

Many Christians, especially among the young, are interested in knowing what pleasures are inconsistent with a Christian's life. What sacrifices in this respect does God ask us to make? God does not ask us to make sacrifices for its own sake. When he asks us to give anything up, it is because he knows it would be harmful to us to keep it. In all our thoughts about God we must hold with a firm grip the great fundamental truth that he loves us. We cannot think rightly or feel comfortable without starting here. Because he loves us he wants us to be happy. He does not want to take away our happiness but to give us more. And he knows that we can be happy only as we love and serve him. He really asks us to give up nothing, except to give ourselves to him. When we realize that we belong to him we also realize that certain things harm us, and that certain other things may have a harmful influence upon others. We are living for him, and for the people for whom his Son died. All these questions settle themselves quite easily then. There are many unobjectionable pleasures, but we should shun those that waste precious time; that lead to evil companionships; that involve acts and associations which interfere with our spiritual progress; that are inimical to health or reputation, and also those that, by setting a bad example, may operate as a stumbling-block to others. In this way we will find more happiness in the consciousness that we are pleasing and helping him than we could ever have found in any form of self-indulgence.

458 How may I pray acceptably to God?

This is a question asked by many earnest people. This is the natural state of one in whom spiritual life has not yet been fully awakened. Prayer, like belief, is not an act that can easily be made clear to the unenlightened. If you go to God as a child to its father, when you are in trouble, and ask him in simple faith to help you for Jesus' sake, you will be better able to understand why others believe in prayer and find it one of the principal mainstays of their lives. Seek the side of some aged Christian and put the question as to his belief in prayer, and you will immediately receive the answer that a large part of his life rests upon daily communion with God, and that very many of his petitions, presented in the name of Jesus, have been answered. There are tens of thousands of good Christian people throughout this land who can testify to the efficacy of prayer. Very many of these believers make it a rule to honor God by acknowledging before the world the answers to their prayers. We would advise any one who doubts and who sincerely wishes to be helped, to drop all argument and apply the test to his own case, and then give God the glory before the brethren. We would not, however, advise any one to pray for mere material blessings, or worldly honors, or wealth or luxuries, but to pray in the right spirit and to study that he does not pray amiss. Every petition should be presented in Jesus' name.

459 What does redemption do for us?

"Ye are bought with a price," says Paul (I Cor. 6:20, 7:23). This price is the blood of Christ and he was sent to effect our redemption with it (Acts 20:28; Gal. 4:4, 5). And what were we redeemed from? From the bondage and curse of the law, the power of sin and of the grave, from all troubles, iniquity, evil, enemies, death and destruction (Gal. 4:5, 3:13; Rom. 6:18; Ps. 49:15, 25:22; Tit. 2:14; Gen. 48:16; Ps. 106:10, 11; Hos. 13:14; Ps. 103:4). This redemption procures for us justification, forgiveness, purification and adoption through the precious, plenteous and eternal power and grace of God (Rom. 3:24; Eph. 1:7; Gal. 4:4, 5; Tit. 2:14). To those who partake of it there is opened up a new life and existence, for they are the property of God, a peculiar people, are first-fruits of God and are sealed unto the day of redemption. They are zealous of good works, walk safely in holiness and shall return to Zion with joy (Is. 43:1; Rev. 14:4; II Sam. 7:23; Eph. 4:30; Eph. 2:10; Is. 35:8, 9; Is. 35:10). This redemption man cannot effect, nor can corruptible things purchase it, but it is the free gift of God by Christ.

460 What is regeneration?

Regeneration is being born again, and is the work of the Holy Spirit, by which we experience a change of heart. It is perhaps better expressed as being "born anew from above" (John 3:7), being "awakened" (Eph. 2:1), Christ coming into the heart (Gal. 4:19), "renewing of the mind" (Rom. 12:2), the "purifying" (Titus 3:5). Man is not the author of his own regeneration. The change consists in the recovery of the moral image of God upon the heart, leading us to love him supremely and serve him as our highest end. It is wholly the work of the Holy Spirit. The change is in the heart and the will—in our moral and spiritual faculties; and the natural faculties, being dominated by the will, while they may resist for a time, ultimately follow the change. The evidences of regeneration are conviction of sin, sorrow and repentance, faith, love and devotion to God. In regeneration we *receive* from God, whereas in conversion we *turn* to God.

461 Is regeneration different from the baptism of the Holy Spirit?

They are part of one process—the work of the Holy Spirit. Regeneration is the new birth by which we experience a change of heart, and it is the work of the Holy Spirit. Titus 3:5 speaks of "the washing of regeneration." We are made members of the visible Church of Christ by baptism and renewed in the Spirit by the Holy Ghost. The "higher baptism," or the bestowment of the Spirit upon faithful believers, often differs greatly in degree, but it is identical in character and is the universal privilege of all Christians.

462 Is remorse a discipline?

We should bear remorse until by God's grace a happier state of mind is produced. You remember that significant record (Mark 14:72) about Peter's denial of Christ: "When he thought thereon he wept." When you rejoice over sin forgiven, and are overcome with wonder and gratitude at God's magnanimity in forgiving you, it is quite natural and proper that you should grieve that you had ever offended a Being so good and kind. The forgiveness should lead you to love God more than others do, and to rejoice in his marvelous goodness and mercy. It should also lead you to be very watchful against relapsing into sin, and to make great exertions to render service to One who has forgiven you. You should also be very tender and charitable toward others. Do not let remorse incapacitate you for labor, but rather operate as an incentive to service.

463 Where is restitution taught?

See Matt. 5:26; Luke 16:10, 12; Luke 19:8, 9; Rom. 13:8; Philemon 18. The Roman law (in Christ's day) directed a fourfold restitution, which explains Zaccheus' statement in Luke 19:8. His generous addition of "the half of his goods," though not demanded by the law, was evidently heard with approval of the spirit which prompted it. Moralists hold that we are bound to restore the thing owed, in kind, if possible, with the natural increase added. This seems to have been the view adopted by the early Christian Church.

464 Is it right for a Christian to retaliate?

A Christian should never retaliate; nor should he suffer himself to be imposed upon, when possible to avoid it. Between retaliation and the suffering of imposition, he should, however, accept the latter, if retaliation implies his committing any act of vindictiveness unbecoming a Christian. Our Lord's words upon the subject are plain. Read the fifth and eighteenth chapters of Matthew. St. Paul says repeatedly, "Love is the fulfilling of the law." Retaliation is contrary to the spirit and letter of this. But while we are told to love our neighbor as ourself, we are not told to love him better; and self-protection, in a wise and proper spirit, is a duty.

465 Should the Christian work for reward?

The New Testament makes it very clear that the motive of our work should be love for Christ, love that springs from gratitude for his salvation. But the Christian is also reminded of the great rewards that shall come to him in the future life if he is faithful and if his work is of a high order. Study particularly I Cor. 3:1-15. The thought of these rewards helps us to be faithful, constant, and careful. The conception of what the rewards will be varies with different stages of civilization. The best idea of these rewards seems to be that every good deed done is in itself the reward. Somebody was helped, was saved, was made glad, was given power and inspiration for helping others; these facts are eternal, and will bless forever those who are responsible for them. Then, too, the reward implies power to do still greater things. If there is joy in accomplishing things for the Master now there will be greater joy when we find ourselves furnished with the new, heavenly powers for doing still greater service. But more and more the Christian should train himself to keep his eyes and his heart fixed on Christ, eager to please him. He has called us into his friendship, into his fellowship, into co-operation with him in his great tasks. We must not disappoint him.

466 Is a saved person sure of his salvation?

Many good men of whose salvation there can be no question, have at times had doubts, and have suffered acute distress. In some cases the doubts have a physical origin resulting from a gloomy disposition. In others, they arise from too much introspection. In others again, because their conscience reminds them of sins not yet overcome. You must remember that you are not saved because of your feelings, but because Christ died for you. If you have sincerely repented and are trusting entirely in Christ to save you, and are living in his strength a godly life, you have the right to thank God for saving you, in spite of your doubts. If you cannot take his word that those who come to him through Christ have eternal life, you should ask him to forgive you for doubting him. You may be quite sure that he will keep his promise, whether you have the joy of assurance or not.

467 What is the Christian's duty as to Sabbath observance?

Paul gave this advice to people who were troubled by legalists in his day: "Let no man judge you in meat or in drink or in respect of . . . the Sabbath days" (Col. 2:16). In every generation since Christ and before his time, there were people who laid more stress on days and forms and ceremonies than on essentials. The Pharisees found it much easier to give tithes of their kitchen-gardens than to do justly and refrain from robbing widows and orphans. You as a Christian are not under the law at all. When Gentiles were first admitted to the Church it was expressly declared that they were not required to observe the Jewish code of laws. The question came up at a solemn council at which the Apostles were present and was decided once for all. You will find the result of the discussion in Acts 15. In the name of the Holy Spirit the decision was given as stated in verses 28 and 29, and it was expressly stated that no other burden was laid upon them. They naturally and properly celebrated the day on which Christ rose from the dead, not the Jewish Sabbath, with which they had nothing to do, and we follow their example.

468 What is the true theory as to Sunday observance?

The Sabbath was divinely ordained as a day of cessation from labor. In the Jewish Church, the restrictions were most rigid and profanation of the day was severely punished. It was a day of rest, reconciliation, worship and religious festivity. (See Is. 58:13, 14.) Christian Sabbath observance recognizes the same general obligation to abstain from regular vocations and to devote the day largely to rest and worship. Jesus himself rebuked the slavish Sabbatic restrictions of the Scribes and Pharisees, and showed them that the Sabbath was made for man, meaning that it was designed and instituted for our common humanity, and to conduce to our highest good. He pointed out that there were various acts which in themselves were not sinful, but meritorious, and such as might be done on the Sabbath. These were the works of necessity or of mercy. This is the attitude of the Christian Church of today on Sabbath observance (Col. 2:16). It may be briefly said that no labor should be performed on that day which can be done on secular days, and that works of charity and mercy are justified on that day. We have the divine example for abstention in Gen. 2:2, 3.

469 Is it possible to get beyond God's willingness and power to save?

There is none who can go beyond the reach of the Divine mercy. Jesus saves "to the uttermost" (Heb. 7:25). God will always hear and answer the prayer of the earnest, penitent heart. Christ's offering of himself was once *for all* who accept him; and his intercession, which is continuous, assures us that we cannot be separated from his love if we take him into our hearts and lives.

470 What is the way of salvation?

It would probably disappoint if we answered in the Scriptural way: "Believe on the Lord Jesus Christ and thou shalt be saved." Yet that is the only true answer. Stripped of theological phraseology, the way of salvation may be described as committing your case to Christ, much as you would commit your case to a physician if you were sick, or your trouble to a lawyer if you were in danger of imprisonment. "Believing on him" is the complete trust you place in him and the profound conviction that he can and will save you. This is the decisive thing, the turning point. That done, several results flow from it. One is sorrow for sin previously committed and a renunciation of it for the future. A second is the endeavor, in the strength that Christ imparts, to follow his example, to cultivate his spirit, and to live his life of purity, holiness and helpfulness. This involves prayer and submission to his will in all things. Then you should join a church to confess him openly. There are other matters that will call for your attention as you go on, but these we have mentioned are the plain, simple duties that you have to do in order to become a Christian.

471 How, if God works in us, must we work out our own salvation?

There is no contradiction in the passage Phil. 2 :12, 19. It is very true that we must work out our own salvation; and it is equally true that it is God who worketh in us. A certain part is ours to do, which God cannot do for us; another part is God's to do which we cannot do for him. In the first place we must do the believing. Mr. Moody used to tell how he prayed for faith until he noticed the passage: "Faith cometh by hearing, and hearing by the Word of God." Rom. 10:17. God has given the Word; we must do the believing. Again, God gives us the power, but we must use it. God may give his Spirit to enable a Christian to testify or to preach, but the Christian must use his lips and tongue and voice. God dwells in us and works in us and we have his power; but by using his power and accepting his help we increase our capacity for more, we gain mental, spiritual and physical strength and skill for our work. Our bodily life bears a perfect analogy to the spiritual life in this respect; God starts our hearts beating and keeps bestowing the gift of life. In this sense he dwells and works in us. But we must work and exercise that we may grow stronger and more efficient and accomplish the work we find to do.

472 How are we to accept Christ as Saviour?

Though salvation by faith is such a simple thing, many souls stumble at it. It seems too simple to be true, so they go about trying to find a harder way to be saved, and of course they do not find it because there is no other way. This is what we should say to every seeking soul: The first step toward Christ is to realize what it is that keeps you away from him, that is, your sin. Christ is very near you, nearer than your closest friend; but your sin separates your soul from him. You must confess your sin, acknowledge that you have sinned; you must repent of your sin, making restitution if you have wronged any one; you must determine to forsake your sin. But these things are not faith; they are only the necessary steps to faith. Faith is the definite belief that Christ died for your sins and that he actually forgives them now. "He tasted death for every man." If that is so, then he really, literally died for you. It is very easy to believe Jesus if you will just let yourself do it. Faith is an extremely simple thing; doubt is difficult. In your brain you know that he died "for every man." How can you doubt, then, that he died for you? You know that he died for the sins of the whole world; this must include you. Nothing in the history of the world is a surer, steadier fact than that Christ was crucified to save you from sin. The moment any one will stop doubting that fact and begin to believe it he will find peace, and find Christ. "Be not afraid—only believe." "Believe in the Lord Jesus Christ, and thou shalt be saved." Have you not proved that the way of doubt is hard and sad? Will you not try now the way of trust, and find how sweet and light and glad it is?

473 What distinction is to be made between the false shepherd and the true?

The test that Christ gave (Matt. 24:24) whereby we may know the false prophets, and the true as well, is practical for every age. "By their fruits ye shall know them." The Scriptures specify the characteristics of the "false shepherd" in part as follows: They serve only themselves, mind earthly things, feign piety and sanctity, fear persecution, respecters of persons, deceitful workers, prophesy false peace, wrest the Scriptures, deny the Lord that bought them, preferring questions of vain philosophy to truths of Scripture, etc. The "true shepherd" preaches the Word that is able to save and build up; he watches for souls, seeks the wandering, reclaims in love those repelled by uncharitableness, is willing to make personal sacrifice, sympathetic, faithful in warning and reproving, tender in treatment of young and burdened Christians, persevering if by any means he may save souls. Thus it is grace, producing character, and not talents, that distinguishes the true from the false.

474 Does God allow Satan to punish us with sickness?

Do not make the mistake that Job's friends made, of assuming that sickness, trouble, or bereavement may necessarily be punishment. You will find a different theory, not in John only, but in Hebrews. The writer of that epistle says (12:5-11) that chastisement is sometimes to be regarded as a proof of God's love. He evidently regarded it as being inflicted by God, but to be in the nature of discipline and education rather than punishment. On the other hand, Paul said his "thorn in the flesh" was the messenger of Satan (II Cor. 12:7). It does not make much difference to the sufferer whether God inflicts or permits Satan or men to inflict. In either case the affliction must be endured, and if it is borne with patience and equanimity, God is pleased, because then the world sees how his children love and honor him. The statement often made that all sickness and affliction are sent as a punishment is not true, but on the contrary, is a hideous libel on God and a cruel outrage on the sufferers. Sickness is sometimes a punishment for disregarding the laws of nature, but it is not God's punishment for sin. The book of Job was written to show how false and cowardly was the theory that those worst afflicted were the worst sinners. Job insisted and God confirmed him, that we have no right to infer that the afflicted man has been a heinous sinner. Christ also indignantly repudiated the idea (see Luke 13:2-4, and again John 9:1-3). Sickness often comes as a discipline to develop spirituality, to lead to greater faith and patience and sometimes to give an example of Christ's sustaining power. People have often wondered at the patience and endurance of the afflicted Christian and have gained from the spectacle a deep impression of the power of religion.

475 Does "falling into sin" prove that conversion has not yet taken place?

That is not a reliable test. Unhappily, even converted men fall into sin at times. There is, however, this difference, that before conversion, sin occasions little if any sorrow, whereas after conversion it is sincerely mourned and deplored and God's help is sought not only for pardon, but for strength to avoid it in the future. There are many signs of conversion. One is that just stated in the soul's attitude toward sin. Another is love for Christ, through whom all blessings come. There is, too, an intense desire to know him and be like him and a complete dependence on him, and a resolve that if his will is recognized it shall be obeyed at any cost. There is also a change of feeling toward others, especially toward all who also love Christ. The soul that has been born again is full of love to men and women and there is a desire to render them service. These are among the most conspicuous signs of conversion, but they are not always all present at the beginning of the Christian life, but develop later.

476 If past sins harass the mind, is it evidence that God has not forgiven them?

No, it is sometimes an evidence of lack of faith. But generally it arises from a very proper sense of the heinous nature of our sin. Though God forgives, and we rejoice in the fact and adore him for his marvellous magnanimity, we cannot forgive ourselves. There is a very touching expression in Mark 14:72 which intimates that Peter's memory of his denial of Christ was life-long: "When he thought thereon, he wept." The other Evangelists speak of his weeping at the time, but Mark, who probably knew him well in his later years, phrases it differently. Yet, though Peter may have continued to weep at the thought, he could never have had any doubt as to his being forgiven.

477 Are we punished for sins while yet here on earth?

It might be difficult to prove that there is direct punishment, but experience proves that the results of sin are often very bitter and painful.

Sometimes they are felt in the body, when the sins of youth bring on disease which lasts all through life. They are often seen in the cases of Christians who set a bad example before their conversion, and they grieve when they see young people, whom they led into evil, grow worse and worse. The results of the sin of neglecting the training of children are frequently very sorrowful. The child grows up and falls into sin, and then the parent suffers remorse, as he feels that if he had only done his duty before it was too late, the child might have been saved. In many other ways, by natural law, sin works its own punishment.

478 Does willful sin exclude a Christian from pardon?

No; we firmly believe that there is no passage that excludes him from pardon. The writer of the Epistle to the Hebrews (who, by the way, was probably not Paul), simply taught that there was no further sacrifice for sin than that which had been offered in the person of Christ. (See Heb. 10:26.) He was writing to Hebrews, who, under the old dispensation, could bring another sin-offering when they sinned again. The Christian must revert to the cross, for there remained no other atonement, and if he put that away from him, he was without resource. The backslider who sincerely repents is encouraged to return and is sure of welcome. It is the one imperative duty he is bound to perform. Peter, who denied his Lord, was tenderly welcomed. The wicked member mentioned in I Corinthians, you will see if you look to the second epistle (2:7), was to be forgiven and comforted. As a father receives a beloved child, who goes to him with confession and repentance, so God will receive the Christian who has fallen, but has renounced his sin and humbly pleads for forgiveness through Christ.

479 How does religion help one to get over a besetting sin?

There is first the direct power which God promises to give through Christ to those who sincerely and earnestly seek it. Then, there is the subjective power that comes from a soul turning decisively to God. This Chalmers called "The expulsive power of a new affection." It is an over-mastering impulse which leaves no room in the mind for the old enemy. When a man falls again under the power of the sin, he need not conclude that God has not given him the aid. He has more reason to think that the aid was given, but not used. Man must work with God in such a case and must must expect to be delivered without striving, but to be delivered through striving in the new strength that God gives him. But above all there must be firm belief in Christ and his redeeming love. A mere intellectual belief is not sufficient. As James remarks, "The devils believe." Belief in the sense of trusting, confiding, is required. It is the kind of belief that a patient has in his physician when, in a critical illness, he trusts his life to a physician and calls in no other. Or, as when a man charged with murder puts all his reliance on his lawyer and believes in his power to secure his acquittal. Or it is the belief of an outlaw who trusts to a ruler who has issued a proclamation of amnesty. The man who puts himself in Christ's hands for salvation will try to resist all evil and will obey Christ's commands and will seek from Christ the help he stands ready to give to enable him to lead a holy life.

480 Are the regenerate sinless?

In the regenerate, the higher nature, as begotten of God, does not commit sin (I John 3:9). This principle within him is at absolute variance with sin and makes him hate all sin and desire to resist it. Luther, referring to this condition, wrote: "The child of God receives wounds daily and never throws away his arms, or makes peace with his deadly foe." His life is a continual warfare against sin, but he is kept by divine power from falling, although if he even momentarily permit his spiritual weapons to lie idle, he will feel the sharp attacks of sin. The ruling principle of his life is God's law, but the old nature may sometimes rebel. The passage from Hebrews 27 does not conflict with this. The passage in Hebrews 6 was written to urge advancement in the spiritual life and to warn them that the decline of spiritual energies would inevitably lead to a "falling away" and perhaps to ultimate apostasy. The warning was addressed not to the elect but to the lukewarm, who had shown a temporary faith, only to be followed by indifference.

481 Are children punished for parents' sin?

There is in the minds of many a misunderstanding of Scripture on this point. (Ex. 20:5.) Good authorities hold that it does not mean that God punishes a man for the wrongdoing of his parents, but that he is punished by the acts of the parents themselves. It is inevitable that we should be affected by what our parents have done. We enjoy the privileges of our free country because these privileges were won by our forefathers; we have freedom of worship because they fought and suffered and died to secure it. Having received good, do not we inherit evil the same way? The children of a spendthrift must lack the good start in life that they might have had; the son of a father who has disgraced his name is under a reproach. That the character, habits and wickedness of an evil parent must influence his progeny is generally admitted. Natural laws cannot be escaped, and the characteristics of a progenitor may be traced sometimes through several generations. The children who were born in Babylon, suffered in exile because their fathers had deserted God. It is a law of the natural life that the results that flow from a parent's wrongdoing are entailed on his children; but the children are not held morally accountable for the sins of their parents.

482 Is sinlessness possible?

It frequently happens that confusion arises concerning the apparent conflict of statements in the passages in I John 1:8 and 3:9. In the first of these, every one is represented as sinning, and in the latter it is clearly stated that "Whoso is born of God cannot sin." To suppose that none who sin are begotten of God would exclude every one, as John himself admits in the first passage we quote. One explanation is that the writer is speaking of the divine nature implanted in the believer. It never commits or condones sin, but always protests against it. A second explanation is that the man who is begotten of God does not continue in sin. If betrayed by his fleshly nature into sin, he repents, seeks pardon, and watches against a repetition of it. However high the Christian may set his ideal as a follower of Christ, he realizes, after all, that his efforts are sadly short of the Great Exemplar and that his imperfections are beyond dispute. At the same time, he can be said truly to be no longer under the bondage of sin, since, having laid his burden on the Great Burden-Bearer, sin is no longer imputed to him.

483 Is every sin willful and thus
every backslider doomed?

The subject is discussed in Heb. 6:4, 5, 6, and Heb. 10:26, 27. In one sense every sin is willful, because the sinner would not do it without the consent of his will; but the word has another meaning. It implies a deliberate and intentional act, which is different from an act to which a man is lured or deceived, or an act which he commits under some sudden and strong temptation. There was, for example, a marked difference between the sin of Judas and of Peter. The Apostle Paul, too, bade the church at Corinth restore the wrongdoer who had been expelled (II Cor. 2:6-8). Be sure of this, that any backslider repenting and turning to God for pardon, resolutely putting his sin away, will be welcomed and forgiven (See Ezek. 33:14-16, and many other passages).

484 Are all sins pardonable?

Divine mercy extends to the uttermost. The invitation is that "whosoever will may come." The "unpardonable sin," which was frequently spoken of in the early days of the Church, is believed to have been attributing the works of the Holy Spirit to the powers of darkness. With this exception, there is nothing in the category of human offenses that is beyond the reach of divine forgiveness. "Although your sins be like scarlet, they shall be white as snow," is the ancient promise given by God to men; "though they be like crimson, they shall be as wool." This is not to be interpreted, however, as an encouragement to sin, but rather as an inducement to repentance. If the sinner truly repents, imploring God's forgiveness for Jesus' sake; if he accepts him as Saviour and endeavors, with divine help, to live thereafter a Christian life, he will not only be forgiven, but will be kept from falling back into sin. This is the teaching of the Gospel, and it is exemplified in innumerable cases today. We have many instances everywhere of great sinners who have forsaken their evil ways and who are now living the new life, sustained by divine power.

> "There's a wideness in God's mercy
> Like the wideness of the sea."

We have the Saviour's distinct assurance, "Him that cometh unto me, I will in no wise cast out." There is no punishment for sins that are forgiven. "Jesus paid it all."

485 Is the unpardonable sin possible today?

In ancient times, it was generally held that the unpardonable sin (Matt. 12:32) was attributing the works of the Holy Spirit to Satanic agency. If there be a modern counterpart of the unpardonable sin, we should think it is to be found in the case of the person who uses the livery of God to serve the devil in; who enacts the role of the shepherd of the sheep, while he is nothing but a ravening wolf in disguise; who assumes the attitude, language and demeanor of a saint while his exterior covers a heart black with sin and foul with guilt; who brings to the altar of God's house hands that are stained with crime, and who keeps up this show of religion and utters the language of Christian invitation while he himself is not a Christian. It is a terrible picture and one which is almost unimaginable in the case of any sane and responsible person.

486 Is it sinful to do what one considers wrong even though there is no wrong about it?

That is Paul's teaching, as he particularly outlines and emphasizes it in Rom. 14; I Cor. 8 and I Cor. 10:23-33. He said himself that he did not consider it wrong to eat meat which might have been offered to idols (I Cor. 8:4, 8; I Cor. 10:25, 27), but that if he knew of any one who might be offended by his doing so he would eat no meat at all (I Cor. 8:13). In Rom. 14:20 he says: "All things indeed are pure, but it is evil for that man who eateth with offense"— that is, for the man who eats, even though it troubles his conscience. The same thought is in Rom. 14:23: "Whatsoever is not of faith is sin." But our reason bears out this New Testament teaching; we know that it is wrong for a man to do something which he believes to be wrong. The whole spirit of the New Testament is away from legalism and toward a spontaneous, affectionate eagerness to please God and serve our neighbor. Where no command or prohibition is specified, each Christian is left free to follow his own enlightened conscience. To violate this is sin.

487 Is it natural or unnatural to ⁻in?

Judging by the prevalence of sin and the early age at which children usually begin, we should say it was natural. David seemed to have that opinion (see Ps. 51:5). It was not much better before the fall. Adam and Eve do not appear, according to the account in Genesis, to have made much resistance to temptation. The fact of its being natural accounts for a new nature being necessary, as Christ explained to Nicodemus (John 3:1-21).

488 How may we win souls?

"How can I win souls" is a frequent question from beginners in Christian life. They remember the injunction: "He that winneth souls is wise." (Prov. 11:30.) The first impulse which comes to the newborn soul in Christ is to tell some one else of the glad experience and to bring some one else to the Saviour. The first requisite for the work of soul-winning is to have a definite experience which makes its possessor long to have others share it. The most important element of soul-winning is simple testimony to the grace of God. There must be consistent and careful living, for it is difficult or impossible to win others to Christ when one's own life does not exemplify the teachings of the Master. The Bible must be mastered by one who would be a successful soul-winner. He must have in his mind, or be able to reach quickly, passages which will meet the difficulties of those whom he tries to win. There must be also a sympathetic study of human nature. The soul-winner must understand the workings and problems of the hearts and minds he tries to reach. Then, there must be continued activity. Mr. Moody made it a rule to speak definitely to at least one person about his soul's welfare every day. Above all, the power of the Holy Spirit must be sought and found to give wisdom and power, by which alone real success in soul-winning is to be found.

489 Is a Christian justified in suing to recover a loan?

It depends upon circumstances. If his debtor is able but refuses to pay, there is nothing in Christ's meaning to prevent the Christian from appealing to law to recover what is justly his, after all peaceable means have failed. The Revised Version of Luke 6:35 reads? "Lend, never despairing" (margin, "despairing of no man"). We are to be kind to those of whom we can expect no return in sort. God will repay us, though man does not. "It is meant of the rich lending to the poor a little money for their necessity to buy daily bread or to keep them out of prison; in such a case we must lend with the resolution not to demand interest for what we lend, as we may most justly from those that borrow money to make purchases withal or to trade with; but that is not all, we must lend though we have reason to suspect that what we lend we lose; lend to those who are so poor that it is not probable they will be able to pay us again. This precept will be best illustrated by that law of Moses (Deu. 15:7-10) which obliges them to lend to a poor brother as much as he needed, though the year of release was at hand." This is an old commentator's explanation, but it is good and true.

490 Does temptation come from God?

Human nature is weak and temptations to wrongdoing are abundant. Occasionally we hear, at a church meeting, or elsewhere, some dissatisfied soul complaining that he has been tempted and he is disposed to lay the blame for his condition on the Heavenly Father. Now, God does not tempt any one. He permits us to be placed in positions where, if left to our own resources, we would fail; but he does not tempt us to evil, and if we call for his aid, we will assuredly receive it. It is the evil spirit within us and the evil influences about us that bring us into temptation. In I Cor. 10:13 and James 1:13 it is explicitly stated that while God may permit us to be tested, he is not the tempter, and that he "tempts no man." The withdrawal of the Holy Spirit exposes us to temptations by leaving the heart open to the attack of the tempter; but nothing is more erroneous than to assume that temptation, or the placing of any agent in man's spiritual path which may cause him to fall, comes from God.

491 Is it a sin to be tempted?

We are not responsible for our temptations, but for yielding to and encouraging them. The sin consists in asquiescence. Christ himself was tempted. God tempts no man, but the evil spirit in our own hearts tempts us. If you will ask God, in Christ's name, to free you from these temptations and to purify your mind and heart, the temptations will have no power over you. They will come again and again, but will retire baffled and defeated. It is the only way. Christ's prayer (taught to his disciples), is better interpreted: "Abandon us not in temptation" (the power of the tempter), and not "remove us from temptation." It is a part of our earthly discipline.

492 What are tithes?

The question of tithing has been frequently discussed and is ever a fruitful one. A tithe is a tenth of the increase over and above all administrative expenses and not a tenth of the principal. In early days, when agriculture was the almost universal calling, it was generally a tenth part of the produce of the land or the flocks. Later it became a tenth of the profits of personal industry of any character. (See Deu. 14:22, 28, 16:12; II Chron. 31:5, etc.) There is evidence, however, that at certain times it may have meant a tenth of one's entire possessions. The modern interpretation would limit it to a tenth of the increase. There are many good people who still hold that a tenth of one's income should be set aside for the Lord's work. Under the ancient Jewish economy, tithing was regulated by a code of laws which were amplified and made still more complex by the rabbins; but under Christianity, the supreme law of love has been substituted and is applicable to the tithing problem quite as well as to others. We are to give according as God has "prospered us," and from a generous and loving heart. One who wishes to tithe his estate should reckon on the increase in value, or number, or whatever form his available assets may assume, excluding of course the necessary expenses of conducting his business. As to household expenses, these are elastic, and one's domestic and personal expenditures are liable to increase with every augmentation of income, such increase frequently being one of extravagance rather than of necessity. It is quite conceivable that the whole income might be thus swallowed up. But if we act conscientiously, we will not "rob God" by multiplying our expenditures until nothing is left for his work. "The liberal soul shall be made fat," and this especially applies to the character of our gifts to God's work. While we are not to devote to that work money which we may rightfully owe to our creditors, we can exercise self-denial in many things, so that our tithable "increase" (or, if no increase, then our surplus over and above all proper expenses) may be such as to assure a liberal gift to the cause of religion.

God is a creditor, too. A very large per cent of the people of the United States are in debt. Surely, it would not be right for them to stop all payments to the church and to charity till they are out of debt. While they and their families are getting the benefits of the church they ought to pay their church dues just as they pay their taxes and their rent. Your creditors would not expect you to neglect to pay for the food which your body needs; they should not expect you to neglect to pay for your soul food. Remember, however, that a tithe is required not on the gross earnings or income, but on the "increase."

When Jesus stood by the treasury, he called attention to the fact that while the rich had cast in gifts of their superfluity, the poor widow had done better than they, for she had cast in "all her living" as a love offering, and it was an acceptable one. If we are to lavish all our prosperity on ourselves and our families, leaving nothing for the Lord's work, may we not be "robbing God"? Practically all of the difficulties involved in the problem would be solved if we followed the method of many Christians, who have been rich both in prosperity and good works. They gave freely from the *increase* of their wealth which remained after absolutely necessary business expenses were covered, making the Lord a partner in all that remained.

An offering we do not feel, and which is simply of our surplus, is a gift of comparatively little worth, no matter how large the sum, while one that involves self-denial and even sacrifice, given with a cheerful heart, is rewarded with blessing. Still, the spirit in which we give is what counts. We should not plan so that our gifts to God return to ourselves or inure to our material benefit. Whatever is given to the Lord's work, whether administered personally with our own hands or through the church or its subsidiary organizations, or through any other channel, should be put wholly away from us so that we cannot derive any material benefit from the outlay. It is not giving to the Lord at all, if we attach a string to the gift.

493 In what sense are we to understand Scriptural "inspiration"?

In II Tim. 3:16 the statement is clear that the Scripture is given by divine inspiration—that the perceptions and work of the writers were divinely influenced. The Holy Spirit filled the hearts of those men with a message and led them to write that message for the world. This is what inspiration means. The inspired writers were holy men, prophets, evangelists and spiritual leaders who lived close to God and were in constant communication with him through prayer and meditation, and who, by their hearts and lives thus consecrated, were endowed with the power to convey to men his Word, sometimes in one form, sometimes in another. They were the chosen channels of divine communication, interpreting God's purposes in authoritative language, which could be understood by those for whom it was intended.

494 What significance was John's Baptism?

John's baptism was not regarded as conferring an immediate consecration, but as being preparatory; and the disciples of Jesus, taking this view, rebaptized the followers of John (see Acts 19:3-5).

495 Did Jesus baptize?

Whether our Lord personally baptized has been doubted. The only passage which may bear on the question is John 4:1, 2, the explanation of which is presumed to be that John, being a servant, baptized with his own hand, while Christ as Lord and Master "baptized with the Holy Ghost," demonstrating the outward symbols through his disciples. Whether he baptized personally or not, the fact remains that, during his earthly ministry, baptism was the accepted mode of entering his service.

496 What does the Bible teach about borrowing and usury?

The most radical reference to money lending is that of Christ himself (Luke 6:35), "Do good and lend, hoping for nothing again." But it must be remembered that the words were spoken to a people very differently situated from ourselves. In our society the convenience of loans at interest is a benefit to lender and borrower alike. If the practice of taking interest were absolutely forbidden, both borrower and lender would suffer, as the capitalist would be little likely to lend money if he had no compensation, and the borrower would be unable to get the capital he needs for carrying on his business. The general tenor of Bible teaching seems to be that the lender has no right to take advantage of the borrower's necessities to exact more than a fair rate of interest. Many loans are in the nature of a limited partnership, and the borrower is simply paying the lender a share of the profit he makes out of the capital supplied by the lender, which is a legitimate transaction. References to usury in the Old Testament are found in Ps. 15:5; Nehem. 5:11; Prov. 28:8, and Leviticus 25:35-37.

497 How can Christians justify war?

How do you think Joshua, Gideon, David and other Old Testament saints felt about it? Do you suppose they did not know of the commandment "Thou shalt not kill" ? They do not appear to have found any difficulty in reconciling their duty with it. Samuel could scarcely have been ignorant of it, yet he did not hesitate to hew a man to pieces in cold blood (I Sam. 15:33); Saul was blamed for sparing him, as Ahab afterwards was blamed (I Kings 20:42) for similar lenity. Elijah appears to have been a good man, yet he butchered 450 men (I Kings 18:40) in spite of the Commandment, "Thou shalt not kill." If you insist on literal obedience to the Commandment, we do not see how you can justify the butcher in his trade, since the Commandment (Exodus 20:13) does not limit the prohibition to human life. The ablest authorities agree that the Commandment is to be understood in its spirit. It prohibits murder, in the sense in which the word is commonly used. It does not prohibit wars of defense or war in a righteous cause. Men like Washington, Havelock and Chinese Gordon, and Stonewall Jackson, were conscientious men and eminent Christians, yet they went to war without compunction when their duty required it. On the other hand war is universally acknowledged as an evil and the logical outcome of evil conditions. It is the duty of the Christian to make war on war and to hasten to bring about peace with all men. The ideal condition is that which is pictured in Is. 2:4.

498 Why were women commanded
to keep silence in the church?

In I Corinthians 14:34 Paul was dealing specifically with the case of a church which he himself had founded. He had received intelligence from the household of Chloe, a pious member (see 1:11), that serious schisms had arisen and that advice was sorely needed. From other sources he had learned that the church had sunk into corruption and error. Apparently four distinct factions had sprung up, all quarreling over their respective teachers. There was much bitterness in the situation, and, besides, he had learned that immorality and disorderly practices had crept in; also that their meetings were brought into disrepute by the women appearing in them unveiled (in defiance of the common usage among decent women of that time) and that the feasts of the church were often scenes of gluttony and excess. His epistle was written to correct these disgraceful conditions, to set matters right, to rebuke the offenders and to set before them all anew the essentials of the Gospel. We can only infer, from the general contents of the entire epistle, that certain women who had been active in fomenting the trouble had merited a share of his chastening message, which doubtless produced the desired effect. Elsewhere in the Epistles we find full recognition of the character and abilities of Christian women, although it is unquestioned that they did not in those days take as prominent a part in religious affairs as they did later. Thus, for instance, there is no mention of women in Acts 2:16-18, but this does not necessarily imply their exclusion. There are many passages in the New Testament which show that godly women had a good share in the activities of the early church, but it was not customary for them to teach or preach (see Acts 16:40, 17:12, 17:34, etc.). Paul's injunction was not intended as a message to all the churches, but to the one particular church at Corinth, and it is a mistake and a grievous injustice to apply it to women in general. They have borne too noble and useful a part in the progress of the Christian religion to be subjected to any needless criticism that could only be based on a misunderstanding as to the actual conditions in the Corinthian church which rendered such a message necessary. There are many instances of godly women in both the Old Testament and the New Testament. The ministry of Jesus was to both men and women equally. Many of his most devoted followers were women. They were the last to comfort him on the way to Golgotha, the first to visit his tomb and the first to whom he appeared at his resurrection. So why should good women today be excluded from taking part in any Christian activity?

499 Is it proper to "make a gladsome noise" in worship?

Christianity is a religion less of the head than of the heart, and it is not surprising that the joy of the heart should find expression in songs and even at times in shouting. These are the natural, unrestrained outlets of a soul filled with deep religious fervor and spiritual gladness. Scripture literally teems with invitations to God's people to such expressions of feeling. Ezra 3:13 tells of the "noise of the shout of joy" at the laying of the foundations of the Temple. In Psalm 33:3, the congregation is urged to sing new songs and make a "loud noise," and in Is.

42:10, we read "let them shout and declare his praise"; Job 38:7 relates that the "sons of God shouted for joy," while Psalm 65:13, describing the condition of the righteous who had been blessed with prosperity, says, "they shout for joy . . . they also sing." "Let them that put their trust in thee rejoice," says the Psalmist (Ps. 5:11), "let them shout for joy." In marked contrast is the picture in Is. 16:10, of the unrighteous from whom the Lord has turned his face, "There is no singing, neither shall there be any shouting." Surely the Christian who feels his heart overflowing with joy and gratitude to God, has the best of all warrants for publishing his gladness to the world, if he be so minded. We quite understand, however, that there are many natures so quiet and reserved that they do not relish any exuberance and prefer to be moderate in their manifestations. In a majority of cases, religious enthusiasm is a matter of temperament, each kind proper in its own place.

500 What precedent do the Scriptures furnish for solos, duets, and choir singing in church?

In I Cor. 14:26, Paul, referring to the forms of worship of the Corinthian church, wrote: "When ye come together, every one of you hath a psalm, etc." This verse, especially when read in connection with verse 15, "I will sing with the spirit and I will sing with the understanding also," implies that certain members sang alone. Tertullian and Augustine refer to this custom: "Every one," says Tertullian, "was invited in their public worship to sing unto God according to his ability, either from the Scriptures or one indited by himself." These songs were often extemporaneous. From the time of the Song of Miriam, who either sang alone in response to the other women, or led off their singing (Ex. 15:20, 21) there have been special singers and groups of singers to lead the music in the worship of God. The organization of the ancient Hebrew choirs was very elaborate. (See II Sam. 6:5; I Chron. chapters 15, 16, 23, 25, etc.) The congregation of Israel was so enormous that it was difficult if not impossible for all the people to sing at once; and the songs were learned first by the great choirs and must have been sung first by them before the people learned them; but there is no reason for believing that all the congregation joined in all the songs. Many consecrated Gospel singers are rendering acceptable worship and service to God in solos, duets, quartets and choruses. One is undoubtedly right in holding that such music should be really spiritual, should be sung without show, simply, clearly, earnestly to the glory of God. The body of church singing should be by the congregation as a whole, but the special solos and choir numbers also have their place.

TEXTS, FAMILIAR AND OTHER

**501 What is conveyed in the statement,
"God is no respecter of persons"?**

It may seem peculiar for Peter to have made this statement (Acts 10:34, 35) as to the vast majority of reverent minds it goes without saying. But to Peter, brought up as he had been among Pharisees and Sadducees and other religionists of the Old Dispensation, whose central belief was that God *was* a respecter of persons, the discovery of the great truth that God cares for all alike, came as a great awakening. The Pharisee who loved the uppermost seats in the synagogues and greetings in the market-places; who deliberately shunned contact with a publican, a woman or a Gentile, represented that self-righteous and exclusive Judaism in which no one else counted, but in which he was a favorite of the Most High. This exclusive Judaism Peter annihilated with the one sentence of the text, and thereby established the belief in that great, universal Fatherhood which, while it is all to all, is especially kind to the lowly and the meek; which watches even a sparrow and numbers even the hair of our heads. And because of this universal Fatherhood, everyone in every nation "that feareth him and doeth righteousness" is acceptable to him. He makes no distinctions of creeds, of theologies, of usages and customs, of observances and differences of opinions.

**502 In what sense is it true that, "The Lord
giveth and the Lord taketh away"?**

When we use the customary phrase that God takes away any of our friends from this world, it is simply a familiar form of acknowledging submission to his will as the Disposer of all things. Life and death are in his hands. There is nothing irreverent about such an expression. All our blessings come from him and if trial and discipline also come we should accept them in the proper spirit. We should learn to bow to his will, even though it may sometimes try our hearts sorely to do so.

**503 What is meant by the passage, "Seek ye
the Lord while he may be found"?**

It is a wholesome warning that a probable contingency may arise when the seeker, who postpones his search, may lose his power or disposition to seek. There are many instances of men who have put off seeking until they have made a fortune, or done something else, and then the time they set, having arrived, discover that business habits and long-time associations absorb them. They are out of touch with God. Even in church their thoughts are running on worldly concerns. It is very rare for an old man who has been indifferent, or careless, or wicked, to turn to God. Not that God is unwilling to be found, but the man has become incapable of seeking him. None who really seek ever fail to find.

504 What is the extent of the parallel between Christ and Adam?

"As by the offense of one, judgment came upon all men to condemnation, even so by the righteousness of one the free gift came upon all men unto justification of life" (Rom. 5:18). In this passage, Paul is comparing the influence of Adam and Christ. His argument begins with verse 12: "By one man sin entered into the world, and death by sin." (Dr. Denny says: "By Adam the race was launched upon a course of sin.") Paul goes on to state that sin was in the world before the written law was given, but declares that sin is not counted as sin where there is no law. God does not condemn a man for breaking a law of which he is ignorant. But even where sin was not imputed, death reigned, because death had come into the world as the result of Adam's sin, and became a universal experience, affecting even those who broke no specific and plainly stated command, as Adam did. But the grace that comes from Christ is even greater than the doom that came through Adam. One man sinned, and many were condemned; grace, through Christ, pardons many sins. Death reigned because of one man; now abundance of life and grace reign by one, Jesus Christ (verse 17). Verse 18 (quoted above) sums up what has gone before. Adam's disobedience made many men sinners; Christ's obedience shall make many righteous (verse 19). The law was given so that sin might be revealed. Sin was in the human heart, but men did not realize what it was till the law came. The law showed them that they were disobeying God. "But where sin abounded, grace did much more abound;" there was sin for everybody, there is grace for everybody—and more grace than sin. The reign of sin brings death; the reign of grace brings eternal life.

505 What is meant by, "As many as were ordained to eternal life believed"?

This passage in Acts 13:48 has been much discussed. Those Gentiles did not all become believers, but only those in whom the preaching of the apostles had awakened faith and who, being taken into the congregation, had striven earnestly to "make their calling and election sure." It forcibly reminds us that salvation is the gift of God and not in any sense something we can obtain by our own merit or acts; but at the same time, in order to attain this gift (which is divinely ordained to all those who comply with certain conditions), we must put ourselves in the attitude of faith and belief. Further, throughout the whole Scriptures, there is a pervading sense of the fact that many are specially called to be saints and to perform a certain work, who are obedient to the summons and yet who were not in such attitude before. The case of Paul is an illustration in point. He was called right out of the midst of his sinful life of persecution. Some commentators hold that in the case of these Gentiles, God had chosen for himself certain men to become witness-bearers and to be set apart for a special work. Still other translators make the passage read: "As many as disposed themselves to eternal life believed," referring to I Cor. 16:15. We may add, by way of further explanation, that while the call to salvation is a universal one, the call to *special service* is one that comes only to the few.

506 Did the Baptist doubt Jesus' messiahship?

John's message, asking through his disciples whom he sent to Jesus, "Art thou he that should come, or look we for another?" (Matt. 11:3), was the result of impatience, almost of desperation. It must have seemed hard to him that his Master should let him lie so long in prison, after having been honored to announce and introduce him at the beginning of his mission. He tried to get Jesus to speak out his mind, or at least to set his own mind at rest. The conclusion of the incident, however, shows that his transient doubts were set at rest by the message he received.

507 What is meant by, "Buy the truth and sell it not"?

The passage in Prov. 23:23—"buy the truth and sell it not"—is not to be interpreted as meaning that both the buying and selling must be wrong. On the contrary, the meaning is that we should get the truth, whatever it may cost us, and that we should not part with it for any consideration, money, pleasure, fame, etc., for it is more precious than all of these. (See Prov. 4:5-7.) The inspired teacher urges us to get the principal thing, the truth, wisdom, understanding; the world's motto is: "Get riches and with all thy getting get more."

508 Are any by nature "children of God"?

There is a large and true sense in which all mankind are children of God. Paul could say to the idolaters at Athens, "We are also his offspring." But there is a higher, closer, nearer sense in which regenerated men only are God's children. John says: "To as many as received him, to them gave he power to become the sons of God." Speaking pointedly to believers, he says, "Beloved, now are we the sons of God." So there is no discrepancy between Paul and John. The one is speaking of God's children in the large human sense, while the other speaks of them in the restricted, adopted sense. We have, in fact, to recognize four grades of sonship. In the lowest grade there is the whole human family. In the next higher grade we have the regenerated children, who are really children in the spirit. Then in the next grade, we have the angels, who in the Book of Job are specially designated the "Sons of God" (38:7). Then, highest of all, in a sense absolute, unapproachable, divine, we have Jesus Christ, pre-eminently God's own Son. There is no need, therefore, to stumble at the doctrine of the Fatherhood of God; only we need to distinguish between what is implied in the more outward and the more inward relationship.

509 Why is there no remission of sin without the shedding of blood?

The thought of a sacrifice for sin underlies the whole message of the Bible. The fact that John 3:17; John 8:11, 12 and other promises do not specifically refer to this does not violate in any way the broad, general principle. The Bible as a whole states the method by which God undertakes to save people from sin. The Old Testament, in law and ceremony and prophecy, looks forward to a great sacrifice that is to be made, of which the sacrifice of animals is but a type. The Epistles of the New Testament explain how the sacrifice of Christ may be applied by faith to the human soul. The Gospels tell the story of the life of the Saviour and give with great detail and fulness the account of his sacrificial death. He himself said distinctly of his death (Matt. 26:28), "This is my blood of the new testament, which is shed for many for the remission of sins." Read with special care the 9th and 10th chapters of Hebrews, the 5th and 6th chapters of Romans; I John 1:7, and the many other passages which state clearly that salvation from sin is wrought by the sacrifice of Christ. The fact of the atonement underlies all the promises of Scripture. It seems idle, as well as dangerous, to speculate whether there may be or might have been some other way of salvation. This way fits in with our knowledge of nature and of life, and has been testified to by multitudes of redeemed souls. We *know* that through the blood of Christ salvation from sin can be found; we certainly do not know that it can be found in any other way.

510 What is meant by "crucifying the Son of God afresh"?

Heb. 6:4-6 is interpreted to refer to those who having begun the spiritual life, instead of persevering toward perfection, allowed themselves to fall away or backslide. Such having already had knowledge of the word of truth and having experienced a measure of peace in the pardoning love of Christ and the bestowal of the gift of the Holy Spirit (though not in all fulness) were doubly to blame for falling away. Paul did not assert that the Hebrews themselves had yet so fallen, but he warned them that if they did not persevere in going on to perfection, they would retrograde and would need to be "renewed" over again. It is the deliberate apostate, however, who sins in the light of knowledge and crucifies Christ anew whom he holds up as an object of execration. The elect abide in Christ and do not fall away, and he who abides not is "cast forth as a withered branch." The marginal reading of verse 6 in the Revised Versions makes this passage harmonize with the whole spirit of the Bible. It is impossible to renew them to repentance "*the while* they crucify the Son of God afresh."

511 What is meant by "laying aside every weight"?

The passage in Heb. 12:1 means that we are to personally apply discipline, and with divine help to thrust from us all temptations to carnal and worldly indulgence, which would impede our progress in the spiritual race. These obstacles are of the character mentioned in Mark 9:42-48; Eph. 4:22; Col. 3:9, 10. In practical terms, we should include undesirable and unprofitable amusements, doubtful associates, foolish pride, habitual ill-nature or worry, planning things far ahead, striving for social show for appearance's sake, deceitfulness, gossip, profanity, exaggeration or untruth—in a word, the "familiar sins," and especially the one which does "so easily beset us," whatever it may be. All of these act as chains and drags to hold us back.

512 Why did David say he had "not seen the righteous forsaken nor his seed begging bread"?

The psalmist (Ps. 37:25) simply stated his own experience. He had never seen it. He did not say it never occurred. If it did not occur in his day, it does in ours. It ought not, and God never designed that it should. There is enough wealth in the world to provide food and clothing and shelter for all, but under our present system some get more than their share, and others suffer and some starve. If a good man, though he be the seed of the righteous, acts imprudently, or is wasteful, or speculates unwisely, God does not interfere to keep him from ruin.

513 Is it possible for one to be over-righteous?

Commentators interpret the phrase "righteous overmuch" (Ecc. 7:16) as descriptive of religious presumption; of that self-made righteousness which would lay the greatest stress upon outward performances and would claim personal credit for results which the true believer recognizes as the gift of divine grace alone. Pharisaism, with its hypocritical assumption of superior virtue, its multitudinous observances and its devotion to form and ceremonial, forgetting the "things of the spirit," was the type of the over-righteous.

514 How was the term *saint* first applied to the evangelists?

During the early days of the Christian Church, there was no authoritative use of the word "Saint" as a title. Wherever the word occurs in our New Testament, it simply means a "devout person," one who has been sanctified and specially consecrated. After the early Christian era, however, the martyrs and apostles were considered as having attained to the dignity of sainthood, although there was no formal canonization until the ninth century A. D., when the Church of Rome introduced formal canonization with special ceremonies. There is no definite rule in the Protestant Church on the use of the title "Saint." The modern Jews have their saints, as well as the Catholics, and the appellation they use is "Kadosh." Their most celebrated saint is Rabbi Judah Hak-kadosh ("Rabbi Judah the Holy"). Protestant writers are not as consistent as they ought to be in this matter, some applying the title and others not at all. The observance of saints' days applies specially to the Roman and the Oriental Catholic Churches. In the Russo-Greek Church the observance of such days has been carried to extremes and they are so numerous as to interfere seriously with business. Under the influence of the Church of Rome in America, saints' days are becoming numerous among Catholics here also.

515 What are we to understand by, "Time and chains happeneth to them all"?

You are not to take all the words of Ecclesiastes 9:11 as true and inspired because, as the writer shows, he found out that what he said at one time was disproved later on. He is relating his experience. He was seeking happiness, with everything in favor of his succeeding. At first he believed he would find it in pleasure, afterward in learning, and later in other ways. And he tells how he found again and again that he had been mistaken. In this particular passage he means that the misfortunes of life are just as likely to happen to the wise and good as to the foolish. We know it is so. In a railroad accident, for instance, a clergyman or a philanthropist does not escape simply because of his life being beneficent.

516 What is meant by, "Cast thy bread upon the waters"?

The illustration in Ecclesiastes 11:1 is taken from the custom of sowing seed by casting it from the boats into the overflowing Nile, or in marshy ground. When the waters recede, the grain in the alluvial soil springs up. "Waters" expresses multitudes, whose seemingly hopeless character as recipients of charity may turn out better than we anticipate, so that our gift would prove at last not to have been thrown away. The day may be near when we ourselves may need the help of those whom we have bound to us by kindness.

517 What does Paul mean in Romans 5:7?

"For scarcely for a righteous man will one die; yet peradventure for a good man some would even dare to die" (Rom. 5:7). The apostle is illustrating the fact of the Atonement by the facts of everyday life. He says it is hard to find one man who will die for another, even if that other be righteous; but that for a man who is really *good* (a stronger, warmer word than *righteous*) some might be found who would be willing to die. Then follows the keen application: Though we were neither good nor righteous, yet Christ died for us.

518 What is meant by, "Where there is no vision the people perish"?

"Vision" (Prov. 29:18) means communion with God and the revelation of his will. When communities or nations get out of touch with God and cease to know his will, they begin to perish. The Hebrew verb means to become "dissipated" and "unbridled" and so perish—in a word, to lose sight of moral and spiritual ideals, as a nation or community. Individual Christians and the organized church should be constantly seeking a clearer sight of God, closer communion with him, and a more perfect understanding both of his revealed will in the Scriptures and his providential will in present-day concerns.

519 What is meant by, "All things work together for good to them that love God"?

This passage (Rom. 8:28) means that the events of life, including things that we call misfortunes, will be over-ruled to spiritual advantage. The Christian is not promised immunity from trouble, but that his troubles will tend to make him a better man. He is not encouraged to seek discipline, or to act recklessly, with the idea that howsoever an enterprise turns out, it will benefit him. But if after he has sought divine guidance and if after he has carefully considered a matter, it turns out disastrously, he is not to be cast down, but to expect that in some way God will make the disaster a blessing to him.

520 How can "one vessel be chosen unto honor and another unto dishonor"?

This passage (Rom. 9:21, 23) brings up the discussion of the whole subject of "election." The Jews seem to have gotten the idea, from their long habit of exclusiveness, that God had no right to offer salvation to the Gentiles. Paul is here trying to make them see that God has a right to offer salvation to any one. No one can dispute the fact that just as the potter has the right to form one vessel for high and honorable use and another for more humble service, so God has the right to create some souls for prominent and important and honorable service and others for more lowly tasks. However we may interpret the doctrine of election, we must not for an instant forget that God is just. "He is not willing that any should perish." He desires that every soul should have salvation and that every soul shall be fitted for successful service.

521 What did Paul mean by "delivering" an offender unto Satan?

As the apostle himself states explicitly it was that the offender might be saved (see I Cor. 5:5). The man, a member of the Corinthian Church, had fallen into grievous sin, and was living a vicious life. Paul, hearing of it, decides that he must be excluded from the church. He repented, as the event proved, for in his second epistle Paul directs that he shall be tenderly received, lest he be swallowed up by over-much sorrow (II Cor. 2:7). The exclusion was leaving the man without means of grace, and Paul tells the object of it, namely, that the flesh, that is, the lusts and passions of his nature, might be purged from him, so that his soul might be saved. The casting of him out of the Church meant, in Paul's mind, the giving him up to punishment and the will of the enemy, not for his eternal destruction, but for temporary chastisement. Some commentators have thought that Paul's sentence included the infliction of some malady, which he certainly did inflict in another case (Acts 13:11), but that is not directly stated. The words imply discipline that would render the man less under the influence of his fleshly appetites. The man is put out of the church, the fold of God, temporarily, on account of his wrongdoing. It was probably so persistent and inexcusable that the apostle despaired of Christian influences effecting a change. He must be made to feel how wicked he was, and by the church expelling him they practically gave him up for the time. This was probably regarded as delivering him to Satan. They ceased to bring Christian love to bear upon him. In at least one case, it is thought, the discipline had a good effect, if, as is probable, the offender is the one referred to in II Cor. 2:6-8.

522 What is meant by showing "the Lord's death till he come"?

This passage in I Cor. 11:26 has been variously discussed. Is it the Lord's presence, the coming to take away his followers by death, or his coming to judge the world that is here meant? The best expositors hold that the apostle clearly referred to the significance of the Lord's Supper as a perpetual memorial of the Lord's death, to be observed by the Church until the end of this dispensation, or in his own words, "till he come." It could not have had reference to the Lord's spiritual presence, or to the believer's death, as Paul implied that the "coming" would terminate the observance. It must have referred to the coming he describes in I Thess. 2:1-8 and other places, when Christ will appear to call his waiting people to himself, and afterward descend to destroy his enemies and set up his millennial kingdom on the earth.

523 What did Paul mean by "caught up to the third heaven"?

Paul was familiar with the learning of his age, and was a "master" in literary expression. He sat as a pupil "at the feet of Gamaliel," who was celebrated in the Talmudist writings as one of the seven teachers to whom the title "rabbin" was given. In II Cor. 12 (which contains the passage in question) Paul speaks of his vision when he was "caught up to the third heaven." In the Jewish teaching of the time, the first heaven was that of the clouds or the air; the second that of the stars and the sky, and the third was the spiritual heaven, the seat of divine glory. The word "heavens" is used in the Bible in varying senses, which must be gathered from the context, the most familiar being the visible heavens, as distinguished from the earth and as a part of the whole creation. (See Gen. 1:1.) Paul's "third heaven" was thus higher than the aerial or stellar world, and cognizable not by the eye, but by the mind alone. The word "world" is generally used in Scripture in the purely material sense to refer to the habitable earth and its people. The passages in Heb. 4:3, 9:26, 9:5, 11:7, 11:38, etc., have thus material significance. In John 14:2, however, many interpreters recognize an implied recognition of other worlds, the whole universe being a "house of many mansions."

524 What are we to understand by, "Work out your own salvation"?

Grace is inactive without our will, hence the order as to "work." "Fear and trembling" simply mean the holy reverence which accompanies obedience (see Eph. 6:5; I Cor. 2:3; II Cor. 7:15); not slavish fear, like the terror of a mind in danger of condemnation, but anxiety to do what the Lord would have us do, and the realization that our own merits are insufficient and we must trust him to give strength for our weakness. The last clause of the sentence (verse 14) confirms this interpretation.

525 What is meant by being "baptized with the Holy Spirit"?

The Holy Spirit is received at conversion, but the baptism with the Holy Spirit is a further enduement, an experience which comes usually at some time after conversion. The disciples were regenerated men when Jesus told them to tarry in the city of Jerusalem until they should be baptized with the Holy Spirit (Acts 1:4-5). This was the experience to which he had previously referred as the coming of the Comforter (John 14, 15, 16). God's Spirit is constantly trying to get into a man's heart. He speaks to him in many ways, convicting of sin, urging to repentance, etc. The impressions leading to a wise and safe course of action, which a man may receive before he is converted, are really the messages of the Holy Spirit. God is very good, and tries to help us in every way. But it is not until one has become a child of God and received the fullness of the Spirit that he can expect to have the clear guidance of the Holy Spirit.

THE HEREAFTER

526 Were the Jews taught to look forward to a heaven or hell?

From the first mention of the tree of life in Paradise, the eating of which would make immortal, the idea of a continued existence has had a place in Jewish theology. Many passages might be quoted to show this belief. See the Mosaic injunctions against necromancy, or the invocation of the dead, Deu. 18:9-12; I Sam. 28; Ps. 106:28 and other passages. Moses wrote that God "took" Enoch (Gen. 5:22, 24), because he had lived a pious life. David speaks of his child in another life when he says, "I will go to him, but he shall not return to me," (see II Sam. 12:23), Job says (Job 19:26 and 27) that he "will see God for himself and not another" in the future life. Ecclesiastes, which doubtless echoed faithfully the theology of that day, shows very clearly the belief in a spiritual life (Ecc. 12:7); see also the allusions in the Psalms (the Jewish Psalter) to expectations of reward and punishment after death (Ps. 17:15, 49:15, 16, 73:24, 26, 28). These and other passages which might be quoted, make it certain that the ancient Jews did believe in a future life; but it is equally certain that they had only dim and uncertain views on the subject, and that the full knowledge was not attained by any race or nation on earth until Christ himself came to "bring life and immortality to light."

527 Did there exist a belief in immortality before the Christian era?

Although before the dawn of Christianity there were nations who undoubtedly had glimpses of immortality, it was not until Christ came, "bringing life and immortality to light" (II Tim. 1:10), that the world began to realize the glorious future which was assured to those that love God and follow obediently the teachings of his Son. The Hindus, Egyptians, Chinese, Persians, and even the American Indians, Polynesians, Australian aborigines and Greenlanders believed in a future life, but all more or less dimly. The ancient Greeks had a clearer conception of immortality, which was well defined by Socrates in his last speech. There are hints of the same belief in the Jewish teachings also, although they are indefinite (see Gen. 5:22, 24, 37:35 and other passages). Jesus lifted the veil. Some, today, deny the inherent immortality of the soul, while admitting that it is conferred as the "gift of God" upon those who are accepted. The Church of Christ today, however, teaches immortality— a future life of bliss or of woe, to be decided at the judgment. The duty of Christians is, as Paul urges, to strive to "win the prize" and so to begin to live eternally, here and now, in the realization of God's pardon and acceptance promised through his Son.

528 What does *damnation* mean?

Damnation, or condemnation, does not always imply the final loss of the soul. Thus the passage in Rom. 13:2 clearly means condemnation from the rulers, "who are a terror to evil-doers." I Cor. 11:29 means that the offender would be exposed to severe temporal judgments from God and to the censure of good men. Rom. 14:23 means that such a one is condemned already by the Word and by his own conscience. The final loss of the soul of the impenitent, however, is clearly taught in many passages, including Rom. 6:23; Matt. 25:41; Jas. 1:15; Matt. 10:28; II Thess. 1:9; Matt. 25:30; Luke 16:23, 26.

529 What of one who lives nobly, yet who is not a Christian?

He will not be as one who lived a purely selfish life, because he will not suffer those reproaches of conscience, which may be expected to torture the selfish man. If, however, he has heard the Gospel and rejected it, we do not see how he can expect recognition of, or reward from God on account of his good deeds. Christ said emphatically, "no one cometh unto the Father but by me." If, therefore, a man rejects Christ and takes his stand on his own merits, he plainly intimates that he considers his way better than God's way. He makes Christ's life and death, so far as he is concerned, unnecessary. If a man who is bringing a suit in a court wilfully and contemptuously ignores the rules of the court, he is not likely to be heard, no matter what are the merits of his case. So a man who rejects Christ puts himself out of court. We are not to judge, however, in such cases.

530 What is the "second death"?

Spiritual, or "second death," implies "everlasting punishment" (Rev. 21:8)—the utter lack of all spiritual hope of restoration or reclamation. It means entire separation from God. Death, in the destructive sense, applies to the entire man and every part of his nature. We speak even now of men as "spiritually dead" while they yet live in the body, just as we speak of men who may be already in the grave, as "spiritually alive," and who shall never die. Spiritual death may begin even in this life. Death, therefore, need not imply extinction and annihilation. One commentator writes: "The proper life of the spirit lies in the harmony and subjection of its powers and disposition to the nature and will of God; its death in contrariety and enmity to him. This involves the disruption of a holy and dutiful relation with the Father of spirits, and by inevitable consequence a deprivation of the fruits of his love and favor on which life and blessedness depend. The whole man shall go away forever from the glory and joy of God's presence."

531 What does death do to the body?

When life ceases, the body as an individual organization is said to be dead; that is to say, death is the cessation of organic life. Matter, however, is indestructible; when it loses one form it appears in another. The matter of which the body is composed does not perish on the death of an organized being; it undergoes various changes which are known by the names of decay and putrefaction and which are the preparation for its becoming subservient to new forms of life. What becomes of the mind or thinking principle in man, otherwise the soul, is altogether a matter of religious faith or philosophic conjecture on which science has been unable to throw the slightest light. But it should not be forgotten that "there is a natural body and there is a spiritual body" (I Cor. 15:44). God has revealed the truth in the Bible, and particularly in the historic fact of Christ's resurrection, that the soul which is in harmony with himself will live forever. For the Scripture teaching concerning the resurrection of the body read I Cor. 15, which has been recognized from the earliest Christian times as the expression of the Christian's faith about the future life. Note particularly verses 35-44, 50-54.

532 Will our resurrection bodies rise with us on the judgment day?

See this whole subject fully set forth in I Cor. 15th chapter. A vast amount of philosophic conjecture has been expended and many books have been written about it; but the fact remains that nowhere is it more clearly and comprehensively stated than in this chapter. The belief in the resurrection of the human body has apparently been fortified by the well-known passage in Job. 19:26, which in the old version was mistranslated, but is corrected in the Revised to read "yet without my flesh shall I see God." All the evidences go to show that while the body to be raised shall be such as to preserve identity, it will be a purified, changed and spiritualized body, with the grosser material elements removed or so transformed as to render them fit for heaven and immortality. It shall become a glorified body like unto that of Christ. (See I Cor. 15:49; Rom. 6:9; Phil. 3:21.) The bodies of those who are alive at the last day will undergo a similar miraculous purifying transformation without death (see II Cor. 5:4; I Thess. 4:15; Phil. 3:21).

533 Does a person go directly to heaven or hell after death?

There is no passage that asserts it explicitly. There are, however, passages from which the inference is made. One of these is the assurance of Christ to the dying thief on the cross (Luke 23:43), "This day shalt thou be with me in Paradise." Another is the Parable of the rich man and Lazarus (Luke 16:19-31), in which Dives is represented as being in torment and Lazarus in Abraham's bosom, while the five brothers of Dives were still alive on the earth. A third passage is Philippians 1:23, in which Paul says he desires to depart and be with Christ, implying that his death would give him that felicity, but he prefers to abide in the flesh because he can do good in the world. From these passages and a few others the deduction is made that there is no interval between death and the eternal state; but some eminent Christians now and in past times have thought that there is an interval long or short, and some that it lasts till the resurrection. In Matt. 22:31, 32; Mark 12:26, and Luke 20:37, 38, Christ insists that the righteous who are called "dead" are still alive. The appearance of Moses and Elijah with Christ at the transfiguration was an actual demonstration of this fact. Even at the very beginning of the Bible (Gen. 5:24), there is the implication that Enoch continued in another life the walk with God which he had begun in this. And Heb. 12:1, including all the faith heroes mentioned in the eleventh chapter, states that they are alive and conscious now, witnessing the conflicts of the saints still on earth. Many books have been written concerning the state of the soul between death and the resurrection. Catholics have the doctrine of purgatory, but the early Christians held no such belief. They believed that there was a judgment immediately after death and a final judgment later, and that in the intermediate state (not "place"), every believer's soul would find a foretaste of the greater joys to come. Some non-Catholic authorities have held that the soul after leaving the body remains inert until the resurrection. The best authorities, however, hold that it retains its active powers, and is assigned to a condition which is suited to its degree of spiritual development until the final change. Dr. Tuck points out that Hades, the abode of the departed, was regarded by the Hebrews as divided into two sections: one for the good; the other for the wicked. "Both together made up the abode of the dead"; one Paradise, the other Gehenna. Paradise was to the Jewish theologians a state of future bliss with lower and higher stages; yet it is not the final stage. See also II Cor. 12:4; I Pet. 3:19; II Cor. 5:6-8. On the other hand, there are passages that are capable of a different construction. See Job 7:21; Dan. 12:2; I Cor. 15:51; I Thess. 4:14. In these passages, it is probable that "sleep" may refer to the body and not to the spirit.

**534 If the saved go directly to heaven
after death, why a resurrection
followed by a judgment day?**

In dealing with spiritual things, one must guard against materialistic conceptions of the after life which prevailed previous to the Messianic advent. Only as associated with the physical and material is spirit cognizant of time and place. Jesus had to use these forms of speech in order to make his teachings comprehensible to the people; but on many occasions he strove to raise and enlighten their minds to a clearer spiritual understanding. God is Spirit, incomprehensible, indescribable. God is in heaven, yet God is everywhere, hence heaven is everywhere. See Matt. 6:33; Luke 17:20, 21; Luke 23:43 and other passages. From these it must be evident that by the term "heaven" is meant a state or condition of existence. Resurrection and final judgment were taught in Egypt centuries before the days of Moses; were in a modified form incorporated in the teachings of the Hebrews, and so passed down into the doctrines of the Christian Church. They are an appanage of the belief in immortality, and mark the boundary to which the human mind can soar. But when we come to question the why and wherefore, we are seeking a deeper revelation of God's purposes than he has been pleased to give us. John 3:13 must not be separated from its preceding verse. No one can explain or throw light on spiritual conditions without having first entered into such spirituality for himself or herself, neither can such teaching or explanation be understood or accepted by any who themselves have not so entered. This is why materialistic ideas of a future state still so universally prevail. See Eph. 4:9, 10.

**535 Should a Christian dread
the thought of a hereafter?**

One who does should pray for more faith, and keep the fact constantly in mind that he who has promised cannot lie. Professor David Smith expresses this attitude very clearly and convincingly. He says: "If we were truly Christian, we would be less concerned about this question of the hereafter, for we would have a larger and braver trust in God. There is nothing more calming than recognition of the fact that it is not God that condemns, but sin. God is our Saviour, and his thoughts towards every creature of his hand are thoughts of good, and not of evil. If any perish, it is in spite of him. He is the Father of us all; and when I think what has been shown us of his heart by his eternal Son, our Brother and Lord, Jesus Christ, I am not afraid of anything that he may do, and I am well content to leave my future in his hands. He will do for every child of his undying affection the best that love can devise. Why should we fret or fear? God knows, and he is our Father."

536 Will more souls be lost than saved?

It is impossible to answer with any degree of authority. God alone knows who are lost or saved. One factor, however, that may tend to a solution of it is, that we are assured that there will come a time when the whole world will acknowledge Christ's sway. As the population of the world increases from year to year, we may assume that at that time, whenever it occurs, there will be more people on earth than at any preceding period in the world's history, which will materially add to the total number who are saved. The question is not one that is of profit. Christ did not encourage speculation on the subject. When the question was put to him he would not answer it, but gave the questioner practical advice. (See Luke 13:23.)

537 Shall we know each other in the future life?

We find the assurance of heavenly recognition in a number of passages both in the Old Testament and New Testament. David said of his dead son: "I shall go to him, but he shall not return to me" (II Sam. 12:23). See also the parable of Dives and Lazarus, which teaches recognition. See Phil. 3:20; Heb. 12:1; Matt. 17:3; Rev. 6:9, 10; Rom. 14:12; Luke 16:23; Rev. 6:9, 10; I Thess. 4:13-18; Heb. 13:17; Matt. 8:11; Eph. 3:15. These and other passages indicate the preservation of identity. We have no reason to doubt that the redeemed will know each other, that pure friendship begun on earth will there be perfected, that we shall know the saints and our own dear ones. Heaven is the Christian's fatherland, where we shall see our friends and know them.

538 What will heaven be like?

Of heaven itself and the blessedness in the life to come, we know only what is revealed in the Scriptures, and it is not possible, from such limited knowledge, to form any adequate conception. The Bible describes the happiness of heaven in general terms. See Rom. 8:18, 22; II Cor. 4:17, 18. It is described as a kingdom (Matt. 25:1); as a place of rest; as a place where knowledge will go on to perfection, and as a state in which the saints will dwell together. It will be a place of complete felicity, where the enjoyment will be heightened by friendly intercourse. It is further described as having a city with everlasting foundations; a place of innumerable homes (see John 14:2); a place where we shall meet our loved ones and our children (see II Sam. 12:23; Luke 16:25). John in Rev. 22 tells us of the "pure river of water of life" and "the tree of life with its abundance of fruits." Beyond these little is disclosed; but we have enough to assure us that it is a place of great happiness (see I Cor. 2:9); of blessed reunions where there are eternal youth and strength and where sorrow, sighing, pain and the afflictions that wound us in this life are unknown.

539 Will we have work to do in heaven?

A life without occupation is inconceivable. One of the great equipments for such occupation will be the enjoyment of perpetual youth—implying strength for service. Unquestionably it will be a life of intense activity—a busy place, with high avocations suited to the varied degrees of skill and to the endowments of the redeemed. Throughout the Scriptures, all evidences point to the conclusion that it is to be a life of activity, progress and spiritual development on the highest lines, when we have the assurance that God is himself a ceaseless worker (see John 5:17). Besides, in Heb. 1:14, it is clearly intimated that the redeemed will be actively engaged in carrying on the Lord's work, by a ministry to those who need help and consolation. They serve God continually (Rev. 7:15), and doubtless in a great variety of ways. "There is not the least reason to suppose," writes an able commentator, "that God will abolish this variety (of talent and abilities) in the future world; it will rather continue there, in all its extent. We must suppose that there will be, even in the heavenly world, a diversity of tastes, of labors, and of employments, and that to one person this, to another that field, in the boundless kingdom of truth and of useful occupation, will be assigned for his cultivation, according to his peculiar powers, qualifications, and tastes." This is the view now generally accepted by the Christian Church throughout the world.

540 What of wives and husbands in heaven?

A similar question was put to Christ (Matt. 22:23-30). You will see how he answered it. We know very little of the conditions of life in the spirit. We cannot easily conceive of life apart from the body, yet it is obvious that there is such life. Christ's answer to his questioners appears to imply that the material relationships of life are left behind, and that while we shall recognize one another, there will be such a purification and elevation of being that all idea of marriage will be lost in the sublimity of spiritual life. In Luke 20:27-40, Jesus was questioned on a similar topic and was replying to questions about the resurrection. Marriage was ordained to perpetuate the human family; but as there will be no breaches by death in the future state, the ordinance will cease and man will be *like the angels* in his immortal nature. This immortality, however, referred only to "those who shall be counted worthy."

541 How can one be happy in heaven
if he knows his dear ones are lost?

It is difficult, in view of the very little we know about heaven and the life of those admitted there, to conceive of their feelings and condition. All that we do know indicates a condition of happiness; that is certain. It may be that in the presence of God righteousness becomes so paramount a consideration, and sin is seen to be so dreadful and heinous a thing that the redeemed and purified soul shrinks from it as utterly loathsome, even when it exists in persons he loved in his earthly life. Pure souls may seem nearer to one in heaven than impure souls, though they may have had an earthly relationship. Christ being told that his mother and brethren desired to speak to him, said (Matt. 12:50): "Whosoever shall do the will of my Father the same is my brother and sister and mother," as much as to say that spiritual likeness counted for more with him than physical relationship. Redeemed souls, in becoming like him, therefore, may not suffer such poignant sorrow as to us now seems inevitable.

542 Will we see God in heaven?

There are several passages in the Bible which make clear statements on this subject. See Luke 1:19; Rev. 5:8, 11; Jude 24; Matt. 5:8; Isaiah 33:17; Job 19:26, 27; I John 3:2, and others.

543 Are there degrees in heaven?

There are several passages that would seem to indicate the probability of degrees. Daniel's famous passage relative to the soul-winners who will "shine as the stars forever" is one; Paul implies a similar diversity when he speaks of one star differing from another in glory; so did Jesus in his reply to the two disciples for whom it was asked that they should sit at his right and left hand in his kingdom. The parable of the talents also bears a kindred interpretation.

544 Will infants be saved?

In the passage in Rom. 5:18 the sin of Adam and the merits of Christ are pronounced as co-extensive; the words in both cases are practically identical: "Judgment came upon all men" and "the free gift came upon all men." If the whole human race be included in the condemnation for original sin, then the whole race must also be included in the justification through Christ's sacrifice. Children dying in infancy, before the age of understanding or moral responsibility, are all partakers of this inclusive justification. Were it otherwise, a very large proportion of the human race would have no share in this "free gift," but would be condemned for sin which they never committed, which is contrary to the divine characteristics of love and justice, contrary to the apostolic teachings, and contrary to the spirit and language of the Master himself, who said of the innocent children: "Of such is the kingdom of heaven." This is the general attitude of theology today on this matter. Faith always presupposes knowledge and power to exercise it, and as a little child has neither, it has no moral responsibility. Even so stern a theologian as Calvin held practically this view. Any other conception of God would make him a Moloch instead of a loving Father.

545 What will be the status of infants in heaven?

The only pertinent passage we recall is the incident of David and his infant child (II Sam. 12:23), in which he expressed the belief that he would go to him. Evidently he expected joy in meeting the child and expected recognition. Christ made an enigmatical remark about the angels of children (Matt. 18:10), as if implying that children had angels as their guardians in heaven. Then, too, he took a child and set him before his disciples with the words: "Of such is the kingdom of heaven" (Matt. 19:14). In the spiritual state, when the body is left behind, there is no question of growth. It is a matter of development. What condition then is so favorable to a beautiful development as the atmosphere of heaven? That must be a very beautiful nature, which never having sinned, has grown up in heaven in such society as exists there. There is no reason to suppose that the future life will be other than one of progress, and this would imply progress in growth in every direction. We can only conjecture, however, what that growth will mean in the spiritual world.

546 Will the heathen be lost? What does Scripture teach on the subject?

The greatest minds in religion and philosophy have discussed the fate of the unevangelized heathen. Justin Martyr and Clement held that they were called justified and saved by their philosophy and their virtuous lives under natural law. Zwingle contended that the heathen who had never been evangelized would be forgiven through the merits of Christ, although they had never heard of him. Christ himself said (Matt. 11:20-24) that the wicked but ignorant people of ancient Sodom and Gomorrah (who lived long before the Gospel age) would be more tolerantly dealt with than those who had heard the Gospel and rejected it. Paul (Rom. 2:14, 26, 27) shows that those not having either the law or the Gospel "may be a law unto themselves." We cannot therefore assert that the heathen who died in ignorance of Christ are beyond the reach of the Divine mercy, although we may not know in what form that mercy may be extended. In every age and every land God had his witnesses in the person of good men and women, whose upright lives, even under natural law, were a blessing to those around them. Who shall say that such are not acceptable to him? (See Acts 10:35.) The whole question of heathen salvation is one concerning which no one has a right to dogmatize. It should be left in God's hands. John Wesley wrote on this subject: "We have no authority from the Word of God to judge 'those that are without'," and he also wrote, toward the close of his ministry, "He that feareth God and worketh righteousness according to the light he has, is acceptable to God." (See Rom. 4:9.) God, who will judge all, will not judge unjustly. Every person will be judged according to the light he has had. There is no explicit statement as to the condition of the heathen who died without hearing the Gospel, and there was no reason why God should tell us what he does in respect to them. As, however, we are told that there is no way of attaining eternal life except through Christ, there is abundant and urgent reason for the church to make earnest effort to carry the Gospel to those who have not heard it. The heathen are in God's hand, it would be presumption on our part to say what he will do with them. It is sufficient for us to know that it is our duty to preach the word of salvation "to every creature." We can see no way in which salvation can come to those who died without the Gospel; but that does not prove that, in the infinite resources of God's compassion, there is no way.

547 Does not the revelation of God's love make the doctrine of hell incredible?

Not in all its aspects. God has not revealed definitely what kind of place the abode of the lost is, but merely that it is a place of weeping, gnashing of teeth and intense suffering, typified by burning. The idea is not inconsistent with what we know of sin here. We know the kind of a life a young man will lead in his premature old age if he gives himself to vice in his youth. However loving his father may be, he cannot save the lad from physical suffering if he persists in evil courses. He can only warn him, and God does that with his children. We have no ground given us for expecting that God will give another opportunity, although he may do so, for there are no limits to his mercy; but it is an awful risk to run. Our duty is to accept the opportunity that is offered now and not to speculate on the possibility of there being another. The terms of the offer read to us like those of a final offer. We cannot conceive of God being inconsistent. The punishment of the impenitent seems to be not so much an infliction by God, as the result of choice on the part of the sufferer. You may have seen a boy at school, in spite of all warnings and all advice, neglect his lessons and give his time to play and idleness. Can he blame his teacher or his parents, if at the end of his school life he is ignorant and is unfit for a profession? If a young man voluntarily associates with men of foul life and coarse manners and acquires their habits, do you blame a refined lady if she excludes him from her home? If a child who has been warned against touching a hot stove and has had the consequences explained to him, avails himself of a brief absence of his mother to lay his hand on the glowing metal, he must not blame his mother when he suffers. If he is so badly burned that he loses his hand, he goes through life maimed because of that momentary act. We do not blame the mother, or charge her with being inconsistent. All her love cannot save him from the consequences of his own perversity. When a man deliberately chooses sin after being warned of the consequences, and refuses the offer of pardon and regeneration, what is to be expected as to his future? Still, we are not to judge others, and above all we should not attempt to set limits to the Divine mercy.

548 Is there any Biblical warrant for believing in repentance after death?

The well-known passage "That at the name of Jesus every knee should bow, of things in heaven and things in earth and things under the earth" (Phil. 2:10), has been construed by some to imply that there may be repentance after death. It rather implies a confession of Christ's supremacy and triumph. We can imagine a man dying impenitent, realizing afterwards how foolish as well as how wicked he has been. You remember that in the parable of Dives and Lazarus (Luke 16:27, 28), the rich man was so convinced of his folly that he begged for his brothers to be warned, lest they, too, should be lost. James, too (2:19), says that the devils believe and tremble. It is not so much a question of whether there is repentance after death, as whether repentance avails then. It is not for us to limit the mercy of God, but there is nothing in the Bible to encourage the hope of there being an opportunity of gaining salvation after death. Any man postponing repentance till then, runs an appalling risk against which he is emphatically warned. That there is no chance for repentance after death cannot be absolutely proved, but the trend of Bible teaching is in that direction. The passage (Ecc. 11:3), "If the tree fall toward the north," etc., is often quoted in proof, but the inference is not decisive. So also is Rev. 22:11, "He that is filthy, let him be filthy still," etc., which is more to the purpose, but not absolute proof. Another passage implying the hopelessness of the lost is Luke 16:26, "Between us and you there is a great gulf fixed, so that they which would pass from hence to you, cannot," etc. The burden of proof, however, seems to be on those who contend that there is opportunity of repentance after death. Where there are such momentous issues at stake, a man must have very positive assurance of there being the opportunity before he decides to run the risk, and he does not appear to us to have any ground at all.

549 What is the paradise which Jesus promised the repentant thief?

Jesus' answer to the appeal of the penitent thief on the cross "gave him what he needed most—the assurance of rest and peace. The word 'paradise' meant to him repose and shelter, the greatest contrast possible to the thirst and agony and shame of the hours upon the cross." Paul speaks of degrees of heavenly exaltation (II Cor. 12:3), and the religious teaching of the Jews of that day taught this. The promise spoken by the Saviour, however we may interpret it, conveyed to the penitent the assurance that his future place would be one best fitted for him, and beyond this it is useless to speculate.

550 Does the soul exist apart
from the body after death?

Paul evidently looked forward to such a condition when he said that he was willing to be absent from the body and present with the Lord (II Cor. 5:8). He refers to the subject again in I Thess. 4:14, when he speaks of Christ bringing with him before the resurrection them who sleep in him. John saw (Rev. 6:10) the souls of the martyrs under the altar, clearly without their bodies. The parable of Dives and Lazarus (Luke 16:19-31) implies that the resurrection had not taken place when Dives made his petition to Abraham, inasmuch as the five brothers were still living. The corrected translation of the well-known passage in Job 19:26, makes it read, "Yet *without* my flesh shall I see God." These are a few of the passages directly implying the doctrine, though there are teachers, very sincere in their belief, who put another construction on the passages, and others making them harmonize with the doctrine that the soul has no separate existence.

551 Will there be a millennium
and what will it be like?

There are some Christians who do not look for a personal reign of Christ on the earth. Those who do so, base their belief chiefly on such passages as Rev. 20:4-6: "They shall be priests of God and of Christ, and shall reign with him a thousand years." Isaiah 2:3, which describes the extent of Christ's dominion. Isaiah 11:9, which describes the change of disposition in the animal creation. Zech. 14:16-21, which predicts the supremacy and purity of his reign and Heb. 8:10, 11, promising the universal acceptance of Christianity. Besides these, there are the promises to Abraham of the possession by his descendants of an area they have never yet possessed, and those that Christ would occupy the throne of David. The Scriptures do not give clear or definite accounts of the conditions of life in the millennium, but we infer that it will be a time of extraordinary conversion, and that great multitudes will be born again in a day. (See Micah 4:2; Is. 2:2-4.) See Rev. 20:4, 5. The apostle appears to teach (I Cor. 15:35-52) that a new spiritual body will be given in place of the one that has turned to dust.

552 Do angels have wings?

There is little positive Scriptural authority for the popular conception of the angelic form as endowed with wings. The "angels" of the Bible, who visited men, seem to have appeared in the human form, and were often accepted and entertained as men until, through the utterance of some remarkable prophecy or the manifestation of some supernatural quality, their spiritual nature was disclosed. The fact that they were "messengers" of God, may have supplied basis for the idea that they have wings as a means of swift and ethereal progression. The winged cherubim and seraphim seem to belong to a higher order of celestial beings than those designated "angels," since they are always represented as standing in the immediate presence of God in heaven or guarding his dwelling-place on earth. The golden cherubim watching over the mercy-seat in the ark of the covenant were four-winged, so were those mighty figures under whose outstretched pinions the ark was placed in Solomon's Temple. Four-winged were the "living creatures" of Ezekiel's dream, "who every one went straight forward whither the spirit was to go." Six-winged were the seraphim of Isaiah's vision, who stood above the "Throne of the Lord," crying; "Holy, holy, holy is the Lord of hosts"—almost the same song which later the four-winged "beasts" of Revelation cried day and night before the Throne.

553 What is meant by "a new heaven and a new earth"?

Rev. 21 gives a vivid description of the "new heaven and new earth." It has been a fruitful subject of comment, some holding that the earth, having been cursed by sin, will be redeemed, regenerated, purified, and transformed by the "second Adam" and made a fit dwelling-place for the righteous, where the law of love shall prevail and God shall be all in all. The "new heaven" is interpreted to mean the firmament above us. Thus the "new creation" is interpreted to mean the restoration of the physical universe as the final abode of glorified, deathless and sinless humanity. Others hold that the teaching is clear that the present earth is to be literally destroyed, and that the promise of a new heaven and a new earth will be fulfilled, as he hath said: "Behold I make all things new."

554 What is to be understood by the silence mentioned in Revelation 8:1?

While the whole book of Revelation is of that literary character which may be described as mystical, dealing extensively in types and metaphors, there are occasional passages in which the writer descends to simpler language for the purpose of more clearly conveying his meaning. The half hour of silence in heaven; at the breaking of the last seal is not to be reckoned by minutes and seconds, but is purely a figure of speech. It is meant to convey to the mind a long, solemn pause by way of introduction to the joys and activities of the eternal Sabbath rest of God's people, which begins with the reading of the sealed book. The preceding chapters have run through the course of Divine action, where everything unites in a solemn hush for the final act. In the ancient Jewish temple, the instrumental music and singing, which formed the first part of the service, were hushed immediately before the offering of the incense, so this pause immediately precedes the adoration of the blessed spirits and the angels and the imminent unfolding of God's judgment. See similar figurative expressions in Rev. 17:12, 18:10, 19.

555 What becomes of the soul in the interval between death and the resurrection?

There are three passages from which an inference may be drawn, in the absence of an explicit statement in the Bible. The first of these is Christ's assurance to the penitent thief (Luke 23:43): "This day shalt thou be with me in Paradise." We are not sure what Paradise meant, but it was evidently a place of conscious existence, if it was not heaven itself. A second passage is contained in the parable of Dives and Lazarus (Luke 16:19-31). Some allowance must be made for the form of picture teaching Christ used, but he certainly described the rich man as being conscious and being able to see, hear, speak and feel at a time when his brothers were alive upon earth. This indicated a conscious existence for the soul prior to the resurrection. The third passage is Paul's expression of a desire for death (Phil. 1:23). He wished "to depart and to be with Christ." It is not likely that he would have had such a wish if he expected to sleep until the resurrection. So active and energetic a man would have wished to live and work for Christ rather than to lie unconscious in the grave. He clearly expected that as soon as he died he would be with Christ. These are a few of the statements from which the inference is drawn that man goes immediately after death to his reward and does not wait for the resurrection. It is not clear that Paul expected a resurrection of the body at all. He expected to receive a new body (I Cor. 15:37)—not the body that was laid in the grave.

FACTS ABOUT THE BIBLE

556 What is one to do who, in the light
of modern scientific education, cannot harmonize
the Bible stories of the creation, etc.?

We do not know of any denomination but one which would insist that its members regard as inspired every paragraph of our present version of the Bible. For instance, one or two passages of the Authorized Version are omitted in the American Revision and one or two more are indicated as having been omitted from the earliest manuscripts. Under such circumstances it would hardly be fair for any church (except the Catholic) to excommunicate a person who found it difficult to accept one or two more paragraphs of the present version. The new emphasis in regard to the Bible is that it is not a text-book of science, or geography, or history—but of salvation. It shows how God has dealt with the souls of men in the past and promises that he will do even greater things for those who will trust him now. It gets us acquainted with Christ as Saviour and Friend and shows how we may live in his companionship and service. But again, we must not be too sure of our own scientific knowledge. Science is constantly being compelled to shift its position. The most scholarly attitude is that of the greatest humility. It is never necessary to violate one's " better judgment," but it is necessary, in order to find salvation, to be humble and reverent and to be willing to receive into one's soul the light and truth of the Holy Spirit.

557 What are the specific objections of Jews
and Catholics to having the Bible read
in the public schools?

The Jews, so far as we know, would be willing to have the Old Testament read in the public schools and also some of the ethical passages of the New Testament. It would be difficult to win the consent of Catholics to more than the purely ethical and perhaps the historical passages. The Jews, of course, object to the Bible as it is because it recognizes Christ as the Messiah and teaches the doctrine of the Trinity, whereas they are strict Unitarians. The Catholics object to its use in the public schools because they hold that the church, as represented by its priests, must interpret the doctrines of the Scriptures. They object, of course, to the use of the King James and Revised Versions because they were prepared under Protestant auspices. The Catholic Church uses the Douay Version, which differs in a number of details from the Protestant. Catholic doctrine makes the church's interpretation of the Scriptures of as great value as the Scriptures themselves, hence that church has not, we believe, definitely encouraged the private reading of the Bible, unaccompanied as that must be by priestly interpretation. There is noticeable, however, a marked change in Catholic opinion on this point, for Catholic periodicals now carry advertisements offering Bibles for sale, while authorized selections of Scripture passages are also recommended for private and family use.

**558 How many different kinds of laughter
     are mentoned in the Bible?**
1. Laughter of incredulity (Gen. 18:12). 2. Laughter of joyful wonder (Gen. 17:17). 3. Laughter of defiance or conscious security (Job 5:22). 4. Laughter (or, in modern parlance, smile) of approbation (Job 29:24). 5. Hollow laughter, with undertone of sorrow (Prov. 14:13). 6. Laughter of derision or scorn, applied by strong anthropomorphism to God (Ps. 2:4). 7. Laughter of rapturous delight (Ps. 126:2).

**559 What have famous men, not known
     as active Christians, said about the
     Bible and its teachings?**
Many men have paid unfaltering tribute to the Scriptures. Thus Benjamin Franklin said: " Young man, my advice to you is to cultivate an acquaintance with and firm belief in the Holy Scripture, for this is your certain interest. I think Christ's system of morals and religion as he left them with us the best the world ever saw or is likely to see." Professor Huxley wrote: "I have always been strongly in favor of secular education without theology, but I must confess that I have been no less seriously perplexed to know by what practical measures the religious feeling which is the essential basis of moral conduct is to be kept up in the present utterly chaotic state of opinion on these matters without the use of the Bible." Even Goethe must say as follows: " It is a belief in the Bible which has served me as the guide of my moral and literary life. No criticism will be able to perplex the confidence which we have entertained of a writing whose contents have stirred up and given life to our vital energy by its own. The farther the ages advance in civilization the more will the Bible be used." And the great Napoleon pays this tribute: "The Bible contains a complete series of acts and of historical rule to explain time and eternity, such as no other religion has to offer. If it is not the true religion, one is very excusable in being deceived, for everything in it is grand and worthy of God. The more I consider the Gospel, the

more I am assured that there is nothing there which is not beyond the march of events and above the human mind. Even the impious themselves have never dared to deny the sublimity of the Gospel, which inspires them with a sort of compulsory veneration. What happiness that Book procures for those who believe it." Diderot says: "No better lessons can I teach my child than those of the Bible," and Matthew Arnold: "To the Bible men will return because they cannot do without it. The true God is and must be preeminently the God of the Bible, the eternal who makes for righteousness, from whom Jesus came forth and whose Spirit governs the course of humanity."

560 What do the Scriptures tell us about various animals?

Beasts of all kinds were created by God and they exhibit God's power even as they are made for the praise and glory of God (Gen. 1:24, 25; Gen. 2:19; Jer. 27:5; Ps. 148:10). He gave them the herbs of the field for food and as power over them was given to man they instinctively fear him. Adam gave them their names, but they remain the property of God and the subjects of his care (Gen. 1:30; Gen. 1:26, 28; Gen. 9:3; Gen. 2:19, 20; Ps. 50:10; Ps. 36:6). They are described as devoid of speech, understanding and immortality, but possessed of instinct, and though wild by nature, capable of being tamed (II Pet. 2:16; Ps. 32:9; Ps. 49:12-15; Isa. 1:3; Ps. 50:11). They are found in deserts, fields, mountains and forests and inhabit dens, caves and deserted cities (Isa. 13:21; Deu. 7:22; So. of Sol. 4:8; Isa. 56:9; Job 37:8; Isa. 13:21, 22). They were divided into clean and unclean and to this day the distinction is observed. The clean beasts were ox, wild ox, sheep, goat, hart, roebuck, wild goat, fallow deer, chamois (Ex. 21:28; Deu. 7:13; Deu. 14:4, 5), while among the unclean were counted the camel, dromedary, horse, ass, mule, lion, leopard, bear, wolf, unicorn, ape, fox, dog, swine, hare, mouse, mole, weasel, ferret and badger (Gen. 24:64; I Kings 4:28; Gen. 22:3; II Sam. 13:29; Judg. 14:5, 6; So. of Sol. 4:8; II Sam. 17:8; Gen. 49:27; Num. 23:22; I Kings 10:22; Ps. 63:10; Ex. 22:31; Lev. 11:7; 6:5, 29, 30; Ex. 25:5. The domestic animals are to enjoy the Sabbath, are to be taken care of and not to be cruelly used (Ex. 20:10; Lev. 25:7; Num. 22:27-32).

561 What do we learn from the Bible about various birds?

Birds were created by God for his glory (Gen. 1:20, 21; Ps. 148:10). The power over them given to man and they instinctively fear him; man may learn lessons of wisdom from them (Gen. 1:26; Gen. 9:2; Job 12:7). They are called fowls of the air, fowls of heaven, feathered fowl, winged fowl, birds of the air (Gen. 7:37; Job 35:11; Ezek. 39:17; Deu. 4:17;

Matt. 8:20). Many kinds are granivorous, many carnivorous; they all have claws and are propagated by eggs (Matt. 13:4; Gen. 15:11; Gen. 40:19; Dan. 4:33; Jer. 17:11). They have each their peculiar note or song, are migratory and inhabit mountains, deserts, marshes, deserted cities, trees, clefts of rocks and dwell under the roofs of houses (Ps. 104:12; Eccles. 12:4; Jer. 8:7; Ps. 50:11; Isa. 14:23; Isa. 34:11, 14, 15; Ps. 104:17; Num. 24:21; Isa. 34:15; Ps. 84:3). They were divided into clean and unclean. Among the clean were reckoned the dove, pigeon, quail, sparrow, swallow, cock and hen, partridge, crane (Gen. 8:8; Lev. 14:22; Lev. 1:14; Ex. 16:12; Lev. 14:4; Ps. 84:3; Matt. 23:27; I Sam. 26:20; Isa. 38:14), and among the unclean the eagle, vulture, glede, raven, owl, cuckoo, hawk, owl, swan, pelican, stork, heron, bat, ostrich, peacock (Lev. 11:13; Lev. 11:14, 15, 16, 17, 18, 19; Job 39:13; I Kings 10:22).

562 How are we to strengthen our belief in the Scriptures?

The first step is to stop all anxious worry about this matter. God is going to take care of you. Christ is a very kind physician, and his first treatment for one who is all worn out and weary with fruitless mental effort is rest. "Come unto me, and I will give you rest," he is urging. He would say to you, as he said once to his disciples: "Come ye yourselves into a desert place, and rest a while." The mental effort you have been making is in the wrong direction. One does not find the Christian life as one masters the multiplication table, by mental effort and application. It is as if you were longing to hear a beautiful piece of music; and instead of going to hear the music when you were near the place in which it was being rendered, you should spend your time and strength studying the scientific meaning and methods of melody, harmony, etc. To delve into these studies does not make you hear music. You must go where the music is being made and *listen* to it. While you are listening you will not be puzzling your own brain, or trying to understand anything. It is in some such way that the soul finds and touches Christ—by ceasing to struggle, by ceasing to figure things out, by yielding the soul to him in complete abandonment. You will be greatly helped by going among the most intensely spiritual people you know. You may shrink from this. You may find their ways and their sayings distasteful, because your heart has not yet been put into tune. But go to their meetings; give yourself up to the atmosphere of them; be reasonable enough to admit that God would like to do for you what he has done for them, to bless you as he has blessed them. We can get help reading our Bibles alone, but we get added help in understanding the Bible and in getting acquainted with Christ by associating with spiritually minded people. Above all, begin and begin now, to trust Christ himself. Test him. Accept the fact of his divinity and his power to forgive and cleanse you and become your friend as a mathematician or logician accepts a "hypothesis." Take it for granted it is true, and as you take it for granted you will begin to find the evidence in your own heart and mind that it is true indeed. Then begin at once to help others. Forget yourself in helping them, and the light of Christ will keep growing brighter and brighter in your life.

563 Can a person be a Christian and not study the Bible?

The Christian should go to the Bible just as a sheep goes to pasture or a thirsty man to water. We should cultivate the feeling that in the Bible God is speaking to us personally, and read it for ourselves, expecting to find definite, personal messages for our own souls. Hearing others talk about the Bible or explain it or preach from its texts can never take the place of reading it for ourselves. But we ought ever to be mindful of the fact that preaching and teaching are the most important functions of ministers and preachers. They are highly trained, are specially endowed to that end, and their explanations of texts and passages, being the result of careful and prayerful preparation and research, have the weight of authority and should be accordingly valued. Helps and commentaries are also useful, but we should not get into the habit of relying upon them or of reading them to the exclusion of the Bible itself. Many people, particularly young Christians, are apt to become discouraged about their Bible reading because they begin with the most difficult instead of the simplest parts. A good book to begin with is the Gospel of Mark. This is a straightforward account of the life and death and resurrection of Jesus. After reading this several times you will become interested in reading Matthew's and Luke's accounts of the same events, and will read John to get the deeper and more spiritual conceptions of the Master and his wonderful conversations reported at greater length here than in the other Gospels. At the same time be reading the book of Acts, which is plain and intensely interesting. Read Isaiah and the Psalms for devotional use. In Paul's epistles a good place to start is the letter to the Philippians, which is full of joy and contains plain and important teachings about the person of Jesus. Ephesians and Colossians contain rich spiritual teaching, and Romans and Galatians give the foundations of Paul's doctrine. Starting with this foundation you will be better able to understand and enjoy all the other epistles of the New Testament. Gradually you will grow familiar with the Old Testament, history and prophecy alike, and will soon come to find Bible reading a delight, particularly if you have passed through a definite experience of conversion through faith in Christ's blood and are seeking all the time to come, through faith and obedience, into closer fellowship with him.

564 Is its antiquity the best reason we have for believing the Scriptures?

Some ancient writings, like the Vedas, for instance, are almost as ancient as the Bible. And many tablets and monuments are in existence containing words written as long ago as the writings of the Scriptures. There are many powerful arguments for the Bible, but the greatest is that every person who will really study it finds that it does tell the truth about the human soul. When a man reads in an arithmetic that two and two make four he does not stop to ask himself why he should believe the arithmetic. He knows instinctively and intuitively that the arithmetic is telling him the truth. So when an honest man studies the Bible he finds it full of truths about himself. The Bible tells him he is a sinner; and he knows that is true. The Bible tells him about God, and he finds in his heart a deep conviction that just such a God exists. The Bible offers forgiveness and the man knows he needs it. Step by step and point by point, the Bible shows the man what he is and what he needs and points the way to finding the fulfilment of his needs and desires. People find in the Bible help for bearing their trials, power to resist temptation, assurance of immortality and friendship with God. A man who never saw the Bible before, when he reads of God in it, realizes that he always needed and longed for God but did not know how to find him till the Bible showed him the way. Particularly does it show him how to find God in Christ. That, after all, is the supreme mission of the Bible—to lead men to Christ.

But again, taking the Bible as literature, we find that it hangs together, that it bears within itself the evidence that it is true. Start with the writings of Paul. Here is a level-headed, highly educated, practical man who has left to the world's literature certain letters to groups of friends. These letters tell about Paul's personal knowledge of Christ, his personal friendship for him, his personal endeavors to forward the work of Christ which he had formerly antagonized until Christ himself appeared to him and set him right. Paul tells of becoming acquainted later with men who had known Christ in the flesh—Peter, James, John and others. We find that these men also wrote about Jesus; John writing three letters and a narrative of his life, Peter writing two letters, and apparently giving much of the information to his nephew Mark, who wrote another version of the life of Jesus. Luke, another friend of Paul and probably also a personal friend of Jesus, wrote another version of his life and wrote the history of what the apostles did through his power after he had risen from the dead and gone back to the heavenly world. These were all good, honest, intelligent men. We may believe what they wrote about Christ and his salvation, just as we believe what Caesar wrote about the Gallic wars. Further, we find that Christ came from a people whose history is recorded in the books of the Bible and whose prophets uttered messages from God, many of them foretelling the coming of Christ. Peter connects the messages of the prophets with those of himself and the other apostles in II Peter 3:2: "That ye may be mindful of the words which were spoken before by the holy prophets, and of the commandment of us the apostles of the Lord and Saviour." The Bible holds together about the person of Christ the great divine-human document which reveals him to the world.

565 Is the Bible grammatical?

In the authorized version, prepared in the reign of King James (seventeenth century), many of the forms and phrases used by the earlier translators were retained, and these have not all disappeared even at the present time. The relative pronoun is frequently used in the A.V. instead of the personal, the word "let" for "prevent," "mine" for "my," "an" for "a" (before the aspirate), "bewray" for "betray," etc. Amid the changes which every language undergoes these ancient forms (now obsolete) seem out of place; but the veneration in which the Bible is held has been the means of preserving them. At the time they were first employed they were not only thoroughly grammatical but elegant in a literary sense and even today they cannot be regarded as a violation of grammar. The Revised Version has substituted modern phraseology for very many of the old forms employed in the King James Bible.

566 What are the more prominent
New Testament manuscripts?

1. The Codex Sinaiticus now in St. Petersburg, or Petrograd. It contains the whole New Testament, and was discovered by Tischendorf in 1859 in the monastery of St. Catherine on Mount Sinai. It was written not later than the fourth century.

2. The Codex Alexandrinus, now in the British Museum, was written in the fifth century and contains the whole Bible.

3. The Codex Vaticanus, known as Vatican M.S. No. 1209, and now in the Vatican library. It was written in the latter part of the fourth century and contains the whole Bible with some exceptions.

4. The Codex Ephraemii Rescriptus, so called because part of the original writing had been erased in order to use the parchment to write some of the work of Euphraem, a Syrian father, thereon.

5. The Peshito Syriac version, considered by some scholars as spurious.

567 Can the entire Bible be considered
as good literature?

The Bible is all good literature. It stands high in the narrative, the didactic, the oratoric, the allegoric, the lyric, the dramatic and the epic. Much of it is poetry of the highest order; much is praise sublime in character and expression; a good deal of it is philosophy of a kind that appeals to the minds of all the ages; it is replete with tragedy, in both the Old Testament and the New. To classify all the finer passages from a literary standpoint would be a large task, and one to be undertaken only by able and reverent scholarship. It would have to be gone over by literary experts, book by book, chapter by chapter, verse by verse.

568 What became of the book of Nathan the prophet, and of Gad the seer mentioned in I Chronicles 29:29?

They are lost. That is to say, if they are in existence anywhere no one knows where they are. The titles of nineteen books which are missing, are mentioned in the Bible, such as the Book of the Wars of the Lord mentioned Num. 21:14 and the Book of the Acts of Solomon mentioned I Kings 11:41. There is no doubt that the historical books of the Bible as we now have them were compiled from older books or documents which were not preserved.

569 Who are the "unnamed persons" in the Bible?

Among the unnamed persons in the Bible, so far as any clue to their identity can be found from legendary or traditionary sources, were these: Jannes and Jambres, the magicians who withstood Moses in Pharaoh's court; Veronica, the woman who touched the hem of Jesus' garment; Ben Ezra, the son of Marianne (sister of Philip the disciple), the lad who held the basket of loaves and fishes; Longinus, the soldier who pierced the Saviour's side, and Dismas and Gestas, the crucified thieves (to the former of whom the promise of Paradise was given). Nearly all of these names are to be found in the apocryphal "Gospel of Nicodemus."

570 Who first collected the Scriptures of the Old Testament?

Popular belief as well as tradition credits Ezra and his learned associates of the "great synagogue" with the task of collecting the Scriptures of the Jewish Church. It is generally held that the foundation of the present Hebrew canon is due to him. The work of assembling the writings which made up "The Book of the Lord" must have begun before Isaiah's time, since he mentions it as a general collection (Isa. 34:16), to which his own were to be added. It is not clear that there was any definite collection either of psalms or the prophets before the Captivity. Daniel, however, refers to "the books" (Dan. 9:2), which in his day had apparently been collected as a whole. It is considered quite probable that Nehemiah had a share in gathering the books. Ezra lived about 460 B. C. All that is known of him through Scripture is contained in the last four chapters of the book of Ezra and in Neh. 8 and 12:26.

571 Is not the Bible in part obsolete?

Not so. It has in every part of it its lessons even to the present day, though of course not all its merely local laws are binding on all men. So, for instance, while God does not now ask us to offer sheep and bullock and other material sacrifices, yet those requirements have their deep lessons for us. The sin offering, the trespass offering, the burnt offering, the peace offering teach deep lessons of how much is necessary to atone for sin and how great was the work of Jesus in doing penance once and for all for all sin. The deluge has no warning at the present time, but who can doubt the lesson it taught and who would be without the rainbow which followed it? The Ten Commandments, who would do away with them, even though Christ has fulfilled all law? Are they not ever the never-failing reminder of what is required of us and the ever-reflecting mirror in which to view our misdeeds and shortcomings?

**572 Was the the art of printing
known in Biblical times?**

Not in the sense in which we understand it. Printing is first mentioned in the Bible in the book of Job, chap. 19:23, where he says "O! That my words were now written! O! That they were printed in a book!" Although this has been taken by some as indicating the existence of the printer's art in the earliest times, the obvious fact is that Job intended to refer to manuscript or writing on papyrus rolls and that the translator gave the passage a modern aspect which is misleading. Engraving on stone and wood and metal was done in very ancient times, but the honor of discovering the "art preservative" as we now interpret it seems to belong to China, where printing long antedated Guttenberg's discovery.

**573 Is it right to secularize the Scriptures or any part
of them by putting their characters or the person
of our Lord into imaginary story environment?**

The prejudice against such form of literature as *Ben Hur, The Prince of the House of David*, etc., is a mistaken one. You would rob literature cruelly if you took out all the resettings of Scripture narratives and teaching, and all the beautiful stories, poems, parables and idyls that have grown up about the person of Christ. The works of the great poets, like Dante, Milton, Tennyson, Browning, are full of Scripture allusions, the retelling of Scripture incidents and the restatement of Scriptural lessons. The incalculable amount of good done by such parables as Bunyan's *Pilgrim's Progress* and *Holy War*, in which the person of Christ becomes a character of the story, proves that their writing was justified. The very books *Ben Hur* and *The Prince of the House of David* have done untold good, serving to make the person of Christ and the facts of the spiritual life more real. Of course all within limits. We do not approve of many of the modern dramas and photoplays where the person of Christ is brought in, but in books like those you mention only good can be done by treating of Christ in a "familiar" way. Many of us are oftentimes unmindful of the fact that the "Word was made flesh" with all that that implies to us; became as we are, had our body, our physical and psychic functions and ills (all, however, minus sin and its consequences), and thus was one of us, our Brother, whose very likeness makes him near and dear, as indeed he wants to be. Many traits of his character, many peculiarities are not mentioned in the Scriptures; much that he said and did is not there recorded. Why, then, not idealize, so long as we stay within bounds of due reverence and truthful likelihood? "Lo, I am with you alway" (Matt. 28:20). Glorious words! If he is with us always, and everywhere, why not picture him as with those who figure in *Ben Hur*, etc.?

574 Is the Bible opposed to woman suffrage?

The language of I Tim. 2:11-15 and I Cor. 14:34, 35 is frequently quoted by the opponents of woman suffrage. The attitude of the church in Pauline times was clear and emphatic. The apostle evidently was of the opinion that there were callings for which a woman was unfitted by nature, that she had a well-defined sphere which she could fill with grace and satisfaction. We cannot reconcile this view with present-day ideas. It may be, however, that there was a necessity for such teaching at that time, especially in Corinth, where a certain class of women (non-Christians) was very much in evidence. Paul naturally desired that Christian women should be in marked contrast with the conduct of the pagan women. In this view his rules might have an application more local than general. Paul stands practically alone, among the early writers, in the rigidity of his attitude toward women. He believed in wifely obedience and modesty in behavior and apparel, and he did not wish to see the women of the Christian Church emulate the brazen conduct of a certain class of Greek women. At the time when Paul wrote, the morals of Corinth and Ephesus were of such a character (with loose living and false teaching) that he deemed it advisable to urge the Christian women to a quieter and more seemly mode of living than their heathen contemporaries. His epistles were suited to the time and place and conditions. Paul's suggestion in I Tim. 5:11 was with relation to the choice of suitable women for membership on the presbytery rolls. He drew the line at lightheaded, worldly minded persons whose fondness for pleasure and society was pronounced and who were more likely to seek marriage again than to devote themselves wholly to the service of the church. Second marriages he regarded with disfavor. Moreover, widowed presbyteresses, when taking their vows, engaged to remain single because the interests of the church made this desirable.

575 What do the Holy Scriptures say about themselves?

They are given by inspiration of God and the Holy Ghost (II Tim. 3:16; Acts 1:16; Heb. 3:7; II Pet. 1:21). Christ sanctioned them by teaching out of and appealing to them (Matt. 4:4; Mark 12:10; John 7:43; Luke 24:27) . They are called "The Word," "The Word of God," "The Word of Christ," "The Word of Truth," "Holy Scripture," "Scripture of Truth," "The Book," "The Book of the Lord," "The Book of the Law," "The Sword of the Spirit," "Oracles of God" (James 1:21-23; Luke 11:28; Col. 3:16; James 1:18; Rom. 1:2; Dan. 10:21; Ps. 40:7; Isa. 34:6; Neh. 8:3; Ps. 1:2; Eph. 6:17; Rom. 3:2).

They contain the promises of the Gospel, reveal the laws, statutes and judgments of God, record divine prophecies and testify of Christ (Rom. 1:2; Deu. 4:5, 14; II Pet. 1:19, 21; John 5:39; Acts 10:43; Acts 18:28; I Cor. 15:3).

They are full and sufficient, an unerring guide and able to make wise unto salvation through faith in Christ Jesus (Luke 16:29, 31; Prov. 6:23; II Tim. 3:15). They are pure, true, perfect, precious, quick and powerful (Ps. 12:6; Ps. 119:160; Ps. 19:7; Ps. 19:10; Heb. 4:12), and are designed for regenerating, quickening, illuminating, converting the soul and sanctifying (James 1:18; Ps. 119:50, 93; Ps. 119:130; Ps. 19:7; John 17:17; Eph. 5:26). They produce faith, hope and obedience, cleanse the heart, convert the soul, make wise the simple (John 20:31; Ps. 119:49; Rom. 15:4; Deu. 17:19, 20; John 15:3). They should be the standard of teaching, believed, appealed to, read and known; they should be read publicly to all, received as the Word of God with meekness, laid up in the heart and obeyed (I Pet. 4:11; John. 2:22; I Cor. 1:31; Deu. 17:19; II Tim. 3:15; I Thess. 2:13; James 1:21; Deu. 6:6); while all should desire to hear them, they should be not only heard but obeyed and be used against our spiritual enemies (Neh. 8:1; Matt. 7:24; Matt. 4:4, 7). Saints love them exceedingly, delight in, long after, stand in awe of and esteem them highly (Ps. 119:97; Ps. 1:2; Job 23:12; Ps. 119:82; Ps. 119:161). Therefore they hide them in their heart, hope in them, meditate, rejoice, trust in and obey them (Ps. 119:11; Ps. 119:74; Ps. 119:162, 42, 67), also speak of them and praying to be conformed to, plead their promises in prayer (Ps. 119:172; Ps. 119:133, 25, 28, 41, 76, 169).

OLD TESTAMENT SUBJECTS

576 Is there any truth in the assertion that when Abraham offered up his son he was following the example of his idolatrous neighbors who offered up their children in sacrifice to Moloch?

The record in Genesis, 22d chapter, is clear and unmistakable. It was a test of Abraham's faith in God. It is probable that human sacrifices already existed among the heathen, but Isaac was a "child of promise," and therefore doubly dear to his parents, and there is no warrant in Scripture for inferring that Abraham, of his own free will, made the deliberate choice to offer him up. Indeed, verse 2 dismisses such a supposition altogether.

577 Was the covenant with Abraham intended as a continuing covenant?

The covenant with Abraham was, in a spiritual sense, to be an everlasting covenant. It applies to the church in all ages (to "Abraham and his seed," Gal. 3:29). Circumcision was a sign and symbol of spiritual blessing. The covenant, however, applied only to those who lived up to its requirements. In the Christian Church baptism conveys the same significance.

578 What are the leading dates from the call of Abraham to the birth of Christ?

Students who try to construct a chronology exclusively from the Bible records are practically in accord on the date of the beginning of the reign of Saul, the first King of Israel, as being 1093 or 1095 years before the Christian era. Counting backward from that date the question arises how long the country was ruled by the Judges. If the Judges mentioned were successive the period between the death of Joshua and the accession of Saul was about 500 years. But if some of those Judges governed contemporaneously the period may not have been more than 334 years. So that some students place the death of Joshua at 1593 B.C., and others at 1427 B.C. Others again, taking Paul's statement (Acts 13:20), make the date 1543 B.C. The results, according to the long reckoning, are as follows: Call of Abraham, 2164 B.C.; migration of Jacob to Egypt, 1874; birth of Moses, 1738; the exodus, 1658, and the death of

Joshua, 1593. Deduct 166 from each of these dates, and you have the dates assigned by students who believe that the "times of the Judges" was not more than 334 years. The later dates are: Accession of Solomon, 1013; dedication of the temple, 1003; revolt of the ten tribes, 973; fall of northern kingdom, 722; capture of Jerusalem under Nebuchadnezzar, 587; decree of Cyrus for the return of the Jews, 537; completion of the second temple, 517; Antiochus subjugates Palestine, 218; Antiochus Epiphanes profanes the temple, 170; Jerusalem taken by Pompey, 63.

579 How can the incident of Abraham's prevarication be explained (Genesis 12:11-13)?

We must not think that all that the Bible records of the doings of good men must all be good. Abraham was only human, after all, and had human failings. Scripture, being truthful, records the bad in a man with the good. Abraham did not succeed in being always faithful. He did not trust God to the extent that he could preserve both himself and Sarah from the perils to be met among the Egyptians. So he hit upon a scheme of passing off his wife as his sister, thereby endeavoring to run the lesser risk of having her merely confined for a time in a harem. His desire seems to have been intended merely to gain time during which he might take measures for securing her return to him. The *Speaker's Commentary* draws this conclusion: "We see in the conduct of Abraham an instance of one under the influence of deep religious feeling and true faith in God but yet with a conscience imperfectly enlightened as to many moral duties, and when leaning to his own understanding suffered to fall into great error and sin. In this practical difficulty Abraham's faith failed. He fell back upon devices and lost his trust. The man who is consciously in divine hands need not plan and plot, need not devise and equivocate, he may simply follow the divine lead with assurance of perfect safety."

580 Was Adam created before Eve?

Some scientists have contended that the first human pair appeared simultaneously and that if there could have been priority it would have been with the female. The account in Genesis 2:22 most certainly implies that man was created before woman. The apostle Paul evidently believed that it was so (see I Tim. 2:13). The other account of the Creation (Gen. 1:27) indicates a simultaneous creation. Whether we are to accept the account in Genesis 2:22 as a fuller and more detailed narrative, or whether we must regard it as an attempt to prove the close and intimate relation of husband and wife, is not clear.

581 If the physical man in Adam did the eating of the forbidden fruit, why should his soul have suffered?

While it is true that there is a soul in man which is a distinct entity, you cannot separate the responsibility for sin, apportioning some sins to the soul and some to the body. There is no need to argue about Adam, when our own experience is so much more pertinent, and in this Adam was only a type of ourselves. Luther used to tell the story of a bishop who was also an archduke. One day he uttered an oath, and when some one looked astonished he asked why the man stared. "To hear a bishop swear," was the reply. "I swear," said the bishop, "as a prince, not as a bishop." To which the other replied: "When the prince goes to perdition, what will become of the bishop?" The soul is a consenting party to the sins of the body. It is defiled and degraded by bodily sin, and is justly punished for not maintaining order. The soul should be supreme, and when the body, which is allied to the animal world, craves indulgence in forbidden things, the soul ought to restrain it. If it does not, it has abdicated its functions and deserves punishment. God gave man a soul that he might rise out of his brutal origin, and gave it power over the body and stands ready to give it more power if more is needed.

582 Who was the mother of Asa?

In I Kings 15:2-10 there seems to be a contradiction as to the relation of Maachah to Asa. Was she his mother or his grandmother? She appears to have been his grandmother. Her name is mentioned probably to show Asa's title to the throne. Rehoboam, his grandfather, enacted that of all his children only those of whom Maachah was the mother should be in line of succession to the throne. She is spoken of loosely as his mother just as in the next verse to the one quoted (I Kings 15:11) David is described as his father, though he was really Asa's great-great-grandfather. Nor was Maachah the daughter of Absalom, but his granddaughter.

583 When was the ark of the covenant last heard of?

No reference is made to the Ark after that of II Chron. 35:3, when Josiah ordered it to be restored to the Temple. It may have been carried away by Nebuchadnezzar with the other sacred articles when he plundered the Temple. No reference being made to the Ark by Ezra, Nehemiah or Josephus subsequent to the Captivity, it is believed that there was no Ark in the second Temple and that the Holy of Holies was empty. The Jews, however, have a tradition that before Nebuchadnezzar plundered the Temple the priests hid the Ark and that its hiding-place will be revealed by the Messiah at his coming. His knowledge of it will, they declare, be a proof of his claims. No specific search is being made for the Ark, but the Exploration Society would be little likely to neglect a clue to its hiding-place, if one could be furnished.

584 How was it possible for a structure with the large dimensions of the Tower of Babel to be erected in the time and by the few people who lived directly after the flood?

It is clear, from the Biblical account, that in the considerable period which must have elapsed between the Flood and the confusion the race had multiplied rapidly and spread out over the land (see Gen. 10). Josephus, the Jewish historian (in *Antiquities*, Book I, chap. 4), says that they were "a multitude" when they followed Nimrod's advice to build the tower. He adds "by reason of the multitude of hands employed on it, it grew very high sooner than any one could expect." All the evidence points to the conclusion that the period intervening was much greater than is indicated in Ussher's chrolonogical notes found in the margin of the Bible. Those calculations are not in any sense a portion of the text itself, but were made about the year 1650.

585 Who was Balaam?

Balaam, first mentioned in Num. 22:5, belonged to the Midianites. Pethor, where he dwelt, was in Mesopotamia, a considerable distance from Moab. He himself speaks of "being brought from Aram out of the mountains of the east" (Num. 23:7). Josephus, the historian, calls him "a diviner" (soothsayer), a man of great skill in prediction and magic. Balak's language to him in Num. 22:6 was meant to flatter him and make him compliant with his will. It is evident, however, that Balaam had knowledge of the one true God. One commentator writes: "He was possessed of high gifts and had the intuition of truth—in short, he was a poet and a prophet. He himself confessed that he derived his gifts from God. But he, elated with his success, had become proud and believed the gifts were his own and could be used for his own purposes, to make merchandise and acquire riches and honors. But when he received the message of the elders of Moab and Midian, and was tempted to seize the great opportunity to his own advantage, he was divinely warned that his actions would be overruled. As the Bible story shows, God did interfere and the genius of the self-willed, stubborn prophet, under divine influence, became the instrument through which came a message of great power and beauty, bearing upon the destiny of the Jewish nation, and which is cherished by the church throughout the world.

586 Was the prophecy regarding Babylon's fate fulfilled?

The prophecy in Isa. 13 regarding Babylon has been literally fulfilled. It is a heap of ruins; it has never been rebuilt and is uninhabited, save by wild beasts. Its extensive ruins are traced on the east bank of the Euphrates River. The region, once fertile, has become a sterile waste, largely marsh. Explorers have made many excavations, but no one, we believe, has ever suggested the *rebuilding* of Babylon.

587 Why was the beetle worshiped by the Egyptians as an emblem of eternity and resurrection?

The scarabaeus was worshiped because of its supposed mystical virtues. The number of its toes (30) represented the days of the month; its time of depositing eggs had reference to the lunar month, and another of its peculiarities had reference to the action of the sun on the earth. As it was of one sex (as supposed) it represented the eternal, self-existent, self-begotten principle of deity, and there were still other parallels which the Egyptians discovered to connect the sacred beetle with their gods. During its life it was worshiped, and after death embalmed.

588 Where did the black race originate?

Noah and his family being all that were saved from the Flood (Gen. 6:17), the black race must have originated in this family. Noah had a son named Ham. The name *Ham* signifies *swarthy* or *sunburnt* and Noah's youngest son was undoubtedly so named prophetically as the progenitor of the sunburnt Egyptians and Cushites and all the dark-skinned servile races who are to-day designated sons of Ham. Ham was married when the Deluge occurred and with his wife and four sons, Cush, Mizraim, Phut and Canaan, was saved from general destruction. It is a notable fact that Noah did not curse Ham for his offense (see Gen. 9:25), but he cursed Canaan the youngest son of Ham, and prayed that he might be the slave of Shem and Japhet and their descendants. The punishment involved in the curse was perpetual servitude.

589 Where was Daniel when the three Jews were thrown into the fiery furnace?

The question concerning the events described in Dan. 3:12-21 has often been asked, but no authoritative answer can be given as the Bible is silent. It may be that he was in some distant province of the kingdom. Nebuchadnezzar would know enough of Daniel's character to be aware that he would not bow to the image and as he valued his services may have purposely dispatched him to a remote part of the kingdom to avoid the risk of such a conflict as ensued with the other three Jews.

590 How can we explain the seeming inconsistency between I Samuel 16:18, where it said David was a mighty valiant man, and I Samuel 17:33, where Saul says, "Thou are but a youth"?

It would appear that David's talents were already well known and this statement "by a servant" (tradition says it was Doeg) probably magnified his prowess intentionally, to make a good impression. Still, he was only a youth, though stout of limb and fearless of heart. In I Sam. 17:55, Saul's question to Abner was probably prompted by jealousy. A few years had passed since the shepherd minstrel was the king's harpist and these years may have produced such a change in his appearance—from the smooth-faced youth to the bronzed and bearded young soldier—that for the moment he was not recognized by Saul. Or the king might simply have pretended not to know him. In either case, it is not necessary to regard the statements in the Book as inconsistent, since they are clearly capable of reasonable explanation.

591 Did David give Araunah fifty shekels of silver for his land as stated in II Samuel 24:24 or six hundred shekels of gold as stated in I Chronicles 21:25?

The discrepancy has often been pointed out. The probable explanation is in the attitude of the two writers. The writer of Chronicles is believed to have been an officer of the Temple, perhaps a singer. In all his work he goes into the most minute details about the Temple. It evidently engrossed his life and filled his thoughts. The Temple, as you know, was built on this ground of Araunah's. David probably purchased the threshing floor, as Samuel says, for fifty shekels; but afterward deciding that the Temple should be built there, he bought the whole hill, as the chronicler says, for six hundred shekels. The chronicler, with his mind on the Temple, makes the latter payment his record.

592 What are we to think of the spirit of personal revenge that animates some of David's Psalms?

The passages in Ps. 119:20; Ps. 5:8-10; Ps. 7:11-17; Ps. 25; Ps. 88:10 and Ps. 69 appear to need explanation as coming from so good a man as David. We must remember at the outset that these Psalms are accounts of "the free outpouring of a man's feelings and wishes to God in a time of great excitement and not the outpouring of curses upon, or even in the hearing of, the man's enemies." And even in that these Psalms may well be an example to us. Divine love wants our perfect confidence and openness, wants us to be just ourselves, open and just as we are. If in a bad mood, as David was, we can do no better than to pour out our bad moods before God to show him how badly we feel and how much we need his help against those who would harm and hurt us. To be entirely open with God, even to the sharing of our faults and weaknesses, is a great stride in the right direction, and to tell him how badly we need him and how desperate is our position is the beginning of that true relationship with him who fully understands even our frailties and shortcomings.

The *Speaker's Commentary* says: "The Psalmist, contemned and despised by those to whom he had done good and by whom he had been cursed often and persecuted to death, betakes himself at first to prayer as his single refuge; then addresses himself to God, with whom is vengeance, and hurls back the curse which his foes had imprecated upon him upon themselves with a fire and energy which seem to some surprising in this divine collection of hymns. But is a Christian spirit to be expected always in the Psalms? Would the words of Christ have been uttered (Matt. 5:43, 44) if the spirit which animated the Jewish people and is exhibited not infrequently in their annals had been always that which he came to inculcate? Under the Old Covenant calamity, extending from father to son, was the meed of transgression; prosperity, vice versa, of obedience; and these prayers of the Psalmist may express the wish that God's providential government of his people should be asserted in the chastisement of the enemy of God and man."

593 Did not David sin in deceiving the priest (I Samuel 21:1) and eating the shewbread? If so, did Christ approve his act (Matthew 12:3)?

David's deception was sinful and his eating the shewbread was a technical violation of the law. Christ did not express approval of his conduct; he was being assailed by the Jews on questions of the observance of the strict letter of the law and he referred to the incident as an illustration. He reminded them that their great king whom they so highly venerated had broken the command in that particular. He was constantly reproving the Jews for their bondage to the letter of the law and their disregard of its spirit.

594 What is the Book of Enoch?

The only Scriptural reference to the book of Enoch is that found in Jude, verses 14 and 15, but it is not known whether Jude derived his quotation from the written book itself or from tradition. Several of the early fathers of the Church mention the "writings" and "books" of Enoch as though there were several productions. Justin, Irenaeus, Anatolius, Clement and Origen all make such mention, and Tertullian quotes the book as one which was not admitted into the Jewish Canon. It seems to have been known as late as the eighth and ninth centuries, and then all trace was lost until three manuscript copies of an Ethiopic translation were brought to England by Bruce from Abyssinia in 1773. It has since been translated into English, French and German. The book consists of a series of revelations given to Enoch and Noah. In the fourth part of the book the Messiah is predicted and the final redemption of the world. It should be added that the ablest scholars agree that the composition of the book could not have been earlier than a century before Christ, and possibly only half a century. Dillmann assigns the chief part of it to some Aramaean writer about 110 B.C., and believes it was greatly added to by translators afterward.

595 Did the curse of Ham apply to all his descendants?

Ham, the youngest son of Noah, had four sons, Cush, Mizraim, Phut and Canaan (Gen. 10:6). The name, race or nationality of his wife is nowhere given. From Ham were descended the Ethiopians and probably the dark-skinned nations of Africa, as well as the Canaanites of Palestine and Phoenicia and even the Egyptians themselves. Like his brothers, Ham was married at the time of the Deluge, and was saved in the ark, together with his wife, from the general destruction. Egypt is recognized as "the land of Ham" (see Ps. 78:51 and other passages). Thus among Ham's descendants there was a wide variety of races and different grades of complexion, from the primitive Chaldeans to the blacks of the equator. The Bible narrative shows that Noah's denunciation was directed not against Ham, but against his fourth son, Canaan, and some have held that the curse (Gen. 9:25) was accomplished by the subjugation and extermination of the Canaanites by the Jews during the Palestinian conquest.

596 Did God approve of Jacob's duplicity in dealing with Esau?

His conduct is nowhere approved in the Bible. In fact it was most unjustifiable. The Bible does not conceal the faults or wrongdoing of good men. It tells the story of David's awful crimes without reserve. Jacob's wrongdoing led to his banishment from home and separation from his mother, between whom and himself there appears to have been a very tender affection. He suffered retribution too in being tricked by Laban and in the terrible anxiety he suffered later on, when he heard that his brother was coming to meet him with four hundred men; and still later when his own sons deceived him about Joseph. The whole story of his life shows that he was continually learning by hard experience the evil of his early vices of duplicity and hard bargaining.

597 Who are the descendants of Esau?

They are by many believed to have been the successors of the original inhabitants of Idumea and of the Horites. Esau has been called "the father of the Edomites" (Gen. 36:43). With his immense family he retired to Mount Seir, from which they gradually dispossessed the existing population, and held it for many generations. In the course of the Maccabaean wars, the children of Esau lost their independent existence and became merged in the house of Israel.

598 Where was the Garden of Eden?

According to many Biblical authorities Eden, described in Gen. 2:8-10, was located in that region of Asia in the neighborhood of the Euphrates, and not far from the supposed site of Babylon. There are, however, several other regions indicated as the probable site of Eden. These include Armenia, the country near the Caspian Sea, the region of the Oxus, Cashmere in upper India, Ceylon, etc. Many attempts have been made to identify various rivers with those mentioned in the story in Genesis. Probably the preponderance of scholarship points to that section where the Euphrates and Tigris unite.

599 Why did Moses quit Egypt?

There is a seeming discrepancy between the accounts of this event in Ex. 2:14, 15 and in Heb. 11:25-27. The reason mentioned in Hebrews operated first and that in Exodus later. They are two stages in the same process. If he had been ashamed of his race and without faith in God he would have kept away from the Hebrew quarters and posed as an Egyptian. He went to look after his brethren, though he must have known how deeply it would exasperate the Pharaoh. The writer of Hebrews is fully justified by the account given in Exodus for his contention that Moses showed his faith and courage in what he did. When the crisis developed from his interference and there was ground for a definite charge against him, then he fled as stated in Exodus.

600 Is immortality taught throughout the Old Testament?

In the Old Testament there are many passages which deal with the natural order of events: birth, life, death, the grave, etc. The great question of immortality was one of which the ancient races had only a dim foreshadowing, although they were by no means ignorant of it, as numerous passages show. Thus, it was written of Enoch that, because he had lived a pious life, God took him, so that he was no more among men. Paul, speaking of Jacob, says he regarded life as a journey, and that all the patriarchs looked forward to a life after death (see Heb. 11:13-16). In Ex. 3:6 the implication is clear that Jehovah is the God of the living patriarchs still, although they had long been dead (see also Isa. 14:9; Job 19:25-27; Ps. 17:15; 49:15; 73:24; Isa. 26:19; Dan. 12:2, and Eccles. 12:7). It remained for Christ, by his teachings, his death and his resurrection, to bring "life and immortality to light" in the fullest measure. It is only in the clear light of the Gospel that we find the veil removed and the future life fully illuminated.

601 What were the grievances that induced the ten tribes to revolt?

Only the question of taxation appears on the surface, but there had been jealousy on the part of Ephraim from the beginning of the monarchy. Ephraim was a more powerful tribe than any of the others, and wanted to lead. The Ephraimites were reluctant to accept David as king, because he belonged to the tribe of Judah, and yielded only after seven years of disastrous quarreling. David's removal to Jerusalem of the national capital from Shechem, and the religious capital from Shiloh, was another grievance against the house of Jesse. Solomon's magnificence must have involved heavy taxation on the whole country, while the South alone derived benefit or gratification from it. The compulsory attendance at Jerusalem for the annual feasts would also increase the jealousy which culminated when Rehoboam gave his imprudent answer at his coronation.

602 What was the discontent and dissatisfaction that spread among the people of Israel in the desert?

The explanation of the discontent that spread among the people of Israel (see Num. 11:1-5) is given in the statement that among them there was "a mixed multitude that fell a-lusting." Among this multitude were many who were probably of Egyptian blood and descent, and who recalled the abundance of animal and vegetable food to which they had been accustomed in Egypt (see their plaint in verses 4-6). Their discontent was aggravated by the fact that they were in a gloomy, desolate region, far away from any prospect of the rich abundant country that had been promised. Their dissatisfaction was communicated to the Israelites themselves, and the diet of manna became monotonous. They were thoroughly ungrateful for the heavenly gift and demanded a change of fare. They had entered the desert with large flocks and herds (see Ex. 12:38); but these had evidently been greatly reduced until they would not have long sufficed to feed such a multitude. The hope was to preserve their flocks, as far as possible, for the new country whither they were bound; but if they consumed them now they would be forced to enter the land of promise empty-handed.

603 Were the children of Israel justified in borrowing from the Egyptians silver, gold and jewels?

The transaction was not regarded on either side as a loan. The Revised Version (Ex. 12:35) correctly translates the words, "They asked of the Egyptians," etc. It was the custom at parting of friends, or on the leaving of a servant, to make a gift. The idea is much like the backsheesh in Oriental lands at this day. The Israelites had fully earned the gifts by long years of unrequited labor, and the Egyptians in the panic were heartily willing to give them anything if they would only go, and go quickly.

604 How many times did Israel fall back into idolatry?

It would be difficult to answer with absolute accuracy. The first allusion to their idolatry is found in Gen. 31:19, when Rachel stole her father's seraphim. Afterward, we find that the Israelites gave evidence of idolatrous practises on the way from Shechem to Bethel; they defiled themselves with idols in Egypt; later, they worshiped the golden calf, images and stars (Ex. 32); Moloch, Remphan, Chiun, and Baal-Peor, Baal, Baal-berith, Ashtoreth Chemosh, Milcom, the sun, the moon, were all worshiped in succession. Even after possessing Palestine they went astray after the idols of the land times without number.

605 Were any of the kings of Israel and Judah crowned?

Yes; there are frequent references in the Old Testament to both crowns and diadems, the latter sometimes being used for both. The high priest wore a plate of gold in front of the mitre. It was tied behind by a ribbon (see Ex. 29:6; 39:30, 31). The same word used to describe this in the original is used to describe the diadem which Saul wore in battle and which was brought to David (II Sam. 1:10). It was used at the coronation of Joash (II Kings 11:12). David took a crown of precious stones from King Ammon at Rabbah, and it was used as the state crown of Judah (see II Sam. 12:30).

606 Why was Israel ruled by Judges?

In the days of the Judges in Israel the rule was patriarchical. They were chosen for their moral fitness, their experience and their rectitude; yet none of the most notable among them was of priestly lineage. Some were appointed to do particular services, for which they were specially qualified, or to correct evils that had arisen in the community. One commentator writes: "God allowed them Judges in the persons of faithful men, who acted, for the most part, as agents of the divine will—regents of the invisible King—who would be more inclined to act as loyal vassals Jehovah than kings, who would develop notions of independent right and royal privileges, which would draw attention from their true faith in the theocracy. In this greater dependence of the Judges upon the divine King, we see the secret of their institution." That Israel enjoyed more liberty and happiness under the Judges than under the monarchy is shown in the record; yet they were led by the example of the nations around them to clamor for a king. Read the warning written to them by Samuel in I Sam. 8:10-19—an experience which was literally fulfilled.

607 Who composed the armies of Israel?

In these warlike times it may be interesting to learn something about the armies of Israel. They are first mentioned in Ex. 7:4. They were collected by the sound of trumpets (Judg. 3:27), by special messengers and extraordinary means, and enrolled by the chief scribe (Judg. 3:27; Judg. 6:35; Judg. 19:29; II Kings 25:19). Called the "host" and the "armies of the living God" (Deu. 23:9; I Sam. 17:26), they were composed of infantry and later had horsemen and chariots (Num. 11:21; I Kings 1:5; I Kings 4:26). They were divided into three divisions, van and rear, and were divided into companies of thousands (Judg. 7:16; Jos. 6:9; Num. 31:14; II Kings 1:9, 11). Though commanded by the captain of the host they were often led by the king in person (II Sam. 2:8; I Sam. 8:20; I Kings 22 ch.). All males from twenty years and upward were liable to serve, while those who had builded a house, were lately betrothed or newly married were exempt (Num. 1:2, 3; Deu. 20:5; Deu. 20:7; Deu. 24:5). Sometimes the armies consisted of the whole nation and they were supplied with arms from public armories (Judg. 20:11; II Chron. 11:12; II Chron. 26:14). Before going to war Israel's armies were numbered and reviewed, were required to keep from iniquity and to consult the Lord (II Sam. 18:1, 2,4; Deu. 23:9; Judg. 1:1). The Ark of God was frequently brought to lead these armies and they were attended by priests with trumpets who led in the singing of God's praises, who directed their movements (Josh. 6:6, 7; Num. 10:9; II Chron. 20:21, 22; Josh. 8:1, 2). Thus with the aid of God they were all-powerful, but without him they were easily overcome (Lev. 26:3, 7, 8; Lev. 26:17; Num. 14:42, 43).

608 When the prophet Isaiah brought the shadow ten degrees backward, did that not interfere with the movements of the other planets?

The dial of Ahaz, it is assumed, was in the form of a staircase upon which a shadow was made to fall from a pillar, the declination or elevation of the shadow measuring the hours of the day. There is no need to imply, as some have done, that the earth retrograded on its axis; for the miracle might have been produced by the miraculous refraction of the sun's rays on the dial in question without disturbing the divinely appointed order of nature. This might have been effected by a partial eclipse, or by simple refraction through the interposition of a different medium. It is a fact known to scientists that refraction takes place when the rays of light pass through a denser medium.

609 What became of the prophet Isaiah?

Little is known respecting the circumstances of Isaiah's life. His father's name was Amoz (not the prophet Amos). Isaiah resided in Jerusalem, not far from the Temple. He was married and had two sons, whose names are given in Scripture, and he called his wife "a prophetess," showing that she was in active sympathy with and had a share in his spiritual vocation. There is a tradition that he suffered martyrdom under the wicked king Manasseh by being sawn in two, and the scene of his martyrdom is even pointed out under an old mulberry tree, near the Pool of Siloam. Josephus (in *Antiquities* 10:3, 1) mentions the massacre of the Hebrew prophets by Manasseh, although Isaiah is not named among them. It has been maintained, however, by several good authorities that Isaiah lived to a great age and died from natural causes. His prophetical office began in his twentieth year and was continuous until his eightieth year.

610 Was Joseph's wife Asenath converted from the Egyptian heathenism before he married her?

Presumably not. She was the daughter of the priest of On, and was no doubt a believer in the religion of her fathers. She was even named after one of the Egyptian deities, *Neith*. It is fair to assume, however, that after marriage she took the religion of her husband. She became the mother of Ephraim and Manasseh.

611 Did Jacob really see God face to face when at the Brook Jabbok?

Jacob's mysterious wrestling has been a fruitful source of difficulty and misinterpretation. Jacob had left the land of Canaan, full of guilt and liable to wrath, and he was to enter it amid sharp contending, such as might lead to great searchings of heart, deep spiritual abasement and renunciation of all sinful and crooked devices. This was the conflict he had to undergo with "the angel of the Lord's presence." Jacob's inquiry for the name of his antagonist was unanswered. But he called the place *Peniel* ("the Face of God") in token of his nearness to Jehovah while the great struggle was going on. He had been overcome, yet, through the strength of his faith, he had prevailed and got the blessing.

612 What were the prominent Jewish feasts such as the Feast of the Passover?

The Jewish feast days were appointed by God as appointed, solemn, eucharistic meetings (Ex. 23:14; Isa. 1:14; Lev. 23:4; II Chron. 8:13; Isa. 1:13; Ps. 122:4). All males and children from the twelfth year on were required to attend and did so gladly, going up to them in large companies, though they often encountered difficulties and dangers in so doing (Ex. 23:17; Luke 2:42; Ps. 122:1, 2; Ps. 42:4; Luke 2:44; Ps. 84:6, 7). The feast times were seasons of joy and gladness, sacrificing and entertainments (Ps. 42:4; I Sam. 1:4, 9; I Kings 9:25).

The Feast of the Passover was ordained by God to commence the fourteenth of the first month at even (Ex. 12:2, 6, 18) and lasted seven days (Ex. 12:15). It was called the Feast of Unleavened Bread (Mark 14:1) from the circumstance that no leavened bread was to be eaten or kept in the house during it (Ex. 12:15; Deu. 16:3). On the first day the Pascal lamb was to be eaten and the feast was to be observed as commemorating the passing over the first-born and the deliverance of Israel from bondage (Ex. 12:6, 18; 13:17).

613 What was the Feast of Pentecost?

This feast was held the fiftieth day after offering the first sheaf of barley harvest (Lev. 23:15, 16) and was called Feast of Harvest, Feast of Weeks, Day of Firstfruits, Day of Pentecost (Ex. 23:16; 34:22; Num. 28:26; Acts 2:1). It was to be perpetually observed and all males were required to attend as a holy convocation and time of holy rejoicing (Ex. 23:16, 17; Lev. 23:21; Deu. 16:11, 12). At this feast the firstfruits of bread were presented and sacrifices were made (Lev. 23:17, 18, 19). The law from Mount Sinai was given upon the Day of Pentecost, as was the Holy Ghost to the apostles on one of these days (Ex. 19:1, 11; Acts 2:1-3).

614 What was the Feast of Tabernacles?

The Feast of Tabernacles, held after harvest and vintage, began the fifteenth of the seventh month and lasted seven days (Deu. 16:13; Lev. 23:34, 39; Lev. 23:41; Deu. 16:13-15). It was called the "feast of ingathering" (Ex. 34:23). The first and last days were days of holy convocations at which sacrifices were offered (Lev. 23:35, 39; Lev. 23:37). It was to be observed with rejoicing and perpetually. During the feast the people dwelt in booths, bore branches of palms, drew water from the Pool of Siloam and sang hosannas, all to commemorate the sojourn of Israel in the desert (Lev. 23:42; Lev. 23:40; Isa. 12:3; Ps. 118:24-29; Lev. 23:43).

615 What was the Feast of the New Moon?

This holy day was observed on the first day of the month and was celebrated with blowing of trumpets and the making of sacrifices (Num. 10:10; Ps. 81; 3, 4; Num. 28:11-15). It was a season for inquiring of God's messengers and worship in God's house, also for entertainments (II Kings 4:23; Isa. 66:23; I Sam. 20:5, 18). The feast was observed with great solemnity, therefore the mere outward observance thereof was hateful to God (I Chron. 23:31; Isa. 1:13, 14).

616 What was the Feast of Trumpets?

The Feast of Trumpets was held the first day of the seventh month as a memorial of blowing of trumpets. It was a holy convocation and that at which sacrifices were made (Lev. 23:24, 25; Num. 29:2-6).

617 What was the Feast of Purim, or Lots?

This feast, instituted by Mordecai, began the fourteenth of the twelfth month, and was held to commemorate the defeat of Haman's wicked design (Est. 9:20; Est. 3:7-15; Est. 9:17). It lasted two days and was made the occasion of much joy, of rest and of sending presents (Est. 9:17-19, 21). The Jews, after it was confirmed by royal authority, bound themselves to keep the day (Est. 9:27, 28, 29).

618 What was the Feast of Dedication?

The Feast of Dedication was held in the winter month Chisleu, to commemorate the cleansing of the temple after its defilement by Antiochus (John 10:22; Dan. 11:31).

619 What was the Feast of the Sabbatical Year?

Every seventh year the Jews kept the Feast of Sabbatical Year. It was a sabbath for the land at which all field laborers stopped, the fruits of the earth were common property, debts were remitted, all Hebrew servants were released (Lev. 25:2; Ex. 23:11; Lev. 25:4, 5; Ex. 23:11; Deu. 15:1-3; Ex. 21:3). For neglecting this feast the Jews were threatened, and the seventy-year captivity was a punishment therefor. After captivity it was restored to them (Lev. 26:34; II Chron. 36:20, 21; Neh. 10:31).

620 What was the Feast of Jubilee?

The Feast of Jubilee was held every fiftieth year and began on the Day of Atonement (Lev. 25:8, 10; 25:9). It was called "Year of Liberty," "Year of the Redeemed," "Acceptable Year" (Ezek. 46:17; Isa. 63:4; Isa. 61:2). It was specially holy. Respecting it there were these enactments: cessation of all field labor, the fruits of the earth to be common property, redemption of sold property, restoration of all inheritances and release of all Hebrew servants (Lev. 25:12; 11, 23-27, 10, 13, 28; Lev. 27:24; Lev. 25:40, 41, 54).

621 Of how many days was the Jewish year composed?

By Num. 14:34 and Ezek. 4:4-6 the application of a day for a year in prophecy is authorized. A Bible month, according to Gen. 7:11; 8:4, is thirty days. The beginning of the Deluge is placed on the second month and seventeenth day; the ark rested on the seventh month and seventeenth day, and Gen. 7:24 shows this period to be just 150 days, a period of five months, at thirty days to the month. Twelve of such months would constitute a year of 360 days. The year of twelve months is indicated in I Kings 4:7; I Chron. 27:1-15.

622 Were the kingdoms of Judah and Israel totally distinct?

The separation of the monarchy into two took place shortly after Solomon's death, as described in I Kings 12. After the downfall of the ten tribes, the southern branch, consisting of Judah and Benjamin, continued to occupy the land they had formerly occupied until they too were carried away captive.

623 Who were the Maccabees?

The family of Maccabees, which is treated of in the books of the Maccabees, derives its name from Judas, the third son of Mattathias, who was called Judas Maccabeus—that is, Judas the Hammerer. This appellation was given him because of his mighty assaults on the Syrians. The family were leaders against an attempt on the part of Antiochus Epiphanes to force Greek worship upon the Jews in the year following 175 B. C. The trouble arose in the town of Modin, where Mattathias and his five sons lived. In 167 B. C. the leadership in the revolt fell upon Judas, and by the support of loyal Jews he was enabled to restore the temple worship. In subsequent battles for political independence he became prominent as a general, but fell in 161 B. C., in the battle of Eleasa. His brother Jonathan succeeded him. They were rulers in a way, but dependent on Rome. The books of the Maccabees relate the history of those times and are not considered inspired. Though Judas Maccabeus and his followers were brave men imbued with high ideals, they are in no wise guides for us, and the books of the Maccabees contain much that is at least questionable theology and not in harmony with the teaching of inspired Scriptures.

624 Was Moses the author of the first five books of the Bible?

The question has been argued now for many years. The present tendency is to a belief that Moses left records which, after his death, were woven into the continuous narrative we now possess. The references of

Christ and his Apostles to "Moses and the prophets" imply that the belief that Moses was the author of the books that bear his name was prevalent at that day. There are, however, expressions scattered through the five books which were certainly not written by Moses. A specimen instance is Genesis 36:31: "These are the kings that reigned in the land of Edom before there reigned any king over the children of Israel." That verse was evidently written after there had been kings in Israel. Whether these passages indicate that the books were not written by Moses, or whether they were inserted after his death, is a disputed question. There is, however, good reason to believe that the work of Moses formed the basis of the books, even if he did not actually write them in their present form.

625 Who was the mother of Moses' children?

Moses' children were by two wives, one an Arabian woman (Ex. 2:21 and 3:1) and the other a Cushite woman (Num. 12:1). His sons, whose careers were comparatively obscure, he evidently regarded as unfitted to succeed him as leader of the host, so he chose Joshua (Deut. 34:9), and "laid hands upon him" in token of divine approval of the choice (see Josh. 1:2). All that we know of the home relations of Moses is what Scripture relates, which is comparatively meager. Read the more detailed account of Moses' life in Josephus' historical work.

626 What was the method of reckoning time in antediluvian days so as to account for the long lives accredited to the patriarchs?

The method of reckoning time in antediluvian days is uncertain. Bible students are divided in opinion, but the leading commentators are led to conclude that Moses meant *solar* and not *lunar* years, averaging practically as long as ours. Josephus, the Jewish historian, writing on this point, says in his *Antiquities* (1:3:3): "Let no one, on comparing the lives of the ancients with our lives, make the shortness of our lives, at present, an argument that neither did they attain so long a duration of life." This was the Jewish view. On the other hand, Pliny, Scaliger and others assert that the ancients must have computed time differently. The ancient Babylonian year seems to have consisted of twelve lunar months of thirty days each, intercalary months being added at certain periods.

627 Who were the Pharaohs of Joseph's time?

Joseph, it is reckoned by authorities, was born about 1913 B.C. He was sold into Egypt about 1895 B.C. He died 1802 B.C. As to the identification of the Pharaohs of his time there are various opinions. Wilkinson identifies the first Pharaoh of Joseph's experience with Osvitesen I, while Bunsen holds that the monarch was Osirtesen III, and Osborn claims he was Apophis. McClintock and Strong believe that the Pharaoh of the period of Joseph's imprisonment was one of the eighth (Memphitic) dynasty whose names are all unrecorded, but who were contemporary with the twelfth (Diospolitic) dynasty and the fifteenth (Shepherd) dynasty. The time of Joseph's deliverance from prison, according to the chronology adopted by many scholars, falls under the reign of Apophis, one of the shepherd kings (the fourth ruler of the fifteenth dynasty); but it is believed that by this time their power was declining and that they were then in possession of only a part of Egypt, the rest being governed by two other monarchs of different dynasties.

628 Did God employ evil spirits to trouble King Saul?

In I Sam. 16:14, 15, Saul's servants said: "Behold, now an evil spirit from God troubleth thee." The ancients did not know the difference between cases of mental disease from cases of demoniac possession and hence they attributed many maladies to the influence of evil spirits that had their origin only in physical or mental ill health. We can readily receive the truth that diseases affecting the body may be tolerated by God as useful for judgment and correction, and thus also diseases of the mind may be used by God for a like purpose. The evil spirit of God afflicting Saul was some form of melancholia. Matthew Henry says: "He grew fretful and peevish and discontented, timorous and suspicious, ever and anon starting and trembling."

Bishop Wordsworth says: "Saul became melancholy, gloomy, irritable, envious, suspicious and distracted as a man wandering about in the dark." Elliott's *Commentary* says: "It was a species of insanity, fatal alike to the poor victim of the malady and to the prosperity of the kingdom over which he ruled." But be it what it may have been, it certainly had some perfectly natural cause and was not a judgment of God through the agency of evil spirit.

629 Who founded the school of the prophets?

There were schools in ancient Israel taught by the prophets, and the pupils were called "sons of the prophets." The earliest mentioned are those established by Samuel, at Gibeah and Naioth, to which there are vague references in I Sam. 19:20 and other places. The prophets whom Obadiah hid from Jezebel were probably the pupils in such schools as these. Another school at Bethel is mentioned in II Kings 2:3, and still another at Jericho in the fifth verse of the same chapter. The reference to a school at Gilgal (II Kings 4:38-44) would seem to indicate a kind of college where there was a common table. In II Kings 6:1-4 we have the account of the building of such a college. There are the Bible references. If you want further information the rabbis give it, but you must take it for what it is worth. They say that Methuselah established a school before the Flood; that Abraham was a student at three years of age, and that in his young manhood he studied under Melchizedek, and they relate other legends of a similar kind.

630 What were the different questions with which the Queen of Sheba tested King Solomon's wisdom?

There is no record, but there are traditions which cannot be verified at this late day. According to these traditions, the queen produced two bouquets, one of which was of natural flowers and the other of artificial flowers, so excellent in imitation that an ordinary observer could not tell which was the natural. She challenged the king to distinguish without leaving his throne. He ordered his attendants to let bees into the room, and as they alighted on the natural flowers he rightly indicated the bouquet. Another was the challenge to fill a cup with water that came neither from earth nor sky. This Solomon did by collecting the perspiration from a hard-driven horse. A third was to thread a jewel. This the king did by inducing a small worm to crawl through the minute perforation. Lastly, to decide which of two groups of children, dressed exactly alike, were boys and which girls, Solomon ordered bowls of water to be placed before them that they might wash. He rightly decided by the way each group turned up their sleeves before washing. These are some of the questions tradition attributes to the queen.

631 Where did Solomon die?

The Bible record of his death is in I Kings 11:43 and II Chron. 9:31. It simply relates that he slept with his fathers and was buried in the City of David. Farrar narrates the tradition current among the Jews as to his death. It is that Solomon went up to the Temple to worship. He stood there engaged in prayer, a picturesque figure with his long, white hair floating over the imperial mantle, and wearing the gold crown that Bathsheba, his mother, gave him. As he stood leaning on his staff death came to him, but the staff supported the corpse. The priests saw that he was dead, but feared to touch him, because on his dead hand was the famous ring with which he had worked wonders of sorcery. But a mouse ran out from its hole and gnawed at the leather at the foot of the staff until it slipped and the great king fell on the floor and his crown rolled in the dust.

632 Was the lament of Lamech that of a penitent person?

In Gen. 4:23 the outburst of Lamech showed a proud and presumptuous self-confidence: "The boast of a bold, bad man, elated with the possession of arms," which his son Tubal-cain had invented, and with which he had just found that he could take life at will. It cannot be determined whether Lamech was speaking of an actual occurrence, or merely asserting what he would do if opportunity offered. The translators, however, seem to agree that Lamech had already avenged himself on some young descendant of Cain who had wounded him, and that in this speech he was attempting to justify the homicide on the ground of self-defense.

633 Was Cain repentant when driven out after the murder of his brother?

Gen. 4:14 gives the lament of Cain when he was driven out, an exile and wanderer, after the murder of his brother. He was overwhelmed with a sense of the severity of the sentence, but there was no sign of penitence, no cry for pardon, no expression of regret or sorrow. It was the cry of a selfish soul about to be deprived of all its material belongings and driven forth into the wilderness. Cain was afraid that some of the kinsmen of Abel would find him and slay him in revenge. It is evident from various passages that the population had multiplied considerably since the expulsion from Eden, although the record of Genesis deals only with a few individuals until we reach the latter part of chapter 4.

634 Did Solomon repent before his death?

There is no record in the Bible of his having repented, but there is a tradition to that effect. Dean Farrar relates a tradition current among the Jews also as to the circumstances of his death. It is that he died while worshiping in the Temple that he had built. It is said that as he stood there, leaning on his staff, the gold crown on his head Bathsheba, his mother, gave him, his long white hair flowing over the royal mantle, death came to him. He still stood, supported by his staff. The priests saw that he was dead, but feared to touch the body, because on his finger was the ring which was believed to possess magical qualities of terrible potency. But a little mouse ran out and gnawed at the leather at the foot of the staff, until it slipped. Then the great king fell, and his crown rolled in the dust.

635 Did the patriarch Jacob wrestle with an angel or with God?

The passage in Gen. 32:30, notwithstanding Jacob's expression, is interpreted elsewhere in Scripture as referring to an angel (see Hosea 12:5), the conclusion of commentators being that he was the "Angel of the Covenant." Jacob was favored with visions, and Calvin, Hessenberg, Hengstenberg and others have held that this experience was of a similar character to that of the vision of the ladder. The majority, however, interpret it as an actual event, the object of the revelation being to revive the spirit of the patriarch and arm him with confidence in God.

636 What were the "Urim and Thummin" and what was their significance?

Various commentators and translators have differed concerning the real meaning of the words. Some translators give its equivalent as "light and perfection." "Urim" is synonymous with "Teraphim" ("lights" or "fires"). Josephus identifies the Urim and Thummim with the sardonyxes on the shoulders of the ephod, which were bright when all was auspicious and dark when disaster threatened. Others held that they were the Divine Name, one in forty-two letters, the other in seventy-two letters. Still others asserted that they were prophetic symbols, and there were many who held that the Urim and Thummim were identical with the twelve stones upon which the tribes' names were engraved, and that they were employed in oracular consultation, the stones becoming illuminated in rapid succession, according to the character of the message and the order in which the letters or engraved symbols were employed. Michaelis writes that the Urim and Thummim were three stones, on one of which was written "Yes," on another "No," while the third was left blank or neutral, and these were used in lot-drawing and in the deciding of evidence. Kalisch identifies them with the twelve tribal gems in a condition of illumination. The high priest, by concentrating his thoughts on the qualities they represented, passed into a prophetic trance. Lightfoot and others took the same view. It is quite clear that the Urim and Thummim were well known to the patriarchs as an appointed means of divination.

NEW TESTAMENT SUBJECTS

637 Why does the Book of Acts close so abruptly, saying nothing of Paul's death?

The suggestion has been made that Luke intended to write a third work recounting the events subsequent to his second work, but was prevented, or that he did write it and it has been lost. The more natural supposition is that he died during or at the close of Paul's imprisonment, and that he concluded in his history all the events up to the end of his own life. It is reasonable to suppose that if he had lived to see Paul acquitted he would have recorded the fact. The close of the book has the appearance of a work interrupted by death. It is evident, however, that Luke was with Paul when the second epistle to Timothy was written (see II Tim. 4:11), and at that time some kind of trial had taken place which Luke does not record (see II Tim. 4:17). The Acts was probably written during Paul's imprisonment at Rome or completed at that time and was sent out before the final issue of Paul's case was determined. The general opinion is that after Paul's acquittal he went on another missionary journey, penetrating as far as to Spain, and that only on his second imprisonment was he martyred. Luke's silence on these matters leads to the conclusion that he died about the end of those two years mentioned in his concluding verses.

638 Did the apostles forgive sins?

There is no record in Scripture of any of the apostles exercising in a literal and authoritative sense the power of personally forgiving sins. They all, without exception, preached the forgiveness of sins through faith in and acceptance of Jesus Christ as Saviour. The passages in John 20:21-23 is one that is frequently cited by Catholics in support of the claim of their church of the power to forgive sins. But it has no relation to the Roman Catholic Church, which did not exist until long after apostolic times. Further, the best commentators hold that "in any literal or authoritative sense, or as a personal act," this power of forgiveness of sins was never exercised by any one of the apostles, and plainly was never understood by them as a power which they possessed or which had been conveyed to them. All they were authorized to do, or ever did, was in a ministerial or declarative sense to interpret the offer of divine clemency to repentant sinners. No Catholic can point to a single text of Scripture to prove that there is any other mediator than Jesus Christ, or a single text to prove that priests can personally forgive sins. There are, however, other commentators and large church bodies who hold differently (see Augsburg Confession and Lutheran Catechism). These latter believe that there exists in the church of God "a peculiar church power which Christ has given to his church on earth to forgive the sins of penitent sinners unto them, but to retain the sins of the unpenitent, as long as they do not repent"; that the called ministers forgive sins and absolve those who repent and in so doing act as the instruments of God or in virtue of the external office of the ministry and that "this is as valid and certain in heaven as if Christ dealt with us himself."

639 What was the contention between Barnabas and Paul?

The contention referred to in Acts 15:39 is believed to have grown out of the fact that Mark "had either tired of the work, or shrunk from the danger and fatigue that yet lay before them." Barnabas had expressed the desire to take Mark with them (Col. 4:10), which Paul opposed. Barnabas was probably unwilling to adopt Paul's severe attitude toward the young worker, and desired to give him another trial. In this view, Barnabas seems to have been justified, since Mark did retrieve his character later, and he and Paul became fully reconciled (Col. 4:10, 11; II Tim. 4:11).

640 Was Cornelius converted before Peter was called to visit him?

Cornelius is reckoned by Julian and other noted writers as one of the few persons of distinction who embraced Christianity in its earliest stages. His religious position before his interview with Peter has been the subject of much debate. It has been contended that he was a Gentile who, having renounced idols, worshiped the true God, but not after the manner of the Jews, and that he gave much alms. He probably belonged to the same class as Queen Candace's Treasurer, and who had benefited by their contact with the Jewish people so far as to have become convinced that theirs was the true God. Cornelius was regarded as having been selected of God to become the firstfruit of the Gentiles, but he was not converted until his meeting with Peter. In Acts 10 we are told of his vision, and of the divine instruction to him to send to Joppa for Peter, who had already been prepared by the noonday vision on the housetop for the messengers. It was not until Peter reached the house of Cornelius and explained his mission that the Holy Ghost fell on all present and they were baptized.

641 What was the location of the "upper room," where the first gathering of disciples and converts took place?

The "upper room" mentioned in Acts 1, where the first gathering of disciples and converts was held after the ascension, may have been in the house of one of the apostles (or of John Mark, as some suppose), but the general view is that it was probably the upper chamber in a house, the owners of which made it a custom to hire out such rooms for meeting purposes. This custom, it is claimed, was known in Jerusalem long before Christ.

642 How long a period of preparation did John the Baptist undergo before beginning his public mission?

There are no data from which to determine how long a period of preparation was passed by John the Baptist before his public mission began. Banus, one of his instructors (mentioned by Josephus), records that he was with John three years in the wilderness, sharing his austerities. He doubtless spent a much larger period in preparation, however, but the whole of his life from childhood until about his thirtieth year is hidden in obscurity. His public ministry began about A.D. 25, and his death occurred in A.D. 38.

643 Who was the "elect lady" to whom John addressed his second epistle?

Her name is not known, unless the Greek word "Kyria," translated "lady," be a proper name. Some have regarded it as the Greek form of Martha. She was evidently a woman well known to the apostle. He had, as we infer from the epistle, been at the house of her sister, where he met her children. The idea formerly entertained that under this name the apostle was writing to a church is now generally abandoned.

644 What hymns were in use in the Christian church in apostolic days?

That hymns were in use in the Christian Church in apostolic days we gather from Matt. 26:30; Mark 14:26; Acts 16:25; Heb. 2:12, etc. These were probably adaptations from the old Hebrew psalms. The hymn which Jesus and his disciples sang at the Last Supper is believed to have been the latter part of the *Hallel*—the psalms sung by the Jews on the night of the Passover—and which included parts of Ps. 113, 114 and 118. But it is made clear, by other passages, that very early in the history of the Christian Church another class of vocal music came into use in worship (see Eph. 5:19; Col. 3:16). These "psalms, hymns and spiritual songs" were what Professor Schaff has termed "a lyrical discourse to the feelings"—a metrical form chosen for the expression of experiences that would excite pious emotions and draw the hearer to the source of joy and blessing. The revival hymn, as we know it to-day, had its prototype in those early Christian spiritual songs, which it may be reasonably supposed held forth the Gospel of a free salvation through Christ and the joys and rewards of heaven as compensation for the sorrows and sufferings of the persecuted believers here on earth.

645 Was John's dress of camel's hair and a leather girdle the distinctive dress of a prophet?

Some have seen in John's dress a designed imitation of that of the great Elijah, but there is as much reason against this contention as there is for it. In the towns great attention was paid to dress and many fine garments of beautiful texture and colors were worn; but in the desert districts and among the tribesmen a much simpler mode of dress was in vogue. It was often made out of homespun cloth out of the materials provided by flocks of camels, sheep or goats. The shirt, or tunic, was fashioned of the long hair of the camel. It has been suggested that the expression "camel's hair" was a recognized trade term for a certain kind of cloth. The leathern girdle was provided from the skin of the animals, and the mantle, or cape, was, in all probability, a sheep skin with the wool left on—a kind of dress still worn by the peasants of Palestine. Kitto says of John's dress: "He was clad in raiment which would wear well and required no care—such as Elijah and other ancient prophets wore, not as distinctive of their profession (for John had not yet been called to be a prophet), but as the dress of poor men, and best suited to their condition. It is a dress which may still be seen every day in the Syro-Arabian countries: a rough but stout and serviceable robe of camel's hair, or of camel's hair and wool combined, bound about the waist by a broad girdle of stiff leather."

646 Was John's baptism of divine authority?

John himself regarded his mission as a lower one and as not having the divine authority of the Saviour's work. He considered the existing Judaism as a stepping-stone by which the Gentiles were to arrive at the Messianic kingdom. He taught with the authority of a prophet who in his long wilderness sojourn had received spiritual inspiration and guidance for his work. "Repent and be baptized" was the order of his mission. His baptism, however, was not regarded as conferring an immediate consecration, but as being preparatory; and the disciples of Jesus, taking this view, rebaptized the followers of John (see Acts 19:3-5). Commentators explain that the point of contrast between the baptism administered by John and that by Jesus was not a personal one, but was between water baptism unto repentance and the promised baptism of the Spirit unto a new life. John himself said (Matt. 3:11): "I indeed baptize you with water . . . but he shall baptize you with the Holy Ghost and with fire." As to the significance of Christ's baptism, these simple disciples had not yet been enlightened. They were accordingly baptized by Paul himself "unto the whole fulness of the new economy as now opened up to their believing minds."

647 Who was the John whom Jesus loved?

John was the younger of the two sons of Zebedee, a Galilean fisherman. His father appears to have been in comparatively good circumstances, owning a vessel and having hired servants. John had not the natural vehemence of his brethren, but was of a mild and gentle disposition, thoughtful and affectionate. Nor did he join in their strifes for leadership. His whole heart seemed to be centered on Jesus, and our Lord, recognizing this supreme attachment, made him his "bosom disciple." The disciple, in his writings in later years, referred to himself as the one "whom Jesus loved." His Gospel and Epistles all breathe a deeper spirituality, a more complete absorption and a higher degree of inspiration than those of other writers of the New Testament books. Wholly different was the character of David. He was the warrior and soldier-king as well as the sweet singer. His love and his hate were both ardent; hence we find him in Ps. 139 "hating his enemies with a perfect hatred"—the language of zeal untempered by moderation or forgiveness. It was the expression of human feeling, and not like that of John, whose feelings were inspired by personal contact with the Saviour, who taught us to forgive our enemies.

648 In view of his being espoused to Mary, what relation was Joseph to our Saviour?

"Espoused" means "betrothed." Joseph was the nominal father before the Jewish law, but it is expressly stated in the Scripture that Jesus was begotten of the Holy Spirit. James the Younger and Joses, according to the usual interpretation, were the sons of Salome, the sister of Mary and wife of Cleophas (see John 19:25; Acts 1:13; Matt. 27:56; Mark 15:40). This is the view of many commentators, who hold that the term "brethren" was applied to cousins and others of the same kindred. On the other hand, there are not a few who hold that the brothers in question were later sons of Mary herself.

649 Do we know what became of Mary the mother of Christ?

The New Testament records go no further than the fact that Jesus on the cross commended his mother to the care of the apostle John, and to mention her later as a member of the company of believers who continued together in prayer before Pentecost (Acts 1:14). Traditions vary as to the length of her life after this, some saying two, some saying twenty-four years. Many traditions grew up about the later years of Mary's life. Her death is variously reported to have occurred at Ephesus and Jerusalem. Catholics came later to hold the belief that she did not die but was translated bodily into heaven. While belief in the "Assumption," as this is called, has not officially been made a point of Catholic doctrine, Catholic theologians generally class it among those truths which it would be "rash to deny." The feast of the Assumption has been celebrated since the fifth or sixth century. Of course there is no historic or Scriptural ground for thinking that Mary died in any other than the natural way, or that her body escaped the ordinary natural processes of destruction.

650 What was the offense for which the Nicolaitans were condemned?

The offense for which the Nicolaitans were condemned has given rise to much conjecture. They are believed to have attempted to graft on the Christian faith pagan licentiousness and idolatry. One writer says: "They made their liberty a cloak for cowardice and licentiousness and united brave words with evil deeds. They mingled in the orgies of idolatrous feasts, and brought the impurities of those feasts into the meetings of the Christian Church. All this was done as part of a system, supported by a doctrine, accompanied by the boast of a prophetic illumination" (II Pet. 2:1, 2).

651 When did Joseph, the foster-father of Jesus, die?

Commentators do not claim to be able to fix the date of Joseph the Carpenter's death. Some hold that it must have taken place before Jesus began his public ministry. In support of this they point to the fact that Joseph is not mentioned in connection with the wedding feast at Cana. Others believe that Joseph must have passed away before the crucifixion, otherwise he would have been at the cross with Mary. Under the circumstances nothing definite can be stated on the matter. Christian tradition asserts that Joseph was over eighty when espoused and that he lived to be a very old man.

652 Who was Onesimus?

The epistle of Paul to Philemon is linked very closely with the apostle's epistle to the Colossians, and both were carried by the same messenger, Onesimus, who was the slave of Philemon and a fugitive from justice. Under Paul's teachings he was converted to Christianity, and, being induced to return to his master, was made the bearer of this letter, in which Paul recommended him as no longer a mere servant but also a brother in Christ. Apphia, mentioned in verse 2, was the wife of Philemon, and Archippus, the Colossian pastor, is supposed to have been a near relative, dwelling in Philemon's house. The epistle was regarded by the ancient church as the unquestioned work of Paul himself. It was written, as authorities believe, by the apostle early in the year A.D. 62, during his first captivity in Rome, and its whole object was an appeal for the restoration of Onesimus to Philemon's favor. While the longer epistle to the Colossians was dictated to an amanuensis, this message to Philemon was wholly in Paul's own handwriting. The last line, "Written from Rome to Philemon, by Onesimus, a servant," does not mean that Onesimus was the writer but the bearer. It was as though a letter-writer to-day should write on the envelope, "To Mr. So-and-So, per kindness of Mr. Smith."

653 Was Paul acquitted at his trial before the emperor at Rome?

It would appear from II Tim. 4:6 that Paul was condemned. There is good reason, however, for believing that Paul was acquitted at the end of the two years mentioned (Acts 28:30). He then appears to have gone to Ephesus and other places, penetrating as far as Spain. Clement, the apostle Paul's disciple, mentioned in Phil. 4:3, says that he went to "the extremity of the West," which at that time would mean Spain. He was harassed and worried by errors creeping into his churches, and did not, it is thought, stay long in one place. Jerome says that Paul was "dismissed by Nero that he might preach Christ's Gospel in the West." Returning, he appears to have again visited Ephesus and Crete. A passage in his Epistle to Titus (3:12) indicates an intention to spend a winter at Nicopolis, a city on the western coast of Greece. It is believed that he did so, and was arrested there and taken again to Rome. His second imprisonment, as we gather from the two epistles to Timothy, which, it is thought, were written at this time, appears to have been much more severe. Nero's persecution of the Christians was raging, and Paul could not, and did not, expect to escape condemnation. It is believed that he was put to death late in May or early in June, 68, five years after he was released from his first imprisonment.

654 How could the Apostle Paul be a Roman and also a Jew?

Roman citizenship was bought and sold at high prices in the reign of Claudius. Paul, born a Jew, also inherited the rights of a Roman citizen at his birth, either by the purchase of citizenship by some ancestor or as a reward granted to his father or grandfather for services to the state. The rights of citizenship, freedom to be considered equal to Romans, was sometimes granted to whole provinces and cities, and frequently to families. In the latter case it was transmitted from father to son in the direct line.

655 Was Paul led of the Holy Spirit to go up to Jerusalem that last time when he was arrested?

We are aware that a prominent teacher has urged the view that Paul's last journey was made contrary to the will of the Spirit and in opposition to definite warning, but it does not seem to us tenable. Paul evidently believed it was his duty to go. Previously in so many instances he had yielded to the intimations of the Spirit that we have a right to believe that he would have done so in this case if any had been made. The mere threat or prediction that he would suffer would not deter him. He was ready, as he said (Acts 21:13), not to be bound only, but to die at Jerusalem for the name of the Lord Jesus. Those are not the words of a man wilfully and perversely opposing the Holy Spirit. Agabus professed to be speaking in the name of the Holy Spirit (Acts 21:11), but we do not think he was, otherwise he would have been more accurate. He said the Jews would bind Paul and deliver him to the Gentiles. The event shows that it was the Gentiles who bound him, and the danger was lest they should deliver him to the Jews. The last thing the Jews were disposed to do was to deliver him to the Gentiles. They wanted to deal with him themselves. Prophecies inspired by the Holy Spirit are not so inaccurate in details.

656 What authority is there for the belief that Peter died in Rome?

It is held as a settled point, by the oldest writers, that Peter went to Rome in the last year of his life. The statements of Eusebius and Jerome that the apostle remained many years in Rome do not seem to rest upon accurate information. But concerning his actual visit there, there is no room for doubt. Clement of Rome, writing before the close of the first century, mentions it. Ignatius, in an epistle to the Romans, refers to Peter in terms that show his special personal connection with their church. Papias also refers to Peter's Roman experience, and Dionysius of Corinth, writing to Soter, Bishop of Rome, in the second century, explains the intimate relations between the two churches by the fact that Peter and Paul both taught in Italy and both suffered martyrdom there. Irenaeus bears distinct testimony to Peter's presence in Rome. Caius, the Roman presbyter, in the next century, also gives similar testimony and speaks of Peter's tomb in the Vatican. Besides, there is the additional evidence of Origen, Tertullian and the ante- and post-Nicene fathers as to Peter's presence in Rome. None of those authorities mentioned, however, assert that he was the sole founder and head of the church, as the Romish clergy contend. As to Peter's martyrdom, we may cite Origen, who declares that the apostle himself chose crucifixion. St. Ambrose and Tillemont also give corroborative testimony.

657 When was Peter converted?

We have no record of the period in Peter's life when the change took place. It may have been when he left all to follow Christ. His doing so was stronger evidence of conversion than some converts now would give. Or it may have been when he confessed Christ and was commended for it (Matt. 16:17). In the passage which has probably prompted the question (Luke 22:32) the word is better translated "restored" or "turned again" than "converted."

658 Why is it that the Abyssinian church proclaims Pontius Pilate a saint?

Many strange legends concerning Pilate have been preserved. Concerning these one commentator writes: "The disposition to represent Pilate as himself becoming a Christian explains, perhaps, the belief of the Coptic Church that he died a saint and a martyr." His wife, Claudia Procula, according to the tradition, had already become a convert to the new faith, and on that account she is honored as a saint by the Greek Church. Some of the early Christians seem to have identified her with the Claudia of II Tim. 4:21; but this is by no means definite. Tertullian wrote that Pilate, "at or immediately after Christ's death on the cross, was already a Christian in his own convictions." The Copts have canonized both Pilate and his wife and honor them on the same day, June 25. The Abuna or patriarch of the Abyssinian Church receives his investiture from the Coptic patriarch of Alexandria, who is the nominal head of the Ethiopian Church. The Abyssinians have no doubt adopted their notion of Pilate's canonicity from this source. Jesus' estimate of Pilate, however, as recorded in John 19:11, is the verdict of history. The governor was a worldly man, weak and ambitious and unsupported by moral principle, who made a great crime possible by his feebleness of character.

659 Who was Pilate's wife?

Pilate's wife, she who had "suffered many things in a dream," and hence sought to prevent the execution of Jesus, was, according to tradition, a proselyte, named Claudia Procula. Though nothing is known of her origin, the tradition as to her becoming a Christian is as old as the time of Origen. The Greek Church has canonized her. Her dream has been interpreted by some as a divine interposition, and by others as a suggestion of the devil, who wished to prevent the Saviour's death, and by still others as the unconscious reflection of her interest in the reports which had reached her regarding Jesus.

660 Was Salome a sister of Mary, the mother of Jesus?

She was apparently the wife of Zebedee (compare Matt. 27:56 with Mark 15:40). Some modern critics hold that she was that sister of Mary the mother of Jesus to whom reference is made in John 19:25, while others believe the passage refers to Mary, the wife of Cleophas, who is mentioned immediately afterward. This passage has been the subject of much dispute among Bible commentators.

661 Why did the Samaritans reject Jesus as their Messiah?

The fact that Jesus had set his face toward Jerusalem (Luke 9:53) led the Samaritans to reject him as Messiah, because they had been taught that their Messiah would come to Mount Gerizim (compare John 4:20, 21). The Samaritans still consider Mount Gerizim the most sacred place in the world.

662 Who was Theophilus?

He is referred to in Luke chap. 1 and Acts chap. 1, and is variously regarded by commentators, some holding that it was a name applicable to every lover of truth. Thus, Origen, Salvianus, Epiphanius and others held that all who are beloved of God are "Theophil." Others assert that he was an actual person in high official position, some contending that he was a Roman governor or senator at Antioch or Achaia, with whom Luke was intimately acquainted and whom he had baptized. It is obvious that he was a Christian. Another view is that he was addressed by Luke as the head of the Jewish nation. Later commentators reject the impersonal view and hold that Theophilus was a native of Italy, probably a convert of Luke or Paul, to whom the former dedicated his beautiful Gospel history. He lived about 56 A.D.

663 Who was Titus, to whom Paul addressed one of his epistles?

Titus was of Greek origin and was thought to be a native of Antioch. Paul after converting him called him his own son. This is all that is known of the early history of Titus. Some writers have endeavored to identify him with Timothy, but the evidence all goes to show that they were two distinct individuals.

664 Does the New Testament gift of tongues exist at the present time?

The "Gift of Tongues" at Pentecost was given because of an urgent need. It was speaking not in unknown tongues, but in the current languages represented in that great throng of different nationalities. There was no confusion, no misunderstanding, no Babel of uncouth or unintelligible sounds. It was the method chosen by the Holy Spirit to bring into the Gospel fold the strangers from other lands who were soon to depart. That the gift may still be bestowed in modern times is not questioned; but that it has been bestowed in some instances where emotional and uninstructed persons are concerned is questionable. We should "try the spirits" to see whether they be of God or otherwise. He is not the author of confusion and he gives no message to his children that is wholly lost through being unintelligible.

Because of the gift of tongues, we have no doubt that in the days of Paul there was a great deal of trouble in the church on that account and many conflicting opinions. All the spirits are not of God, and it is well to try them, as the Bible suggests. Writing of tongues, Paul says distinctly in I Cor. 14 chapter: "Let all things be done unto edifying. If any man speaketh in a tongue, let it be by two or at the most three, and that in turn; and let one interpret: but if there be no interpreter, let him keep silence in the church, and let him speak to himself and to God." In other words, any message claiming to be in a tongue, yet which could neither be understood nor interpreted, was, in Paul's view, unfitted for delivery in the church or in public at all. God is just as able to bestow the gift of tongues to-day as he was at Pentecost; but we want to be sure that it is the divine gift and not a counterfeit, sent to delude and mislead.

665 Who was Veronica?

Veronica was a pious woman of Jerusalem, the story of whose kindness to the Saviour when he was being taken to crucifixion has been preserved in tradition. She is not mentioned by name in the Gospels. She is supposed to have been the woman mentioned in Matt. 9:20.

666 Were there degrees of importance among the apostles?

Matt. 18:18 grants to all of the apostles the same power with regard to admission to and rejection from the membership of the church, which had already been given to Peter, so that all were equally recognized and equipped with the same authority. The apostles were never empowered, as the Roman Church claims, to personally forgive, but simply to declare God's will and readiness to pardon the repentant sinner. (*See Question No. 83.*)

667 Why did Paul after his conversion go into the temple to purify himself?

Paul's action in going into the Temple and purifying himself with the Jews (Acts 21:26) was a conciliation to Jewish prejudice. To the Jews he became as a Jew that he might gain them to Christ.

**668 What kind of death did Herodias
and her daughter die?**

Josephus in *Antiquities*, Book 18, chapter 5, refers to the closing career of Herodias. She went with Antipas to Lugdunum and there shared his exile and reverses until death ended them.

CHRISTIAN LIVING

**669 Is it right to purchase prize packages
or to set aside articles to be won by the
greatest number of votes at church fairs?**

Prize packages, as popularly understood, are a lottery, wherein the value and sometimes even the character of the contents are unknown. They are a species of gambling, and an imposition upon credulous people. Better select what you want, buy it in the regular way, and leave all games of chance alone. The more you are acquainted with such games the poorer you will become. There are many counterfeit methods of giving and they cultivate bogus benevolence. All methods of raising money for the Lord that are contrary to the precepts and examples of his Word are to be condemned. The simple method of free-will offerings alone is approved (see Ex. 35:5, 21, 29; II Cor. chaps. 8 and 9; Matt. 10:8). Lottery and grab-bag and similar devices involving the gambling principle are all "works of the flesh" and a distinct desecration of the Lord's house.

**670 What attitude should a Christian take
on the subject of dancing?**

In the great discussion which is now agitating our churches, as to "letting down the bars" on the question of amusements, dancing occupies a prominent place. There are, doubtless, many good, well-meaning people who, never having fully considered the subject, are disposed to be tolerant regarding the dance, and do not sympathize with the strenuous opposition that is displayed toward it by many in and out of the pulpit. We think, however, that the attitude of the earnest Christian toward dancing should be the same as that toward cards—no compromise. A thing is either right or it is wrong, and even in its least objectionable aspect dancing is a physical dissipation, a waste of time, an invitation to doubtful promiscuous acquaintanceship, and an association which is difficult to describe as other than immodest. "Dancing," says an authority, "breaks down the bounds of modesty." Late hours, crowded rooms, unnatural excitement, and peril of colds from exposure are among the other objections which any sensible person might urge. In the Christian it is enough to know that the ballroom has been the first step to ruin for countless multitudes. It has never helped one soul, and has destroyed many. These considerations should make the earnest inquirer shun such follies and avoid even the appearance of evil. Though he himself might not fall, his example might be the means of leading weaker souls to destruction.

On the other hand, no one has ever heard of a single instance where dancing could be regarded as morally helpful. On the general principle that any amusement which is in the nature of a stumbling-block to spiritual growth should be avoided, the Christian would do well to omit dancing altogether from the list of innocent recreations. Any father who wishes his daughter well does not wish her to be subjected to the promiscuous acquaintanceships, the doubtful companionships of the ballroom, where she must inevitably meet persons at times who would never be considered fit to be invited to her home. If you desire to keep your children pure and honorable, keep them from evil associates, who are common in every dancing and card-playing community.

671 Is it wrong to play chess, dominoes, and authors?

The whole question of amusements must be relegated to the individual conscience. "To him that thinketh it is sin, it is sin." There are some men whose idea of duty and the necessity for devoting all the time available to work for God is so exalted that they would consider any amusement a sinful waste of time, and such men are to be admired. There are others, however, who find in relaxation a means of increasing their power for labor. They wisely take relaxation in some form. Certain games have by association with gambling become disreputable and these for example's sake should be eschewed. Cards, roulette and many that might be cited belong to the category. The games mentioned in the question cannot strictly be called games of chance and it would be uncharitable to condemn as inconsistent those who engage in them for relaxation.

672 What is the correct attitude of the church on the film question?

The church is just beginning to realize that moving pictures can be made one of the most valuable of its accessories. This new art, which has unquestionably come to stay, is capable of being adapted to the teaching of the grandest lessons of history, sacred and secular. Protected from moral blemishes, it will prove one of the church's most powerful coadjutors in reaching the multitudes for good. It lends itself admirably to the uses of instruction and inspiration. Labor, travel, exploration, science, history are all within its reach. It can be made tributary to religion and good citizenship and to instruction in all that relates to the progress and betterment of the race. We believe the time will come, and soon, when our churches, schools and lyceums will employ the new art as one of the main adjuncts of their work, which will simplify and greatly add to its value and efficiency.

673 Is it right for ladies' aid societies to give entertainments in the church and employ professional talent?

Many churches adhere to what seems to be the only Scripturally sanctioned method of raising money for church purposes, namely, that of direct, voluntary giving. Gradually, however, the idea that certain church societies may legitimately "earn" money by arranging some social event or entertainment has gained ground, and in some cases it does not seem to hinder spiritual work. Then, too, the idea is growing that it is the duty of the church to meet and direct not only the spiritual but also the intellectual and social needs of the people. Lectures may very appropriately have a place in the program of a church, and there seems to be no reason why the best vocal and instrumental music may not also be rendered. Many churches are making extensive use of the motion-picture machines for educational and wholesomely entertaining exhibitions. Some denominations still have a strong prejudice against using the church edifice or auditorium for anything but purely spiritual functions and use a second building or the church basement for these other affairs. Others feel that God's house is also, by his choice, the people's house and that anything which ministers to the physical, mental, moral or spiritual welfare of the people may be given in it.

674 Can a Christian conscientiously play cards?

A Christian cannot conscientiously play cards, because even looking at the matter simply for his own sake cards are the common instruments of gambling; because by its very nature card-playing excites the gambling propensity, and is therefore most dangerous to morality. For the sake of others to whom his example may give scandal, and who might be led by that example to their ruin, a Christian should avoid cards, for by their use, even innocently, he might become responsible for a brother's destruction. Card-playing has been the first step to ruin of countless multitudes.

The true Christian will do nothing whereby he may place a stumbling-block in the way of another. While the mere act of card-playing may in itself be innocent enough, it is a practise which has proved the first step to ruin to countless multitudes. On the other hand, man's moral, spiritual or mental character has never been improved in the slightest degree by card-playing. It is not an accomplishment that wins for a man esteem and confidence either in business or in private life, but the reverse.

For the professed follower of Christ to attempt to justify this dangerous and evil pastime is an incomprehensible inconsistency (see Rom. 14:15-21). Apply the fixed principle that "it is good not to do anything whereby thy brother stumbleth," and you will never touch another card, lest by example you may lead weaker ones into sin and possibly be the means of their spiritual destruction.

675 Is it right for a Christian to attend social gatherings of non-Christians?

A Christian is supposed to be a light in the world, and therefore he should not exclude himself from the world. He must make it a matter of conscience how far he can share in social amusements without violating his principles. There are many amusements that are innocent. Even Jesus attended a wedding feast.

676 In order to live up to Christ's teaching, is it necessary that we give up everything which furnishes an occasion for sinful thoughts or emotions?

The texts Matt. 5:29-30 and Mark 9:43, 47, "If thy right eye offend thee pluck it out," etc., etc., may seem at first blush to mean more than they really do. Suppose, now, we start all over again, remembering that when one wants to do right Jesus is his friend, not his enemy. Suppose now that one, for example, has a good voice or some other accomplishment which may lead to foolish pride or vanity. Or if vanity is aroused by something which is not a talent but a natural gift, like beautiful hair. Should we give up our accomplishment and cut off our beautiful hair? Are we quite sure of the kindness of Jesus? Remember that everything Jesus ever said he said to help people, to help them to happiness. Now we seem to be missing happiness, and Christ comes along to help us. If you will stop to reason, to let your fundamental common sense, your God-given faculty of thought, do its appointed work, you will know perfectly well that Jesus does not want you to do any of the frightful or uncomfortable things suggested above. In the words quoted here he was making a point, was stating a principle. He was saying that eternal life and happiness are of incomparably greater importance than earthly life and happiness. We must stand ready to give up anything at the command of God; our only complete happiness is in complete surrender to him. But Jesus loved beautiful children and sweet music and fragrant flowers; he believed in friendship and sociability and human gladness. He wants his friends to be beautiful and winsome and happy. Even the austere Paul spoke of woman's hair as her "glory." Your trouble is that you are doubting Christ instead of trusting him, fearing him instead of loving him. Tell him at once that you will obey him in everything that he makes *unmistakably clear*.

One would do very wrong to make any great sacrifice on a guess. When he speaks his message is plain: "My sheep know my voice," he said. Every gift and power and grace God has given you can be used in making others happy and in glorifying Christ. Ask him to cleanse your heart from all sin, to fill it with love for himself and others, to help you forget yourself in loving and serving him. Then your life will be full of gladness and beauty and usefulness, and you will wonder that you could ever have been afraid of so kind a Saviour, who wants to make us all glad.

677 Can a Christian conscientiously attend theatrical performances?

The Christian is one who has the Christ spirit, who is trusting in him, seeking to be like him and to know and do his will. We cannot understand how such a one can find pleasure in theatergoing and should expect that his thoughts and feelings would lead him to very different places for enjoyment. But that is a matter for his own conscience. It is not for you, or us, or any church, to say that he will be excluded from heaven for any such cause.

You must consider the effect on yourself, and the effect on others, of your going. Even if you are not injured yourself, your example may be injurious. There are many kinds of theaters, but your friends may not discriminate. A person who goes to see a vicious play may quote your example in defense of himself, because he, like you, went to a theater, though you may detest the nastiness of such plays as he delights in, and you may go only to pure and elevating performances. As to the effect on yourself, you must judge. We think if the love of Christ and his divine life are in your soul, you will not care to go to the theater. You will be so much in earnest in seeking growth in grace that you will not have patience to watch a theatrical performance. You will have no disposition to spend in that way time that may be used in Christ's service.

678 Is it right for church societies to have suppers and picnics?

We devoutly wish that those stern Christians who insist that certain detail acts of conduct are wrong and certain others right would study carefully and prayerfully St. Paul's words about judging and about liberty (Rom. 14; I Cor. 8; I Cor. 10:19-33). The very heart of the Christian system and the new dispensation is that people, after having love for God and love for their neighbor implanted in their souls, are *free*; free to use their sanctified judgment in all matters of conduct not definitely prescribed by the moral law. If a church society wishes to go to the labor of arranging a supper and takes the proceeds for the church, no one should find fault, though it is true, on the other hand, that if all the members of the church contributed as much as they should, these functions would not be necessary. As to picnics, what possible objection could any one have to the children of a Sunday school getting together with their parents and teachers for a pleasant day in the woods or by the lake shore or the sea.

679 Do angels visit people and talk to them as they did in ancient times?

The reference to angels in Heb. 1:14 implies that God still employs them to minister to his children. Our not seeing them does not prove that they are not around us. Elisha's servant was at first unaware of their presence though the mountain was full of them (II Kings 6:17). In the Christian dispensation, however, the Holy Spirit is the recognized channel of communication between God and man. Jesus said that he would be our guide into all truth (John 16:13) and he is to abide with us forever (John 14:16). The laws of God being unchangeable it would seem that there should be now as formerly visions, miracles and angelic appearances as of old.

In one sense, of course, God's laws are unchangeable; they are always wise, beneficent and righteous; but it does not follow that he always deals with men in the same way. There is an obvious growth in the development of his revelation of himself which you can trace in the Bible. Moses and Samuel and David and the prophets had not so clear an idea of him as we get in Jesus Christ. It is as with the education of a child. In his early years we teach him by pictures and stories, but as he grows older we leave all that behind. Christ was clearly hurt by the craving of the people to see miracles performed. Paul had but a low estimate of the value of the tongues (see I Cor. 14:19). God in our age is dealing with men in preaching and by the Holy Spirit. As Abraham said to Dives: "If men believe not Moses and the prophets, neither would they be convinced though one rose from the dead."

We are told that God is a spirit and he is therefore invisible to mortal eyes. All that we read of his revelations leads us to believe that he assumed a form for the purpose of communication with the Old Testament saints. That form they saw, but God himself they could never see. In the same way the very writers who declare that God could not be seen were well aware that they had seen him in Christ. In a very solemn manner Jesus told them that they who had seen him had seen the Father. Yet even in him the glory of God was veiled by his flesh; but there was such a manifestation of his presence as a human being could bear to see and no more. The Old Testament writers doubtless believed that they saw God, but in the New Testament light it was realized that God could not be seen, being a spirit.

**680 What is the doctrine of assurance?
Must we have it?**

Various schools of theology differ about this doctrine of "assurance." Some saints and scholars are so impressed with the frailties and vagaries of the human mind that they cannot understand how a human being can be *sure* of certain things relating to the infinite and divine. Others, and this is, we think, the position held by most Protestant bodies, hold that faith will lead to assurance. "Know," "knowing," "knowledge" are favorite New Testament words. The apostles were absolutely sure that Christ had redeemed them and was their friend. Many other souls have had and many still possess this same experience. They know God has forgiven them just as they would know that a debt had been paid that they owe. They say with the once-blind man: "One thing I know, that whereas I was blind now I see." They know they used to dislike and distrust God; now they know they love and trust him. They began by believing his promises because others had found them true; now they believe them because they have found them true. Study II Tim. 1:12; I John 2:3; 3:14, 3:19, 4:13, 5:13, 5:19; Rom. 6:6, etc. Assurance is produced by faith, Eph. 3:12; made full by hope, Heb. 6:11, 19; and is confirmed by love, I John 3:14, 19. Saints are privileged to have assurance of various things. Such as their election, Ps. 4:3; I Thess. 1:4; their redemption, Job 19:25; their adoption, Rom. 8:16; their salvation and eternal life, Isa. 12:2; I John 5:13. They are also sure of the unalienable love of God, Rom. 8:38, 39; of union with God and Christ, I. Cor. 6:15; Eph. 5:30; of peace with God by Christ, Rom. 5:1; of preservation, continuance in grace, comfort in affliction, support in death and a glorious resurrection, Ps. 3:6; Phil. 1;6; Ps. 73:26; Luke 4:19; Ps. 23:4; Job 19:26; Phi. 3:21. They should therefore give diligence to attain assurance and strive to maintain it (II Pet. 1:10, 11; Heb. 3:14, 18) .

**681 Is a Christian bound to strive constantly
after the highest possible attainments?**

The injunction of Paul, I Cor. 9:24, has been interpreted to mean that a Christian is bound to live, as it were, constantly living, in a constant strain.

There can be no doubt that a Christian must seek the highest spiritual attainments. But there are many misconceptions of what those highest attainments are. They certainly do not mean that a Christian should be under a "constant strain," if by that is meant a restless, anxious, troubled life. It is from precisely this kind of spiritual "strain" that Christ came to relieve us. A great Bible word is "rest." Christ came to substitute God's strength for our strength in spiritual efforts. "Come unto me, and I will give you rest." The writer of the Epistle to the Hebrews says (4:10): "He that is entered into his rest, he also hath ceased from his own works as God did from his." Whittier prays:

> *"Take from our souls the strain and stress,*
> *And let our ordered lives confess*
> *The beauty of thy peace."*

But as the soul enters into those higher places of rest and peace there will be still great activities in *service*. The best saints are those who are under the *strain* of a great, passionate desire to serve and help others. But such a life is delightfully "normal," and also usually "healthy." To be free from anxieties about self, and lost in service for others in the name of Jesus, that is the life not only of highest duty but of highest delight.

682   To what extent can a Christian, a saved and sanctified person, engage in a mercantile or speculative business?

Such a person may engage in business to any extent, providing his spirit be that which Christ demanded and his conduct in accordance with Gospel principles. There never was a time when honesty in business was so vigorously demanded as now. At a great convention of advertising men recently held, the watchword adopted for future work was "Truth." The old method of misrepresentation is rapidly losing ground. And while competition is still recognized as one of the principles of business, yet the spirit of co-operation and service is rapidly gaining. A Christian merchant may compete with his rival, but his *motive* need not be to get the better of the other man, to defeat him, but to do his work well, to serve his customers faithfully and retain a fair profit for himself. It is in this matter of profit that the real trouble arises. People's eyes are open as never before to the injustice of many of the present and time-honored standards of profit. They realize that capital has had too great a share and physical labor too little. This is the thing that must be adjusted, and the men of the church should be in the forefront of those making the adjustments, even at great sacrifice. Of course a Christian must not and cannot do a single dishonest thing. He must always represent his side of every bargain honestly, and demand only fair prices. As to speculative business, much of this so-called business is simply gambling. But bonds or stocks may be purchased outright, and the fair profits due to natural changes in legitimate business be retained. Each Christian must determine in his own conscience what it is right for him to do, but he should keep his conscience tender and his determination strong to do right. It is a matter for deep regret that some professing Christians appear to consider practises justifiable which many so-called worldly men would scorn to follow. The whole business world needs to be brought face to face with Christ's great ideal of sacrifice, service, co-operation and brotherhood.

683 Can a Christian be successful in business when there is competition?

There is an ever-widening and ever-deepening conviction that some of the fundamental methods and principles of the business world are irreconcilable with the teachings of Christ. The motive of most work in the world of business is profit, or gain. The motive of Christ is service. For instance, the world says: "Let us make shoes so that we may get a profit by selling them." Christ would say: "Let us make shoes because people need them and will suffer without them." Further, as business is at present organized, an unjust proportion of the gains of manufacture go to the owners of the manufacturing plants, many of whom may have no other connection with the business than the holding of stocks and bonds, rather than to the people who actually do the work of the industry. While Christians should try earnestly to reorganize the business world to bring it into conformity with Christ's laws of helpful service, they may individually adopt his spirit for their own and do their work with the motive of service rather than the motive of selfish gain.

684 Are Christians expected to wear only the poorest and commonest clothes?

We do not believe that the blessing of God would be withheld from one who wears decent clothes corresponding with the position occupied in society. The sin to be most earnestly avoided is pride in such things. No one has a right to dictate in such trivial matters as the quality of another's clothes. The Christian is a law unto himself. As he consecrates himself unto God he will be more and more disposed to curtail his expenditure on himself, that he may have the money to devote to religious and philanthropic work. But how far he shall carry this selfdenial his conscience must decide.

685 What influence should a Christian have on his community?

By his upright and exemplary life, his helpfulness, his readiness to give counsel and aid to those who need it, his generosity to the poor, and his practical faith, as shown by his works, he can exert a good influence on all with whom he comes in contact. He should never miss an opportunity to "let his light shine," so that men may know that he is a follower of Christ. He is a living evangel and by his influence and example attracts others to the source from which he himself draws courage and strength for the struggle of this life and assurance for the life to come.

**686 If the soul's great battle to decide
its eternal destiny must be fought
out in solitude, how are we to regard the
conversions that take place in times
of great public revival?**

We can no more assign bounds to the operations of the Holy Spirit than we can set limits to God's mercy. In many instances, no doubt, the public confession of Christ at a revival is the fruition of a silent struggle that may have been going on in seclusion. Paul, for example, had such a twofold experience. After Christ had been revealed to him on the road to Damascus, he went away in retirement to Arabia for a season. Conviction had come and actual conversion; but he needed the seclusion of the desert, that he might commune alone with God and readjust his future life to new spiritual conditions. Similarly, Moses, after his call from the burning bush, sought the desert for communion. So the convert in modern days finds seclusion with God the only satisfying way to get his new spiritual bearings. There is always a part—generally the principal part—of the great battle which must be fought out alone. In our deepest troubles, we seek the seclusion of our closet; and there, where no human eye can penetrate, we make the fight and God gives the victory. We cannot gauge the operations of the Holy Spirit by human rules; it goeth where it is sent. Whether it be in the church gathering or on the street, in the railroad car or in the privacy of our own home, the shaft of conviction finds us wherever we may be. It may happen that this has been preceded by a long and arduous struggle, or the soul's ordeal may follow it. Hence we have no right to assume that conversions in revivals are not the legitimate work of the Spirit. Often the seeker, though he may be surrounded by others, is really in spirit alone with God. The world itself may know nothing of the beginning of the struggle, or whether it is still going on. Besides, individual experiences vary. Some come easily through the struggle, while others undergo a longer siege. This may be largely due to temperament or other reasons; but in all cases it may be safely averred there comes a time of crisis, when the soul seeks solitude with God, and it is then that it receives its largest measure of strength and assurance. The great thing in revival experience is the reaching of the turning-point, when the soul makes its decision. This, while it may be the work of an instant, is deepened and strengthened by opportunities for spiritual retirement afterward. We cannot go to the desert, but many good Christian people choose opportunities for seclusion at regular seasons, from which they emerge with deepened and strengthened faith and better equipped for leading helpful and spiritual lives.

687 What part should reason, authority, experience, instinct, common sense and advice of friends play as guides in matters of Christian conduct?

Common sense and reason may be considered fundamental, because if a person is unbalanced mentally he is unable to receive correctly the messages from the Bible, the Holy Spirit, or friends. This is why it is so necessary that people who are eager to obey the Master literally and to please him in all things must take care that their brains and nerves are kept normal and strong. Many people who are greatly distressed over some spiritual problem need first of all a wise physician and careful treatment for their bodies before they are in a condition to consider them seriously. It is to such that Jesus would say: "Come ye yourselves apart unto a desert place, and rest a while." Common sense, reason and instinct make a basis; experience and custom help; advice of friends, particularly Christian friends, is important. Authority is, for the Protestant, probably least important of all, for the very principle of Protestantism is that each soul deals directly and freely with God. A safe rule is to get our guidance from three main sources, and defer action until those three agree the Bible, the voice of the Spirit (or conscience) and the counsel of our closest spiritual companions. The Bible must be interpreted to us by the Holy Spirit, and it is part of the plan of God that we should receive help from our companions in Christ in prayer and counsel. Above all, in deciding on matters of conduct we must remember that Christ wishes to be our Friend rather than our Master; that he wants our love. The motive in every decision ought to be a desire to please him and to help others. Often a problem which is very difficult when approached from the standpoint of self becomes easy when we remember that it is he who must be pleased, and others, not ourselves, who must be helped and made glad.

688 How will a Christian conduct himself?

A true Christian will endeavor to live and act in accordance with Christian principles. He will do nothing that "may cause his brother to stumble or offend"; he will avoid even "the appearance of evil"; he will not stifle the voice of conscience or compromise with sin; he will cultivate temperance in his own person and will help others to do likewise. He will engage in no business that involves the impoverishment or moral or physical degradation of his brother man.

689 Can one be a true Christian and disciple of Christ and never join a church?

It may be said, in general terms, that for one to claim to be a follower of Christ and yet to stand aloof from association with his church and decline to take any part in its activities is a strange and seemingly irreconcilable attitude. There are some church bodies that hold it absolutely essential to Christianity that one hear the Word wherever it is possible to do so. If we really belong to the Lord's army we should fight in line with our fellow soldiers in our own proper place in the ranks and under the flag so that all the world may know where we stand. Not once but many times do the Scriptures emphasize the duty of assembling ourselves together, of living up to our privileges as God's people before the whole world, of meeting for prayer, praise and worship, and of working in harmonious relationship with the church in all that tends to advance Christ's kingdom on earth. One who misses these privileges and all the spiritual satisfaction and the social and moral uplift that come from their exercise misses much of the joy of Christian living. There are people, indeed many of them, who, however much they may exalt the spiritual mission of the church in their minds, make little or no effort to have a share in its work. They overlook the great fact that the church of Christ is the divinely ordained agent for the extension of his kingdom. And having no personal part in its work, they miss the great blessing of being among those of whom it was said by Daniel: "They that turn many to righteousness shall shine as the stars for ever and ever."

690 May a person refuse to go to church simply because there are those in it who do not live right?

If this theory had been correct Peter and John would have left the group of apostles because Judas was a member of the group. They were there not for the sake of associating with Judas, but for the sake of associating with Jesus. They could get the benefit of the words of Jesus; they could receive the power of his presence for their own spiritual needs and for the work they had to do; they could help him in his work and help other people, as they went about with him and for him; they could derive help from the characters and experiences of the faithful disciples. Judas could not hinder or lessen any of these things by his own unfaithfulness. Now your problem is precisely the same. You can find Jesus in your church; you can worship him and enjoy his friendship there; you can help others and by your faithfulness and earnestness can help him. By standing for all that is right and noble and pure; by being firm in declaring that those who are not true should not be advanced to positions of responsibility; by trying in every way to be like Christ and to help others to be like him you can serve and honor him in any church. Paul's statement in I Cor. 5:11 certainly does not mean that good members should leave the church rather than keep company with evil members, but that they should not countenance their evil deeds by personal, social intimacy.

691 Should a church change as the people change to keep up with the times?

In some respects a church must change as the times change. For instance, its members change their mode of dress with the changing centuries; they change their language, as new countries are discovered and the races mingle and develop. The Roman Catholic Church has made a great mistake in clinging to a dead language for so much of its ritual. (Paul made clear the advantage of talking in a language the people understood. I Cor. 14:6-11, 19, 27, 28.) The essential truths and principles of Christianity do not change, but the church must adapt itself, so far as it can without violating any of its changeless principles, to the changing conditions of civilization in order that it may win the greatest possible number to the fold of Christ. The apostles walked; Wesley rode horseback. If they were alive to-day they would use trains. We light our churches by electricity, not with candles or crude lamps. We use the newspapers to advertise our services, spreading thus the Gospel invitation. As better musical instruments are manufactured the church uses them for its work. All the modern helps in Sunday school work and church life can be made a means of grace if the old power of the truth is not surrendered. It is pitiful to see a church trusting to these new appliances and methods for results when it has lost the glow and power of God's Spirit, but a Spirit-filled church can make use of these things to forward the progress of the "everlasting Gospel." Paul said: "I am become all things to all men that I might by all means save some" (I Cor. 9:19-22).

692 What is "worldly dress"?

The wearing of ornaments seems to be forbidden in I Pet. 3:3. Let us bring this problem back to our never-failing test of love. Suppose some one whom you greatly loved were in need of food, or were lost, or in great distress which a message from you would relieve. You would make any sacrifice to send the food or the message, or to find the wanderer. This is the Christian's attitude toward life. He loves those for whom his Saviour died, and will make any sacrifice to serve them. But there are nearer circles of friends and more immediate duties of home and community life, and in these we must bear our part happily and helpfully. We have a right to look, or try to look attractive, and to please those who are near us. A Christian cannot, must not be extravagant, but he may dress correctly and tastefully. There is no sin in the wearing of ornaments as such; the only sin can be in placing one's thought on these rather than on spiritual things and in using money needlessly which could be spent in service for others. A Christian woman's dress does not need to be ugly; it simply should not be extravagant. Peter, in the passage mentioned, links the wearing of gold with braiding hair and putting on apparel. He does not mean that any of the three is wrong, but that the *thought* and *care* must be on inner rather than outward things. As for gifts of gold, many of these, such as wedding rings, for instance, are a precious part of the inner life itself, and their possession is a constant help in one's work. Do not get under bondage. The Christian is free to follow his own conscience in these matters. God wants us to be happy, beautiful and free. But all the time there will be at our hearts the tug of our brothers and sisters and the little ones who are in distress, and we will do what we can to save and help and cheer them.

693 Is public confession necessary to forgiveness by God?

We do not think it is required of you. If you have wronged any one and can make restitution you ought to confess your sin to the person wronged and make restitution, but there is no need of public confession. We can easily conceive of offenses in which confession would make greater trouble and do positive harm. If you have made your peace with God your own conscience must guide you as to further steps. Unless it is a wrong which can be rectified, or its consequences alleviated by confession, we do not think you are required to make confession.

694 Can one's conscience be taken as an infallible guide to right living?

Not in its natural state, because it may be misled. A man may do wrong, as Paul did, when he persecuted the church, with a conscientious belief that he is doing right. The conscience needs to be informed and enlightened. The converted man often discovers that habits and practises which his conscience approved before his conversion it condemns afterward when it has been quickened and educated by the Holy Spirit. Light and knowledge are necessary in order that the conscience may do its duty efficiently.

695 How can we consecrate our hearts and lives to the Lord?

The question of consecration is one that frequently arises, yet when we stop to analyze it, it seems strange that there should be any difficulty about it. If you possess anything which you wish to give to another, you simply give it to him; it is just as simple as that to give your whole heart and life to God. We already belong to him absolutely; in consecration we are only returning what is his. The question how we can take ourselves out of God's hands should really be more difficult than the question how we may submit ourselves to him. Remember that God is always reasonable, always kind. Many of the things sometimes suggested to our minds when the subject of consecration is brought up are not the suggestion of the Holy Spirit, but of our own minds, or of disturbing spirits. There is no uncertainty about the voice of God. He only asks us to obey him when he makes duty clear, and has promised to give us grace and power always for the duties he gently lays upon us. There surely should be no unwillingness to submit our lives to him; he can care for them and direct them much better than we. Consecration becomes easy when we approach the cross of Christ. We realize there that he gave himself for us because we were sinners—because of this very unwillingness in our hearts to surrender ourselves to him. Knowing this it is not hard to commit ourselves absolutely to his love, trusting him to forgive our sins, to cleanse our hearts, to guide and to keep us.

696 Can there be such a thing as unconscious conversion?

There are doubtless many excellent Christian people who, having been brought up in Christian homes, were so thoroughly surrounded by religious influences in their childhood that they might be said to have been believers all their lives. This is the result of ideal Christian training. Such persons might have no remembrance of any time when they were not believers, and they might have no impression of any special change, although conscious of steady growth and progress in the spiritual life. Even in such cases, however, there must come a time when fuller realization begins through regeneration by the power of the Holy Spirit, who preaches true repentance and by faith works conversion. Then the desire for more thorough consecration and larger or more definite service makes itself felt, and such a period marks the true spiritual awakening and new birth.

697 How can we get relief from spiritual darkness and doubt?

The only way out of any form of spiritual darkness is a firm faith in Christ. Spiritual darkness always means that in some way or other we are doubting him. We are often tempted to think that something else is necessary to be done before we begin to trust him, some sacrifice to make, some duty to perform, some problem to be solved. But these things come after faith, not before it. Of course if some positive wrong has been committed this wrong must be righted before we can believe that Christ fully saves us. But where no such positive wrong has been done and no clear duty neglected, the first and indeed the only requirement is to trust in Christ. You will be tempted to turn away from this advice because you have heard it so often; but any other advice would be false. "Christ died for the ungodly." There is our only place of peace and light. When you believe that he died for you, that he died to make possible the forgiveness of your sins and the cleansing of your heart, when you believe that because he died your sins are forgiven and your heart is cleansed, you will have peace, and you will find the Saviour near you, with his light and comfort and power. After all, it is no wonder that we feel sad while we are doubting him. You would feel sad if you were doubting your friend, your brother, your parent. And remember that he, too, is saddened by our doubt. Read again some of the rich promises of God's Word, and refuse any longer to doubt that they were written to you as well as to any other of his children: Isa. 55; Ezek. 36:25-27; Matt. 5:8, 10; Matt. 7:7-11; John 7:38, 39; John 8:36; Acts 2:1-4, 16-21, 39; Rom. 6; Rom. 8; II Cor. 7:1; Gal. 3; Eph. 3:14-21; Col. 3; I Thess. 5:23; Heb. 4:9-11; 7:25; 9:11-14; Heb. 10:1-22, 35; Heb. 11; John 3:1-9, 22; I John 5:4; Jude 24:25.

698 How can we get a strong will power to resist evil?

"How can I acquire a stronger will power?" Now the Bible promises all have a different emphasis. What God wants is that we should not count upon any power in ourselves, but rely altogether upon his power. So long as we are trusting in any power of our own we shall fail; but while we are trusting in his power we do not fail. Notice the wording of this typical promise. Ezek. 36:25-27 (see how God wants to substitute his great self, his "I," for our sinful, weak and failing self): "Then will *I* sprinkle clean water upon you, and ye shall be clean. From all your filthiness, and all your idols will *I* cleanse you. A new heart also will *I* give you, and a new spirit will *I* put within you; and *I* will take away the stony heart out of your flesh, and *I* will give you a heart of flesh. And *I* will put my Spirit within you, and *cause* you to walk in my statutes and ye *shall* keep my judgments and do them." The secret of being kept is to let God keep us. At the time you realize your weakness most keenly, then is the time God will give his power most abundantly. Paul says: "When I am weak then am I strong" (II. Cor. 12:10). We wonder, and struggle, and fret, and try to find some new way, when, after all, there is only one way. "Trusting Jesus—that is ALL!" Avoid being introspective. Take it for granted God is going to keep you; put all your dependence upon him; then plunge ahead and try to forget all about yourself in service for others.

699 Is it ever right to pray for deliverance from evil by death?

Many sufferers pray that death might come to relieve them of their sufferings and ask their friends to help them in such prayer. It is not right to do so because it is probably true that no human intelligence can be absolutely certain that any individual case is absolutely hopeless, except, perhaps, in cases of terrible wounds in which vital organs have been destroyed or large portions of human tissue detached. But in cases of sickness, no matter how severe, the old saying is generally true: "While there is life there is hope." Medical and surgical sciences now accomplish feats which would have been considered miracles a few years ago. And beyond the powers of these miracles of science are the miracles of God, which he is still willing to perform. It is right to pray for relief from pain, and for deliverance from death. But it would not seem right, except in most extremely rare cases, to pray for death itself. Those last days or hours of life might bring the richest soul experience of the years and might, indeed, be necessary to put the finishing touch upon God's preparation of the soul for heaven. If the trouble is other than physical, if it involves the conduct of friends, or financial difficulties, it is still easier to see how God might find ways of relieving the distress. Hearts are changed and blessings received in most undreamed-of ways in response to fervent prayer. These friends would do well to ask, not for death, but for God's "very best" for them and theirs, and particularly that, before death comes, they be made absolutely and jubilantly submissive to his will. This will make their entrance to heaven more glorious, and all eternity for them more glad.

700 Is it right to have a shrinking from thoughts of death?

Many feel a strange shrinking from death. You must not chide yourself too severely for this, for it is something experienced by many good people. A man may be truly brave yet have a shrinking from pain. He goes straight ahead toward the pain without the slightest thought of wavering, yet dreads the pain that waits him. Then, too, many shrink from the mystery of death. But there should be no real fear. Christ can and will save us from that. He conquered sin, which gives death its sting; and he went through death and the grave triumphantly, and promises to be with each of us when our time comes to die. As a matter of fact, however, there is apparently much less distress connected with the experience of death than people generally think. Nature usually provides a physical soothing and partial stupor which make the passing easy. When to this kindness of nature is added the infinite grace of Jesus, who takes us by the hand to lead us into the new home, there should be no apprehension at all. The deathbed of many believers has been truly glorious. In these cases there was no numbness of nature, but a keenness of intellect which seems to pierce the veil and observe the realities of the spirit world. It should be our chief concern now to let God cleanse our hearts from all sin and to bring us unto a rich experience of his love. With this blessing and this companionship we may face death triumphantly and, both now and when our hour comes, shout with Paul; "O death, where is thy sting? O grave, where is thy victory?"

**701 How can we attain the consciousness
of being a child of God?**

Our spiritual problems are made simpler if we stick close to the question of sin. (Happiness or unhappiness, success or failure, safety or danger, all relate back to the fundamental problem of sin.) When any soul is in distress it should force itself back to a plain and emphatic settlement of the sin question. Now, are your sins forgiven or are they not? You have asked God to forgive you; what does he say? Your fears say he has not forgiven you; Satan says he has not; unbelief says he has not. But God himself says he has. Christ is saying to you, as he said to those who sought help from him long ago: "Thy sins are forgiven thee." Are you going to trust all these false voices and refuse to believe him? Would he deceive you? Take him at his word. You will feel instantly the peace of forgiveness in your heart. The promises of cleansing from sin are just as emphatic. "He is faithful and just to forgive us our sins, and to cleanse us from all unrighteousness." "Then will I sprinkle clean water upon you, and ye shall be clean." Now, as you take God at his word in these matters of forgiving and cleansing, you will find yourself rejoicing. His presence will be a reality. You will know he is your Saviour and your Friend. Future clouds will be dispelled by that heroic determination to trust his word about saving you from sin. Then, as you grow more and more busy in telling others about your gladness and leading them to trust him too, the light will grow brighter and brighter, your faith stronger, your strength for service greater. Don't worry about whether you have done right to stay in the church. You are in it. Now make yourself a strong, efficient, faithful member by believing that the name of Jesus really means that "he shall save his people from their sins."

**702 Is alliance and society with the enemies
God desirable for Christians?**

No, it is not, for it is forbidden and provokes the anger of God (Ex. 23:32; Josh. 23:6-7; II Cor. 6:14-17; Eph. 5:11; Deu. 7:4; II Chron. 19:21; Isa. 2:6). It also provokes God to leave men to reap the fruits of them (Josh. 23:12; Judg. 2:1-3). Such associations are ensnaring, enslaving, defiling, degrading and ruinous to spiritual and moral interests (Ex. 23:33; II Pet. 2:18, 19; Ezek. 9:1, 2; Isa. 1:23; Prov. 29:14; I Cor. 15:33). They are a proof of folly, have evil consequences and are a sin to be confessed, deeply repented of and forsaken, and as they involve saints in their guiltiness and punishment and being unbecoming to saints, they should shun all inducements thereto (Prov. 12:11; Jer. 51:7; Ezek. 10th chap.; II John 9-11; Jer. 51:6; II Chron. 19:2; Prov. 1:10; II Pet. 3:17). The Bible exhorts us to shun all inducements to such associations, to hate and avoid them, calls us to come out of them and shows us the means of preservation from them (Prov. 1:10; II Pet. 3:17; Rom. 16:17; I Cor. 5:9; Num. 16:26; Jer. 51:6, 43; II Cor. 6:17; Prov. 2:10). There is great blessedness in avoiding and forsaking them, therefore saints grieve to witness such associations in their brethren, pious parents prohibit them to their children and persons in authority should denounce them. The evil of such associations is exemplified in Solomon (I Kings 11:1-8), Rehoboam (I Kings 12:8, 9), the Israelites (Ezek. 9:1-21), Judas Iscariot (Matt. 26:14-16). Let these and many others we know of be a solemn warning to us.

703 How can we overcome feelings of envy and unkindness?

You need to pray to be strengthened in temptation, and to be given power to overcome those feelings. Envy and unkindness and worldliness are loath to loose their hold on the heart, but they will go if you ask for divine help in repelling them. We would advise you to connect yourself with some form of Christian work, either in the church organization or out of it. Visit the poor and the sick and do what you can to help them. Contrast your lot with theirs. Count your blessings and share them with others. You will find happiness and spiritual help in such a course. No matter how little you can do, do it gladly and with a joyful spirit. Do not allow yourself to mope and bemoan your own condition and shortcomings. Leave it all in God's hands, "who knoweth all our infirmities." Hold fast to the great fact that Jesus "saves to the uttermost" and that means *you*, since you have accepted him. Confess him before men and go on in his service and the blessing will not fail to come. Forget yourself and he will take care of you, as he has promised.

704 How did fasting come to be a common religious custom, so that even our Lord gives rules about it?

In Matt 6:16 we read: "Moreover when ye fast be not as the hypocrites of a sad countenance; for they disfigure their faces that they may appear unto men to fast." Moses made no regulations in relation to fasting, and the custom does not appear to have been known before his time. In Judg. 20:26 we find the earliest Bible reference to fasting, and from an examination of the Old Testament passages bearing upon it, it would seem to have been a national and not a religious custom. The religious character of fasting seems to have been evolved out of the national fastings which the Jews inaugurated during the Captivity. The reign of the rabbis over Jewish affairs made national fasting into a religious ordinance and made it a burden. "The spirit of priesthood which claims the guidance of men's consciences and lives must work their minute and multiplied requirements; and is sure to delight in schemes which put men's bodies and bodily habits under painful restraints." No man is required by New Testament teaching to fast—to do so is no part of religious duty. What Christ urges is simply this: "If you must fast, do so for God's knowledge and do not make a show of it." Geikie says of the extravagancies and insincerities against which the Lord protested: "When fasting the Pharisees strewed their heads with ashes, and neither washed nor anointed themselves, nor trimmed their beards, but put on wretched clothing and showed themselves in all the outward signs of mourning and sadness used for the dead. Insincerity made capital of feigned humiliation and contrition." It was this that Christ condemned.

705 Does not the injunction again being conformed to the world (Romans 12:2) apply to fashions, such as shaving the hair from the face and the wearing of fashionable dress?

The injunction applies to the mind, as you will see by the context of the passage quoted. The Christian must not adopt worldly principles, nor be governed by worldly motives. His life should not be conformed to the world. There is no virtue in wearing old-fashioned clothes, or in a man making himself conspicuous in any way. Extravagance in dress and eccentricity in manner should be avoided. If the world had nothing by which to recognize a Christian but his manner of shaving, the man must be living a very poor life. If he is showing Christ's spirit in loving helpfulness, in magnanimity, kindness, forbearance, charity, he is more usefully serving Christ and fulfilling his obligations than he would be by shaving or not shaving. You remember that the Pharisees were irreproachable so far as outward appearance and observance were concerned, but Christ denounced them.

706 Is it wrong for Christian people to read fiction?

The early prejudice among the Puritans and some of their followers against the reading of fiction was caused by the fact that so much of early fiction was vicious. It seems very unwise now to hold to this idea, because so many works of fiction are distinctly helpful. When the prejudice against fiction as such is analyzed it seems difficult to find anything true or solid about it. Christ himself was famous for his parables, which, aside from their authoritative spiritual value, were among the very best pieces of the world's literature. *Pilgrim's Progress* is fiction, and has probably done more for the cause of Christ than any other one book except the Bible. Christian people should, however, use great care in selecting books to read, and should be quick to discountenance any book which has a harmful influence. While it is not necessary to cast aside all books which depict evil, yet any book in which evil is made to appear attractive, any book written by an author who seems to like sin—an attitude that it is not unfair to say some modern writers seem to have taken—should be condemned There are many excellent novels—so-called—some of them conveying spiritual truths, others full of interest because of their delightful portraiture of human character and action, and still others attractive no less for their brilliant ability than for the vivid description of scenes and events. There is also a very large class of novels that may be called worthless and even vicious. The habit of indiscriminate novel reading is generally admitted to be one that has a deteriorating result on the intellectual powers of the reader. Those who read many novels acquire a passion for such literature; they become creatures of wax, molded successively by every character they encounter, and partaking of the nature of all. The habitual novel reader ceases to think or originate for himself. Worse still, he gradually loses all taste for more solid literature, and cannot peruse or absorb anything that calls for the slightest mental effort. This applies to the vast array of publications which have no other aim than to excite the imagination and stir the emotions. If one will read novels, let them be only the best—standards of their class, by authors who write with a high purpose, and convey a wholesome as well as an interesting lesson.

707 Does God grant forgiveness to those who declare that they only forgive when forgiveness is asked?

It would be hard to make any such principle fit in with these words of Jesus: "I say unto you, Love your enemies; bless them that curse you, do good to them that hate you, and pray for them that despitefully use you and persecute you" (Matt. 5:44); or the words of Paul, quoted from Proverbs: "If thine enemy hunger, feed him; if he thirst, give him drink" (Rom. 12:20; Prov. 25:21). In the passage in Matthew about forgiving "until seventy times seven" (Matt. 18:22) nothing at all is said about forgiveness being asked, though in Luke 17:3, 4 mention is made of the repentance of the trespasser. The point is that a Christian who has been wronged must have the forgiving spirit, whether forgiveness is asked or not. He cannot cherish bitterness and resentment in his heart. He must be like his divine Master, who prayed: "Father, forgive them," even while he was being crucified (Luke 23:34), and like Stephen, who prayed for his murderers as he died: "Lord, lay not this sin to their charge" (Acts 7:60). But in the nature of the case, forgiveness cannot actually be received by the offending party until he has a sense of guilt and a desire for pardon. An offer of forgiveness would be meaningless to one who has no feeling of having done wrong. God has pardoned us long ago, but we really do not get that pardon into our consciousness until we feel our need of it and ask for it. So while we must love those who wrong us and must forgive them instantly and fully in our hearts as soon as the wrong is done, they cannot possess and enjoy our forgiveness until they desire and welcome it. Yet S. H. Hadley used to say, in telling about his work for the drunkards and outcasts: "If a man cheats me nineteen times I shame him out of his frauds by trusting him the twentieth." Certainly one who has not this forgiving spirit cannot expect nor receive God's forgiveness. Forgiveness is a detail of the greater feeling of love. We must love every one; and in doing this we automatically and instantly forgive all who wrong us.

708 How does a "forgiving spirit" manifest itself toward the one who did the wrong?

A "forgiving spirit" means, first and last, a loving spirit. While we cannot prevent a feeling of deep grief where we ourselves are wronged, the greater grief ought to be for the one who has done wrong. If a son should wrong his mother she feels more sorry for the boy who has done wrong than for herself who suffers the wrong. The same ought to be true of husband and wife, brother and sister, neighbor and neighbor. There is love and forgiveness in the heart the moment the wrong is done. In some respects, however, it is quite impossible to have the same feeling toward the wrongdoer before forgiveness is asked. Our affection for him, before the wrong, was largely based on what we believed him to be; when we find that he is not the person we thought him to be our feelings of delight in his association and admiration for him necessarily undergo a change. Our great desire must be to bring him back to the purity which he has lost. And he himself cannot regain that lost purity till he has confessed his wrong and asked forgiveness. So, while, for our own sake, we freely forgive, and continue to feel and act kindly, yet for his own sake we must seek to lead him to a recognition and acknowledgment of his wrong. All these considerations will unavoidably affect the details of our conduct. While every act must be kind, we must not allow the wrongdoer to think that we are insensible of the fact that he has done wrong, but we must show him that we are earnestly desiring his repentance and restoration.

709 Is to be oppressed by a sense of sin for which one has asked pardon proof of non-forgiveness?

By no means. You should rather regard it as an evidence of a lack of faith. You must remember that you are not forgiven because of your consciousness of pardon, but because God for Christ's sake has blotted out your sins. God does not break his promises. Those who repent and plead to be forgiven for Christ's sake, at the same time renouncing their sins, are assuredly forgiven, whether they realize the fact or not. If you owed a debt which you could not pay, and your creditor canceled that debt, you would not worry about your own consciousness, but would accept his assurance. Put the gloomy thoughts away from you, and, rejoicing in God's promise, go forward, carefully avoiding a repetition of your sins. Assurance will come in time.

710 Does God only forgive as we forgive?

The passage in the Lord's Prayer relative to the divine forgiveness of trespasses as we ourselves forgive others who have trespassed against us is to be interpreted spiritually. We are debtors to God on account of our sins against him. We have neglected his worship, have not honored him with our substance, have transgressed his holy law and have abused the blessings he has bestowed upon us. We ask him to pardon these offenses for which we in our own hearts feel that we cannot atone, for we are spiritually insolvent, and he forgives us not as a right, but as a gift of his divine grace freely bestowed. So we, in turn, are to forgive others, and all the more that they are unable to render us the material satisfaction which the world exacts in such cases. If misfortune has overtaken a man, so that he is unable to pay his honest debts, we must include him in the category of those entitled to our forgiveness; but one who has the means to pay his just debts is not entitled to claim or expect consideration of this generous character, nor was the Lord's Prayer intended to convey such an impression. Elsewhere we are told to "owe no man anything," and to "pay that thou owest." We are to show a merciful and forgiving spirit in all cases where it is needed, to forgive freely, but our Lord himself has recognized the validity of honorable obligations. To counsel otherwise would have been to encourage dishonesty and to put a premium on wrongdoing. The whole problem is a spiritual one—that of mercy and the exercise of a forgiving spirit in cases where it can properly be applied. We ourselves are not to ask God for that mercy we refuse to others who ask it at our hands.

711 Once a sin is forgiven will God remember it?

God utterly blots out the record of the sin he has forgiven. This is very distinctly and emphatically promised in many passages of the Bible. Perhaps the most explicit is Ezek. 33:16: "None of his sins that he hath committed shall be mentioned unto him: he hath done that which is lawful and right: he shall surely live." There are, however, warnings to the pardoned man that he must quit his sin. Having once been pardoned, he must be careful not to abuse God's magnanimity under the impression that God will continue to pardon. There are many warnings of the peril that a man incurs who returns to an evil life after once being delivered from it.

712 Does the Bible commend generosity?

There are so many passages in the Bible commending the generous heart that one may gather from a comparison of those noted below what may be called the Bible estimate of a model giver: Lev. 25:35; Deut. 15:7; Ps. 68:5; Ps. 10:14; Isa. 1:17; James 1:27; Deut. 14:29; Deut. 15:10; Prov. 19:17; II Cor. 8:12; Luke 21:3, 4. etc. He who gives gladly, generously, unostentatiously, with kindness and consideration for the feelings of the recipient; he who gives in his name who gave his life for us and through whom we have the gift of eternal life; who gives expecting no return, not even thanks; who gives that he may have a heavenly treasury instead of accumulating a big bank account here to leave to others when he passes away; who regards his wealth as a stewardship which he must use to the glory of God and the good of his fellow men—he is the model giver. We should not judge others, however, who may have a single great and worthy object in view. Those men and women who enrich the whole world by their gifts to noble causes that advance humanity should not be left out of the category of model givers. We know personally some who devote their means systematically to the support of missions and the spread of the Gospel, or to the reclamation of the fallen, the amelioration of poverty, the cause of the sick, etc. America is rich in model givers of this class.

713 Does every good desire come from God?

It is impossible to say just what impulses proceed from self and what are the direct influence of God in the unconverted soul. Some impulses to kindness seem purely natural, such as the instinctive care of a mother for her child, which is found in beasts as well as in human kind. The affection of animals for people, like the affection of a dog for his master, is sometimes tremendously strong. While all these noble and beautiful things come from God, they do not necessarily indicate the presence of God in the soul. He has planted certain admirable traits both in the instincts of animals and the minds of men; he also has, of course, the power of communicating with men, speaking to their minds and consciences by his Spirit and by his Word. Reason is higher than instinct and conscience is higher than both, but even conscience may not mean that God is dwelling in the soul. Conscience seems to be not so much the voice of God as the human faculty of hearing that voice. But at conversion God's Spirit comes into a man's soul. He is no longer outside, but within; mystically though actually linked to the man himself. The great change then is that a man finds himself loving God, eager to get his messages, anxious to please him. The impulses to do good, instead of being vague and weak, become definite and intense. The converted man feels that God is within him, making suggestions, awakening holy, unselfish, beautiful desires, and giving him power to carry out these good desires in vigorous and successful action,

714 Must we keep on trying to do good even though it is unappreciated?

Those who are of the household of faith are admonished "not to be weary in well-doing; for in due season we shall reap if we faint not." And this applies even to the small details of every-day life. There are many things that are discouraging, viewed through the lenses of the world's estimation, and the lack of appreciation for kindness or of gratitude for help rendered to others is not the least of these. Yet this need not trouble one who is doing good not for praise or reward and not even for thanks, but for the sake of him who "went about doing good." A truly noble spirit, inspired by the love of Christ and humanity, will not seek any reward beyond the approval of a good conscience and the knowledge that he is serving the divine will. The real merit in a good act largely lies in the fact that we do it from a spirit of brotherly love, without thought of recompense, and all the better if it can be done quietly and unostentatiously, even so secretly that the left hand does not know what the right hand doeth. (Matt. 6:3, 4.) God's secret service is the richest in spiritual rewards.

715 Is the neglect to do good, sin?

Yes; we are commanded to do good, and not to do it is disobedience. The man who had one talent (Matt. 25:24-30) was punished not for losing it but because he did not employ it. The people on the Lord's left hand (Matt. 25:41-46) were not punished for doing wrong but for neglecting to do good.

716 How can one who fell from grace be restored to grace?

Any one who desires to return to the Lord or to a special state of grace once enjoyed can certainly do so. No one need ever fear that such a return is impossible so long as the desire is there; it is those who have lost this desire who are in the most grievous danger. The way back is by exercising faith again. "Praying and feeling very repentant" will not accomplish the result unless you also believe. You must believe that "Jesus Christ is the same, yesterday, to-day and forever." You must believe that anything he did for you once he can do for you again. You must literally and positively trust him to do for you now what he did for you in those happier days. You see, what causes all the trouble is doubting him. Doubt seems a slight thing, but it is enough to fill the whole spiritual sky with darkness, to take away all spiritual strength, and to make the spiritual path full of overwhelming difficulties. Trust Jesus again.

Trust him to forgive your sins, and then cease worrying about them. Trust him to cleanse your heart, and then cease worrying about that. As you trust him to forgive and cleanse you, you will realize how near he is to you; this will awaken the old-time feelings of love and friendship for him, and with the returning love will come returning joy and power.

717 Can one be a true Christian without any special evidence of growth in grace or progress in the spiritual life?

Such an experience may, and doubtless often does, happen in the case of those who, though sincere believers at heart, have never taken the first step toward those Christian activities which are the road to spiritual growth and development. Going to church is only a part of the Christian's duty. Having found the truth himself, he should strive earnestly to give it to others. There are many ways in which he can do service. By kindness and upright example; by quiet, unostentatious charity, seeking out the needy, who are to be found in almost every community; by visiting the sick, the prisoners, the shut-ins; by reading to the aged and infirm; by taking an interest in missions, and, last but not least, by striving, in tactful and kindly ways, to arouse the same spiritual desire you feel in your own heart, in the hearts of your church fellows. Many a Christian makes an excellent team-worker who cannot work well alone. Take the minister into your confidence. Tell him to help you to "get busy." If you feel led that way, connect with some Gospel mission and get right into the work. Don't hesitate to confess Christ at every fitting opportunity; it will strengthen you and give you confidence. Ask the Lord to open the way and to give you equipment and the power to reach the hearts of men and lead them to the cross. Ask in Jesus' name, nothing doubting, and you will receive. Do not be overambitious at the outset. Take the humblest opportunity that offers and make the most of it, and hope for better things. Once entered in that service, whatever talents you may possess will be in no danger of rusting through idleness.

718 Is it right for a Christian to joke with his fellow employees?

Innocent mirth is not a sin, nor should it be confounded with wicked levity or godless conversation. If your fellow employees are non-Christians, their mirth will probably be of the latter sort, and should be avoided. There is a good-fellowship and wholeheartedness which is pleasant and agreeable, and many very good people are noted for their wit and humor. But mere worldly merriment, vain and empty conversation, and, above all, that species of wit which is low, coarse and debasing, should be shunned by any one who desires spiritual growth and a "pure heart."

719 Is it possible to be truly kind without being a Christian?

We must not judge others, especially on general principles, and where we do not know the facts. There are many people who, while not professing Christianity, are yet full of sympathy for those in suffering. Kindness and generous helpfulness were prominent features of Christ's teachings while here on earth. He taught his followers to love one another and to cultivate the spirit of kindness to all who came within their influence and who needed help. He regarded any kindness shown to the needy, the sick, the prisoners, the destitute as done to himself, and, equally, any indifference shown to the sufferers he condemned in the words "Inasmuch as ye have not done it to the least of these, ye did it not unto me." There was nothing in his language to convey the lesson that kindness was to be confined exclusively to those who were of the faith. His own love and pity went out to the whole world. When the case is that of a believing brother who needs our help such a one has a double claim upon our practical sympathy as being a member of the household of Christ.

720 Is it a lie not to tell the whole truth to one who has the right to know the whole truth?

It depends upon the circumstances of the case. By keeping back a portion of the truth one may give to a particular statement the color and effect of a lie, even though it should be literal fact. Conveying a wrong impression by whatever means is indirect lying. On the other hand, we can imagine a case in which one might be silent from laudable motives as to certain facts, the bringing out of which might serve no good purpose, but would involve others in sorrow or disgrace. Even in such a case the motive must be unimpeachable. As to the "right to know," there is none who has the right to know the innermost secrets of the heart save God.

721 Should a person keep a matrimonial engagement at all hazards?

It is an old and perhaps fairly true proverb that "a bad promise is better broken than kept," but its too general application gives opportunity for a fickle excuse for promise-breaking, where all the obligations of honor and duty point to a different course. If, however, it should be clearly shown that the promise was a bad one, calculated to make two lives miserable, and given impulsively and without experience, wisdom would suggest its reconsideration by both parties. While there is nothing more contemptible than a disregard for an honorable pledge, there is nothing more foolish than to hesitate at an honorable avowal of one's mistake before it is too late.

722 Would a Christian girl be justified in marrying an atheist?

Try to answer Paul's question (II Cor. 6:15): "What part hath he that believeth with an infidel?" The Christian girl who married such a man would be separated from him in the highest, holiest and best part of her nature by a wide gulf. Her husband would have no communion with her in the emotions and principles which should be the chief part of her life. We cannot imagine a union more uncongenial and unpropitious. We do not know what the penalty would be beyond the grave, but we believe it would be misery for the wife on this side of it.

723 Should a Christian minister attend a circus?

We do not believe that a minister, any more than a layman, is to be condemned because he pays a visit to a circus. As a rule, such entertainments are instructive and amusing, and free from objectionable features. There are probably very few men or women who haven't some pleasing recollection of the circus. There might be occasions, however, when, for various sufficient reasons, it would be obviously improper for a preacher of the Gospel to attend such a performance.

724 Can the custom of stated salaries for ministers be defended on the basis of of New Testament teaching?

Under the Levitical law due provision was made for the maintenance of the priests and teachers in the Jewish church, but nothing of this kind was known in the primitive Christian Church. It is distinctly implied, however, in various passages of the New Testament that the church had a duty to maintain its religious teachers (see Matt. 10:10, I Cor. 9:14, etc.). In the apostolic age this maintenance consisted in supplying their immediate personal wants (II Cor. 11:7, 8 and Phil. 4:16-18). In those early days the church owned little or no property, but later specific provision was made for the support of the clergy. This included fees for particular services, firstfruits, voluntary offerings which probably supplemented any meager allowance from the church's treasury. There is no specific rule laid down in the New Testament on the subject. The ancient Jewish law is regarded by some as a precedent. It is very clear that, even in apostolic times, it was a recognized principle that the laborer was "worthy of his hire." In our own day a congregation would be considered very unappreciative of God's message to men if it did not support its own minister.

725 Are the methods of preachers who use slang and colloquial language in the pulpit to be approved?

If Christ was right and if the professed belief of all the evangelical churches of our country is right, viz., that man possesses a spiritual part which neither time nor death can efface, then and in that event the one fact which must forever overtop all other facts is this: that man's soul, or the spiritual part of a man—call it what you will—must be awakened to the consciousness that to "fear God and keep his commandments is the whole duty of man." There is one thing that, in a Christian sense, is like the light of the sun compared with the light of the millions of stars which the sun's light hides absolutely, and that one thing is this: the soul's eternal salvation. If this is not true, then the professed belief of all of our so-called Evangelical churches is a farce, and the teachings of Jesus Christ are simply so much idle talk. If this is true—if the consequences are fraught with such awful destinies—then the kind of preaching which is most productive of bringing the most people to this consciousness is the best kind of preaching, view it from whatever standpoint you will. When a preacher of the Gospel delivers his message with strength and courage, dealing with the evils of his time, he doubtless does his duty as a servant of Christ, as he understands that duty. The battle against sin is not one to be fought with kid gloves nor to be settled with polite speeches or elegant phraseology. Paul and Silas, when they preached in Thessalonica and were accused of "turning the world upside down," met with the same kind of criticism that is visited upon some modern preachers and evangelists. That preacher or evangelist who never strikes fire, or arouses opposition, is an indifferent servant. We need to-day zeal and earnestness in the pulpit, even more than literary or oratorical ability. Simplicity and directness, strength and gentleness, fervent persuasion and humble appeal—each has its proper place. Luther's words have been described as "half battles" in their intensity and forcefulness; Weaver used the dialect of the coal-pit; Jerry McAuley, that of the prison and slums, and Sunday that of the ball-field and the thoughtless multitude. There are times when the modern minister or evangelist feels that he is dealing with an antagonist, to cope with whom he can use at times only the homely sling of David and a vulgar pebble of the brook. God in his wisdom uses many diverse instrumentalities in reaching the hearts of men, and multitudes are moved and won by methods that would not influence and might even repel others. The real test lies in the result of the work. If it finds acceptance and souls are won who then should be against it?

726 Should a man going into the ministry have always possessed the highest character, or doesn't it matter what he has been?

The Lord chooses his own instruments, and sometimes makes what seems to mortals a strange choice. Saul was a persecutor and "the chief of sinners" before he became Paul the faithful apostle. Thousands have been taken from the ranks of sin and after undergoing a change of heart have become valiant captains in God's army. John Bunyan, the converted tinker; John Newton, once infidel and libertine; Richard Weaver, the drunken pitman, and thousands on thousands of others have been called from the depths of sin to become active workers for souls. Every mission in the land can point to once notorious sinners now redeemed and laboring as preachers and evangelists, and not a few as regular pastors. The fact that some of our ablest spiritual leaders, in all ages, have been thus chosen demonstrates that a man's past sins, when pardoned through redeeming grace, should not weigh against him among Christians, since all are sinners and under condemnation by law.

727 What is the basis for the respect and confidence which we accord ministers?

In I Thess. 5:12, 13 the apostle commends the leaders in church work—pastors, elders and teachers—to the respect and confidence of the congregation. They were to recognize their office and treat them with respect, giving attention to their admonitions and responding liberally to their requests for material aid in the Lord's work. The church in Thessalonica had been lately organized; some of the ministers were probably new to the place and the people and Paul urged that they be cordially received. They were specially chosen laborers in the vineyard and were entitled, if for no other reason than that they had been selected for places of such importance and responsibility in the Gospel ministry and to work for the salvation of souls, to reverent love and cordial support. Above all this they should be well received "for the very works sake." It was advice which might be taken by many congregations to-day with great advantage, especially in dealing with any new spiritual leader who comes among them.

728 Is it right for a Christian to enjoy more than the bare necessities of life?

It is perfectly right that one should enjoy all the good things of life in moderation, always keeping in view what is due from himself to others, and the duty of helping those who are in need; but indulgence in luxuries, extravagance in any form, and all pleasures that are other than innocent, educative, recreative and healthful, are to be avoided. There is nothing to be gained by living the life of an ascetic or a misanthrope. The Almighty gives us life to make the best of it we can, and it is better to walk in the brightness of the sunshine than in the gloom. One who diffuses sunshine and happiness is more likely to be serviceable in the upbuilding of the kingdom of righteousness than one who takes existence here as a penance.

729 May a Christian take an oath in the witness box without transgressing Christ's injunction, "Swear not"?

The judicial oath or solemn asseveration or promise, as in the presence of God, that you will tell the truth, should not be confounded with oaths of another character. An oath to take vengeance, uttered in the name of Deity, is an illustration of the perverted use of a solemn adjuration. So, also, is an oath taken in levity. An appeal to God, or to any sacred thing, was a custom among the ancient Hebrews, who used such oaths in private and official business. The Christian custom of taking judicial oaths was founded upon the Jewish, the oath on the Gospels in court being the legitimate adaptation of the Hebrew mode of placing the hands upon the Book of the Law. There are certain sects, including the Mennonites, Quakers and Moravians, who apply literally the words of Christ, "Swear not at all," and therefore regard all oaths as unlawful. In view of all the facts, the taking of a judicial oath, or promise before Deity to tell the truth and render exact justice in the cause at issue, must remain a matter to be decided by the conscience of the individual.

730 How can we feel assured of and experience God's pardon?

It is so simple and so easy that many people miss it. They seem to think it is impossible that so much joy can come from such a simple thing. That thing is to trust God. Doubt and unbelief shut out all the glory and peace of salvation; faith lets them in. But before you can trust God you must be certain that you need him. Only sinners need him, those who are appalled by the enormity of their failings and faults as seen in the light of him to whom sin is impossible. Only he who has been frightened by the lightnings of divine wrath and who has been stunned by the accompanying terrifying thunders of "thou shalt!" "thou shalt not" of Mount Sinai can fully appreciate the certainty that the lightning has spent its force on the cross and the rumblings of anger have been stilled on Calvary, never more to harm those who flee there in childlike helplessness. They trust the Father who so loved them that he gave his only begotten Son to be that Brother and Friend who constantly holds out welcoming strong arms while he soothingly assures: "Fear not, I will comfort thee." Let us think of our children, infants if you please, or even grown-ups. Think how miserable and unhappy they would be if they were all the time wondering whether or not we loved them; if when they had asked us to forgive them for doing something that displeased us and we had assured them that we did forgive them they should wonder whether or not we meant it, and should keep coming to us again and again asking forgiveness for the same offense. Theirs would be a very unhappy childhood; so we are unhappy when we do not utterly trust the love of your father God.

What more can he say than to you he hath said,
To you who for refuge to Jesus have fled?

731 Are we to address our prayers to
God the Father or to Jesus?

One of the very greatest arguments for the deity of Jesus is that he allowed people to kneel and worship him. The apostles were horrified when dwellers in pagan cities attempted to worship them, and even the angel who talked with John refused to be worshiped. "See thou do it not," he said. But Jesus accepted worship as his due. He forgave the sins of the man sick with palsy (Matt. 9:2), and of the woman who came to anoint his feet (Luke 7:48). Others objected to his exercise of this power, but he would not retract. One of the earliest historical-characterizations of Christians was that "they offered prayers to Christ as God." This has been done all through the history of Christianity. And the results prove that it is a right thing to do. People ask Jesus for forgiveness and help and receive what they ask for. That was the simple prayer which changed the life of S. H. Hadley: "Lord Jesus, can you help me?" "I and my Father are one," Jesus said. The form of address makes no difference. The ordinary form is to address the Father in Jesus' name; but it is helpful rather than otherwise to vary this form occasionally with a direct address to Christ.

732 What should be our attitude in prayer as to
whether God's will or our will should prevail?

We must always remember in praying that God knows everything and we know very little. We often deny the earnest requests of our children because we know that what they ask will do them harm rather than good. It has sometimes happened that when friends have prayed insistently for the recovery of loved ones, other calamities and sufferings, perhaps worse than death, have overwhelmed them. So our prayers should end like Christ's own prayer: "Nevertheless, not my will but thine be done." What is most important in prayer is to enter into such close fellowship with God, to have such intimate conversation with him, that we come to have something of an understanding of what he himself desires. No matter how strong our own wishes may be, there should always be the stronger and deeper wish that God's will be done. And we must remember that his will is our best welfare and that of all our friends. Sometimes when a Christian is praying for something not specifically promised in the written Word, he seems to receive an "assurance" that God wishes to do certain things for or through him. After such a deep, clear, unmistakable assurance he is justified in praying vehemently, battling against the forces of doubt and wrong, holding fast to the promise and remembering that God "cannot deny himself." Especially can we pray in this manner when the prayer is for the forgiveness of our sins, the cleansing of our hearts, or our endowment with the Holy Spirit, for these things are plainly, specifically promised in his

Word. In cases of sickness, while there are many promises for health, we know that we and all our friends must some time die. While using all the human means and skill available we should pray, always in the name of Christ, that health may be restored. And while there is no doubt that many sicknesses would be healed if God's people had more faith, yet we must be willing to let God choose the time when he takes our loved ones to himself. And when they go we should not grieve but rejoice to know that they are safe with him, awaiting our coming in the new home.

733 Are we to take all our troubles to the Lord in prayer?

We are assured that if we seek first the spiritual blessings—"the things of the kingdom"—all the rest will be added unto us, since he knows we have need of them. We should be satisfied, therefore, to put faith in God for all our daily needs, and to do the best we can to help bring this about, relying on his blessing to crown our efforts. There are many things we need not enumerate in our petitions. Mr. Spurgeon, when his church committee met to consider appeals for help, would pick out a few letters and, after glancing at their contents, would say: "We won't trouble the Lord about these; I'll attend to them myself." God loves to be helped, and he has endowed us with reason and other faculties for that purpose. He will always bless the efforts of the believing, self-reliant Christian who goes ahead on simple faith. There are, however, many good people who take comfort in laying all their troubles before him and who will take no step without prayer. They find it a daily and almost hourly necessity. We have no word of adverse criticism for these dear ones, who live in an atmosphere of prayer. There are others who submit the conduct of their lives to him, but without taking up those things that seem small and trivial. It is a matter of temperament and doubtless both are right. But if we have the broader, deeper faith, we will learn to trust him and to ask in our prayers only those things that are spiritually or materially vital. We have an unquestionable right to take all our real troubles to the throne troubles of temptation, of doubt, of anger, of ill health, of want and distress, of friends who need to be prayed for, etc. If we choose to omit the trivialities, trusting him for them, it is better so. He knows all about us and we should have faith that he will supply all our needs as he has promised (Phil. 4:19).

734 What steps must we take to pray more effectively?

Prayer is simply the wire that brings the electricity of God's power down to our needs. It is true that we have no "power," no spiritual power, in ourselves. All we can do is to make way for God's power in us. "It is God that worketh in you, both to will and to do of his good pleasure." You say you seem to have lost your power in prayer. It may prove to be a very helpful and useful thing to you to feel just that way. You are finding out what we must all find out before God can do greater things for us and through us, that you have no power of your own. "When I am weak, then am I strong," wrote Paul. The best way to pray is to realize that we have not only no power of our own, but not even any wisdom of our own to ask for the things we need most. We must seek God directly; get into touch with him; ask him what he wants us to have, what he wants us to do. This leads us to a new conception of God's will. We begin to realize how strong it is; we begin to feel sure that God will work out his will in our lives. We cannot compel the wills of other people to yield to God; but when our own wills are absolutely surrendered to him, and our faith takes hold upon him, he will not only work out his own will in us, but will show us how best to persuade others also to yield their lives to him. Do not worry; do not fret; do not doubt. Leave everything to the infinite power of God, and trust him to do the very best for you, and, through you, for those you love.

735 In what way can we do everything to the glory of God?

This exhortation in I Cor. 10:31 refers to our motive, our purpose in life. The one supreme purpose of every Christian life should be to glorify God—that is, to reflect credit and honor upon him. A patriot wishes to bring honor to his country, a wife to her husband, a pupil to his master, a friend to his friend. If we truly love God we shall be anxious that he shall be understood and obeyed and honored and loved by the world. The whole matter becomes simpler when we relate it to Christ. In Col. 3:17, where Paul repeats this same idea, his words are: "Whatsoever ye do in word or deed, do all in the name of the Lord Jesus." The true friend of Jesus wishes to please him in all things, and earnestly desires that all men should love and honor him. Therefore, since he is known as a Christian and bears the name of Christ, he must do nothing un-Christlike, nothing that will bring reproach to the name of Christ. Instead of taking pleasure out of life this way of living brings vast pleasure into life. All pure and wholesome pleasure is increased infinitely by the thought of Christ's love. As the song of birds and blossom of flowers reflect the beauty and glory of God, so do the innocent, natural joys of a Christian show the world God's kindness, his beauty and his goodness.

736 Should we persist in prayer, though to all appearance God does not answer?

We need constantly to guard against being selfcentered in our prayers. Of course, God wishes us to tell him what we want in the same simple way that a child tells his parents. But it is necessary to be entirely willing that God's will shall be done, not ours. If we truly love him we shall come to be anxious, not so much that we shall be gratified as that he shall be gratified. What we shall be particularly eager about is to get better acquainted with him; to learn more of his will; and to seek by our efforts and our faith to have his will done in the world. But if the gift is something good and pure and worthy and we cannot help desiring it for ourselves, then we may keep on asking for it, either until it is received or until he makes us sure that it is not his will that we should receive it. At the same time we must remember that God is omniscient, all-wise. He sees into the future where we cannot. His ways are past finding out, and his design for us oftentimes beyond even our most sanguine hopes. He alone, however, knows the time and the circumstances under which his blessings and the answers to our prayers are best calculated to meet our requirements. He is our omnipotent Father, our kind Counselor and Friend. What more can we ask? All the way through we must trust him, never doubting for a minute that he loves us, that he longs to give us everything that will make us truly happy. Perhaps he wants you to believe more positively that this gift is his wish for you and that he will actually bestow it. "According to your faith be it unto you." "He that spared not his own Son but delivered him up for us all, how shall he not with him also freely give us all things?" We have a right to look to our Father to supply all our needs, physical and spiritual—not to grant us luxuries or such things as the world esteems most, but to give us what we really stand in need of. There is, however, a supreme request which we ought to make and even to be importunate until we get it, namely: a clean heart, a contrite spirit, a soul at peace with God through the love of his dear Son who died for us. If we ask these in all faith and sincerity, he will surely grant us forgiveness. It is not necessary to continually urge for pardon of the old sins—the old life; incessant pleading shows our lack of faith. Take God at his word; then, having once established this new relationship and having begun the life of the kingdom, we have the Master's promise that "all things will be added unto us." Our dear Father knows what we need. He knows, if we are sick, how we long for health, and if we have pain, how we sigh for relief. Then, too, we have a right to ask him to bless such means as are being used for our physical restoration. We should not forget that now, as of old, he is still able to "pardon all our iniquities and to heal our diseases." He is still the great Physician, who cures both the soul and body, if we only have faith in him; and he it is who gives us strength to bear our afflictions, and transforms the furnace of trial into a place of blessing.

737 How can I learn to pray?

The important thing about prayer is not to ask for what we want, but to find out what God wants. We are urged to bring our requests to God, but with every prayer there must be the willing assent: "Not as I will, but as thou wilt." Unless we are very careful our prayers will be selfish. We ask for things simply because we desire them, forgetting that in many cases God cannot answer our prayer without taking the thing we ask away from some one else. In praying we should think always of others, and how the granting of our petition will affect them. We must try to get God's point of view and understand what bearing the granting of our prayer would have on the whole progress of his kingdom. The first essential in praying is to come into definite personal communion with God himself. Often in prayer there comes the definite revelation of God's will, so that we seem to know what he plans and purposes. With this assurance will come a definite faith that the thing we ask will come to pass because it is God's will. We must pray in the name of Christ; we must become part of the great plan he is working out; we must pray that certain things be done because we love Christ and know that Christ wishes to have them done. So the way to become effectual in prayer is to come closer to Christ; to trust him to forgive all our sins and cleanse our hearts; to become intimate friends of his so that we shall understand his wishes and long to have them carried out; to let him so change our hearts that we shall love others more than we love ourselves, and shall pray chiefly not that we shall be made happy but that others shall be blest; to have such a clear vision of his love and power as will lead us to a faith that his will shall be carried out in our lives and that our prayers must prevail because they coincide with his almighty will.

738 Is there any limit to the prevailing power of prayer?

Jesus placed no limitations on the prevailing power of prayer. He has said, however, that we ought to seek first the things of the kingdom, and all the rest will be added; that is, a sufficiency for our needs. We should strive to know what are the things for which we should pray, and that are according to his will. Thus, to pray for wealth or for power could not be considered as coming in this category. The granting of such desires might be followed with evil to ourselves and others. Hence, it is right to say that we should pray for those things that he knows to be best for us, and which are in accordance with his will. The reference to praying for the removal of mountains is a figure of speech designed to show the vastness of God's munificence when our faith rises to meet it. The prayer of faith can remove mountains of difficulty from our path, and can overcome the seemingly insurmountable. The believer, therefore, should ask to be led that he may not pray amiss, through a wish to indulge in mere worldly desires. Many good Christians who live by faith have acknowledged in their experience instances in which their prayers have been denied, and they have been able to see later what a calamity it would have been to them had their desires been granted.

739 Does God punish in this life with sickness and other misfortune?

The Bible does not teach that all trouble comes from God as a punishment. It recognizes the fact that trouble is in the world, and, while it has some very definite things to say about it, it does not attempt to give a complete solution of the whole problem. Heb. 12:5-11 declares that God does in some instances discipline or "chasten" those whom he loves, but this could hardly be called punishment (see also Dcu. 8:5; Ps. 94:12; John 15:2). Sometimes, however, calamity is a definite punishment, as in many cases during the history of Israel, and particularly in their exile. The book of Job is a beautiful explanation of a form of suffering which has the double purpose of disciplining the soul and glorifying God. Nothing can bring such credit to God as the demonstration made by a soul that trusts and praises him in the midst of misfortune. Paul and the other apostles gloried in their opportunities to suffer for Jesus' sake. They rejoiced "that they were counted worthy to suffer shame in his name" (Acts 5:41). They felt that he had borne so much for them that they wanted to bear something for him. The Bible nowhere encourages people to dodge suffering; it exhorts them to bear it, while at the same time it exhorts them to lessen the sufferings of others, and help them bear their woes (see James 1:2-5; I Pet. 4:12-19; Gal. 6:2).

740 What is the true doctrine of restitution?

It is very clearly set forth in the Scripture that restitution should follow repentance. The change of heart may come before or after the act of restitution takes place, but in either event the convert will feel bound to make restitution at the earliest possible moment and in the fullest manner. It is expected of us that we shall make it right with our brother and we have no right to ask God to bestow on us the fulness of his gracious pardon until we do this (see Neh. 5:10, 11; Luke 19:8; Rom. 13:8). In his Gospel work Evangelist Moody emphasized restitution wherever practicable as a necessary adjunct to complete salvation. A few principles, however, are fixed, and apply without exception to all such cases. In the first place, you must bring yourself to agree to obey God at any cost. This is precisely what Jesus meant by his stern words about the right eye or the right hand. He probably did not mean that a circumstance would ever arise in which a man should pluck out his eye or cut off his hand. He thought too much of efficiency for that. He wants two-eyed and two-armed men in his army. But he did mean that it is far more important to obey God than it is to have two arms and two eyes. We must become so desperately in earnest to be right with God that we promise him that *when he makes his will clear we will obey*. Now that does not mean that we must go right off and do some fantastic or un-reasonable thing before God has made his will clear. We must wait till his will is clear. That is all the consecration he ever asks from anybody: to obey, step by step, as he makes the way unmistakably plain. "My sheep know my voice," he said. If you are not sure it is his voice speak-ing, wait till you are sure before taking the step. Where any property is involved, even if the amount is very small, it should be returned to the owner or his heirs. You will find such a procedure easier than you fear. People do not ridicule the "conscience fund." They admire a man who is trying to do absolutely right. In the case of conduct in which others are involved the matter is more difficult. If your confession involves another make very sure that the offense was really a serious matter and confer with those involved before making any statement. As to making financial restitution out of funds absolutely needed for present use, that problem is more difficult. In such a case it would be wise to make con-fession to those who were wronged, and ask them to give you time to make full restitution. Above all, think of God as a friend, who is trying to lead you to a place of perfect happiness, not as a tyrant demanding obedience to harsh and arbitrary rules. He is our best friend. You may win peace by trusting him. Then he will guide and strengthen you in untangling the problems and undoing the mistakes of the past.

741 May we pray with the same assurance for another's salvation as we do for our own?

We know that God is concerned for those who are still rejecting him even more than we can be, and loves them even more than we can love them. We can have greater influence to bring our dear ones to Christ if we have a cheerful, bright, trustful experience. We must remember, however, that God does not save people against their wills. In all our in-terpretations of Scripture we must be reasonable, interpreting each pas-sage in the light of all the rest. The promise in John, then, cannot mean that God will save one who refuses to be saved. So we cannot always pray for others with the same assurance as we pray for ourselves, for we have not control of their wills, as we have of our own. But sometimes the assurance may come from the Holy Spirit that a friend is going to yield, just as evangelists often have assurances in prayer that certain campaigns will result in great spiritual victory. Keep on praying; keep on trusting that God will do every possible thing to win your friend's love; let him see in you a peace and joy and confidence that will attract and win him. There will probably still be seasons of intense, passionate intercessory prayer, and in some such season you may receive the assurance that your friend is about to yield to the Saviour. Don't say or think that the case is "hopeless." There are no such cases. Christ can reach and save and forgive and bless "whosoever will."

742 What is meant by keeping the Sabbath day holy? After one has gone to church, what else is required, and what in the line of pleasure is permissible?

Paul, who apparently had to answer many questions concerning Sabbath observance at a time when legalists were urging the most rigid conformity with the strict Jewish laws on the subject, wrote: "Let no man judge you in meat or in drink or in respect of . . . the Sabbath days" (Col. 2:16). When the question of the obligation of the Gentile converts in the new church to observe the forms of the old religion was discussed by the apostles in council for the first time, the whole subject of legalism was simplified in two verses (see Acts 15:28, 29). Jesus himself rebuked the old slavish restrictions which were so prominent a part of the teachings of the Scribes and Pharisees, and showed them that the Sabbath was made for man, meaning that it was designed for our common humanity and for the doing of those acts which would conduce in largest measure to the general good. An act which is not in itself sinful but rather commendable, such as a deed of kindness, of charity, of urgent help and even of absolutely indispensable labor (which if left unattended too might entail loss or suffering), might thus not only be regarded as justifiable on the Sabbath but even as a duty. In general, the observance of the day may be summed up in rest and worship. No labor that can be done on other days should be performed on the Sabbath, but it is not to be a day devoted to social pleasure or amusement. It is the Lord's day, and we ought to spend it in a manner becoming its character. The question of visiting must be one for the individual conscience. There may be visits that come within the range of Sunday proprieties. Even the rigid Jews were permitted a "Sabbath day's journey," presumably for recreation and exercise, and we cannot believe that they shut off all social intercourse. There is a wide difference, however, between such happenings and the carrying out of a deliberate purpose of spending a portion of the day on social calls.

The gravest danger that confronts Christian parents in regard to Sunday conduct is that by a too strict regulation they will make the day actually distasteful to the children. The day should be literally happy, and any plan that tends to make the children gloomy and dissatisfied does more harm than good. Story-telling is always a delight to children. They like to hear a good book read aloud. Get them to take turns in reading aloud. Winter and summer alike, long walks are in order, and always delightful. Do not be afraid to let them run and laugh. Explain to them that it is best not to indulge in games because the habit of playing games on Sunday is coming to be a real national peril, and is taking people away from God and the church. Provide some refreshments for them; let them help in preparing them. There could be no harm in carrying the refreshments on their walk and eating them at the walk's end. Show them how they can find God in nature. Make them feel that Christ is the "God of the open air," and that he loves health and happiness. In such an atmosphere they will grow to love Bible talks and will come to realize that Christ is a delightful friend and Sunday a delightful day. Give them something to do. If they can take flowers or fruit to the sick or poor, or go to sing for shut-ins or at some afternoon service, they will find the day still fuller of blessing.

743 How should the Sabbath day be spent in an area where no church privileges are available?

It should be spent in prayer to God, in praise and in meditation on his Word. This is to be done, where possible, either in the privacy of one's own apartment, in the family, or in the assembly of the faithful. Where public worship in the sanctuary is not practicable, its substitute is to be found in the assembling of a few in the home and there reading and expounding the Scriptures, first asking a blessing on the effort. There are in isolated parts of this great country many sections without church buildings. Little gatherings of friends and neighbors are held for worship and often a sermon by some devout minister of the Gospel is read aloud by some one present to the edification of all. All labor should be set aside and everything that will distract the mind from the sacred duties of the day. The children, too, should not be forgotten. Their instruction in the Word is an essential part of the duties of the Sabbath.

744 Does a Christian always feel the same as to his salvation and its fruits?

Suppose we begin, in trying to find an answer for this problem—which could be matched in countless lives—by quoting these words from Paul: "God is able to make all grace abound toward you, that ye, always having all sufficiency in all things, may abound to every good work" (II Cor. 9:8). That's comforting, isn't it? Whatever our problems are, then, we are not going to worry about them, because God's grace is so abundant. Almost every difficulty in life is solved by just getting a little more of God's grace. He is going to take away your anxiety, and make you happy; you can count on him for that. But not even perfect Christians "feel" the same all the time. Another word for feeling is *emo-*

tion, and that very word implies motion, change, fluctuation. Our feelings are affected by many things—health, sleep (or the lack of it), conditions of the air, etc. In bad health, and, especially in cases where nerves are overstrained and the brain overwearied, there is very likely to be depression and oversensitiveness. Now let us analyze and see what makes us Christians. You hate sin; you love God; you wish every one well; you long that others shall love God's Word. Now thank God for all the grace he has given you, and ask him for more. Read his wonderful promises of cleansing and believe he means them for you. Then, disregarding your feelings and living actively for others, keep on believing that he keeps his promises for you, moment by moment (see Ezek. 36:25-27; II Cor. 7:1; I Thess. 5:23, 24).

745 How can we overcome fear as to the certainty of our salvation?

Many good people are troubled by fears and selfaccusations which come from own imaginings or from the tempter, rather than from the Holy Spirit. It may be some comfort to know that there are many cases where sensitive souls have suffered great torment because of similar accusations and fears. Do you not see, in the first place, that these feelings cannot be reproofs from God, because if they were they would be definite and emphatic? When God accuses us of anything we know exactly what he means. He does not tease and perplex us by talking in riddles and in enigmas. Jesus said: "My sheep know my voice." It is one of the offices of the Holy Spirit to "convict," but conviction is a plain, definite thing that tells us when we have done wrong and just what the wrong is. What God regards is the motive of our act, and it is very plain from your letter that at every step you meant to do the right thing. All you need to do now in order to have peace is to stop doubting God and begin to trust him. Remember that what saves you fully is not anything that you do or promise, but what God has done in the gift of his Son and what he has promised in his Word. Do not grieve God any longer by distrusting him and wondering whether or not he is kind. You would feel deeply grieved if your children doubted and feared you in this way. Even the strange, evil thoughts which come to you do not condemn you because they are hateful to you and you try to banish them. Wesley said: "I cannot prevent, the birds from flying over my head, but I can prevent them from building nests in my hair." So we can not prevent evil thoughts coming to us, but we can drive them away as we look to God for speedy deliverance. It is not necessary to "go forward" before you can receive the gift of the Holy Spirit. No! Nothing is necessary except to believe at once that God does give us this gracious gift, "for the promise is unto you and unto your children and unto all that are afar off, even as many as the Lord our God shall call" (Acts 2:39). Read the wonderful promises for cleansing and for the filling with the Holy Spirit: Ezek. 36:25-27; Zech. 13:1; II Cor. 7:1; Rom. 6 (the whole chapter); Heb. 10:1-23; I Thess. 5:23, 24; and Heb. 13:20, 21. Take your stand firmly upon these and other promises, believe that God meant them for you, and refuse any longer to live in fear and distress. He is *abundantly able* to save and will save "to the uttermost."

Do you remember that the first word of the angel who announced Christ's coming to the shepherds was "Fear not"? You are being tormented with fear. This fear is the cause of your spiritual distress. You must deal with yourself just as you would deal with a child who is afraid of ghosts. Tell him there are no ghosts; there is nothing to be afraid of. Now the thing that torments you is just as untrue as the child's thoughts about ghosts. Your ghost is the thought that God is not kind. This is not true. He is so kind that he sent Christ to save you. Since he did so, why should you fear and doubt any longer? "Believe on the Lord Jesus Christ and thou shalt be saved" is just as true for you as it was true for the Philippian jailer and for the millions more who have tested it. But if you will not believe, if you insist on fearing instead, you will continue to live in torment. Do not wait for a "right feeling." That cannot come till you stop fearing and begin to trust. Perhaps you do think of yourself too much. Fix your eyes on Christ. Realize his great love and power, and remember that he loves you just as much as he loves anybody. He surely will save you. Take him by faith as your Saviour. Begin to live for others. Spend what strength you have in service for others, and he will give you more (Isa.40:29-31).

746 Can a true Christian willfully sin?

This question usually revolves about the passage: "Whosoever is born of God doth not commit sin; for his seed remaineth in him; and he cannot sin, because he is born of God" (I John 3:9). As we have stated many times the whole volume of Scripture must be taken together in answering any question. Now the whole message of the Bible seems to be built upon the assumption that it is possible for any one to sin. The temptation of Christ seems to imply even he could have yielded; otherwise temptation would have no meaning. Paul said he was conscious of the possibility of becoming "a castaway" (I Cor. 9:27). While this passage from John is extremely difficult, we may, perhaps, interpret it in this way—that while a person is loving God he cannot sin. The love must drop out of his consciousness first. Righteousness means the desire and effort to obey God; so that while we are loving him we are not sinning. Sin is "a wilful transgression of a known law"; and God does not account an act sinful when we do it believing that it has his approval. The way to keep from sinning is to keep this love for God ever present in our consciousness. While we have it our deeds will not be sinful.

But we may at any time put it away, or allow ourselves to lose it, and then we shall yield to sin. A wilful sin means that one sins, saying: "I know that God does not wish me to do this, but I am going to do it." And certainly it is not an extravagance of language to say that while one is conscious of loving God he cannot say that.

747 Is it true that the closer we live to God the more trouble he sends us?

We think that God's treatment of his children is directed to their development. If he sees that trouble and suffering will lead to that end he will administer them; if prosperity will best promote development he will send that. The same difference is made by judicious parents and teachers in the treatment of children. Some children develop better by kindness than by severity, while others would make no progress if they were not treated severely.

748 Is uncharitableness compatible with Christianity?

No one should go into the business of judging others. But a Christian who is unkind and cross is certainly an anomalous creature. If the New Testament teaches anything it teaches that the fruit of the religion of Jesus is kindness, charity, friendliness, neighborliness, love. Love is not incompatible with sternness and an earnest opposition to everything that is wrong. But the real Christian ought to convince every one who knows him that his heart is tender and kind. We ought, however, to recognize the fact that often persons with thoroughly kind hearts have a gruff and rugged exterior and manner. Also, intense pain, long-continued sickness, overstrained or disordered nerves will sometimes make an individual appear impatient who might otherwise be most patient. We ought to recognize these differences of temperament and the unusual strain put by circumstances upon certain souls. We should believe and experience and teach that the grace of God is great enough to remove all petulance and unkindness from the soul, but while advocating and urging this belief we should ourselves be most patient with those whose faith has not yet grasped the truth that complete deliverance from unpleasant tempers is possible.

749 How can we reconcile the doctrine of good works as taught by James with that of St. Paul?

There is an apparent contradiction between Rom. 3:28, "Therefore we conclude that a man is justified by faith without the deeds of the law," and James 2:24, "Ye see then how that by works a man is justified and not by faith alone." In order to harmonize the apparently opposing doctrines it is to be remembered that the two apostles were writing for two different classes of readers, both of whom were liable to run to extremes. Paul wished his hearers to understand that good works did not avail to save a man whose heart had not been changed. It was through his faith in Christ that he was accepted and that he could not earn salvation. James, on the other hand, was writing for people who were disposed to do no good works at all, but to rest contented with their own salvation, claiming that faith was sufficient. He told them that such faith did not avail. Faith without works was dead—was in fact no faith at all. The explanation which reconciles the two is that true faith always leads to good works, and if there are no good works we are justified in inferring that the faith is not genuine.

750 What do the Scriptures teach us about good works?

As with all things that are good, Christ was an example to us in good works (John 10:32; Acts 10:38). Good works called good fruits, fruits meet for repentance, fruits of righteousness and works and labors of love (James 3:17; Matt. 3:8; Phi. 1:11; Heb. 6:10) are by Jesus Christ wrought by God in us to the glory and praise of God (Phi. 1:11; Isa. 26:12). The Scriptures are designed to lead us to do them in Christ's name, but only they who abide in Christ can perform them (II Tim. 3:16, 17; Col. 3:17; John 15:4, 5). Though heavenly wisdom is full of good works, justification and salvation are not attainable through them (James 3:17; Rom. 3:20; Eph. 2:8, 9; II Tim. 1:9). Saints created in Christ unto good works and exhorted to put them on are full of and zealous of them (Eph. 2:10; Col. 3:12-14; Acts 9:36; Tit. 2:14). They should not only be so but should be rich, stablished, fruitful and perfect in them, ready and prepared unto all of them which they are to manifest with meekness and to which they are to provoke each other without ostentation (I Tim. 6:18; II Thess. 2:17; Col. 1:10; Heb. 13:21; II Cor. 9:8; Tit. 3:1; Heb. 10:24; Matt. 6:1-18). God will remember these good works which shall be brought into the judgment and there will be an evidence of faith (Neh. 13:14; Eccles. 12:14; Matt. 25:34-40).

751 How much of the Lord's work ought a Christian to do—one who has home duties to attend to?

God expects his people to give their lives unreservedly and absolutely to his service. Whether one is at work in the home or in the church, there should be the consciousness that the work is being done for God. "Whatsoever ye do, in word or deed, do all in the name of the Lord Jesus" (Col. 3:17). The question of how much time should be given to God's service in the home and how much to God's service in church and community must be settled in the individual conscience. "Duties *never* conflict." There is always one thing to do which is the thing God wants done at that particular time. It is probably true that a mother's first duty is to her home, though there are exceptional cases in which a woman may be called to leave her home for broader work, and every mother must cultivate a deep interest in the needs and sufferings of those outside the home circle and do all she can to relieve them. But women who are kept close at home should not feel that their lives are being wasted. They are training lives which may bless multitudes. Susanna Wesley was a true mother and homemaker, doing her work there and giving to the church and the world two great spiritual leaders. Home must be kept bright, neat, happy, cheerful, worshipful. Church and community duties which unfit women for their work at home, or take them too much away from their children, should not be undertaken.

752 What is the best way to worship and serve the Lord?

The best worship is a faithful, loyal, adoring, prayerful service; an upright, reverent walk before men, "bringing forth fruits of righteousness" for his glory. The Samaritan woman asked the same question of Christ, and you will find his answer in John 4:21-24.

753 How can we reconcile the widely differing views of equally well-meaning Christians?

In the passage, John 7:17, "If any man will do his will he shall know the doctrine." Jesus is speaking simply of the question of the divine source of his teaching. He was constantly repeating the assertion made in the preceding verse: "My doctrine is not mine, but his that sent me." The Jews thought he spoke with his own human authority; he asserted that his authority came from God. And he told them that the reason they could not perceive this was the sinful stubbornness of their hearts. "If you were really willing to do God's will," he told them, "you would know that my teaching comes from him." It is this fact that makes faith in Christ a fair spiritual test; those who reject him are not really willing to obey God; those who are really on the lookout for God's guidance and who will actually submit their wills to him will learn the truth about Jesus. While not implied in this particular verse, the question involves another problem, which is why "equally well-meaning Christians" differ so widely on religious matters, when the promises of divine guidance are so numerous and so emphatic. One would reasonably think, if God promises to guide every one who will allow him to do so, that all who do yield themselves to him would see everything alike. Briefly, we may say that most of the things Christians differ about are not essential. God does promise to guide in vital matters, but not in non-essentials. Read Paul's statements about the charity Christian believers ought to manifest toward one another concerning matters about which they differ. Then, too, many people think they disagree concerning things about which they really do agree. They all see limited parts of one great truth, like the two knights who, coming up to an inn from different directions, fell into a dispute as to whether the shield hanging before it was of silver or gold. They began to fight, and in the struggle reversed their positions, whereupon each saw that both had been right, the shield being gold on one side and silver on the other. Not only our points of view but our mental capabilities differ widely; some can understand a specific truth or fact, others cannot. We must be tolerant and charitable, believing that God is blessing and leading those who differ from us as well as those who agree with us. But there are certain great vital principles, upon which all Christians can and do agree.

754 How can a Christian escape the criticism of those who do not agree with his methods?

Christians need not expect to escape unjust criticism at times. There are good, well-meaning people who take the narrow view, and would compel all Christians to be of one type—their type, of course—and to believe precisely what they believe and worship in all respects as they themselves worship. This is altogether wrong. You may remember what Jesus said to some of these faultfinding folk who desired him to rebuke an independent worker (see Mark 9:40). Our heavenly Father looks at the hearts of men and regards their inmost thoughts and desires as of far greater consequence than outward forms and ceremonies. Moses had trouble in his time with the formalists, and see how he answered them (see Num. 11:26); and Paul, in the midst of his great apostolic missionary work, had occasion to rebuke some of his followers whose overzeal led them to criticise a few good people who did not choose to copy their methods, but struck out a path for themselves (see Phil. 1:15-18). If you go on energetically doing your best in a humble way, and asking divine guidance daily, you can afford to overlook the critics. Keep in constant touch with your church and get on friendly terms with your fellow members. Try hard to put aside all feeling against individuals, no matter what their attitude has been in the past. We think you might cultivate the social side of church membership to advantage. One who holds aloof certainly misses much in the way of Christian fellowship and sociability.

755 What shall I do to become the good Christian worker I used to be?

"I am not as good a Christian or worker as I used to be," is a complaint often heard. Thousands of professing Christians could make this same complaint. Removal to a new home, the death of consecrated

Christian friends who encouraged and guided us in other years, gradual yielding to the influence and pressure of other interests and desires— these are among the countless causes of inactivity and unconcern on the part of those who were once zealous Christian workers. Further, one's views or one's tastes may change with passing years, and the tasks one once delighted in may not be so congenial as before. Or, more seriously, one's faith in some of the details of the creeds of earlier years may have been weakened, and this weakened faith has caused a hesitancy about trying to guide others. What shall be done? In the first place we must come resolutely back to Christ. Whatever may have happened to our old faith we are still sure that he is the Master of our souls. We must confess our shortcomings, ask his forgiveness, and ask him to set us at work again. We must be strenuous and uncompromising in making right whatever wrongs have crept into our lives during these years of neglect. He will freely forgive. He will give us a new vision of himself, a new vision of old truths. He will show us what he wants us to do now. Opportunities will open—it may be to take up the very tasks we laid down; it may be to take up new tasks more in line with our present interests. But we must begin *at once* to do some definite thing for Christ, and when that is done another task will surely be at hand. We dare not delay another hour to return to our fidelity and our zeal. We must think not only of Christ's disappointment during the faithless years and of the loss to our own lives, but of the burdens we might have lifted, the heartaches and tears we might have prevented, of all the people who have had sad hours or wrong hours that we might have saved them from, or who are wrong now because we were unfaithful. We dare not add another moment to those unfaithful years.

756 Can one be saved and yet be unkind?

Salvation by faith does not release a Christian from the duty of being kind. That is a dreadfully distorted view which some people appear to take. Our faith in Christ should be a faith that brings a cleansing from unkindness, selfishness and impatience, and that fills the heart full of love. Among the fruits of the Spirit Paul names "love, peace, longsuffering, gentleness, meekness." The wonderful 13th chapter of I Corinthians gives a vivid picture of what a Christian's life among others should be. As for overwork and weariness, it is perfectly true that they may so strain our mental and nervous system as to put it into an abnormal condition. In our rapid, high-tension American life this condition is very common and we should do all in our power to avoid it. God's command to rest is as definite as his command to work. Between our work times we must take what rest we can, and then trust God to keep us sweet and patient and kind during the hard hours of work.

757 What cure is there for one living under the cloud of spiritual doubt?

Suppose you had lost your sleep for two or three nights. This would put your brain into a thoroughly abnormal condition. You would probably have all sorts of doubts and fear and misgivings, and what you would need to rid yourself of these would be not prayer but sleep. God made your body according to certain laws, and to keep it in correct working order you must conform to these laws. If you break the laws, even innocently, your first religious duty is to repair the physical damage. If our brains are overstrained or the delicate nervous system is overstrained or deranged in any way our brains will manufacture queer and abnormal and distressing thoughts and feelings. First of all insist upon getting well. You have faith enough in Christ to tell him simply and frankly that you cannot figure these things out in your present state, and ask him to make it possible for you to rest. Then as your mind and nerves grow stronger associate with the most spiritually minded people you can find; attend their religious services. Accept whatever of their teaching you can without mental effort and leave the rest till you get enough stronger to consider it. Do the same with your Bible reading. Accept what is plain and easy and simple, and leave the difficult passages till you are better. Above all, remember that of all kind and gentle and sympathetic friends Jesus is the best. He wants to make you well; he wants to drive away the clouds. Just let him be the friend he wants to be, and his light will drive the darkness away (see II Cor. 4:6).

758 How can one have harmony between one's higher and lower selves?

David prayed a beautiful prayer in the 11th verse of the 86th Psalm: "Unite my heart to fear thy name." Charles Wesley prays for

> "A heart in every thought renewed,
>   And full of love divine;
> Perfect and right and pure and good,
>   A copy, Lord, of thine."

Scripture promises for the cleansing of the heart from sin are numerous and positive. But the fact remains that even after the heart has been cleansed by the power of the Holy Spirit a struggle goes on with one's lower or animal nature. The heart itself, that is, the will and the affections, may be united and consistent, but the body has tendencies away from the right. So long as life lasts there will be this battle between the body and the soul, the battle described in Paul's strenuous words in I Cor. 9:27 (American Version): "I buffet my body and bring it into bondage." But the struggle with the bodily impulses need not disturb our

Christian peace. It is different from the struggle James speaks about in his reference to the "two-souled man." This is a good translation of his phrase, "double-minded man." That is a terrible and grievous situation, in which a man's inmost soul is divided, part set on the good and part set on the evil. But when we receive the blessing of a "united heart," when we have what Jesus called the "single eye," then we may set ourselves jubilantly to face the struggle with all the forces that would oppose us, including our own physical nature, knowing that we shall be constantly "more than conquerors through him that loved us."

759 Does a Christian ever have evil desires?

The word "desires" hardly covers the problem. It deals not so much with desires as with the question of love or good feeling toward another, or the lack of such good feeling. In discussing these problems it helps us to remember Jesus' summary of the law, "Thou shalt love God; thou shalt love thy neighbor," and Paul's statement, "Love is the fulfilling of the law." Whenever we have an unloving or unkind feeling toward another we have sinned. Whenever we are indifferent as to whether or not an act pleases God, particularly when we persist in an action after we know it to be displeasing to God, we have sinned. The Scriptures teach very clearly that God, through Christ, provides a grace which will keep our hearts kind and loving all the time and will keep alive there the sense of our love to God. Of course, when another commits an act that is hurtful to ourselves or to others, there can be displeasure at the act, there can even be indignation; but in the perfect Christian the very displeasure or indignation would be connected in some way with love. This was the case with the anger of Jesus; he was angry that people were trying to thwart his works of love. But, as stated before, there is sin the moment one persists in an action while believing that it is displeasing to God. A person may be a Christian and still have such lapses, but he may also press on to a higher Christian state in which the soul is so filled with love that such lapses do not occur.

760 Must a converted person give up the use of tobacco?

If you have come to the conclusion that you ought to give up the use of tobacco it is your duty to do so. You remember the principle laid down by the apostle Paul for similar cases: "There is nothing unclean of itself; but to him that esteemeth a thing to be unclean, to him it is unclean" (Rom. 14:14). The serious feature, according to this rule, is not the use of tobacco, but is that you are doing something you believe you ought not to do. A Christian who is convinced that a certain thing is wrong ought immediately to abandon it, without any question as to what the penalty of wrongdoing is. You will suffer, but is it not worth suffering to put yourself right with God? You may be sure that if you ask God for strength it will be given you. There are multitudes of men who have been delivered from rum, tobacco and other enslaving habits who could tell you that an honest, sincere, persistent effort made in God's strength is sure to be successful.

761 Can a person be a Christian and use liquor moderately?

Liquor, like everything else in this world, poisons included, has its uses, but these are mainly medical. It is not an article of food nor a necessity, and there is no excuse for the indulgence of a habit which, even in its most temperate aspect, is pernicious, morally and physically, like all other sinful indulgences. The Bible admonishes us to avoid all such practises, and especially to avoid drink. The "temperate drinker," who believes he is doing no wrong in tampering lightly with this great evil, should remember that he is incurring a double responsibility—risking the wreck of his own soul and body, and also leading others by his bad example to a like fate (see Cor. 8:9-13 and 10:21, 31, 32; Rom. 14:21; Matt. 18: 6, 7, and other passages).

762 How are we to drive away harrowing thoughts of our past misdeeds?

Even David had these troubles. Does he not say in Ps. 51:3: "My sin is ever before me"? But God has promised to forgive our sins, and we must try to do the same. It should not be hard to believe that he forgives our sins when he has stated so often and so emphatically that he will do so: "I, even I, am he that blotteth out thy transgressions" (Isa. 43:25); "Though your sins be as scarlet, they shall be as white as snow" (Isa. 1:18); "As far as the east is from the west, so far hath he removed our transgressions from us" (Ps. 103:12). After you have trusted Christ to forgive your sins you should give yourself so earnestly and energetically to service for others in his name that you will have little time to think about the past. Some converts make a mistake in dwelling too much on past sins in telling about their redemption. It is sometimes helpful to others to tell of our sins in testifying to God's pardon, but we must be careful not to do it too much. As for responsibility for our thoughts, we have quoted a number of times Wesley's saying: "I cannot prevent the birds from flying over my head, but I can prevent them from building nests in my hair." Thoughts of evil are suggested to us, but we can repel them by our will power, helped by the grace of God.

763 What was the origin of the mite box?

The mite box is supposed to have had its origin in the suggestion furnished in the New Testament story of the widow's mite (Mark 12:42). A mite was equal to about half a mill; hence the idea of furnishing a receptacle for offerings of the smallest denomination. Just when mite boxes were first used is unknown.

764 On what scale should we give to the Lord's work?

There is no definite scale laid down in the Gospels for our gifts toward the Lord's work, although there are various passages on the subject. Many good people even today adhere to the tithing system and find satisfaction in it, while others, who give "according as God has prospered them," find that where love stimulates their generosity their gifts are blessed to themselves and others. If we lavish all our prosperity on ourselves and our families, leaving little or nothing for the Lord's work, we are "robbing God." It is well, therefore, to make him a partner in all our increase, and a sharer in all our benefits. Since everything we have comes from his hands, we should not hesitate to acknowledge it by a generous return. We know of several worthy people who systematically plan to devote a good share of their income to the church, to missions, to charities, and to various philanthropies. One of these friends carries a list of some sixteen missionaries in foreign fields, whom he supports, and with whom he is in more or less regular correspondence. Nor does he let other good causes suffer, although the one dearest to his heart—the spread of the Gospel—may receive the largest share. Another person devoted a large percentage of the profits of an immense business to the support of a chain of home missions. He did not neglect church work or other causes, and prosperity always stood by his side. We believe in systematic giving, however much or little may be our gift, and whatever we give let it be done without ostentation, but modestly and gladly, and it will not fail to bring a blessing.

765 Is it possible for a Christian to be deeply interested in some earthly work and ambition, music for instance, and to be equally interested in personal work for souls?

It is not at all likely that the Master wishes you to give up your music. The history of Christianity and the history of music are closely intertwined. In fact, it is hard to conceive what Christianity would have been without music. Many a soul has been won to Christ by the singing of a hymn. And even instrumental music at the hands of Spirit-filled performers may bring positive spiritual blessing. God has special need of consecrated masters of music now for two specific tasks—to oppose the tendency to make music contribute to the baser instincts, and to raise the standard of music used in Christian work. This does not mean that a Christian musician should be interested only in what is called sacred music. The best secular compositions, vocal and instrumental, may be studied and rendered. But for the Christian there will always be the thought of God in his work and the desire that souls shall be spiritually blest. Be sure to think of Christ as a great Friend rather than a great taskmaster. Get on the closest possible terms with him, asking him to cleanse your heart and fill you with his Spirit, and make you feel his anxiety that people shall be saved and blest. Then he will show you how to use his gift to help forward his work.

766 What pleasures must one sacrifice in joining a church?

God does not ask us to make sacrifice for its own sake. When he asks us to give anything up, it is because he knows it would be harmful to us to keep it. In all our thoughts about God we must hold with a firm grip the great fundamental truth that he loves us. We cannot think rightly or feel comfortable without starting here. Because he loves us he wants us to be happy. He does not want to take away our happiness, but to give us more. And he knows that we can be happy only as we love and serve him. He really asks us to give up nothing, except to give ourselves to him. When we realize that we belong to him we also realize that certain things harm us, and that certain other things may have a harmful influence upon others. We are living for him, and for the people for whom his Son died. All these questions settle themselves quite easily then. Wholesome athletics make our bodies stronger to do his work. But we know that dancing has injured the moral and spiritual life of many, and that the great majority of plays have objectionable and harmful features. So the sacrifices that seemed hard at first are seen to be really not hard at all, and we find more happiness in the consciousness that we are pleasing and helping him than we could ever have found in any form of self-indulgence.

767 Is it right to accept "tainted" money for church work?

When Christian institutions accept ill-gotten wealth for any purpose, knowing how such means have been obtained, they give quiet sanction to the crime. The early Christians were forbidden to eat the flesh of offerings made to idols; then how much should Christians abstain from money obtained as the price of crime. Christianity would better die than become a partner of sin and an abettor of distress. No doubt every dollar the saloonkeeper offers is blood money taken from the mouths of starving women and children.

768 What is the difference between law and grace?

The clear and definite teaching of the Scripture is "Believe on the Lord Jesus Christ and thou shalt be saved." Divested of all theological phrases, the way of salvation is pointed out in these plain words. Man, as a sinner, is under condemnation by the law; but the Gospel opens the way to pardon and to rehabilitation in righteousness. Salvation is of God's free grace and comes through no merit of our own. Christ has satisfied the law and paid the penalty in our behalf. He is to be accepted as Saviour, Atoner, Advocate, Counselor, Friend. Not in the strength of our own righteousness, but with his righteousness covering our imperfections, and his shed blood washing away our sins and his divine intercession pleading for our forgiveness, we place our whole life, here and hereafter, unreservedly in his hands. We must first confess our sins with sincere repentance, and then determine, with his help, to forsake sin hereafter. If we have wronged any one we must show the sincerity of our repentance by righting the wrong. We must ask help to overcome all assailing doubts and to have our faith strengthened daily. We have his assurance that such prayers will never be unanswered. In all of this process there is nothing concerning works. We must ask help to overcome all assailing doubts and to have our faith strengthened daily. We have his assurance that such prayers will never be unanswered. In all this process, there is nothing concerning works. If men were saved by virtue of their works, what would become of those who, sunk in the lowest depths of sin, have no works to plead for them? Yet he "saves to the uttermost." He has already fulfilled the law and done all the works needful for our salvation, and it only remains for us to accept his sacrifice and rejoice that Jesus has "tasted death for every man," and that he died for us. Regeneration follows conversion, and the regenerated heart, in grateful and glad obedience, brings forth those fruits of the Spirit that are described in Gal. 5:22, 23; Eph. 5:9; James 3:17, 18; Phil. 1:11. They are the things that make the life rich and abundant, in contrast with the barren and unproductive nature of the unregenerated life. Thus fruit (or works) logically follow, for it is inevitable that a living faith must be productive; hence our faith is literally known by the works we do in token of the love that gave us as a free gift that new and larger freedom which otherwise we could never have attained (see Rom. 8:2; Gal. 5:1; Rom. 6:18; John 8:32, 36).

769 At what date and what season of the year was the Saviour born?

According to the leading modern authorities, and many others of former times, the birth of Christ took place four years before the opening of what is known as the Christian era. Dionysius Exiguus, a monk who made the calculations upon which the Christian calendar is based, lived in 526 A. D., and it has long been conceded that he erred to the extent of four years in fixing the date of the Nativity. The date, however, is unimportant, as far as it affects Christ's mission or character, although it has been a subject of discussion for centuries. There was no agreement as to the date, in the primitive Christian Church, nor as to the season. Clement of Alexandria regarded the 20th of May as the date of the Nativity, others the 20th of April. Modern chronologists differ, some holding it probable that either June or July (when the fields are parched from want of rain) was the time; Lightfoot names September; Lardner and Newcomb, October; Strong, August; Andrews and many others between the middle of December, 749, and the middle of January, 750 (dating after the founding of Rome). Church historians and popular tradition have fixed on December 25. One clue is found in the fact that Zacharias was officiating in the Temple when the angel announced to him the future birth of his son, John the Baptist. It is known that the course of Abia, to which Zacharias belonged, was serving in the Temple in October of that year. Another clue is in the fact of the shepherds being in the fields, which was more likely to occur in December than in June, which latter is the alternative month.

JESUS' LIFE AND DEATH

**770 Is there any authentic portrait
of Christ in existence?**

Perhaps the oldest and supposedly the most authentic is a cameo, said to have been cut in the reign of Tiberius, but it may not now be in existence. The Christs of the great artists are the highest ideal to which human art can attain. There is the divinely noble yet sad Christ of Ary Scheffer; the placid Christ of Raphael; the strenuous Christ of Da Vinci; the suffering, thorn-crowned Christs of Guido Reni, Quentin Matsys, Rembrandt, Titian, Correggio and Albert Dürer; the ascetic Christ of Munkacsy, and the later presentations of the Dutch, French, Spanish and English schools. Each artist has given to the world his highest conception according to the standards of his nation. But the real face of the Saviour, glorious with its fulness of power and majesty, yet inexpressibly tender with love and sympathy, has eluded them all. Isaiah (53:2) gave a prophetic glimpse of him that was to come.

**771 Why do artists represent Jesus and his disciples in a sitting
posture at the institution of the Lord's Supper
when all sacred writers say it was customary
in those days to recline at the table?**

Artistic conceptions have certainly varied greatly in the treatment of this subject. Some painters have apparently discarded Oriental forms and customs, in order to produce a picture that would be less strange, yet no less impressive in the eyes of their own countrymen. A few, like Tissot, have adhered closely to the Eastern standards. Italian painters have given us the Last Supper as a classic Italian scene, and German, Dutch and English artists have each given their own national interpretation of the subject. They painted for their own time and their own people, and unless they had had the advantage of travel and study in the Orient they could not have done otherwise. Strict accuracy was apparently held as of less importance than a noble and beautiful ideal.

**772 Was Jesus as a baby like an ordinary baby,
or did he know all things?**

It is difficult if not impossible to comprehend the union of the divine and the human in Christ's nature. He could not have been an ordinary babe, as the divine nature must have been potent in him even in infancy. But that he knew all things in the sense of secular knowledge cannot be believed. In fact Luke says explicitly (Luke 2:52) that he increased in wisdom. Even after he commenced his ministry he admitted that he did not know all things (Mark 13:32). His divinity must have been restricted by its fleshly environment.

773 What evidence is there outside of the Bible of the existence of Jesus Christ?

A number of the most eminent historians, both Jewish and Roman, mention Jesus in their writings. Tacitus, who lived in the first century, wrote "this sect (of Christians) came from Judea and was founded by Jesus Christ, who was put to the death of the Cross." Suetonius, a Roman historian, who wrote the lives of the Cesars, mentions the sect "under one Christus." This writer, although an enemy to Christianity, still recognized it. Lucan, who lived near the close of the first century, mentions the Christians and describes their belief. He tells us "of all the great men Judea has brought forth, their crucified Master exceeds in his philosophy and teaching all before him." A magnificent tribute from a heathen! Josephus, the greatest of Jewish historians, writing about the middle of the first century, says: "Now, there was about this time Jesus, a wise man—if it be lawful to call him a man—for he was a doer of many wonderful works, a teacher of such men as received the truth." He further relates his preaching, trial condemnation, crucifixion and resurrection, and refers to the prophecies concerning him as having been fulfilled in all these matters. Thus is established, outside of Sacred Writ, the existence of Jesus on earth.

774 In what sense can Jesus be regarded as descended from David?

You will notice that there is a divergence in the lists of his ancestors, as given by Matthew and Luke. Matthew gives Joseph's father as Jacob (Matt. 1:16). Luke says (Luke 3:23) his father was Heli. We cannot think that either was mistaken. It is suggested with some plausibility that Heli was Mary's father, and Joseph was really his son-in-law, not his son. The Jews followed the genealogy in the male line, which may account for Joseph's name being inserted instead of Mary's. If that is the explanation it is Mary's ancestry which Luke gives. Her accompanying Joseph to Bethlehem to be counted seems to imply that, like Joseph, she could claim descent from David.

775 What text of Scripture may be presented as the most definite and powerful assertion of the Diety of Christ?

In John 10:30 Christ says: "I and my Father are one." This is his own unqualified assertion of his oneness with the Father. He also prayed to the Father in these words: "And now, O Father, glorify thou me with thine ownself with the glory which I had with thee before the world was" (John 17:5). St. John, in his Gospel, opens his record of Christ with words used by Moses in introducing God upon the scene. "In the beginning God," says Moses. "In the beginning was the Word," says John, and adds: "And the Word was with God, and the Word was God." We identify this Word as Christ as we read John 1:14: "And the Word was made flesh." The writer of the Epistle to the Hebrews declares that God made the worlds through his Son and that to the Son he saith: "Thy throne, O God, is for ever and ever." And again: "Thou, Lord, in the beginning hast laid the foundation of the earth and the heavens are the work of thy hands." Paul, in writing to the Romans, speaks of Christ, "who is over all. God blessed forever."

776 How was Jesus' childhood spent?

All we know of the childhood of Jesus is what the Scripture relates. There are, however, various traditional writings on the subject, more or less apocryphal, which have been preserved, but to these little importance is attached. The life at Nazareth, though quiet and obscure and passed over in a few lines by the evangelists, was unquestionably a life of preparation for the great work to follow. While Jesus "must have been at all times marked out by his higher spiritual nature," writes Dr. Geikie, "yet in his human nature there must have been the same gradual development as in other men, otherwise they would not have felt the wonder at him which they afterward evinced. Year after year passed and still found him at his daily toil, because his hour had not yet come." It is in various ways made evident that, even in childhood, he had distinct convictions of his divine nature, and that these grew with the years, until the time was ripe for beginning his public ministry.

777 Were the Jews, or were the Romans, responsible for Christ's death?

At that particular time the Jews were not allowed to inflict the death penalty. Afterward, as in the case of Stephen, they did inflict it, and they carried it out by stoning. Their responsibility, however, is undoubted. Pilate did not want to kill Jesus. The Jews placed Pilate in a technical difficulty by denouncing Jesus as a rival to Caesar. If he had refused to punish him the Jews would, as they covertly threatened, have denounced him to Caesar. He could easily have cleared himself of such a charge, but there were other matters in his career which would not so well have borne investigation, and these would naturally have been cited if the Jews had impeached him. Pilate consented to the execution reluctantly under Jewish pressure, and therefore, though the actual execution was conducted by Romans, the Jews were responsible.

778 Is there any way of reconciling an apparent discrepancy in the narratives of the evangelists as to the thieves at the crucifixion, Matthew and Mark speaking of both thieves reviling Christ, while Luke speaks of one thief reproving the other for doing it?

Augustine and others who have dealt with the subject (for the difficulty was considered centuries ago) contend that the penitent thief did not revile Christ. They think that Matthew and Mark were in the habit of using the plural form of a word where the singular was the correct form, and they refer to other instances of the habit. Matt. 26:8; Mark 14:4 compared with John 12:4 is one of them. On the other hand, it may have been that both thieves reviled Christ, but the spectacle of magnanimity and patient suffering so affected one of them, as he drew near death, as to produce a penitent frame of mind. We may infer also, from the form in which he presented his petition, that he must have previously had some instruction either from Christ or his disciples, which had remained in his memory without, until his dying hour, affecting his heart or life.

779 Who was regarded by the Lord as his foremost disciple?

John was called the "disciple whom Jesus loved" (John 13:23, 21:7 and 21:20). The Saviour commended Mary to the keeping of John, while he hung on the cross (see John 19:26, 27). Peter, however, by many is regarded as having been the leading spirit of the band.

780 Did Jesus gain by experience?

In becoming man Christ voluntarily subjected himself to certain human limitations. He was made in all things like unto his brethren and yet without sin. Luke explicitly states (2:52) that he increased in wisdom. He took upon himself the human form and with it the conditions of its life, among which would be the need of being educated like other boys. We can imagine that if in his boyhood he was conscious of his divinity the human life must have been very strange to him. Experience alone could enlighten him and it is that fact which specially fitted him to be a High Priest who could sympathize with our infirmities. His temptation in the wilderness was a human temptation. In passing through the ordeal with a human body he learned the misery of being tempted and consequently he "gained by experience" the power to succor those who are tempted.

781 What was the purpose of Christ's forty days fasting?

It was immediately after his baptism by John that Jesus was led by the Spirit into the wilderness. He had just received the outward acknowledgment of his mission and authority, and now he was to prepare for the more public work before him by a period of prayer, fasting and deeper spiritual experience and communion with the Father. It was, in effect, a higher consecration, if such were possible. During those forty days "the plan and future of his work must have been always before him." Nowhere in the Scripture are we led to conclude that he had not always been clearly conscious of the outline of his mission, although its comprehensiveness and detail could only become apparent as the work proceeded.

782 Was Jesus on earth and in heaven at the same time?

The passage in John 3:13 is to be taken in connection with the immediately preceding verse. Jesus had told his hearers of earthly things and they believed not. Would they believe if he told them of heavenly things? Yet such knowledge of heavenly things could come only from One who had himself been in heaven, since no other hath ascended, to return with such knowledge, and none could know these things save he that hath descended, even the Son. Many ancient authorities omit the last four words of the verse, "who is in heaven," regarding them as a later interpolation, unnecessary and tending to confuse the text.

783 Is there pardon possible for Jesus' executioners?

Jesus' words, "Father, forgive them; they know not what they do," were spoken as his executioners were completing their dread task. But the prayer was not limited to them alone, but included all who had a hand in it, for the apostle could afterward say, with truth, "had they known it, they would not have crucified the Lord of Glory." In a still wider sense the prayer was a fulfilment of the Messianic prediction in Isa. 53:12. The world, in every age, owes much to these few words. We have no right to question the validity of Jesus' prayer, that what these fanatical and misguided men did in their ignorance and anger should not be laid to their charge in the final account.

784 Is it possible to harmonize the two genealogies of Christ given respectively by Matthew and Luke?

Many efforts have been made to do so and several hypotheses have been suggested which are reasonable. The one that commends itself to the largest number of scholars is that of Dr. Barrett, who contends that Matthew gives the genealogy of Joseph and Luke that of Mary. The husband and wife belonging to the same tribe would naturally have in their genealogical lines some ancestors common to both. After a great deal of research he discovered that the Jews had a habit, in tracing the female line, of speaking of a woman's husband as the son of her father, when really he was the son-in-law. Thus Luke speaks of Heli as the father of Joseph, when he was Mary's father and Joseph's father-in-law. If that theory is correct Jesus could trace his genealogy through Mary to David and Abraham. That there was no flaw in it we may be sure, otherwise the Jews would surely have pointed it out when his Messiahship was claimed. It is matter of history that this question was never raised during his life or for a hundred years after his death.

785 Did God ever speak to Jesus as he did to Moses, Abraham, Jacob and others?

At the baptism the Father said to Jesus: "Thou art my beloved Son. In thee I am well pleased" (Luke 3:22; Mark 1:11). The utterances at the Transfiguration (Mark 9:7; Luke 9:35) seem to have been addressed not to Christ himself, but the disciples. [In Matthew's account of the baptism the same form is used (Matt. 3:17).] But whatever kind of communication Jesus had with the Father, it was altogether different from that which any other human being ever had had, or could have. No one could say, as he said, "I and my Father are one" (John 10:30), or, still more startlingly, "He that hath seen me hath seen the Father" (John 14:9). We know that Jesus had long periods of communion with the Father. What mystic and beautiful messages passed between them in those prayer vigils we can only wonder. We know that he was, in fact, in constant communion with the Father, for he said: "The Father hath not left me alone" (John 8:29). Only upon the cross was this perfect communion interrupted. It was from the anguish revealed in that cry from the cross that he had pleaded in the garden to be delivered: "My God, my God, why hast thou forsaken me? "

786 Who was Joseph, the foster-father of Jesus, our Lord?

There are many traditions concerning Joseph, the foster-father of the Saviour. One that is generally accepted by early Christian writers is that he was quite old when espoused to Mary, and had by a previous marriage four sons and two daughters. Epiphanius mentions this, and Theophylact and Eusebius give further detail, and state that Joseph's wife was the widow of his brother Cleophas, who died without issue, Joseph marrying her according to the old Jewish law. Nicephorus gives Salome as the name of Joseph's first wife. The origin of all these assertions by the early fathers is found in the apocryphal gospels, and particularly in the *Protevangelium of St. James*, which is supposed to have been written by a Christian Jew in the second century, and which is referred to by Origen, Clement of Alexandria and Justin Martyr in their writings. The Bible gives nothing of them. It should be added that Jerome, and several other eminent authorities, hold that "our Lord's brethren" referred to in the Gospels were his cousins, and that Joseph was not married before his espousal to Mary.

787 At what meal did Jesus institute the Lord's Supper?

There has been much discussion concerning the meal at which the Lord's Supper was instituted, as to whether it was the Paschal supper, according to the Jewish law. The first three Gospels indicate that the use of the guest chamber was secured in the manner customary with those who came from a distance to keep the festival. The three evangelists state that "they made ready the Passover," and Jesus himself calls the meal "this Passover" (Luke 22:15, 16). After a thanksgiving he passed around the first cup, and when the supper was ended there was the usual "cup of blessing" and a hymn was sung, presumably the last part of the *Hallel*. John's Gospel, however, would seem to imply that the Lord's Supper took place the day preceding the usual Jewish Paschal meal (John 13:1, 2). In John 19:14, when our Lord was before Pilate and about to be led out to Calvary, we are told that it was the "preparation" of the Passover, and again, after the crucifixion (verse 31), the Jews were solicitous because it was still "the preparation." Further, the law of Ex. 12:22 was that none should go out of the door of his house until the morning after the Paschal supper, although this law may have come into disuse. Lightfoot, a leading authority, claims that the supper was held two days before the Jewish Passover, while Bengel held that it was eaten the evening *before* the Passover. The question is an open one, and in view of conflicting opinions of commentators it will probably so continue.

788 What would be the present value of the thirty pieces of silver for which Judas betrayed the Saviour?

The thirty shekels of silver, it is estimated, would equal about $20 of our money, a shekel being worth about 62 cents. Thirty shekels equaled 120 denarii, and a denarius was the price of a day's work. The present purchasing power of the money would be perhaps ten times its value in those ancient days.

789 Was there a Roman census of Judea at the time when Jesus was born?

The passage in Luke 2:1-3, which was formerly so frequently quoted by a certain class of Bible critics as a "blunder" on the part of the Gospel historian, has in recent years received unexpected confirmation. It was claimed that Luke's statement regarding a Roman census of Judea was a pure invention and that Cyrenius was a myth. Now, however, it has been discovered by historians and excavators that the entire passage which has occasioned so much controversy is literal fact. Sir William Ramsay, the noted archeologist, while excavating at Antioch of Pisidia (in Asia Minor) in 1912-13, unearthed inscriptions which revealed that Cyrenius was the name of the governor of Syria at the period of the Advent. Further, it has been established by careful investigation of ancient historical sources that the Roman authorities took a regular fourteenth-year census, and that under the prevailing law every one at some time within the year had to go and personally register in his native city.

790 What became of Lazarus and the son of the widow of Nain after they were resurrected?

There is no authentic record. According to an old tradition, mentioned in Epiphanius, Lazarus, who was thirty years old when he was restored to life, lived thirty years afterward. One account was to the effect that, with Mary and Martha, he traveled to Provence in France, and preached the Gospel in Marseilles. Nothing further is mentioned concerning the subject of the resurrection at Nain.

791 Why is so much stress laid on the Lord's Supper and so little on foot-washing?

Because people have come to hold the spirit in more reverence than the letter. In Christ's time foot washing was a common act of hospitality performed by a servant. In doing it himself for his disciples he took the servant's place. The command is obeyed by any one who is willing to render a humble service to a brother for Christ's sake. The words about the Lord's Supper, "ye do show the Lord's death till he come" (I Cor. 11:26), sufficiently explain why this loving memorial has survived.

792 Why was no contemporaneous record made of the public ministry of Jesus?

Doubtless the thought has occurred to many that it is somewhat remarkable that no contemporaneous record was made of the public ministry of Jesus. It has been suggested by certain writers that such a purpose does not seem to have occurred to any of his immediate followers at the beginning of his ministry, although as it developed, and more especially toward the close, it is reasonable to assume that some of his disciples may have kept records of a more or less fragmentary character. John, in the close of his Gospel (21:24, 25), says distinctly "this is the disciple which testifieth of these things and *wrote* these things." All four evangelists made records, although at what time cannot be learned, and Jerome states that Theorhilus arranged these records into one harmonious work. The Gospels, as we now have them, are to be traced chiefly to the oral teachings of the apostles as their original source; that is, they were proclaimed orally before being committed to writing. It was an age of oral traditions rather than writing. In Luke 1:1-4 there is a very clear intimation that an early effort had been made—probably shortly after the ascension—to set forth a formal statement of Christ's ministry, and that the facts had been related by eye-witnesses and ministers (disciples), who were familiar with the events from the beginning of the public career of Jesus. Westcott writes: "So long as the first witnesses survived, so long the (Gospel) tradition was confirmed within the bounds of their testimony: when they passed away it was already fixed in writing."

793 What miracles did Jesus perform during his childhood?

The Evangelists pass over the boyhood of Jesus with the simple remark that his obedience, intelligence and piety won the affections of all who knew him (Luke 2:40, 50, 51). There is no authentic record to show that he performed miracles during his childhood, although the Romish Church preserves certain traditions to that effect.

794 Were the Old Testament prophecies respecting Christ fulfilled?

Yes, as will be seen by comparing the following passages:
As the Son of God, Ps. 2:7; fulfilled, Luke 1:32, 35.
As the Seed of the woman, Gen. 3:15; fulfilled, Gal. 4:4.
As the Seed of Abraham, Gen. 17:7; fulfilled, Gal. 3, 16.
As the Seed of Isaac, Gen. 21:12; fulfilled, Heb. II:17-19.
As the Seed of David, Ps. 132:11; fulfilled, Acts 13:23; Rom. 1:3.
His coming at a set time, Gen. 49:10; fulfilled, Luke 2:1.
His being born of a virgin, Isa. 7:14; fulfilled, Matt. 1:18; Luke 2:7.
His being called Immanuel, Isa. 7:14; fulfilled, Matt. 1:22.
His being born in Bethlehem, Judea, Mic. 5:2; fulfilled, Matt. 2:1; Luke 2:4-6.
Great persons coming to adore him, Ps. 72:10; fulfilled, Matt. 2:1-11.
His being called out of Egypt, Hos. 11:1; fulfilled, Matt. 2:15.
His being preceded by John the Baptist, Isa. 40:3; fulfilled, Matt. 3:1-3.
His being anointed with the Spirit, Ps. 45:7; fulfilled, Matt. 3:16.
His ministry commencing in Galilee, Isa. 9:1, 2; fulfilled, Matt. 4:12-16.
His entering publicly into Jerusalem, Zec. 9:9; fulfilled, Matt. 21:1-5.
His poverty, Isa. 53:2; fulfilled, Mark 6:3.
His meekness, Isa. 42:2; fulfilled, Matt. 12:15.
His tenderness and compassion, Isa. 40:11; fulfilled, Matt. 12:15-20.
His being without guile, Isa. 53:9; fulfilled, I Pet. 2:22.
His zeal, Ps. 69:9; fulfilled John 2:17.

His bearing reproach, Ps. 22:6; fulfilled, Rom. 15:3.

His being betrayed by a friend, Ps. 41:9; fulfilled, John, 13:18-21.

His disciples forsaking him, Zec. 13:7; fulfilled, Matt. 26:31, 56.

His being sold for thirty pieces of silver, Zec. 11:12; fulfilled, Matt. 26:15.

His price being given for the potters' field, Zec. 11:13; fulfilled, Matt. 27:7.

His being numbered with the transgressors, Isa. 53:12; fulfilled, Mark 15:28.

His intercession for his murderers, Isa. 53:12; fulfilled, Luke 23:34.

His death, Isa. 53:12; fulfilled, Mat. 27:50.

That a bone should not be broken, Ex. 12:46; Ps. 34:20; fulfilled, John 19:33, 36.

His being pierced, Zec. 12:10; fulfilled, John 19:34, 37.

His resurrection, Ps. 16:10; fulfilled, Luke 24:6, 31, 34.

His ascension, Ps. 68:18; fulfilled, Luke 24:51.

His sitting on the right hand of God, Ps. 110:1; fulfilled, Heb. 1:3.

**795 Was there any real virtue in the waters of the
Pool of Siloam, or was it a superstition?**

In the account in John's Gospel, fifth chapter, it is made clear that there was a popular belief that the pool possessed certain healing qualities at the time of the "moving" (or inflow) of the waters from the hidden springs. This may or may not have been based on superstition or on some tradition concerning the pool. It should be noted, however, that Jesus (in John 5:6-8) said nothing about any wonderful virtue in the waters of the pool; if there was a tradition or superstition on the subject he simply set it aside and cured the infirm sufferer where he lay. In the case of the blind beggar at the pool of Siloam (John, 9th chapter) there is frequently a misconception in the mind of the reader. Jesus did not tell the blind man to wash "in" the pool, but, having anointed his eyes with clay and spittle, directed him to wash "at" the pool—to cleanse his eyes of the moistened clay with which, under the divine touch, the miracle of restoring his sight was accomplished.

**796 What was the origin of the custom
of releasing a prisoner at the Feast as
mentioned in Matthew 27:15?**

There is no mention of the practise in secular history, but it is easy to see how it may have arisen. In a conquered country it is to the interest of the conquerors to conciliate the people, and a governor wishing to make himself popular would please them if, at a time of public festivity, he granted them such a concession. Generally, the man whose release was asked for would be some leader who had made himself obnoxious to the government by espousing the cause of the subject people. The English government has several times tried to win the support of Irish members of Parliament by releasing some prisoner who has been sent to prison for sedition and has not served out his sentence.

797 Did the child Jesus attend school as an ordinary boy?

Of the first thirty years of his life little is recorded beyond the incident of his visit to Jerusalem with Joseph and Mary, when he was twelve years old. Usually both parents of a Jewish child took an active part in its early education. It was incumbent on the father to teach his offspring the Law and the other Scriptures, which constituted the essentials of Jewish education. Josephus, the historian, states that, at fourteen, he himself had so thorough a knowledge of the Law that the high priests and first men of the town sought his opinion. Christ's earlier years, after he had passed from the first lessons of Joseph and Mary, were doubtless spent in school, with other children of the little Galilean village.

798 While on earth did Jesus at any time suffer from sickness?

That Christ was wearied we know from the inspired record of his life. There is no such record of his being sick at any time. In Matt. 8:17, Revised Version, we read: "Himself took our infirmities, and bare our sicknesses." Reference is apparently made to Isa. 53:4: "Surely he hath borne our griefs and carried our sorrows." In verse 3 of the same chapter we read that he was acquainted with grief. The words griefs and grief might be rendered respectively sicknesses and sickness; still, there is no assertion in these texts that Christ suffered disease of any kind, any more than the statement that he bare our sins implies that he sinned. His obedience to all law, sanitary included, undoubtedly served to keep him in health.

799 What was the name of the soldier who smote our Lord with his spear?

It has been preserved to us by tradition as Longinus, a Roman. The tradition still further adds that the spear was brought by Joseph of Arimathea to King Pellam, who was of Joseph's time, and Balim, a savage, seized the spear and wounded Pellam nigh unto death.

800 Where were the stable and manger in which Christ was born located?

The account of the humble birthplace of the Saviour in Luke 2:7 is all we know about the immediate surroundings of our Saviour's birthplace. The manger is believed to have been in one of the exterior buildings of a public khan or caravanserai. His entrance into the world in Bethlehem was an express fulfilment of the prediction in Mic. 5:2.

801 Was Simon of Cyrene a white man or a black man?

He is believed to have been a native of North Africa, and hence black as was Philip's convert, the Ethiopian eunuch, and Apollos, the great preacher of Alexandria. The early history of Christianity furnishes many illustrious examples of men and women of color who suffered and died for the faith. Onesimus, one of Paul's most devoted converts, was probably black, and there were many blacks holding exalted positions in the Christian Church in Africa, the whole northern countries of which, in the early ages, were Christian.

802 Where was the spirit of Jesus during the three days his body lay in the tomb?

There is little in the Scriptures to throw light on the question "Where was the spirit of Jesus during the three days his body lay in the tomb? " Among the early writers, and by many of later days, the subject has been discussed. The Apostles' Creed says: "He descended into hades" (the place of departed spirits). Some theologians, Dean Alford among them, in discussing the passage in I Pet. 3:19, 20, contended that Christ, in the interval between his death and resurrection, preached or announced his finished work to the spirits "in prison"; but the passage is mysterious and has always puzzled Bible students. In the early days of the Christian Church, there were several writings on the subject professing to describe the exultation of the saints and the pre-Christian fathers whom he delivered from hades and brought into paradise; but these writings have long ago been stamped as uncanonical and apocryphal.

803 Why was Jesus, though having no property and not engaged in any trade, required to pay taxes?

In Matt. 17:24 we read that the tax collector came to Peter saying: "Doth not your master pay tribute? " The Revised Version renders this passage in such a way as to bring out the particular tax which is referred to: "And when they were come to Capernaum, they that received the half shekel came to Peter and said, Doth not your master pay the half shekel? " Following this rendering we learn the tribute or tax referred to to be the gift required by the Mosaic law from all Jews, to meet the expenses of the tabernacle or temple service. Josephus tells us that this tax had come to be collected annually from all Jews over twenty years of age. The tax being for religious purposes, all men shared in it irrespective of their trade or calling and the tax was paid by our Lord as a worshiping Jew who "fulfilled all righteousness."

804 What were the names of the two thieves who were crucified with Christ?

The names, as preserved by legend and tradition, vary according to different writers, and there is no absolutely authentic record on the subject. One early writer (in the Apocryphal Gospel of Nicodemus) gives the name of Demas or Dismas as the penitent, who hung on the right hand of the Saviour, and Gestas as the impenitent. Bede gives the names of Matha and Joca, respectively, as those that prevailed in his time. The first, however, have been preserved, and in the hagiology of the Syrian, Greek and Latin churches Dismas is recognized as the penitent malefactor. Bengel asserts the belief that Dismas was a Gentile and Gestas a Jew.

805 Of what kind of plant was Jesus' crown of thorns made?

The crown of thorns which was placed upon the brow of Christ is believed to have been either of the thorny species known as the coppares spinosae, or the Arabian nubk. Some writers hold that it may have been the plant known as the southern buckthorn. There is a legend that Empress Helena recovered the thorny crown and preserved it as a sacred relic. Several treatises have been written about it, but nothing definite can be stated.

806 In what sense is Christ "royal"?

When Christ said "Follow me," and when he told his disciples that the test of their affection for him was that they keep his commandments, he took a position that is not even now fully realized by men who call themselves by his name. We are so accustomed to speak of Jesus as being meek and lowly that we are apt to forget how high were the claims he put forth and how implicit is the obedience he requires.

Christ insisted that he was a King, and, at the very last, when clothed with the royal robe in mockery, he would abate not one jot of his claim, even when he knew that he was furnishing Pilate with an excuse for putting him to death. He firmly believed in his own royalty, and, in simple majesty, he performed its functions.

Christ was a king in the sense of establishing a kingdom. He proclaimed the kingdom of God. People scoffed at him, but he was right, and his claims have been substantiated. They would have understood him had he set up his throne in Jerusalem and defied the Roman power. But how much higher was his ideal! He conceived of a kingdom which should embrace all nations and be above all governments. He has established such a kingdom. Throughout the world are to be found men loyal to their respective rulers, good citizens and law-abiding men, who in a day would be turned into rebels if the claims of those rulers ever became antagonistic to the claims of Christ. He is to them King of kings, and their allegiance to him transcends all others.

He is also king in the sense of legislation. He does not argue or explain. His is no limited monarchy. His word is "I say unto you." He expects unfaltering, unquestioning obedience. Personal attachment, personal loyalty are the principles of his kingdom. Men may hold different creeds, may worship him by different ceremonies, but there must be no division, no diversity in allegiance to him. He issues his commandments, and it is only as we obey that we can have any valid claim to call ourselves by his name. Only so can we enter the kingdom of heaven.

807 Why did Jesus drive the money-changers out of the temple?

When Jesus drove the money-changers out of the Temple he gave the reason in Matt. 21:13, Mark 11:17. They had profaned and defiled it with their merchandise. Their occupations were worldly, and had no proper place in the Lord's house.

808 How much wine did Jesus make at the wedding feast in Cana?

The only source of information is the Gospel narrative. The Evangelist estimated the capacity of each of the six waterpots at "*two or three* firkins." The firkin, according to Smith's *Dictionary of Classical Antiquities*, was equal to eight gallons and seven-eighths of a gallon. Thus the Evangelist's estimate gives us as the capacity of each jar somewhere between seventeen and twenty-six gallons. Nothing is told us about the vessel in which it was borne to the governor of the feast. It was probably a pitcher. There is an ancient picture on ivory in existence which represents the miracle. It is believed to have been painted not later than the seventh century. In this the jars are represented as wide stone jars as high as the breast of the man who is drawing from them. He holds in his hand a drinking-cup which apparently would hold about a pint. This, however, is only the conception of the miracle formed by an artist who lived about six hundred years after the miracle was performed.

809 What have famous men, not known as active Christians, said about Jesus?

Napoleon Bonaparte expressed the following view of Jesus: "I know men, and I tell you Jesus Christ was not a man. Superficial minds see a resemblance between Christ and the founders of empires and the gods of other religions. That resemblance does not exist. There is between Christianity and other religions the distance of infinity. Alexander, Caesar, Charlemagne and myself founded empires. But on what did we rest the creations of our genius? Upon sheer force. Jesus Christ alone founded his empire upon love; and at this hour millions of men will die for him. In every other existence but that of Christ how many imperfections! From the first day to the last he is the same; majestic and simple, infinitely firm and infinitely gentle. He proposes to our faith a series of mysteries and commands with authority that we should believe them, giving no other reason than those tremendous words: I am God." "Jesus is the most perfect of all men that have yet appeared," said Ralph Waldo Emerson, and Thomas Carlyle wrote of him: "Jesus is our divinest symbol. Higher has the human thought not yet reached. A symbol of quite perennial, infinite character: whose significance will ever demand to be anew inquired and anew made manifest." Lord Byron paid this tribute: "If ever man was God, or God man, Jesus Christ was both."

Rousseau, greatest in his line, writes as follows: "Can it be possible that the same personage whose history the Scriptures contain should be a mere man? Where is the man, where the philosopher, who could so live and so die without weakness and without ostentation? When Plato describes his imaginary righteous man, loaded with all the punishments of guilt, yet meriting the highest rewards of virtue, he exactly describes the character of Jesus Christ. What an infinite disproportion between the Son of Saphronisius and the Son of Mary. Socrates dies with honor, surrounded by his disciples listening to the most tender words—the easiest death that one could wish to die. Jesus dies in pain, dishonor, mockery, the object of universal cursing—the most horrible death that one could fear. At the receipt of the cup of poison Socrates blesses him who could not give it to him without tears; Jesus, while suffering the sharpest pains, prays for his most bitter enemies. If Socrates lived and died like a philosopher Jesus lived and died like a God." Benjamin Disraeli, mighty and honest Jew, pays this tribute to our Lord: "The wildest dreams of their rabbis have been far exceeded. Has not Jesus conquered Europe and changed its name to Christendom? All countries that refuse the cross wither and the time will come when the vast countries and countless myriads of America and Australia, looking upon Europe as Europe now looks upon Greece, and wondering how so small a space could have achieved such great deeds, will find music in the songs of Zion and solace in the parables of Galilee."

SAYINGS OF JESUS

**810 Where is Chorazin, in which Jesus
said he had done mighty works
(Matthew 11:21)?**

There is no record of Christ having visited Chorazin. This mention of
the place shows how far the Gospels are from being complete narratives
of Christ's life. He had evidently been there and worked miracles, yet
none of the four evangelists describes the visit. The author of the Fourth
Gospel admits the incomplete character of his own work (John 21:25)
and says that if all Jesus said and did had been written the books
needed would have been more than the world could contain (that is
could profitably use). The site of Chorazin was unknown until recently,
when Dr. Robinson identified it with Kherza, a ruined town three miles
from Capernaum.

**811 What was the "cup" which
Jesus desired to have pass from
him in Gethsemane?**

In Matt. 26:39 the "cup" undoubtedly referred to the whole sum of
Christ's suffering in making the atonement for sin, particularly the suffering on the cross. There have been many explanations of the garden
agony. The explanation that Jesus was afraid he would die in Gethsemane does not seem convincing. Nor does the answer sometimes given,
that Christ shrank from the mere suffering, seem adequate, considering
his splendid and unfailing courage. His words on the cross, "My God,
my God, why hast thou forsaken me? " imply that there was a real separation from the Father in this dreadful experience. There is a depth of
mystery here before which the most thoughtful and reverent may well
pause. Yet it seems reasonable to believe that, although Christ's soul
was to the last absolutely untainted by sin, he suffered, in some real
way, the results of sin in his own spirit. It was this horrible, unspeakable experience of alienation from God from which he shrank and which
gave rise to the agonizing prayer that at the eleventh hour some other
method might be found of making atonement for sin.

812 What kind of action is necessary for a Christian to fulfill Jesus' command, "If any man will come after me, let him deny himself and take up his cross and follow me"?

This passage in Matt. 16:24 has been often discussed. It would be impossible to state just what details for each individual life are involved in this sacrifice. Christ definitely commanded the rich young ruler to sell all his property and give it to the poor. He refused, and, so far as we know, lost his soul. But Christ left no specific command that every follower of his must do that same thing. What he did demand, and still demands, is that every follower must acknowledge that all his possessions belong to Christ, must cease to use them selfishly, and begin and continue to use them for the welfare of others. It is true enough that radical changes would take place in society if all professed Christians should really live on this principle. But it is the clear teaching of Christ, and we cannot do otherwise without forfeiting our discipleship. We must deny ourselves for the sake of others, we must "take up our cross," that is, must do the thing that is hard or will cause us loss, because our loyalty to Christ demands it; and we must follow him in paths of self-sacrifice and sympathetic helpfulness.

813 What did Jesus mean when he said that the least in the kingdom of heaven is greater than John?

The Saviour, in Matt. 11:11, was referring not to John's personal character, but presumably to his official standing or position in the economy of grace, in which, although he was above those that went before him, he belonged to the old dispensation and was therefore behind the humblest worker in the new order of things. See Matt. 11:15; Luke 16:16, which further illustrate the meaning of the passage.

814 What was Christ's definition of the word *everlasting*?

We have before noted the fact that Christ uses the same word when speaking of the duration of the life of the righteous and the punishment of the wicked. The literal rendering of the speech word (aionios), translated sometimes "eternal" and at other times "everlasting" in the New Testament, is age-lasting. If, with the help of a concordance, you will look up the two words "eternal" and "everlasting," wherever they occur in the New Testament, you will be able to form a reasonable opinion of Christ's meaning of the word. In Eph. 3:11 and I Tim. 1:17 the word "everlasting" comes from a slightly different word, and in Rom. 1:20 and Jude 6 the word "everlasting" is quite a different word. Omit these four passages, therefore, in your study.

815 What did Christ mean by saying that his people were the "light of the world"?

Being taught elsewhere that Christ is the light of the world we cannot well understand Matt. 5:14, "Ye are the light of the world," unless we consider that his people were lights in view of the Spirit of Christ which was in them. When Christ left the world they were to take his place. In Prov. 4:18 you have the same figure, "The path of the just is as a shining light." They were to give the light to the world. Some men who would never be impressed by a sermon or by reading the Bible are attracted to God by the lives and goodness of Christian people whom they know.

816 Is Jesus' command, "Swear not at all," in conflict with other Old and New Testament Scriptures?

There are many Old Testament passages that apparently condone swearing (e.g., Lev. 5:1, 19:12; Num. 30:2-15; Deut. 23:21-23). Other passages describe God Himself as having sworn (e.g., Deut. 1:8; Ps. 110:4: Isa. 14:24). These references, at first consideration, seem to be in conflict with Jesus' admonition, "Swear not at all." Jesus was pointedly focusing on the hypocrisy of the scribes and Pharisees and their evasion of responsibility when they declared that only oaths sworn "to the Lord" were to be strictly enforced. Oaths "by heaven" or "by the earth" or "by Jerusalem" or by one's head were of lesser importance, implying that the keeping of such oaths was really not a matter of great consequence. To those who held this view, Jesus said, "Swear not at all." One could possibly rephrase Jesus' directive to the scribes and Pharisees as follows: Better not to swear at all than to live as if some oaths carry less weight than others.

817 Whom does the widow represent in the parable of the unjust judge?

The story of the importunate widow related in Luke 18 is a parable which is designed to follow as a continuation of the subject treated in the previous chapter—the coming of the Son of man, which, however long it might be delayed, should yet be the theme of our prayers and our hopes. Commentators on the parable hold that the Christian Church is represented as a widow, desolate, oppressed and defenseless, and exposed to all manner of indignities and wrongs from which the Judge of all can alone set her speedily free. Her incessant crying, even when he seems to have turned a heedless ear, shows her faith, and ultimately produces the desired result.

**818 Why did Jesus give us the parable
of the unjust steward (Luke 16:1-9)?**

The conduct of the steward was dishonest, but Christ did not hold up his dishonesty for imitation. He was inculcating the same lesson that he taught in Matt. 25:34-40. Those who ministered to the poor and the afflicted, especially to the followers of Christ, would receive a reward out of all proportion to their services. If they knew how great that reward was they would not let the opportunity escape them. The children of the world were more crafty, and then he tells of one of them who worked a device at his master's expense to effect this object. He placed his master's debtors under an obligation, so that they might feel bound to help him, when he needed it, as he had helped them. It was not Christ who commended him, but his own lord, who admired the shrewdness of his dishonest scheme.

**819 To whom did Jesus refer
when he asked Peter,
"Lovest thou me more than these?"**

The question in John 21:15 is somewhat obscure. It is just as impossible in Greek as in English to tell whether the word "these," as it is used here, refers to persons or to things. In some cases it would be evident, because the form of the pronoun differs in different genders and numbers. But this is the genitive plural, and the form is alike for all genders. It is likely that Jesus indicated by his question that he meant "More than these other disciples." That is, "Do you love me more than they love me? " He probably refers to Peter's boast that although all the rest should forsake the Master he himself would remain true, implying that he loved him more than any of the rest. But in answering the question now Peter does not repeat his boast. He merely says: "Thou knowest that I love thee." There is the possibility, however, that Jesus meant: "Do you love me more than you love these other men? " or "Do you love me more than you love these earthly things and tasks? "

**820 Why did Jesus employ parables in much of his
teaching?**

Jesus himself gives us the clue in Mark 4:12. He did not begin to do so until his miracles were malignantly ascribed to Satanic agencies. His enemies saw his works, yet closed their eyes to their source and spiritual meaning. They heard his words, for he "spake as never man spake"; yet they were deaf to the life-giving message conveyed. They voluntarily refused to accept the Gospel and at length became morally incapable of doing so.

821 What custom did our Lord object to when he blamed the Pharisees for praying in the streets?

The passage in Matt. 6:5, "They love to pray standing in the synagogues and in the corners of the streets that they may be seen of men," has reference to the desire of the Pharisees to parade their outward show of religion. A rigid Pharisee prayed many times daily and had certain set hours for doing so. Many of them took pains to show their praying customs to the public for its admiration, and thus allowed their hours of prayer to overtake them while at the street corners in full view of any who might be about. They sought the praise of men and would not scruple at any methods for attracting public attention. What the Lord desires to impress on us here is that our religion should be of the heart and not of the market-place. Our religion should be of that sort that is satisfied when he that seeth in secret knows about it. "If a man's religion be a round of forms and ceremonies," says one commentator, "then he will be sure to want somebody—some fellow man—to look on and admire, and he will soon come, more or less consciously, to adjust and arrange his doings so as to win men's admiration." This, however, is not Christ's religion and, therefore, he warns against it.

822 Have Christ's prophecies of persecutions been fulfilled?

The persecution of Christians dates from the beginning of Christianity. According to McClintock and Strong, there were ten pagan persecutions of the Christian Church, viz.: Under Nero (A.D. 74), when great multitudes perished; under Domitian, when in one year (A.D. 95) 40,000 suffered martyrdom; under Trajan and his successor Adrian, when vast numbers were accused and executed, mostly without even a pretense of legal trial; under Antoninus, when the persecutions took a wide range. Then came the persecutions under Severus, Maximinus, Decius, Valerian, Aurelian and Diocletian. In the last decade of this inhuman period hundreds of thousands were slain, 140,000 in Egypt alone, while 700,000 succumbed to the hardship and fatigue they were compelled to face. Persecutions by Catholics form a long and dark record. In Germany, Poland, Lithuania, Hungary, Bohemia and Holland the victims were almost innumerable. The Belgic martyrs who died for their faith are estimated at 100,000. In France in the reign of Charles IX the St. Bartholomew's Day massacre, it is variously estimated, had from 30,000 to 100,000 victims. But all previous atrocities seem to have been eclipsed by the hideous persecution of Protestants in France in the time of Louis XVI. Few countries were free from such visitations. England, Ireland, Scotland, Spain, Italy, all experienced them in turn, some much more heavily than others.

823 What did Christ teach as to the difference between the righteousness taught by him and that preached by the Pharisees?

In Matt. 5:20 he shows that the righteousness of the Scribes and Pharisees was formal; it did not spring from the heart. Christ's plan of righteousness is that it should be the spontaneous fruitage of a meek, worshipful, affectionate spirit; that it should spring from an ardent, self-forgetful love to God and man. In verses 29, 30 he shows that righteousness and salvation are such priceless things that nothing in the world must be allowed to stop our pursuit of them. The eternal values are here contrasted with earthly values; better suffer any loss or sacrifice here than to miss eternal life. He wished to impress on his hearers the terrible importance of spiritual and eternal things; then they would learn that eyes and hands must be used, not for the gratification of self, but for service to men in the name of Christ. The Jews thought they had exclusive rights to salvation, but Jesus shows in Matt. 8:11, 12 that many Gentiles shall enter the kingdom of heaven while many of the chosen people shall be cast out. It is another insistence that real religion must be of the heart; membership in the Jewish race will not save unless the heart is right. This righteousness must, however, meet the test, as did the Master who promulgated it. Christ made the extreme sacrifice in coming to earth (see Phil. 2:6-8 and II Cor. 8:9). His followers, therefore, must realize their obligation to make any sacrifice for his sake, even to disregarding all outside "considerations in which latter the Pharisees and other ritualists find much righteousness." Therefore, he asked his followers, in Matt. 8:22, to disregard a sacred duty. Under ordinary circumstances he wants his followers to fulfil their obligations to households and friends, but in this case he probably saw that the man had not definitely made up his mind to put Jesus first in his life. If he could have trusted him he would probably have directed him to attend the obsequies of his father and then return; but he feared that if the man got back among his old acquaintances he would lose his determination to be a follower of Jesus. Christ everywhere insists that he must be first; then he directs his followers to fulfil their social obligations in his name, serving others for his sake.

824 Does the command, "First be reconciled to thy brother and then come and offer thy gift" (Matthew 5:24), mean that God will not accept our gifts if our lives are not consecrated to him?

There is in these words of Jesus no intimation that the gift will not be accepted. "First be reconciled to thy brother, and *then come and offer thy gift.*" He is insisting that we cannot pacify God with gifts if there is injustice in our lives. An extreme case will illustrate this point: Suppose a thief wishes to get right with God. He cannot do so by making gifts. He must make every possible effort to return to its rightful owners the property he has stolen before his gifts can be acknowledged in heaven. In other words, we cannot straighten out injustice by charity. Justice should precede generosity. There is something splendid and regal about the uncompromising demands of Jesus. A prominent Free Methodist pastor has a favorite motto: "Nothing is made right until it is made right." If God commands us to do one thing we cannot fulfil his requirement by making a substitute proposition and doing something else. He demands that we live on terms of justice and honor with our neighbors. He is so insistent upon this that he cannot be pleased with our worship or service until we have established our lives upon this basis. At every step we need his divine grace, grace to help us to live justly with our neighbor and grace to worship and serve him acceptably. We must be careful not to judge others in this matter, except in cases where we know that positive wrong has been done. The final answer to the question depends upon what we mean by the word "consecrated." There are many Christians who feel that while they wish to serve God there are certain sacrifices and services so difficult that they shrink from making this full surrender. While God is very stern in such cases he is also very gentle and patient. He will receive our services and gifts, hoping that we shall soon be led to make the full surrender. The passage referred to does not deal with this phase in Christian life, except so far as it relates to the matter of making right the wrongs we have done to others. In this there must be no delay. Indeed, there should be no delay whatever in making the complete, glad surrender to God which will bring us the fulness of his power and put us in line with his richest blessings.

825 Does the Lord, in the parable of the fellow servants (Matthew 18:25), favor slavery?

No, he does not. We must remember the distinction between compelled personal service in the East and the slavery in which the blacks among us suffered. In the East man is often treated as property and such treatment well agrees with the tribal idea in which the chief is the owner of all the members of the tribe. "Easterners do not punish by perpetual imprisonment or by penal servitude, but consider selling a person, and even his family which was dependent on him, along with him, for debt, a more hopeful way of punishing him. A man who proved himself unable to manage money was wisely sentenced to work all the rest of his life for another. Knowing these facts, it was but natural that Jesus should employ them in his parables, the more so as he always spoke in the terms familiar to his age. We must clearly see that he referred to the slavery which he knew of, and not to the slavery which had disgraced the late Christian centuries."

826 What did Christ mean by his statement that he would come before the disciples had gone over the cities of Israel?

The statement in Matt. 10:23, "Ye shall not have gone over the cities of Israel till the Son of man be come," has caused much discussion. It is not clear whether Christ referred to the time of persecution, which followed his revelation of himself in his resurrection, or to the taking of Jerusalem, or to his final coming at the end of the dispensation. Probably if we had a verbatim report of his words his meaning would be understood. It is not important.

827 What is the true meaning of "poor in spirit" as it occurs in the Beatitudes?

Poor in spirit denotes, not circumstances, but inward character; not a condition of life, but a state and temper of mind. To be beaten utterly out of conceit with one's own strength, goodness and wisdom; to feel that apart from God's grace we are nothing, can do nothing. It is he who feels most poignantly his need of all, who will most heartily hail the promise of the free gift of all. Our Saviour says we are happy, blessed, in proportion as we feel our own want, our own emptiness, in things spiritual. The more we are poor, the more we are rich. This poverty of spirit being the condition of every blessing, therefore to it is attached the promise of the kingdom of heaven, which is inclusive of all blessings.

The word for "poor" means utter destitution, and "in spirit" defines the sphere of destitution. Some interpret this, "destitute of the wealth of learning and intellectual culture which the schools offered, because men of this class readily gave themselves up to Christ's teaching, and proved themselves fitted to lay hold of the heavenly treasure." Others make the idea more inward and ethical, that is, destitute of spiritual blessings. This is better. But shall we read, "poor in the spirit," that is, poor in spiritual treasures, or "poor in their spirit," that is, conscious of their spiritual need? There is no virtue in poverty. The church at Laodicea was "poor, and blind, and naked," but was rebuked by Christ. They thought they were rich and had need of nothing. So it is better to read, conscious of their spiritual need. It is this consciousness of need that leads one to seek the grace of God in Jesus Christ. The publican who prayed, "God be merciful to me a sinner," is a good illustration of those "poor in spirit," whose is the kingdom of heaven.

828 What is meant by Christ's figure of speech about the salt that has lost its flavor and is therefore cast out to be trodden under foot of men?

The passage in Matt. 5:13, "If the salt has lost its savour, wherewith shall it be salted? it is thenceforth good for nothing but to be cast out, and trodden under foot of men," is based upon actual facts of Eastern life. It is well known that salt under certain conditions loses its saltness. Dr. Thomson, in *The Land and the Book*, tells this story to substantiate this contention: "A merchant of Sidon having a large supply of salt filled sixty-five houses in a mountainous district with it. These houses had merely earthen floors and the salt next the ground was in a few years entirely spoiled. This salt, becoming insipid and useless, effloresced and turned to dust, not to fruitful soil, however. It was not only good for nothing itself, but it actually destroyed all fertility wherever it was thrown, and this is the reason why it is thrown into the street. So troublesome is this corrupted salt that it is carefully swept up, carried forth and thrown into the street. There is no place about the house, yard or garden where it is tolerated. No man will allow it to be thrown onto his field, and the only place for it is the street; and there it is cast to be trodden under foot of men."

829 What is meant by, "If thy hand or thy foot offend thee, cut it off"?

The words of Jesus in Matt. 18:8-10 point out—among other things—the wickedness of those who, by evil example and by their impure inclinations, their quarrelsome and revengeful dispositions, their unworthy aims and ambitions, stand in the way of others and prevent them from seeking salvation. It is as though he had said there would be stumblings and pitfalls enough through the world's treatment of young and inexperienced souls without any addition from the disciples, and he warns them not to share in such wickedness, as the one who, after having himself received light, wilfully caused others to stumble was doubly an offender. Far better were it for him to make any personal sacrifice than to be the means of causing a weaker brother or sister to stumble and lose faith.

830 What language did Christ use when he said, "Eloi, Eloi, Lama Sabachthani"?

The passage in Mark 15:34 is identical with Ps. 22:1, and commentators express the opinion that it was uttered by the Saviour on the cross not in the current Greek, nor in the Hebrew original, but in the native Syriac, the mother tongue of his earthly life. It was the crisis of his sufferings, the moment in which he "must taste the bitterest of the wages of sin, who did not sin." Contrast this with the cry "It is finished," in which "the mighty voice of the expiring Redeemer was nothing else but the exultant spirit of the dying victor," perceiving the fruit of his travail and nerving the organs of utterance to an ecstatic expression of its loftiest feelings in the one glorious sentence.

831 What is Jesus' testament?

John 14, and it is one of the most sacred chapters in the Gospels, being a record of the last moments passed by Jesus among his disciples before the great crisis. Love filled his heart and flowed from his lips. His language assumed even a loftier strain than usual. In his intercessory prayer he poured out his soul in behalf of those who were already his own. To the disciples it was a discourse both of cheer and sorrow. He seemed to open heaven's gates, to give them a glimpse of the heavenly home, the "house of many mansions" that awaited them, and whither he was now going. More than ever before he expressed with clearness and simplicity his close and loving relations to them. He strengthened their faith, promised them an endowment of spiritual power and the coming of the Comforter to be their guide and adviser. In dignity, significance and supreme affection, it was a parting address whose equal never fell from human lips.

832 What did Jesus mean when he said, "But when thou doest alms, let not thy left hand know what thy right hand doeth" (Matthew 6:3)?

Can a person really keep his left hand from knowing what his right hand is doing? When one stops to think about it, can a hand *know* anything? It is the mind that *knows* something. Obviously, we cannot interpret this saying of Jesus literally. What, then, was the intent of these words?

This saying of Jesus is paradoxical, that is, it is seemingly contradictory. It seems that Jesus is telling us to make an effort to avoid knowing what we are consciously (knowingly) doing (in this case, the giving of alms).

Our hands often work together. Often they work in consort: lifting, carrying, catching, driving, and many other activities. What one hand does, the other "knows." Both are controlled by the same mind.

What Jesus is advocating describes the opposite; so his directive must be symbolic exaggeration, urging us not only to keep our giving a secret from others (Matt 6:1, 1), but also not to dwell upon it ourselves. We are to forget about our offerings and gifts; we must not pat ourselves on the back for our charitable contributions; we must not rehearse in our minds our acts of generosity. The message of verse 3 of Matthew 6 is essentially the same as the admonition in verse 2: Don't advertise your generosity; don't call it to the attention of others; don't fall prey to the sin of seeking the admiration of others.

A similar line of thought is found in Jesus' words recorded in Matt. 25:37-39, where Jesus tells us that the righteous on the Day of Judgment will be quite unaware of the benevolent deeds they had performed while living on the earth. They will respond to the Judge, "Lord, when saw we thee ahungered, and fed thee? or thirsty, and gave thee drink? When saw we thee a stranger, and took thee in? or naked, and clothed thee? Or when saw we thee sick or in prison, and came unto thee?" Thoroughly unaware were they of their good deeds.

The Apostle James also warned against the sin of pride (4:6), reminding his readers that "God resisteth the proud, but giveth grace to the humble" (Prov. 3:34)

833 In what sense are we to understand the quotation from the Psalms applied to Christ in John 2:17, "The zeal of thine house hath eaten me up"?

It simply implies an intensity of zeal that absorbed him. His disciples were astonished at their teacher's conduct. He was usually so gentle and inoffensive that they were amazed at this sudden ebullition of indignation. They could scarcely recognize Jesus as he took the scourge and drove the traders out of the Temple. It was so vigorous a thing to do that it probably seemed to them inconsistent with his character. When, however, they remembered the words quoted, they understood how his whole soul was stirred when he saw the building consecrated to his Father used as a common market.

WORDS AND TERMS

834 What is adoption?

Adoption, in the theological sense, is "that act of God's free grace by which, when we are justified by faith in Christ, we are received into the family of God, and become heirs to the heavenly inheritance" (see Rom. 8:17; II Cor. 6:18; Rom. 8:15, 16). The certainty of one's adoption and of the inheritance warranted by it are counted among the attributes of the new birth. This adoption is according to promise, is by faith, is of God's grace through Christ (Rom. 9:8; Gal. 3:29; Gal. 3:7, 26; Ezek. 16:3-6; Rom. 4:16, 17; Eph. 1:5, 6, 11; John 1:12; Gal. 4:4, 5; Eph. 1:5; Heb. 2:10, 13). Saints are predestined unto adoption and even the Gentiles are selected for it (Rom. 8:29; Eph. 1:5-11; Hos. 2:23; Rom. 9:24-26; Eph. 3:6). The adopted are gathered together in one by Christ, their new birth is connected with it and the Holy Spirit is not only a witness of our adoption but the very fact that the said Spirit leads us is an evidence of our adoption (John 11:52; John 1:12, 13; Rom. 8:14; Rom. 8:16). This adoption is a privilege of saints and by it they become brethren of Christ, but while waiting for the final consummation we are subject to the fatherly discipline of God, which, however, is not to be feared as God is longsuffering and merciful to the partakers of his adoption (John 1:12; John 20:17; Heb. 2:11, 12; Rom. 8:19, 23; I John 3:2; Deu. 8:5; II Sam. 7:14; Prov. 3:11, 12; Heb. 12:5-11; Jer. 31:1, 9, 20). Our adoption should lead to holiness and produce likeness to God, childlike confidence in God together with a desire for God's glory, a spirit of prayer, a love of peace, a forgiving and merciful spirit (II Cor. 6:17, 18; II Cor. 7:1; Phil. 2:15; Matt. 5:44, 45; Eph. 5:1; Matt. 6:25-34; Matt. 5:16; Matt. 7:7-11; Matt. 5:9; Matt. 6:14; Luke 6:35, 36. Those who receive this adoption are safe and are entitled to an inheritance (Prov. 14:26; Matt. 13:43; Rom. 8:17; Gal. 3:29; Gal. 4:7; Eph. 3:6).

835 What are we taught about baptism with the Holy Ghost?

As distinguished from the baptism with water as practised by the apostles and the church after them, there is a Holy Ghost baptism. It was foretold by the prophet Ezekiel (36:25): "Then will I sprinkle clear water upon you, and ye shall be clean; from all your filthiness and from all your idols will I cleanse you." This baptism is through Christ as we read Tit. 3:5: "But according to his mercy he saved us by the washing of regeneration and renewing of the Holy Ghost." As John (Matt. 3:11) prophesied that he that cometh after me shall baptize you with the Holy Ghost and with fire, so when Christ had come he said of him (John 1:33): "He that sent me to baptize with water the same said unto me, Upon whom thou shalt see the Spirit descending and remaining on him, the same is he which baptizeth with the Holy Ghost." This form of baptism is promised to saints (Acts 1:5; Acts 2:38, 39), and they all partake of it (I Cor. 12:13) because it is necessary. Christ himself says of it (John 3:5): "Except a man be born of the Spirit he cannot enter the kingdom of God," and Paul assures us that Christ saves "by the washing of regeneration and renewing of the Holy Ghost" (Tit. 3:5), also Peter (I Pet. 3:21) writes to like effect when he says "ever baptism doth also now save us," and draws the distinction that it is the Holy Ghost baptism rather than the water baptism that renews and cleanses the soul. To the attainment of this baptism the word of God is instrumental, yes, essential. "That he might sanctify and cleanse it with the washing of water by the word," says Paul to the Ephesians (Eph. 5:26), and in Acts 10:44 we read that "While Peter yet spake" (of Jesus and his works) "the Holy Ghost fell on all them which heard the word."

836 What is belief?

"Belief" has been defined as "the assent of the mind to the truth of a proposition." In the spiritual sense it means the "unreserved acceptance of God's plan of salvation, as expressed through the Gospel teaching, the life and atonement of his divine incarnate Son, Jesus Christ, and the acceptance of Christ as a personal Saviour." This belief does not come through any intellectual operation, but is the result of faith, which enables us to lay hold of that which the mind itself cannot achieve by any of the ordinary intellectual processes. Yet it is not a blind and superstitious assent, but rather a "saving grace whereby we receive and rest upon Christ alone for salvation." As the child believes in his earthly parent, nothing doubting, so we are to look to our heavenly Father, who will give us this faith if we ask it in all sincerity. He will refuse it to none who come to him in this spirit and with an earnest desire to forsake sin. Our faith may be weak at first, like that of the man who cried out: "Lord, I believe; help thou mine unbelief," but he will strengthen it until we can realize what it means to "walk by faith." Being quickened by the power of the Holy Spirit, we learn to trust wholly In God's love for us as expressed in the redemptive work of Christ "the Author and Finisher of faith," for the salvation of a fallen world. Throughout the whole experience of the earlier stages of the Christian life we should remember that faith is God's gift, and that "whosoever receiveth not the kingdom of God as a little child shall in no wise enter therein."

837 What is the new birth?

Why new birth? Because the corruption of human nature requires it (John 3:6; Rom. 8:7, 8), and none can enter heaven without it (John 3:3). This new birth is effected by God through Christ and the Holy Ghost (John 1:13; I John 2:29; John 3:6; Tit. 3:5). He effects the new birth by the word of God, preaching the resurrection of Christ and his redeeming grace (James 1:18; I Pet. 1:3), and is of the will and mercy of God and to his glory (James 1:18; Tit. 3:5; Isa. 43:7). The Scriptures describe it as a new creation, a spiritual resurrection, a new heart, new spirit, as putting on the new man, partaking of the divine nature (II Cor. 5:17; Rom. 6:4; Eph. 2:1, 5; Ezek. 36:26; Rom. 7:6; Eph. 4:24; Rom. 7:22; II Pet. 1:4). The new birth produces likeness to God and Christ, knowledge of God, hatred of sin, victory over the world and delight in God's law and is evidenced by faith in Christ, righteousness and brotherly love (Eph. 4:24; Rom. 8:29; Jer. 24:7; I John 3:9; 5:1; 2:29; 4:7; Rom. 7:22.

838 What is the second blessing?

Many persons who have long been identified with the church come to feel the need of a definite experience which shall make them conscious of loving God and really desirous to please him. The experience of peace found by such a seeker is the same as that which comes to any unconverted person who has never made any profession of religion. When one has been soundly converted feelings of dissatisfaction are almost sure to follow the first weeks or months of peace. They point the way to a still higher and better experience to which the Holy Spirit would lead us. It is not necessary to bother with explanations and definitions about this "second blessing." The Bible and Christian experience unite in summoning all converts to this "higher ground," into this inner circle. God certainly can keep you "in all things" as well as in some. You must trust him for cleansing and keeping and energizing power, as well as for pardoning and regenerating power. Study carefully such passages as Ezek. 36:25-27; II Cor. 7:1; Gal. 3; Eph. 3:14-21; Col. 3; I Thess. 5:23; Heb. 4:9-11; Heb. 10:1-23; Heb. 13:20. Appropriating these and God's other "rich promises" to your own soul's needs, go forward vigorously in helping and serving others, and you will find the Christian life an ever-deepening satisfaction and delight, and the second blessing will follow.

839 What was the position and office of an elder, according to Scripture?

According to the accepted definition, "the office of elder was the only permanent and essential office of the church," under both the old and new dispensations. The elders of the New Testament church were pastors (Eph. 4:11), bishops or overseers (Acts 20:28), leaders and rulers (Heb. 13:7; I Thess. 5:12) of the flock. They were also the teachers of the congregation, expounding and preaching and also administering the sacraments. Doubtless many were elders who did not leave their temporal occupations. In the modern church their duties are somewhat modified, although the same general characteristics remain.

840 What is faith?

Faith is defined by the apostle (Heb. 11:1) as the substance of things hoped for and the evidence of things not seen. If there were any doubt as to its desirability, the command of Christ (Mark 11:22), "Have faith," should be enough of an incentive. The objects of faith are God and Christ as revealed to us by Moses, the prophets and the Gospel (John 14:1; John 6:29; Acts 20:21; John 5:46 ; II Chron. 20:20), and God's promises (Rom. 4:21; Heb. 11:13). Faith in Christ, that precious, most holy and fruitful gift that is accompanied by repentance and followed by conversion, is the gift of God through the Holy Ghost, produced through the Scriptures and teachings therefrom (Rom. 12:3; Acts 11:21; II Pet. 1:1; Jude 20; I Thess. 1:3; Mark 1:15; Acts 20:21; I Cor. 12:9; John 20:31; John 17:20. Through this faith we obtain remission of sins, justification, salvation, sanctification, spiritual light and life, edification, preservation, adoption, access to God and eternal life with rest in heaven (Acts 10:43; 13:39; Mark 16:16; Acts 15:9; John 12:36; John 20:31; 3:15; Heb. 4:3; I Tim. 1:4; I Pet. 1:5; John 1:12; Rom. 5:2). Without faith it is impossible to please God, it is essential to the profitable reception of the Gospel, necessary in the Christian warfare since justification is only by it (Heb. 11:6; Rom. 4:16; Heb. 4:2). It produces hope, joy, peace and confidence, makes Christ precious to those who have it and makes him to dwell in their hearts (Rom. 5:2; Acts 16:34; Rom. 15:13; Isa. 28:16; I Pet. 2:7; Eph. 3:17). By faith saints live, are supported, stand, walk, obtain a good report, overcome the word, resist the devil and they should be sincere in it, abound therein, continue in it, be strong in it, stand fast in and have full assurance thereof (Gal. 2:20; Rom. 11:20; 4:12; Heb. 11:2; I John 5:4, 5; I Pet. 5:9; Eph. 6:16; Ps. 27:13; I Tim. 1:5; II Cor. 8:7; Acts 14:22; Rom. 4:20; I Cor. 16:13; Col. 1:23; I Tim. 1:19). True faith is evidenced by its fruits, is dead without fruits, overcomes all difficulties and is a shield and breastplate against all danger (James 2:21-25; 17:20-26; Matt. 17:20; Eph. 6:16; I Thess 5:8).

841 What is the difference between faith and absolute determination?

The person who is absolutely determined to quit sin and lead a godly life may be supposed to be depending on his own strength. He is resolved to change his ways and to be a Christian. The person who exercises faith depends on the strength of Christ. He is convinced that he cannot change himself; he has learned from experience that good resolutions are apt to be broken, and he places himself in Christ's hands to be saved. He is sure that Christ is able to save him from punishment for past sins, and to keep him from falling into new sins. He is also sure that Christ is willing to save him and he trusts, not in his own resolves, but solely and only in Christ. The difference, you see, is radical.

842 Is the Biblical term *hell* used in a symbolical or literal sense?

There is a tendency among a certain class of critics to symbolize many things in Scripture even where the text is clear and explicit. The Bible language concerning future punishments and rewards cannot be explained away by such methods. While the Bible abounds in metaphor and similitude, these are used in their proper places, and to the diligent student, who searches with faith and an open mind, they are not confusing. Certainly, where it refers to God the Creator, the loving and merciful Father, to his Son the Saviour, and to the plan of salvation for the redemption of the human race, it is sufficiently clear to have convinced countless multitudes and have transformed their lives.

843 What are heresies in the Biblical sense of the term?

The Greek word translated "heresies" in Gal. 5:20 means either an opinion or a party. As used in the New Testament it stands for an opinion "varying from the true exposition of the Christian faith" (as in II Pet. 2:11), or a body of men following mistaken or blameworthy ideas, or, as a combination of these two meanings, "dissensions." This latter definition "dissensions" is the rendering given by Thayer of this passage. The American revision translates the word "parties," leaving, however, the expression "heresies" as the marginal reading. The three last words of the verse, "strife," "seditions," "heresies," are, in the American revision, "factions," "divisions," "parties."

844 What is justification?

Justification was promised in Christ by the prophet Isaiah when he said (Isa. 45:25): "In the Lord shall all the seed of Israel be justified and shall glory," and is the act of God (Rom. 8:33). Justification was necessary because there was required perfect obedience, which man cannot attain (Lev. 18:5; Rom. 10:5; Job 9:2, 3, 30; Ps. 130:3). Thus some other way had to be found. It is of grace by the imputation of Christ's righteousness earned by the shedding of his blood and sealed by his resurrection. This righteousness we may only take as our own by faith, not by our works, or by faith and works united, but purely by grace through faith (Acts 13:39; 15:1-29; John 5:24; Rom. 3:24; I Cor. 6:11; Isa. 61:10; Rom. 5:18; 5:9; 4:25; I Cor. 15:17). The blessedness of justification is apparent when we consider that it frees from condemnation, entitles to an inheritance and assures glorification (Ps. 32:1, 2; Isa. 50:8, 9; Tit. 3:7; Rom. 8:30).

845 Have scientists honored the Bible?

They have. Professor Huxley says: "I have always been strongly in favor of secular education without theology, but I must confess that I have been no less seriously perplexed to know by what practical measures the religious feeling, which is the essential basis of moral conduct, is to be kept up in the present utterly chaotic state of opinion on these matters without the use of the Bible."

846 What is redemption?

Redemption is defined by Paul (I Cor. 6:20; I Cor. 7:23) as being bought with a price. It is of God by the blood of Christ, who was sent on earth to effect it for us (Isa. 44:21; Matt. 20:28; Acts 20:28; Heb. 9:12; I Pet. 1:19; Gal. 4:4, 5). And from what are we redeemed? From the bondage of the law and its curse, the power of sin and the grave; all troubles, iniquity, evil, enemies, death and destruction (Gal. 4:5; 3:13; Rom. 6:18, 22; Ps. 49:15; 25:22; 130:8; Gen. 48:16; Jer. 15:21; Hos. 13:14; Ps. 103:4). By reason of our redemption we have justification, forgiveness, adoption and purification and believe it is precious (Rom. 3:24; Eph. 1:7; Gal. 4:4, 5; Tit. 2:14; Ps. 49:8). By it God manifests his power, grace, love and pity (Isa. 50:2; Isa. 52:3; Isa. 63:9; John 3:16). When we have been redeemed we become God's property, his firstfruits, a peculiar people, sealed unto the great day, zealous of good works and walking safely in holiness, commit ourselves to God while awaiting the completion of our redemption, when we shall return to Zion with joy (Isa. 43:1; Rev. 14:4; II Sam. 7:23; Job 19:25; Eph. 4:30; Eph. 2:10; Isa. 35:8, 9; Ps. 31:5; Rom. 8:23; Isa. 35:10).

847 What is the origin of the title "Reverend" as applied to ministers?

Its origin is obscure. It is known to have been in use as early as the thirteenth century. It was a recognized title at the Reformation. The Puritans applied it and Richard Baxter addressed his colaborers in the ministry as "Reverend Brethren." In the early church the ministers were designated as "leaders." The title "reverend," which came into use later, referred to the character of the office rather than to the individual. It dignifies the work rather than the worker. Paul, in calling himself an apostle, glorified his ministry (Rom. 11:13) and this, rightly understood, is the case with "reverend," which, however humble the worker, honors the labor that is performed with a single eye to God's glory and the salvation of men.

848 What is sanctification?

Sanctification is that act of the Holy Spirit in which he calls us through the Gospel, enlightens us by his gifts, sanctifies and preserves us in the true faith and moves us to holy works which are pleasing to God (Acts 15:9; Gal. 5:6; Eph. 2:10; Tit. 2:14; I Thess. 4:3; Rom. 15:16; I Cor. 6:11). This sanctification is effected through the atonement of Christ and the work of God, and saints are elected to salvation through it (Heb. 10:10). Sanctification is making sacred, a consecration or devotion of times, places, things or persons (Matt. 23:17, etc.). To sanctify is to render morally pure, to cleanse from sin, to render holy (John 17:17; I Thess. 5:23). This moral purification is in two distinct stages: Its commencement, called regeneration or new birth, and its progressive accomplishment unto ultimate perfection, which progress is sanctification. Regeneration and sanctification mark the progress of the real moral change wrought in the soul by the Holy Ghost. The means of sanctification are internal, the indwelling Holy Spirit, faith and the co-operation of the regenerated will with grace and external, as the Word of God, sacraments, prayer, Christian fellowship, and the providential discipline of our heavenly Father. Sanctification should lead to mortification of sin and to holiness (I Thess. 4:3, 4; Rom. 6:22; Eph. 5:7-9).

849 What is the meaning of Psalm 51:4, "Against thee, thee only have I sinned, and done this evil in thy sight, that thou mightest be justified when thou speakest and be clear when thou judgest"? Did David sin for such a purpose?

No; his meaning appears to be that his confession was the justification of God's sentence, whatsoever it might be. Suppose a man was on trial for some heinous offense, and the judge pronounced a severe sentence. Some one might say, "That was too long a term," or "I do not believe that man is guilty; the Judge should have been more merciful in view of doubt of his guilt." The verdict of the jury might not satisfy such a critic; but if the man had made a full confession of his guilt the judge would be justified or clear. Doubt would be removed, and it would be seen that he had done right in punishing the self-confessed criminal. We know that some commentators hold that David was permitted to sin in order that God's mercy might be exhibited to the world, but we do not believe that David meant any such thing. Ps. 51 illustrates David's true repentance. It embraces all the stages through which a soul can pass, from conviction of sin to confession, sorrow, prayer for mercy and expression of a lively faith and a strong purpose of amendment. David's character was a complex one; he had many faults and many virtues. His offense, which was the subject of the plea in this psalm, was a very grievous one; but his repentance was deep and thorough. He attempted no concealment of his business, but made full confession before the Lord, and presumably before his own people, who must have understood the meaning of his plea for forgiveness. It is one of a series of prayers for pardon and purifying. He was punished even while he was pardoned.

850 Are the chronological figures in the margins of Bibles reliable?

The chronological figures which you read in the marginal notes of many Bibles are not an integral part of the Scripture by any means. They were the result of the computations of Archbishop Ussher, an Irish church prelate and distinguished scholar, who lived 1580-1656. They have been both a help and a vexation to Bible students. Taking the birth of Christ (A.D. 1) as a starting-point, Ussher reckoned backward as far as authenticated history permitted. He had no other purpose than to assist scholars in getting a right perspective of historical events prior to that date. Many of his calculations have been upset by the later light thrown on ancient history through archeological discoveries, the translation of ancient inscriptions, etc. As to fixing the date of Creation, the first verse of the opening chapter of Genesis still remains unchallenged as the only reference the Bible affords on the subject, viz.: "In the beginning." The Mosaic books nowhere claim that the world was created in 4,000 B. C. In the New Testament John's Gospel opens with the identical phraseology of the Old Testament, showing that in both dispensations the fact is recognized that the date of world creation is beyond human computation.

851 What are the cardinal sins?

The term usually employed is "mortal" or "deadly" sins. The distinction between mortal and venial sins has no Scripture foundation. The seven deadly sins, according to this classification, are pride, anger, envy, sloth, lust, covetousness and gluttony.

852 What is sinlessness?

What is sinlessness? The state of being free from sin. What is sin? "Whatsoever is not of faith is sin" (Rom. 14:23). "The thought of foolishness is sin" (Prov. 24:9). "Sin is lawlessness" (I John 3:4). John Wesley, *Ser.*, Vol. 1, p. 15, taught: "Ye are saved from sin. This is the salvation which is through faith. This is that great salvation, foretold by the angel before God brought his first-begotten into the world: 'Thou shalt call his name Jesus, for he shall save his people from their sins.' And neither here nor in other parts of Holy Writ is there any limitation or restriction. All that believe in him, he will save from all their sins;

from original and actual, past and present, sin of the flesh and of the spirit. Through faith that is in him they are saved both from the guilt and power of it." Sinlessness is gloriously possible. Adam and Eve, as they came from the hand of God, were sinless (Gen. 1:27-31). If man cannot regain that pristine purity, then Satan has wrought a ruin that Christ cannot repair. "Where sin abounded, grace did abound more exceedingly." II Cor. 5:21: "Him who knew no sin he made sin [offering] on our behalf that we might become the righteousness of God in him." Jehovah had respect unto Abel and to his offering, "through which he had witness borne to him that he was righteous, and he being dead yet speaketh" (Heb. 11:4). "Enoch was translated that he should not see death; for he had witness borne to him that before his translation he had" (Gen. 5:22) "been pleasing to God" (Heb. 11:5). Enoch walked with God three hundred years. Joseph was a sinless man. "How can I do this great wickedness and sin against God?" (Gen. 39:9; 49:22-26). Daniel, Shadrack, Meshach and Abednego (the first Y. M. C. A.) were lion-proof and fire-proof against sin. Zacharias and Elisabeth "were both righteous before God, walking in all the commandments and ordinances of the Lord blameless." Most of these were married and had offspring. Celibacy is not sinlessness (see I Thess. 5:23, 24).

853 What is the soul?

This term has been used in a variety of senses by the writers of the Bible. The Old Testament word *nephesh*, literally "that which breathes," corresponds to the New Testament word *psyche*, which is translated soul or life. (1) It means physical life under natural conditions. "They are dead that sought the young child's life" (Matt. 2:20); "Is not the life more than food?" (Matt. 6:25). (2) It means the life of emotion and desire, including the appetites of hunger and thirst, and the feelings of kindness or hatred. "My soul doth magnify the Lord." Here the word *soul* is used synonymously with *spirit*; they both refer to the emotional life and in a sense correspond to *heart*, which is the seat of all thinking, feeling and willing (Luke 1:46, 47). The word is used in a bad sense as in James 3:16, where jealousy is shown to be a sensual trait, that is psychical, of the soul. (3) It means the self, that which distinguishes one individual from another. "I will say to my soul," that is to myself (Luke 12:19). "Let every soul (person) be in subjection to the higher powers" (Rom. 13:1). (4) It is also used in a religious sense: Paul and Barnabas confirmed the souls of the disciples (Acts 14:22). Hope is an anchor of the soul (Heb. 6:19). In these two instances soul is used synonymously with spirit; but in most cases the distinction is clearly drawn between soul which is natural and spirit which is akin to God. This distinction was first emphasized by Jesus, who helped men to realize the divine life in them and invited them to deepen this spiritual faculty by responding to the gracious appeal of the Spirit of God. But it was Paul who in his Epistles emphasized the supremacy of the spirit.

The soul then is that conscious existence which is made up of desires, impulses, emotions and volitions. It refers to man in his natural state, untouched by the revelation of grace. It is his personality, what he is in himself, as distinct from all other people. It is the moral man who supports his family, attends to his business, pays his debts and is a respectable member of society. He has, however, not yet reckoned with God who has been revealed by Jesus Christ and so he remains outside the temple of divine fellowship. His life will continue to be imperfect, until he is born again and permits the Spirit of the Eternal, which is the Spirit of Christ, to take possession of him. When this takes place the whole man undergoes a transformation. He feels that the spiritual occupant of the temple of flesh is indeed an immortal guest within, reflecting, in thought, desire, act and disposition, the nature of God. Thus we know that the living soul in man, though undefinable by human terms, partakes of the divine nature and is imperishable.

854 What is the difference between soul and spirit?

The terms are frequently used interchangeably and it is not easy to define the difference. Indeed some philosophers hold that man is composed of only the two elements—soul and body. But others recognize the distinction which is confirmed by several passages of Scripture, such as I Thess. 5:23. Broadly defined, the soul usually stands for the life, the affections, the will, the consciousness; while the spirit stands for the higher elements by which we apprehend spiritual truth.

A CHRISTIAN'S PROBLEMS

855 What evil power tempted some of the angels to rebel?

While the Scriptures are explicit as to the apostasy of the angels, of whom Satan was the leader, they tell us scarcely anything as to the time, cause and manner of the fall (see Rev. 12:7, 9; II Pet. 2:4; Jude 6; Matt. 25:41; Luke 10:18; I Tim. 3:6). From these and other collateral evidence it would appear that pride and ambition were the causes. There is, however, a wide difference of opinion among theologians on the matter. Milton, treating the subject from a poetic standpoint, declares that ambition was at the root of the angelic rebellion.

856 Does the mere belief that Jesus Christ as the Son of God save the soul?

The soul cannot be saved by belief in any doctrine or truth whatsoever. Nor can it be saved by works. It is Christ and he alone who saves the soul. He has given himself as a ransom for it and by him men may be saved. He who believes this fact has taken the first step. But the step by which the man avails himself of the benefits of Christ's sacrifice is the crucial one, just as a man may believe theoretically in the skill of a physician, but the decisive point is reached when he knows that he is suffering from a mortal disease and commits himself to the care of that physician, staking all his hope of life on the physician's power to cure him. The soul that trusts Christ to save him, as the sick man trusts the physician, has the faith of which it is said "by grace are ye saved through faith" (Eph. 2:8).

857 Is it possible to get along spiritually without the new birth?

Jesus' interpretation of the "new birth" was that it made people like little children. "Except ye turn and become as little children [R.V.], ye shall in no wise enter into the kingdom of heaven" (Matt. 18:3). This corresponds with his remark to Nicodemus (John 3:3): "Except a man be born again he cannot see the kingdom of God" The spirit of childhood is the spirit of his kingdom. He said again (Matt. 19:14; Mark 10:14, and Luke 18:16): "Suffer little children to come unto me, for of such is the kingdom of heaven" [or "of God"]. The humility, the simplicity, the sincerity, the trustfulness of childhood, these are the things that mark the true citizens of Christ's kingdom. In the face of Christ's statement, then, that children do belong to his kingdom, it is impossible to say that they do not. Unless they lose this state of childhood innocence by unrepented sin, they may continue in his kingdom without a definite crisis of return to it, such as is necessary in the case of adults who have forfeited that innocence. There seem to be well-authenticated cases of men and women of great and undeniable Christian piety who cannot point to any such crisis of regeneration. Such seems to have been the case of young Timothy, to whom Paul wrote: "I call to remembrance the unfeigned faith that is in thee, which dwelt first in thy grandmother Lois, and thy mother Eunice, and I am persuaded in thee also" (II Tim. 1:5). What seems to happen, however, in the majority of instances is that the child loses that first innocence by sin, and this awakens a feeling of repugnance toward God and toward spiritual things. In this way the episode of the garden of Eden is repeated again and again; after the child has disobeyed he hides away from God. But if he is led to repent at once he need never have that long, sad experience of wandering which is common to most individuals and which makes necessary the return to God and the restoration of spiritual life in the soul which we call conversion and regeneration.

858 Does the Biblical command to put the convicted murderer to death apply to this age?

It has been contended by the advocates of capital punishment that, though the command (Gen. 9:6) antedated the Mosaic code, it was intended to survive it. That inference, however, is rather a doubtful and insubstantial ground for so important a matter. It seems probable that if God had intended the practise to continue as a permanent obligation, throughout all time, some more definite and explicit intimation of that permanency would have been given. Whether it is advisable to continue the penalty is a larger question, and there are many weighty reasons for and against it. We ought, however, to have some surer and better reason for putting the murderer to death than that at that early age of the world God ordered it to be done. If, therefore, any state or nation arrived at the conclusion that the interests of the community might be better served by punishing a murderer in some other way we think it need not be deterred by the ancient command from making the experiment. The statement in Rev. 13:10, "That he who kills with the sword must be killed with the sword," does not constitute a law, but it refers to the period of persecution that was to come upon the church. The persecutor would himself suffer, as he had caused the saints to suffer. Nothing would prevent punishment overtaking him. Christ, however, said the same thing (Matt. 26:52) with a more general application. His people were not to depend on warlike weapons for their preservation, for those who relied upon them would perish by the powers they evoked.

859 Is there any sanction for capital punishment in the New Testament?

The whole spirit of the New Testament would seem to be decidedly against it. Jesus referred to the old standard, "An eye for an eye and a tooth for a tooth," and replaced it by a higher standard of forgiveness and service (Matt. 5:38-42). By his spiritual discernment and authority he prevented the stoning of a woman convicted of a crime punishable under the Mosaic law by death (John 8:1-11). Paul refers in Rom. 13:4 to the bearing of the sword by the civil power, but this does not necessarily sanction the killing of offenders. He is merely urging Christians to keep the civil law, saying that if they do righteously they will not come into conflict with it. There is a wide diversity of opinion concerning capital punishment. In certain countries it has been nominally abolished; yet it is questioned whether in such countries capital crimes have therefore decreased. Under the old Mosaic laws capital punishment was provided for certain classes of offenses. A century ago many crimes were so punished which are now visited by imprisonment instead. The argument against capital punishment is that man has no right to take away that which he cannot either give or restore, and that in depriving a criminal of life we may be also depriving him of the opportunity of repentance and salvation. Many books have been written on the subject, and both sides have been thoroughly canvassed.

860 What commandment is the greatest?

When the Pharisees asked, "What is the greatest commandment in the law? " Jesus replied, "Thou shalt love the Lord thy God with all thy heart, with all thy soul and with all thy mind This is the first and greatest commandment, and the second is like unto it. Thou shalt love thy neighbor as thyself. On these two commandments hang all the law and the prophets" (Matt. 22:36-40).

861 What does the Bible teach us about care?

Care, overmuch, about earthly things is forbidden (Matt. 6:25; Luke 12:22-29; John 6:27), for God's providential goodness should keep us from it (Matt. 6:26, 28, 30; Luke 22:35), as his promises should prevent it in us (Heb. 13:5), and trust in God should free us from care (Jer. 17:7, 8; Dan. 3:16). Our cares should all be cast on God as Peter eloquently advises (I Pet. 5:7), "Casting all your care upon him, for he careth for you," and the Psalmist triumphantly directs (Ps. 37:5), "Commit thy way unto the Lord, trust also in him; and he shall bring it to pass." Care is an obstruction to the Gospel (Matt. 13:22); is unbecoming in saints (II Tim. 2:4); is futile and in vain (II Tim. 2:4; Matt. 6:27; Ps. 39:6). It is sent as a punishment to the wicked (Ezek. 4:16; 12: 19), and the saints are warned against it (Luke 21:34): "Take heed lest at any time your hearts be overcharged with cares of this life."

862 Why should innocent children suffer for the sins of the father?

This particular passage is often misunderstood and misinterpreted. The denunciation in Ex. 20:5 does not refer to physical evils, arising from the sins of progenitors, although it is a well-known fact that these, too, through the inflexible law of nature, are visited upon the helpless and innocent. It has a special reference to idolatry. Under the Jewish law, as under all wise and equitable governments, fathers were not permitted to suffer for the children's sins, nor the children for the fathers' offenses, but every one should suffer for his own sin. In the case of idolatry, however, it would seem that God appropriated to himself the execution of his own law, which was designed to discourage that special sin. National rewards and punishments seem inevitably to extend over a single generation, in order to produce any permanent effect.

863 How do children who die before reaching the age of responsibility get into the kingdom?

In the passage in Rom. 5:18 the sin of Adam and the merits of Christ are pronounced as coextensive; the words in both cases are practically identical; "Judgment came upon all men" and "the free gift came upon all men." If the whole human race be included in the condemnation for original sin, then the whole race must also be included in the justification through Christ's sacrifice. Children dying in infancy, before the age of understanding or moral responsibility, are all partakers of this inclusive justification. Were it otherwise a very large proportion of the human race would have no share in this "free gift," but would be condemned for sin, which they never committed, which is contrary to the divine characteristics of love and justice, contrary to the apostolic teachings, and contrary to the spirit and language of the Master himself, who said of the innocent children: "Of such is the kingdom of heaven." This is the general, though not exclusive, attitude of theology today on this matter. Faith always presupposes knowledge and power to exercise it, and as a little child has neither, it has no moral responsibility. Even so stern a theologian as Calvin held practically this view. Any other conception of God would make him a Moloch instead of a loving Father.

864 What does the Bible teach of the second coming of Christ?

That Christ is to come a second time was foretold by the prophets and by Christ himself, as well as by the apostles and the angels (Dan. 7:13; Matt. 25:31; Acts 3:20; Acts 1:10, 11). It is called, among others, "time of refreshing from the presence of the Lord," "of restitution of all things" and glorious appearing of the great God and our Saviour (Tit. 2:13; Acts 3:19, 21). The time thereof is unknown, but the signs which are to precede it are fully set out (Matt. 24:36). In his second coming Christ shall appear in the clouds, in his own glory and that of the Father. He shall come suddenly, unexpectedly, with a shout and voice of the Archangel, with power and great glory and accompanied by angels and his saints (Matt. 24:30; Mal. 16:27; Matt. 25:31; II Thess. 1:8; Matt. 24:30; I Thess.4:16; Mark 13:36). At his coming the heavens and earth shall be dissolved and those who sleep shall rise, they who shall have died in Christ shall rise first, while the saints alive at the time shall be caught up to meet him (II. Pet. 3:10, 12; I Thess. 4:16, 17). The purposes of the second coming are to complete the salvation of saints, to be glorified in them, be admired by them that believe, judge the earth and reign over it after bringing to light the hidden things of darkness (Heb. 9:28; II Thess. 1:10; I Cor. 4:5; Ps. 50:3, 4; Rev. 20:11-13). The saints being assured of this second coming, love it, look for, await, haste unto, and pray for it. They shall therefore be preserved unto it, shall be blameless at it, shall be like him, shall not only see him but shall reign with him (Job 19:25; II Tim. 4:8; Phil. 3:20; I Cor. 1:7; II Pet. 3:12; Matt. 24:24, Matt. 24:42, 44; Phil. 1:6; I Cor. 1:8; Phil. 3:21; I John 3:2; Col. 2:4; Dan. 7:27). The wicked who scoff at it and presume upon its delay shall be surprised by this second coming and shall be punished while the man of sin is to be destroyed (II Pet. 3:3, 4; Matt. 24:48; Matt. 24:37-39; II Thess. 1:8, 9).

865 Will all the world be converted before the second coming of Christ?

We need not expect to see the world converted before the Lord's return. This is the age of the Gentiles. The age during which God is seeking out a people for his name. The calling out of the church to become the bride of his Son (Acts 15:14). Again, the conditions which the word of God describes to precede his coming are not what we would find in a converted nation. His disciples asked him for a sign of his coming. He did not tell them, when you see a converted world. No. His answer was: "Ye shall hear of wars and rumors of wars." "Nation shall rise against nation." "Love of many shall wax cold." "False prophets shall arise, and deceive many." "As the days of Noah were," etc. (Matt. 24:34-41). Again, Paul speaks of the great apostasy which shall mark the time of the end; also of the Antichrist, the man of sin (II Thess. 2:3; I Tim. 4:1. See also I John 2:18). Remember, "All these are the beginning of sorrows." Christ's coming will bring with it the millennial reign. He will introduce the age when nations will beat their swords into plowshares and their spears into pruning-hooks (Isa. 2:2-4). This seems to have been the view of the primitive church. It has among its many able supporters Dean Alford, Prof. Delitzsch, Dr. Tregelles, and Dr. Bonar. Others, however, think otherwise. Thus it has been suggested that our faith in God should lead us to believe that the world will be converted before Christ comes. To believe otherwise would imply the thought of such a failure in God's plans as is inconceivable. The predictions in the Epistles and the Revelation appear to favor the opposite view, but perhaps they were not intended to be accepted literally. One reason for thinking so is that they imply battle and wholesale destruction of Christ's enemies, which is inconsistent with his character. The conversion of the world seems an achievement so stupendous as to be impossible; but so did the situation today seem to be nineteen hundred years ago. Who could have thought that the little company of a hundred and twenty unlettered, obscure men and women, who gathered together after Christ's death, would grow into the enormous number who today own him as their Lord? The influence of Christian nations is growing at a prodigious rate, and it is not inconceivable that, when it culminates, there may be such an outpouring of the Holy Spirit that millions will be brought into the kingdom in a year. God is not willing that any should perish, and we believe that, having undertaken the work of redemption, he will succeed in his own way and time, and that eventually there will be a generation which shall be entirely Christian, and there will be a time when every knee shall bow and every tongue own Jesus as Lord.

**866 Is a person a Christian who has never felt any
   sudden conviction of sin or emotional
   change which could be called conversion?**

Sorrow over sin and an effort to amend are Christian duties, but do not make a person a Christian. Neither do the sudden conviction of sin and emotional change, though they may accompany, or precede, the new birth, by which a person becomes a Christian. As you will see by Christ's own explanation to Nicodemus (John 3:3-21), the new birth is the work of the Holy Spirit, which is given freely to all who seek. When a person ardently desires to become a Christian he asks Christ to save him, not only from future punishment, but from present sin. He should believe in Christ's power to do so, and should confidently place his case in Christ's hands as he would place his case in the hands of a physician if he were sick. The effort to amend will then take new shape, because Christ's life and strength will be imparted and victory assured. Christ promises to dwell in the heart of any who desire his presence and will yield themselves to him. With Christ in the heart there will be new life, and by union with him the person becomes a Christian.

867 Why was it necessary for Christ to come into the world if men were being saved before he came?

The fact of Christ's coming and suffering and dying should preclude all thought of such a question. If God so loved the world as to give his only begotten Son, you may depend that there was supreme need for it. In Christ the types and sacrifices of the Jewish dispensation found their fulfilment as well as their culmination. Without him and his life and death they would have been empty, meaningless forms. Besides all this Christ came to reveal the Father to the world. If all that we owe to Christ and his Gospel to-day were eliminated from the world, the gloom and poverty and hopelessness of life would be appalling.

868 What state of society would prevail if the Christian ideal of hope was realized and every one now living were to become true Christians?

In the ideal Christian commonwealth there would be an end to trade competition of the sort which drives many to the wall that a few may thrive. Employers would treat employees equitably and even generously, and the latter would return this treatment in faithful, intelligent service. There would be no corners, pools or combinations. No speculative market to rule the prices of crops, coal and other commodities; no stock speculation in the Wall Street sense, and no vast fortunes would be possible, since each member of society would employ all his energies and resources for the uplift and improvement of the whole community. Interest and usury would be unknown. Taxes would be such only as were needed to administer the community's affairs and do its actual work. Legitimate enterprise would develop the highest resources of nature for the benefit of all. Love would make each the servant of the whole, and the servant would be honored by all. Art, science and a varied culture would flourish, and the general intellectual horizon would widen, as the hard struggle no longer engrossed man's time, strength and physical and mental energies. Leaders and followers there still would be, of course, but there could be neither a rich nor a poor class. Money might and possibly would survive the change, but it would no longer be the magnet of mankind and the source of so much evil. And the love of Christ and his service would sweeten the new life to all who were participants in it.

869 Is there a point beyond which Christ cannot save?

In Heb. 10:26 the apostle describes the hesitancy of certain people (professing Christians) in reference to their confidence of faith. Professor Bernhard Weiss, commenting on this passage, says this lack of faith and hesitancy "to the consummation of redemption Paul regarded as a sinning against better knowledge and conscience, in the case of those who have received the knowledge of the truth of redemption. For sinners of this kind the Old Covenant already had no sacrifices; how much less did the New Covenant have such, in which there is only the one sacrifice of Christ, in which those who do not trust this sacrifice with the confidence of faith have no part at all."

870 Is it true that no one is won to Christ except through the efforts of some other person?

We think not, in the literal sense. Take the case of the sudden conversion of Paul as an illustration. Certainly it could not be said that he was brought to a saving knowledge of Christ through the efforts of any person. Dr. L. J. Birney, in an address some time ago before a religious gathering at Indianapolis, spoke of Dr. Durbin as having laid down the same general proposition. There are doubtless many who come into the light through the reading of the Scriptures and prayer; yet, in a remote and impersonal sense, they may be said to have been influenced, perhaps unconsciously, by the experience and example of others. Hence, if we critically investigate each case of conversion within our knowledge, it will be generally found, except in very rare instances where the connection is untraceable, that they have been led by the influence of others. By way of illustrating the remarkable and far-reaching power of human influence, Dr. Durbin on one notable occasion made this statement: "If Peter had won three thousand souls every day after Pentecost, and if his apostolic successors had had religion enough to do the same thing, it would have taken a thousand years to bring the world to Christ as the world was in Peter's day, and there would have been thirty new generations unaccounted for; but if each of the three thousand had gone out to save one a year, and each new disciple had done the same, the entire world would have been reached for Jesus Christ a whole generation before the Gospel of John was written."

871 Will God cast away anyone who confesses his sins to him?

"Him that cometh unto me I will *in no wise* cast out." Look up those words, in John 6:37; read them till they are so vividly photographed upon your inner eye that they shall keep repeating themselves to your brain and finding their healing way down to your troubled heart. Already you *know* they are true, but your will refuses to let go and rest upon them. They are surer than anything else in the world. Even standing alone they are wonderful enough to bring any soul to peace, but they are backed up by the whole story of the life and death of Jesus, by the gracious messages of his apostles and the promises of his prophets. That is the kind of a God we have, "who forgiveth *all* thine iniquities." We cannot repeat too often our universal remedy for troubled souls:

"Trusting Jesus, that is ALL!" It is understood that before we can really believe that he forgives us we must be willing so far as possible to make right any wrongs we have done to others (see Matt. 5:23), and to determine to forsake our sins. But to the soul who will "confess and forsake" his sin there is nothing so sure in all the world as that God will "abundantly pardon."

872 Is it possible for any one, in the gospel dispensation and not believing in Christ, to be saved?

We can set no limit to the mercy and pardoning power of God. In all ages and in every nation he has raised up witnesses to himself. If the question refers to one who, living in Gospel times and having heard the message of salvation, wilfully ignores or rejects it, we might have reasonable doubts, although we are not to judge in such matters; but if he be in a portion of the world still in heathen darkness the case is different. To deny the possibility of salvation to the heathen who have never heard the Gospel is opposed to the spirit of both the Old Testament and New Testament. The earliest Christian teachings held that the Holy Spirit exerted an influence upon the unevangelized by means of reason, and that those who lived pure, upright lives before God might be called, justified and saved. Justin Martyr, Clement, and still later Zwingle, taught this doctrine, and believed that the moral and pure among the heathen might be accepted for the sake of Christ's finished work and atonement. Job was an Arab, of a heathen race; yet he is represented as a man of perfect integrity and under divine protection and blessing. See Paul's exposition in Rom. 2:14, 26, 27, which holds that those not being under the law (of Christ) may be a law unto themselves.

873 Is a man who is spiritually dead responsible for not accepting Christ?

A man is responsible if he rejects the offer of Christ, because he is physically alive and knows what he is doing. The offer of Christ is "Arise from the dead and Christ shall give thee life" (Eph. 5:14). The Holy Spirit is a quickener and it will be given to those who ask for it. Suppose a man is dead to art. The most beautiful picture or statue does not appeal to him. Some artist makes his acquaintance and shows him the beauty of color, teaches him how to recognize the perfection of form. That side of his nature becomes alive and he learns to appreciate the beauty of art. The influence of Christ is infinitely greater. The man who desires to be saved mourns over the deadness of his nature and prays to be quickened, and Christ speedily quickens him. It is true that salvation is God's work, but he does not force it upon an unwilling man. Christ came that men, though they were dead, might have life (John 11:25).

874 What can we say to those who seem unreconcilable to the loss of a dear one through death?

What can we say to these friends? In the first place, they must quickly and with intense determination seek God. They may feel that their minds are almost shattered by the crushing blow, but the one steady fact upon which to rest in the midst of all the anguish is God himself. Or it may be that instead of sharp agony some feel a terrible weariness and bewilderment. They, too, must seek God for his rest. It is a time for creeping into "the secret place of the Most High, and abiding under the shadow of the Almighty." They will begin to realize something of the depth and strength of God's great love for them, a love even greater than their love for the dear one who has gone. They will think of the cross of Christ, where God showed so unmistakably his love for mankind. They will see Christ going through that strange experience of death, and coming out untouched by it, untouched except to be glorified. Then they will see Christ "sitting at the right hand of God"—and know that out in that other world their loved ones are safe with him. They will realize again that the abiding things in human life are thought and love and character; they will know that their dear ones have not lost those things which made them dear, but have only laid aside the garment of flesh and gone out into the world of the spirit, their true home and ours. Most wonderful and blessed of all, they may come to feel, as many have come to feel, that those whom we call dead are nearer to us than ever before—no one knows how near. A young man who recently lost his wife bears testimony that he is sure she knows what he is doing and how he and the children are getting along. May we not find, after all, that the real world is not the world of clay and stones and wood and flesh, but that all the atmosphere and ether are the real abiding places and working places of human spirits, that even the stars are nothing but the golden nails in God's home and that the house itself is all that we call "space," in which there is ample room for all the spirits who have ever lived and shall live hereafter? But at any rate we may know Jesus, Master of life and death, and know that our loved ones and ourselves are safe in his strong and sympathetic keeping. Tell these friends that "his grace is sufficient" even for their time of bitter anguish. Tell them to come close to him and thus get in closest possible communion with those who have passed out of sight. Tell them he will give them strength to bear this burden of grief, and enable them to lead others to the rest of faith they have found.

875 Are disasters, such as great fires, storms, floods and destruction, judgments from God?

Although all human experience and divine revelation teach us that God punishes the wicked who do not repent and turn to him, we are not justified in assuming that visitations of the character referred to are in any sense to be regarded as in this category. Indeed, Christ plainly rebuked such a conclusion, when he referred to the persecution of the Galileans, and the disaster at Siloam (Luke 13:1-4). Nature has her divinely adjusted laws; and the world moves in obedience to these laws. Greater wisdom would teach us not to live in localities that are obviously liable to be inundated, or overwhelmed by landslides; and to build of such material, and in such manner that risks from conflagration will be minimized. In a majority of cases, however, human foresight seems utterly powerless to provide against or to escape from such happenings, and we must be content to regard them as the result of natural law, to which the righteous and the wicked are alike subject, "as the rain falleth on the just and the unjust." There have been instances, as in a railroad disaster, in which good people have been killed and wicked people have escaped. Christians must not expect immunity from injury and accident, nor must the wicked conclude that because they escape, God is indifferent to their evil deeds. God expects us to trust in him and wait the time when all these mysteries shall be explained. In the meantime, as in the case of Job, we should be adding cruelty to misery if we hastily assumed that those who suffer most have sinned most grievously. The opposite is often true. God is not settling accounts with men in this life. That will be done at the judgment. In the same way, the wars, accidents, wrecks, etc., may be the direct result of human negligence or wrongdoing, but we must not regard God as an indifferent spectator of the events in his world. There is an overruling Providence that turns evil to good results in spite of evil intentions on man's part. We cannot always explain it, and some providences seem mysterious, but we cannot be surprised at our not being able to fathom God's purposes. From what we do know, we must conclude that those we do not know are also good and wiser than we can conceive.

876 Do the Scriptures sanction divorce for any cause?

It would seem as if there were a discrepancy between the doctrine as enunciated in Mark 10:11, 12 and that in Matt. 5:32. The rule of interpretation is that when two writers report the same speech and one is fuller than the other, the one who gives the fullest report is to be deemed the more accurate. It is more likely that the one writer omitted a sentence than that the other inserted something that never was uttered. Following this rule, Matthew's report is more likely to be accurate than Mark's. If you will turn to Matt. 5:32 you will see that Christ made an exception in the case of a person who had been false to the marriage vow. He did not require one partner to live with another who had been unfaithful. Then we may also ask whether the Scriptures sanction divorce on the ground of desertion. This is a disputed question.

The only passage dealing with it is I Cor. 7:10-15. Whether the apostle there means that the person who, he says, "is not in bondage" is entitled to marry again during the lifetime of the deserting partner, is doubtful. It seems unreasonable, however, that a man deserted by his wife, or a wife deserted by her husband, should be precluded from making a second marriage by the misconduct of another. It generally happens; too, that there is good reason for suspecting that desertion is not the only offense against the marriage tie that the deserting partner has committed, but as it is sometimes impossible to furnish proof of the fact, while desertion can be easily proved, most of the churches sanction divorce for desertion; but direct and explicit sanction from the Scriptures there is none.

877 Are ecclesiastical entertainments permissible as a means of raising money for church support?

Our churches should be sustained by voluntary offerings. "Freely ye have received, freely give." Throughout the Bible God's acceptance of gifts, whether for the Temple service or in apostolic times, seems to have been in proportion to the willingness with which they were offered. In Ex. 25:1, Moses is told to accept whatever is "offered willingly with the heart," and in Christ's commendation of the poor widow who gave two mites the teaching clearly is, that it is the spirit in which the gift is made more than the value of the gift itself that makes it acceptable to God. "For if there be first a willing mind, it is accepted according to that a man hath, and not according to that he hath not," and so far is this willing spirit to go that we are even to provide in advance for our gifts. "Upon the first day of the week, let every one of you lay by him in store," etc. Ecclesiastical entertainments for raising money ignore this truth so plainly taught, being based on the assumption that we are not willing to give to God's cause without getting something in return for ourselves. So questionable a method of raising money has first an evil effect on outsiders, in that it leads to the belief that one branch of the church's work is to make money and another to provide entertainment. A further argument against these entertainments—such as bazaars, etc.—is that they are not even conducted on sound business principles, which goes far to belittle the church in the eyes of the world. Second, this class of entertainment has an evil effect upon the church itself, as it brings to the front the members least spiritually minded and gives them a controlling interest in its affairs; it diverts attention from the legitimate work of the church; it arouses jealousies; it accentuates class distinctions; it places too much stress upon the value of money for conducting religious work; it cannot compete with similar attractions held by secular organizations; it obliterates the line that should always exist between the church and the world.

878 Is it right for a church to open its doors for fairs, concerts, and suppers when the building has been dedicated to God for pure worship?

While the social side of church life should be cultivated, it is desirable that fairs, suppers and similar matters having in no direct sense a spiritual side should be held elsewhere. There are, however, some social features that may with perfect propriety be held in the church building, such as concerts of a proper character, lectures and the like. If we apply the test of conscience in such matters and ask ourselves whether the holding of any special gathering within church walls is derogatory of the sacred purposes to which the building is dedicated, a decision will not be difficult to reach. The good sense of pastor, elders and managers should be exercised to prevent the use of the church rooms for anything that savors of levity or disrespect, or that has not for its object the furtherance of God's purposes and the spread of the Gospel.

879 Is the use of unfermented wine at Communion in accordance with the teaching of Christ?

There is no record of Christ having said anything on the subject. The broad principles he laid down, however, apply to many questions that at that time were not pressing. Concern for the welfare of others he certainly regarded as a duty. That concern at the present time may surely take into account the position of a man who was formerly a drunkard, and who may find his desire for intoxicants aroused by tasting fermented wine at communion. Sympathy with him and a desire to shield him from temptation, and save him from the pain of a struggle with his old enemy, is thus in accord with Christ's principles, and may legitimately find expression in using unfermented wine at the sacrament.

880 How often are we to forgive a person who has wronged us?

Our duty is to cultivate a forgiving disposition. There is no doubt that when the wrongdoer repents, we ought to forgive him, even though it be seventy times seven times that he has offended. Toward the hardened offender who does not repent, we ought to feel more pity than animosity. It may be that for his own sake forgiveness should be withheld. It is good for some men that they should be taught by a sharp lesson that they must not misbehave. But under all that, the Christian ought to exercise a kindly feeling toward the wrongdoer, ought not to be vindictive, and should be ready to forgive when he shows contrition. We believe that God loves the sinner while hating his sin, and we should try to be like him in that. We, who have done so much for which we hope God will forgive us, can surely afford to forgive those who have injured us. The man who has done the injury and is not penitent is in the greater need of forgiveness, though he is not entitled to it. We should pity him.

881 Is there forgiveness for the person who sins over and over again after having been forgiven?

In Isa. 55:7 we are told that God will abundantly pardon, and that means that God will forgive just as long as there is sincere repentance. The danger for one repeatedly sinning is not that God will not forgive, but rather that by sinning one places himself where there is no more conscience of sin. God's mercy is unlimited both as to time and quantity and is well told in Matt. 18:21-35; Luke 17:3, 4; Isa. 1:18; Mic. 7:18, 19. But constant sinning against conscience hardens the heart and benumbs the conscience. There may be, to the end, sorrow exercised because of the consequences of sin, but to him who continues to sin the conscience becomes at last benumbed, so that while it mourns over the results, it still loves the sinning and is not offended by it. Continuous sinning should lead one to self-examination and humility. "Him that cometh to me, I will in no wise cast out," says Jesus. God will abundantly pardon all those who forsake their ways and return to the Lord—but we must come, must return and we must come as did the Publican—humble.

882 Is the doctrine of the second work of grace a true Scriptural teaching?

We should be assuming an unwarrantable authority if we answered the question categorically. Brethren whom we honor and who are undoubtedly sincere believe that it is Scriptural. Who are we, that we should say it is not? We can only give you our opinion which you must take for what it is worth. Our belief, then, is that sanctification is a gradual process, lasting all through our lives; that we are always receiving new light, new strength to overcome temptation and new grace to live more like Christ. We believe that at no time is it safe to relax our vigilance and that the time never comes when we attain absolute perfection, or immunity from the possibility of falling into sin. We believe that progress in the divine life is not uniform in its rate, but under favorable circumstances such as a season of special retirement and prayer and association with godly brethren we may make greater progress than at others. But we do not believe in sudden miraculous changes which would make the soul impervious to sin.

883 What is the fate of the Jews who have passed away since the death of Christ?

It would be pure speculation to answer a question concerning the ultimate fate of the Jews who have passed away since the death of Christ. We have no right to judge men; judgment belongs to God alone. Besides, in all ages he has raised up witnesses to himself in the persons of godly men and women who, although they might never have heard the Gospel message, have lived according to their highest lights in a way that may have been acceptable, and whose faith has been accounted to them for righteousness.

884 Do the promises as to immunity from snake bite and poison belong to all believers now as in Christ's time?

Though the passage in Mark 16:17, 18 appears to refer the promises to all believers, the facts prove that they do not. A Christian taking up a venomous serpent or drinking poison would undoubtedly suffer as a man would who is not a Christian. In the days when the promise was given, a handful of unlettered men were going out to preach to an unbelieving world and needed special miraculous power to help them in their testimony. These powers were granted for that special purpose. If you are thinking of making a personal test we would strongly urge you to consider before doing so whether Christ's words (Matt. 4:8) do not apply in the case. At the same time there is no doubt that one who accidentally gets into difficulty of this kind may well call upon the Lord and reminding him of his promises, expect and receive absolute relief.

885 Are we still under the law?

It is impossible to explain the teachings of the New Testament on this subject such as Gal. 3 and 4 without recognizing two distinct meanings of the word "law," as applied to the old dispensation. It meant both the *moral* law and the *ceremonial* law. The New Testament is very clear in teaching that from the ceremonial law the believer in Christ is set free. Christ put an end to the sacrifices and ceremonies of the Temple when he became the sacrificial Lamb for the sins of the whole world. The 15th chapter of Acts shows how the first church council set the Gentile Christians free from the obligations of the ceremonial law, even the fundamental ordinance of circumcision. When we come to the moral law the explanation is more difficult. Paul says: "Do we then make void the law through faith? God forbid. Yea, we *establish* the law" (Rom. 3:31). The moral law was never abrogated. Paul's argument is that law in itself has no power to make a man good; but Christ has that power. Christ takes the law and fills it full of life and love. He transforms the soul so that it loves the Lawgiver and loves every individual for whose protection the law was given. For instance: is the Christian *under* the law against murder? He has no such sensation, no such consciousness. He does not want to murder anybody. By Christ's power he has been made to love his neighbor and he knows that he must continue to love him. Love solves the problem of the moral law; love gives the law a power it never had before. "Love worketh no ill to his neighbor; therefore love is the fulfilling of the law" (Rom. 13:10). In a sense this was taught in the Mosaic law, as both Christ and Paul pointed out, but Christ brought a new interpretation and a new power. So we may be said to be living under his law, as Paul expressed it: "Bear ye one another's burdens, and so fulfil the law of Christ" (Gal. 6:2). We are in the dispensation of the Holy Spirit, who brings to our hearts the experience of loving God (Rom. 5:5), and who makes us truly love our neighbor.

886 Why does the Lord seem so much nearer and dearer at certain times and not at others?

Even perfect Christians are sometimes "in heaviness through manifold temptations" or trials. The human brain is such a delicate organ, and the human body so imperfect, that many times the things we are surest about become obscure; in sleep, for instance, or in extreme fatigue, or suffering, or even nervousness. Our chief concern must be to keep free from sin. We may be cleansed and kept clean by the blood of Christ; and while we are trusting him for cleansing, we shall be, under normal conditions, conscious of his presence.

887 Are there any people without conception of a supreme being?

Missionaries and other travelers affirm that nowhere on the globe is there a people who have no conception of worship of some sort, the sole possible exception being the natives of the Solomon Islands, who are said by some writers to have been absolutely without any idea of a Supreme Being, or any kind of worship, when first discovered by white men. Even idolatry must be regarded in a sense as an apprehension of an overruling Power, though a perverted one. The contention of skeptics that we have no right to enlighten the heathen cannot be maintained; for, if it be conceded that it is our duty to help our fellow men in any degree, we certainly should strive to enlighten them on the most vital of all questions: that which affects their happiness here and hereafter. Besides, Christians are commanded to "preach the Gospel to all the world."

888 Is anything too hard or difficult for God?

The day of miracles is not past. The question, "Is anything too hard or impossible for God?" is apt to be misleading. While it is true that nothing is impossible for God, yet it is also true that God seems always to work according to method, or law. When the flying machine was invented, no laws of gravity were superseded; they were simply recombined with other laws, just as the magnet seems to break law, but does not. So with radium; it appears to break and change other principles, but in reality only readjusts and reapplies them. In his miracles Christ made use of a new power, but did not set aside the laws of the universe.

We never hear of a lost limb or member being made to grow again. Christ restored the ear of the high priest's servant not, doubtless, by making another ear grow, but by rejoining the severed member to its place—a thing which surgeons now occasionally do in their regular practise. An eye injured could probably not be restored to normal condition, any more than if the eye had been lost another could be made to grow in its place. But foreign growths have been removed; germs dislodged; weak organs strengthened—by Christ's miraculous power in response to the prayer of faith. And, while not neglecting any human skill or aid or material means, we should be constantly expecting from God greater things rather than less, and may come to find that even things we had called impossible are after all included in his plan.

889 Is there intercession needed between us and God?

The full price of the world's salvation was paid by Christ on the cross. After a soul has once heard of Christ and his atonement, he needs no other help in approaching God than that of the divine Saviour. The New Testament is full of emphatic statements of the absolute sufficiency of Christ's sacrifice. There is "one Mediator between God and man, the man Christ Jesus." This is the message of the whole book of Hebrews. Read especially the first seven chapters (see also I Cor. 1:30; Rom. 5; II Cor. 5:18-21; Gal. 1:3-9; Gal. 3; Gal. 5:1-6; Gal. 6:14, 15, etc.). After we are regenerated, no one can possibly be nearer to us than Christ is. It surely seems, to say the very least, extremely foolish to ask any one else to convey a message to him for us when he himself is nearer than any one else can be.

890 Is an official marriage ceremony of any real value?

In Gen. 2:22 God brought about the first marriage by bringing Eve to Adam. By what ceremony this was done we are not told, but that there was some sort of preliminaries to the union there can be no doubt as is indicated by the injunction in verse 24 and the solemn enunciation of the principles of the bond. In early times one of the essential things in marriage seems to have been the coming of the bride from her father's house to that of her husband or his father. Betrothal accompanied by more or less ceremony preceded this. In Ezek. 16:8-14; Mal. 2:14; Prov. 2:17; Gen. 24:57-60; Ruth 4:9-13 we have examples of the customs common to the occasions. In Jesus' time the ceremonies appear to have been observed as is indicated by his numerous references to wedding feasts; for instance, such as are found in Matt. 22:3; Matt. 22:11; Luke 12:36; 14:8; and by his participation in a wedding feast at Cana. The right of wife and children and the demands of good government necessitate such formality in the marriage ceremony as will give to the married state that dignity and solemnity which is essential to the inviolability of the act. The use made of marriage as a symbol of union between Christ and his church (Rom. 7:4; Gal. 3:27; Isa. 54:4-6; 61:10; 62:3-5; Rev. 21:1; 19:7-9) indicates that there is more to the marriage than a mere contract between two parties and that in God's sight it is the holiest state. Such holy relation should, in deference to posterity and the public good, be initiated by a ceremony of public character and record.

891 Is the marriage of a Protestant with a Catholic advisable?

Marriage with Christians is not merely to be a physical union, but a union and communion of souls. This is the essential requirement and only sure guarantee for a happy marriage. Difficulties and disagreements do and must arise, if the marriage is blessed with children and a decision is to be made in which church and faith they are to be reared. Disagreeing, as Protestants and Romanists do, in the most fundamental truths of the Christian religion, they lack all mutual basis for religious exercise, even prayer, and particularly in the days of adversity must suffer grievously because of the cleavage existing between them in the things of highest moment in their spiritual life. Read Rom. 16:17; II Cor. 6:14-18; I Cor. 7:16 and ponder whether these admonitions do not also apply to the entering into so close a union as that of marriage by those who in their religious conceptions and convictions, and hence in their entire view of life, are so far apart as are Romanists and Protestants. Experience proves that what is stated in Gen. 6:2 with reference to the children of God uniting in marriage with the children of the world applies also to marriages of Protestants to Romanists, *i.e.*, that such unions very frequently result in both falling into religious indifference, spiritual death. Either there will be a persistent effort by one or the other spouse seeking to convert the other to what is held to be the true faith, or for the sake of external peace both will drop all religion. If the Protestant agrees to a Catholic marriage he by that very act acquiesces in the Roman Catholic doctrine of marriage being a sacrament which none other than a Roman Catholic priest can validly perform and that every other marriage is at best a legal concubinage. Thereby he places the stigma of concubinage upon his own parents if their marriage was not solemnized by a Roman Catholic priest, and confesses himself illegitimate. On the other hand, the Catholic party to such marriage must ever hold her marriage to be nothing else but concubinage and her entire marital life a sin in the sight of God, should her marriage not have been consecrated by a Roman Catholic priest. Surely no stedfast Protestant could ever promise to have his children brought up in a church and faith whose most fundamental teachings he holds to be a denial of divine truth depriving Christ of his true glory and sinful mankind of all true peace, the assurance of reconciliation with God and of that precious liberty wherewith Christ has made us free.

892 What are the limits of ecclesiastical proscription of marriage?

By Levitical law the prohibited degrees included direct relatives in both ascending and descending lines, of the whole and of the half blood, children who had the same parents or parent, the brothers and sisters of fathers or mothers, brothers' wives, daughters-in-law, a woman and her daughter, or other descendant, in the third generation and the sister of a wife during her lifetime. By Lev. 18 where these degrees are set out, the analogy to relatives there mentioned may be applied to others equally close of which, however, nothing is said. In the early church a still stricter rule of prohibited degrees was a part of canonical law. Thus the Emperor Theodosius I forbade the marriage of first cousins which the earlier Roman law permitted. The Greek and Roman churches went even further. The Roman Catholic Church carried the prohibition to the seventh degree, but in 1216 Innocent III cut it down to the fourth, and a little while after Gregory IX modified Innocent's rule that a marriage between a third and fourth cousin was allowable. The council of Trent further mitigated the restrictions. According to the canons of the Greek Church a man may not marry his second cousin's daughter, his deceased wife's first or second cousin nor his deceased wife's first cousin's daughter. Two brothers may not marry two sisters, an aunt and a niece, two first cousins. A man may not marry his wife's brother's wife's sister, his brother-in-law's wife nor can his own brother marry her. The feeling lying at the bottom of all these prohibitions was the pretension of a moral principle to promote chastity. Another consideration is that the marriage of near relatives promotes neither the health nor the multitude of offspring. Besides these reasons it might be urged that to marry out of one's near relationship binds families together and diffuses the feeling of brotherhood through neighborhoods and tribes. Besides enacting laws against the marriage of blood relations, states have sometimes prohibited men from connecting themselves with women who sustain toward them the closest degrees of affinity. Some countries make it unlawful to marry a wife's sister. There are no valid arguments against such unions from Scripture, but rather, when it is said (Lev. 18:18) that a man shall not have two sisters as his wives, the inference is that Jewish law allowed marriage to one of them after the death of the other and preceding wife. Marriage to a brother's widow or deceased husband's brother is more doubtful. Yet in the canonical law the Pope can probably give a dispensation. Such was the case of Henry

VIII of England. Some church bodies, however, inhibit marriages between both of these affinity degrees.

893 Is a religious marriage ceremony absolutely necessary?

Early in the history of the Jewish race (as their sacred books show) it was considered advisable that a priest or rabbi should perform the marriage ceremony, as important religious questions had to be put to the bridal pair which only a learned man could do. In the first centuries (A.D.) Christian marriages were solemnized by the clergy, but there were many exceptions. There was no prescribed form, and the public ceremonies apparently were not regarded as essential by the early Christians. There is no record preserved of the first marriage by a minister. Marriage ceremonies that are not performed by regularly ordained pastors in the case of a religious ceremony, or by the authorized official in civil marriages, are irregular and unrecognized by the courts and the community. Such ceremonies, if undertaken in jest, are a mockery of the sacred ordinance, and in the worst possible taste. No Christian can afford to have a share in such follies. "Mock marriages" are usually prolific of evil to all concerned, and unsolemnized, irregular marriages usually result in leaving the wife at the mercy of one who should have begun the new relation by surrounding her with every honorable safeguard and protection.

894 Were miracles wrought by other men of God before and since Christ?

Yes, indeed. By Moses and Aaron as follows: Rod turned into a serpent and restored again; hand made leprous and restored again; the various plagues in Egypt, such as water turned into blood; frogs, lice, flies, boils, locusts and darkness brought; the first-born destroyed; the Red Sea divided (see Ex. 4-12). Joshua divided the waters of Jordan, took Jericho, stayed sun and moon and destroyed the Midianites (Josh. 3, 4, 10 and Judg. 7:16-22). Samson killed a lion and Philistines, carried away the gates of Gaza and pulled down the house of Dagon (Judg. 14 and 16). Elijah brought on a drought, multiplied meal and oil, restored a child to life, brought rain and divided the waters of Jordan (I Kings 17, 18; II Kings 2:8). Elisha divided the waters of Jordan, multiplied oil, restored a child to life, healed Naaman, caused iron to swim and restored a man to life (II Kings 2:14, 21; II Kings 4:17; 32-35; II Kings 5:10, 14; II Kings 6:6; II Kings 13:21). The apostles and seventy disciples performed miracles (Luke 10:9, 17; Acts 2:43; Acts 5:12). Peter cured a lame man, healed the sick, made Eneas whole and restored Dorcas to life (Acts 3:7; Acts 5:15, 16; Acts 9:34; Acts 9:40). Stephen and Philip wrought miracles (Acts 6:8; Acts 8:6, 7, 13), and Paul cured a lame man, cast out an unclean spirit, made the bite of a viper harmless, restored Eutychus to life and healed the father of Publius (Acts 14:10; Acts 16:18; Acts 20:10-12; Acts 28:5, 8).

895 Have all the prophecies been fulfilled?

All the prophecies have not yet been fulfilled, notably those that refer to the restoration of the Jews and other far-reaching predictions of the Old Testament prophets. The Messianic prophecies, especially those relating to the coming of the kingdom, are now, commentators hold, in process of fulfilment. The Gospel has not yet been preached to all the nations of the world. There are parts of Central Asia, some parts of China and almost all of Tibet, together with portions of Central Africa, the Sahara tribes and parts of South America, still unevangelized. It is the imperative duty of the church of Christ to hasten this work, which Jesus himself laid down as one of the principal tasks of his followers.

896 When furnishing references to a prospective employer, am I morally bound to disclose facts derogatory to the person under consideration?

You should either answer the questions fully and truthfully, and give any other essentially important facts as far as your personal knowledge goes, or else be silent altogether. The appeal to you by another employer, for a reference, is a purely private matter, and as the prospective employer is bound in honor to keep the information you furnish strictly private, so you are equally bound to be truthful with him, and to keep back no vital fact, since he places his interest wholly in your hands, trusting you implicitly. If you, by a too generous recommendation, impose upon him a worthless employee, you will very likely have reason to regret it afterward. I have suffered more than once from engaging domestic help on the strength of fulsome and even enthusiastic recommendations from mistresses who apparently made it a rule to give to every servant whom they dismissed for incompetency or other cause a certificate of the highest character, and who said nothing of faults which were certain to prove very objectionable. A single qualifying word would have been sufficient, in such cases, to avert the trouble that followed. You must bear in mind that business men who ask questions about persons they intend to employ ask the important questions they want answered. They better than many others know man's weakness and do not expect to find perfection. Then by all means refrain from tearing down what might be the opportunity of a lifetime, remembering that wealth throws a protection around the business man, and he who works for him must stand or fall on the character his friends give him, before trial. If you do anything, go to the party you are recommending;

if he has a fault, tell him of it, and warn him that it might cost him a position sometime. Unless the person under consideration had committed some grave wrong and was entirely unworthy of the position offered, your answering the questions asked would be sufficient. But if you believe he can and will perform the work required, even though he has not always done the right thing, it would be wrong indeed to say anything that would debar such a one from the expected position. The tendency of the world in general "to kick a man when he's down" is unchristian. When a man is trying to be somebody, lend a helping hand and treat him as a true Christian should—it matters not how low such a person had fallen previously. God help us to lift our fallen brothers!

897 Is there more than one way of salvation?

During his earthly ministry, Jesus set before his hearers the way of eternal life and also showed them the way that leads to perdition and the means of escape. There were many among the Pharisees and Sadducees who, having heard the message, still persisted in their unbelief. He warned them of the fate that awaited the impenitent wicked. He had come to save the world, and those who rejected him must bear the burden of their own rejection. The record of the Scriptures cannot be altered or done away with. God is a God of love and ever ready to forgive; but if we reject his Son and continue in sin after having received the Gospel invitation, we should blame ourselves alone for what may befall us. We bring our punishment upon our own heads and are self-condemned by our own act.

898 Can a Christian find anywhere in the Bible justification for self-defense even though his life is at stake?

We presume you mean defense by force. If a man were accused of murder, or any capital offense, he could find justification for defending himself in court in the example of Paul, Peter, Stephen, etc., who defended themselves by speeches. Paul also availed himself of the provisions of the law of citizenship to save himself from injustice (see Acts 22:25). We believe that if Paul had been attacked by robbers when he was carrying to Jerusalem the money subscribed by the Christians for the relief of the poor, he would not have given up the money without a fight. But direct justification for taking up arms in self-defense, there seems to be none. Perhaps none was needed. It may have been regarded as the natural course, and as there is no direct prohibition of it, that course may be followed. We do not think that Christ's command that "ye resist not evil" (Matt. 5:39) applies to self-defense so much as to retaliation.

899 Why were early Christians urged to anoint the sick with oil (James 5:14)?

There are those who explain James 5:14 by associating the anointing of the sick with the official anointing of priests, kings and perhaps prophets. In this way they have given a sacramental and symbolical character to what is really a simple custom of ordinary family life. Now oil is in familiar use in the East as an article of the toilet. It takes the place of our pomades and scents and its use is regarded as a sign of health. Just so the neglect of oil is the sign that a man is out of health. Those who are sick are not allowed to be anointed, nor are those who are passing through a time of mourning. When, therefore, James enjoins the elders to anoint the sick—that is, at once make his usual toilet—after prayer for his restoration, he really means that they are to pray for him with full faith and show the strong faith by acting toward him as if he were in fact recovered— that is, ready for his daily anointing. The elders were to give expression to their faith by their works, the particular works which would best show it in the case of the sick that they should at once proceed to wash, dress and anoint the sick man as if he were quite sure that God had heard their prayer and made him well.

900 Is there no sinlessness because God is not able to keep from sin those who trust in him?

God is able to do many things that he will not do. He is able to keep men from sin, but it is not his habit to treat them as automatons. He could save the whole world by any act of his will, but he takes the slower, more noble course of drawing men to himself. He would have men choose him and seek him. As in the parable of the Prodigal Son, the father might have locked his son up and prevented him from going to the far country; but he would not do so with his son. The son might go if he wished and when he wished to return he was welcomed back, but no compulsion was used. God deals so with men. He will not by an act of his power relieve his children of the necessity of watchfulness and resistance to temptation, making them as it were sin-proof. They must watch and pray, and he will help them to resist. The question of men leading a sinless life is one of fact, not of their ability to do so. God could keep us from committing sin, no one disputes; but as a matter of fact, he does not. The man does not live who does not commit sin. If he is a child of God he deplores it, repents of it, and strives to keep from it in the future, and beseeches God to keep him from falling. Sometimes he is brought to this condition by God's discipline: God interferes to prevent him continuing in sin and brings him back to himself by a road of sorrow and suffering. No child of God will say, "May I commit a sin a day or one sin an hour?" He will be anxious to avoid it and not to regard it as a privilege.

901 What proof have we outside of the Bible that man has a soul?

Man's conviction of immortality, even outside of the Bible, is world-old and world-wide. He is the only being who desires a hereafter or who has conceptions of another life. Wherever man is found, he has the in-born conviction of the existence of a Supreme Being and another world. He feels within him an influence that is not mortal or material. No other being on earth can rise above the mere allurements of sense; no other aspires to a future. Man feels that his state here is a preparatory one; that it is a step to a higher education. The soul, in all its aspects, is its own prophet of immortality and has been so in all ages. From the days of the earliest philosophers, from Socrates and Cicero down to Baxter and Liddon, this fact has been stamped upon the history of the world, and despite materialists and skeptics, it is stronger and more universal than ever.

902 Is there any ground for the opinion that God makes men suffer in the very way in which they have made other men suffer?

There are those who hold with Adoni-bezek (Judg. 1:6) that "as I have done so God hath requited me," and there are undoubtedly retrib-utive providences, but such cases are so rare as to be negligible. When such cases occur men's love of the sensational leads them to take note thereof and attach undue importance thereto. The great majority of God's judgments are not retaliatory. "It was an ethical maxim exten-sively accepted among ancient nations that men must suffer the same pains that they have inflicted on others. The later Greeks called this the Neoptolemic Tisis from the circumstance that Neoptolemus was pun-ished in the same way in which he had sinned. He had murdered at the altar and at the altar he was murdered. Phalaris had roasted human be-ings in a brazen bull, and the same punishment was inflicted on him-self." Dr. Farrar says of the punishment inflicted on Adoni-bezek: "This kind of punishment was not uncommon in ancient days. The cutting off of the thumbs would prevent a man from ever again drawing a bow or wielding a sword. The cutting off of his great toes would deprive a man of that speed which was so essential for an ancient warrior." But though retributive punishments of this kind are not recognized in mod-ern times it is peculiar how the old sentiment still prevails so that great satisfaction is felt in hearing of cases where Providence deals the blow to men which they have dealt to others.

903 Would a converted person, by committing suicide, lose his inheritance in heaven?

Persons who are united to Christ by faith and have become heirs of God would not commit suicide, as no murderer (and a suicide is a self-murderer) has eternal life abiding in him (see I John 3:15). If such a person took his own life it is certain that his reason must have become unbalanced by grief, or trouble, or anxiety, and that he was irresponsible. Any person who, having his reason and his mental powers unimpaired, deliberately kills himself would give evidence by his act that he was not a true Christian, and therefore had never an inheritance in heaven. The condition of the suicide's mind prior to his committing the fatal act has to be taken into account. There is no doubt that a large proportion of persons who commit suicide are of unsound mind at the time. The brain is unbalanced, and the person is not responsible for his act. You may be quite sure that if a Christian loses control of his faculties, and in that condition kills himself, he will not by that act lose his interest in Christ. God will receive him, as he would if he died by accident or disease. In thinking of a suicide, we must bear in mind the possibility of dementia, and not sorrow as those who have no hope.

904 Who is the Holy Spirit, and what is his work?

The Holy Ghost is the Third Person in the Trinity and equal with the Father and Son in power and glory. He is the divine helper, assistant, counselor and instructor, and his office is to carry forward the great work of teaching and saving men which Christ began. He is to the disciples of Christ what Christ himself was to them while on earth (see John 15:26; I Cor. 12:4-11). He is the divine Spirit commissioned to guide, inspire and energize believers for doing the work of God on earth, interceding, directing, bearing witness and giving "gifts" (special spiritual qualifications). It is by the power of the Holy Ghost working through consecrated men and women that souls are won and the Gospel is made effective. It is apparently impossible fairly to interpret the Scripture references to the Holy Spirit and the experiences of Christian people in regard to him in any other way than by accepting this doctrine of the Trinity. Jesus said he would send the Holy Spirit. Peter declared on the day of Pentecost that he had come, and explained that Christ, after he had been exalted to the right hand of God, had sent him in fulfilment of the promise (Acts 2:16-33). His work is to convict of sin, to lead to repentance, to guide the believer, to reveal Christ, to be the Comforter in trouble, to strengthen and to sanctify the soul, to be the Guide, the Energizer, the Sanctifier of the Church.

905 Does the Lord send evil spirits?

The statement in I Sam. 16:14 must be understood and so must many others in the Old Testament from the standpoint of the writer. The historians who wrote the books of Samuel and Kings were men of intense spirituality and deep piety. They looked at every event in its relation to God. Our modern histories reverse this method, and relate the circumstances which, in the opinion of the writers, suffice to explain events.

Just as the ancient writers described thunder as the voice of God, and we explain it as the impact of the clouds. We should regard Saul as a man subject to periodical attacks of insanity; but the historian of the Old Testament regards him as under the displeasure of God, who sends an evil spirit to torment him.

906 Why, if God is so wise and loving, did he make man so liable to physical suffering?

Do you not think that so delicate and wonderful an organism as the human body has less pain than might have been expected? Of course, there is no limit to God's power to do anything, but he has himself set limits to his mode of operations. He works through natural laws, and he seldom interferes between a violation of them and the penalty. Whatsoever a man sows that he reaps. A watchmaker produces a watch that he is sure will keep good time and will wear for years. But if a boy owns the watch and is fond of inspecting the works, altering the regulator and occasionally dropping it on the floor, the watchmaker's skill fails of its purpose. Even good men who should know better are not sufficiently careful of the laws of health, and they have to suffer and they often transmit enfeebled constitutions to their children. There are, however, evidences of the foresight and goodness of God even in pain. One of them is that singular provision in excessive suffering which we call "fainting." It is like the safety valve of a steam engine, operated by the very power that brings danger. When pain becomes so extreme that nature cannot bear it, the man faints, that is, becomes unconscious of what he is suffering. That is a very merciful provision indicating the kindness and foresight of the Creator

907 May Christians consistently pray for wealth?

According to the old Hebrew formula, it was not sinful to ask for an increase of substance or for prosperity for flocks and crops. The Christian view of prayer, however, has modified this, and while there is no express prohibition against praying for riches, there is a direct promise that, having sought and obtained the divine blessing and pardon for sin, all things will be added. Probably the best answer to the question is furnished in the prophecy of Agur (Prov. 30:8) wherein he says: "Remove far from me vanity and lies; give me neither poverty nor riches; fill me with food convenient for me, lest I be full and deny thee and say who is the Lord, or lest I be poor and steal." Riches, as well as any other earthly good, are the gift of God, and deserve to be considered in this light. If one desires riches, that he may have more power to do good, there seems to be no just ground why he should not consider it proper to pray for them. We know that riches are a source of great temptation, and that, as a matter of fact, they are frequently, if not almost con-

stantly, misused, so that great grace is needed in order to their proper
use. But the thoroughly consecrated soul will pray that he may be kept
from perverting God's gifts. If we pray for riches to use them for our
own pleasure alone, we do wrong. But many a man has prayed for
riches, that he might have the means to benefit the world, and help toward the advancement of Christ's kingdom. If these things are kept in
view, we see no reason why one should not pray for riches. We have
many evidences that God is pleased with such petitions, when they are
offered in the right manner. Jabez called on the God of Israel, saying:
"Oh, that thou would bless me indeed and enlarge my coast." This was
a prayer for increase of worldly possessions, and we are informed that
God granted the request. From this we may infer that God was pleased
with his petition. But when prayer is offered for riches, three things
should be borne in mind: First, that we must work as well as pray. If a
man prays for riches, and then folds his hands waiting for God to add
to his possessions, he does wrong. Second, when he has not properly
used what he has already in his possession, it is wrong to ask for more.
Third, temporal things are never good unless they are to be used for
good ends, for the glory of God and the advancement of his kingdom.
Riches are to be sought, and it is not improper to pray for them. But it
should be remembered, when asking for them, that they are the smallest
of the Christian treasures.

908 Is the world getting better or worse?

"The question of whether the world is getting better or worse is a
much mooted one. It is discussed from many angles, and upon it many
of our best thinkers differ. The answer must rest upon what kind of improvement is in the mind of the student of the question. Scientifically,
we know the world is moving forward by gigantic strides. When we
think of the huge drink bill, the white slave traffic, the oppression of the
helpless poor, etc., in the light of present enlightenment, perhaps in the
minds of the majority, there is a question as to whether the world is better or worse morally. It seems to me, however, that the basis upon
which God decides that question is that of relationship to him. The
question which determines eternity with the soul is what we do with Jesus Christ. If the world is being drawn into closer fellowship with the
Lord Jesus Christ, in the sight of God, we must believe it is growing
better. If not, the opposite must be true. From this viewpoint, the question cannot be settled by world conditions, but by the spiritual condition of the visible church of God. If the professing believers in Christ
are more spiritual, shining brighter, a greater power in the world and
leading souls to Christ at a greater ratio than the physical birth rate,
then, and only then, can we believe the world is growing better, as God
sees it." Our correspondent is right as to the real character of the test of

world betterment. It must be a spiritual one, not regulated by our advancement in knowledge, art and science, nor by the multitude of our inventions, but by our loving obedience to God's laws, our closer union with him through his Son, and by our application of the teachings of Jesus in our daily lives. The Gospel standard of Christian efficiency is not one of wealth or intellectuality, but of rightness with God and love for our fellow man.

909 What is the comparative value of human and divine wisdom?

The first three chapters of I Corinthians contain the argument that all human wisdom and power are valueless and insignificant as compared to the power and wisdom of God. The passage (I Cor. 3:22, 23) marks the climax of this argument, and is one of Paul's exalted flights of thought and language. He is exhorting the Christian to a right sort of pride in his splendid possessions. The possessions and powers of other men are not worth being proud of. But everything in the universe belongs in a sense to the Christian because it belongs to Christ. This does not of course mean that any man would have a right to claim the possessions of another in the name of Christ. But the Christian's riches are in Christ. Christ is the Creator and Ruler of everything, and since the Christian is the heir of Christ he has a share in all the power and wisdom and richness of God. This chapter also contains Paul's urging against divisions: followers of the various teachers formed different groups in the Corinthian Church. The apostle wanted to get their minds up above all these human matters to the infinite source of all wisdom. It is a plea for Christian unity as well as for a spiritual and heavenly, a bold and buoyant frame of mind.

910 Can we justify a devotion to religious work so close that it is maintained at the sacrifice of health?

While religious principle is of more value than health or even life itself, God does not ordinarily require a devotion so close that bodily illness will follow. A devotion which would deliberately sacrifice health would belong to the same category as the penances, flagellations and mutilations, self-inflicted by followers of other religions than the Christian. To violate the natural laws set up by God is a sin, yet even such a violation may be justifiable in cases of great emergency.

911 What do the Jews of today believe in regard to Jesus?

Many educated Jews believe thoroughly that Jesus of Nazareth lived and that he was the teacher of a high, pure and true philosophy. They reject those passages of the New Testament which claim divinity for Jesus and which narrate miracles, though many of them still accept as historic the miracles of the Old Testament.

912 If God has power to do all things, why doesn't He banish starving, or send food from the sky, as He did long ago? If God loves us and has power to do all these wonderful things, why does He let sin and evil continue?

Taking the second part of the question first, we must remember that the whole spiritual world is based on the freedom of each individual to choose between right and wrong. There would be no such thing as character if every act and choice were forced. A choice that is forced has no moral value or quality whatever. So because God wants to develop a race of beings who are really good, he leaves us free to choose right or wrong. It is terrible to imagine that God is the author of sin. He is the author of freedom, and many of the creatures to whom he has given this priceless gift and opportunity of freedom use it in making shameful choices and doing shameful deeds. We get a little light upon the first part of the question by this consideration of the second part. The whole universe seems to be in the midst of titanic agonies, struggling toward perfection. Paul declares: "The whole creation groaneth and travaileth together in pain." The mystery of pain no one can solve, except that we know that just as freedom produces character, so pain produces moral, mental and spiritual strength and purity. Man seems to be the highest point in nature, and everything in nature is subordinate to the main business of producing that race of beings who are to be really good. Starvation is simply a part of the vast woe of the universe. But to conquer starvation is not God's duty but man's. It is man's fault that some people starve. There is enough food for all, but man has devised laws and instituted customs which deprive part of the human race of the means of subsistence and give others more than they need. And it is man's duty to find a way whereby the world's bounty can be so distributed that all shall have the means of life.

913 What did Daniel Webster say about Jesus and the Bible as a real help to good citizenship?

Daniel Webster says: "If we abide by the principles taught in the Bible, our country will go on prospering and to prosper; but, if we and our posterity neglect its instructions and authority, no man can tell how sudden a catastrophe may overwhelm us and bury all our glory in profound obscurity. The Bible is the book of all others for lawyers as well as divines, and I pity the man who cannot find in it a rich supply of thought and rule of conduct. I believe Jesus Christ to be the Son of God. The miracles which he wrought establish in my mind his personal authority and render it proper for me to believe what he asserts."

914 Is it right to hold Sunday school in a hall used at other times for dancing?

It would be far better not to have the Sunday school meet in such a hall. If it were a hall to which the community looked as a center of social and civic life, and dances were only occasionally had there, the situation would not be so bad. The thought of the children about the building would be of its lectures, concerts, debates, forums, conferences, or possibly its athletic contests, or reading rooms; the dancing being only incidental would not be largely in their minds, but would be thought of in a matter-of-fact way as something which some of their elders sanctioned and others disapproved. Again, the fact that other interests centered in the hall would tend to keep even the dancing parties within the limits of decorum. But a hall used exclusively for dancing must possess an atmosphere of sensuality and irreligion that makes it entirely unsuitable as the meeting-place of a Sunday school. If the public school is available for the Sunday school sessions they ought by all means to move back to it.

915 Can there be any moral standard without a knowledge of and recognition of a supreme being?

Races that have not received the Gospel are judged according to the light they have. Missionaries tell us of heathen peoples who have a certain standard of morals and conduct, notwithstanding their ignorance of the Gospel, and all races, however unevangelized, have some knowledge or intuition of a Supreme Being whom they must obey. The Bible tells us that those not having either the law or the Gospel may be "a law unto themselves" (Rom. 2:14). We have no warrant for assuming that the heathen who died in ignorance of Christ are beyond the reach of God's mercy. In every age he has had his witnesses—good men and women who have lived clean, upright lives, even under natural law. We are not justified in holding that they are not acceptable (Acts 10:35; Rom. 4:9). You will find in Rom. 2:12-14 the passage which explains that those who have neither the law nor the Gospel "may be a law unto themselves." This obviously means that men and women who have never heard of Christ are not beyond the reach of the divine mercy, if they have lived good lives even under natural law, and have been a blessing to those around them. John Wesley wrote toward the close of his ministerial career: "He that feareth God and worketh righteousness according to the lights he has is acceptable to God." In Rom. 4:9 it is clearly stated that faith was reckoned to Abraham for righteousness. The Judge of all will not judge unjustly. For those who know the Gospel, there is the immediate responsibility to accept it, and live it in their lives.

916 With so many denominations extant, who can say which one is right?

It has been very aptly said that, while no one church or denomination has a monopoly of the truth, all have more or less of the truth. We have never believed in the attitude which denounces others simply because they do not agree with us in matters of detail. When they hold the great essentials of the Christian faith, they are Christian, irrespective of differences in creeds or ceremonies. There are doubtless many who find themselves in doubt with respect to certain Scriptural interpretations; but even this difference may not be vital. Further, many find that they receive more spiritual benefit in one church than in any other, and if that church holds the essentials, then it is the best church for such people. We sometimes hear doubts expressed as to the orthodoxy of the teachings of certain pastors; but this, after all, is a matter which soon settles itself. If any man's work is of God, it will be acknowledged by him and will stand; if otherwise, nothing under heaven can make it permanent. It may flourish for a little time, but will ultimately pass away and be forgotten.

917 What should be the attitude of Christians on the question of war?

Under the old dispensation, war was regarded as having the divine sanction when it was waged in a righteous cause. Under the Gospel, however, we are taught to love our enemies and to be on terms of friendship with all men. Yet, even in the teachings of Jesus, we are told that wars will continue to the end of the age (see Matt. 24:6; Mark 13:7). The Apocalypse is full of it. The enlightened portion of the race regards it as an evil, yet as one which is inevitable as the outcome of human conditions. Under these circumstances, it is the duty of the Christian to fight war with all his power and influence; but, being compelled to recognize its actual existence, must distinguished between wars that have justification from a human standpoint and those that have no justification. All war is bad, but some wars are far worse than others. The ideal condition for which we should work and strive is described in Isa. 2:4.

918 Does God permit evil that good may result?

That he permits evil, or removes the restraint of the Spirit from evil-doers who are flagrant and persistent, is shown by many instances in Scripture and even in modern history. If we accept as true the Scripture statement that God "maketh the wrath of man to praise him," we see no reason to doubt that he many times overrules the evil acts of men for ultimate good.

919 Has the Bible found favor among non-Christians?

This is best answered by quotations from such men as Goethe, the great German poet and writer, who wrote as follows: "It is a belief in the Bible which has served me as the guide of my moral and literary life. No criticism will be able to perplex the confidence which we have entertained of a writing whose contents have stirred up and given life to our vital energy by its own. The farther the ages advance in civilization the more will the Bible be used."

920 Can there be healing without medicine?

We have stated on a number of occasions that we believe the prayerful use of medicine to be right and Scriptural. Isaiah put a fig poultice on King Hezekiah's boils. The bacteriological theory of disease has made the use of medicine all the more reasonable. We have found that many diseases are simply attacks made upon the bodily tissues by living organisms, quite like minute animals. It is no more wrong to attack these diminutive animals with poison than it would be to attack, with club or gun, a mad dog who would threaten one's wife or child. Medicines produce a chemical reaction in the body which has curative or nutritive value; indeed, many medicines are foods, and to take them is just like regulating one's diet to meet physical conditions. Many skilful physicians are firm believers in prayer, and pray for the success of their treatment. God gives wisdom and skill to combat disease, and after we have availed ourselves of all these means we should ask his blessing upon them. When, however, we speak of persons divinely healed being sufferers from functional and not organic disease, we do not restrict divine power. We have no doubt of God's being able to heal organic disease. We believe, however, that some of the cures attributed to divine healing are really effected by other means. We can understand that if a man has all the organs of his body in a healthy condition, but some of them not performing their functions, he may be cured by a mental process. If he believes thoroughly and sincerely that God will cure him in answer to prayer, his faith will save him. It may give him an impulse which will start the sluggish organs into activity. A sudden fright will sometimes do the same thing. This is not divine healing, but it is faith healing, and it explains the cure of many of the people who think that God has healed them. There are other cases, however, which cannot be explained in that way.

921 Was there any other way possible for remission of sin except by the shedding of blood?

The thought of a sacrifice for sin underlies the whole message of the Bible. The fact that some promises do not specifically refer to this does not violate in any way the broad, general principle. The Bible as a whole states the method by which God undertakes to save people from sin. The Old Testament, in law and ceremony and prophecy, looks forward to a great sacrifice that is to be made, of which the sacrifice of animals is but a type. The Epistles of the New Testament explain how the sacrifice of Christ may be applied by faith to the human soul. The Gospels tell the story of the life of the Saviour and give with great detail and fulness the account of his sacrificial death. He himself said distinctly of his death (Matt. 26:28): "This is my blood of the new testament, which is shed for many for the remission of sins." Read with special care the 9th and 10th chapters of Hebrews, the 5th and 6th chapters of Romans, I John 1:7 and the many other passages which state clearly that salvation from sin is wrought by the sacrifice of Christ. The fact of the atonement underlies all the promises of Scripture. It seems idle, as well as dangerous, to speculate whether there may be or might have been some other way of salvation. This way fits in with our knowledge of nature and of life, and has been testified to by multitudes of redeemed souls. We *know* that through the blood of Christ salvation from sin can be found; we certainly do not know that it can be found in any other way.

922 Does not Isaiah 58 teach the duty, not since abrogated, of observing the seventh day as the Sabbath?

To our mind the chapter seems to teach exactly opposite. It was a reproof to the formalists who were more careful about the letter than the spirit. The fasts and observances on which they prided themselves were an offense to God while they were not fulfilling the law in the spirit. It was righteousness and deeds of kindness and mercy that God required of his people, not the minute literal observances which were easy to render. The command to observe the seventh day has not been repealed so far as we know, nor has the command to observe the Passover, nor the law of circumcision. We keep the spirit of the command in consecrating a seventh portion of our time and at the same time we celebrate the resurrection of Christ which to us is a much more important reason for holding a day sacred than the reason given in Ex. 20 for observing the seventh day. The very question of longitude precludes the possibility of uniform observance. If you travel westward around the world and observe the natural days, you would find yourself at the end of the first voyage observing Saturday as Sunday and at the end of the second voyage observing Friday, and so on unless you dropped a day in each instance to bring yourself in line with the rest of the world. The people who think they are pleasing God by going back to the seventh day observance make the mistake of conceiving of him as having a mind as small as the human mind, which is far too apt to attach importance to trivialities.

923 Can an individual unknowingly be a hypocrite?

There is in the essential meaning of the word "hypocrite" the idea of deceit, of making an effort to mislead others about one's character. This can only be done consciously. So in this sense there can be no such thing as an unconscious hypocrite. But there is a practical danger, namely the danger of unconscious inconsistencies between one's character and one's profession. The true Christian should always strive eagerly to make his conduct tally with his profession. He must make no compromises with his conscience. He must not only insist upon conquering, by divine grace, the inconsistencies he is aware of, but he must try to discover these "unconscious inconsistencies," these things in his life which appear wrong to others or may have a hurtful influence, and gain their eradication also.

924 What chance is there for true and lasting church union?

In the study of the religious conditions of the present time it is very disappointing to find so much lack of sympathy for each other's views among Christian people of the different sects. It is not as acute as in former years, but too much of it exists for the upbuilding of the Christian life in the community. However, to lament because all bodies of Christians are not of one mind in all things, and do not all have one form of worship and one denomination, is illogical under present conditions. The church is steadily drawing closer together. There is a growing disposition to meet on common ground and make common cause in many branches of Christian work; yet it may be a long time before denominational distinctions are surrendered and all are merged in one flock with one Shepherd, as we have the divine assurance will ultimately be the case. There have been distinctions ever since apostolic times (see I Cor. 1:12; also I Cor. 12); still the church has grown amazingly; the little group of 120 mentioned in Acts 1:15 has become a vast army of 564,000,000. In this mighty host there are many battalions, each with its own distinctive insignia and history, many of them of glorious memory. Yet all serve under one Commander, the great Captain of Salvation, and all march under the banner of the Cross. Jealousy there has been, and there has been also much of that emulation in well-doing which was the characteristic of the early churches; but the march of the army as a whole has been steadily onward, always keeping in view the ultimate goal. This is a time when the church needs to be helped rather than criticized. It may be that it needs new trials and sufferings to prepare it for the new Pentecost for which the whole Christian world is earnestly praying and watching.

TEXTS FAMILIAR AND OTHER

925 Can there be true forgiveness without confession?

If the wrong was done to some particular person or persons, God's forgiveness cannot be claimed until the wrong has been confessed to the person or persons concerned, if they can be found, and until it has been, so far as possible, made right. Many sins are between the soul and God alone, and these sins it is not necessary to confess to any one but God. Many Christians lose their peace by taking the attitude of unwillingness to confess, when they are probably under no obligation to confess. What robs them of their peace is not their failure to confess, but their refusal to say to God that they will do anything he wants them to do. Do not be afraid of God. He will not hurt you; he will not ask you to do anything grotesque or unreasonable. Tell him you will confess as and when he wishes. Then search the past, with the Holy Spirit's help, and see if there are any people to whom you should confess personal wrongs or with whom you should make certain matters straight. God will give you grace and courage to make the confession and restitution frankly and fully. But remember we are saved not by confession nor restitution, nor even repentance, *but by faith in Christ.*

926 Are all the Christian virtues or characteristics fruits and gifts of the Holy Spirit?

James writes (James 1:17): "Every good gift and every perfect gift is from above." That is, among others, all the Christian graces or characteristics are direct gifts of the Holy Spirit, and then they are the fruits or results of these gifts. The Holy Spirit implants them and then develops them to stronger and higher degrees. It has been the experience of multitudes that after trying in vain to secure such soul qualities as love, joy, peace, gentleness, meekness, patience, they have received these gifts directly through the blessing of the Holy Spirit. It is also true, however, that many people who are not professed Christians, indeed, some in pagan lands, have seemed to attain many of the graces of Christianity, such as meekness, gentleness, humility, kindness, self-control. It is impossible to explain all the subtle workings of the Holy Spirit, who, as Jesus said, is like the wind, of which we hear the sound, but cannot tell whence it comes nor where it goes. But knowing the Gospel and its results, it is our duty to persuade others to attain heavenly character by receiving the Holy Spirit, and, for ourselves, to give the Spirit right of way in our souls as he strives to make us more and more like Christ.

927 Where was Jesus "delivered unto the Gentiles to be mocked and spitefully treated"?

The passage in Luke 18:32, 33 was absolutely fulfilled. The Jews arraigned Jesus before Pilate, the Roman governor, and he was delivered over to the Roman soldiers and taken by them to Calvary. It was Roman soldiers who carried out Pilate's sentence by crucifying Christ, Roman soldiers who parted his garments among them, who kept guard by the cross and who pierced his side, and they did not leave until their duty was fully accomplished (see Matt. 27:27 and 54; Luke 23:47 and rest of the chapter; John 19:23, 32, 33, 34).

928 If "everyone that asketh receiveth," according to Matthew 7:3, how does God act when two or more Christians ask for the same object?

There are cases in which it would be clearly impossible for each of two Christians to get the same object, for which both might pray. A certain position might be vacant, and two Christian men might each pray to secure it; or a prize might be offered and each of two Christian students might pray to receive it. Or, as indeed has not infrequently happened, two good men might each love the same woman and each pray for success in winning her. In any such case God cannot answer the prayer of one without depriving the other of the gift. These are all amplifications of the same general principle which the Lord illustrated in the case of Paul and his "thorn in the flesh" (II Cor. 12:7). Paul's prayer was answered, but not in the way he wished for. He asked for relief from the thorn; he received instead the promise of superabounding grace. So in every case in which God must refuse the literal answer to a prayer, he will, if the soul is submissive and trustful, make up for the disappointment by bestowing direct and personal blessing, and not infrequently even a better material gift than the one requested. Again, in the case of two Christians praying for the same object, it is probable that only one could have prevailing faith. All the Scripture teaching about prayer must be massed together in studying any phase of it. We are to ask "according to his will" and "in faith." God would not give to two of his children the assurance that each was to receive a certain single object, nor would both of them reach the plane of prevailing faith. This was the message of the paragraph quoted. It was a warning against selfish praying. When we pray for an object we should stop to ask ourselves whether or not our receiving the gift means that it must be taken away from some one else.

929 In what sense did Paul fear that he might become a castaway?

In the well-known passage in I Cor. 9:27 Paul implies that if he, with all his labors for others, still needs to apply self-denying watchfulness and strenuous effort, and might still fall short of the special reward for which he strove, how much more should the Corinthians, who were going recklessly to the extreme of Christian liberty, apply the lesson to their own lives? It is to be noted that the Revised Version, instead of using the word "castaway," adopts the preferable translation "rejected," *i.e.*, a loser in the special contest for the reward of those who "turn many to righteousness."

930 Has the prophecy in Ezekiel 4:3 of a city besieged by a wall of iron ever been fulfilled?

It was not a prophecy at all, but a picture sermon. The situation was this: A number of Jewish exiles in Babylon were naturally concerned about what was happening at home in Jerusalem. There were no newspapers, and they went to Ezekiel's house to learn what he thought. He was a man of eminence and piety. Some of the exiles did not believe that Jehovah would allow the city and temple to be hurt; others thought that nothing could resist the Assyrian armies. Ezekiel believed that the city would be destroyed. To impress the conviction upon them, he made a clay model of the city and set up an iron wall before it. Perhaps he talked to them, too, but the symbol would tell the story whether he did so or not. As you know, Jerusalem was taken and the temple burned.

931 What is the meaning of the statement that Christ was "made perfect" by his sufferings (Hebrews 2:10)?

There can be no doubt of Christ being perfect. His life in the flesh proved that. But in order that he might be specially prepared for the work he is now doing, as the Head of his Church, the High Priest of his people, he had to undergo temptation and suffering, that he might be able to help the tempted and comfort the sufferer. What they bear, what their struggles are, he could learn only from experience. That he did learn, that he bore all so nobly, was a proof of his being perfect. The man who has encountered temptation and has triumphed belongs to a higher order than the innocent man who has never been tested. His holiness has been proved by his trial. The physician who knows how to treat yellow fever is better able to deal with the disease after he has passed through an epidemic of it than he was before he put his theories to a practical test.

932 What is the meaning of the phrase "offense of the cross"?

By the "offense of the cross" (Gal. 5:11) Paul means the contempt and antagonism felt by both Jews and Greeks toward the idea of being saved by the death of Jesus. The Jews thought they would be saved by keeping the law; the Greeks hoped to be saved by seeking wisdom. But Paul insisted that we are saved, not by keeping the law nor by being wise, but by believing that Jesus Christ died for us (see I Cor. 1:18-24). It is hard for us in these days to understand precisely the controversy Paul was having with the Jews and the way they felt toward him. They looked upon him as a bad man. That was the reproach that he had to bear. They felt that to be "good" one had to be circumcised and to keep the ceremonial law of Moses. Paul said that was not the way to be good. He said it was not necessary to be circumcised or to keep the ceremonial law. The Galatians to whom he writes in the passage mentioned had accepted this teaching of his, but had been influenced to return, to some extent at least, to the bondage of the Jewish law. Paul sternly rebukes them for this. They have been refusing to bear the "offense" of the cross; they were refusing to state and live the testimony that they were saved not by any effort of their own but by the fact that Christ died for them. The "offense" of the cross also means the self-sacrifice, the humility, the brave service for others which are included in the self-abandonment which the soul must make at the cross of Jesus.

933 What is the "faith verse"?

What is known as the "faith verse" (Heb. 11:1) is a description of faith in its widest sense, not restricted to faith in the Gospel alone. "The substance of things hoped for" is interpreted to mean that faith gives substance to God's promises by enabling us to take hold of them with absolute confidence, and making them present realities to us, although yet unfulfilled. By the assent of faith, we already enter into the enjoyment, in a spiritual sense, of those things that are promised; or, as one expositor has expressed it, "through faith, the future object of Christian hope in its beginning is already substantiated." By faith we are sure of eternal things that they *are*, and by hope we are confident that we shall *have* them. The clause, "the evidence of things not seen," refers to the soul vision that enables us to see what the eye itself cannot perceive." Calvin wrote on this subject: "What should we do if we had not faith and hope to lean on, and if our minds did not emerge amidst the darkness, above the world, by the shining of the Word and Spirit of God?"

934 What was the "host of heaven" which the children of Israel worshiped?

In Acts 7:41, 42 Stephen was describing the idolatries of the Israelites which had driven them into the wilderness as a punishment, where they were abandoned to the worship of the "heavenly bodies"—the stars. During their long stay in Egypt they had become accustomed to the idols of that land and the golden calf was one of these. Possibly Apis, or

Mnevis, was the Egyptian model of the calf they set up in the desert. They had also learned the worship of Moloch and Remphan, heathen deities representing the divine powers ascribed to nature.

935 To whom does Paul refer by the title, "James, the Lord's brother"?

There has been a bitter dispute as to this passage in Gal. 1:19 and as to the identity of this James and indeed as to whether Christ had a brother at all. Scholars, however, outside the Roman Catholic Church, are now generally of the opinion that this James was a son of Joseph and Mary; that he did not believe in Christ until after the resurrection; that he was a man greatly respected by the Jews on account of his blameless life, until he became a Christian; that he became the bishop of Jerusalem, and was president of the council mentioned in Acts 15:13 and was the author of the Epistle of James.

936 What is the meaning of the phrase "the testimony of Jesus"?

The term "the testimony of Jesus" (in Rev. 19:10) means, as it is used frequently in the Revelation, the testimony of the Christian *to* Jesus or *about* Jesus. It is his "witness" for Jesus, his statement as to who and what Jesus is and what he has done for his own soul. All Christians should certainly have this testimony. They should be able to state, humbly, firmly, simply, frankly, what Christ has done for them and what he means to them. In the New Testament it means chiefly this speaking for Jesus or giving Christian exhortation or instruction under the inspiration of the Holy Spirit.

937 What is meant when Isaiah said that God would shave with a razor that is hired (Isa. 7:20)?

The passage is its own explanation. It is that God would use Assyria to chastise and punish his people. The loss of the beard among the Jews was considered an indignity and a disgrace. Evil was to come upon them, and Assyria would be the instrument in God's hand of inflicting it. The Assyrians were not his servants, and did not know that in attacking Israel they were doing God's will. They were hired, in the sense that they received compensation in plunder, not as God's children obeying him, but as strangers who were hired and paid for performing a special task.

938 What is meant by Noah being "perfect in his generation"?

The passage in Gen. 6:9 means that Noah, as living by faith, was just and perfect; *i.e.*, sincere in his desire to do God's will (Gal. 3:2, Heb. 11:7). In a world teeming with wickedness, and amid universal depravity, he had stood alone, exercising faith in the testimony of God and condemning the sins of men to which his own virtuous life offered a remarkable contrast.

939 How is the statement that God did not command sacrifice (Jer. 7:22) to be reconciled with the elaborate legislation of Leviticus?

The apparent discrepancy is due to the Hebrew idiom in which the negative has the effect that the comparative has with us. To render the passage in Jeremiah freely, we might say: It was not of sacrifice and burnt offering that God spoke when he brought the people out of Egypt, but of something much more important, namely, righteousness and obedience. By some it has been doubted whether God ever did command sacrifice, or only regulated a practise in existence from the earliest times. The peculiar phraseology of the first verses of Leviticus gives color to that theory. "If any man of you bring an offering," is a different way of introducing legislation to that of the Decalogue.

940 What is the meaning of, "We know that to them that love God all things work together for good, even to them who are called"?

The passage in Rom. 8:28 in the original is more striking: "We know that to them that love God all things work together for good, even to them who are called," etc. This is an assurance that, whatever may come to us, he will cover us with his loving providence and will not suffer his beneficent purpose in our behalf to be turned aside, if we fully trust him.

941 Is it possible to live as perfect a life as Adam did before he fell?

We know so little about Adam's life that it is difficult to answer the question categorically. The circumstances of our lives are so different from those described as existing in the garden of Eden, that they do not admit of comparison. Our inherited proclivities would make it more difficult for us than for Adam to live a perfect life. Theoretically it is, of course, possible to live without sinning, but as a matter of experience we know that no one attains that ideal. Some come nearer to it than others, being of a more spiritual nature, or by being kept more rigidly from temptation, or in having the help of the Holy Spirit in larger degree than others. Absolute sinlessness is the Bible ideal to which we are repeatedly exhorted to aim.

**942 What is meant by Jacob's prophecy, "The sceptre shall
not depart from Judah nor a lawgiver from between his feet"?**

The passage in Gen. 49:10 is one which has ever been regarded by Christians and by the Jews themselves as indicating the Messiah. In ancient Egyptian monuments of important personages the position of the secretary or scribe who records the prince's or ruler's decrees or laws is a kneeling one, almost literally "between his feet." The Targum renders the passage thus: "One having the principality shall not be taken from the house of Judah, nor a scribe from his children's children, until the Messiah come whose the kingdom is." Still another version from the same source is: "Kings shall not fail from the house of Judah, nor skilful doctors of the law from his children's children, until the time when the King's Messiah shall come." The allusion to Judah is interpreted to refer to the primacy of that tribe in war, which was to continue until the promised land was conquered and the ark of the covenant deposited at Shiloh. Some of the ablest expositors point out that the descent of our Lord from Judah is not conveyed in the words "from between his feet," hence the question of lineage is not involved.

**943 Who is the "King of the South"
referred to in Daniel 11?**

The "king of the south" (literally, "king of midday") was Ptolemy Soter (of Egypt), the son of Lagus, who took the title of king, although his father was merely a governor. In Dan. 12:1 "at that time" is interpreted as referring to the time of Antichrist, and the great persecutions that were to precede the final deliverance. Like many other prophecies, however, this one has the double vision, the first having reference to the time of Antiochus, the persecutor of the Jews, and the second or further interpretation relating to the last persecutions which are to precede the final deliverance of Israel.

**944 What is the meaning of Paul's statement
that nothing is unclean of itself?**

Paul was sweeping away all the dietary and ceremonial laws of the Jewish code. They were so much rubbish from his standpoint. At the same time, he did not wish to hurt any one's prejudices. If a man had honestly and sincerely come to the conclusion that a certain practise was sinful, and yet indulged in it, he would be committing sin, because he would be doing what he believed to be wrong. The practise might not be really sinful, but it would be sinful for him, because it was a violation of his conscience. The Talmud gives a case in point. If a Jew in traveling lost count of the days of the week and was found working on the Sabbath, he was blameless; but if knowing it was the Sabbath he was working, he would deserve to be stoned.

945 What is the meaning of, "If any man's work shall be burned, he shall suffer loss but he himself shall be saved yet so as by fire"?

There has been much discussion concerning the passage in I Cor. 3:15. Dean Alford gives the sense as "if any teacher's work consist of such materials as the fire will destroy," loss will be suffered, and he adds that the meaning is as though the structure reared by a builder (not the foundation) is consumed by the fire, yet he escapes, but with the loss of his work; or as Bengel puts it, as a shipwrecked merchant, though he loses his merchandise, is saved though having to pass through the waves. It is really a crucial test of the value of the man's work; all those parts that will not stand the ordeal of burning investigation will perish, although the man himself may be saved, salvation being a free gift and not a reward. These perishable portions may be interpreted as doctrines that are valueless in themselves and which have been superadded to the essentials. They are frail handiwork and cannot stand the fierce heat of the furnace of trial. Thus it follows that there are some who, stripped at the last of all their assumption of personal merit, will stand naked before God and yet receive the precious gift of his clemency.

946 Who was the poet to whose writings Paul referred in his speech at Athens?

The poet to whom Paul referred in his speech at Athens (Acts 17:28) when he made the quotation, "For we are also his offspring," is believed by some commentators to have been Aratus, who had the same sentiment expressed almost identically in an astronomical poem entitled *Phenomena*. Others claim to have discovered the source of the quotation in different writers, among them Cleanthes and Pindar. The real source is uncertain, and it is quite probable that Paul spoke from general recollection, rather than in the precise language of any particular author.

947 What is meant by someone leaving "the first love"?

These words were addressed to the Christian believers at Ephesus. The "first love" does not refer to any person or influence other than Christ, but simply means that the Ephesians had lost the intensity of their affection and zeal for Christ. The Ephesian Church had had special opportunities and blessing. Under Paul's ministrations its members had received the gift of the Holy Spirit (Acts 19:1-6); the apostle had resided with them for three years (Acts 20:31); he had later written to them what is perhaps his most spiritually exalted epistle. Their experience of love for Christ had been warm and keen. In his message sent them through John the Master is reproving them for having allowed their love for him to grow weak and cold.

948 What is meant by Paul when he speaks of Jesus "being made better than the angels"?

The passage in Heb. 1:4 means that the Son, through his exaltation to the majesty of God, had attained to complete dominion over the world, and was thus, in both power and dignity, greater than the angels. In the second chapter Paul is dealing with the significance of the redemptive message, and all the circumstances connected with it. The Hebrews to whom he was appealing doubted whether Jesus, who was crucified, was really their Messiah, and he addresses himself to dispelling this doubt. In Heb. 2:9, he shows that Jesus, for a short time in his humanity, was subordinated to the angels ("in all things as we are") (see verse 7); but with the completion of his sufferings and death, he is again crowned with exaltation in honor and glory. It was only by his voluntary humiliation that he could become the Mediator of salvation.

949 What is the meaning of the greeting, "Peace be with this house"?

The greeting in Luke 10:5 was the ancient form of salutation in the East and prevails unto this day. "But from the lips of Christ and his messengers," writes a commentator, "it meant something far higher, both in the gift and the giving of it, than the current greeting." It meant the spiritual peace which is the gift of God through Jesus Christ. There are many homes in our own land to-day in which such a salutation from the lips of Christian friends would not be regarded as out of place but would be welcomed.

950 What is meant by the Jews having a "veil over their hearts"?

The passage in II Cor. 3:14 means that the Jews have a veil upon their hearts, because they have allowed their allegiance to the old dispensation to keep them from believing Christ. It is he who brings light. The Jews let the old ceremonial law remain as a veil between themselves and the light of God which is in Christ.

951 What is the meaning of, "Whosoever shall keep the whole law and yet offend in one point he is guilty of all"?

This passage in James 2:10 is on the principle (maintained by the Jewish rabbis) that the law is one seamless garment and if you rend a part you destroy the integrity and perfection of the whole. It is as though one discord spoiled an entire harmony, one broken link ruined the chain. The law is a whole, and by breaking any part you break its *wholeness*, though you may not have broken the whole law. God requires perfect, not partial, obedience, and we are not to choose parts of the law to keep and parts that we may break.

**952 What is meant by being "caught up
to the third heaven"?**

The passage "caught up to the third heaven" in II Cor. 12:2 has been variously interpreted. Some say that the birds live in the first heaven, the clouds are in the second, and the third is the home of the soul. Others claim that childhood is the first heaven, the church the second, and the third is the home of the soul. According to the ancient writers, there were several degrees of spiritual elevation, these being revealed in visions. The "first heaven" (the first of these degrees) was that of the clouds and the air, the "second" that of the stars and sky, and the "third" was above both of these, where God's glory continually shines (see Eph. 4:10). Paul was familiar with the learning of his age, and was a "master" in literary expression. He sat as a pupil "at the feet of Gamaliel," who was celebrated in the Talmudist writings as one of the seven teachers to whom the title "rabbin" was given. In II Cor. 12 (which contains the passage in question) Paul speaks of his vision when he was "caught up to the third heaven." In the Jewish teaching of the time, the first heaven was that of the clouds or the air; the second that of the stars and the sky, and the third the spiritual heaven, the seat of divine glory. The word "heavens" is used in the Bible in varying senses, which must be gathered from the context, the most familiar being the visible heavens, as distinguished from the earth and as a part of the whole creation (see Gen. 1:1). Paul's "third heaven" was thus higher than the aerial or stellar world, and cognizable not by the eye, but by the mind alone. The word "world" is generally used in Scripture in the purely material sense to refer to the habitable earth and its people. The passages in Heb. 4:3; 9:26; 9:5; 11:7; 11:38, etc., have this material significance. In John 14:2, however, many interpreters recognize an implied recognition of other worlds, the whole universe being a "house of many mansions."

**953 What does John mean by the statement that the
world could not contain the books necessary to
report all Jesus said and did?**

The words in John 21:25 were probably written when the writer was overwhelmed at the thought of how much there had been in those three wonderful years that had never been written, and never could be written. He may, too, have had the idea that there were some things which the world could not appreciate or understand if they were written. The word "contain" may have been used in that sense.

**954 What is meant by the statement in
I Corinthians 7:13-15 about wives being
sanctified by husbands?**

This was Paul's answer to certain Corinthian Christians, who wanted to know whether they should continue living with pagan partners. If the pagan wife or husband refused to live with the Christian husband or wife, Paul said they were not to be hindered but allowed to go. But where the pagan was willing to stay, the Christian was not to move against them. The Corinthian Church seemed to fear that the Christian might be drawn back into heathenism by the heathen wife or husband. Paul does not fear that, and he thinks, on the contrary, that the Christian, having divine help, would be the stronger, and would sanctify or save the pagan partner.

955 What does Paul mean by saying that a woman ought to have power on her head because of angels (I Corinthians 11:10)?

By the abstract word, *exousia*—power—Paul plainly designates the hood covering her head. With this view the marginal reading accords: "A covering in sign that she is under the power of her husband." It is even possible that the Greek word was the name of the hood, as the Latin word *imperium*, of the same meaning, was at one time the name for a woman's headdress. As to "angels," they are doubtless often present at the worship of the church below. See I Tim. 5:21: "I charge thee . . . before the elect angels"; and I Cor. 4:9, we are "a spectacle to angels and to men." Bengel says that "as angels veil their faces before God, so would they require that the female face should veil before man." It was in accordance with Jewish and Roman custom that women's heads be covered in worship. The uncovered female head in Paul's day expressed the moving of woman from her sphere and assimilated her to the disreputable class. Of course, at the present day, the apostle would not consider the hood as possessing any religious significance. Women now can sit or stand before men with heads uncovered, either in social circles or large assemblies, with no violation of womanly modesty.

956 What is meant by being "ready always to give an answer to every man that asketh you a reason of the hope that is in you"?

This passage in I Pet. 3:15 is one of encouragement to the sincere but timid Christian. Fearing God, and having nothing else to fear, we should not be afraid to honor him whenever the occasion serves, by confessing him before men and by giving a testimony to the saving power of the Redeemer and the assurance of immortality. It means that we should run up the flag whenever occasion demands. This is a holy duty and one need not be afraid nor even agitated in revealing what is in the heart—in showing "the reason of the hope" that is in us in order that others may know that we are Christ's followers.

957 What is the beast that was and is not, yet is?

This passage from Rev. 17:8 has been the subject of much discussion. The language of Revelation throughout is mystical and figurative. The time when the beast "is not" is the time when it has the "deadly wound"—a time when the seventh head became Christian externally, while the beastlike character was only temporarily suspended. Enough books to make a fair-sized library have been written on Revelation, many of them with special reference to the "beast," which typifies the Antichristian world power which, after a period of quiescence, returns worse than ever. Its semblance of Christianity is spurious and is quickly followed by open anti-Christianity. Some have held that the mark of the beast was the brand of the ivy leaf with which Antiochus Epiphanes branded the Jews; others interpret it as the sign of popery and point out that the Greek letters of the word "*Lateinos*" contain the mystical number 666. Still others believe that the mark or sign was that of Balaam, the false prophet. Again, there are not a few who hold that the "ark" may not be a visible one, but something symbolical of allegiance.

958 Who were the Epicureans and Stoics whom Paul encountered?

Epicureans followed the teachings of Epicurus (342-270 B.C.), a Greek philosopher. They relied on sense experiences for knowledge, rather than on reason, and were concerned with natural evidences—with the amount of pleasure or pain in life. They were not devoted to sensual pleasures and luxury, as is commonly thought.

The Stoics were also philosophers. The Greek Stoics were solely concerned with the origin of natural things and natural laws. The good life, they said, was controlled by reason, not emotion. Later Roman Stoics were also concerned with ethical and political matters. In general, stoicism refers to indifference to external circumstances.

959 What is meant by Paul's injunction to "speak evil of no man"?

It is the duty of the Christian to repress in himself and to discourage in others the tendency to unduly criticise other people. Indeed, we are expressly commanded to "speak evil of no man" (Tit. 3:2; James 4:11). This of course applies equally to both sexes. The universal proneness to gossip, to "running down," or "knocking," is one of the evils of our time. It may arise from thoughtlessness, but it is prompted by a bad spirit. There are legitimate occasions when reproof may be necessary. The pastor who would hesitate to administer a judicious rebuke at a fitting opportunity would be neglecting his duty, and there are times when any good man or woman may have the duty to perform of speaking "a word in season," in reprobation of evil conduct. Even in such cases, we should act with moderation and judgment, aiming rather to convince than to irritate. But ill-natured, envious, disparaging talk, judging others unheard, shows an un-Christian spirit and is unworthy of one who professes to serve him who hates the sin, but loves the sinner. Wholly apart from its inconsistence with the Christian profession, there is something radically wrong with the mind and heart of the man or woman who persistently indulges in ill-bred, uncharitable and injurious remarks about other people.

960 What is the meaning of "scarlet" and "red like crimson" in the well-known passage in Isaiah 1:18?

"Though your sins be as scarlet they shall be white as snow; though they be red like crimson, they shall be as wool," said the Lord through his prophet. Why these colors, and not for instance black? These terms are used because red is such a vivid color, making such deep stains. Smith's Bible dictionary states: "The only fundamental color of which the Hebrews appear to have had a clear conception was red." An other authority states: Certain scarlet cloth is first dyed in the grain and then dyed in the piece; it is thus double-dyed. In contrast with this our souls are to be washed *white*, like the "undyed wool," and even like the snow. The contrast is between a deep stain and purity.

961 What is meant by, "And it repenteth the Lord that He had made man on the earth and it grieved him at his heart"?

Gen. 6:6 is a passage which has puzzled many Bible students. God cannot change (see Num. 23:19; I Sam. 15:29; Mal. 3:6; James 1:17); nor can he be affected by sorrow or other feelings common to humanity, but it was necessary on the part of the inspired writers to use terms comprehensible to the minds of men; hence he is described as "repenting" and "being grieved." Commentators here explain that the only adequate interpretation of the passage would be that the Creator was about "to show himself a God of judgment, by employing the power and agencies of the system in which they had been placed as the instruments of their punishment." They had "filled up the measure of their iniquities," and now the divine justice which his law had provided for such contingency was to go into operation. They had brought their punishment on their own heads by their persistent violation of the laws he had laid down for the government of the world—a judicial system which was self-operative and from which there could be no escape save through divine grace, granted in answer to sincere repentance. From the beginning, the wages of sin has been death. The passage in Acts 15:18, in stating God's foreknowledge, in no wise conflicts with this view. His fixed laws are beneficent to the obedient, but stern and inflexible to the unrepentant sinner.

962 What is meant by the psalmist's plea, "Bring my soul out of prison"?

In Ps. 142:7 the phrase, "Bring my soul out of prison," is held by commentators to refer to the prison house of trouble and affliction (see Ps. 143:11). There are several passages in the Psalms in which the same figure of speech is employed.

963 What is meant by the statement, "Sin lieth at thy door"?

Gen. 4:7 was a favorite text with Spurgeon, "Sin lieth at thy door." Cain's sin began as all other sins begin, with disobedience to God. Some people will tell you that "it does not matter how you worship God as long as you are sincere"; but there are right worship and wrong worship and only the right, given in the right spirit, is acceptable. Cain saw that Abel's perfect obedience was accepted, and he was angry and jealous. God is not unjust. Sin does not come upon a man unawares; there is a sentinel to warn of its approach. If it be indulged at the first advances and if the warnings be unheeded, serious danger follows. If, knowing the right, Cain sinned in the face of such knowledge, the sin would lie at his door, *i.e.*, he would be held accountable for it.

964 What is meant by the passage that says the Lord sought to kill Moses?

The passage in Ex. 4:24 is obscure. The Lord could kill Moses if he wished, but we infer that Moses was stricken down with sudden illness and was in danger of death. He and his wife appear to have thought that it was a judgment on them for deferring in the case of one of their sons the rite by which the boy was initiated into the Hebrew nation. Moses had, we imagine, postponed it at his wife's request. Her conduct seems to imply blame of him for yielding to her wish.

965 How can we reconcile the statement that Asa hated God with the explicit statement in another book that Asa's heart was perfect with the Lord all his days?

The latter statement in I Kings 15:14 is not explicit. You must remember that Asa had already been reproved for taking matters in his own hand and showing distrust of God (see II Chron. 16:7-10), and had been very angry with the prophet who reproved him, putting him in prison and punishing others who apparently were of the same mind as the prophet. He repeated his fault in his sickness, and perhaps if we knew the kind of physicians he consulted we should understand why God was so angry with him. As the prophet told him in the first instance, he, of all men, had reason to look to God in an emergency, as God had come to his rescue in a sore strait. The temper the king showed under reproof justifies the statement that he hated God, though in his earlier years he had done some very good things. The writers of Chronicles and Kings were doubtless grateful to him for these things, and in courtly fashion praised him for the good he had done, and overlooked the evil.

966 What does the psalmist mean by "presumptuous sins"?

Presumption, as used in Ps. 19:13, when having reference to conduct or moral action, implies arrogance or irreverence. When it relates to religion in general, it means a bold and daring confidence in God's goodness, without obedience to his opposition to the warnings of conscience, and with the delusive idea that they can be repented of afterward, when God will surely pardon them. Among presumptuous sins may be enumerated these: to profess religion without principle; to ask God's blessing and yet go on in sinful living; to search out and run into temptation; to be self-confident and complacent concerning one's spiritual condition, though no effort has been made to set the heart right with God, and to arraign the goodness and justice of the Almighty, instead of finding in our own sinful hearts the cause of our misfortunes. Persistent drunkenness, profanity, Sabbath-breaking and licentiousness are properly classed as presumptuous sins, when the sinner is one who knows the law and wilfully violates it, excusing his offense on the ground that God is too good and kind to punish such doings on the part of his mortal children.

967 What are symbolical expressions?

There are many expressions in Scripture that are figurative or symbolical, and which are not to be interpreted literally. Again, there are passages relating to the spiritual world which, in order to be comprehensible to our minds, must be expressed in human terms. The passage in Rev. 7:17 belongs to this class, and conveys to our minds in the only terms we can understand that there will be neither sorrow nor tears in heaven. See I Cor. 15:41-45, in which Paul tells of the natural and the spiritual body—the latter not conformed to the lower and animal life, but to the higher and spiritual life. Flesh and blood (verse 50) cannot inherit the kingdom. The passage in Revelation simply means that all the old earth sorrows and persecutions, the thirst, the heat, the hunger, cannot enter that heavenly realm.

968 If God is omniscient, why did he say to Abraham, "For now I know that thou fearest God"?

This statement in Gen. 22:12 may be taken merely as the announcement that Abraham had stood God's test. The old problem of foreknowledge is an extremely difficult one, and discussion about it is usually fruitless. But we know that such an experience as this that Abraham had gone through is like the testing or proving of any instrument. It demonstrates what it is made of and how strongly and well it is made. God in this case speaks of the test as if it had been his own experiment. He proved Abraham and found him sound.

969 What is meant by the reference in Revelation to Babylon, seeing that the city of that name is now only a heap of ruins?

In Rev. 18 there is a detailed account of the fall and desolation of the mystic Babylon. Some writers on prophecy believe that when the ten kingdoms of the ancient Roman Empire become confederated in the last years of this dispensation, a federal city will be needed, and then Babylon will be rebuilt and will be destroyed as described in the chapter referred to. Other expositors, however, identify Babylon with papal Rome. The Romish ritual contains many striking resemblances to the heathen rites of ancient Babylon, which is a fact cited in confirmation of the theory. Similar denunciations to those in Rev. 18 will be found in Isa. 13, 21, and other places, where they apply to the literal Babylon of the Captivity.

970 What is meant by, "laying aside every weight" (Hebrews 12:1)?

The allusion is to the races and athletic contests of the Olympian games. He is trying to stimulate Christians to strive after the higher attainments of the Christian faith. Every believer has some special and peculiar hindrance to his progress. When he is saved by faith in Christ, he should endeavor to reach perfection. If his mind is set on wealth, or if there is some indulgence which he is fond of, which divides his attention and prevents him concentrating his energies on higher spiritual attainments, he should lay it aside. It may not be sinful, but if it is a hindrance, it should be given up by one who is striving to rise. Though it be harmless, it may be a weight which must not be carried by one who is running the heavenly race.

971 What is meant by "the just living by faith" (Romans 1:17)?

The apostle is quoting Hab. 2:4, in which the prophet points out that even in the approaching calamities, the righteous people would be supported by their confidence in God. The apostle, quoting the passage in Romans, shows that faith is not a new principle of life, as it was prominent in the Old Testament. Beyond the fact of faith being the channel by which men enter into life, it persists all through the Christian's career. If the Christian lost his faith, his means of maintaining his spiritual life would be cut off. There are many Christians so worried and harassed that they would succumb if they were not sustained by their faith in him who is invisible.

**972 What does Paul mean by speaking of delivering
certain people to Satan (I Timothy 1:20)?**

It appears that the apostles possessed some mysterious power, unknown to us, of disciplining unworthy members of the church. There is
a still more circumstantial reference to this power in I Cor. 5:5. It appears to have included, in addition to excommunication, some form of
physical suffering which it was hoped would operate as a discipline to
bring them to repentance. This suffering the apostle attributes to Satan,
as he did his own affliction of the thorn in the flesh which he says (II
Cor. 12:7) was a messenger from Satan to buffet him.

**973 What is meant by the question, "Is there no balm
in Gilead" (Jeremiah 8:22)?**

The *balm* or *balsam* is a common name used for many oily and resi-
nous substances flowing from certain trees or shrubs and used in medicine and surgery. Gilead (Num. 32:39) was famous for its balm, which
was of the species called *opobalsamum*. This particular balm is mentioned by Pliny, Strabo, Tacitus and other famous historians, as being
found in that part of Judea alone. Josephus says the trees or shrubs
were originally brought by the Queen of Sheba to Solomon. It is believed, however, that the *balsam* or true balm of Gilead has long disappeared, although there are still trees belonging to the same class. The
gum of the balm tree of Gilead was very precious, especially for healing
wounds, hence the expression applied by Jeremiah (8:22): "Is there no
balm in Gilead, is there no physician there?"

**974 What is the difference between calling a man blessed
who has committed no wrong and one who,
having committed many, has repented?**

There is no conflict between the "blessed" of Ps. 1:1 and the "blessed"
of Ps. 32:1. Blessed means happy, a mental state of contentment and
joy, a condition of comfort and safety upon which a man is to be con-
gratulated. Now both these classes of men are in this state—both the
man who either as his life habit or at any particular crisis or instance
has done no wrong, or the man who has done wrong and is pardoned.

975 What is the "divine right" of kings?

Belief in the divine right of kings is largely the result of Old Testament interpretations, though it is also found among peoples who do not
possess our Scriptures, as in Japan, where the orthodox Shintoists believe not only in the divine right of kings, but that the king is actually of
divine ancestry. Indeed the close connection between spiritual and temporal power is found in many pagan tribes and from the earliest times.
In some savage tribes the "medicine man" is supreme, holding religious
and secular authority. In the time of Abraham we find Melchizedek

both priest and king (Gen. 14:18). In Egypt the powers of the priesthood were vast, and the kings, being anointed by the priests, were thus supposed to receive their power from the gods. It was perhaps to get away from this very tangle of priest and king that Jehovah took his chosen people out of Egypt. They were to have no king but him, and when the people, influenced by the memories of Egypt and by the prosperity of the kingdoms about them, demanded that Samuel anoint a king for them, Jehovah expressed his great displeasure and warned them of the terrific evils which would follow the establishment of a throne (I Sam. 8:10-18). Notwithstanding all this, it was largely the influence of the Jewish Scriptures that perpetuated the theory of the divine right of kings in modern civilization. Since the Christian Church took over many of the ideas and forms of Judaism the kings of Christian countries are still crowned by representatives of churchly authority, in some cases "holy" oil being used for the anointing. The New Testament writers advised Christians to recognize civil authority where matters of conscience were not involved, but were bold in defying that authority whenever it led contrary to what they believed to be the will of God. Indeed even the Old Testament writers were frank in depicting the crimes of the kings and were free to declare that evil kings were displeasing to God. So that the deeper message of the Bible, Old and New Testaments alike, is a refutation of this very theory it has been supposed to teach. What the Bible really teaches is the divine right of the people, the preciousness of every individual life in the sight of God, the principle that every soul is responsible directly to God for his acts, the principle that no man should be *master* of another, but that each shall be the comrade and helper of all. It is this revolutionary power of the Bible which gave the world the Magna Charta and the new hopes of real democracy. As for David, while he could not have attempted to justify his crime by his kingship, it is very likely that Bathsheba believed that in obeying the king she was really doing right. History is full of instances in which kings have presumed upon the old theory of the divine right of kings to do unjust and wicked things.

976 What is the difference between "the kingdom of God" and the "kingdom of heaven"?

The expressions "kingdom of God" and "kingdom of heaven" are used in different senses in the Scriptures. At times the "kingdom of God" is meant to include the whole universe; again, the "kingdom of heaven" is applied to the celestial regions, where divine Majesty sits enthroned. In the Jewish church it was taught that there were various degrees or heights in the heavenly kingdom (see II Cor. 12:2). The old rabbinical doctrines made the distinction of three heavens, viz., the firmament, the starry heavens and the "heaven of heavens," which is the abode of the omnipresent God and of the highest of his spiritual creation, and it is this latter heaven which Christ called "the house of his Father" (John 14:2). Still further, the phrase "kingdom of heaven" is frequently used in the Gospels as meaning that wherever the rule of Christ is set up in the hearts of men, "the kingdom of heaven is within you." When we pray "Thy kingdom come," we look forward to the time when the ends of the earth will acknowledge God's supremacy and his rule will be universal.

977 What is the "gift of tongues"?

The gift of tongues at Pentecost was the miraculous method employed to bring strangers from distant lands into the Gospel fold. That the gift became later a cause of deep concern to the spiritual teachers of apostolic times is evident from such passages as I Cor. 12:10, which are not meant to depreciate the gift, but to warn believers not to be misled by unprofitable or doubtful manifestations of it. God is not the author of confusion. He never sends a message to his children that is totally unintelligible, and it may well be held that a message to which there is no key should be regarded as extremely doubtful.

978 What is conversion?

Conversion is the "turning" of the sinner to God, following the conviction of sin by the power of the Holy Spirit, bringing a change in the thoughts, desires, dispositions and life of the sinner as the result of the exercise of a saving faith in the atonement by which he is justified. In a more restricted sense, the word "conversion" is often used to mean "the voluntary act of the soul consciously accepting Christ in faith as Saviour." "Regeneration" is the creation of a new condition of the heart and is not a personal act of man, but that work of the Holy Spirit by which we experience a change of heart. It is being born anew "from above" (John 3:7), a "renewing of the mind" (Rom. 12:2), "a putting off of the old man and a putting on of the new" (Eph. 4:22, 24). The change in regeneration lies in the recovery of the moral image of God in the heart—"a condition which enables us to love him supremely and to find our highest joy in his service." It is right to believe that one who is willing to do God's will and to give up everything to him—one who holds himself and all he has at the Lord's disposal—is regenerated and ready to be used by the Lord in his work.

979 Why was Nehemiah "sad"
before the king?

The incidents in the first two chapters of Nehemiah are the record of a series of events which show how the narrator had found a way providentially opened to him to state the request he wished to make to the king. He was cup-bearer in the royal palace. The queen referred to was probably Esther, whose presence would doubtless tend to encourage him in making his request, as it was known throughout the kingdom that she exercised great influence and was in strong sympathy with any movement for the benefit of the Jews. The monarch was Artaxerxes Longimanus, then in the twentieth year of his reign, or about B.C. 437. Josephus, the Jewish historian, relates how Nehemiah, while walking around the palace walls, overheard several persons talking in his native tongue, and, finding that they had lately come from Judea, he spoke to them and learned all about the unfinished and desolate condition of Jerusalem and the helpless state of the returned exiles. It was this knowledge that made him sad before the king.

980 When were churches first used?

Temples and places of worship have been a feature of the world's civilization from the very earliest times. The erection of Christian churches may properly be said to date from about the time of Constantine the Great, when Christianity superseded paganism and became the controlling spirit in the architecture of the Christian world. The first assemblies of the primitive Christians, however, were not held in churches, but in the rooms of private houses, or in the open air. In Acts 1:13, 15 we have an account of the first church meeting indoors in an "upper room" in Jerusalem, where about 120 persons gathered for the first Christian service. Within the next half century, as the result of the apostles' missionary efforts, churches sprang up in many places, and some buildings began to be devoted almost exclusively to these services.

981 Who were the Philistines?

The origin of the Philistines is not expressly stated in the Bible. However, Amos 9:7 speaks of them as "the Philistines from Caphtor," and "the remnant of the maritime district of Caphtor" (Jer. 47:4). It is believed by some authorities that they were the people who expelled the Avim and occupied their territory (Deu. 2:23) and that they were the descendants of Mizraim (Gen. 10:14). Some eminent scholars hold that they belong to the Semitic family, as the names of their cities and their proper names would indicate. The island of Crete is believed to have been the Caphtor of ancient times. The Philistines were a warlike race, superstitious and idolatrous. In the time of Saul they were evidently superior in the arts of life to the Israelites (see I Sam. 13:19-21).

982 What is "the great tribulation"?

The "great tribulation" referred to in Dan. 12:1 ("there shall be a time of trouble, such as never was since there was a nation") is also implied in other prophecies, and in the utterances of the Saviour himself on various occasions. There is a remarkable concurrence in the view that the time of world salvation and regeneration is to be preceded by a period of phenomenal world trial and suffering. This is an essential part of the great drama—the Messianic hope, which, according to the Jewish prophets, is to find its climax in the complete restoration of the Palestinian kingdom to its ancient glory, while the Christian teaching is that it will culminate in world-wide Messianic dominion.

983 What is fellowship with God?

Fellowship with God is the essence of the Christian life. He is Light, and as in the natural world all material life and growth depend on light, so all spiritual life and growth must depend on God, "in whom is no darkness at all." "Walking in the light," therefore, is descriptive of the intimate fellowship and close dependence of the believer, who keeps in touch with God and with Christ, who is the "true light" (see I John 1:5-9). If we are in the light, we will be divinely helped and guided in our inward and outward actions, and in all things to which we apply ourselves. Indeed, this is the test of our fellowship. "He that saith he abideth in him ought himself also so to walk, even as he walked." Such companionship brings not only spiritual development but enlarges our Christian fellowship one with another and gives a new joy and fulness to life. It is not an imitation merely, but a union and oneness in all things with him with whom we walk.

984 Is the story of the rich man and Lazarus a parable?

Although the story of the rich man and Lazarus is the only one of its kind in the New Testament in which a proper name is employed, it is universally regarded as a parable. Lazarus was a familiar name in the country where Jesus spent the years of his ministry. It is true, there are traditions still preserved which give the name of the rich man as Dobruk, and that of the beggar as Nimeusis, but these are unauthentic. Jesus used the two characters to illustrate two different types of men, the helpless and friendless poor and the heartless, selfish rich.

985 What was a Sabbath day's Journey?

A "Sabbath day's journey," the distance which according to Jewish ecclesiastical law might be traveled without violating the sanctity of the day, was approximately 2,000 yards, or 12,000 handbreadths. The distance was not to be measured from any point according to whim, but in obedience to definite and minute rules. It is assumed that the distance was originally fixed in relation to the distance between the ark and the tents of the people in the wilderness (Josh. 3:3, 4). To assemble near the ark was a duty on the Sabbath, therefore walking that distance was no violation of the day and it was taken as the measurement of a lawful Sabbath day's journey. The spirit and purpose of the prohibition were to forbid traveling on ordinary business on that day, and to afford rest

for beasts of burden, as well as men. The Mount of Olives is stated in
Acts 1:12 to be a Sabbath day's journey from Jerusalem.

986 What is the meaning of, "The heart of David was perfect"?

To understand the Bible use of words in I Kings 11:4 we must remember that God's thoughts are not man's thoughts (Isa. 55:8), neither
does God see as man sees. He looks not upon the outward appearance,
but upon the heart (I Sam. 16:7). God's dealings with nations or individuals has but one standard for character—righteousness of intention and
desire of "the heart"; to do his will only.

We find other Bible characters described as "Perfect with (notice the
word 'with') the Lord"; "Upright"; "Eschewing evil"; "Righteous";
"Walking with the Lord"; yet all guilty of sinning in times of weakness
and temptation; some falling into degrading transgressions.

It may be asked: "How can this be explained?"

When the Scriptures testify they were "perfect with God" it does not
assert they were sinless, in the absolute meaning of sinless perfection.
When we are told "the heart of David . . . was . . . perfect with the
Lord his God," it is not saying that in his efforts to serve him he was an
expression of all God required him to do and be.

"Perfect" has various shades of meaning. In Bible usage it may imply
full development, or growth into maturity of godliness and perfect holiness. It denotes perfection of action toward a finish. A child may be
perfect as a child but short of all perfection of manhood. Control of
spiritual and mental and physical powers must be acquired through
growth in experiences. God knowing man's frame to be but sinborn
clay, remembers it (Ps. 103:14). Therefore, he must rescue his creatures
through spirit and heart affections by a love and faith developed unto
the measure of the stature of the fulness of Christ. Perfection of God's
children consists of a ceaseless growth into a knowledge of God and
Christ.

THE HEREAFTER

987 Will the future state be one of material or spiritual glory?

The future state will be one in which our personal identity will be preserved. We will have what may be called resurrection bodies, not greatly unlike that of our Saviour after his resurrection. The book of Revelation being prophetic and highly figurative, is to be interpreted accordingly. As the resurrection body will be spiritual, so will the abode of these bodies be spiritual—a state of indefinite development of our highest powers, chiefly the moral, intellectual and spiritual. It will not be a disembodied state. The qualities seen in the spiritual bodies of those who have reappeared on earth (such as Moses, Elijah and Jesus himself) are, very likely, but properties superior to those we now possess Read and compare Job 19:25-27; Ps. 17:15; I Cor. 13:12; I Cor. 15:44, and entire chapter, and I Thess. 4:17, etc. Many believe that the earth will be refitted, for the abode of the righteous in this exalted state. To others, it appears that then all the universe will form the theater of that existence, as we shall have powers of locomotion commensurate with all our other conditions.

988 Is sanctification complete at death, or does it continue in heaven?

We cannot dogmatize about the state of the believer in heaven. So little is revealed to us about that state, that absolute knowledge is impossible. Judging by what we do know, we infer that there must be a vast increase in knowledge of God and divine things which must have its effect on the character. Then, too, to be in the presence of God, and associated with pure and holy beings and liberated from the gross influence of the flesh would, we should imagine, tend to elevate and ennoble and develop the spiritual nature. Perhaps it would be more accurate to describe the progress we expect as growth and development rather than sanctification.

989 Did the Jews believe in the immortality of the soul?

While the belief is nowhere directly stated in the early Jewish writings there are many passages which appear to indicate that it was general. The laws in the Pentateuch against holding communication with the dead imply a prevalent belief that the soul lived on after the death of the body. Saul's application to the witch of Endor (I Sam. 28) shows that he believed in the continued existence of the soul. In Heb. 11:16 the statement is made that the patriarchs expected to enter a heavenly country. Christ also referred to the belief as existing in the days of Moses (see Luke 20:37).

990 What becomes of those who die in ignorance of the true God and his Word?

God has his witnesses in every land and every nation. There is no race, as far as known, which has not a definite idea of a Supreme Being and of right and wrong. The Jews held that the heathen were lost, but Christianity has always held that they will be judged under God's natural law and may be accepted as being a law unto themselves (see Rom. 2:14, 26, 27). No one can set limit to the divine grace and forgiveness, and no church or creed can dogmatize concerning those who, not having the Gospel, have yet lived according to their lights. If Christ's atonement was made for all mankind, it is logical to believe that it includes the virtuous and upright in pre-Gospel days as well as those who come afterward.

991 Will every one be saved?

The statement (I Tim. 2:6) that Christ gave himself a ransom for all, and other statements of like import might be taken to imply that all will eventually be saved in the next world if not in this, but it would be very rash to depend on such an interpretation. It would be an awful thing for a person who did so to find that it was wrong. If a king were to offer amnesty to all rebels who laid down their arms within a given time, the offer would be made to all, but only those who complied with the conditions would be benefited. Salvation is offered to all who accept Christ and there is no limit. If the whole world would accept him, his sacrifice would avail for all. Thus it is universal. But what is to be said of those who neglect it or reject it? There is no further sacrifice. It is not for us to limit God's mercy, but he gives us in his Word no ground for hope that another opportunity of accepting Christ will be afforded after death.

992 Is the desire for immortality a universal one, or must we regard it as one that appeals only to the enlightened or spiritualized heart?

The belief in immortality and the desire of it are world-wide. Yet when we look around us and see the vast majority of the human race with their affections strongly concentrated on material things, we may well doubt whether the problem of a future life is receiving the supreme attention it merits. There are three classes, *i.e.:* 1. Those who really desire immortality and who try, with divine help, to mold their lives accordingly; 2, those who shrink back from the great question; and, 3, those who apparently never think of it. This last is a very large class. What they hear on the subject seems to make no impression. Christ came to bring life and immortality to light, but there is no outward evidence that these darkened minds have ever heard and understood the message. The pursuit of riches, of pleasure, of luxury, of sinful indulgence, and of the prizes the world offers is fatal to spiritual development. Yet even such persons, once thoroughly awakened, often become the most zealous of Christians and the world's allurements seem to them a very little thing in comparison with the life to come.

993 Will a Christian who has studied and cultivated his mind here upon earth be any further advanced in heaven than if he had not?

All that has been revealed to us concerning the other life justifies the conviction that it is a state of vastly enlarged activities and uninterrupted progress. There the spiritual life, which has been kindled in the soul while here, will find amplest room for expansion, and all those noble qualities of heart and mind that go to the formation of the best type of character here below, and which are elementary forms of the perfect manhood, will doubtless survive after our spiritual enlargement, since they have a close affinity to the spiritual life. To efface all intellectual culture in the next life is as great an improbability as would be the effacement of individuality. Consequently, one who while on earth has cultivated the nobler faculties will probably begin the heavenly life with that advantage.

994 Who and what are the angels?

Although much has been written concerning the nature of angels, very little is really known, beyond the fact that they are Gods messengers, endowed with spiritual bodies (see I Cor. 15:44), and employed as the ministers of the divine will. The Bible sheds little light on the nature of angels, although it mentions them many times. One commentator writes: "They are represented as being in the widest sense agents of God's providence, natural and supernatural, to the body and to the soul; thus the operations of nature are spoken of as under angelic guidance fulfilling the will of God." The ministry of angels is mentioned in various passages, including Matt. 13:41-49; 24:31; Luke 16:22, etc. Jewish rabbinical literature has preserved the tradition of the rebellion and fall of the apostate angels, and the reference in Isa. 14:12 has sometimes been interpreted as related to this tradition. In Jude 6 there is a well-known passage on the same subject. Milton in *Paradise Lost* described the fall of Lucifer in a famous poetic passage (see also Luke 10:18). The angels are ministering spirits who while themselves obeying the will of God, communicate God's and Christ's will and execute their purposes and judgments (Neh. 9:6; I Kings 19:5; Ps. 68:17; Dan. 8:16; Matt. 2:13, 19; Luke 1:19, 28; Ps. 103:20; Num. 22:22; Ps. 103:21; II Sam. 24:16). Their duties are to minister to Christ, extend his purposes and to watch over us, especially over the children and helpless (Matt. 4:11; Matt. 13:41; Matt. 18:10; Ps. 34:7; Ps. 91:11).

995 What will be the reward of saints?

The reward of saints prepared by God and Christ for the servants of Christ is of God's good pleasure, not given us on merit but by grace (Rom. 2:7; Rom. 4:4, 5; Matt. 20:14; Heb. 11:16; John 14:2; Col. 3:24). It is described as "being with Christ, beholding the glory of him and of God and of being glorified with Christ" (John 12:26; Ps. 17:15; Matt. 5:8; John 17:24; Rom. 8:17, 18; Col. 3:4). In this state we shall sit in judgment and reign with Christ for ever and ever (Dan. 7:22; Matt. 19:28; II Tim. 2:12; Rev. 22:5). This reward is an incorruptible crown of righteousness, glory and life and joint heirship with Christ and all saints of an immovable kingdom and all things (I Cor. 9:25; II Tim. 4:8; I Pet. 5:4; James 1:12; Rom. 8:17; Rev. 21:7; Acts 20:32; Heb. 9:15; I Pet. 1:4; Matt. 25:34; Heb. 12:28). In this glorious state we shall shine as the stars with everlasting light and live in a home eternal in the heavens and in a city which has foundation and enter into rest and fulness of joy (Dan. 12:3; Isa. 60:19; Luke 18:30; Heb. 10:34; II Cor. 5:1; Heb. 11:10; Matt. 25:21; Heb. 4:9; Ps. 16:11). Such reward is great, full, sure, satisfying and inestimable and saints may feel confident of attaining it but should be careful not to lose it (Matt. 5:12; II John 8; Prov. 11:18; Ps. 17:15; Isa. 64:4; Ps. 73:24; II John 8). And therefore the prospect thereof should lead to diligence, pressing forward, enduring suffering for Christ and faithfulness unto death (II John 8; Phil. 3:14; II Cor. 4:16-18; Rev. 2:10).

996 Is there Scriptural authority for the claim that Christ will rule on earth?

The passage in Rev. 11:15 has its parallel in Dan. 2:44. It is the visible setting up of heaven's sovereignty over the earth—that sovereignty which was rejected before by the world's rulers. This done, the distinction of the worldly and the spiritual shall cease. The whole earth, with all of its affairs, will at once be worldly and Christian, but worldly in the transformed sense, all being ordered in accordance with the divine will and in perfect recognition of and obedience to God's laws. But it should not be forgotten that the kingdom has its first beginnings in the hearts of God's true children here and now. This is repeatedly emphasized by Jesus in his talks with his disciples. These beginnings, though only a faint foreshadowing of the ultimate development of the kingdom, are nevertheless real and their earnest cultivation is a duty laid upon all believers. Christ ushered in the kingdom; his followers, like a little faithful flock, maintain it perseveringly and we look forward to the day, in the fulness of time, when it shall be proclaimed in divine majesty and power over the whole earth.

997 Does memory of the earthly state continue after death?

In the parable of Dives and Lazarus (Luke 16:27, 28) it is clearly shown that memory of the earthly state continues after death. This is so because the soul being freed from earthly obstacles sees clearly through space. Death is only a veil and transparent to those on the other side are the things here. In two distinct passages (I Cor. 13:12 and II Cor. 3:18) Paul employs a figure of speech to convey the idea that our mortality is an obstacle to spiritual vision—a veil. Death is the shedding of the garment of mortal flesh. As the believer nears the close of life, his hold on material things becomes feebler and his spiritual perception grows clearer. The soul is preparing to loosen its material environment; it is ripening for release—the putting off of the tabernacle of this flesh (II Pet. 1:13, 14; II Cor. 5:1). As the end of the journey comes into view, the spiritual vision is enabled to perceive and understand many things it could not do before. With regard to the knowledge of those on the "other side" of what is going on here, we have Scriptural evidence in support of it. Heb. 12:1 tells us that we are encompassed with "a cloud of witnesses." All heaven is looking on and watching our struggles here, although our own eyes are still holden. There are other texts in Scripture which go to show that those who have passed "beyond the veil" are not indifferent to us who are left behind (see Luke 16:19-25).

998 Will the final judgment be of two parts or kinds?

All that we read about the final judgment indicates that it will be of two kinds. There will be the great separation of the sheep from the goats (Matt. 25:32) and there will also be another and more joyful judgment, in which rewards are distributed among the children of God in proportion to the work each has done for Christ (Luke 19:22-26). These rewards will not be given according to the prominence Christians have attained in the world, nor according to the quantity or conspicuity of the work done; but on Christ's principles of fidelity to him and his spirit. The apostle teaches that many a servant of Christ will miss a reward, because his work has not been done in the right spirit and motive. He will be saved if he is in Christ, but his work will not be accepted (see I Cor. 3:13, 14). To cite examples: Can you conceive of a Christian man doing good works from an impure motive? Suppose a clergyman has lost the high ideal he had when he entered the ministry, and now his aim in preaching is to increase his popularity, or to get more money. Suppose a man gives a public library to the city, or pensions a widow, and his real motive, if he would honestly analyze it, is to get a reputation for charity and beneficence, or to promote his election to Congress. The clergyman's preaching may be earnest and effective and the other man's gifts may be well applied, but God, who reads the heart, knows that he has had his reward in getting the applause, or the money, or the position which was sought. Having had it he deserves no other, and he gets none. He suffers the loss of the reward God would have given him for work done for his sake.

999 There being no marriage in heaven, will husband and wife recognize each other in heaven?

Recognition does not imply a resumption of the old relations. Christ's words were a reply to a question which assumed that there might be a dispute between husbands of the same woman as to the right of one of them to treat her as his wife. He reminded them that in heaven people would not have their fleshly bodies. After the resurrection they will have spiritual bodies (see I Cor. 15:44). The husband may and doubtless will recognize his wife and the wife the husband, and it will be a loving recognition; but they will be so absorbed in the spiritual delights of the new condition that the old relations will be gross and coarse in their eyes.

1000 Will there be a resurrection of the wicked?

In the earlier stages the resurrection doctrine was evidently taught as a hope which applied to righteous Israelites, and it was afterward extended by degrees to others, including the Gentiles. In Luke 14:14 a distinction seems to be made between the resurrection of the righteous and that of the wicked, and in Luke 20:35, 36, those who are accounted worthy to attain the resurrection from the dead are spoken of as "the children of God"—the inference drawn by some commentators on this point being that the resurrection of the righteous is to be separate from that of the wicked (see John 5:29 and Acts 24:15; also I Thess. 4:16; I Cor. 15:23, 24). Compare also John 6:40, in which the resurrection of the righteous is represented as an act of grace, as also in John 5:21; and in John 6:44, 54 Jesus says: "And I will raise him up at the last day." Paul also, in Rom. 8:11, teaches a resurrection of the righteous. With regard to the second resurrection, whether it will be simultaneous with the first, or after an interval, commentators differ. Rev. 20:4-6 has been held to imply an interval of a thousand years, but this is merely conjecture. There has been a great deal of discussion concerning the two resurrections, and many books have been written on the subject.

Index

Index

Index

Index

confession of sin (Ps.51:4), 849
eating of the shewbread, 593
and execution of Joab and Shimei, 58
imprecatory psalms, 592
a "mighty valiant man," 590
name of his mother, 28
"perfect" heart, 986
progenitor of Jesus, 774
wives, 60
a "youth," 590
Day of Atonement, 620
Death
accidental, 332
of children, 863
comfort after loss of a loved one, 874
and dread of hereafter, 535
and existence of body and soul, 550
in ignorance of the true God, 990
interval before resurrection, 555
"let the dead bury their dead," 327
"not dead, but sleepeth," 285
and the physical body, 531
repentance after? 548
second death, 530
thoughts about, 700
Deliverance to Satan, 972
Demons
cast out, 165
possession by, 175
Denominationalism, 916, 924
Depression, 697
Desires, evil, 713, 759
Devils. *See* Demons; Satan
Devotion to God, 439
Disciples in the Garden of Gethsemane, 226
Discipleship
"I am come to set a man at variance . . . ," 262
"Let the dead bury their dead," 258, 327
Discipline in the Christian life, 511
Disease, 418
Dispensations, 354
Divine right of kings, 975

Divorce, scriptural view, 362, 876
Doctrinal differences, 198
Doing good, 714, 715
Doubt, cure for, 419, 757

E

Earth and its "passing away," 278, 306. *See also* Eschatology
Ecumenism, 924
Eden, garden of, 598
Edomites, their origin, 62
Egypt
cultural rejection of shepherds, 103
death of Pharoah, 93
great famine in, 30
Jacob's arrival in, 33
Joseph's arrival in, 31
Pharaohs, 621
worship of the beetle, 587
Elders, 839
Elect, 177
Elect lady, 643
Election, 178, 325, 505, 520
Elias, 263
Elijah
death, 63
second appearance, 117
Endor, Witch of, 109
Engagement, 721
Enoch, Book of, 594
Entertainment in the church, 673
Envy, 703
Epicureans, 958
Esau
descendants, 597
and Jacob, 596
Eschatology. *See also* Heaven
arrival in heaven or hell after death, 533
desire for immortality, 992
the future state, 987
Jewish belief in immortality, 536, 989
judgment day, 534
resurrection of the wicked, 1000
rule of Christ on earth, 996
Essenes, 142
Everlasting, defined by Christ, 814

Index

Index

Index

Index

Index

Index

Index

Index

Index

Index

Index

Index